THE NEW MIDDL

M000189146

BONNIE WHEELER, *SERI.*

The New Middle Ages is a series dedicated to pluridisciplinary studies of medieval cultures, with particular emphasis on recuperating women's history and on feminist and gender analyses. This peer-reviewed series includes both scholarly monographs and essay collections.

PUBLISHED BY PALGRAVE:

Women in the Medieval Islamic World: Power, Patronage, and Piety
  edited by Gavin R. G. Hambly

The Ethics of Nature in the Middle Ages: On Boccaccio's Poetaphysics
  by Gregory B. Stone

Presence and Presentation: Women in the Chinese Literati Tradition
  edited by Sherry J. Mou

The Lost Love Letters of Heloise and Abelard: Perceptions of Dialogue in Twelfth-Century France
  by Constant J. Mews

Understanding Scholastic Thought with Foucault
  by Philipp W. Rosemann

For Her Good Estate: The Life of Elizabeth de Burgh
  by Frances A. Underhill

Constructions of Widowhood and Virginity in the Middle Ages
  edited by Cindy L. Carlson and Angela Jane Weisl

Motherhood and Mothering in Anglo-Saxon England
  by Mary Dockray-Miller

Listening to Heloise: The Voice of a Twelfth-Century Woman
  edited by Bonnie Wheeler

The Postcolonial Middle Ages
  edited by Jeffrey Jerome Cohen

Chaucer's Pardoner and Gender Theory: Bodies of Discourse
  by Robert S. Sturges

Crossing the Bridge: Comparative Essays on Medieval European and Heian Japanese Women Writers
  edited by Barbara Stevenson and Cynthia Ho

Engaging Words: The Culture of Reading in the Later Middle Ages
  by Laurel Amtower

Robes and Honor: The Medieval World of Investiture
  edited by Stewart Gordon

Representing Rape in Medieval and Early Modern Literature
  edited by Elizabeth Robertson and Christine M. Rose

Same Sex Love and Desire among Women in the Middle Ages
  edited by Francesca Canadé Sautman and Pamela Sheingorn

Sight and Embodiment in the Middle Ages: Ocular Desires
  by Suzannah Biernoff

Listen, Daughter: The Speculum Virginum and the Formation of Religious Women in the Middle Ages
  edited by Constant J. Mews

Science, the Singular, and the Question of Theology
  by Richard A. Lee, Jr.

Gender in Debate from the Early Middle Ages to the Renaissance
  edited by Thelma S. Fenster and Clare A. Lees

THE LOST LOVE LETTERS OF HELOISE AND ABELARD

PERCEPTIONS OF DIALOGUE IN TWELFTH-CENTURY FRANCE

SECOND EDITION

Constant J. Mews

With a translation by
Neville Chiavaroli and Constant J. Mews

THE LOST LOVE LETTERS OF HELOISE AND ABELARD
Copyright © Constant J. Mews, 1999, 2008. Translation, "From the Letters
of Two Lovers," Copyright © Neville Chiavaroli and Constant J. Mews,
1999, 2008.

First edition published in 1999 by PALGRAVE MACMILLAN® in the
US—a division of St. Martin's Press LLC, 175 Fifth Avenue, New York, NY
10010.

Where this book is distributed in the UK, Europe and the rest of the world,
this is by Palgrave Macmillan, a division of Macmillan Publishers Limited,
registered in England, company number 785998, of Houndmills,
Basingstoke, Hampshire RG21 6XS.

Palgrave Macmillan is the global academic imprint of the above companies
and has companies and representatives throughout the world.

Palgrave® and Macmillan® are registered trademarks in the United States,
the United Kingdom, Europe and other countries.

ISBN-13: 978-0-230-60813-9

Library of Congress Cataloging-in-Publication Data is available from the
Library of Congress.

A catalogue record of the book is available from the British Library.

Design by Letra Libre.

Second edition: September 2008
10 9 8 7 6 5 4 3 2 1
Printed in the United States of America.

Transferred to Digital Printing in 2008

For Maryna

CONTENTS

INTRODUCTION

This book is the product of a journey that began in 1976 when I first came across Ewald Könsgen's edition, *Epistolae duorum amantium: Briefe Abaelards und Heloises?* (Leiden: E. J. Brill, 1974) in Auckland University Library, New Zealand. I was attracted by the subtitle and was curious to find out how those letters related to the more well-known correspondence between Heloise and Abelard. As things turned out, the direction of my studies changed after I went to Oxford to pursue doctoral research. I heeded the suggestion of Sir Richard Southern that I turn my attention to Abelard's *Theologia*, a treatise which Abelard continued to revise for over twenty years. That research, guided by David Luscombe, brought me into direct contact with one of the most subtle minds of the twelfth century. Between 1980 and 1985, I was fortunate enough to attend the seminar of Jean Jolivet on medieval philosophy at the École pratique des hautes études (V^e section), in Paris. Jolivet played a key role in helping me understand the evolution of Abelard's thinking about logic as well as about theology. I was able to complete a critical edition of Abelard's *Theologia Summi boni* and *Theologia Scholarium,* initiated by Fr. Eligius-Marie Buytaert, while working on a research project funded by the Leverhulme Foundation and directed by David Luscombe at the University of Sheffield. My research into the *Epistolae duorum amantium* is the fruit of these scholastic labors. To all my teachers, I owe an enormous debt of gratitude.

This book also draws on interaction with many colleagues, students, and friends here in Australia. They made me aware how important issues of gender are to understanding Latin tradition and to putting in perspective the skills that I had absorbed in the schools of Oxford and Paris. Becoming interested in the writing of Heloise's direct contemporary, Hildegard of Bingen, also enabled me to see more clearly how the ideas of both Abelard and Heloise were shaped by the deeper structures of the society in which they lived.

It was when reading afresh the *Epistolae duorum amantium* in 1993, this time with greater awareness of Abelard's vocabulary as a logician, that I encountered words and ideas that sent a shiver down my spine. Terms like "without difference" (*indifferenter*) and "knowability" (*scibilitas*) were words to which Abelard paid great attention in his logic. Could an incomplete copy have been made in the fifteenth century of the lost love letters of Heloise and Abelard? I put aside my research into Roscelin of Compiègne and his influence on Peter Abelard to explore the significance of these letters. Heloise demanded attention in her own right. The relatively recent capacity to search large quantities of Latin text on CD-ROM now makes it much easier to pursue such research. Comparing these love letters to a wide range of other Latin texts, literary, philosophical, and theological, I gradually became persuaded that, for all the limitations of the fifteenth-century transcription, they were indeed written by Heloise and Abelard. They made me consider the *Historia calamitatum* in a new light. Over the years I had identified a number of anonymous texts as written or inspired by Abelard in the domain of either logic or theology, but here I was dealing with texts that dealt with human relationships at a much more profound level.

At an initial reading, the love letters present such an idealized picture of a relationship, far removed from the details of everyday life, that it might seem impossible to identify their specific context. Könsgen made an important step in arguing that they were written by two articulate individuals who lived in the Île-de-France in the first half of the twelfth century and were fully conversant with the classical authors known at that time. I argue that while Könsgen's insights are fundamentally correct, they can be taken much further. I believe that this transcription has much to contribute to our understanding of the early relationship between Heloise and Abelard and the literary climate in which it evolved.

This book focuses not just on the authorship of these letters, but on the broader issue of relationships between educated women and men in twelfth-century France. Heloise and Abelard have long occupied a key role in the collective mythology of European civilization as epitomizing values of love and reason respectively. The protracted debate over the authenticity of the famous letters of Abelard and Heloise is part of an ongoing process of re-interpretation of their legacy. By looking at the wider phenomenon in the twelfth century of men and women communicating with each other through the written word, always through the filter of the manuscript record, I hope to show how the relationship of Abelard and Heloise brings to a head many central tensions within French society in the twelfth century.

My argument is presented as a journey. I begin by inviting the reader to discover the letters that Johannes de Vepria copied at Clairvaux in the late fifteenth century and to gauge the context in which he did so. To answer the questions these letters raise, we need to go back in time. In a second chapter, I consider the more well-known exchange of letters between Abelard and Heloise discovered by Jean de Meun in the thirteenth century, and their role in shaping the way their relationship has been remembered. Debate about the authenticity of the famous letters of Heloise has often been influenced by assumptions that her professions of love for Abelard are incompatible with monastic tradition. Such claims, I argue, are based on a profound misunderstanding of Heloise's reflection on love. The third chapter considers the relationship of Heloise and Abelard from a range of historical records other than the *Historia calamitatum*. It cannot be understood outside the context of a volatile political environment, in which ecclesiastical authority was anxious to assert itself over the clerical community as a whole, and over women in particular. The love letters preserved at Clairvaux constitute perhaps the richest surviving example of educated women and men writing to each other. While there will always be debate about whether such women are invented by men, I argue in the fourth chapter that Heloise was not so unusual in reflecting in prose and verse on the demands of love. In a fifth chapter, I compare the vocabulary of the love letters to that of the known writings of Abelard and Heloise. Here I argue that these textual and stylistic parallels are so complex that it stretches plausibility to argue that the letters were written by anyone other than Abelard and Heloise. In a final chapter, I sketch out what this implies for our understanding of the subsequent evolution of their relationship and of their thought. Abelard so often commands attention by the sheer output of writings on logic and theology attributed to him by his disciples that those unseen voices to whom he responds are often concealed. These anonymous love letters enable us to listen more attentively to voices long hidden from view. They deserve far more critical attention than they have hitherto received. The translation offered of these letters in the second part of the book is not intended to be definitive, but rather is provided to waken interest in a remarkable set of texts from the twelfth century.

Heloise's concern that words should not mouth empty rhetoric echoes a wider interest among reforming circles in the twelfth century that meaning is more important than verbal convention. These shared concerns help explain why it may not be so extraordinary that a record which she kept of her early exchange with Abelard should surface in the abbey of Clairvaux, a community founded in 1115 in a wave of enthusiasm for living out the true meaning of the monastic life. The conversations of Abelard and Heloise about love are part of a larger dialogue taking place among a literate elite in early twelfth-century France about the nature of authentic relationships. There have been no shortage of books written about Abelard this century. Two new studies of Abelard appeared too late for me to give them detailed attention: John Marenbon, *The Philosophy of Peter Abelard* (Cambridge: Cambridge University Press, 1997) and Michael T. Clanchy, *Abelard: A Medieval Life* (Oxford: Blackwell, 1998). Only after this book was completed did I learn from C. Stephen Jaeger that he had suggested, quite independently of my own research, that the love letters were those of Abelard and Heloise in a forthcoming book, *Ennobling Love: In Search of a Lost Sensibility* (Philadelphia: University of Pennsylvania Press, 1999). It is a measure of the richness of this subject that so many good new studies can be written. I was delighted to discover that Marenbon and Clanchy argue that Heloise was a major intellectual influence on Abelard. I wish to take their arguments further, and consider Heloise as a major figure in her own right. At the same time, I have been anxious to show that both Abelard and Heloise need to be understood within the broader context of cultural change in twelfth-century France. It is only by penetrating the mythology which surrounds both Abelard and Heloise that we can begin to look at the deeper structures which shape their thought.

By training, I am a historian rather than a philologist or literary critic. In the course of this study, I have inevitably trespassed into a variety of disciplinary traditions that are not my own. I believe, however, that it is imperative for historical and literary disciplines to learn from each other and transcend the factionalism by which they have sometimes been divided. I acknowledge a particular debt to Ewald Könsgen for the painstaking attention that he has given to my arguments and to the translation of the letters, as well as for allowing me to reproduce his critical text. I also register a great debt to Peter Dronke for doing so much to demonstrate the ongoing vitality of Latin literature in the eleventh and twelfth centuries. The translations of Latin texts offered here are often indebted to his readings. Inevitably, many nuances of meaning can still be debated, new sources discovered, and new questions posed. If, however, I can encourage readers to study the Latin language and engage in dialogue with neglected strands of Latin tradition, both secular and religious, it will have been worthwhile. At a time when the study of Latin is disappearing from many universities, it is imperative that literary and philosophical treasures jealously guarded by devoted scholars continue to revitalize cultural debate.

The practical process of engaging in detailed research into the twelfth century from an Australian standpoint has been much assisted by many institutions and individuals. Invitations from the Institute for Advanced Study, Princeton, in 1990 and the École pratique des hautes études, Paris, in 1993 enabled me to pursue research into Abelard's scholastic milieu, the basis for my subsequent inquiry into the love letters. This book has also benefited from the financial support of Monash University and the Australian Research Council, sponsors of a larger project on gender and religious life in the twelfth century. My special thanks go to the graduate students with whom I have discussed many aspects of this study, in particular to Neville Chiavaroli, to whom I proposed the project of translating the letters in 1993. Many ideas germinated in our discussions of how to translate the letters. The chance to present a reading of these love letters at a Melbourne restaurant in 1994 enabled us to appreciate their impact in the public domain at an early stage in the project. I am immensely grateful to Jocelyn Wogan-Browne, John O. Ward, Julie Hotchin, Juanita Ruys, Jeremy du Quesnay Adams, and John Lewis for their comments on drafts of this book, Marjorie Mitchell for typing the Latin text, Kathryn Mews for discussing the translation, and to Hilary Davies and Sebastian Barker for sharing ideas about Abelard and Heloise, while benefiting from their hospitality to me in London. I am grateful to the many librarians who have made their collections available to me. Bonnie Wheeler has played a particularly important role in this book's development, offering advice and guidance throughout. Rick Delaney of St. Martin's Press has been ever patient with the process of its production. Responsibility for error is of course entirely my own. I am grateful to Oxford University Press for giving permission to reproduce Frances Horgan's translation of part of *The Romance of the Rose* (1994), and to University of Pennsylvania Press for reproducing Gerald Bond's translation of the poem by a scholar-nun in *The Loving Subject. Desire, Eloquence, and Power in Romanesque France* (1995). I also thank Michel Lemoine for introducing me to the vast lexicographic resources of the Comité Du Cange, available to medievalists at the Institut de France, Paris and the staff of the Institut de recherche et d'histoire des textes (Section latine) for their unstinting assistance over the years. Many other friends and spiritual guides, too numerous to name, have shaped my thoughts about Heloise, Abelard, and the schools of Paris. I must conclude by singling out my debt to the one person who has contributed more than anyone else to understanding the issues of dialogue and communication that lie at the heart of this book: Maryna. Only she can know what it is really about.

ABBREVIATIONS

BNF	Bibliothèque nationale de France.
CCCM	Corpus Christianorum Continuatio Mediaeualis (Turnhout: Brepols, 1966–).
CCSL	Corpus Christianorum Series Latina (Turnhout: Brepols, 1954–).
Checklist	Julia Barrow, Charles S. F. Burnett, and David Edward Luscombe, "A Checklist of the Manuscripts Containing the Writings of Peter Abelard and Heloise and Other Works Closely Associated with Abelard and his School," *Revue d'Histoire des Textes* 14–15 (1984–85): 183–302.
Constable	Peter the Venerable, *The Letters of Peter the Venerable*, ed. Giles Constable (Cambridge, Mass.: Harvard University Press, 1967).
CSEL	Corpus Scriptorum Ecclesiasticorum Latinorum (Vienna-Leipzig: Teubner, 1866–).
CSS	Cistercian Studies Series.
DHGE	*Dictionnaire d'histoire et de géographique ecclésiastique*, ed. A. Baudrillart et al. (Paris: Le Touzey et Ané, 1912–).
Dronke, *ML*	Peter Dronke, *Medieval Latin and the Rise of the European Love Lyric*, 2 vols., 2nd ed. (Oxford: Oxford University Press, 1968).
Dronke, *WW*	Peter Dronke, *Women Writers of the Middle Ages. A Critical Study of Texts from Perpetua (†203) to Marguerite Porete (†1310)* (Cambridge: Cambridge University Press, 1984).
Dufour	*Recueil des Actes de Louis VI roi de France (1108–1137)*, ed. Jean Dufour, 4 vols. (Paris: Diffusion de Boccard, 1992–94).
HC	*Historia calamitatum*, ed. Jacques Monfrin (Paris: Vrin, 1959).

Hicks	*La Vie et les epistres Pierres Abaelart et Heloys sa fame,* ed. Eric Hicks (Paris: Honoré Champion, 1991).
Könsgen	*Epistolae duorum amantium: Briefe Abaelards und Heloises?,* ed. Ewald Könsgen, Mittellateinische Studien und Texte 8 (Leiden: E. J. Brill, 1974).
Luchaire	Achille Luchaire, *Louis VI le Gros: Annales de sa vie et de son règne* (Paris: Piccard, 1890; repr. Brussels: Culture et Civilisation, 1964).
MGH SS	Monumenta Germaniae Historica. Scriptorum Series
PL	Jacques-Paul Migne, Patrologia Latina (Paris: Garnier, 1844–).
Radice	*The Letters of Abelard and Heloise,* trans. Betty Radice (London: Harmondsworth, 1974).
Recueil	*Recueil des historiens des Gaules et de la France,* ed. Martin Bouquet et al., 24 vols. (Paris: [various publishers], 1738–1904).
SBO	*Sancti Bernardi Opera,* ed. Jean Leclercq, 8 vols. (Rome: Editiones Cistercienses, 1957–75).
SC	Sources chrétiennes.
Vita Ludovici	Suger, *Vie de Louis VI le Gros,* ed. Henri Waquet (Paris: Les Belles Lettres, 1964); *The Deeds of Louis the Fat,* trans. Richard C. Cusimano and John Moorhead (Washington D.C.: Catholic University of America, 1992).

Note. Medieval scribes observed a variety of orthographical conventions. Editors of texts vary in the extent to which they reproduce conventions like *e* for *ae* or *ci* for *ti.* Latin texts are cited in this book according to the edition being followed. Names also present a problem. Although *Abaelardus* was originally pronounced as five syllables (Aba'elardus), I use "Abelard" for the sake of consistency with a corrupt orthographical tradition, aware that "Abaelard" may get lost in a computer search. Twelfth-century names are generally cited in their English form. "Heloise" is written without the diaresis employed in the French spelling (*Héloïse*), but should still be pronounced with three syllables.

The love letters are cited by the numbering of Könsgen's edition, rather than by page numbers, the man's letters being numbered in italics. My numbering of the famous letters of Abelard and Heloise follows that established by André Duchesne in the 1616 edition of the *Opera Omnia,* reprinted in PL 178: 113–314 and followed by Victor Cousin in *Petri Abaelardi opera hactenus seorsim edita,* 2 vols. (Paris: Durand, 1849, 1859), 1:

1–213: The first, second and third letters of Heloise are thus *Ep.* 2, 4 and 6, the replies of Abelard *Ep.* 3, 5, 7 (on the religious life) and 8 (the Rule for the Paraclete). Radice identifies these letters as 1–7, rather than as 2–8 in her translation, *The Letters of Abelard and Heloise* (Harmondsworth: Penguin, 1974), following the numbering used by J.T. Muckle: "Abelard's Letter of Consolation to a Friend," *Mediaeval Studies* 12 (1950): 163–213 [*HC*]; The Personal Letters between Abelard and Héloïse," *Mediaeval Studies* 15 (1953): 47–94 [*Ep.* 2–4]; "The Letter of Héloïse on the Religious Life and Abelard's First Reply," *Mediaeval Studies* 17 (1955): 240–81 [*Ep.* 5–7]; T. P. McLaughlin, "Abelard's Rule for Religious Women," *Mediaeval Studies* 18 (1956): 241–92 [*Ep.* 8]. I refer to the page numbers of the Radice translation, even though I might offer my own translation, to convey the particular nuance of the Latin. I use . . . to indicate my own shortening of a quotation, as distinct from ..... to indicate a scribal ellipse in the manuscript copied by Johannes de Vepria.

I

Perceptions of Dialogue

CHAPTER 1

THE DISCOVERY OF A MANUSCRIPT

Clairvaux, 1471. A young monk is rummaging through cupboards full of manuscripts. He is looking for examples of good Latin prose to include in an anthology of letters from Christian antiquity to the present that he is compiling. There is no complete inventory to help him find his way through the mass of parchment that has accumulated at the abbey during the three and a half centuries since it was founded by St. Bernard in 1115. Most of the official letters he finds begin with a standard formula: "To X, Y: greeting (*salutem*)." His eye then falls on the rhyming phrases of a very different kind of letter, one that does not identify the sender by name:

> [Amori suo precordiali] omnibus aromatibus dulcius redolenti, corde et cor- heart and body ↗
> pore sua: arescentibus floribus tue juventutis viriditatem eterne felicitatis.

> [To her heart's love,] more sweetly scented than any spice, she who is his in
> heart and body: the freshness of eternal happiness as the flowers fade of your
> youth.[1]

Who is this woman whose voice is preserved in an abbey to which women are denied access? Is she real, or is she the creation of a vivid literary imagination? Who is the man whom she imagines to be so wonderful? Is it not fiction to imagine that one can eavesdrop on a dialogue of the heart from so many centuries ago?

The monk begins by transcribing only the extravagant greetings that they send each other and their farewells. Meticulously, he makes sense of his text by adding *M[ulier]* or *V[ir]* to the margin to distinguish whether a woman or a man is speaking, sometimes just adding a paragraph mark. The early letters reveal little of the identity of the two lovers. She praises him in letter 21 as "glory of young men, companion of poets" (*o decus juvenum, consors poetarum*). The word *iunvenis* is applied to men aged between twenty-one and forty-eight.[2] Only in letter 49 does the woman reveal more about the identity of the man to whom she is writing. Here she employs extravagant language, with carefully sought out literary allusions, in order to apologize for daring to address such a famous teacher:

> magistro inquam tanto, magistro virtutibus, magistro moribus, cui jure cedit francigena cervicositas, et simul assurgit tocius mundi superciliositas, quilibet compositus qui sibi videtur sciolus, suo prorsus judicio fiet elinguis et mutus.

> a teacher so great, I declare, a teacher of virtue, a teacher of character, to whom French pigheadedness rightly yields and for whom at the same time the haughtiness of the whole world rises in respect, that anyone who considers himself even slightly learned, would be rendered completely speechless and mute by his own judgment.

In letter 49 she discusses at length the nature of the true friendship that she considered to bind them both. Our first clue to her identity occurs in his reply (50), when he calls her the only female student of philosophy among all the *puellae* of his day:[3]

> Soli inter omnes etatis nostre puellas philosophie discipule, soli in quam omnes virtutum multiplicium dotes integre fortuna conclusit . . .

> To the only disciple of philosophy among all the young women of our age, the only one on whom fortune has completely bestowed all the gifts of the manifold virtues . . .

He praises her as so skilful in arguing about the laws of friendship that she seems not to have read Cicero, but instead to have taught him. She identifies him as her teacher on two further occasions: in her first major attempt at metrical verse within the exchange (66), when she asks the Muses to bestow favor on a teacher with whose light "the throng of the clergy shines" and in her final letter (112), when she addresses him for the first time as her teacher rather than as her lover. Although there are more letters from him than from the woman with whom he is in love (sixty-five, compared to forty-eight), the exchange presents itself as initiated by the woman. It closes with a short note (112a) from her, saying that she no longer wants to reply to him, and a poetic lament from him (113), begging forgiveness and explaining that he had been seduced by her beauty.

The monk who transcribed these letters and poems identifies himself at the end of the letters of Sidonius Apollinaris, a previous item that he had copied in his anthology: "In the year 1471, the day after the feast of the Magdalen [23 July], by me, brother Johannes de Vepria."[4] We can only presume that Johannes de Vepria copied the love letters sometime after this date. It is not even absolutely certain that he discovered this exchange of letters and poems at Clairvaux. What is certain, however, is that his transcription of those letters survives in an anthology of various letter collections that he compiled, now in the possession of the municipal library of Troyes (MS 1452, fols. 159r–167v). This workbook was one of over a thousand manuscripts of the library of Clairvaux transferred to Troyes during the French Revolution. It did not attract scholarly attention until Dieter Schaller suggested to Ewald Könsgen that he edit the Latin text of these love letters for a doctoral thesis. In his edition, published in 1974, Könsgen presented a remarkable set of texts from the twelfth century. By studying other transcriptions Johannes de Vepria made, copied from known manuscripts of Clairvaux, Könsgen established that this hitherto unknown monk was an accurate scribe with a wide knowledge of often very rare Latin texts.

The subtitle attached to Könsgen's edition of these letters (*Briefe Abaelards und Heloises?*) raises a tantalizing possibility: are these letters of Abelard (1079–1142) and Heloise (d. 1164)? Although Könsgen was more concerned to establish a reliable critical edition than to resolve questions of authorship, the question remains. Could these be the love letters that Peter Abelard says he composed in order to seduce Heloise when he was teaching at the cathedral school of Notre-Dame? Abelard mentions these letters in passing:

Tanto autem facilius hanc mihi puellam consensuram credidi, quanto amplius eam litterarum scientiam et habere et diligere noveram; nosque etiam absentes scriptis internuntiis invicem liceret presentare et pleraque audacius scribere quam colloqui, et sic semper jocundis interesse colloquiis.

I believed that she would consent all the more easily to me, the more I knew that she both possessed and loved knowledge of letters, and that even when separated, we could be present to each other through intermediary messages and that it was more daring to write about many things than to discuss them; thus we could always enjoy delightful conversations.[5]

Heloise refers to these letters as great in number at the end of the letter she wrote to Abelard after reading his *Historia calamitatum:*

Cum me ad turpes olim voluptates expeteres, crebris me epistolis visitabas, frequenti carmine tuam in ore omnium Heloysam ponebas: me platee omnes, me domus singule resonabant. Quanto autem rectius me nunc in Deum, quam tunc in libidinem excitares? Perpende, obsecro, que debes, attende que postulo; et longam epistolam brevi fine concludo: vale, unice.

When you sought me out for shameless pleasures, you showered me with incessant letters, you placed your Heloise on the lips of everyone through frequent song: I resounded through every market-place, each house. But how much more rightly might you now arouse me in God, as then you aroused me in lust! Consider, I beg you, what you owe me; listen to what I demand; and so I finish a long letter with a brief conclusion: Farewell, my only one.[6]

Könsgen argued that the differences between the style and vocabulary of the man's letters and those of the woman were so great that the exchange could not be a rhetorical exercise, but had to be a record of correspondence between two distinct individuals. His analysis of literary allusions in the letters led him to date them to the first half of the twelfth century. He mentioned some obvious parallels between these anonymous lovers and Abelard and Heloise, but avoided saying any more than that they were written by a couple "like Abelard and Heloise."[7] More concerned to establish that they were written by two distinct individuals than to examine the significance of the contrast between their arguments, Könsgen claimed that both were writing about worldly love (_amor carnalis_) rather than spiritual love (_amor spiritualis_). Expressions like "I hold God as my witness," frequent in the woman's letters, he interpreted simply as formal turns of phrase. He did not relate the contrasting perceptions of love in these letters to wider discussions of love in other twelfth-century literature. If these love letters were written by a couple other than Abelard and Heloise, the question remains as to who these individuals could be. I argue for the simplest solution, that they are indeed written by Abelard and Heloise.

Könsgen's edition attracted relatively little notice in the two decades following its initial appearance, appearing too late to be examined within a study of love letters as a literary genre in the twelfth and thirteenth centuries.[8] The letters were translated into Italian and (in part) into French, but in both cases without extending Könsgen's analysis to any significant degree.[9] Anonymous texts rarely attract the attention accorded writings by "big name" authors. The most common response of reviewers has been to steer away from making any firm judgment about the authorship of these love letters.[10] Some excellent recent biographical studies of Abelard and

Heloise either do not mention them or dismiss them as problematic.[11] Perhaps the most influential comments made about Könsgen's letters have been those of Peter Dronke. While accepting that they originated from a genuine exchange, he was skeptical about the possibility that they could be letters of Abelard and Heloise.[12] He judged them to be stylistically closer to a set of love letters from Tegernsee, comparing them to the record of a similar liaison between a teacher and a student preserved in a manuscript from Regensburg.[13] Dronke subsequently suggested that the love letters could not have been written by Abelard and Heloise because "it emerges from one of her letters that his high bond of love, though full of erotic intensity, had not yet led—or perhaps would never lead—to physical fulfilment."[14] He interpreted a phrase in letter 84, in which the woman conflates two Pauline texts (1 Cor. 9.24 and 2 Tim. 4.7), as being about sexual consummation: "Thus far you have remained with me, you have manfully fought the good fight with me, but you have not yet received the prize." Dronke suggested that this was an unconsummated relationship, very different from that which Abelard describes in the *Historia calamitatum*. Wolff similarly judged the love letters as characterized by "absence of sensual allusion."[15] Such hypotheses are fragile. The differences between the two sets of letters can better be explained in terms of the contrast between the way a relationship is seen by lovers and the way it might be remembered by a couple reflecting on a past affair.

The reluctance of scholars to engage in the issues raised by the exchange is certainly related to an ongoing controversy about the authenticity of the Abelard–Heloise letters, particularly intense in the late 1970s and early 1980s. If this famous exchange has generated so much debate, what hope is there of resolving such issues in relation to a much less well-known exchange? Within a short paragraph about these letters, Jean Charles Payen has confidently asserted that they form "an epistolary novel from the period, perhaps written by a disciple of Abelard." Another scholar has claimed in passing that the exchange is a literary collection giving an artificial sense of temporal development, "like Elizabethan sonnets." In neither case was any argument offered to substantiate the claim put forward.[16]

The problem is particularly acute in relation to women's writing. If one cannot be sure that a woman wrote the letters of Heloise, how can one make any comment about the extent of women's writing in the Middle Ages? Heloise is not mentioned in some important repertories of medieval authors, except under the rubric "Peter Abelard."[17] Even if her authorship of the famous letters is recognized, she tends to be subsumed within discussions of Abelard. Georges Duby is only one of a number of scholars who have thought that the letters of Heloise were probably written by a man. He argued that twelfth-century writing about love was essentially a male invention by which young men sought to escape the constraints of feudal society. His views are related to a larger debate about the literature of *fin'amor*, or so-called courtly love.[18] The suggestion that medieval texts attributed to women may have been written by men is often driven by assumptions that medieval women could not exercise their own voice. Peter Dronke has played an important role in arguing that between the second and the twelfth centuries there is a continuous tradition of women writing in Latin. A common feature of this tradition, he argues, is that they demonstrate an immediacy not found in their more erudite male contemporaries.[19] Debate about the interpretation of the letters of Heloise touches on the larger issue of women's involvement in literary culture in twelfth-century France. In recent years there has been growing awareness of the extent of female literacy in medieval culture, as well as of the way women are presented as objects of admiration.[20] The letters copied by Johannes de Vepria can contribute significantly to these discussions.

The *Historia calamitatum* provides such a detailed narrative of Abelard's affair with Heloise that it is often assumed that their early relationship was an explicitly carnal affair, at odds with the spiritual direction of their later lives. Do the letters copied by Johannes de Vepria at the abbey of Clairvaux enable us to reconsider that relationship, or are they simply an imagined fiction, conceived in the silence of the cloister? How do they relate to the flowering of interest in love in the twelfth century? What are secular love letters doing in a monastic library? Before addressing these questions, we need to examine the trustworthiness of the monk who copied this exchange, the gatekeeper through whom these letters survive. He was himself someone who saw no difficulty in crossing between secular and religious literature.

Johannes de Vepria (ca. 1445–ca. 1518)

Little is known about Johannes de Vepria other than that he took monastic vows at an early age at Châtillon, transferred to Clairvaux sometime before 1471, and was its prior between 1480 and 1499. He died sometime between 1517 and 1519.[21] In 1471/72 Johannes de Vepria compiled for abbot Pierre de Virey (1471–96) the first major catalogue of the library of Clairvaux, a task that required him to explore the vast collection of manuscripts preserved at the abbey.[22] It had been decided in 1459 that all abbots of the Order of Cîteaux should see to the cataloguing of books and papers in their communities.[23] Like Pierre de Virey, Johannes de Vepria was a lover of books. His transcription of the love letters was part of a wider process whereby monastic communities in the late fifteenth century rediscovered the literary treasures which they owned. Johannes de Butrio (d. 1522), a fellow monk of Clairvaux and a doctor of theology in Paris, remembered him in 1511 as a Latinist of great sophistication who devoted himself to the study of secular as well as religious texts. He recalled that Johannes de Vepria was generous in passing manuscripts to others to be printed, a detail that might explain why the manuscript from which he copied the love letters has not survived at Clairvaux.[24]

The only non-epistolary text that Johannes de Vepria included in his anthology was Cicero's *De Officiis,* placed after extracts from the *Variae* of Cassiodorus. He then attached excerpts from the correspondence of less well known early Christian authors (Sidonius Apollinaris, Ennodius, and Cyprian) and anthologies on the art of letter writing by Transmundus, a papal notary (d. 1216), and John of Limoges (d. ca. 1250), both monks of Clairvaux.[25] These he followed by excerpts from the *Epistolae familiares* of a Louvain humanist, Carolus Virulus (ca. 1413–93), extended with his own comments on particular words and phrases from a range of authors, ancient and modern.[26] On a separate gathering he copied out extracts from the *Gesta Regum Anglorum* of William of Malmesbury (d. 1143) and two letters of William to David of Scotland and the Empress Matilda, found otherwise only in a twelfth-century manuscript of Clairvaux.[27] He transcribed the love letters on a single gathering (fols. 159r–167v), leaving its last leaf (fol. 168r) blank. On its reverse side he copied out five other letters relating to complaints about the condition of the Cistercian Order and of the Church.[28] Könsgen established that Johannes de Vepria copied many of these items from manuscripts belonging to Clairvaux. He probably came across them while compiling the inventory of 1471/72.[29] Only his transcription is recorded in the catalogues of Clairvaux, not the original manuscript from which he copied the love letters.[30] He copied out these letters because he wanted to remember a dialogue that impressed him for its literary merit and interest.

The workbooks kept by Johannes de Vepria reveal him to be a discerning student of both classical and medieval literature. A comment he appends to Gerson's *On the Consolation of Theology* provides us with a rare insight into his thinking. Inspired by Petrarch's explanation that the figure of Monicus in his first Bucolic Eclogue refers to his brother Gerard, Johannes comments that the word *monachus* should be spelled *monicus* as meaning one who flies: "A *monicus* is a meditative and inquisitive intellect."[31] The breadth of his literary interests is amply illustrated by an anthology that he completed in 1475. It contains Latin poems by Petrarch and later Italian humanists as well as by ancient authors, including Ovid's *Sappho to Phaon* and the *Art of Loving*.[32] Johannes de Vepria supplied Josse Badius Ascensius (1461/62–1535), the Parisian printer of both religious and classical texts, with manuscripts of Pierre Bersuire's *Ovid Moralized* and Jean de Hauville's *Architrenius*. This latter verse epic, a masterpiece of twelfth-century satire, relates the pilgrimage of a young man initiated into the pleasures of Venus and of Gluttony, who advances through the schools of Paris to arrive at Ambition and Presumption before Lady Nature gives him a wife, Moderation.[33] In 1482 Johannes de Vepria transcribed another Latin epic about amorous adventure that he found at Clairvaux, *On the Deeds of Knights,* composed in the mid-thirteenth century by Hugh of Mâcon. This epic was unknown to scholars until Könsgen edited both this work and a medieval commentary on it.[34] The only publications attributed to Johannes de Vepria are a collection of French proverbs, published in 1495, and a translation into French of the divine office for the use of Cistercian nuns.[35]

Johannes de Vepria was an admirer of Aeneas Sylvius Piccolomini (1405–64), the humanist scholar who became Pope Pius II in 1458. He transcribed Aeneas' treatise on educating the young in 1474.[36] There is no evidence, however, that Johannes was familiar with *Eurialus and Lucretia,* an epistolary novel about two lovers that Aeneas Sylvius composed in 1444.[37] Johannes de Vepria was a humanist scholar rather than a creative writer. His only comments on the love letters are a scribbled *diffinicio* added alongside a philosophical definition of love in letter *24,* and a *Nota* added to a comment in letter *75* about loving wisely. The bulk of his annotations reflect a desire to establish correct Latin syntax. By studying Johannes de Vepria's transcriptions of known Clairvaux manuscripts, Könsgen established that he was an accurate philologist who took great care to indicate whenever he was abbreviating a text that he had come across with the sign // (reproduced in Könsgen's edition and the translation attached to this study as .....).[38] It is most unlikely that he composed these love letters as a literary exercise.

By copying out rare and unusual texts, Johannes de Vepria was able to distance himself from a raft of problems then besetting the Cistercian Order. His interest in writing about love between man and woman stands in sharp contrast to the frequent complaints issued by the general chapter about the worldliness of Cistercian monks and nuns, "caught up in pollution of the flesh." A ruling of 1461 decreed that an abbot or abbess found guilty in this way had to face a year in confinement, a monk or nun, six months. Abbots were urged to raise educational standards in the Order by sending two young monks to Paris each year to study at the Collège Saint-Bernard, and to take care that they did not fall victim to sexual temptation. We do not know for certain whether Johannes de Vepria was one of those young monks sent to Paris in order to improve educational standards within the Order. After arriving at the age of sixteen or seventeen, a monk might spend six years studying the liberal arts and then another three studying theology.[39] In 1476, Jean de Cirey (d. 1503) became the new abbot of Cîteaux and launched a campaign against what he perceived to be laxity in the Order. Besides centralizing finances, he issued stern warnings about the tendency for young monks studying in Paris to be led astray from their manner of life and insisted that they study only at the Cistercian College there.[40] In 1488 Johannes de Vepria's abbot, Pierre de Virey (abbot of Clairvaux 1471–1496; d. 1504), was condemned by Jean de Cirey for seeking the arbitration of the Parlement of Paris (the body entrusted with governing the University of Paris) in the dispute between Clairvaux and Cîteaux. Jean de Cirey succeeded in imposing strict reforms on the College Saint-Bernard in 1493, suppressing what he considered as dissolute behavior among its students. Pierre de Virey resigned as abbot of Clairvaux in 1496. Johannes de Vepria resigned as prior three years later. Both monks of Clairvaux defended a humanist tradition within the Cistercian Order, under attack in the late fifteenth century from centralizing reformers like Jean de Cirey. The humanism of monks like Johannes de Vepria has tended to be overshadowed by more prominent critics of the religious orders like François Rabelais (ca. 1494–1553), himself a former monk. Johannes de Vepria did not see a contradiction between his interests in secular Latin writing about love and in religious literature.

Letter Collections and Epistolary Fiction

In many ways, it is impossible to separate literature and history in the study of medieval epistolography.[41] Letter writing was a craft learned by imitation of different kinds of literary models. The poetic letter could also be a literary device for developing ideas about love. These love letters draw extensively on the writing of Ovid (43 B.C.E.–17/18 C.E.). In his *Art of Loving*, Ovid instructed both men and women about the letters and verses they should craft. Ovid also composed the *Heroides*, fictive poetic letters from a variety of mythological heroines to their absent lovers.[42] In letter 45, the woman proclaims that her love for him was greater than that of various lovers described by Ovid, Biblis for Cauno, the nymph Oenone for Paris, or Briseis, a captive concubine, for Achilles.[43]

Although the principles of the art of letter writing were not theorized systematically until the late eleventh and early twelfth centuries, the art of learning how to write letters was a traditional skill. It was learned by studying and imitating letters written in the past.[44] Letter collections provided not just models of literary style, but guidance about the various kinds of relationships that could exist between people, from the most formal to the most intimate. Most surviving letters preserved within manuals from the twelfth and thirteenth centuries offer guidance about how students or clerics should communicate either with each other or with their superiors.[45] By the second half of the twelfth century, sample love letters are beginning to surface in anthologies serving as models of epistolary composition.[46] A twelfth-century anthology from northern Italy, for example, contains alongside examples of letters by famous people, a brief exchange between a young man and the girl whom he is wooing. Begging for the opportunity to talk to her, the young man refers to the judgment of Tiresias, as told by Ovid, that women obtained more pleasure in love than men, to express regret that she had not yet allowed her lips to be joined with his. She replies that she is not opposed to further conversation.[47] Whether or not this is an imaginary exchange, the fact that it is offered as a guide for epistolary composition is significant. Perhaps the most original example of such a treatise is the *Rota Veneris* (*Wheel of Venus*) of Boncompagno da Signa (ca. 1165–ca. 1240).[48] It offered guidance as to how men and women should communicate with each other, as well as reflection on the rules of love. Over the centuries, collections of letters came to provide a basis for fictional writing.[49]

The popularity of letters as literature inevitably raises the question of their authenticity. From the early nineteenth century, positivist scholarship has sought to distinguish historical from literary elements not just within the canon of Christian scripture, but within other key texts of the Western canon. The question is particularly acute in relation to Heloise, perceived so often as selfless in her love for Abelard, that questions have been raised about whether she really composed the letters attributed to her. Similar questions can be raised about the letters copied by Johannes de Vepria. As they do not refer to identifiable events, they cannot be authenticated by conventional means. His transcription offers a record of two contrasting voices, both of which seem at first sight to be very different from the conventional voices one expects to encounter in a monastic library. In a sense this exchange offers a multiplicity of voices such as one might find in a novel. Johannes de Vepria, however, was a scholar rather than a creative writer. His transcription articulates not just the literary interests of a fifteenth-century monk, but the concerns of a twelfth-century teacher and student.[50] Attempts to relate love literature to social context are inevitably controversial. Paul Veyne has argued that Roman love poetry is a record of male fantasy, not of actual relationships between men and women. Duby makes a similar claim about writing about love in the twelfth century.[51] In the nineteenth century, Jules Michelet argued that phenomena like the writings of Heloise, Robert of Arbrissel's foundation of Fontevrault, and the rise of courtly love literature all manifested a new prominence accorded women in the twelfth century. This interpretation implied that cultural change was a result of men changing their attitudes toward women. Feminist critics have often argued that eulogies of ideal women may conceal a tendency to reduce them to passive objects. They point out that the literature of "courtly love" developed at the same time as patriarchal authority asserted itself with new vigor both in feudal society and in the Church.[52] In the light of such criticisms, is it possible to make any claims about educated women in twelfth-century France?

The Process of Writing Letters

It has been claimed that no private letters from the medieval period exist "in the modern sense of the term."[53] Yet a degree of privacy was secured by affixing a seal to a wax tablet or parchment letter. This helped authenticate a confidential message.[54] In 1120 Abelard was using a seal showing two heads, which Roscelin of Compiègne construed as that of a man and a woman.[55] The letters copied by Johannes de Vepria seem originally to have been written on wax tablets, fixed with a seal, and then carried by a male messenger (mentioned in 37). In letter 14 the man says that he would write much more if he could hold on to her tablets. It was normal practice for the person sending a message on a wax tablet to keep a record on parchment of that message, to which she or he would add the message received in reply. The tablet was then ready to be used again for a separate message. In the case of the love letters, the exchange seems to have been kept by the woman, from whom the opening greeting comes. The fact that Johannes de Vepria was not always able to distinguish one letter from another suggests that he was copying from a continuous record of a correspondence, in which there was not always a clear break between one letter and the next. The transcription of another intimate exchange, rather less sophisticated than the love letters copied by Johannes de Vepria, is preserved in an early twelfth-century manuscript from Regensburg. It also seems to be the record of an exchange originally conducted on wax tablets, either by the teacher or by the female student with whom he was engaged in dialogue.[56]

Wax tablets provided essentially the same medium of communication between men and women as was customary in the ancient world.[57] Parchment was simply too expensive and slow to prepare for quick communication. Baudri of Bourgueil (1046–1130) describes how he would enclose his wax tablets in an embroidered bag, which were sometimes sent as letters, and then wait for them to be returned in order to write something else. He would have a good copy made of the text he had inscribed on the tablets.[58] Every medieval student was in possession of wax tablets with which to record lectures and send messages to his teacher. A thirteenth-century manual advises a student always to keep such tablets (generally two tablets on a hinge) by his side, so that if he was for any reason not in his teacher's presence, "he can carefully inscribe what he feels to be revealed to his conscience and to ask for clarification of what is uncertain."[59] The brevity of letters 1–21 may have been influenced by the limited size of their tablets. Longer letters, like 22–25 and 49–50, may have needed additional tablets. A transcript of messages conducted in this way represents a record of a relationship, perhaps edited or improved for posterity.

At a very basic level, these love letters function as a device by which the two parties develop their skills in the art of composition (*ars dictaminis*). This was more than the art of simply writing well. It is about communicating matters of substance with style and grace. It would have been normal for Heloise to have used such tablets for her study with Abelard. This most intimate form of communication between teacher and student only survives when the student preserves a copy of the dialogue. Our knowledge of medieval correspondence, as indeed of school literature in general, derives only from edited copies of dialogues otherwise lost from the record. In their way, the love letters are as much an exercise in the art of composition as a genuine communication of ideas.

Although Johannes de Vepria entitled his transcription *Ex epistolis duorum amantium*, the lovers describe what they send each other as *litterae*, a term that embraces poems (as in 69) as well as letters, rather than the more formal *epistolae*.[60] Some are simply short messages of greeting, others metrical poems without a formal salutation. They do not necessarily adhere to the prescriptions of theorists about the constituent parts of the standard letter, as is not uncommon in letters from the early twelfth century.[61] They serve to stand in place of the sender (6). Unlike *Eurialus and Lucretia*, they do not tell a continuous story. They do not always address each other directly and sometimes seem to respond to spoken conversations. The only way to evaluate Könsgen's argument that the transcription is a record of letters exchanged between two distinct individuals is to examine their content. While they are not arranged according to any formal structure, certain distinct phases can be observed in the relationship.

The Formulae of Greeting (Letters 1–21)

Johannes de Vepria was not interested in matters of historical substance or practical information. His initial concern was simply with the elaborate greetings in these letters, very different from the sober Ciceronian style advocated by Petrarch. This epistolary technique is a characteristic feature of letters in the age of Abelard and Heloise. In an important study of greetings in medieval letters, Carol Lanham has shown how the practice of replacing the greeting (*salutem*) with more personal and elaborate expressions developed in the eleventh and twelfth centuries. These more elaborate phrases served to define a more intimate form of relationship.[62] Ivo of Chartres, St. Anselm, and St. Bernard all experiment with the device when writing to women, although never with the intimacy of the greetings in these love letters. In this exchange, they single out the other person as unlike any other. In the first letter that Johannes de Vepria copies, the woman preserves the formal structure of a polite greeting (To X, Y: *salutem*), but describes herself as "She who is his in heart and body" (*sua corde et corpore*). She draws on imagery from the Song of Songs (4.10), "Your breasts are more beautiful than wine and the scent of your perfumes beyond every spice," to transform the standard greeting into half-rhyming phrases of unusual originality. She offers him "the freshness (*viriditatem*) of eternal happiness."[63] In return, he replies (2) by emphasizing the comfort she gives his mind:

> Singulari gaudio, et lassate mentis unico solamini, ille cuius vita sine te mors est: quid amplius quam seipsum quantum corpore et anima valet.

> To the singular joy and only consolation of a weary mind, that person whose life without you is death: what more than himself, in as much as he is strong in body and soul.

His greeting assumes that he is active, while she represents peace and tranquility.

The letters do not all address each other directly. Rather they offer ever more elaborate greetings from one lover to the other. For the first seventeen letters or so, they strive to outdo each other in the originality of their greetings. In many of these letters (3, 5, 7, 9, 21, 25, 27) she does not identify herself at all in her greeting, whereas her teacher tends more often to follow standard epistolary format. Frequently he addresses her as his "lady" (*domina*) to whom he is bound (*6, 8, 36, 61, 72, 87, 108*). The most important issue that they write about is the "love" (*amor*) and "joy" (*gaudium*) they share. She in particular is interested in defining the nature of their relationship. He tends more to express his feelings for her than to analyze them, except when she prompts him to do so. As early as letter 9, she speaks of her desire that their true "friendship" (*amicitia*) be strengthened, a term he does not use until *12*. By contrast, he speaks in letter *6* of his being driven "by the burning flame of love," imagery diffused by Ovid in the *Amores* and *Art of Loving*. He often describes her as a source of eternal light and develops sometimes elaborate astronomical imagery to present her as his star (*4, 6, 20*), his moon (*91*), and his sun (*22, 33, 80, 108*). She comes to share in this rhetoric, addressing him as her star (76) and as both her light and solstice (92) and moon (94). Each is led on by the other's light.[64]

From letter *14* on, Johannes de Vepria starts to transcribe much more of the substance of the correspondence. He does not indicate any omissions in *14, 15, 16, 17,* 18, *19,* 20. In 18, she adopts a daringly original tone that she does not often repeat. Instead of employing the polite convention of an inferior writing to a superior, she opens with a formula that deliberately challenges any idea of her inferiority: "An equal to an equal, to a reddening rose under the spotless whiteness of lilies: whatever a lover gives to a lover." Although she had twice addressed him as her love, this is the first time she speaks of her breast burning with the ardor of love (*amor*). This prompts him to reply that he has read her words many times. He then sends her his first metrical poem (*19–20*). She reverts to this bold formula of parity in 48, "a lover to a lover: the freshness of love," in which she also says that she has been kindled by the fire of love. She addresses him similarly in 62 as "a beloved to a beloved" and in 100 as "Faithful to faithful: The knot of an intact love never untied." He never reverses the order of a polite greeting like this. Only in 112, the last major communication preserved from the woman, does she change to a traditional greeting devoid of any particular intimacy.

The Discussion of Love and Friendship (Letters 22–53)

The first letter that Johannes de Vepria transcribes at length is letter *22*, in which the man replies to the woman's (not wholly successful) attempt in

21 to employ philosophical terminology in her greeti
by the way she transcends words by the richness of
words he directs to others are not as important as the
to her. She responds with an equally lengthy letter (2
ticulates an inner conflict within herself between the b
spirit (*animus*), and the dryness of her talent (*ingenium*).
provoked by some criticism that her teacher had made of her letter 21.[65]
Where Gregory uses the image of a boat, she uses that of *linter* about to
cross a stormy ocean. Isidore describes *linter* as a skiff or shallow boat used
to cross the marshes of the river Po.[66] In reply (*24*), he marvels at the richness of her letter, which he claims offers proof of overflowing faith and
love, according to the saying of scripture (Luke 6.45; Matthew 12.34):
"The mouth speaks from the abundance of the heart." This is not an epistolary novel in which each letter responds to the one before. He mentions
in letter *24* that she often asked him about the nature of love (*quid amor
sit*). Her letters are preoccupied with defining their relationship. He bases
his answer not on the Ovidian texts that he had previously used to protest
his affection, but on Cicero, whose definition of friendship as a union of
selves he applies to *amor*. Letter *24* provides a rare moment when he moves
beyond articulating his passionate desire for her to thinking philosophically
about the nature of love. His discussion enables us to see him as a philosopher as well as a lover. Where Cicero had spoken of love creating an identity of minds, he specifies that love makes two wills the same "without
difference" (*indifferenter*). They cannot be essentially the same as they are
two individuals, but they are not different. His elaboration upon the wording of the *De amicitia* betrays a distinct philosophical position on an important issue in dialectic. While following the Ciceronian theme that
friendship brings about union, he rephrases Cicero's definition to explain
that two individuals bound by love are not different (as distinct from being
essentially the same). He argues that *amor* is a "universal thing" that exists
only among themselves. The teacher's argument that love makes two souls
the same "without difference" recalls that which Peter Abelard early in his
career forced William of Champeaux to concede in a public debate and
which Abelard adopted in his early writing on dialectic.[67]

In reply (25), she launches into her own reflections on love, drawing on
both scriptural themes and Ciceronian ideas to explain her conviction that
"true love" (*verus amor*) had not yet been reached. Love that quickly disappeared was not true love. While he had employed dialectic to interpret Cicero's definition, she relates *amor* to *dilectio*, which she understands not as a
synonym for *caritas*, as common in Christian tradition, but as a special form

ove. *Dilectio,* used in the Latin Vulgate translation of the Song of Songs
nd St. John's Gospel (13.34–17.26), evokes a more deliberate idea of conscious esteem and choice than *amor,* love from inclination or passion. Augustine considered *amor* to be a carnal form of *dilectio,* a purer form of love.[68]
Cicero considered that it was a natural tendency for all creatures to bind with
one another and that friendship was a particular form of this natural state.
The woman on the other hand is influenced by a Christian sense that *caritas* needs to be displayed to all; where Cicero had related *caritas* to special
friendship, she prefers the term *dilectio* to denote a special form of the general category of *caritas.* She sees herself as his *amica,* a friend in both the classical sense and his beloved, as used in the Song of Songs (1.8, 2.2, etc.). This
is a different perception of *amor* from the capricious affairs of the heart about
whose vicissitudes Ovid had written with such biting wit. It is also subtly
different from the Ciceronian ideal of friendship that her teacher had invoked to define *amor.* In her perception there did not yet exist the true identity that he has claimed did exist "without difference" between them. Her
love is one of longing. She is moved by the songs of the birds and the greenness (*viriditas*)of the woods. Above all, her desire is for stability and loyalty.

The contrast between their perspectives is vividly apparent in his reply
(*26*) to her letter. Unlike her, he does not connect *amor* to *dilectio* and never
mentions *caritas.* Instead he begs her to reveal herself more fully, praising
her body as "full of moisture" (an allusion to the classical idea that the feminine body was always more moist than that of the male). He identifies her
love for him not as *dilectio,* but as "all your love" (*amor tuus totus*). She replies
with a cryptic note (27), offering him "The spirit of Bezalel, the strength
of three locks of hair, the beauty of the father of peace, and the depth of
Ididia."Whereas he yearns for physical union, she urges that he absorb the
qualities of great men in scripture, referring to Samson, Absalom, and
Solomon by coded allusion.[69]

Difficulties become apparent in their relationship after letter *28.* He
complains about jealousy creating problems for them. After he experiences
some illness, she expresses joy at his recovery in a letter that talks of snow
melting and a springtime thaw (32). In *33* he urges that they begin a new
eagerness for literary composition (*33: novus dictandi fervor sumendus*). By
letter *34,* she is advising him that careful delay is better than incautious
haste of the mind. The first sign of a major rift occurs after letter *35,* when
he says rather enigmatically that she has not sinned. He then addresses her
(*36*) in the formal *vos* rather than the intimate *tu.* His letter *37* concludes:
"Ask the messenger what I did after I wrote this letter: there and then I
threw myself onto the bed out of impatience."

After a group of messages (*35–44*) to which she does not reply, apart from a few verses (38b), and after some illness on his part, she offers a long letter (45) in which she gives thanks to God that he is well. Her comparing herself in this letter to heroines portrayed by Ovid is of great importance, as the *Heroides* circulated in a relatively restricted literary circle in the early twelfth century.[70] As if showing off her classical learning, she alludes to the pleasure she hopes to offer him by referring to the lovers in Terence's play *The Self-Torturer* (*Heautontimorumenos*): "I send you as many joys as Antiphila had when she welcomed back Clinia. Do not delay in coming; the quicker you come, the more quickly you will find cause for joy."

Letter 49 is far longer than any of the previous letters. She develops further her ideas about the nature of love and asks him to engage in a fuller discussion of the subject. She insists that her relationship to him is based not just on *amor*, but on a firm friendship founded on uprightness, virtue, and *dilectio*. This was a love that did not consider pleasures or riches or any self-concern. She sees their *dilectio* as not like that which bound people who loved each other for the sake of things and had no permanence. Her thoughts are inspired by Cicero's ideals of true friendship, transposed onto the level of love between a man and a woman, but also fused with the vocabulary of scripture. The literary polish that she applies to this letter, her extravagant praise for his greatness, coupled with her protestations about her own lack of ability, serve to build up to a more important complaint, that his letters were not satisfying her completely, that they were not long enough. This is the first letter in which she addresses him as a great teacher, a device to get him to respond to her with intellectual seriousness. It succeeds in winning a reply in which he addresses her as "the only student of philosophy among all the young women of our age." There is an element of truth in his exclamation that she had not just read Cicero, but given Cicero instruction about the laws of friendship. For the first time in his letters, he refers to their love as *dilectio*, but does not continue the discussion that she had initiated. In letter 53, on the other hand, she stretches language to the limit to express what she feels in her spirit, "if a droplet of knowability trickled down to me from the honeycomb of wisdom," she still could not find words "throughout all Latinity" to express the intent of her spirit, as she loves him with a special love.

Crisis and Resolution (Letters 54–98)

References to "the consuming envy of evil men" (*edax malorum hominum invidia*) preventing them from coming together as they wished begin to surface in letter *54*, although they were alluded to in *28*. He suggests that it would be better to communicate in writing. She refers to malicious gossip and enforced separation in letter 57, possibly written after a lapse of time. Some issue must have arisen by letter 58, as she uses the formal plural (*Valete*) rather than the intimate singular (*Vale*) for the first time. When he explains in letter *59* that he is guilty of some sin, she protests that there is nothing to forgive. This provokes great distress on her part (60). This is the first major crisis in their relationship. He has not returned her devotion to him. Unlike her teacher (*35, 59, 61*), she never uses the verb "to sin" (*peccare*) or "sin" (*peccatum*) and speaks of "sinners" (*peccatores*) only once, when reciting a liturgical blessing of forgiveness at the end of letter 60. His mention of sin and blame in *59* and *61* suggests that he is not fully at ease with his own behavior. At one level, he invites her to reveal herself fully (as in *38a*), while at another he accuses himself of committing a sin.

In letter 60 the woman brings the crisis in their relationship to a head. Her unusual greeting to him, difficult to translate, suggests that she was frustrated with the nature of their relationship: "To one till now faithfully adored, hereafter not to be loved with the chain of an infirm passion: the firm guarantee nonetheless of love and faith." She opens a letter of great importance by combining allusion in her greeting to three different degrees of love. She then reflects on her ideals about love, invoking her preferred notions of *caritas* and *dilectio* in a scriptural context: "I had revealed myself to you with a great pledge of loving care, while your true love was founded on a firm root; for I had placed all my hope in you, as though you were an invincible tower." Her image picks up the vocabulary of Ps. 60.4: "Because you have become my hope, a tower of strength in the face of the enemy."[71] She insists that she had never been duplicitous to him. She cannot describe how strongly, how quickly "I began to love you" (*te cepi diligere*). She did not want the "bond" (*foedus,* another word he never uses) between them to be broken again. She had hoped for many good things, but only tearful sighs of the heart had arisen. At the end of her letter, she recites an ecclesiastical blessing from the liturgy of Good Friday and then asks for all written communication between them to cease (*propterea omnis nostra amodo pereat scriptura*).

His response is to send a tearful letter (*61*) in which he speaks again of his having sinned. He initially insists that he does not blame her, saying only that everything was his fault. He then accuses her of adding further to his wounds: "If you loved me, you would have said less" (*Si me amares, minus locuta fuisses*). As if to add insult to injury, he goes on to argue that she has sinned more against him than he against her and that she was being cold to him. These are harsh words, very different in character from anything the woman might say. He closes the letter by exclaiming that he sends it "with tears."

Johannes de Vepria unfortunately omits two passages from the letter that she sends in reply. She fears that he risks incurring danger for himself, while she faces scandal. She simply wants to see him. From this point on in the exchange, she begins to express herself in metrical verse. Her first long poem (66) follows her plea that they cease from mutual recrimination against each other (62), an appeal to the Muses to serve the great master. She composes two further poems (69 and 73) before her most emotionally powerful composition (82) about the purity of her love, in which she voices her fears about the future. Her sense is that grief and mourning will follow their love, which will end up burning to death as on a funeral pyre. She creates the image of a tragic heroine of Roman antiquity, not unlike that of Dido as Aeneas leaves her or perhaps of Cornelia at the cremation of Pompey.[72] There is a steady intensity to her affection, idealistic and ultimately self-denying, very different from his enthusiasm and mood swings. He apologizes for overhasty words by explaining himself in letter 74 with the terminology of dialectic. He had spoken words that meant nothing and carried no weight. What mattered were not his words, but his deeds (*facta*), a frequent theme in his writing (*12, 22, 74, 75, 105*).[73]

He subsequently (*75*) becomes very concerned about their public reputation (*fama*): "But we shall be able to love wisely, because we shall shrewdly look out for our reputation while mixing our joys with the greatest delight!" In her reply (76) she has decided that they should stop exchanging harsh words with each other. Growing fear of external opinion drives him in letter *101* to say: "If you care to note, I am now speaking to you more cautiously, and approaching you more cautiously; shame tempers love, modesty checks love, lest it rush out in its immensity. This way we can fulfil our sweet desires and gradually stifle the rumor (*famam*) that has arisen about us."

She never expresses concern about their public image. Rather, she constantly affirms the constancy and purity of her love for him, as in letter 84, in which she employs scriptural imagery to say that he had stayed with her, manfully fought the good fight, but had not yet received his reward. She promises to reward him for a prologue he had written with "the obedience of love" (*cum amoris servitute*). He protests that behind the weakness in himself of which he is aware, his love is sincere (*85*). It is never clear how long a period of time might have passed between messages. In a long poetic reflection (87), the man reflects on the year that has passed. He regrets those words which had provoked tears. In letter 90 she is still protesting her love but reflects more openly on the troubles she is enduring. He too (93) is aware that love (amor) and shame (pudor) are pulling them in opposite directions. Their emotional distress is provoked by the conflicting demands of public image and private passion. Although he starts to define his relationship to her more consistently as dilectio in these last letters (85, 96, 101, 103, 105), there is still a sharp contrast in how they view their relationship. He speaks of himself as conquered by amor; she speaks of their amor as based on dilectio firma. Whereas his dominant image of love is that of a passion by which he is overtaken, her preferred image is that of a true and lasting friendship (98).

The Breakdown of a Relationship (Letters 94–113)

The final letters (94–113) bring to the surface tensions already evident midway in the exchange. She takes particular exception to his remarks about being pulled in two ways, by love and shame. She accuses him of not sharing her ethic of total, committed love and throws at him the gibe that "you throw words to the winds" (Verba das ventis, from Ovid's Amores 1.6.42). He is not worthy to be a friend if he throws such stones (94). His words come too easily. In letter 95 she is even more harsh, describing him as a tottering ship without anchor. With limpid conciseness, she expresses how "suspended in hope, I barely kept hoping: "Pendula expectacione vix expectavi." He defends himself by claiming that he is still the same person. She never doubts the constancy of love for him (102), but cannot hide the sorrow in her heart (104).

Something serious must have happened to prompt letter 106, in which the man says that he is "paying the price for stupidity" and that he has not been able to keep "that good thing" which he ought. The woman is similarly distraught, but develops a totally new idea in letter 107 in the form of advice given to her by a wise woman (an image adapted from the opening of Boethius' Consolation of Philosophy), that beauty and noble family were as nothing without the grace of the Holy Spirit. The man alludes to her physical absence in a poem (108) composed in her honor. While he is happy to see her again, her reply (109), wishing him to be clothed in virtue, wisdom, good behavior, and "adornment of style," is more measured in tone. She then answers his professions of continuing devotion (110, 111).

Her last major letter (112) is the only one in the exchange in which she addresses him as her teacher rather than as her beloved. The shift in tenor of the greeting, so important in defining the relationship that a letter writer seeks to establish with someone, suggests a subtle shift in the way she interprets her relationship toward him. He is no longer simply her beloved, as in previous letters: "To her most noble and most learned teacher: well-being in Him who is both salvation and blessing." Unfortunately, Johannes de Vepria's unusually limited transcription of letter 112 makes it also one of the most enigmatic in the exchange. Why does she address him as her teacher? The meaning of her first complete sentence is itself far from clear, and has been corrected by the editor to read: "If you are well and moving among worldly concerns without trouble, I am carried away by the greatest exultation of mind."[74] Does she mean that she is carried away by great joy if he is faring well, or is she contrasting his situation of going about daily business without problem with her own mental exultation? The first alternative seems less likely, given that the rest of the letter as transcribed by Johannes de Vepria explores the inexpressible joy that she feels.

Unfortunately so many omissions are indicated in his transcription of this letter that it never becomes clear what is the cause of the joy she speaks about. In the second and third sentences she explains that in the past she has been carried away by his letters and lifted to the third heaven (2 Cor. 12.2) "through a certain agility of mind" (quadam agilitate mentis).[75] She seems to be deliberately contrasting this intellectual delight in the past with her present exultation. She seems to be happy not just because he is well. Crucial sentences are missing which may well have explained more fully the rejoicing she now feels. Ever faithful to his practice of indicating whenever he is abbreviating his text, Johannes de Vepria picks out just two separate sentences from the passage that follows: "nourished at the hearth of philosophy, you have drunk at the fountain of poetry" and "To thirst for God and to cling to him alone is necessary for every living creature." The first comment belongs to a passage in praise of her teacher as immensely gifted in both philosophy and poetry. She speaks about the pleasure his letters had given her in the past. Johannes de Vepria then resumes his transcription with her comment on the glorious future she sees for him: "I already see the mountaintops bowing down before you," a future that she is sure will be fulfilled by divine providence. Again she speaks about him in terms of his public career. By mountaintops she may be alluding to the greatest teachers of her day who will in time recognize his genius. She contrasts this with her own situation, one of a great joy that she cannot put into words. Her language is again veiled in a literary image: "Secure and not ungrateful, I am reaching the haven of your love." In letter 78, the man had used the image of being secure, "coming to port" and "sitting in port" after he had received a letter which he interpreted as implying that the difficulties in their relationship were over.[76] Religious texts frequently speak of the soul reaching the *portum salutis,* "the haven of salvation." She uses the image of "coming to port" to refer to a new stage of happiness, that she cannot describe in any words, greater than any pleasure that his letters had brought her in the past. Is the woman here referring to her joy at conceiving a child?

The sentences that Johannes de Vepria omits from letter 112 make it impossible to know whether the woman explained her meaning more fully in the rest of her letter. His transcription of this letter is most unusual in that it does not provide the customary farewell. Johannes follows it with a marginal annotation *Ex alia,* "from another [letter]," to introduce the line *Ubi est amor et dilectio, ibi semper fervet exercicium* (Where there is desire and love, there always rages effort). Her parody of the great Maundy Thursday hymn *Ubi caritas et amor, deus ibi est* (Where charity and love are, there God abides) captures precisely the tension evident throughout the correspondence, between the Ovidian idea of *amor,* the man's favorite term for his feelings for her, and *dilectio,* the term for love enjoined by scripture. She finds it an effort to marry the two understandings of love. She then adds a note (112a) which has none of the exultation of the previous missive: "I am already tired, I cannot reply to you, because you are accepting sweet things as burdensome, and because of this you sadden my spirit. Farewell." These sweet things (*dulcia*) seem to refer to the source of exultation about which she speaks in the previous letter (112).

The final item in the exchange (*113*) is a lament from the man, explaining that he has been tricked by love (*amor*). He begs for forgiveness. "Love urges me to enlist in its service, to respect its laws." He confesses that he has been obsessed with her and still longs to embrace her, but he is afraid of popular gossip. To distance himself from these feelings he explains that he has been dazzled by her beauty and demeanor, which make her "outstanding in our city" (*Urbe te nostre conspicuam faciunt*). He does not pick up the woman's message about the demands of true love. Instead he retreats to the mock heroic language of Ovid's *Amores* about being driven on by love without an act of free will on his part. The military metaphor employed by Ovid in jest is seen by him to be peculiarly appropriate to his situation. He has been conquered by love, a victim of what he judges to be fascination for what is ultimately superficial. He thinks of love more as a game of the heart than the woman, who is more interested in combining the passionate aspect of *amor* with the high seriousness of *dilectio*. Her desire to fuse the ideas of Ovid, Cicero, and scripture about love is not something which her teacher readily grasps.

The vicissitudes in the relationship presented in this exchange follow an inner logic, crystallized in the final letters. While his understanding of his relationship to the young woman is shaped by Ovid, she is developing a much more refined idea of her relationship to him as based on an ideal of selfless love. Her idea of *amor* is that it is founded on true *dilectio* for him. He is concerned for his own reputation. At times, she sees his caution as a sign of lack of sincerity. The relationship threatens to come apart by letter 60. Her ideals of love were not satisfied by his often confused claims of ardent feeling for her. Her final note in the exchange (112a) suggests that she does not wish to speak to him further because he considered burdensome something sweet which had given her cause of great joy. His response is to consider that he had been tricked by *amor* into falling in love with a seductive beauty that was ultimately based on superficial attraction. He never rises to her sense that love is an ideal which embraces both *amor* and *dilectio*.

The Location and Authorship of the Letters

The city to which the teacher refers in his final poem (*113*) is never explicitly identified. One valuable clue about the place where this teacher is prominent occurs in her description of him in letter 49 as so famous that he is able to subdue "French pigheadedness" (*francigena cervicositas*) and "the haughtiness of the whole world" (*tocius mundi superciliositas*). While Könsgen thought the relationship could have unfolded anywhere between the Île-de-France and the region around Clairvaux, Clairvaux in the twelfth century was in Champagne, not *Francia,* a relatively small landlocked region stretching from north of Paris to south of Orléans, roughly equivalent to the modern Île-de-France.[77] The technical sophistication of the man's letters in the vocabulary of dialectic, coupled with the allusions to him confronting the arrogance of the whole world, suggests that the action takes place in the schools of Paris, preeminent in dialectic in the early twelfth century. The other city in the Île-de-France where the study of Ovid was strong was Orléans, but there was no tradition here of expertise in dialectic.

The contrast between the prose style and vocabulary of the man's letters and those of the woman make it difficult to believe that these letters

are all written by a single person. Two distinct identities emerge in this correspondence: a famous teacher with a command of dialectic, who is also a
poet, and an articulate young woman, very familiar with classical literature
and unusually gifted in the study of philosophy. She is particularly interested in ethical issues, above all, the nature and demands of love. Könsgen's
observation that these letters are about *amor carnalis* rather than *amor spiri-
tualis* does not distinguish sufficiently between the contrasting attitudes toward love of the man and the woman. She develops the more original
synthesis between ideas of Ovidian *amor,* Ciceronian *amicitia,* and scriptural
dilectio. By contrast his vision of *amor* is that of passionate love, not refined
by some higher ideal. He sees love more as an escape from a professional
career. The letters document the disintegration of a relationship, as well as
unfulfilled potential on the part of the young woman.

The absence of any overarching argument in these letters makes it difficult to consider this exchange as a work of fiction. As Könsgen argued,
the differences in prose style and vocabulary between the letters of the
man and the woman are simply too great to make this a likely possibility.
There are too many letters which do not respond directly to each other,
but refer to conversations outside the literary dialogue. This does not
mean, however, that an editorial process has not taken place. One of the
two parties, more likely the woman, seems to have kept a running record
of an exchange originally conducted on wax tablets. Johannes de Vepria
came across such a continuous transcription, endeavoring to identify the
two parties as "Man" and "Woman." Johannes de Vepria was interested
above all in the stylistic merit of these letters, and so did not transcribe
them in their entirety. His transcriptions of known Clairvaux manuscripts
leave us in no doubt, however, that he was an accurate scribe, who always
noted whenever he was omitting a passage.

As Könsgen observed, the figures presented in these love letters are very
like Abelard and Heloise. Far more parallels can be adduced than he mentioned in his edition. The duration of the correspondence, perhaps over a
year, matches what we know about the affair of Abelard and Heloise. There
is no doubt, however, that it presents the relationship between a teacher
and his female student rather differently from the way Abelard presents his
affair with Heloise in the *Historia calamitatum.* Before we can examine the
authorship of these love letters, we need to look closely at the more famous letters attributed to Abelard and Heloise, discovered in the thirteenth
century by Jean de Meun and the subject of much debate over the centuries. How do these love letters compare to other discussions about love
and human relationships in the early twelfth century?

These love letters offer a remarkable insight into twelfth-century reflection on love. While they are rich in imaginative expression, they seem at first sight to be plagued by a lack of precise context. The obvious question that arises concerns their authorship. Are these the lost love letters of Abelard and Heloise? Any discussion of the love letters must come to terms with the better known correspondence of Abelard and Heloise, exchanged some fifteen or so years after the end of their physical relationship. Is Abelard's account of his liaison with Heloise fundamentally at odds with the record presented in these love letters? The debate that surrounds the famous exchange between Heloise and Abelard has great significance for how we are to interpret the letters copied by Johannes de Vepria at Clairvaux.

CHAPTER 2

MEMORIES OF AN AFFAIR

> She herself was not ashamed to write in her letters to her beloved, whom
> she loved so well that she called him father and lord, strange words that
> many people would think absurd. It is written in her letters, if you examine
> the chapters carefully, that even after she became abbess she sent an explicit
> letter to him saying "If the emperor of Rome, to whom all men should be
> subject, deigned to marry me and make me mistress of the world, I call God
> to witness that I would rather," she said, "be called your whore than be
> crowned empress." But, by my soul, I do not think that there has ever been
> such a woman since; and I believe that her erudition enabled her better to
> conquer and subdue her nature and its feminine ways. If Peter had believed
> her, he would never have married her.[1]

In this passage of *The Romance of the Rose,* an allegorical epic about the
nature of love, Jean de Meun (d. 1305) introduces his readers to an exchange of letters between Abelard and Heloise, very different from that discovered two centuries later by Johannes de Vepria at Clairvaux. Jean de
Meun was particularly interested in Heloise's declaration of love for Abelard
in a letter that follows the *Historia calamitatum,* addressed to an anonymous
friend. He picks out from Heloise's letter a sentence which he reads as articulating the selflessness of her love for Abelard, that she would rather be
called his prostitute (*meretrix*) than empress (*imperatrix*) of Caesar. He subsequently translated these letters (although not the Rule) into French.[2]

Jean de Meun discovered the Abelard–Heloise letters sometime before
1278. He was not a monk like Johannes de Vepria, but a secular cleric committed to creating a literature in the French language from the wealth of
examples and literary devices familiar to him from Latin tradition. Little is
known about his life other than that he was born at Meung-sur-Loire, became an archdeacon of the diocese of Orléans, but also owned a house in

Paris. Apart from the letters of Abelard and Heloise, he translated into French *On Spiritual Friendship* by Aelred of Rievaulx, Vegetius's *On Chivalry,* Gerald of Wales's *The Marvels of Ireland* and Boethius's *Consolation of Philosophy.*[3] Jean de Meun was most remembered, however, for *The Romance of the Rose,* a poem that transformed twelfth-century celebration of *joi* and *fin'amor* into a didactic synthesis of epic proportions.[4] By including Abelard and Heloise within his poem, he ensured that they were remembered as mythic lovers existing beyond the constraints of human existence rather than as figures of history.

Any attempt to understand the love letters copied by Johannes de Vepria must come to terms with the debates surrounding the more famous monastic correspondence of Abelard and Heloise discovered by Jean de Meun. Over the last two centuries, great controversy has been provoked by the suggestion that these letters are themselves a literary fiction, composed either by Abelard or by a third party. With such a long history of debate over these letters, how can we establish the authorship of an anonymous collection of love letters? Such debates about the authenticity of the Abelard–Heloise letters deserve attention for what such arguments reveal about the way the figure of Heloise is interpreted. At issue is not so much the authenticity of the text as the authenticity of the image being presented. Jean de Meun created a powerful myth of Heloise by presenting her as the object of a lover's pursuit, even before copies began to circulate of the Latin text of the letters. He effectively turned the correspondence into a great work of fiction.[5] Jean de Meun's idealization of Heloise is not unlike that by which the man in the love letters elevates his beloved into a fictional creature, the embodiment of dazzling light. In this perspective, the same relationship can be seen at different times both as an expression of *amor* and as one of carnal lust.

Ever since the thirteenth century, our perception of Abelard's love affair with Heloise has been filtered through the lens of the *Historia calamitatum* and the associated exchange with Heloise, as well as through a set of assumptions about the love which Heloise professes for Abelard as profoundly at odds with the monastic environment in which she lives. This assumed contrast between an image of Heloise as a patron saint of worldly love and her public reputation for piety and religion (lauded by Peter the Venerable) has been used to argue that a medieval abbess like Heloise could not have written the letters attributed to her. Even those who accept the authenticity of her letters have often viewed the first two letters as outpourings of the heart, at odds with the monastic concerns of her third letter. Yet the exchange between Heloise and Abelard can also be interpreted as serving a moral purpose, as an account of how worldly love has to be subservient to spiritual love. Not the least intriguing aspect of the way in which Abelard and Heloise have been remembered through the centuries is the way in which Heloise's professions of love for Abelard have been assumed to assert "worldly" love at odds with "spiritual" love. This distinction is dangerous. Before comparing Heloise's love letters with those copied by Johannes de Vepria, we need to understand the extent to which Heloise has been mythologized over the centuries, and why doubts have been raised about whether she wrote the letters attributed to her.

Abelard's Report of the Affair

The opening document in the exchange which Jean de Meun had discovered was the *Historia calamitatum,* more correctly titled a letter of consolation to a (male) friend. Abelard subsequently addresses this friend as "dearly beloved brother in Christ, most intimate companion from the religious life."[6] Whether or not this friend is a real person, Abelard addresses him by the personal *tu* rather than the more formal *vos* such as he employs in less intimate correspondence, such as to Bernard of Clairvaux.[7] Abelard's professed intention is to relate how the consoling power of the Holy Spirit had enabled him to survive many difficulties and turn from a life of arrogance and debauchery to one devoted to the will of God. Abelard implies that the friend to whom he addresses the *Historia calamitatum* was personally familiar with the great financial reward and reputation he gained as a teacher in Paris, as well as the fact that his love songs were still being sung "by those who enjoyed that sort of life." This friend serves as a literary device to whom he can address his story. Abelard imagines his reader as fundamentally sympathetic to the presentation of his life as a moral example. He shapes events to fit in with his theme of how a successful, but morally profligate teacher turned to a life lived for God. Even though he does not accept Augustinian beliefs about original sin, Abelard still accepts the traditional assumption, inherited from classical antiquity, that the truly philosophical life transcends carnal sexuality. He is not interested in the complex political situation in France, which had so much shaped his career. His principal concern is to dispel the many rumors still circulating about both his religious orthodoxy and his affair with Heloise. While he recognizes that he had been guilty in the past of both debauchery and pride, he insists that many of the accusations being made about him are quite false. Writing that treatise provided a way of making sense of the past and of instructing others (perhaps including Heloise) about how they ought to remember the past.

Still the most widely remembered aspect of his career is his affair with Heloise. Impossible to render easily in English is the distinction Abelard draws in the *Historia calamitatum* between the way Fulbert loved (*diligebat*) his niece and his own desire to win her love (*in amorem mihi copulare*) by capitalizing on her love (*diligere*) of letters. Abelard presents the affair as beginning with an act of deliberate seduction for which he alone was responsible:

> There was in the city of Paris a certain young woman by the name of Heloise, niece of a canon called Fulbert. Just as he loved her, so he devoted himself assiduously as far as he could to having her advance in the study of letters in general. Not undistinguished in appearance, she was outstanding in the abundance of her literary gift. This asset, namely knowledge of letters, made the girl all the more attractive and all the more famous in the kingdom, given that it is rather rare among women. So, considering everything that traditionally delights lovers, I thought it would be more agreeable to bind her to me in love. I believed I could do this very easily. I then enjoyed such a great reputation, youth and good looks, that I was not afraid of being rejected by any woman to whom I might offer my love.[8]

In translations of this passage, *adolescentula* is frequently rendered as "young girl" even though Abelard describes himself as an *adolescentulus* when he started to teach at Melun ca. 1102, at the age of twenty-three or so.[9] In medieval usage, the word refers not to "adolescent" in the modern sense, but to anyone between fifteen and twenty-eight. The claim that Heloise was aged between sixteen and eighteen at the time of her affair with Abelard does not rest on any firm evidence, but was first circulated in translations of the letters published in the late seventeenth century. Identifying Heloise as a teenager at the time of her affair reinforces a romantic image of her as a sacrificial lamb when she first fell in love with her teacher.[10] Many years later, Peter the Venerable recalled to Heloise that he had admired her literary gift before she became a nun at Argenteuil. He described her as even then a woman (*mulier*) who had already "transcended her sex" through her commitment to the study of secular literature and wisdom. These comments suggest that Heloise is more likely to have been of at least about the same age as Peter the Venerable (ca. 1094–1156) in 1116, in other words in her early twenties.[11] Abelard was then thirty-seven.

In the *Historia calamitatum*, Abelard describes his affair with Heloise as flawed from the outset. He refers only briefly to messages (*scriptis internuntiis*) that he exchanged with her. He devotes more attention to how they abandoned their books for sexual pleasure. He does not dwell on Heloise's desire to engage in literary exchange with himself.[12] He mentions that his lectures became stale as he was more inspired to compose love songs (*carmina amatoria*), still widely sung in many regions, "as you know, by those who delight in that sort of life."[13] Abelard relates the events which followed as the living out of Ovid's fable about the unrestrained passion (*amor*) of Mars and Venus. When Fulbert discovered their intimacy, they were forced to live apart. "Opportunity denied inflamed passion further (*negata sui copia amplius amorem accendebat*)." When she fell pregnant, Heloise wrote to him "in great exultation" (*cum summa exultatione*), asking what she should do. Abelard then sent her in disguise to Brittany to be looked after by his sister. Eventually, he acknowledged to Fulbert that he had been led astray by "the power of love" (*vim amoris*), and offered to marry her, in secret so as to avoid damage to his reputation (*fame detrimentum*). He reports a long speech of Heloise in which she raised pagan arguments against marriage provided in Jerome's *Against Jovinian* which he had earlier quoted in his *Christian Theology* (composed ca. 1122–26) to commend pagan wisdom on the subject.[14] Almost as an afterthought, he adds that she thought it "dearer for her and more honest to be called friend (*amica*) rather than wife, so that grace alone would keep me for her, not the constraining force of any chain of marriage."[15] He was more at ease reporting arguments from patristic authority than those based on the demands of love. He wanted to explain that Heloise knew that marriage was a foolish mistake, punished by harsh consequences, which eventually led to their entering the religious life. Abelard insists that she chose of her own free will to follow his desire that she take the veil. Presenting their affair as a classical tragedy, he reports that when Heloise took the veil from the bishop of Paris, she recited Cornelia's lament that she had brought about Pompey's fall (quoting from Lucan, *Pharsalia* 8.94).

Abelard perceives the male friend to whom he directs the *Historia calamitatum* as sympathetic to the idea that his relationship with Heloise was one of purely physical lust, which deserved to end the way it did. He presents himself as once an excessively arrogant young teacher, in order to reinforce the contrast he makes with his life as a monk. He insists that the punishment meted out to him by Heloise's uncle eventually is part of God's providential plan. He argues that like Origen, he was now freed by castration from the chains of physical desire. He sees the burning of his treatise of theology at Soissons in 1121 as a lesson in humility. Abelard plays up his vices in order to show how they are eventually overcome through divine providence. At the same time, he explains that much of the criticism that he has received is simply the result of jealousy (*livor, invidia*) of his past success, a trope much used by Jerome, Ovid, and other classical authors to protest their innocence against false calumny.[16]

His theme is that true consolation comes not from a woman, but from the Holy Spirit, the Paraclete or Comforter and the very goodness of God. It is in honor of the Holy Spirit that he dedicates the oratory or chapel which he built ca. 1122 on the banks of the Ardusson. He explains that Providence came to his aid again in 1129, when, two years after withdrawing to Brittany, an opportunity arose to re-establish the Paraclete under the direction of Heloise, who had been expelled with her nuns from Argenteuil by abbot Suger (1081–1151). Abelard justifies his decision to re-dedicate his oratory to the Paraclete rather than to the Holy Trinity at some length, and also defends the cause of male concern for the religious life of women. He asks his reader to turn to scripture and in particular to the letters of Jerome to gain comfort in times of adversity, so as to recognize the will of God. The thrust of his narrative is to emphasize that the consolation offered by divine providence is far beyond that offered by carnal pleasure.

Heloise's Memory of the Affair

The first letter that Heloise wrote after reading the *Historia calamitatum* communicates an intensity of passion very different from that of Abelard's narrative. She is wounded that Abelard should think to offer consolation to a male friend rather than to herself and the community of women he had established at the Paraclete.[17] Reminding him of the example of those holy Fathers who had written treatises for women, she expresses astonishment at his neglect of her since their entry into religious life. Whereas Abelard had downplayed the importance of the love songs and letters he had written in the past, she confronts him with the inconsistency between what he proclaimed then and what he was saying in the *Historia calamitatum*. The discrepancy between his declarations of love and his neglect of her after he became a monk provokes her to remind him that her love for him had been completely pure, not concerned with any personal gain or pleasure.

> God knows, I sought nothing in you except you yourself: simply you, not lusting for what was yours. I expected no bonds of marriage, no dowry of any kind, not any pleasures or wishes of my own, but I sought to fulfil yours, as you yourself know. And if the name of 'wife' seems more holy and more binding, the word 'friend' (*amica*) will always be sweeter to me, or, if you do

not object, of concubine or whore; so that, the more I might humble myself because of you, the more I might win your favor, and thus I would damage less the glory of your reputation. You did not completely forget this in the letter you sent to give comfort to a friend; there you did not disdain to present some of the arguments by which I tried to call you back from our marriage, with its doomed union, but you ignored many about how I preferred love to marriage, freedom to chains. I call God as my witness, that if Augustus, presiding over the whole world, saw fit to honor me with marriage and confirmed the whole world on me to possess for ever, it would seem dearer and more honorable for me to be called your prostitute (*meretrix*) than his empress (*imperatrix*).[18]

This passage is often construed as meaning that Heloise was offering Abelard sexual favors outside of marriage. This emphasis is compounded by a tendency to translate *amica* as "mistress" rather than as friend. Heloise's argument here is not that she wants to be a prostitute, but that unfettered friendship means more to her than any derogatory names that might be given to her. She recognizes that he was a great teacher in logic and in theology, but points out that his understanding of ethical arguments was wanting. Words must conform to inner intent. She accuses him of passing over her arguments against marriage based on the purity of love as an ideal. She closes this first letter by reminding him of the many letters that he had showered on her in the past and of the songs that had made her famous. He ought to communicate with her now much as he had during their affair. This is the only time Heloise refers directly to these letters of Abelard in the past; she never mentions any letters or poems she may have sent in reply. The comment she makes in this letter that he was most unusual as a philosopher in being able to compose songs about love as well as to pursue a philosophical vocation echoes the woman's observation in letter 112 of the anonymous exchange: "Already nourished at the hearth of philosophy, you have drunk from the fountain of poetry." Abelard's unusual ability to compose verse as well as to philosophize is also remembered in an epitaph on his tomb and in a poem by Hilary of Orléans.[19] Heloise does not see these two roles as incompatible, as Abelard had implied in the *Historia calamitatum*. As a philosopher, he had been fascinated by the distinction between words and what they signified. Heloise wants to know whether those love letters and songs that he sent her ever meant what they proclaimed. Her first letter recalls the lament of Penelope to Ulysses, as told by Ovid in the first of his *Heroides*. Penelope expresses her concern for the dangers Ulysses faces, but demands that he return, as her love for him has been so faithful. Heloise takes the voice of an Ovidian heroine in order to shape her own reflection on love.[20]

Abelard replies by urging her to forget the past and think of herself instead as a bride of Christ. His emphasis on respectful distance and correct religious devotion reflects his anxiety to distance himself from the image of a wayward teacher that he had acquired in the past. Heloise then sends him a second letter in which she again recalls the purity of her intention towards him, insisting that it had nothing to do with physical lust. She evokes, even more eloquently than before, her demand that Abelard communicate more fully with her than he had in the past. Whereas in her first letter she relies more on classical imagery, in her second she draws on scripture as well to make her point. She laments the hypocrisy of her situation, judged pious by the world, but racked by inner anguish as she cannot forget the pleasures they had enjoyed in the past, even during celebration of the Mass. She describes the reality of physical desire to disclose her human frailty, rather than to condemn it as sinful. Her letter provokes a fuller response from Abelard, in which he urges her to direct her devotion to Christ rather than to himself. Distancing himself from intimate dialogue with Heloise, he recalls past episodes of debauchery and deceit to present physical desire as something which should be left in the past. He reminds her of their physical indulgence in the refectory of Argenteuil during Holy Week, and his forcing her to have sex with him when she was unwilling. Abelard was not interested in talking about the love he had professed for her in the past except as selfish indulgence. "My love which entangled both of us in sins is to be called lust, not love (*concupiscentia, non amor*)."[21]

Heloise never mentions again those "incessant letters" which she says Abelard sent her during the time of their affair. In her third letter, she adopts a different tone. She opens by explaining why she had poured herself out in her two earlier letters by: "the mouth speaks from the abundance of the heart" (Luke 6.45; Matthew 12.34), the same scriptural phrase as the man uses in letter 24 in the love letters to observe how fully the woman would pour herself out in her letters. Heloise gets him to communicate with her and her community by putting forth two requests to which he does respond: that Abelard explain the origins of the religious life for women and that he supply a monastic Rule especially adapted for women. She is appalled by the hypocrisy of living according to rules which women are unable to observe. She observes many details in the Benedictine Rule which simply do not cater to women's needs. She insists that the essential virtue to be observed is moderation. Central to her analysis is the theme of self-knowledge. She is fully aware of the frailty of her body. Extravagant religious ideals are of little use if they do not relate to an individual's situation.

Abelard responds to her third letter by sending her a treatise on precedents for women's religious life in both scripture and classical antiquity, and a Rule for the Paraclete. These two treatises have never attracted the same attention as Heloise's first two letters. Yet they do show how Abelard was forced to think for the first time about the role of women in the religious life. Like Heloise, he emphasizes the primacy of intention in distinguishing between right and wrong behavior, as well as the important role that study should occupy in the lives of the nuns of the Paraclete. Abelard's argument at the end of the Rule that Heloise and her nuns should imitate the example of the holy women around Jerome is very similar to that expressed in his letter 9 "On the study of letters." This is a letter to the nuns of the Paraclete from the early 1130s, transmitted quite separately from the famous Abelard–Heloise correspondence. In a subsequent letter she writes to Abelard, introducing forty-two questions (*Problemata*) about scripture, Heloise expands on Abelard's advice in his Rule by comparing herself to the holy women who put so many questions about scripture to Jerome.

Twelfth-Century Perceptions of Abelard and Heloise

Most twelfth-century chroniclers who mention Peter Abelard do not talk about Heloise. Particularly influential was Geoffrey of Auxerre's account of St. Bernard's condemnation of Abelard's errors at the council of Sens, 25 May 1141.[22] Geoffrey (d. ca. 1188), who had heard Abelard lecture in Paris in January of that year, but had been converted to the Cistercian way of life by hearing Bernard preach, describes Abelard as an arrogant intellectual without ever mentioning Heloise.[23] As the secretary responsible for compiling one of the earliest collections of letters of St. Bernard, Geoffrey was able to shape public perception of his master as hostile to self-important intellectuals. By incorporating Pope Innocent's condemnation of Abelard's errors into his collection of St. Bernard's letters (but not the subsequent lifting of the sentence of excommunication), Geoffrey created the impression that Bernard had succeeded in securing Abelard's condemnation through his letters to various cardinals of the curia, as well as to the Pope himself.[24] Otto of Freising, a Cistercian writer not afraid to criticize Bernard of Clairvaux for his attack on Gilbert of Poitiers in 1148, similarly does not mention the pardon given to Abelard. He also never refers to the Paraclete and alludes to Heloise only indirectly, when he comments that "following certain circumstances well-known enough, he [Abelard], not well treated, became a monk at Saint-Denis."[25] While these words suggest a certain sympathy for Abelard's situation, Otto passes over the name of Heloise in discreet silence.

The information that St. Bernard and Abelard agreed to cease their attacks on each other through the efforts of the abbots of Cîteaux and Cluny to mediate a truce, was not widely known in the twelfth century except through a little circulated letter of Peter the Venerable to Innocent II.[26] The abbot of Cluny also mentions that he was successful in restoring Abelard to apostolic favor in a letter to Heloise, written after Abelard's death.[27] The only other twelfth-century chronicler to report this information is William Godel, an Englishman who spent much of his life as a monk in the diocese of Sens. Writing ten years or so after the death of Heloise (16 May 1164), he is one of the few contemporary historians to be completely uninfluenced by Geoffrey of Auxerre's version of events. Godel recalls Heloise's devotion to Abelard and supplies certain details either distorted or completely suppressed by other chroniclers. While acknowledging St. Bernard's influence as a preacher, he devotes more attention in his chronicle to affirming Abelard's fundamental orthodoxy and to praising the love of Heloise, Abelard's *vera amica,* for the man who had been her husband:

> At this time flourished Bernard, lord abbot of Clairvaux, a flower of the catholic Church in his time, who spread a great perfume of wisdom far and wide. For he was this to many people through the grace of God. There also flourished at this same time master Peter Abelard. Most subtle in genius, he wrote and taught many things. Indeed he was also criticized by some, in particular by the aforementioned abbot Bernard. For which reason he attended an assembled council, and firmly removed a number of things of which he had been accused, and brilliantly demonstrated that very many things claimed to have been written or said by him, were not held by him. Indeed, he eventually denied every heresy and confessed and maintained that he was a son of the catholic Church, and after this finished his life in fraternal peace. He also built a monastery which he called the Paraclete in the region of Troyes, in a certain meadow where he used to read alone, in which he gathered together a number of nuns by epistolary authority. He put in charge over these nuns his former wife, a religious woman, educated in both Hebrew and Latin letters, by the name of Heloise. This true friend of his preserved great loyalty towards him after his death with assiduous prayers. They now rest in this place most honorably in tombs by the holy altar.[28]

Godel's information about the location of the tombs may derive from a direct visit to the Paraclete. He certainly visited other women's religious communities, and saw Hildegard of Bingen (1098–1179) in person in 1172.[29] His reference to Abelard's foundation of the Paraclete from epistolary authority (*ex epistolari auctoritate*) is particularly valuable as it provides precious evidence of familiarity with the Abelard–Heloise epistolary corpus in the twelfth century. The information that Heloise was educated in Hebrew as well as Latin echoes the testimony of Abelard in a letter to the nuns of the Paraclete, that Heloise was competent in Latin, Greek, and Hebrew (a tribute conventionally accorded only to St. Jerome).[30] A few other monastic chroniclers in the twelfth century reproduce imperfectly elements of Godel's account, sometimes merging it with more widely circulated hostile reports about Abelard. Robert of Auxerre changes Godel's *epistolari* to *episcopali*, presumably because he could not understand or accept what Godel meant.[31]

The failure of most twelfth-century chroniclers to recognize Abelard's Rule for the Paraclete may reflect the influence of the II Lateran Council in 1139, which condemned women who called themselves nuns but did not live according to the Rule of either Benedict, Basil or Augustine, as leading lives of shameful depravity.[32] The way of life of the nuns of the Paraclete needed to be authorized by one of the recognized Fathers of the Church. Another ruling of 1139 explicitly prohibited nuns from singing psalms alongside canons or monks in the same choir.[33] For a monastic community to base its existence on "epistolary authority" was irregular to say the least. Heloise's request that Abelard compose a new monastic Rule, as distinct from a commentary on the Rule of Benedict ran counter to received ecclesiastical tradition. The *Institutiones nostrae*, found immediately after Abelard's Rule in the Troyes MS 802 and composed to codify observances at an early daughter house of the Paraclete, reveals that Abelard's Rule was not followed at that abbey as the normative guide for the religious life. Whereas Abelard imagined that the Paraclete could sustain a relatively affluent lifestyle, these observances suggest that life at the Paraclete was more austere than Abelard had envisaged.

Godel's emphasis on the devotion of Heloise to Abelard was also unusual in the light of growing reserve in the Church hierarchy in France towards interaction between men and women in the religious life. There had been a flowering of religious communities embracing both women and men in the first half of the twelfth century. Fontevrault in the Loire valley (founded by Robert of Arbrissel in 1101), Prémontré (founded by Norbert of Xanten in 1120), and Rhineland abbeys like St. Disibod, all accommodated both women and men in the first half of the twelfth century. Concerns about the dangers of proximity between men and women in religious life become more pronounced after the II Lateran Council in 1139. Sometime between 1124 and 1135, Bernard of Clairvaux warned Luke de Roucy, abbot of an early Premonstratensian community at Cuissy, near Soissons, about the risks presented by cohabitation between men and women in the religious life.[34] The nuns at Prémontré, who followed a way of life similar to the women at the Paraclete, moved to a more remote location ca. 1141. At Fontevrault, nuns came to occupy the nave, while monks remained in the choir.[35] By the 1170s, a time of marked reduction in number of new foundations for women, Godel's account of the interaction between Abelard and Heloise was unusual, to say the least.

A few chroniclers in the late twelfth century were familiar with Godel's image of Abelard and Heloise as bound by love and devotion. Sometime around 1200 the chronicler of Tours added a story that when Heloise was laid to rest, Abelard's arms rose from the grave to receive her.[36] Jean de Meun was not the first person to invent the image of Abelard and Heloise as noble lovers, but he did come to learn much more about their relationship than any earlier writer by reading their correspondence.

The Discovery of Abelard and Heloise
(Thirteenth–Sixteenth Centuries)

Heloise had no successor at the Paraclete as fluent in Latin letters as herself. Nothing is known about her library in the twelfth century or any of the books which she may have brought with her from Argenteuil.[37] Although the Paraclete prospered under her guidance, its nuns did not have the economic resources to maintain a large library or scriptorium. The oldest document surviving from the Paraclete is from the late thirteenth century, a translation into French of an Ordinal, giving guidance to the distinctive liturgical practices of the Paraclete. The fact that these instructions and information about burial sites and processions at the Paraclete are given in French suggests that Latin literacy declined among the nuns after the death of Heloise.

It seems likely that Heloise kept her exchange of letters with Abelard at the Paraclete. Our only manuscript of the correspondence to include the complete text of Abelard's Rule for the Paraclete (Troyes MS 802, from the late thirteenth or early fourteenth century) also contains specific observances for the Paraclete drawn up during the time of Heloise, as well as a range of other texts relating to the religious life for women.[38] In the other important early copy of the correspondence (Paris, BNF lat. 2923, from the late thirteenth century), the exchange of Abelard–Heloise letters, without the Rule, is followed by the *Apologeticus* of Berengar of Poitiers. This was a vitriolic attack by Abelard's loyal disciple on St. Bernard for his behavior at the council of Sens in 1141. The manuscript also contains various minor writings of both Berengar and Abelard, notably the *Soliloquium* (from the early 1120s), the *Confessio fidei Universis* (1141), and an otherwise unknown letter to bishop Girbert of Paris (ca. 1120). As Berengar cites a private letter of Abelard to Heloise within his *Apologeticus,* it is possible that Berengar was entrusted by Abelard with transmitting letters to the Paraclete, and subsequently assembled various writings by his master.[39]

In the absence of any twelfth-century manuscript of the famous Abelard–Heloise letters, it is difficult to untangle the early history of their text, but this is not an argument against their authenticity. Most extant copies of the correspondence emanate not from the Paraclete, but from the Parisian region. Robert de Bardi, a canon of Notre-Dame and chancellor of the Sorbonne, bought the Troyes MS 802 from the cathedral chapter in 1347. Petrarch obtained his copy of the correspondence (Paris, BNF lat. 2923) sometime between 1337 and 1343, perhaps from Robert de Bardi, who invited him to Paris in 1340.[40] In Petrarch's manuscript, the Abelard–Heloise exchange (without the Rule) and the Berengar–Abelard anthology are followed by letter collections of Cassiodorus, Stephen of Orléans (1128–1203, abbot of Sainte-Geneviève in 1176 and bishop of Tournai from 1192), and two thirteenth-century letter collections, many from Parisian students.[41]

Petrarch's fascination with Heloise is evident from the many comments that he appended to the margins of her letters in his manuscript. While living as a secular canon at Parma between 1344 and 1349, Petrarch used a flyleaf of his Abelard–Heloise manuscript to record a list of dates, each accompanied by an undeciphered code of dots and dashes, a record of his own struggle at this time with sexual desire.[42] His idealized image of Heloise, evident in marginal notes he made to his copy of the correspondence, has much in common with that of another secular cleric, Jean de Meun. After discovering Cicero's letters to Atticus in 1345, Petrarch cultivated rigorously classical notions of friendship with other male scholars, while writing love poetry in Italian. He singled Abelard out as a philosopher who loved solitude in his treatise *On the Solitary Life* (in which he also observed that there was no poison as destructive to the quiet life as the company of women).[43] Petrarch's fascination with ancient Rome led him to gloss over the extent to which the study of classical letters, vividly exemplified by Abelard and Heloise, had flourished in the twelfth century.

He was interested in the example of Abelard more as a man of learning than as a theologian.

The letters of Abelard and Heloise acquired a mythic status in France during the fourteenth and fifteenth centuries, not least because of the popularity of *The Romance of the Rose*.[44] Petrarch's claim that there were no great writers or poets outside Italy led Jean de Hesdin to remind him in 1369/70 of the example of Abelard.[45] Although Coluccio Salutati asked Jean de Montreuil (1354–1418) in 1395/96 for a copy of the letters of Abelard and Heloise, no manuscripts of the correspondence survive in Italian libraries.[46] Jean de Montreuil was part of an influential circle of humanists loyal to the French king, who defended Jean de Meun's reputation against the criticism of Christine de Pisan and Jean Gerson. Christine had accused Pierre Col, a canon of Notre-Dame, of stooping to the level of Heloise in preferring to be called a *meretrix* (prostitute) in his enthusiasm for Jean de Meun's poem.[47] Christine resented the way that Jean de Meun portrayed women as the focus of male sexual indulgence, effectively offering inspiration only to men. Although she quotes a Latin word used by Heloise, her negative response to Heloise suggests that she had not read much further than Jean de Meun's version of her letter in *The Romance of the Rose*.[48] She saw Heloise as a symbol of a debased form of love.

Abelard and Heloise were seen by educated Parisians in the fourteenth century as embodying values very different from those represented by Bernard of Clairvaux. Gontier Col, brother of Pierre Col and secretary to the king, transcribed Jean de Meun's translation of the correspondence, appending translations of Berengar's *Apologeticus,* Abelard's *Confession of Faith to Heloise,* and the letter Peter the Venerable sent to Heloise after Abelard's death.[49] Nicolas de Baye (ca. 1364–1419), a royal counselor active in the Parlement of Paris, owned an unusually large collection of Abelard's writings, including an unbound copy of the Rule for the Paraclete.[50] In 1396 Benedict XIII, an Avignon Pope in conflict with the Roman Pope Boniface IX, had offered a fifty-day indulgence for all who helped rebuild the Paraclete after its near total destruction wrought by war in the mid-fourteenth century.[51] Notre-Dame came to own a number of manuscripts of Abelard's writing.[52] In vernacular literature, Heloise was associated with the art of love. A fictional guide for lovers, modeled on the *De amore* of Andreas Capellanus, is entitled *Les epistres de l'abesse Heloys du Paraclit* in a manuscript from ca. 1500.[53] From a different angle, Jean Molinet offered the image of Heloise as a repentant sinner in his moralization of *The Romance of the Rose* (ca. 1483).[54]

The history of the Troyes MS 802 of the letters is complex, but reveals much about the way Abelard and Heloise were remembered in the later medieval period. Although it contains a set of texts seemingly put together at the Paraclete, the manuscript itself was bought by Robert de Bardi in 1347 from the cathedral chapter of Notre-Dame. This manuscript, identical in every respect to the *exemplar Paraclitense* obtained by François d'Amboise and André Duchesne from the abbess of the Paraclete, Marie III de La Rochefoucauld, prior to 1616, must have been given to the Paraclete sometime between 1347 and the late fifteenth century (perhaps as part of a program of reconstruction of the abbey).[55] Copied into the Troyes manuscript in a late fifteenth-century hand are various rubrics and epitaphs, as well as Peter the Venerable's formula of absolution of Abelard, all apparently preserved or engraved on the tomb in the twelfth century. These texts, including the formula of absolution, were also added in the late fifteenth century to an important liturgical manuscript of the Paraclete (Chaumont, Bibliothèque municipale 31). It seems no coincidence that these epitaphs were transcribed soon after the solemn opening of the tombs of Abelard and Heloise at the Paraclete on 2 May 1497. Their remains were then transferred from *le petit moustier* or "little monastery" (Abelard's original chapel) to the left and right hand side of the grill, separating the choir from the altar in a new abbey church constructed by Catherine II de Courcelles, abbess 1482–1513.[56] Two other copies of the correspondence containing abbreviated versions of the Rule were also produced in the late fifteenth century.[57] The attention given to Abelard and Heloise as monastic figures in these late fifteenth-century manuscripts reflects a culture of monastic humanism not unlike that which prompted Johannes de Vepria, not far distant at Clairvaux, to transcribe a collection of love letters. This interest in the monastic context of the correspondence was subtly different from the interest of Jean de Meun in Abelard and Heloise as noble lovers.

Between History and Literature
(Seventeenth–Eighteenth Centuries)

Abelard's writings had been included in the first edition of the *Index of Prohibited Books,* issued in 1559, even though they had not yet found their way into print. This made the publication in 1616 of the *Opera Omnia* of Abelard and Heloise an important and potentially controversial event.[58] André Duchesne's still invaluable commentary on the *Historia calamitatum* draws on a wide range of historical sources to provide a far more nuanced picture of Abelard as a theologian and Heloise as an abbess than suggested by Jean de Meun. The doctors of the Sorbonne had their censure of many specific statements made by Abelard (as well as a warning about Heloise's lack of penitence about her past) included in a reprinted version of the 1616 edition, in which an elaborate preface by d'Amboise replaced that of Duchesne.[59] At the Paraclete, no mention was made of Abelard and Heloise in a rigidly orthodox commentary on the Rule of Benedict written for the nuns of the Paraclete and published in 1632 with the approval of the bishop of Troyes. Their fall from honor at the Paraclete was made complete when their remains were transferred from the main church to a small crypt in 1626. The post-Tridentine attitude towards Abelard is exemplified in a study of Abelard's life and thought published by the Cistercian scholar, Juan Caramuel y Lobkowitz, in 1644. He presented Abelard as a heretic who came back to orthodoxy through the efforts of St. Bernard, but hardly mentioned Heloise at all.[60] Duchesne's critical effort to deepen historical awareness was blocked by enduring stereotypes of Abelard circulated by St. Bernard.

Enthusiasm for Heloise as the embodiment of tragic love was re-ignited in the mid-seventeenth century by the first translations of her letters into French to be made from the 1616 edition. In 1642, François de Grenaille included translations of the letters of Heloise within a manual of letters from various women, both fictive and genuine: mythical queens of antiquity, Mary Queen of Scots, and the sixteenth-century actress, Isabella Andreini, to many kinds of lover.[61] De Grenaille explains that he is presenting Heloise not as debauched, but as a "French Magdalen," a true penitent converted to the path of virtue.[62] By implication she was a sinner who converted. His exchange begins with a fictitious letter from Heloise to Abelard warning against marriage, followed by relatively free paraphrases of the first two letters of Heloise as published in 1616.[63] De Grenaille then introduces a letter, deliberately invented "to make Heloise as serious as she seems to be free in the other letters," as well as an imaginary missive introducing Abelard's Confession of Faith to Heloise.[64] He presents Heloise's voice within a framework that makes her respectable in the eyes of the Church. De Grenaille's translation may have stimulated the composition of the Lettres portugaises (Paris: Cl. Barbin, 1669), a collection of letters ostensibly from a Portuguese nun to her lover, in fact composed by Gabriel de Lavergne, vicomte de Guilleragues. In this reworking of the Heroides, a woman's voice was yet again taken over by a man.[65]

Heloise first became widely known as a tragic heroine through a novel attributed to Jacques Alluis, as much about Fulbert as Heloise, imagined as Fulbert's daughter and in her fourteenth year when she met Abelard.[66]

Roger de Rabutin (1618–93), once imprisoned in the Bastille for writing the *Histoire amoureuse des Gaules,* an exposé of morals at the court of Louis XIV, may have been inspired by Alluis' novel to make his own translation of the Abelard–Heloise correspondence in 1687 for Madame de Sévigné, not published until 1697. She admired the way de Rabutin gave *esprit* to Heloise.[67] A French translation of Heloise's first letter to Abelard was published in 1693, the first of a number of translations of the personal letters in the correspondence to gain a wide audience throughout the eighteenth century. It promulgated an influential picture of Heloise as victim of Abelard's passion:"Love is easily persuaded for a girl, especially at the age of eighteen years."[68] Strict censorship during the reign of Louis XIV (1643–1715), particularly severe after 1685, meant that these translations were perceived as subversive of religious life. Like the *Lettres portugaises* and the more explicitly erotic *Vénus dans le cloître,* the letters of Abelard and Heloise were often seized by the authorities.[69] Pierre Bayle praised Abelard's skeptical spirit in encyclopedia articles about both Abelard and Heloise as symbols of resistance to the establishment.[70] Their letters, often printed alongside the *Lettres portugaises,* provided a vehicle for communication between women and men within the salon culture of the late seventeenth century. Although a translation was presented as published "at the Paraclete" in 1696, the Abelard–Heloise letters were not officially allowed to be printed in Paris until 1714.[71] Heloise's letters had acquired canonical status as models of good style by early in the reign of Louis XV (1715–74). In 1724 Malherbe offered Rabutin's translations of the correspondence as the first of a series of models of exemplary prose, along with his comment that in her letters "it is not art, but nature which expresses itself."[72] The monastic context of the Abelard–Heloise exchange was all but forgotten, except at the Paraclete itself.

The 1693 translation inspired the first popular translation of Heloise's letter into English within an anonymous publication, *A Continuation of the Dialogue Between Two Young Ladies Concerning the Management of Husbands. Part the Second. Wherein is a most Passionate Letter Full of Wit and Affection, written by Eloisa (a Young French Lady,) to her Husband, Abelard, who was Emasculated by the Malice of her Uncle* (London, 1696). Its author described Heloise as of "about Sixteen Years, of a quick and sparkling Wit, and of a Beauty able to touch the most Insensible," and of exemplary wisdom in managing a difficult husband.[73] John Hughes translated a fuller version of the correspondence, based only loosely on Abelard's autobiographical narrative which had been renamed the Letter to Philinthus.[74] He inspired Alexander Pope (1688–1744), after translating Ovid's *Sappho to Phaon,* to compose *Eloisa to Abelard* in 1717, and send it to Lady Mary Wortley Montague (1689–1762), then travelling around Europe.[75] Pope's poem provoked an admirer, Judith Madan, née Cowper (1702–81) to compose *Abelard to Eloisa* in 1720, frequently printed alongside *Eloisa to Abelard* and Hughes's translation.[76] A French translation of Pope, originally published in Berlin in 1751, inspired a famous version by Colardeau, presented as published at the Paraclete in 1758.[77] Heloise became an emblem of enlightenment and the focus of literary admiration. Jean-Jacques Rousseau (1712–78) capitalized on this vogue when he published in 1761 *Julie, ou la Nouvelle Héloïse: Lettres de deux Amans.* He had Saint-Preux proclaim to Julie that "Heloise had a heart made for loving" while expressing revulsion for the dishonesty of Abelard.[78] Abelard's career exerted a particular fascination for enlightenment *philosophes,* often critics of clerical celibacy, even though many were not married themselves.[79] Whether in the twelfth, fifteenth, or eighteenth centuries, epistolary dialogue provided a vehicle through which men and women could discuss relationships. The idea that Heloise and Abelard had once exchanged love letters provided an ideal opportunity for writers to present their own version of what such a dialogue should have been like. These translations and paraphrases were read in a literary climate in which Ovid's *Heroides* were still much appreciated as expressions of feminine emotion. They drew on the classical imagery within Heloise's letters, even if they did not understand the monastic context in which they were written.

At the Paraclete, strict Tridentine orthodoxy gave way to enthusiastic devotion to both Abelard and Heloise. In 1701, Catherine III de La Rochefoucauld (abbess 1675–1706) had a memorial to them both erected in the choir, and re-established there a stone statue representing the Trinity, said to come from the time of Abelard.[80] In 1720 Dom Armand Gervaise, former abbot of La Trappe, published a study of the lives of Abelard and Heloise, drawing on a much wider range of texts than earlier accounts. Dedicating it to the new abbess of the Paraclete, Gervaise sought to guide the reader "firmly on the paths of Truth" rather than through the falsifications of contemporaries. Gervaise followed this in 1723 with the first publication to reproduce both the Latin text and a translation of the correspondence, supposedly based on "an old Latin manuscript found in the library of François d'Amboise." (In fact he used only the 1616 edition.)[81] Gervaise presented both Abelard and Heloise as models of Christian humanism and Peter the Venerable as the embodiment of Christian forgiveness. There was such enthusiasm for Abelard and Heloise as lovers at the Paraclete that in 1780 there was a solemn exposition of their remains in the main church.[82] Dom Charles Cajot, last chaplain of the Paraclete and a believer in the need for Benedictines to justify themselves as socially useful, studied the history of the Paraclete. When the abbey was dissolved in 1792, Dom Cajot took with him a number of its printed books (including an annotated copy of the 1616 edition of the works of Abelard and Heloise) to Verdun, where he helped establish its public library. The last remaining manuscripts of the abbey, mostly liturgical in nature, were dispersed among friends of the last abbess, Charlotte de Roucy.[83] While the policy of transferring medieval manuscripts from abbeys like Clairvaux to the municipal library of Troyes occurred without difficulty, the library of the Paraclete was dispersed before the commissioners arrived because of the degree of popular interest in its founders. The house in Paris where Abelard and Heloise were thought to have lived under one roof (first identified as such in 1787) became a place of pilgrimage, as did their new resting place at the cemetery of Père Lachaise in Paris after 1817, the only medieval figures to be accorded such an honor.[84] They were perceived as independently minded spirits, out of sorts with the culture of their time, but united by their love.

The Authenticity Debate
(Nineteenth–Twentieth Centuries)

Abelard, considered a hypocrite by Rousseau, began to be recognized as an important thinker in the early nineteenth century through the research of Victor Cousin into previously unread logical manuscripts of Abelard, transferred at the Revolution to the national library of France. Cousin showed that there was a firm foundation to the claims of the *Historia calamitatum* that Abelard was a great logician in his time. Cousin portrayed Abelard as an intellectual rebel, who laid the foundations of French intellectual tradition long before the more recent achievements of German philosophy.[85] He focused more on dialectic than on ethics, and did not study the writings of Heloise, who remained in nineteenth-century imagination the mythic embodiment of love. Charles de Rémusat spoke in elevated terms about the intensity of Heloise's passion and her outward submission to Abelard, but concentrated on his achievement in philosophy and (unlike Cousin) theology.[86] In their different ways, Cousin and de Rémusat were heirs to those fourteenth-century clerics so fascinated by Abelard. Nineteenth-century readers continued to see Heloise as the embodiment of tragic love, a classical heroine above the cut and thrust of academic debate. It was a fictional image which created its own problems.

The apparent inconsistency between her image as a "patron saint" of love and her reputation for piety and learning has led a number of critics in the nineteenth and twentieth centuries to question whether Heloise wrote the letters attributed to her in the manuscript tradition. Peter von Moos has provided a brilliant account of the ideological issues at stake in that debate.[87] In 1806 Ignaz Fessler, a Capuchin monk who turned protestant and became a professor at Berlin, suggested that a third party might have extended Abelard's *Historia calamitatum* with a fictional dialogue to communicate a traditional theme about the struggle between human love and the values of the cloister. Is the dialogue not like a novel? Did not Abelard's claim to have visited the Paraclete frequently after its re-foundation in 1129 contradict Heloise's claim that he had not offered her personal support, either in person or in letter?[88] Fessler's argument was picked up by Orelli, while Lalanne (editor of Rabutin's correspondence) argued that it was impossible for "compromising passion" to have co-existed with Heloise's reputation for piety and religion, but confusingly argued that original letters "of the heart" had been revised at a later date, by Heloise. Gréard accepted the possibility that the letters had been edited by a third party, but maintained that Heloise "gave them her soul."[89] Enthusiasts for the correspondence effectively created Heloise as an idealized figure, removed from history. This double standard is vividly illustrated by remarks of Henry Adams in 1904:

> With infinite regret, Héloïse must be left out of the story, because she was not a philosopher or a poet or an artist, but only a French woman to the last millimetre of her shadow. Even though one may suspect that her famous letters to Abélard are, for the most part, by no means above scepticism, she was, by French standards, worth at least a dozen Abélards, if only because she called Saint Bernard a false apostle.[90]

While he recognized Abelard to be an intellectual, Adams considered Heloise to be like Isolde, "uniting the ages," more myth than history.

Such attitudes have continued to shape twentieth-century scholarship. Bernhard Schmeidler developed the hypothesis once suggested in passing by Martin Deutsch in 1883 that Abelard composed the entire exchange.[91] Schmeidler's early studies stimulated Charlotte Charrier in the interwar period to devote a monumental study to the fabrication of the legend of Heloise. Following Schmeidler's lead, she identified various Latin phrases (*tanto/quanto, saltem, obsecro*) which occur in the letters of both parties to argue that Abelard had composed the entire correspondence.[92] This interpretation, which emphasizes a conflict between worldly and spiritual love in the correspondence, is often maintained by German scholars, notably Georg Misch, author of a major history of autobiography.[93] D. W. Robertson has espoused a similar interpretation of the letters as part of a wider argument that all medieval literature about *amor* is informed by a sense of irony, and subordinates worldly love to spiritual values. Acknowledging that Heloise and Abelard might have originally exchanged letters, he argued that the existing letter collection was designed for the nuns of the Paraclete as a record of spiritual conversion. He questioned the authenticity of Heloise's letters, doubting whether she could ever have adopted what he calls the "ludicrous" position on marriage attributed to her in the *Historia calamitatum:* "the 'character' Heloise, like the 'character' Abelard, serves as an extreme example, both in degradation and in the final triumph of reasonableness."[94]

Emphasis on the monastic structure of the correspondence also informed an ingenious hypothesis put forward by John Benton in 1972 that the entire correspondence had been invented in the late thirteenth century in relation to a disputed abbatial election at the Paraclete. He subsequently came to accept that Abelard did write the *Historia calamitatum,* but then reverted to Schmeidler's rather shaky argument that similarities in vocabulary and prose rhythm are evidence of a single author of the whole correspondence, namely Abelard.[95] Debate was muddied further by Hubert Silvestre, the only scholar to support Benton's first hypothesis. He suggested that the entire correspondence had been written by Jean de Meun or a colleague and then translated into French as part of a campaign against clerical celibacy.[96] The hypothesis, which reads Heloise's letters as about "free love" at odds with spiritual norms, stretches the linguistic evidence to an impossible degree. Such arguments do not explain the close verbal and thematic interconnections between the correspondence and other known writings of Abelard and Heloise. It has often been argued that the ideals of love touched on in Heloise's letters anticipate theories of pure love (*fin'amor*) in romance literature. Helen Laurie has argued that Chrétien de Troyes was familiar with the correspondence in the second half of the twelfth century.[97] Rather than assessing Heloise's declarations of love as "worldly" and thus incompatible with her situation as a respected abbess, it makes more sense to relate them to new thinking about love being developed by clerics such as Chrétien.

Debates about the authenticity of the correspondence have often degenerated into acrimonious polemic between "believers" and "non-believers." In lectures first delivered at the Collège de France in 1936–37

Étienne Gilson explored the correspondence as evidence of the medieval (and indeed specifically French) roots of values traditionally identified with the Italian renaissance. He considered the correspondence of Abelard and Heloise as a heroic monument to a dialogue between two systems of morality, both endowed with *grandeur*, the fundamentally pagan ethos of Heloise and the Christian ethos of Abelard. Ultimately his sympathy was with Abelard as a genuinely contrite soul.[98] He rebutted skepticism about the authenticity of the correspondence as an attack on texts which were "obviously" true. Peter Dronke has defended the view that Heloise did not repent of her love for Abelard, while also arguing forcefully for reading her letters as sophisticated works of literary art.[99] By contrast, Peter von Moos inherits a line of interpretation that goes back to Fessler, Deutsch, and Schmeidler in arguing that Heloise's silence at the beginning of her third letter about her past cannot be used as evidence of "the state of her soul." Von Moos urges that the correspondence be taken seriously as an *exemplum* of religious conversion.[100] Fascinated by the literature of consolation (of which he has written the definitive study), he reads the correspondence as Abelard might view it, as a rhetorical debate about spiritual ideals.[101] While his arguments offer important criticism of the idea that texts reveal psychological truth, they have been criticized for imposing too much ideological unity on an exchange between dissonant voices.[102] The weakness with both the "unrepentant Heloise" and the monastic *exemplum* hypotheses is that they both interpret the professions of love in Heloise's letters as at odds with spiritual ideals. Indirectly such readings reflect the influence not just of *The Romance of the Rose,* but of the *Historia calamitatum* and a masculine literary tradition which Abelard inherited. The letters can be interpreted as a monastic memorial to the founders of the Paraclete, but this avoids discussion of Abelard and Heloise as thinkers with distinct ideas about love, both of whom present their own lives as *exempla* to make their point.[103]

The mere existence of uncertainty about the authenticity of Heloise's letters has provoked some prominent medievalists to steer away from them. When Georges Duby declared that the correspondence presented a fictitious image of Heloise, he was continuing to read Heloise's letters as about "worldly" love, at odds with the monastic context of the correspondence. This dichotomy mirrors a common theme in historiographical perception of the twelfth century as a time of contest between a secular vision of society, exemplified by perception of Abelard as a kind of secular warrior, and an ecclesiastical model, as defined by Ivo of Chartres and other canonists. Duby is more interested in what knights and clerics have to say about women than in women's reactions to men.[104] Duby's influence underpins the opening statement of a recent essay on women in the eleventh and twelfth centuries: "Women almost never speak for themselves. Scholars are still not sure whether Heloise wrote the letters traditionally attributed to her."[105] This is not a position shared by most English speaking scholars writing on Abelard in the 1990s. David Luscombe in particular has emphasized the close relationship of the correspondence to a range of other historical sources relating to the Paraclete.[106]

The defense of Heloise has been taken up by many feminist scholars since the pioneering studies of Charlotte Charrier and Enid McLeod. Heloise is often seen as struggling against a male ideology. Barbara Newman has defended the authenticity of the letters of Heloise by identifying the absurd consequences that follow from reading Abelard as author of letters critical of himself. She reads Heloise as herself a victim of Abelard's own repressive tendencies, "a failed mystic," devoted to Abelard rather than to God.[107] Peggy Kamuf has looked at Heloise's letters as models of a process by which the narrative of the *Historia calamitatum* is deconstructed. Yet feminist readings of Heloise's letters can also repeat traditional images of an unrepentant heroine, trapped in a male monastic world, recasting a traditional religious/secular conflict as male/female ambivalence. Juanita Ruys has astutely observed that Kamuf's interpretation of Heloise (adopting outward signs of piety while remaining inwardly unrepentant) unconsciously echoes the position taken by Gilson.[108] A number of recent studies consider the artificial nature of any distinctions between public and private in relation to Heloise's letters and the strategies of persuasion and negotiation within the correspondence. Abelard provides a particularly fascinating example of the construction of a masculine identity after his castration.[109]

Heloise's third letter and Abelard's two long treatises about the monastic life have never attracted the same attention as her declarations of love. Yet her third letter provides a brilliantly probing critique of the limitations of the Rule of St. Benedict in dealing with the practicalities of the situation of women in the religious life. As Linda Georgianna has pointed out in an incisive analysis of that third letter, it documents her own search for authenticity within the religious life.[110] Even less well studied than this letter of Heloise is the collection of monastic observances (*Institutiones nostrae*) which follow Abelard's Rule in the Troyes MS 802, rarely included in translations of the correspondence. Chrysogonus Waddell has argued convincingly that this text draws extensively on monastic observances as practiced in Cistercian communities prior to

1147.[111] This finding complemented his earlier discovery that the liturgical manuscripts from the Paraclete lay down prayers and rituals very similar to those practiced in early Cistercian communities, although with the inclusion of certain hymns, sequences, and prayers devised by Abelard.[112] The research of Georgianna and Waddell offers a very different image of Heloise's relationship to monastic life from the romantic picture of a soul arguing with her beloved Abelard, that can be traced back to *The Romance of the Rose*.

Readers of the letters of Heloise have often interpreted them as at odds with the what is assumed to be the predominantly other-worldly focus of medieval culture. This leads to perception of Heloise as either a complete rebel against her society or as a mythic construction devised to contradict the dominant values of medieval culture. The 1988 film *Stealing Heaven*, for example, emphasizes the contrast between carnal and spiritual love rather than the subtlety of Heloise's thought.[113] From a different perspective, Richard Southern has rejected romantic interest in the figure of Heloise and has claimed that she shares the same monastic attitude towards sex as Abelard, "their age not having developed a plausible ethic for the secular life."[114] The difficulty with these interpretations of Abelard and Heloise is that they impose a single ideology on individuals who do not share a uniform concept of ethical behavior. Good poetic fiction about Heloise and Abelard can sometimes grasp these contrasts with more perspicacity than much scholarly writing.[115]

Questions of authenticity have tended to be directed more against the letters attributed to Heloise than those of Abelard. Yet the reliability of the *Historia calamitatum* is just as problematic. In trying to elicit sympathy for his teaching, Abelard presents his career as continually harassed by forces claiming to represent the cause of ecclesiastical reform. His desire to present himself as a teacher who has overcome vices of lust and intellectual arrogance distorts the way he describes his early relationship to Heloise. Framed within conventions of ascetic discourse, the *Historia calamitatum* alludes only in passing to the culture of secular clerics who delighted in amatory verse. Abelard dismisses his love songs as erotic trifles, the product of an inflated ego justly punished through the vengeance of Heloise's uncle. There is an internal repression at work in Abelard's narrative, not just of Heloise, as Barbara Newman has pointed out, but of his own sexuality, consistent with the ascetic milieu to which he belonged. In Heloise's letters, the love lyrics and intimate letters are accorded much more importance as expressions of a love which Heloise trusted and returned in kind. The *Historia calamitatum* seeks to quell the rumors still in circulation about his past by presenting a "true account" of the events leading up to his castration and the burning of his book of theology at the council of Soissons in 1121. She counters his explanation of their past relationship as based on lust alone by affirming that she based her actions on ideals of pure love.

One consequence of the often acrimonious debate of the 1970s and 1980s about the authenticity of the famous correspondence of Abelard and Heloise has been that the *Epistolae duorum amantium,* edited by Könsgen, have been largely neglected by scholars. Yet Könsgen has uncovered a major literary text from the twelfth century. It is part of a larger repertoire of secular Latin writing about love from the eleventh and early twelfth centuries, little known outside a small circle of specialists. Betty Radice, for example, made the confident assertion in a footnote to her translation of the *Historia calamitatum* that "not only do none of the love lyrics composed by Abelard survive, but no love-poems are known in north France from this time."[116] While no love poems in Old French can be securely dated to the early twelfth century, many Latin love poems survive from this period. The letters and poems copied by Johannes de Vepria belong to a wider corpus of exchanges in Latin between educated men and women, and deserve to be more widely known as part of the literature of dialogue.[117]

The *Historia calamitatum* is such a crafted narrative that it is tempting to rely on it as an "authentic" presentation of Abelard's life. Its careful shaping of Abelard's identity only becomes apparent when we consider this narrative and the associated correspondence both in relation to other texts from the twelfth century, and to the particular constellation of political forces at work in Paris in the early twelfth century. The love letters and poems copied by Johannes de Vepria at Clairvaux throw intimate insight into a world normally excluded from view. They create an imaginary space of intimacy and openness very different from that created by the more well-known letters of Abelard and Heloise. They are not concerned with the hurly-burly of political conflict, academic life, and ecclesiastical obligation. Nonetheless, they issue from the same social environment as that from which Abelard seeks to remove himself in the *Historia calamitatum.* In the latter narrative, Heloise is presented in a static form, as both the passive object of his early lust and a saintly abbess. The love letters present a woman much more actively engaged in an intellectual relationship with her teacher. The *Historia calamitatum* is certainly an authentic text of Abelard, but it does not provide an authentic record of his relationship with Heloise.

Conclusion

The exchange copied by Johannes de Vepria records a relationship between an eminent teacher and a brilliant student very similar to that of Abelard and Heloise, although from a different viewpoint. A young woman is dazzled by the attention given her by a famous teacher, and reflects much about the ethics of their relationship. She admires his gifts in both philosophy and poetry. He is someone before whom "French pigheadedness rightly yields," and before whom she predicts "the mountaintops will prostrate themselves." Occasional comments from the teacher suggest that he is worried about his public reputation. He thinks of his behavior more as driven by passion than as the focus of ethical commitment. The exchange concludes with his reflecting that he has been seduced by external charms of a woman "famous in the city." In the *Historia calamitatum*, a teacher similarly wants to affirm that he has now transcended the chains of lust. The woman he once loved challenges this picture, urging him to enter into a dialogue as intimate as that which they once enjoyed. Abelard's ethical schema in the *Historia calamitatum*, based on admiration for the example of ancient philosophers, is challenged by an ethical vision drawing on principles of selfless love.

At the same time as the schools of Paris were buzzing with rumors of scandal in the heart of the cathedral cloister, St. Bernard (1090–1153), freshly ordained by William of Champeaux (d. 1121), was establishing a idealistic monastic community in the woods around Clairvaux. In both places, the favorite topic of conversation was the nature of love, perceived with a new intensity as a force which bound together individuals far more closely than any institutional structure. William of Saint-Thierry (ca. 1075–1148) responded to the question "what is love?" with a treatise *On the Nature and Dignity of Love*, written ca. 1121–24, in which he explains that he is responding to the popularity of Ovid's reflections on the subject.[118] His theme is that *amor* is divine in origin, but embraces many kinds of love, including human love and the love of God. He does not talk at all about love between man and woman. Bernard of Clairvaux shared William's interest in the process of love, but gave more attention to the role of experience and feeling. He was fascinated by the psychology of love, as mediated by the Song of Songs. Bernard was a stronger orator than William. The abbot of Clairvaux could hold an audience spellbound with his reflection on the power of love, and the experience of being visited by the Word of God, the lover of the soul. He saw Cistercian communities as differentiating themselves from old established monastic institutions by their emphasis on authenticity and their rejection of empty conventions. The Cistercian ideal of community based itself on *caritas* rather than authority.[119] The irony was that both Bernard's admirers and his detractors insisted on portraying him as first of all a man of authority.

The letters copied by Johannes de Vepria might be concerned with relationships in a secular rather than a monastic sphere, but they share with the writings of Bernard of Clairvaux a common concern to base ethics on an ideal of true love. The woman in these love letters is concerned with the sincerity of her love, watched over by God. In these letters, she is not having to confront traditional ascetic teaching about sexual relationships. The questions that have been raised about the authenticity of Heloise's letters reflect doubts about whether Heloise could really have been so committed to worldly love while also being a respected abbess. This problem disappears if she is seen as sharing a common concern of her generation to establish a code of conduct not based on empty words. The close interconnections between their correspondence and their other writings leaves no doubt that Abelard and Heloise did write the correspondence attributed to them. Both in these monastic letters and in the love letters copied by Johannes de Vepria, it is the woman who is most interested in developing ethical reflections on the demands of love. Heloise's assertion that she would rather be called Abelard's prostitute than enjoy the wealth of Caesar Augustus puts in more dramatic terms an idea which the woman offers in letter 82, that if she possessed the riches of Caesar, such wealth should be as nothing to her. In both cases, a classical ideal about true friendship is applied to love.

While the historical record is dominated by the achievements of men, we need to consider Heloise not just as the object of a lover's attention, but as an active agent in her society. Tensions about gender surface in many different political and religious debates within twelfth-century France. Just as Duchesne enlarged awareness of Abelard and Heloise by investigating a wide range of historical sources beyond the *Historia calamitatum,* and as Cousin uncovered a previously unknown dimension of Abelard by reading hitherto neglected writings on logic, so it is necessary to relate their correspondence to wider discussions about relationships between men and women in twelfth-century France. The letters copied by Johannes de Vepria may not talk explicitly about political or social events, but they do present a sharp portrait of a woman intellectually independent from her teacher. To understand the situation in which a young woman could define herself in this way, we need to look more closely at the situation of the schools of Paris in the early twelfth century.

CHAPTER 3

PARIS, THE SCHOOLS,
AND THE POLITICS OF SEX

Paris, 1116.[1] On the eastern end of the island stands the cathedral of Notre-Dame, not the Gothic edifice that Maurice de Sully will construct fifty years later but a Merovingian building over five hundred years old. The front porch faces Saint-Étienne, the largest church in Gaul when it was built in the sixth century, now a broken ruin.[2] The canons are proud of being guardians of the cathedral, but they are aware that it needs rebuilding. They want to promote its school as a center of learning. There is a climate of optimism abroad, of many new ideas for the future. The precentor is Adam, a brilliant young poet and musician, whose compositions bring a new vitality to its liturgy.[3] The cloister of Notre-Dame, an area stretching from the north side of the cathedral down to the Seine, outside the jurisdiction of the bishop, is alive with activity.[4] Students lodge in the canons' houses, a practice that leads some to complain that the tranquillity of the cloister is being disturbed.[5]

In 1116 a new teacher is attracting students to the cathedral school from far outside France: from Brittany, Anjou, Poitou, Gascony, Spain, Normandy, Flanders, even Germany, Sweden, and Rome itself.[6] Peter Abelard's appointment there, probably in late 1113, was the responsibility of the chapter rather than the bishop. In particular he has the esteem of canon Fulbert, one of the three subdeacons at the cathedral since at least 1099, who lives in a house near the cathedral school.[7] Although a cleric, Abelard is not ordained to higher orders, and thus does not carry any major liturgical responsibilities. He is a canon, not at Notre-Dame, but at Sens, center of the archdiocese of which Paris is a part.[8] Such positions do not demand residence, but provide both income and status, to the outrage of those who detest such sinecures. Abelard is also making money by charging fees from his students, not a practice followed by teachers who were monks.[9]

A young woman is living in one of the canons' houses in the cathedral cloister. Heloise is from a privileged background, having been raised and educated at the abbey of Notre-Dame at Argenteuil, a richly endowed community on the banks of the Seine with strong connections to the crown.[10] Her mother, Hersende, is from a noble family.[11] Her father's identity is unknown.[12] It is not unusual for cathedral canons to have members of their family living with them. Some canons are married, like Durand, one of the three priests of the cathedral. He and his sons had apparently built a house outside the cloister, which was subsequently pulled down by Louis VI (1108–37). Louis compensated the cathedral chapter for this when he married Adelaide of Maurienne in March 1115, and formally acknowledged that the houses of the canons "inside and outside the cloister" were free from interference.[13] The cloister was a place of legal sanctuary theoretically independent from either the king or the bishop.[14] The independence of the cathedral canons is disliked by Galo, bishop of Paris (1104–1116) and William of Champeaux (d. 1120). In 1109, William had left the cloister in order to establish a stricter religious life not far away, at Saint-Victor. There, canons regular lead a communal life, observing precepts of chastity and austerity, without distraction from any women.

In 1116 Heloise already has a reputation for literary brilliance, but is keen to further her studies. Fulbert eventually agrees that Abelard should offer tuition to his niece, in return for lodging in his house. What then happened is reported by Roscelin of Compiègne in a letter written to Abelard no more than two or three years after the scandal broke. Roscelin had taught Abelard before he came to Paris. He is merciless in his account of what happened:

> I have seen indeed in Paris that a certain cleric called Fulbert welcomed you as a guest into his house, fed you as a close friend and member of the household, and also entrusted to you his niece, a very prudent young woman of outstanding disposition, for tuition. You, however, were not unmindful but contemptuous of that man, a noble and a cleric, a canon even of the church of Paris, your host and lord, who looked after you freely and honorably. Not sparing the virgin entrusted to you whom you should have protected as entrusted to you and taught as a disciple, whipped up by a spirit of unrestrained debauchery, you taught her not to argue but to fornicate. In one deed you are guilty of many crimes, namely of betrayal and fornication and a most foul destroyer of virginal modesty. But *God, the*

Lord of vengeance, the God of vengeance, has acted freely; he has deprived you
of that part by which you had sinned.[15]

Roscelin describes the relationship between Abelard and his student as one
of unbridled sexual indulgence in the same way as Abelard recalls the affair in the *Historia calamitatum.* He considered Fulbert's action in having
Abelard castrated, not an action condoned by ecclesiastical or Roman law,
to be divinely ordained retribution for such debauchery.[16]

Orderic Vitalis, a monk of Saint-Évroul in Normandy, tells an intriguing story about Fulbert, that may be related to his involvement in Abelard's
castration. Sometime between 1108 and 1118, Fulbert traveled to Normandy in order to return "for his own reasons" a complete bone of St.
Évroul stolen from the chapel of Henry I of France, that he had been given
by a certain chaplain as "a pledge of affection" (*pignus amoris*). Orderic does
not reveal what twinge of conscience had prompted Fulbert to betray the
chaplain's trust and return the relic to Normandy, at war with France for
much of this time.[17] This journey fits in with an independent report of
Fulbert's temporary exile from Notre-Dame and loss of property after
Abelard's castration.[18] The fact that Fulbert does not sign documents of
Notre-Dame in 1117 suggests that this was the year of his disgrace. By
1119 Fulbert is back at the cathedral signing charters until 1124, when he
seems to have passed away.[19] By returning the bone of St. Évroul to Normandy, Fulbert was hoping to make peace with God.

Roscelin's account of Abelard's relationship with Heloise reinforces the
image given in the *Historia calamitatum* that it fell far short of serious intellectual exchange. The love letters copied by Johannes de Vepria, on the
other hand, present a picture of a relationship in which teacher and student communicate a great deal in writing and speak for the most part in
very idealized tones. To argue that these differences make it impossible for
Heloise and Abelard to have written the love letters does not take account
of the rhetorical structure of the *Historia calamitatum.* Abelard emphasizes
the carnal aspect of their relationship to bring out his theme that he has
now successfully transcended the lusts of the flesh. Roscelin uses similar
rhetoric to vilify his former student. To understand how idealistic discussions about love could be conducted in a society in which there was also
fierce condemnation of sexual promiscuity, we need to consider the degree
to which educated young women could enter into literary dialogue with
clerics. The relationship between Heloise and Abelard was not just a private matter. It developed at a time when ecclesiastical authorities were endeavoring to prohibit clergy ordained to the rank of subdeacon and above

from any form of unchaste association with women. Relationships between clerics and women could easily be seen as dangerous if correct behavior was not observed.

Cathedral Politics and the
Kingdom of France 1100–1116

Abelard describes his early career in the *Historia calamitatum* in terms of personal hostility between himself and other teachers, in particular William of Champeaux (d. 1121) and other disciples of Anselm of Laon (d. 1117). He glides over the political struggles, still very intense at the time he is writing (ca. 1132/33), that had shaped his career. He wants to explain that he has been unjustly hounded by rivals, while at the same time recognizing that his affair with Heloise was wrong and that it merited the punishment that ensued. His relationship to Heloise he thus presents as an episode in which he allowed himself to be overtaken by *amor* and distracted from his studies. His affair with Heloise was inextricably related, however, to much larger conflicts dividing both the cathedral chapter and the clerical order as a whole within France.

The bishop of Paris during the time of Abelard's ascent to prominence as a teacher was Galo (1104–1116), former provost of the collegiate church of Saint-Quentin, Beauvais. At Saint-Quentin, Galo had led the strict, quasi-monastic life of canons regular, based on the Rule of St. Augustine.[20] Galo was a disciple of its first dean, Ivo of Chartres (ca. 1040–1115), a canon lawyer who wished to return ecclesiastical practice to what he imagined were the norms of the early Church. Galo shared Ivo's insistence that bishops should be elected freely by the canons of a cathedral chapter, without interference from secular authority. When the see of Beauvais became vacant in 1101, Philip I (1060–1108) took an oath never to accept Galo as its bishop. To Ivo's horror, Philip supported the rival candidature of Stephen of Garlande (d. ca. 1147), a relatively young cleric who had been since 1095 one of the three archdeacons of Paris. An archdeacon (not a grade of holy orders, like subdeacon or deacon), responsible for collecting tithes from diocesan clergy and looking after the physical fabric of church buildings, could become very wealthy.[21] Ivo complained to the Pope that Stephen was "not ordained in holy orders, not yet a subdeacon, a gambler, a womanizer, publicly condemned for adultery, and excommunicated for this by the archbishop of Lyons, then papal legate."[22] Nothing is known about this accusation of sexual misconduct, made by an archdeacon of Beauvais who subsequently withdrew the charge, to Ivo's embarrassment.

Abelard rose to prominence in Paris at the same time as Stephen of Garlande and his brothers came to dominate senior positions in the royal court. Stephen's family was not from the old nobility, but had been promoted by Philip I late in the eleventh century to assist in the government of the royal domain. Abelard acknowledges that he was supported by certain powerful enemies of William of Champeaux in establishing a school at Melun (ca. 1102), "at that time a royal palace."[23] The growth in influence of the Garlande brothers coincides with the action of Philip I in casting aside Bertha of Holland, mother of prince Louis (born ca. 1081), and taking as his wife Bertrada of Montfort, until then married to Count Fulk IV of Anjou (1043–1109). This union signaled a shift in royal policy away from Flanders toward the Montfort family and the Anjou.[24] Bertrada's brother, William of Montfort, became bishop of Paris in 1096.[25] Ivo of Chartres and Galo refused to recognize Philip's union with Bertrada, but this went against the tendency of most bishops in France.[26] Bertrada provided two further sons for Philip I, Philip and Florus, and a daughter, Cecile. In his Life of Louis VI, Suger describes Bertrada as "a virago, more powerful than all these others, seductive and clever in that amazing artifice of women by which they boldly trample on their husbands after tormenting them with abuse."[27] Her critics accused her of being a "sorceress" who plotted against the young prince Louis in favor of her own children by Philip.[28] When Philip died (29 July 1108), Ivo of Chartres and Galo were involved in the hasty consecration of Louis VI at Orléans, in order to neutralize the threat from his half-brother.[29] Bertrada and her sons then returned to Anjou. She became a nun at Fontevrault but continued to style herself as "Queen of the Franks" in the first seal to survive in France from a woman, issued in 1115.[30]

After William of Montfort's death in 1103, a new bishop was chosen by the cathedral chapter: Fulco, former dean of the cathedral and supported by Stephen of Garlande and Vulgrin. When Fulco died unexpectedly on 8 April 1104, an outsider to the chapter was chosen much more sympathetic to policies of ecclesiastical reform. Galo had recently returned from Rome, having visited Poland as papal envoy.[31] On 2 December 1104, Galo presided over a council at Paris at which Philip I finally acceded to the demand of the assembled bishops that he renounce "the sin of carnal and illicit union" with Bertrada.[32] Galo's victory over the aging king reflected the pro-Norman policy then supported by prince Louis, who invited St. Anselm to France in 1104/5. Galo gave St. Anselm a relic of the virgin martyr Prisca, acquired in Rome.[33] In 1106, in a ceremony presided over by Ivo of Chartres and Adela of Blois, sister of Henry I of England, Louis' sister, Constance, married Bohemond of Antioch, a Norman prince returned in glory from the first Crusade.[34] The Garlande brothers temporarily lost influence during these years, after Guy of Rochefort returned from Crusade in 1104 and reacquired the post of seneschal. Unlike the Garlande brothers, Guy of Rochefort was of old noble stock. In 1105 the betrothal was announced of his daughter, Lucienne, to prince Louis (a proposal annulled at the council of Troyes in 1107).[35] This period of temporary disgrace of the Garlande brothers coincides with the years (ca. 1104–7) when Abelard returned to his home region, apparently having fallen ill through overwork. Suger blamed the rupture of Louis' relationship to Guy of Rochefort on the influence of the Garlande brothers to whom Louis entrusted the castle of Gournay in 1107 after a prolonged military engagement. In December 1108, Louis came to the assistance of Anselm of Garlande against Hugh of Crécy, who had taken prisoner the count of Corbeil.[36] Abelard returned to Paris by 1108, to take up a position at the abbey school of Sainte-Geneviève.

Stephen of Garlande is first identified as a royal chancellor, responsible for drawing up documents in the king's name, in 1106/7, when Philip and Bertrada visited both Orléans and Angers.[37] Stephen retained this position for most of the reign of Louis VI, apart from a critical period between 1127 and 1132. Not long after 1108, Louis made Stephen dean of Sainte-Geneviève, an ancient abbey on the Parisian left bank that Stephen did much to rebuild. The canons of the abbey enjoyed legal immunity from external influence, being answerable only to the king. Galo gave these canons permission to live with their own households in private houses, but not (in theory) with any women.[38] By 1116, Stephen of Garlande and his brothers dominate all major positions of power within the French kingdom. Anselm of Garlande is seneschal or senior military adviser to the king, and Gilbert of Garlande the king's butler. Stephen subsequently becomes seneschal himself in 1120, holding the position until the crisis of 1127. Stephen's influence prior to this date was so great that the Benedictine chronicler of Morigny described him as effectively controlling rather than serving the king.[39] Such hostile rhetoric creates the misleading impression that Stephen represents a conservative secular tradition. Stephen is in fact a reformer of his own kind, eager to strengthen royal authority through effective administration. The numerous charters that he draws up for the king show him to be involved with establishing and reforming a wide range of important religious houses. Stephen has strong connections in Orléans, where he is dean of Sainte-Croix and several other churches. He is well placed to introduce the cultural traditions of Orléans and the Loire valley into Paris.

William of Champeaux, master of the schools at Notre-Dame when Abelard first came to Paris ca. 1100, is a very different figure from Stephen.[40] Appointed an archdeacon of Paris by Galo soon after 1104, his first and only major recorded action as archdeacon was to assist Galo in May 1107 in expelling the nuns from the ancient abbey of Saint-Éloi on grounds of sexual impropriety and replacing them with monks.[41] Like many old religious houses, Saint-Éloi (physically adjacent to the royal palace) was under the direct control of the crown. Its nuns had long enjoyed the right to accompany the canons of Notre-Dame in procession at Rogationtide and the Feast of the Ascension, and at funerals of members of the cathedral chapter, ceremonies also observed by nuns of the sixth-century abbey of Sainte-Croix, Poitiers.[42] By excluding the nuns from participation in Rogationtide processions, bishop Galo was endeavoring to remove these women from public gaze. Pope Pascal II (1099–1118) had raised rumors about the nuns' sexual behavior to Galo in 1104, presumably in response to information from the bishop.[43] The abbey had been involved in protracted litigation with the monks of Morigny over the sale of some land. Stephen of Garlande and Herluin, tutor to prince Louis, acted as witnesses for the nuns. The monks used archdeacon Rainald as a witness along with canon Fulbert.[44] In 1107 Galo gave this property to monks from Saint-Pierre-des-Fossés. While the monks benefit from taxes paid by residents living in houses that belong to Saint-Éloi, itinerant traders on the site pay rent to the king.[45] The expulsion of the nuns provided a symbolic victory for Galo and William of Champeaux prior to the council of Troyes. The king was also able to enlarge the royal palace.[46] The charter confirming the expulsion of the nuns of Saint-Éloi in 1107 was signed on the king's behalf not by any of the Garlande brothers (then still out of influence in court) but by Hugh of Crécy, son of Guy of Rochefort and for a short time seneschal.[47]

On 23 May 1107 William of Champeaux and Galo attended the council of Troyes, presided over by Pope Pascal II. The bishops implemented a range of measures, including the prohibition of simony (obtaining ecclesiastical office through financial means).[48] Some rulings concern society as a whole, such as the prohibition of fighting that disturbed "ecclesiastical property and people, merchants and pilgrims" between Thursday evening and dawn on Tuesday. Marriage is not to take place between parties of less than twelve years or without legitimate witnesses and cannot be dissolved except in the presence of the bishop. Most relate to ecclesiastical standards, such as the enforcement of sexual continence on deacons and priests. Priests cannot profit from holding two positions at once. There is to be no buying and selling of ecclesiastical benefices, or receiving such property from laymen. Another ruling prohibits deacons and priests "from wearing long hair, beak-shaped pointed shoes, sewn clothes and from having laces on tunics or shirts, or from using games of chance."[49] Like many rigorists, William and Galo advocate a strict ascetic code for priests and deacons, whose dress they complain often differed little from that of affluent lay folk. They think that clerics engaged in public ministry should dress and behave like monks. Ecclesiastical complaints about secular fashions among the clergy reflect wider fears that patterns of behavior often associated with the Angevin court are making deep inroads into both Norman and French society.

The expulsion of nuns from Saint-Éloi in 1107 is one of a number of attempts to reform old-established female communities in the early twelfth century. In 1098 Ivo of Chartres had complained to the bishop of Meaux that he had heard about the nuns of Faremoutiers in the diocese of Meaux having turned their abbey into a brothel where they prostituted themselves "to all kinds of men." He advised that if they could not reform themselves, they should be replaced by monks. Similar arguments were later used to justify expulsion of nuns from the abbey of Saint-Jean, Laon in 1128, and from Argenteuil in 1129.[50] Whether or not communities of nuns were more dissolute than those of monks, rhetoric about sexual pollution provided a common way of asserting ecclesiastical authority.[51]

While the reform of Saint-Éloi in 1107 reflected an attempt to alter the balance of power in the Île-de-la-Cité, no single institution or individual enjoyed complete control over the city. Between the royal palace on the western part of the island and the cathedral on its eastern corner is the central market place, known for over two hundred years as the Jewish quarter (vicus Judaeorum) with its own synagogue, not transformed into the church of Sainte-Madeleine until Philip Augustus expels the Jews in 1180.[52] Unlike Rouen, Paris did not witness any major persecution of Jews during the first Crusade.[53] The population of Paris is growing on the northern side of the river, connected to the Île-de-la-Cité by a new stone bridge. There is much new commercial activity around the Châtelet and along the rue Saint-Denis, connecting Paris to the abbey of Saint-Denis to the north. By 1120 the annual royal fair of Lendit, held every June on this road, is blessed by the bishop with a fragment of the true cross, sent from Jerusalem to the chapter of Notre-Dame.[54] In 1121 the merchants of the city acquire the right from the king to impose a tax on boats carrying wine.[55] The left bank is less commercially developed. Vines still grow on the slopes of the Montagne Sainte-Geneviève, the hill that overlooks the city. Many students attend the public school of Sainte-Geneviève, an abbey outside the bishop's jurisdiction. While the lives of most of the population in and around Paris are hidden from view, the occasional charter hints at a new freedom in relationships. In 1114 Stephen of Garlande draws up a royal charter instructing that serfs of Notre-Dame be given freedom to testify against freemen, as equals.[56] Also in that year he draws up a document allowing Sancelina, daughter of a certain Ascho, to be freed from the yoke of serfdom so that she can marry a man of Notre-Dame, as she wants.[57] Prosperity makes possible a new degree of freedom, but it also demands procedures by which freedom can be regulated.

Paris is not the only important city in the royal domain, a relatively small, landlocked region straddling both the Loire valley and the Seine basin. The other city where the king spends much time is Orléans, which shares cultural and economic ties with the major towns on the Loire under the control of the Counts of Anjou. In 1108, Philip I had been buried at his express wishes at the ancient monastery of Saint-Benoît-sur-Loire, near Orléans.[58] Suger reports that travel between the two cities was difficult until prince Louis took firm action against armed bands from the castle of Montlhéry in 1105.[59] North and east of the royal domain are important cities under episcopal lordship: Beauvais, Laon, and Châlons-sur-Marne, important to the king strategically and economically. Louis has little effective power in regions like Anjou, Blois, and Champagne, whose allegiance to the king of France is largely nominal. Blois was governed for much of the early twelfth century by Adela, daughter of William the Conqueror and close friend of both Ivo of Chartres and St. Anselm. Her son, Theobald of Blois (d. 1152) became count of both Blois and Champagne after Count Hugh of Champagne renounced his inheritance to become a Templar knight in 1125.[60] Suger considered that Louis VI did much to strengthen royal authority over his vassals by recognizing the privileged position of Saint-Denis in the kingdom, and thus the role of Paris.[61] The political ambitions of Henry I of England (1100 - 35) demanded that Louis VI pay more attention to the Seine basin than to the Loire. Economic rivalry between these two regions fuelled the political competition between the Garlande brothers on one hand, and a faction that embraced William of Champeaux, Galo, and Suger of Saint-Denis on the other.

Abelard's Studies in Anjou

Born in 1079 in the western part of Brittany at Le Pallet, near Nantes, Peter Abelard always saw himself as an outsider to France. His cultural associations were formed in Anjou, where he pursued his early studies. When he came to Paris ca. 1100, he brought with him an intellectual and literary culture shaped by the educational traditions of the Loire valley. In the *Historia calamitatum*, he mentions that his father, Berengar (a Poitevin, according to Richard of Poitiers), encouraged all of his sons to pursue an education in letters before acquiring the skills of war, but says nothing at all about his sisters.[62] Abelard's attachment to his mother is suggested by his recollection that "my dearest mother Lucia" obliged him to return home when she was preparing to follow his father in entering the religious life.[63] Lucia was Breton.[64] In a society where Breton and Nantais elements competed for influence, the loyalties of Abelard's father were towards Anjou. The marriage of Alan IV Fergant (duke of Brittany 1084–1112) to Ermengard, daughter of Fulk IV of Anjou ca. 1096, cemented these ties.[65] Abelard had left his family by the age of fourteen, following his father's ambition that he become an educated knight before taking over the family estate. Breton ancestry on his mother's side did not stop him from commenting in his *Dialectica* that the word *brito* was applied to someone who was a brute. When he took up a position in 1127 as abbot of Saint-Gildas, in a more remote part of Brittany, he complained that he could not understand the local dialect.[66] With a Poitevin father, Abelard may have been as familiar with the tongue used by Count William IX of Poitiers in his songs about love as with the French dialect of the Anjou. He was sent to Loches, a major castle of the Counts of Anjou, in order to acquire fluency in Latin and thus become like his father, an educated knight.[67]

The teacher who inspired Abelard to turn away from inheriting the family estate was Roscelin of Compiègne. Roscelin later chided his former student for forgetting what he had learnt at Loches, "where you sat so long at my feet as the youngest of the disciples."[68] Only a few years earlier, Roscelin had been accused of teaching heresy at a council in Soissons ca. 1090 by Fulco, a monk of Bec whom St. Anselm was supporting as bishop of Beauvais. Fulco was then facing accusations from clerics in Beauvais that he had acquired his bishopric in 1088/89 illegitimately from the king of France. After seeking help unsuccessfully from Ivo of Chartres, and being accused for a second time of teaching heresy by St. Anselm, Roscelin was given sanctuary by the Count of Anjou. Anselm labeled Roscelin as one of "those modern dialecticians of our time, who do not think universal substances to be anything but the puff of a word, who cannot understand color to be other than a body, or the wisdom of man different from the soul."[69] Roscelin emphasized that an individual term signified a separate thing. His argument that God the Father could not be described as the same thing as God the Son seemed to St. Anselm's disciples to fly in the face of tradition. It re-ignited tensions which had flared earlier in arguments between Berengar of Tours (ca. 1000–88), supported for a long while by the Counts of Anjou, and Lanfranc of Bec (ca. 1010–89), supported by Duke William of Normandy.

Abelard broke away from Roscelin after arriving in Paris, provoking Roscelin to accuse his former student of gross ingratitude soon after the affair with Heloise:

> If you had savored even a little of the sweetness of the Christian religion, which you chose in habit or were not unmindful of the profession of your order and forgetful of the many and great benefits which I have showered on you, from being a boy to being a young man, under the name and action of being a teacher . . .[70]

Abelard subsequently endeavored to distinguish his thinking about both dialectic and theology from that of his teacher, while extending Roscelin's concern to explain statements about reality as linguistic constructions of human origin.

Roscelin was not the only figure in the Loire valley to make an impact on Abelard. In 1101 Robert of Arbrissel (ca. 1045–ca. 1117) established an abbey for both women and men at Fontevrault, midway between Tours and Angers. The rapid growth of his order (which counted some nineteen priories in 1117) owed much to the support Robert received from Bertrada of Montfort, her son Fulk V (count of Anjou 1109–42), and her step-daughter, Ermengard, married to the Duke of Brittany. Wives and husbands are often mentioned together in charters granting property to the Order. Peter the Venerable's mother was one of those many women who came under Robert's influence as a preacher.[71] Abelard defended Robert as "an outstanding preacher of Christ" against Roscelin's criticisms that Robert encouraged women to abandon their conjugal duties to pursue a religious life.[72] Husbands were apparently complaining about Robert to the local bishop. Roscelin thought that Robert shared the blame if an abandoned husband "sinned from necessity."[73] A contemporary of Roscelin also critical of Robert of Arbrissel is Marbod (ca. 1035–1123), bishop of Rennes from 1096 until his death. Sometime after 1100, an aging Marbod accused Robert of excessive intimacy with women under the guise of religion.[74] Marbod did not believe that Robert could remain chaste, when he was tied to women "by desire, sight, conversation, connection." Antagonism towards Robert of Arbrissel in Anjou was related to the fact that not everyone sympathized with Robert's particular vision of a reformed Church. Geoffrey of Vendôme accused Robert of ignoring the wickedness of women. Geoffrey mentions that Robert was a supporter of bishop Rainaud of Martigné (1102–25), and that he also benefited from the support of "an actress and a public woman" in ousting the aristocratic Geoffrey of Mayenne (1094/95–1101) from the see of Angers.[75] In their old age, Roscelin, Marbod, and Geoffrey of Vendôme all feared that Robert was disrupting the social order by associating with women. Like the early Cistercians, Robert sought to distinguish a true religious life from stultifying convention, although he differed from them in wanting to involve women with men in the process of reform.

Abelard cannot have been unaware of these upheavals taking place in the Loire valley at this time. In the *Historia calamitatum,* he describes himself simply as a kind of knight engaged in an intellectual adventure: "wandering through different provinces in disputation, I imitated the peripatetics wherever I heard that study of that art was flourishing."[76] Abelard may have consciously modeled his vocabulary here on the account offered by Baudri of Bourgueil of the early studies of Robert of Arbrissel:

> He wandered restlessly through regions and provinces, unable not to be concerned for the study of letters. And since France then flourished more richly in scholarly reward, he left his paternal home, like an exile and fugitive, went to France and entered the city which is called Paris, found there the study of letters which he sought for himself alone, to be as helpful as he hoped; and the diligent reader began to live there. . . . He gave back to scholastics because he was a scholastic, and did not meanwhile offer himself any the less to the service of God.[77]

Baudri saw no contradiction between Robert of Arbrissel being educated in the schools and living a life dedicated to God. Writing not long after Robert's death ca. 1117, Abelard sympathized with Robert's interest in opening religious life to women. Fifteen years later, Abelard was more reserved towards Robert's practice of subordinating men to the authority of a woman as "against the natural order." Yet he still raises many of the same arguments as Baudri about the possibility that men can live chastely alongside women, denied by Roscelin and Marbod of Rennes.[78]

Abelard supported the cause of involving women with men in the religious life at a time that some people in France considered such interaction subversive. Guibert of Nogent reports the case in 1114 of Clement and Everard of Bucy, from near Soissons, burned to death by an angry crowd outside the city because they had established communities (*conventus*) outside the Church and were thought to hold heretical opinions.[79] Although Guibert accused them of being depraved in their practices and beliefs, he also mentions that Count John of Soissons considered no one wiser than Clement. They apparently invoked the word of God by some long invocation of words, and rejected child baptism, the eucharist and sacred burial sites. Guibert's comment that they live, "men with men, women with women" may simply refer to both sexes living an ascetic lifestyle as part of a single community. Guibert's lurid stories, familiar to him from rumors which Augustine had reported about Manichaean heretics, serve to pour scorn on the claim that this community at Soissons lives the apostolic life according to the Acts of the Apostles. Like Robert of Arbrissel, Clement appealed to Christ's statement "Blessed are you when men hate you" to justify his vision of an ideal community.[80] The support Clement received from the Count of Soissons was not as powerful as that which Robert of Arbrissel enjoyed from the Count of Anjou. The involvement of both women and men in the movement attracted suspicions of sexual immorality. Abelard stood for a different set of ideals.

The Argument with William of Champeaux

Sometime after the coronation of Louis VI at Orléans on 3 August 1108, William of Champeaux gave up his post as archdeacon to establish a new foundation for canons regular at Saint-Victor on territory adjacent to the abbey of Sainte-Geneviève but outside the jurisdiction both of the abbey and of the cathedral canons. The canons of Saint-Victor followed a stricter way of life in common, similar to a reformed monastic community. Great importance was attached from the outset to the copying of books and to the training of novices in its school.[81] William bequeathed his house in the cloister to the cathedral, a gift witnessed by all the canons (including Fulbert, now the senior subdeacon).[82] William's departure from the cathedral chapter coincided with the return to royal favor of Anselm of Garlande and Louis' appointment of Stephen of Garlande as dean of Sainte-Geneviève. The canons of this abbey followed a less austere way of life than the canons of Saint-Victor.[83] They encouraged external students to attend its public school on the Montagne Sainte-Geneviève, overlooking the city.

Peter Abelard was invited to teach at Sainte-Geneviève at the same moment as Stephen became its dean. Abelard soon engaged in a public disputation with William of Champeaux, forcing him to concede during

lectures on rhetoric that two individuals of the same species or genus could
be described as the same, not because they shared an essence, but because
they were not different from each other. Abelard forced William to recognize that two identical individuals were the same *indifferenter* (without difference) rather than *essentialiter* (by essence). This is the same argument as
appears in the teacher's letter (*24*) in the exchange copied by Johannes de
Vepria, about love making two wills into one *indifferenter* (without difference). Abelard was not the first teacher to question traditional ideas about
language. The biographer of Goswin, who once dared challenge Abelard to
debate at Sainte-Geneviève ca. 1110, mentions that a certain celebrated
commentary on Priscian's *Grammatical Institutes* was then provoking much
controversy because of "the novelty of meanings" students were reading
into Priscian's text.[84] This is very likely to be the *Glosule,* a late eleventh-
century commentary which emphasizes the distinction between the
meaning of individual words and their various grammatical forms.
Abelard's achievement was to make William acknowledge that it was no
longer possible speak about shared essences as St. Anselm had done.
Abelard was not the only contemporary critic of William of Champeaux,
as student notes preserved at Fleury by a disciple of Joscelin of Vierzy (a
teacher in Paris before he became bishop of Soissons 1126–52) confirm.[85]
Joscelin also ridiculed the idea that Socrates could be informed by some
universal thing which could be at Rome and Athens at the same time, and
defined universality as a collection of individuals.[86]

The position which Abelard attacked in 1111 was a traditional assumption which sharp minded dialecticians liked to question. There was also a
political dimension to Abelard's attack on William. St. Anselm's influence
in France had begun to spread after his monk Fulco obtained the bishopric
of Beauvais. St. Anselm was friendly with Walerann, cantor at Notre-Dame
in the 1090s, and later with bishop Galo.[87] After the accession of Louis VI
and the decision of William of Champeaux to move from Notre-Dame to
the abbey of Saint-Victor in 1111, Abelard was ideally placed to challenge
the authority of St. Anselm and his admirers.[88] Not long after St. Anselm's
death (21 April 1109) Stephen of Garlande denounced as unjust the control of certain estates in and around Paris by the Norman abbey of Bec.
Stephen then acquired them from the abbot of Bec through an exchange
for other property.[89] Bec had managed to obtain certain privileges in
France between 1093 and 1108.[90] By 1109 hostilities had re-opened between Normandy and France. Louis VI engaged in a bloody campaign
against Henry in the Vexin, laying waste the lands of Robert of Meulan,
close adviser to Henry I.[91] As an act of revenge, Robert sacked the royal

palace on the Île-de-la-Cité while Louis VI was at Melun, preventing him from coming into Paris by destroying the bridges. Robert is said to have been driven out with the assistance of Parisian citizens.[92] Louis then constructed a new stone bridge to connect the Île-de-la-Cité to the royal domain at Châtelet rather than to property held by the count of Meulan between the Monceau Saint-Gervais and the Grève. After 1111, Louis VI started to spend more time in Paris, although still taking care to spend time at Orléans and other major cities in France.[93] In March 1111 he granted Stephen of Garlande the right for canons of Sainte-Geneviève to answer charges within the chapter of the abbey rather than at the king's court, "in accordance with the just traditions of the Church."[94] Abelard's rise to prominence coincides with that of Stephen of Garlande. Scholastic debate runs along similar lines to a property dispute or a feudal argument, fought out in the classroom or the lawcourt rather than in the battlefield. The disputes in which Abelard participates provide a structure to regulate issues in contention within a masculine world.

Perhaps the most misleading aspect of Abelard's narrative is his claim that William's influence started to decline after that public debate. When Abelard wrote the *Historia calamitatum* (ca. 1132/33) the conflict between the abbey of Saint-Victor and the abbey of Sainte-Geneviève was at its height. Sainte-Geneviève had been put under interdict by the bishop of Paris, Stephen of Senlis, who blamed partisans of Stephen of Garlande for the murder in 1133 of Thomas, prior of Saint-Victor. When Abelard recalled his debate with William of Champeaux he was stoking the fire of an ongoing argument that was as much political as intellectual. Abelard's conflict with William was not just one of personality or of ideas about logic. It related to a struggle between a pro-royal Stephen of Garlande, eager to reform government by strengthening the administration of written law, and a pro-clerical William of Champeaux, who considered that the only legitimate path of reform was by transforming the clerical order into a morally upright, independent force within society.

Conflict at Laon

In June/July 1113 William of Champeaux was elected bishop of Châlons-sur-Marne. Louis VI signaled his support for William by endowing the canons regular of Saint-Victor with much property in a ceremony witnessed by the archbishops of Sens and Rheims, and many other bishops, including Ivo of Chartres and Galo of Paris.[95] William thus became both spiritual and temporal lord of an independent territory outside the royal domain and a valuable ally for Louis VI. This royal patronage marked a turning point in the fortunes of Saint-Victor and the reform movement as a whole in France. While at Châlons-sur-Marne, William befriended Bernard, a young monk who had come to Cîteaux in 1112, ordaining him in 1115 abbot of Clairvaux.[96]

William's departure from Paris provided the opportunity for Abelard to go to Laon to study divinity. The libraries in Laon contained many rare and precious books from the time of Charlemagne. Anselm of Laon was celebrated for his ability to summarize patristic exegesis and to answer a variety of questions about Christian doctrine, all in the cause of ecclesiastical reform.[97] Goaded by his students, but against Anselm's wishes, Abelard started to lecture on Ezekiel. Abelard's difficulties were compounded by a volatile political situation in the city. On 25 April 1112 the bishop of Laon had been murdered during a civic disturbance. Gaudry (also known as Waldric) was Henry I of England's former royal chancellor, and had obtained the bishopric by dubious means in 1106, when prince Louis was temporarily pursuing a pro-Norman policy in France. It was widely suspected that Gaudry had been involved in the assassination in 1110 of Gerard of Quierzy, lay protector of the nuns of Saint-Jean in Laon.[98] Gaudry initially supported the establishment of a commune in the city, but subsequently revoked his promise. Gaudry's assassination followed his action of crushing the commune in 1112, with the support of Louis VI. Although not enthusiasts for communal government, both Guibert and Orderic Vitalis agree that Gaudry was notorious for his exploitation of the financial resources of the city. Anselm of Laon took care to distance himself from the policies of his bishop, but was inevitably tarred by association with the corrupt bishop.

The murder of the bishop made any criticism of ecclesiastical authority look like seditious behavior to the authorities. The situation was complicated by the fact that Hugh, a cleric from Orléans chosen with the support of Stephen of Garlande to succeed Gaudry, died the next year. This led the way to the election of Barthélemy de Jur, a relation of Bernard of Clairvaux, as bishop of Laon (1113–51).[99] The hostility Abelard encountered from Alberic of Rheims and Lotulf of Novara, both disciples of Anselm of Laon, was part of a political struggle shaking the city. Guibert of Nogent is dismissive about Stephen of Garlande's attempt to gain influence in Laon. The violence that followed the crushing of the commune meant that any intellectual who challenged authority could be seen as questioning the established order of Christian society.

The Affair with Heloise

Abelard returned to Paris after only a short time (*post paucos itaque dies*) at Laon in order to take up the position at Notre-Dame that he had long coveted. He reports that he held that office "quietly, for some years" (*annis aliquibus quiete possedi*). There he completed glosses on the prophet Ezekiel, which he had started to compose at Laon. The chancellor of the cathedral at Notre-Dame was Girbert, a colleague of Stephen of Garlande and Galo's successor as bishop of Paris (1116–23).[100] The relative absence of official proclamations from Girbert as bishop suggests that he did not interfere in the traditional privileges of the canons, a policy that made it easier for Abelard to develop his relationship with Heloise. The cause of ecclesiastical reform was still extremely weak across Europe before the election of Pope Calixtus II (1119–24).[101] In Paris, ecclesiastical authority began to assert itself only after the death of bishop Girbert in 1123 and the election as bishop of Stephen of Senlis, an outsider to the cathedral chapter. In 1116 there were still few controls on a successful cleric to prevent him from behaving as he wished.

In the *Historia calamitatum* Abelard explains his affair with Heloise as a consequence of worldly success: "The more I advanced in philosophy or divinity, the more I slipped away from philosophers and divines in impurity of life." The two vices into which he says he slipped were debauchery (*luxuria*) and pride (*superbia*). He wants his reader to learn how divine grace provided a remedy for both those vices "from the affair itself, rather than from hearsay, in the order in which they happened."[102] His debauchery was punished by castration, and his pride by the burning of his treatise at Soissons in 1121. He describes himself as an arrogant rebel in his youth, the intellectual scourge of William of Champeaux, in order to present his life as an example of how pride had to give way to humility. In his account of his early relationship with Heloise, Abelard similarly dwells on his debauchery in order to heighten the dramatic significance of his castration. By presenting his affair as one of carnal lust, he glides over the extent to which it was a literary relationship, developed through the exchange of messages. He has no interest in wanting to present Heloise's attitude to their relationship as one of desire to participate in philosophical discussion.

Abelard interprets his relationship with Heloise as deliberate seduction on his part rather than as the working of mutual desire. He explains how, through the intervention of "certain friends" Fulbert allowed him to lodge in his house as well as to offer tuition to his niece. While Abelard is keen to admit his physical debauchery, he does not explain the actual process by which he maintained his relationship with Heloise. To maintain secrecy from Fulbert, he needed to communicate with her by written messages. There is little psychological subtlety in Abelard's account. He remembers that Fulbert discovered the relationship "after several months had gone by." There then followed an enforced separation, and subsequent communication by letter. Abelard then explains that not much later Heloise discovered that she was pregnant and wrote to him in great exultation to ask what should be done. He decided to send her, disguised as a nun, to his sister in Brittany, where she gave birth to a boy baptized Peter, to whom she gave the *cognomen* Astralabe. (Patrilineal surnames did not become common until the following century.) The astrolabe was an instrument pointed at the stars or at the sun. Heloise's choice of name recalls the astronomical imagery of the man's letters copied by Johannes de Vepria about the woman he loves, as his morning star, his sun.[103] She may have chosen it to signify that the child was the means through which both she and Abelard could gaze at celestial light.

The love letters copied by Johannes de Vepria tell a story not incompatible with the sketchy details Abelard supplies in the *Historia calamitatum*. In the early love letters, the woman is uncertain whether she can respond adequately to her teacher, whom she describes in letter 23 as overflowing "with the riches of your philosophy." His comment in letter *24* that she is accustomed to ask him "what is love?" seems to refer not to any earlier letter, but to spoken conversations. His remark (*22*) that he directs "to others words, to you intention" and stumbles in words because his thought is far from those words echoes Abelard's comment in the *Historia calamitatum* that his lectures became dull and repetitive because he was now thinking only about Heloise. The expression "to direct the intention" is also a characteristic phrase of Abelard's theological writing in the 1120s and 1130s, in relation to directing intention to God.[104] While many letters respond to each other, others could have been written after a period of time had elapsed. In letter *28,* for example, he worries that envy is troubling their "great friendship." He had been much more confident in his previous letter (*26*), in which he professes his ardent desire that she reveal herself to him. She mentions that snow is melting, as if it were spring (32). By letter 57, she refers to the fact that "for a long time" they had not been able to see each other. At the end of letter 84 she promises that she will reward him "with an act of thanks and the obedience of love" for composing for her a certain prologue. While there is no clue as to what kind of treatise this prologue introduced, it is significant that he is sharing academic work with her. The only clue to the passing of time in the correspondence is his comment at the outset of a long poem (87) that it has been a year since he has been conquered by her love. His comment "Now the year is new, and a new love is to begin," need not relate to the beginning of January, but to the beginning of a new phase he wishes to begin in the relationship. In a subsequent poem (108), he refers to the earth "being caressed by flowers" as if it were the season of spring.

Dronke's suggestion that the letters copied by Johannes de Vepria reflect an unconsummated relationship between teacher and pupil and therefore cannot be written by Abelard and Heloise, depends on reading her Pauline allusion in letter 84 as about sexual intercourse: "Until now you have remained with me, you have manfully fought the good fight, but you have not yet received the prize."[105] Even if her allusion is to consummation (far from certain), her overriding concern in this letter as elsewhere is not with sexual union, but with the fulfillment of the relationship itself. In the *Historia calamitatum* on the other hand Abelard deliberately contrasts a sinful past of physical indulgence, with his present relationship to Heloise as based on spiritual concern alone. His suppression of the intellectual aspect of his early relationship to Heloise is the attitude to which she reacts so harshly.

A consistent theme that emerges from the women's love letters is the value she attaches to their correspondence (53, 79). She is overwhelmed by "the riches of your philosophy" and her sense of inadequacy in being able to respond (23, 71). In letter 69 she fears that it exceeds her mental capacity to think of what "sweetness of composition" (*dictaminis dulcedine*) she could use to speak to her beloved. In verses which begin that letter she begs that he remember the tears which he had shed for her and asks why he is coming so infrequently, breaking her heart. She does not want any jealous eye to read these verses. In letter 71 she says that she wants to speak to him for an hour but is distressed that when she should be working, she is thinking completely about him. The man in turn marvels at the quality of her prose and verse, surpassing that of Cicero and Ovid (75). In her last major letter (112), she again recalls the immense pleasure that his letters had given her although she now implies that this was in the past and cannot compare to her present joy. In the letters of Heloise that follow the *Historia calamitatum* there is far more emphasis on Abelard's proclamation of his love for Heloise in song and in frequent letters than in Abelard's own recollection of the past, in which this aspect of his early career is presented as typical of a debauched life. Just as the woman is fascinated by the combination of gifts of philosophy and poetry in her teacher (112), so Heloise also singled out this combination of gifts as making Abelard so unusual.[106]

Abelard's presentation of his seduction of Heloise as the consequence of an insane passion is itself very close to the man's emphasis on *amor* in his feelings for his student in the Troyes love letters. By contrast she often combines the words *dilectio*, an ideal form of love, with *amor*, passionate love, to emphasize the purity of her love. The contrast between the two positions becomes acutely evident in the final poem in the exchange (*113*), in which he laments that he had been driven by love to follow its commands and that he had been seduced by the glamour of "beauty, noble birth, behavior" which "make you famous in our city." Unlike her, he falls back on conventional clichés about love for a woman being ultimately superficial. Both lovers are writers of distinction, each aware of the other's reputation. Their contrasting attitudes to love echo the contrast between the attitudes of Abelard and Heloise in their correspondence. In the *Historia calamitatum* Abelard reports that after Heloise had announced "with great exultation" that she had become pregnant, he explained to Fulbert that to someone who knew the force of love (*amor*) he had not done anything unusual. "Had not women laid low the greatest men since the beginning of time?"[107] Heloise is fully familiar with this argument but is convinced that her love for him was pure and selfless. When Abelard went back to Brittany to tell her of his plan that they should marry, Heloise resisted his plan, but eventually succumbed and they returned to Paris where they were married in secret, so as to protect his reputation. Abelard saw this as at least the semblance of a moral reform on his part. Fulbert was particularly furious when Heloise slipped out of his house at Notre-Dame and took refuge at Argenteuil, where she had been brought up and educated. A plan was hatched to have Abelard punished. Fulbert's change in attitude toward Abelard was complete.

The Rhetoric of Pollution and Moral Decline

The remarks in both the *Historia calamitatum* and in Heloise's response to that text, show how their relationship acquired a significance far beyond the private lives of those two individuals. In the public mind, Abelard and Heloise were seen as crystallizing tendencies which the traditionally minded feared were gaining ground among the young. Ecclesiastics who prided themselves on the cause of "reform" were often profoundly conservative. Heloise's conviction that love was more important than social convention was not simply the concern of an isolated individual. The love letters reflect a tendency to talk about love which Guibert of Nogent complained was widespread among young women of his own day. They dressed extravagantly and no longer respected values of chastity, "the width of sleeves, the tightness of dresses, the curling beaks of shoes from Cordoba, proclaiming everywhere that modesty has been cast aside."[108] Guibert was appalled by the intimacy of communication between men and women, as revealed through their dress and through the way they talked about their relationships. He saw these new fashions as symbolizing an untoward desire by women to throw off established convention. Orderic Vitalis is another monastic writer who associates new fashions with dissolute sexual morality. He singles out the pointed shoe, identified by Guibert as coming from Cordoba, as a symbol of these new vices. He blames their popularity "among rich and poor alike" on Count Fulk of Anjou, husband of Bertrada. Orderic describes in detail what he sees as symptoms of pernicious Angevin influence: curled long hair, the front part of the head shaven but covered by a cap, a trimmed beard, tight shirts, trailing robes and extravagant shoes.[109] Similar complaints about men adopting effeminate patterns of dress and behavior were made in Norman England by William of Malmesbury.[110]

These fashions were not introduced by any single individual. They developed out of expanding trade and travel between regions north of the Loire and territories where dialects of Provençal were spoken. With Christian expansion into the Iberian peninsula, new fashions were coming from Moorish Spain. Conservative chroniclers had long complained that extravagant fashions came into the north from the regions of Auvergne and Aquitaine. Raoul Glaber blamed these new fashions on the marriage of Robert the Pious to Constance of Arles in 1002/3.[111] The marriage of Agnes of Poitou to the Emperor Henry III in 1043 was blamed by Siegfried of Gorze for introducing the fashions of her Poitevin courtiers into the Empire, including trimmed beards and tight-fitting clothes.[112] The fall of Toledo to Christians in 1085 was much more important than the capture of Jerusalem in 1099 for introducing new products and fashions into the Latin West. When Pope Urban II, former archdeacon of Rheims, urged Latin Christians to march towards Jerusalem, he wanted to re-assert traditional Latin values against what many monks saw as a process of moral decline that had crept into the West.

The complaints raised at the council of Troyes in 1107 about the dress and behavior of priests and deacons reflect wider concern about a perceived weakening of traditional divisions between men and women, clergy and laity. In England and Normandy, it was not unknown for a powerful sermon to conclude with the preacher cutting the hair of those present. In 1096 St. Anselm had his congregation have their hair cut after a Lenten sermon. The council of Westminster in 1102 had insisted that clergy have their heads shaved, and that men cut their hair so as not to cover their ears and eyes. Anselm of Canterbury decreed that those who did not wish to cut their hair should not enter a church. If they did enter, a priest need not stop the service, but should warn such long-haired reprobates that they were coming into the church to their own damnation.[113] In 1090 bishop Radbod of Tournai (1068–98) is said to have solemnly cut the hair of a thousand young men and have trimmed robes that flowed down to the ground. This followed a sermon delivered in the cathedral of Tournai during a time of plague. Herman of Tournai, an admirer of St. Anselm and critic of "modern dialecticians," recalled this event in order to contrast such zeal with contemporary vices "of visiting women or of irregularities in hair, dress and the like that we see being practiced everywhere."[114] At Rouen in 1102 it was forbidden for those with long hair to enter a church. Serlo, bishop of Séez, preached a sermon at Carentan in Normandy before Henry I and all his court in 1105, berating them for their long hair "by which they make themselves seem like imitators of women and by womanly softness they lose their manly strength and are led to sin, and often fall wretchedly into hateful apostasy." Henry I, Robert of Meulan, and most of the assembled magnates then had their hair trimmed by the bishop.[115] A similar event occurred at Saint-Omer in 1106 in the presence of Robert II Count of Flanders (1093–1111), one of the heroes of the first Crusade. There is no record of such public rituals taking place in France, despite the efforts of bishop Galo and William of Champeaux to reform clerical dress. Only with the growth of enthusiasm for going to Jerusalem, actively supported by Bernard of Clairvaux and other preachers, was an alternative put forward to fashions which Guibert of Nogent and Orderic Vitalis complained were so widespread.

The original concerns of reformers in the eleventh century had not been with new fashions among the clergy and laity, but with the practice of buying ecclesiastical office from secular rulers: simony or the heresy of Simon Magus. Pope Leo IX had the council of Rheims rule in 1049 that positions of authority in the Church should be chosen by clergy and people, rather than simply bestowed by a secular ruler.[116] Ecclesiastical prebends were frequently passed from father to son, without regard for the capacity of sons of ordained clerics to perform their role. Reformers argued that chastity was essential if clerics occupying senior liturgical and pastoral responsibilities were to command respect from the Christian community. They modeled their vision of a reformed clergy on a monastic ideal, which they believed to have been followed by the early Church.

Such concerns led Pope Nicholas II (1058–61) to call a council which ruled that the Pope had to be chosen by a college of cardinals, representing the universal Church and acclaimed by the people, rather than by the Emperor alone. He instructed the laity to avoid attending the services of unchaste clergy and insisted to the bishops of Gaul that those priests who had taken concubines should not celebrate mass.[117]

The rhetoric of reform became more authoritarian with the advent of Pope Gregory VII (1073–85). It was easier to blame women for introducing impurity into the Church than powerful families, suspected of obtaining ecclesiastical office through illegitimate means. Gregory VII insisted that clerics ordained to higher orders must observe chastity (*castitas*) and a communal way of life, in other words that they live like monks. The key concept in his legislation was not so much celibacy as chastity. He instructed bishops to suspend priests guilty of fornication. The reaction of French clerics to these reforms is revealed in the Life of Walter, abbot of Saint-Martin, Pontoise. When bishops and abbots assembled at a council in Paris (probably ca. 1074), they declared these rulings to be "intolerable and therefore irrational" and attacked Walter for daring to suggest that the decrees of the supreme pontiff should always be obeyed, even if one thought them wrong. The bishops arrested Walter as a blasphemer and had him brought in chains to the king. There were similar disturbances at Rouen and Poitiers, provoked by married clergy hostile to these reforms.[118] Ivo of Chartres once complained to archbishop Daimbert of Sens about a certain senior figure in the Church who had publicly linked himself to two whores and was preparing to marry a third.[119] The problem was equally difficult in Norman England. In 1102 St. Anselm advised that archdeacons and canons who had physically separated from their wives could be tolerated so long as they refrained from sexual intercourse or speaking to them without witnesses. Priests who had not given up their women could not celebrate mass.[120] Treatises were still being written in the late eleventh century in defense of clerical marriage by authors who supported loyalty to secular authority. Particularly controversial was the right of priests' sons to acquire prebends, defended by Serlo of Bayeux against rigorists in the Church.[121] An Oxford master, Theobald of Étampes, criticized the argument of Roscelin of Compiègne that sons of clergy were not to be admitted to holy orders, observing that the genealogy of Christ included Thamar and three other women of whose lives scripture disapproved. He considered it catholic belief to claim: "It is more use to live well than to spring from righteous parents. God considers the life, not the birth, of a human being."[122] Marbod of Rennes was similarly critical of those who censured unchaste clerics.

The prohibition on clerical marriage for subdeacons, deacons, and priests was not firmly imposed in France until the council of Rheims, held in the presence of Calixtus II (1119–24) in October 1119. After a long period of internal weakness within the papacy, the new pope (who happened to be uncle to Adelaide, queen of France) was eager to impose firm discipline on the Church, and resist what he saw as moral laxity and undue secular influence in the Church.[123] One of its rulings was that all subdeacons, deacons and priests who kept concubines should be deprived of their benefices. When this decision was promulgated at Rouen in 1119, priests of the diocese protested about the conflict this provoked between body and soul. One of their number was taken off to prison by the archbishop, leading to a general riot quelled only by force. The responses of those women repudiated by clergy anxious to regularize their situation are not recorded, although it is reported that a number of such women had burned themselves to death in the time of Gregory VII.[124] Whereas accusations of simony often involved challenging influential families, charges that women were a source of sexual corruption for the clergy were easier to make and deflected suspicions that ecclesiastical reformers had reached too close an accommodation with political authority. The sexual scandal associated with Abelard's behavior as a teacher at Notre-Dame provided ample opportunity for his critics to claim that he had been polluted by the fires of lust.

Sexual Mores

Ivo of Chartres included in his *Decretum* the demands of the council of Elvira that sex outside marriage demanded one year's penance (five years if the couple did not marry). He insisted that sex was legitimate only if there was intention to conceive a child.[125] According to the strict letter of canon law, there were severe penalties for sexual intercourse between unmarried persons and for adopting contraceptive measures. In practice, information about contraceptive and abortifacient plants was widely available.[126] There was little stigma attached to a man having a mistress, and offspring could be well looked after. In spring 1117, two years after his marriage to Adelaide of Maurienne, the king allowed his illegitimate daughter, Isabelle, to marry William, son of Osmond of Chaumont.[127] As Louis was born in 1081, he is unlikely to have been more than twenty when he conceived Isabelle by an unknown woman. No less a person than Clemence of Burgundy, countess of Flanders, sister to Calixtus II and aunt to Queen Adelaide, is reported as having used female art so that she would no longer become pregnant after bearing three children in three years. She was afraid of the political consequences of her children fighting over Flanders. Herman construed the early death of all her offspring as divine vengeance for her behavior.[128] For all their desire to speak for the Christian community, canon lawyers were powerless to influence sexual behavior. When both Ivo of Chartres and bishop Galo passed away in 1116, their vision of a chaste clerical elite was an unrealized ideal.

Secular clerics were frequently the butt of accusations about sexual immorality from those committed to a monastic way of life. In a letter written to Abelard soon after his castration, Fulco of Deuil reports rumors that he had frequented the company of prostitutes:

> Whatever you could acquire by selling your learning through speech making, apart from daily victuals and necessary requirements (as I have heard by report) you did not stop throwing into the whirlpool of a fornicating appetite. The rapacious greed of prostitutes robbed you of everything. No age has heard of a prostitute wanting to have compassion on another or to spare the passions which in a certain way they are able to consume.[129]

Abelard's insistence in the *Historia calamitatum* that he did not visit prostitutes may well have been a reaction to rumors of this kind about his reputation.[130] *Meretrix* (prostitute) was a common term of abuse. Heloise's proclamation that she would rather be called Abelard's prostitute than empress of Augustus threw into question one of the most common labels used to define pollution. Later that century Parisian prostitutes, said to frequent the cathedral cloister, were to become significant enough as a group to offer chalices and stained glass windows to the new cathedral. The offer was turned down by Maurice de Sully for fear of giving approval to their profession.[131] Abelard was less critical of such women. He once advised his son that prostitutes were not as bad as sodomites or chaste women who were proud or talkative.[132]

In a clerical milieu from which women were officially excluded, accusations of sodomy served as a way of asserting authority. Homoerotic relations were perceived as a difficult problem by St. Anselm, who complained that sodomy was "so common that hardly anyone is ashamed of it and that many people, ignorant of its magnitude, fall headlong into it." He advised his archdeacon that excommunication was to be considered for this offence, although one had to consider for how long the sin had been practiced and whether the sinners had wives or not.[133] There is a good deal of verse from the eleventh and twelfth centuries which either celebrates or denounces homosexual relationships within a clerical milieu.[134] According to one poem, Orléans was particularly celebrated for sodomy, as well as Paris and Chartres.[135] Ivo of Chartres was so incensed by the behavior of the new bishop of Orléans, nicknamed Flora by his fellow canons because of alleged sexual intimacy with King Philip, that he sent such a poem to the archbishop of Lyons to prove his depravity. He wrote about this episode to Pope Urban II in 1097:

> For some of his boyfriends, calling him Flora, have composed many rhyth-mical songs about him, which are sung by depraved young men through the cities of France at market places and crossroads, a scourge as you know of this land. He did not blush to sing them sometimes himself and have them sung for himself. As proof, I have sent one of them, which I snatched vio-lently from someone singing it, to the archbishop of Lyons.[136]

This archdeacon had successfully competed against Baudri of Bourgueil for the see of Orléans, even though Bertrada had apparently promised Baudri the position. Ivo reported that the real reason was that Baudri did not have as much money as the archdeacon with which to press his case at the royal court.[137] Ivo's comments about the songs of "depraved young men" show how the rhetoric of sexual pollution very often had a political focus, in this case against a bishop, suspected of being too close to the king. The wandering clerics about whom Ivo complains, made fun of the es-tablished ecclesiastical order. They sang about political corruption as easily as about love. Guibert of Nogent recalls that clerics would wander from town to town in search of employment as teachers.[138] This was the cleri-cal milieu of the young Peter Abelard. Sexual mores were fluid. If the bishop of Orléans could be held up to such ridicule, what possibility was there of imposing strict moral standards on cathedral clergy?

What made Peter Abelard so unusual in the eyes of Heloise was his gift for combining his skill in philosophy with a gift for composing and singing songs of love.[139] When she read the *Historia calamitatum*, she reminded him of these public declarations of love and of the incessant letters which he had showered on her in the past. From her perspective, a true relationship was not an illicit sexual encounter but a mutual profession of true love. She professed to be unconcerned about whatever label might be given her, as all she was concerned about was true love. The letters copied by Johannes de Vepria reflect attitudes which Ivo of Chartres and Guibert of Nogent found deplorable among the younger generation. The lovers mock the jealousy of those who would deny them their intimate pleasure. She describes the man she loves as a great teacher, before whom the French have to yield (49), a "companion of the poets" (21) and in letter 112 as one "who is both nourished by philosophy and who drinks from the source of poetry." The technical sophistication of the prose and verse letters, in particular the mastery of certain philosophical terms by the man (notably the allusion to "non-different" identity in letters *16* and *24*) shows that they are far beyond student doggerel. The woman's emphasis on the purity of her relationship to her teacher is very different from Abelard's description of their behavior in the *Historia calamitatum* as one of pure lust. Only in the concluding poem of the exchange copied by Johannes de Vepria does the man suggest that he has been seduced by the charms of her beauty, noble birth, and behavior, as if these are all external qualities. The conventional stereotype of women as the source of seduction, encountered so often in ecclesiastical documents from the twelfth century, surfaces both in this final poem and in the *Historia calamitatum*.

Conclusion

Abelard's account in the *Historia calamitatum* of his early career, culminating in a vivid description of his affair with Heloise, is rich in circumstantial detail about the life of a successful cleric in early twelfth-century Paris. It also glides over much of importance. His affair with Heloise was much more than simply a moral lapse on his part. Heloise was wanting to participate in a culture of intellectual debate, in which many traditional ideas and institutions were being questioned. It is misleading to interpret the early twelfth century as a time of conflict between "reformers" and "traditionalists." Many different ideas for reforming traditional patterns of behavior were being discussed. Ecclesiastical reformers viewed Stephen of Garlande, dean of Sainte-Geneviève, chancellor and eventually seneschal, as a symbol of the worldliness they wished to eliminate from the clerical order. Abelard's early rebellion against William of Champeaux was part of a wider political struggle between Stephen and William. Abelard's liaison with his student can be seen as an act of rebellion against the policies of clerical austerity which Galo and William of Champeaux sought to impose.

Educated in Anjou in the late eleventh century, Abelard had absorbed an intellectual culture very different from that of William of Champeaux and Anselm of Laon. At Loches, a stronghold of the counts of Anjou, he became acquainted with a sophisticated cultural milieu, frequently blamed by some Norman and French ecclesiastics as responsible for a decline in contemporary moral standards and for the popularity of new fashions of dress. The refusal of many ecclesiastical reformers to recognize Bertrada of Montfort as the legitimate wife of Philip I was only one manifestation of their hostility to a culture which they associated with the Angevin court. They preferred the crusading ambitions of the Norman princes as a nobler form of aristocratic culture. The complaints of Guibert of Nogent that men and women devoted too much attention to boasting about love were directed against precisely the sort of people that Abelard says in the *Historia calamitatum* were still performing the love songs which he once composed for Heloise.

The love letters copied by Johannes de Vepria belong to this cultural milieu. The woman in particular articulates very different attitudes from the ecclesiastical moralists. Her letters celebrate the love between a woman and a man as a noble form of friendship, one which combines both *amor,* passionate love, and *dilectio,* a love that actively esteems another person. This woman is very like Heloise, in that she celebrates her teacher as skilled in both philosophy and poetry. She is searching for an authentic relationship, based not on social convention, but on a true love that is known to God. The man by contrast celebrates his relationship to her more as an amorous passion which operates quite differently from his friendships with other people. Although he does once try, at her request, to define *amor* philosophically (24), he is generally less original in the way he explores the obligations of love, which he sees more as an escape from his normal activity. Toward the end of the exchange he becomes worried about his public reputation, and defines his behavior to her as a sin (*peccatum*), a concept she never invokes. Abelard manifests very similar attitudes in the *Historia calamitatum.* He recalled how his lectures became stale and uninspired as he was thinking about the songs he was composing for her. His relationship to Heloise he now interpreted as one of base passion, quite at odds with philosophical inquiry, and meriting the punishment which ensued.

Heloise wanted to share in the atmosphere of excitement which prevailed in Paris in the early twelfth century. Inevitably there was friction between competing visions of an ideal community. William of Champeaux established a community at Saint-Victor, where an all-male community was committed to following apostolic ideals according the Rule of St. Augustine. Stephen of Garlande, by contrast, was more interested in building up schools at the abbey of Sainte-Geneviève, where he was dean. Bernard of Clairvaux, ordained in 1115 by William of Champeaux, saw himself as developing a more authentic community at Clairvaux, defined by simplicity and mutual love rather than by the opulence and hierarchy associated with much traditional monasticism. In their different ways, both Bernard and Heloise sought to define ethical relationships in terms of sincerity and love rather than social convention. In wanting to deepen her relationship with Peter Abelard, Heloise was fascinated by the possibility that a woman and a man could share in the most intimate form of friendship. At the outset Heloise believed that Abelard was a teacher willing to share his wisdom with herself as much as with his other students. The ideal was easier to imagine than to implement in practice. The love letters copied by Johannes de Vepria illustrate what can happen when an educated woman engages in sophisticated dialogue with her teacher, drawing on ethical models provided by classical literature. Heloise is not the first young woman to have an affair with a cleric or to be exposed to the anger of her family. More unusual is the extent of her commitment to the study of literature, through which she hopes to escape the confines of her situation.

CHAPTER 4

TRADITIONS OF DIALOGUE

Vernum tempus est amenum	Springtime is pleasant
et amoris melle plenum;	and rich in the honey of love;
quicquid est in mundo rerum	whatever is in the world of things
novum facit ac serenum.	it makes fresh and clear.
In hoc uere uernant flores,	In spring flowers truly bloom,
quia tellus dat humores;	because the earth gives sap;
puellarum nunc dolores	now girls' sorrows
risus petunt et amores.	chase laughter and love.
Iam qui amat uel amatur	Already he who loves or is loved
illud petit quo letatur,	seeks what makes him happy,
et si locus umquam datur,	and if a chance is ever given
trahit palpat osculatur.	he draws near, touches, gets a kiss.

This simple song, included within an anthology sent to Marbod of Rennes sometime before 1100, relates spring to the delights of love. It provides as good an introduction as any to a world of imagined intimacy celebrated both in the Loire valley and beyond in the late eleventh century.[1] The association of love and nature, a theme as old as the Song of Songs (2.10–12, etc.), often surfaces in the love letters copied by Johannes de Vepria, particularly in those of the woman. Just as she offers her beloved the freshness (*viriditas*) of eternal happiness (1) and of love (48), so this song celebrates an imaginary union of lovers as spring returns. In letter 25 she exclaims that she languishes with love for him, "stirred by the songs of the birds and the freshness of the woods" and relates her love to the passing of winter in letter 32. She refers to flowers and flowering more often than he does (1, 49, 53, 66, 73, 79, 90, 109), although in one of his last poems (*108*) he evokes an Ovidian image of nurturing earth (*alma tellus*): "Mother Earth is caressed with its flowers. / All nature prepares itself for your praises."[2] The song about spring evokes an enthusiasm for both nature and love much developed by the woman in her love letters. Latin writing about love from the early twelfth century provides a cultural context against which we can better appreciate the love letters and poems copied by Johannes de Vepria in the late fifteenth century. The phenomenon of educated men and women exchanging Latin verse and prose about love was not in itself unusual.

The Literature of Love in Anjou ca. 1070–1100

The love letters betray no direct literary parallels with the lyrics of William, ninth duke of Aquitaine and sixth count of Poitiers (1071–1126) and other early troubadours.[3] Latin and vernacular love lyrics from this period share a common concern, however, to define a code of values based around ideals of true or pure love (*fin'amor*). The earliest identifiable authors of troubadour literature are men. Women troubadours (*trobairitz*) do not appear in the written record until the second half of the twelfth century. It has often been assumed that this literature is essentially masculine in initiative, and principally concerned with putting women on a pedestal.[4] Bezzola argued that the poetry of William of Aquitaine provided a secular equivalent to the esteem with which Robert of Arbrissel accorded women within the religious life.[5] It is often assumed that this literature originated in the aristocratic courts of Aquitaine, and was brought to northern France by Eleanor, granddaughter of William of Aquitaine, when she married the young Louis VII in 1137.[6] Denis de Rougemont postulated that the major influence on troubadour ideas of love was the Cathar heresy (disregarding the fact that no troubadour is known to have been a Cathar).[7] René Nelli argued that troubadours emphasized equality with women rather than traditional patriarchal values.[8] All these interpretations assumed that vernacular literature about love had little in common with Latin writing about love or with ethical thought in the late eleventh and early twelfth centuries.[9]

The scholarly debates about the sources of this code of pure love developed in vernacular poetry are too complex to be explored here. By contrast, the originality of Latin writing about love in the late eleventh and early twelfth century has been relatively neglected. One scholar who has done much to interpret vernacular writing about love in the twelfth century in the context of Latin verse is Peter Dronke.[10] In a major two-volume study of medieval lyric poetry, Dronke edited and translated a range of Latin texts about love from the early twelfth century, including women's love letters in a manuscript from Tegernsee and a verse exchange between a teacher and a female student in a manuscript from Regensburg. Dronke placed the exchange copied by Johannes de Vepria within this tradition of men and women writing to each other in Latin.[11] The love letters are considerably more sophisticated, however, than the Tegernsee or Regensburg texts. The woman's concern with the definition of love looks forward to the more elaborate reflection on the ethics and obligations of love developed in vernacular literature later in the twelfth century.

The influence of Latin literature on vernacular writing has begun to attract attention in recent years. Tony Hunt has considered Chrétien de Troyes and Andreas Capellanus as clerics informed by Aristotelian dialectic.[12] Gerald Bond has argued that in the Latin poetry of Baudri of Bourgueil and Marbod of Rennes, as in the lyrics of William of Aquitaine, a new, more secular definition emerges of the individual as "the loving subject." Bond interprets the verse that Baudri of Bourgueil exchanged with his friends throughout the Loire valley as the creation of an Ovidian "subculture."[13] The shared feature of both the troubadour lyrics and this Latin verse is a common concern with the correct behavior demanded by love. The same is true of the letters and poems copied by Johannes de Vepria.

The late eleventh and early twelfth centuries witnessed a sharp growth in the number of "wandering clerics" (*clerici vagantes*), who moved from town to town in search of employment either as teachers or as secretaries to important people. Some clerics acquired a reputation for composing and performing songs, the most famous of whom was Peter Abelard. Hennig Brinkmann paid particular attention to the role of literary exchanges between clerics and women in promoting twelfth-century love literature in both Latin and German.[14] The best-known secular Latin lyrics of the period are the *Carmina burana,* songs about love, drinking, and the corruption of the world, preserved in a thirteenth-century manuscript from Benediktbeuern.[15] The collection seems to have been compiled by clerics at the cathedral school of Brixen in the Tyrol, one of whom spoke French.[16] At least two are by Hilary of Orléans, a cleric educated at Sainte-Croix, Orléans, who taught at Angers 1109–22, before joining Abelard's early community at the Paraclete. Hilary's letters to other clerics living in towns along the Loire valley, from Nantes to Orléans, provide valuable insight into the sophisticated clerical culture with which the young Peter Abelard was familiar. Hilary composed Latin poems in honor of a number of religious women, including the recluse Eve of Wilton (who lived near Angers with a companion, Hervé), two nuns identified as Bona and Superba, and an unknown lady called Rosea.[17]

In a poem about "the pope of the schools," Hilary certainly alludes to
Abelard when he praises a great teacher who is loved by his students and
who composes pleasant songs. Another of the poems in the *Carmina burana*
may possibly be by Abelard himself. It is a lament on the bitterness of separation from the poet's beloved: "The star of joyful countenance is dulled
by [my] heart's cloud" (*Hebet sydus leti visus cordis nubilo*). Its reference to
"the light of Phoebus" has been interpreted by Dronke as a play on both
helios (sun) and *Heloisa*.[18] Its opening verse is strikingly similar to the man's
first poem in the Johannes de Vepria exchange (*20*):

> Stella polum variat, et noctem luna colorat,
> Sed michi sydus hebet, quod me conducere debet.

> The star turns around the pole and the moon colors the night,
> But that star is fading which should be my guide.

Hebet sydus in the *Carmina burana* is more sophisticated than this poem, but
it develops a similar comparison of the beloved to a fading star. It echoes
a more general fascination in the man's love letters with imagery about
heavenly light. Other poems in the *Carmina burana* could possibly have
been composed by Abelard, but it is difficult to be certain about this.

While the exchange copied by Johannes de Vepria is unusual in its
length, it is not the only surviving example of a Latin dialogue between a
man and a woman. Such exchanges are attested to in a number of manuscripts from the late eleventh and early twelfth centuries, although often
only one side of an exchange is preserved.[19] Marbod of Rennes and Baudri of Bourgueil are early pioneers in addressing Latin verse to women,
while Hildebert of Lavardin (1055–1133) became one of the most celebrated practitioners of the genre.[20] In eleventh-century Germany, it became common for clerics to forge friendship networks by exchanging
letters informed by a love of classical literature, Cicero in particular.[21] In
Anjou and France, however, writers were particularly fascinated by the
theme of love, above all as articulated by Ovid. This is the dominant literary tradition from which the Troyes love letters draw their inspiration.

The Ovidian Revival

When the man in the love letters protests his inability to express his feelings fully, he explains that even Ovid would not have been up to the task
in verse, just as Cicero could not have articulated those feelings in prose

(75). Earlier in the correspondence (45), she had compared her love for him as like that of Biblis for her twin brother Cauno, celebrated in Ovid's *Metamorphoses,* or like that of the nymph Oenone for Paris, or the love of Briseis for Achilles, heroines of Ovid's *Heroides.*[22] Her letters, which never allude to the much wider range of Roman love poets familiar to humanists in the fifteenth century, enable us to glimpse a precious moment in the mutation of European literature, before Petrarch fostered perception of cultural decline after an imagined collapse of classical culture. The tradition of writing love poems in Latin never disappeared in the medieval period. The love letters testify to the vitality of an ongoing tradition, that is not always as visible as other forms of literature in the manuscript record.

Their debt to Ovid is not simply a matter of borrowed images or phrases. The very practice of exchanging letters and verses was itself shaped by the advice that Ovid gave both men and women in the *Art of Loving* on how they should communicate with each other.[23] Ovid makes fun of love letters written by women in his *Amores.*[24] In *Cures for Love,* he mockingly warns that once a relationship was over, a woman's love letters were best destroyed.[25] The chance discovery of an intimate letter from a woman to a Roman official suggests that women in the Greco-Roman world were more literate than the canon of authors transmitted by monastic scriptoria would suggest.[26] Juvenal mocked the practice of women keeping compromising love letters.[27] Most letters written in Antiquity have been lost. Just as the New Testament leaves only an echo of the voices of the first women followers of Jesus, so the surviving body of classical texts tends to filter out the voices of articulate Roman women.

Ovid was always fascinated by relationships between women and men. In his *Tristia,* he defends himself against the accusation adduced as the reason for his exile by the Emperor Augustus, that his *Art of Loving* had corrupted women. He recalled how he and his stepdaughter Perilla used to read their poetry aloud to each other. He encouraged her verse composition, proclaiming that she would be surpassed only by Sappho, "the Lesbian singer" whom Ovid held in high esteem.[28] In the *Heroides* Ovid invents poems written by mythic women to men (Penelope to Ulysses, Dido to Aeneas etc.) as well as poetic exchanges between a man and a woman (Paris to Helen, Helen to Paris, etc.). The one historical woman whose voice Ovid recreates in the *Heroides* is that of Sappho to Phaon (no. 15). That epistle provided the Latin West with its only major image of Sappho prior to the sixteenth century. It is also the only one of the *Heroides* to have its Ovidian authorship questioned by some critics.[29] The allusions to Ovid's heroines in the love letters are particularly valuable given the relative rarity of the *Heroides* in the twelfth century. They show how an educated woman could invoke a literary fiction to express herself.

By *amor,* Ovid was referring not to passion of the heart in Stendhal's sense of *amour–passion* but to sexual seduction usually outside of marriage. Paul Veyne has argued that Roman love poetry is radically different from that of a later period in Western civilization because amorous passion was not conceived of ethically "as an experience or as a relationship with the loved object but in relation to the subject who underwent it."[30] Certainly many Roman authors dismissed women writers as superficial.[31] Ovid was unusual in writing as much as he did about the interaction of women with men. Juvenal jokes about arguments that literary women would raise about Dido or the relative merits of Virgil and Homer.[32] His *Satires,* widely copied in the eleventh and twelfth centuries, sustained a set of attitudes of great influence in ensuring that women's voices be mocked rather than listened to with respect. While educated Roman women undoubtedly did discuss and write poetry, hardly anything has survived of this writing, apart from a few lines written by Sulpicia, a female contemporary of Tibullus.[33]

Ovid's writing about *amor* was considered potentially subversive of the established order not just by the Emperor Augustus, but by Latin Christian authors influenced by Stoic thought. The Latin Fathers inherited classical assumptions that serious philosophical debate took place only among male friends. Patriarchal themes were read into the canon of scripture to make it conform more closely to the dominant assumptions of established tradition. Only one letter of the many female correspondents of St. Jerome (*Ep.* 46 from Paula and Eustochium) is preserved within collections of his letters. St. Augustine similarly never abandoned traditional assumptions about the superiority of male friendship over relationships with women, although he did reflect much more than Jerome on the psychological roots of uncontrolled sexuality.[34]

Ovid was more appreciated in late antiquity as a source of information about ancient myths than as a commentator on human relationships.[35] Few early copies survive of his writings on love.[36] The first poems to draw extensively on the *Heroides* are two laments, attributed in the surviving manuscript to Venantius Fortunatus (ca. 535–ca. 600), but quite possibly composed by Radegund (ca. 520–587) herself. She was a Thuringian princess who escaped marriage to Clothar I by being consecrated deacon and then establishing a monastic community for women at Sainte-Croix, Poitiers.[37] Venantius may have brought the single manuscript of Ovid, from which all surviving copies of the *Heroides* derive, from Italy to the region of the Loire in the sixth century.[38] It is in the Loire valley that Ovid's verse

epistles inspired Carolingian writers to imitate the genre. Theodulf of Orléans (ca. 760–ca. 820) drew from Ovid the literary topos of Envy unjustly
defaming true genius, used in both the love letters and the *Historia calamitatum*.[39] One of the earliest signs of interest in the *Art of Loving* can be seen
in the brief glosses preserved in a ninth-century manuscript subsequently
belonging to St. Dunstan (909–88).[40] Our earliest witness to the *Tristia* and
the *Heroides* is an anthology of often rare classical texts, including *Sappho
to Phaon* and many works of Cicero, assembled probably at Fleury or Orléans in the mid-twelfth century.[41] The classical allusions in Johannes de
Vepria's love letters are more likely to derive from anthologies than from
complete texts of ancient authors.

The enthusiasm for Ovid in the love letters contrasts with suspicions in
more conservative monastic circles that his love poems were risqué. Guibert of Nogent confesses that as a young monk he used to compose "Ovidian and bucolic" verse about love in the form of epistles that he would
recite to select monastic friends, but now thinks of such activity as at odds
with his religious vocation.[42] A German Benedictine, Conrad of Hirsau
(ca. 1070–ca. 1150), recognizes that Ovid is popular in monasteries, but
warns novices of the dangers of certain of his poems:

> Why, when so many great authors are at hand [Arator, Prudentius, Cicero,
> Sallust, Boethius, Lucan, Virgil, and Horace], the honest reading of whom
> sharpens us in the mind and provokes us to virtue, why is corrupting liter-
> ature to be sought out, the sense of which refuses to allow the mind to be
> exercised? Why does the Christian novice dumbly submit his mind to Ovid-
> ian books? Although gold can be found there amidst filth, the stench next
> to the gold soils the seeker, although he may be eager for gold.[43]

In Conrad's dialogue, the master then explains that while certain works of
Ovid were morally acceptable, others were of lesser value: "who can put
up with his cawing about love, his sordid digressions in different letters, if
he has a taste for what is healthy?"

Abelard offers a subtly different perspective in his *Christian Theology*,
written in the early 1120s. Here he quotes from Ovid's *Amores* to prove
that pagan authors glimpsed the same insight as St. Paul into the frailty of
human nature: "We always strive for the forbidden and desire what is refused."[44] Ovid's presentation of himself as a literary exile, expelled from
Rome because of unjust jealousy of his genius, appealed to Abelard. He
quoted Ovid's *Cures for Love* to describe how as a young but brilliant
teacher he had been pursued by jealous rivals: "Envy attacks the highest, as

winds scour mountain summits."[45] Just as Ovid wrote the *Tristia* to win back his public reputation in Rome after being unjustly persecuted by jealousy of his genius, so Abelard sought to restore his own reputation in Paris against the "gnawing envy" of his rivals.[46] This Ovidian theme of "the jealousy of evil men" recurs in the letters copied by Johannes de Vepria (*54: edax malorum hominum invidia; 69: ne versus oculus legat invidiosus*). In her third letter to Abelard, Heloise quoted the *Art of Loving* of Ovid, "master of sensuality and shame" to support her point that hospitality could easily provide opportunity for fornication.[47] She countered traditional monastic ambivalence towards Ovid by judgment that he provided a fount of wisdom on human relationships.[48]

Enthusiasm for Ovid became strong in the twelfth century in the schools of Orléans, doubtless facilitated by the access of its teachers to rich monastic libraries in the region, such as Fleury (Saint-Benoît-sur-Loire). Anthologies were compiled of many rare classical texts.[49] By holding important positions at both Orléans and Paris, Stephen of Garlande was well placed to promote access to these texts in Paris. Ovid's poetry in particular provided a stimulus for much new writing in Latin and then in French in the twelfth century.[50]

Marbod of Rennes (ca. 1035–1123)

One poet whom Könsgen considered to manifest a direct influence on certain of the letters and poems copied by Johannes de Vepria was Marbod of Rennes, a teacher and then archdeacon at Angers, appointed bishop of Rennes in 1096.[51] The parallels that he identified all occur within the woman's writing (including her one allusion to *natura*).[52] Marbod was a prolific writer of both religious and secular poetry, saints' lives, and writings on eloquence.[53] When he came to write his *Book of Ten Chapters* (one chapter of which is about woman as the root of all evil in the world), he rejected much of what he had written as a young man as both indecent and trivial and poorly expressed, but confessed that it was impossible to withdraw what had been uttered.[54] He admitted that in his youth he had been gripped by sexual passion, but now advocated moral rigor.[55] The image he projected of himself in these writings is that of a sophisticated writer who applies his literary skills to defend traditional moral values that he acknowledges he had not always observed.

Precious insight into a less well publicized part of Marbod's output has been provided by Walther Bulst's discovery that certain poems included in the rare Rennes (1524) edition of Marbod's verse, were expurgated from subsequent editions.[56] No medieval manuscript is known of most of these poems, but the printed collection seems to reproduce an anthology of earlier writings, probably put together by Marbod himself. It begins with a commendation of chastity and verses to a dedicated virgin. Poems addressed to Ermengard of Brittany and to Matilda, wife of Henry I, are followed by "Persuasion against venereal love" and other verses of a more erotic nature, some with an introductory rubric "under an assumed persona" (sub assumpta persona). Of particular interest among the poems unique to the 1524 edition are various verses addressed to an unidentified female friend (amica), a girl or young woman (puella) for whom Marbod professes love-sickness. The first is addressed "to a friend preparing to return home."[57] The poet says that this was not the first time that he had loved a girl, but only now did he know what it was to love.[58]

One of the poems expurgated from later editions carries the title "a girl to a friend promising gifts" (puella ad amicum munera promittentem). A girl rejects the advances of a lover as empty of substance. This particular poem also occurs in the anthology of verse sent to Marbod in the late-eleventh century, as well as in a copy of the letters of Walter of Mortagne to various theologians, including Peter Abelard:[59]

> You promise the joys of nymphs, violets, and rose-flowers, lilies of wonderful whiteness, and tasty apples, like that of doves joined by their mother, purple clothes dressed in which I would be able to subdue the woods by elegance and surpass them in appearance, above silver, jewels, and gold. You promise everything, but you send me nothing. If you love me and you have what you promise, things would come first and words would follow. Therefore either it is fictitious and you do not know the blows of desire or you are rich in empty words and empty in things. If you are filled with many riches, you are a rustic who believe that I love your things, rather than you yourself.[60]

As this poem is included in the anthology sent to Marbod, it seems unlikely to have been one of Marbod's own compositions, attributed to someone else. The poem raises the same theme as letter 49 in the exchange copied by Johannes de Vepria, that those motivated by true love loved each other not because of wealth, but because of each other. Heloise insists on the same theme in her first letter to Abelard:

> God knows, I never sought anything in you apart from yourself, desiring purely you, not what was yours. I did not seek the bonds of marriage, any dowry, not even my own pleasures or desires, but I was anxious to implement yours, as you yourself know.[61]

The next poem in the anthology of Marbod's verse is presented as a reply to this young woman:

> Dearest, joyfully I read what was sent by you to me, for it is contained there that I have pleased you. If I knew truly what you are saying, most beautiful of all, I would then be happier than if I became king. I would rather not create the treasures of the great Octavian than not please you, as is mentioned there. The letter which says that I am so sweet to you has conquered me, the kisses which it tells, the heart asks for me.[62]

In a moving poem copied by Johannes de Vepria (82), the woman reiterates the theme that if she possessed whatever had been owned by Caesar, such riches would have been as nothing to her. This image of spurning Caesar's wealth is also raised by Heloise, when she protests that if Augustus had honored her with marriage and endowed her with the whole world, she would rather be called Abelard's prostitute (*meretrix*) rather than Augustus' empress.[63] She is here proclaiming with more dramatic power a moral argument, raised by the *puella* to Marbod and repeated by Marbod in reply, that true love ignores wealth.

In the next poem, "Reply to the reply of the same person," Marbod refers to her having "to put up with words of a father, and quarrels of a mother, because of which you are fasting at nights and keeping vigils."[64] This is followed by "A reply to the girl loved passionately," articulating a new degree of intimacy:

> I am happy at last, because now I know what I have entrusted to you, since I no longer fear that I displease you. What hope beckoned, fear till now used to prevent. I swear through the quiver of Venus, by which you also seem wounded, through the eyes under which you lie: . . . For your appearance has hurt me with a wound in my breast, your face shining again as a cloudless day. Your hair was combed, not folded with any tie, long and golden colored, your forehead white as a swan, your sloping side and smooth belly and what stands from the beginning, a lower abdomen that is too taut, these and what remains create wounds for me; unless I touch them, I cannot live.[65]

A short final poem in the 1524 anthology is addressed "to a female friend placed under protection":

> I can neither live without you nor with you. For fear prevents the latter, love the former. O would that I could live without you or with you. But I would rather live with you than without you.[66]

A comment made by the woman to her lover in letter 13 may also be a direct quotation from this poem: "in you is my death and life."

Bulst thought that these poems were exchanged between distinct individuals. It is impossible to be certain, however, whether the *puella* in these poems is a real young woman or a creation of male poet's fantasy. What matters about these poems, excluded from the most widely-circulated anthologies of Marbod's verse circulating in the twelfth century, is that they open up a space in which a woman's voice is able to be heard, within the rules and conventions of the literary game being played. As much as Marbod might dismiss his early verse as erotic fancy, he did not completely repress memories from the past within his *Book of Ten Chapters*. Erotic poems could serve a moral purpose. Marbod's poems do not just provide occasional phrases picked up in the letters copied by Johannes de Vepria. They furnish their readers with a rudimentary framework for discussion of relationships between women and men. When Heloise argued that she would rather be called Abelard's prostitute than be endowed with the treasures of Augustus, she was taking further an argument about the relationship between love and possessions raised in a poetic (and perhaps fictional) exchange between Marbod and an unidentified *puella,* already part of Latin imagination by the late eleventh century.

Fulcoie of Beauvais (fl. 1070–1100)

Less well known than Marbod's poetry is the verse of Fulcoie of Beauvais, an archdeacon of Meaux and a married priest of the second half of the eleventh century who composed a major biblical epic, rich in classical imagery, on the marriage of Christ and his Church.[67] His verse epistles are much concerned with the sexual proclivities of his fellow clerics.[68] He explains why sexual intercourse was morally superior to sodomy in a verse epistle to Ingelrann, archdeacon of Laon: "We humans drink wine, wear robes, linen; we take the turns of Venus, gentle, sometimes harsh—may we take them, experiencing that by which we become compassionate."[69] In an epistle addressed to Milo, dean of Paris, Fulcoie evokes the love of Mars and Venus and the jealousy of Vulcan to berate him for getting too jealously attached to a nun also being pursued by a rival:

> You cannot escape like Mars. . . . You excuse yourself thus, that you refuse marriage. . . . "I do not know whom I would marry or whom I want to marry, but I want to marry a beautiful girl, for whom I would be the only one. This companion is a burden, nor does he divide up equally. If she be

ugly, she would not be the only one for me. . . . "'Be continent,' you say, but being continent is an effort. . . ." What are you doing with such a one, a virgin, a nun? . . . Many come together, many men and many women students, but which school orders one man to be with one woman? . . . What are these instruments, this pen and polished tablets? Virgil does not take up these concerns with "Of arms and men." They do not make poems worthy to be read. . . . She whom your violence injured has given a reply. By reasoning, know your guilt, not hers.[70]

Fulcoie implies that he is responding to Milo's verses, but claims that he also knew what the nun had written to the dean. He argues that Milo is being unnecessarily jealous about a rival's affections for this nun and sympathizes with her in this affair. As with the anthology of Marbod's verse, it is impossible to ascertain the extent to which Fulcoie is commenting on specific situations. Fulcoie may be satirizing a situation that he finds humorous, a situation in which a senior cleric got into emotional difficulties with an educated nun. Such sexual freedom provoked bishop Galo and William of Champeaux to expel nuns from the abbey of Saint-Éloi. Like Guibert of Nogent and Marbod, Fulcoie mentions having written juvenile verse of which he is now ashamed.[71] His poetry is not of the kind to attract a wide audience. To ecclesiastical authorities trying to impose strict observance of chastity on the priesthood, his satirical inventions could seem dangerously subversive.

Baudri of Bourgueil (1046–1130)

Baudri of Bourgueil engages more seriously than Marbod in reflective dialogue with other women, but his verse never circulated widely in the twelfth century. Baudri shares with the woman in the love letters a common interest in the ethical basis of love.[72] Born eight miles from Orléans at Meung-sur-Loire, Baudri became a monk at Bourgueil, mid-way between Angers and Tours, and its abbot sometime after 1078. He tried unsuccessfully to become bishop of Orléans in 1096 through the help of Bertrada of Montfort. In 1107 he gained the less important bishopric of Dol, a position from which he was suspended in 1120 by the papal legate, Conon of Preneste.[73] Baudri's public reputation as a writer was ensured by a history that he wrote of the first crusade, as well as lives of various saints, including one of Robert of Arbrissel. A more intimate picture of his circle of friends and admirers is provided by a collection of his verse epistles preserved in a single twelfth-century manuscript. Some of these are epitaphs for knights, citizens, and clerics of Angers.[74] While the majority are addressed to various clerical and monastic friends, often in exchange for verses received from them, a number are directed to noble women, mostly nuns at the abbey of Notre-Dame du Ronceray, Angers.[75] Founded in 1028 by Fulk Nerra and his wife, Hildegard, Le Ronceray attracted daughters and widows mainly from the nobility. The wealth of the abbey is amply attested in its charters.[76] Baudri complains when Beatrice has not replied in verse as he had asked and then adds a witty four-line verse about her silence.[77] He praises Muriel for her skill in the recitation of poetry. Explaining that he had not written directly to any other *puella*, he asks her to respond to his verses in like manner. This Muriel is also the recipient of a long poem by a certain Serlo, who describes her verse as better than his own.[78] Describing Emma's poetry as "spiced with nectar," Baudri wants to become her disciple, if her order allowed, "like the other female students who flock to her as to a "queen bee."[79] The women to whom Baudri addresses these verses do not seem to be any less real than his many male correspondents, scattered through the Loire valley and beyond.

Whereas Marbod considers *amor* to be a passion of the heart, sometimes at odds with a chaste ideal, Baudri perceives *amor* to be synonymous with true friendship (*amicitia*). Baudri always emphasizes the purity of true love, even if he uses erotic language to do so. He was inspired in particular by Ovid's writing about sincere love, as articulated by women in the *Heroides*. In his epistle to Constance, he writes:

> Believe me and I want both you and the readers to believe that a filthy love has never driven me to you. I want virginity to live in you as a fellow citizen; I do not want modesty to be shattered in you. You are a virgin, I a man: I am young, you are younger. I swear by all that is: I do not want to be your man. I do not want to be your man, nor you to be my woman: let mouth and heart strengthen our friendship.[80]

Baudri explicitly contrasts the purity of his intentions toward Constance, to baseness of other youths "following the impious deeds of Jupiter." He wants her to pursue virtue, as counseled by pagan authors, so that she may be a virgin spouse truly worthy of God. He repeats Ovid's argument in the *Tristia* that writing erotic verse is not necessarily a sign of dubious morality.

Baudri's poem to Constance is followed by an eloquent profession of delight from her, written after she had received Baudri's poem. Jean-Yves Tilliette has argued that Baudri himself composed the poem attributed to

Constance. Her poem contains the same number of lines as that of Baudri and alludes to passages elsewhere in Baudri's verse. Yet there is a significant contrast in tone between Baudri's poem and her reply, which combines imagery from both the Song of Songs and the *Heroides* to reflect on a theme of great seriousness, the correct relationship between a man and a woman in the religious life. She voices frustration that he is so long absent:

> Woe is me that I cannot often see the one I love! Miserable me! I cannot behold what I desire. I am weakened by desire and day long prayers; in vain I pour out vows and prayers to God.[81]

She expands on Baudri's theme of chastity, but demands that he not play with her emotions. This is not a theme which Baudri articulates elsewhere in his verse.

> I have been chaste, I am chaste now, I want to live chaste. Oh would that I could live as a bride of God. Yet not for this do I detest your love; the bride of God should love God's servants. . . . May law and rule always protect our love. May a modest life grace our games. Let us therefore hold to simplicity as pure as a dove, and do not prefer any woman to me.[82]

At the climax of her poem, she insists that he should visit her, finding some reason why he might come to Angers:

> Your crime is great if you do not feed one hungry, do not satisfy one who pleads. Long awaited one, come, and do not linger long; often have I called you; you who are called often, come![83]

To read this verse as an expression of sexual desire does not do justice to the particular values that she is asking him to uphold: greater communication with Baudri based on a relationship of "dove-like" simplicity. Her poem uses literary artifice to present an ethical demand. It offers the image of an articulate woman quite different from the conventional Mary Magdalene figure constructed by many male authors. Whereas Baudri's verse is about the appropriate physical distance they should maintain, her concern is that he should not hide behind literary jest or the pleasure of the written word. She is able to go along with the literary form of an agreeable diversion, but she does not want the purity of their relationship to be betrayed. The moral seriousness of Constance's poem is comparable to that evident in the woman in the letters copied by Johannes de Vepria. While the man in the exchange remains influenced by Ovidian conception of *amor* as an external force that undermines reason, the woman he loves explains *amor* as *dilectio,* a more deliberate form of love. Like Constance, she identifies more with the ideals of love articulated by women in Ovid's *Heroides* than with the rhetoric of intense passion for a woman, satirized in the *Amores.*

The contrast between the attitudes of Marbod and Baudri toward Robert of Arbrissel's association with women parallels that which divides Roscelin and Abelard in their attitude toward Robert. Marbod suspected that any relationship between a man and a woman could only be sexual. Baudri developed a more sophisticated argument that *amor* was divine in origin. Within an imagined exchange between the exiled Ovid and his male companion, Florus, Baudri has Florus say:

> God has driven our nature to be full of love; nature teaches us what he taught her. If love is to be blamed, the agent of love is to be blamed; for the agent of love will be the agent of the crime. That we exist is a crime if it is a crime that we love; God who gave being, granted me loving. And God himself, who made love, did not make hate; for what is hate is born from vice. You talked about love, but did not create it; no flame was lit by your teaching.[84]

Baudri viewed *amor* as a sublime force rather than as a degrading passion, a conviction that anticipates the ideals celebrated by some vernacular poets in the twelfth century. While the situation of the female student in the love letters is different from that of Constance, they share a common belief that God recognizes true love, a common formula in subsequent troubadour and trouvère lyric. Baudri composed fictive dialogues, modeled on the *Heroides.* He also exchanged poems with a network of friends, including a few women whose literary gift he admired. Like Jean de Meun, Baudri employs the device of fictional speech to explore for himself the nature of love. Baudri believed that the insights of Ovid and other classical authors were fully compatible with the insights of Christian tradition.[85] The woman who exchanged those love letters with her teacher shared the same conviction.

The Regensburg verse exchange and Tegernsee letters

The phenomenon of educated men and women exchanging messages in prose and verse was not confined to Anjou and the Île-de-France in the early twelfth century. The letters and poems copied by Johannes de

Vepria can usefully be compared to the verses preserved in a twelfth-century manuscript, apparently the record of an exchange between a teacher and his female pupil (or pupils).[86] An internal reference to a new boy ruler may allude to the accession of Henry V in 1105.[87] The teacher is from Liège, the woman, probably a nun or a student at one of the old-established Benedictine communities in Regensburg.[88] The exchange may have begun simply as an exercise in verbal dexterity, conducted on wax tablets, but copied onto parchment by one of the two parties. It begins with a poem about the fable of the fox in the vineyard, thinly disguised sexual innuendo.[89] Then follows a reply by a woman who treats the exchange as a game. She protests that "he who is far from sight is far from light of heart. I shall hate if I can, if not I shall love unwillingly . . . nor am I an old woman—let the play go on!"[90] The man becomes more specific in his demand that she yield to him, earning a sharp reply from the woman: "You should be called monkey or sphinx to which you are similar in your deformed face and immoderate hair!"[91] She emphasizes the importance of virtue (*virtus*) in relationships.[92] The lack of form and the quite distinct voices recorded in the manuscript argue against their being the composition of a single author. In one, the girl complains that the teacher is giving his attention to Bertha.[93] In some verses, the girl speaks for a whole group of women. Others convey a private message:

> It is I whom you know, but do not betray your lover. I beg you to come to the old chapel at dawn. Knock lightly, for the sacristan lives there. Then what the breast now hides, the bed will reveal to you.[94]

Her immediate concern is to negotiate a satisfying relationship with her teacher. Not all the letters express glowing fondness for the other. Near the end of the exchange, the man accuses her of fleeing from him, and of not bringing him "whatever secret you have." She accuses him of dallying with another girl, and eventually announces that she is leaving him.[95] He had not lived up to her ethical principles. The exchange concludes with her deciding not to pursue the relationship any further, an ending that parallels the desire expressed in the woman's final note (112a) as copied by Johannes de Vepria. This latter exchange draws on a far wider range of literary sources and elaborates much more sophisticated ideas about the nature of love. Whereas the Regensburg verses are remarkable for their immediacy and openness, the complex literary allusions in the love letters are much more difficult to interpret.

Comparing these love letters to a collection of women's letters preserved in a twelfth-century manuscript from Tegernsee is similarly instructive.[96] The Tegernsee letters are written in the same rhyming prose style as
the woman's love letters, copied by Johannes de Vepria. They do not constitute a continuous exchange, however, and lack any level of formal philosophical analysis. The author of the first letter defines herself not as lover
but as a female friend (*amica*), writing to her male friend (*amico*). Like the
woman in the Troyes love letters, the female writer apologizes for her lack
of sophistication when writing to someone who is more educated:

> Trusted one, accept the reply to your letter. I do not know if I am capable
> of writing what I consider worthy, especially since it is a shame to assault
> the ears of a learned man with uncultivated language, and it would be
> wrong to let it pass in silence. I will reply to you, however, as I can. It seems
> a hard and difficult thing what you are trying to ask from me, namely my
> complete trust, which I have never promised to any mortal. But if I know
> that I shall be loved by you with a pure love, and that the pledge of my
> chastity is not to be violated, I do not refuse effort or love. If it exists with-
> out suffering, it cannot be called love, and thus certainly is the greatest ef-
> fort. Take care that no one sees these words, because they were not written
> by authority.[97]

The closing caution, so similar to the woman's warning in letter 69, provides valuable evidence that such a letter was meant to be private. Literary
communication created a private sphere needing to be protected from the
outside world. She invokes familiar feudal imagery to describe the ethos of
love (*amor*) by which she wishes to be bound. Although the fourth letter
in the collection has no salutation identifying firmly whether the author is
a man or a woman, it could be a reply to the preceding letter, written in
the same rhyming prose.[98] The fifth letter may be written by a woman to
another woman ("C. darling dearest"), as it closes with a final greeting:
"The convent of young women also greets you, sweet pearl." It voices the
conviction that two friends are separated by great distance, but are joined
by "equanimity of souls and true friendship, which is not artificial, but
which is fixed in my heart." The writer protests with the same sort of affection as Baudri reserves for his male friends: "I want to love you until the
moon falls from the sky because before everyone who is in the world, you
are fixed in the depth of my heart."[99]

The second letter in the Tegernsee collection is rather different from
the others in that it is from "an abandoned friend" to a (male) friend. She
berates the man with an intensity not unlike that of the first letter of

Heloise to Abelard. She insists on her innocence, shifting the blame firmly to his quarter:

> My soul is consumed with sorrow and filled with bitterness, because I seem to have been completely wiped out from your memory; I always hoped for trust and love from you to the end of my life. What strength, H., do I have that I may bear this patiently and not weep over what is now and for ever? Is my body bronze, or my mind like a rock or my eyes stony that I may not mourn the evil of my misfortune? What have I done? What have I done? Did I ever reject you first? In what am I found guilty? Indeed, I have been rejected without any fault of mine. If you are looking for guilt, you have yourself, yourself, as the guilty one! For often, indeed very often, I sent a message of mine to you, but I never obtained either in great or even in the least part consoling words from you. May all men depart, not seeking trust and love further from me! Take particular care that no third eye comes between us. Farewell, farewell; follow better ways.[100]

The Tegernsee letters do not present a continuous exchange, as in the Regensburg and Troyes manuscripts. They are preserved in a monastic library not for any spiritual content, but as models of literary style, respected for their command of language. Nothing is known about who wrote them. The two subsequent poems are certainly love letters, although they are written in metrical verse. One sings the physical praise of a woman, "By the plenty [ubere, also meaning breast] of your many delights, dearest, by your looks, see how you punish me endlessly . . ."; another asks why love has grown lukewarm: "It is enough and too much that our letter between us is delayed."[101] Although these letters were preserved at Tegernsee for their literary interest, they originated from outside its confines. They do not share the same complex fusion of literary and philosophical themes as makes the exchange copied by Johannes de Vepria so unusual.

The Zurich anthology

The Troyes love letters are also more sophisticated than a collection of verses preserved in a late twelfth-century Zurich manuscript (perhaps from Schaffhausen), containing some four hundred items, mostly anonymous, but with some poems by Marbod of Rennes and Hildebert of Lavardin and a few texts in German.[102] The anthology contains many verses that illustrate the literary and intellectual concerns of a cleric studying in France in the mid twelfth century when Abelard and Heloise were already well known. Some are satirical, such as those about sodomitical clergy.[103] Others relate to Poitiers and Orléans. One is about a teacher of logic called Galo, perhaps the Gualo who succeeded Abelard at Notre-Dame after 1117, and who came into conflict with bishop Stephen of Senlis in 1127.[104] The compiler of this anthology was interested as much in writing about women as about famous people. One of his verses begins with a similar invocation to the Muse as the first poem by the woman in the Troyes anthology (66), although now addressed by a man to his "sweet friend":

> The Muse of a friend greets you with happy augury. My Muse sings of you, she delights to play for you alone. . . . [105]

This is followed by another poem, employing images sometimes similar to those of the man's love letters: "My sweet friend, more beautiful than Galatea, the glory, flower, mirror, light, and beauty of women, the one hope of my life, sweet friend. . . . As Lucifer is set over the stars, thus you are set over young women. . . . Remember these things, beloved, lest you do not give them to the wind. Live, always fare well, another does not worship you more than me."[106] The comparison to Lucifer recalls an image used by the man in his first poem in the anthology (20); the Ovidian phrase "words to the wind" is also cited in the love letters (75, 94). The next two poems in the Zurich manuscript are epitaphs for Abelard and Heloise, evidence that this part of the anthology must have been completed after 1164. One is an epitaph celebrating the love of Abelard and Heloise; the other is reported in the late fifteenth century as having been engraved on an image above Abelard's tomb. It records that Abelard both composed verse and engaged in the study of philosophy, the same combination of gifts as celebrated by Heloise in her famous letter to Abelard and in the last of the woman's love letters (112).[107]

The Zurich anthology also contains a number of verse epistles in which the poet asks for proof of a lady's love:

> I have often written to you and at the same time have received your writings. I beg you not to be light-hearted towards us; or if your love has turned into boredom with us, write briefly to me what you want. Do not keep our mind further in suspense. If you wish that I love you, I shall always love you, I say; and although you do not, you will always be my concern.[108]

Perhaps the most moving poem in this anthology is addressed "To a fugitive" (*Ad fugitivum*), written in the voice of a woman who feels abandoned by her lover. She has lost her virginity, and complains that she is being beaten by her father or guardian because of her relationship to the man. Its intense lament is worth quoting at length because it parallels the rhetoric employed in Heloise's first two letters to Abelard:

> All things are becoming cheap, my limbs becoming limp with sorrow; there is no need to explain what difficulties of a settler they sustain. Sense weakens, the body, the voice grows silent. Therefore come back, in case you deserve death. . . . I beg the living God that he give you back to me as a friend. Take thought for a delirious mind, already lost. . . . Writings are empty for me, because they bring sad things to the heart. What may I say to one who is absent—woe is me—to a fugitive? What does it help to assault absent ears with verses? You have become harder than stone, until you pine for me: I am not able to overcome your stony self far away. Come with me, let me make you not be with yourself; I wanted to speak many things with you, if I had time and places which suited our tears. May my writings speak these things on my behalf because they are not given, and may parchment stand for my living voice. May I gain what I deserve, by no spoken permission, dwelling with you in hidden places. If you do not want to yield to me in private, at least allow my parchment to say a few things. . . . May the gold streams of the Rhine turn into the Histria before you do not wish to speak to me. By what reason I might be more shameful to you than before, I cannot say at all. This came from you, whatever displeased you in me: Surely you have tested what I am? Why do you weaken me? Then I was a jewel, then a flower, then the lily of the field; then I was unlike any woman in the world. What I was then I am now, apart from being a virgin; nor can I ever be that: over that I weep. I weep over this, night and day, because fate has not carried my life with sweet virginity. To triumph by deceit is nothing apart from wanting praise. Promising me good things, you have often given me much, and in place of good things, I have taken much that is bad. Often because of you, I am given many beatings that my soft limbs can scarcely bear. The reputation of dishonor hurts more than beating of limbs. Suffering beatings is easier than suffering words. What previously gave delight, now makes me burst into tears.[109]

Is this poem an imaginary composition or is it the copy of a genuine letter? It recalls the second letter in the Tegernsee collection in the intensity of its demand that the man return to the woman he once loved. She wants him to be her friend again. She alludes to previous epithets applied to her (like "lily of the field," drawn from the Song of Songs), and asks why he has changed in his attitude. She describes her letter as a poor substitute for her voice. The directness of her complaint makes this poem difficult to imagine as a male invention. Heloise was not the only educated woman in the twelfth century to rebel against the injustice of the way she was treated by the man she loved. Most women who suffer violence do not have their voices heard. This poem was sufficiently eloquent for some cleric to include it in his anthology (if he was not himself the fugitive to whom the poem is addressed).

This poem is followed by five verse epistles (nos. 117–121), of interest for their immediacy rather than any literary merit. The first begins: "No woman can be found, I testify, equal to you . . ."; the second: "May God turn away from punishment and give you pleasant dwelling places, but with me, because I want to live with you." The fourth missive recalls the early protestations of the man in the Troyes exchange: "I put off everything, I love you with my whole breast; you are the living spring of worldly delights. I worship you, I want you, I look for you, I am worn out in my breath. About to die, I sigh for you and look for you. . . ."[110] The fifth refers to poems that a woman sent: "You have sent songs, you have given what my Muse loves; they make bronze and gold squalid, as songs alone they are strong."[111] These poems may form a sequence directed to the woman who wrote the poetic epistle "To a fugitive."

The Fleury poems

Verses about Abelard and Heloise also occur at the end of a twelfth-century manuscript from Fleury, of great interest because they include an exchange in which the rights and wrongs of Abelard's behavior in 1117 are debated.[112] The first poem voices sympathy for Heloise and hostility towards Abelard for his having forced her to enter the religious life unwillingly. Its first line alludes to a detail mentioned in the *Historia calamitatum*, that Abelard came back from Brittany after his mother had decided to enter the religious life:

> Peter set out for Paris when his mother had taken the veil. Nor will the cruel man's beloved come back other than veiled. The mother takes the veil of her free will, the friend unwillingly. It was appropriate for an old woman who is cold in body; it is damnable for a tender and less fearsome girl, whose face had set her above many, whose philosophy had set her above all girls, she through whom alone Gaul has worth. Yet her cruel friend endured abandoning her—if anyone calls him "friend" not because he loves, but is loved: he ordered her whom he had abandoned to be veiled. She obeyed, nor could she have left unfulfilled for her husband whatever love can fulfil.[113]

This poem confirms what Heloise says in her letter to Abelard, that she entered the religious life at his behest. It sympathizes strongly with her predicament.

The next poem sides with Abelard as a philosopher brought low by betrayal, just as women had brought down famous men in the past. It compares Abelard's fate to that of Matthias, probably the count of Nantes (d. 1101), according to this poem castrated because of adultery:

> Two jewels, Gaul, adorned you once: Matthias the consul and Peter the philosopher. One the glory of knighthood, the other the light of the clergy. Envious fate deprived both these exalted men of their genitals; an unlike charge made them alike in the wound. The consul was undone by a just charge of adultery; the philosopher fell by a supreme betrayal. The shameful wound attached the philosopher to the monks, and took study away from you, philosophy. A woman destroyed Adam, Samson, Solomon: Peter alas has been destroyed by a like fall. This was the public downfall of the highest men.[114]

After a missing line or lines, a verse follows that presents a diametrically opposite viewpoint. It defends Heloise on the grounds that she is innocent:

> Only the wife of Peter is free of the crime. There was no consent on her part to make her the guilty one.

The contrast in opinions is difficult to comprehend unless these poems record a verse exchange between two people, like the Regensburg exchange of verses between a teacher and a female student. In the Fleury manuscript, the couplet defending Heloise is followed, after two lines on another subject, by a verse that proclaims the speaker's frenzy of passion and unwillingness to remain a virgin. A shorter version of this verse is also contained in the Zurich anthology:

> Either the frenzy of love will excuse me in my blindness or I will be guilty of a great betrayal. A providing host has given everything to me apart from you: I want nothing but you, nor will I be another Joseph![115]

Taken literally, these four lines present a declaration of passion from a man who does not wish to preserve his virginity, like Joseph. This plea is followed by a verse asking Robert whether he is truly a monk:

> Do you keep the substance of being a monk, Robert, if you dislike the name, or do you rejoice in the name of canon? If I am not mistaken, the cowl alone frightens you, brother.

He then confronts her with a similar accusation:

> Sister, often I ask you to spurn precious clothes, which the one you have
> loved does not love, rather forbids. . . . May your clothing show that you
> have put on Christ, my friend.[116]

These fragmentary verses seem to record repartee between a monk and a
nun, exchanging contrasting views about Abelard and Heloise. The woman
admires Heloise for her great learning, and feels that she has been badly
treated by Abelard, while the man (Robert?) sympathizes with Abelard for
having suffered a brutal punishment. The repartee, much less sophisticated
than that recorded in the Troyes love letters, shows how quickly Abelard
and Heloise acquired legendary status during the time of their early affair.
This exchange is preserved in a monastic library rich not only in works of
Ovid, but also in copies of early logical glosses of Peter Abelard from the
second decade of the twelfth century. They may have been brought to
Fleury by a monk who had studied in Paris at the time of Abelard's affair
with Heloise. Like the exchanges preserved in German libraries, the Fleury
exchange does not show any of the literary sophistication of the Troyes
love letters, but it provides further evidence that the practice of men and
women in the early twelfth century exchanging Latin verse was not in itself unusual.

Letters and friendship

The love letters, as well as the verse exchanges preserved in anonymous anthologies within monastic libraries at Regensburg, Tegernsee,
Schaffhausen, and Fleury, constitute only a small proportion of surviving
dialogues of the period celebrating values of friendship and intimacy. The
vast majority are between men. Yet the tradition of women participating in
literary exchanges stretches back to the early medieval period. In the
eighth century, educated Anglo-Saxon nuns exchanged verse with Boniface, archbishop of Mainz. Lioba asked Boniface to accept her "in place of
a brother" and begged him not to forget her so that "the bond of true
love" (*vere dilectionis ligatura*) between them would remain for ever. She sent
him verses "composed according to the discipline of poetic tradition," a
skill she had learned from Eadburgh, abbess of Thanet, another correspondent of Boniface.[117] The modest revival of religious communities for aristocratic women in the tenth and eleventh centuries enabled these literary
traditions to be preserved into the eleventh and early twelfth centuries.[118]

Nuns and recluses were not allowed to preach, but they did copy manuscripts, for which a high degree of literacy was required.[119] Clear evidence
of the literacy of aristocratic religious communities for women is provided
by the contributions they made to obituary rolls, carried round from one
abbey to the next by a messenger to celebrate the death of an important
figure. The contributions from nuns at Wilton in England, Le Ronceray at
Angers, Sainte-Trinité at Caen, and Sainte-Croix at Poitiers are all of a
consistently high standard, not to speak of those from Argenteuil.[120]

Vernacular verse composed by women is even more difficult to glimpse
than that in Latin, except through the filter of persistent ecclesiastical condemnations of "shameless songs" and "girls' songs." Legislation of Charlemagne in 789 prohibited nuns and abbesses exchanging love songs
(winileodas) with monks.[121] A substantial body of songs in a woman's voice
are preserved in kharjas in Spanish and Galician-Portuguese dialects, and to
a lesser extent in Provençal and Old French.[122] Gerhoch of Reichersberg's
remark in 1148 that both holy women in monasteries and married women
whose husbands were on Crusade were singing new religious songs in the
vernacular, shows how women could be recognized as creative in their
own right.[123]

Exchanges between women and men in the vernacular tend to be
recorded only when they attract negative attention from the authorities.
One such comment is noted by Dronke in the Life of a bishop of Iceland
in the late eleventh century:

> There was a favorite game among the people—which is unseemly—that
> there should be an exchange of verses: a man addressing a woman, and a
> woman a man—disgraceful strophes, mocking and unfit to be heard. Bishop
> Jon had it discontinued—he utterly prohibited the practice. Poems or stro-
> phes of love-song he would not hear recited or allow to be recited; nonethe-
> less he did not altogether succeed in getting them stopped.[124]

While nothing is known about these love songs (mansaungs), these condemnations suggest that the authorities were never able to suppress such
exchanges between women and men. The Cambridge songbook, compiled
in the Rhineland ca. 1050, includes a Latin love poem written as a letter
from a bride to her dearest spouse.[125] Another presents itself as a verse dialogue in both German and Latin between a nunna and a man.[126]

Records of Latin exchanges between women and men survive mostly
from the period between 1050 and 1150. The Troyes love letters provide a
rare example of a literary genre that may have been much more wide-

spread than the surviving record suggests. By the second half of the twelfth century, opportunity for women to practice such literary skills seems to have become more rare, as the education offered by women's monastic communities was unable to complete with urban schools, to which women were denied access. The monastic correspondence of Heloise and Abelard represents perhaps the last great flowering of the genre. It articulates with unusual clarity the tension between traditional perception of *amor* as a lapse from commitment to God, and an ethic based on the obligations of love which Heloise struggles to define to Abelard.

The Poems in the Troyes Anthology

The letters and poems copied by Johannes de Vepria represent a high point in the genre of Latin dialogue within a secular context. They are not just derivative of an existing literary tradition. They manipulate literary themes in a far more complex way than any surviving exchanges from Anjou or southern Germany. The woman's literary skills develop in the course of the exchange. The first metrical poems in the exchange are by her teacher, who initially uses a traditional "leonine" meter, in which the last syllable of the second half of the line (not necessarily the accented syllable) rhymes with the first half. In his old age, Marbod condemned the type of rhyme that he had used in his youth, also found in the Regensburg exchange, as clumsy.[127] This is the style of the first metrical poem in the exchange (*20*), in which the teacher celebrates his beloved as a star who should lead him but threatens to fade (also an image in the poem *Hebet sydus* of the *Carmina burana,* often attributed to Abelard).[128] The key image of the man's poem in letter *20* is that the woman is a light or morning star (*lucifer*) who drives out darkness.

Her first metrical verse occurs in response to verses she receives from him (*38a*).[129] He composes five lines, each with its own internal rhyme, to express his longing to touch her. The woman continues in the same style, insisting that she will be faithful to him, no matter what he thinks, and reiterates a prayer raised in her second letter (*3*). The final verses are from the man, picking up on her profession of fidelity. They proclaim his love for her without her religious allusions. He develops an idea he raised in his first letter to her, that living without her is death (the same idea as used by Marbod). His rhymes fit into the same pattern of literary exchange as the Regensburg verses.

Apart from short metrical lines in letters 48 and 49, the first major long poem from the woman is letter 66, an appeal to Clio and then to each of the Muses to sing their greetings to her teacher, whom she sees as dispelling all darkness. She begins by using a different rhyme in each syllable, although she does not keep this up. Her list of the nine Muses (Clio, Euterpe, Thalia, Melpomene, Terpsicore, Calliope, Urania, Polimnia, and Erato) derives not from Ovid, but from Fulgentius, a fifth-century author.[130] While the convention of invoking the Muses (*Camenae*) for inspiration had fallen out of fashion in late classical poetry, Boethius and some Carolingian writers exploited the convention.[131] Baudri of Bourgueil drew more extensively on Fulgentius to describe each of the nine Muses in a long mythological poem, than the woman in the love letters.[132] Her direct appeal to each of the Muses is closer to a poem of Hildebert of Lavardin that she could have known.[133] She imagines these Muses as still alive. In a sense, she is Sappho singing to her Apollo. Her first major poem in the anthology boldly asserts that she sees herself to be in direct continuity with this antique tradition. The crisis in the relationship that provoked her to insist in letter 60 that all communication between them should cease, seems to have unleashed a new degree of creativity in her. She now sees herself more self-consciously as a poet.

In her next poem (69), she experiments with elegiac distichs: "Go, letter, and take my complaints to a friend" (*Littera, vade meas et amico ferte querelas*), an opening that recalls Ovid's address to Perilla (*Tristia* 3.7). She begs that jealous eyes not read her verses. After a third poem (73), written in the more joyful spirit of letter 66, she composes a lament (82), singled out by Peter Dronke for its arresting quality. Here she protests that Caesar's riches were nothing to her, compared to the treasure that she loved. Like the stones on a funeral pyre "our body completely vanishes in love." She sees herself as a classical tragic heroine, not unlike Dido immolating herself in her love for Aeneas. This is the first time she does not always make both halves of her verses rhyme. Her teacher avoids this practice completely in his first major metrical poem (87), in which he considers how he has been conquered by love in a year that was both short and long, and apologizes if he has brought his beloved at any time to tears. There are three other metrical poems from the man near the end of the exchange. They all avoid those obvious rhymes found in the Regensburg exchange and in the early verses of the Troyes correspondence. The man's mood is different in the last communication (113) copied by Johannes de Vepria, a lament begging forgiveness and explaining how he had been led astray by *amor*. He complains about the obstacle presented by the murmuring of people "which I fear" (*Obstant et populi murmura, que timeo*). With elegiac detachment, he considers his feelings for her to have been ultimately based on deception, precisely that trickery about which Ovid was considered such a wise and prudent guide. The man's style of carefully structured verse is subtly different from the emotional intensity with which the woman invests her letters and poems.

Conclusion

Much more can be said about the letters and poems in the Troyes anthology and their relation to twelfth-century writing about love than indicated in this brief survey of their literary context. While the exchange is remarkable for its size, it builds on an existing tradition of literary dialogue between women and men belonging to an educated elite. Aristocratic monastic foundations for women, like those of Notre-Dame at Argenteuil and Le Ronceray at Angers were able to provide privileged young women, generally from noble families, with the opportunity to study Latin literature. The closest literary connections of the Troyes love letters and poems are to the verse epistles of Marbod of Rennes addressed to an unnamed *amica*. A major difference between the Troyes love letters and these verse epistles, however, is that most of the letters are written in crafted prose rather than in metrical verse. The love letters demonstrate a greater degree of freedom and spontaneity. The woman in the love letters displays a distinct character not found in any of the other exchanges. She has an ardent desire to learn the philosophy which she admires in her teacher, and is particularly keen to discuss the concept of love. She offers her own thoughts about love as an ideal, subtly transforming the thought of Cicero by transfusing it with imagery and idealism drawn from scripture. As the man observes in letter 50, she is unique among all the young women of her time in being a female student of philosophy.

The love letters manifest a view of love infused not just by Ovidian satire but by ideals of *amicitia* normally articulated within an all-male context by Latin writers, whether pagan like Cicero, or Christian like Ambrose and Jerome. Belief that a chaste relationship could develop between women and men was fostered by apocryphal texts like the Acts of Paul and Thecla. The revival of the idea of a chaste union between a man and a woman in the eleventh and twelfth centuries provided an alternative vision of male/female relationships, traditionally viewed as legitimate only for sexual procreation.[134] Ivo of Chartres may have been a strong advocate of the ideal of chastity for the clergy, but he also advocated a greater sense of moral seriousness in relationships between men and women. He saw marriage as based on true consent between two individuals rather than simply on the existence of a physical relationship.[135]

One of the most fascinating features of the letters copied by Johannes de Vepria is the tension they portray between two views of love. While the man is highly educated and speaks of the *amicitia* they share, it is the woman who reflects more fully on the implications of applying ideals of selfless friendship to both *amor* and *dilectio*. She identifies more with the moral seriousness of the heroines about whom Ovid wrote in his *Heroides* than with the flippant wit of the *Amores*. The few Latin verses presented in a woman's voice in poetic anthologies from the twelfth century strengthen the argument that some educated women did engage in exchanging writing in Latin with men. In doing so, these women were participating in a wider cultural phenomenon practiced among an educated elite in the late eleventh and early twelfth century, of exchanging intimate verse and letters in order to forge a friendship network. Just as St. Anselm and St. Bernard broke out of monastic convention by expressing themselves with greater intimacy to their friends, so the teacher and his student create their own secret world, shielded from the gaze of jealous outsiders through a complex web of allusions to scripture and classical literature.

The letters copied by Johannes de Vepria celebrate an imaginary world of idealized love at a time of much questioning about traditional relationships between women and men. They throw precious light on the development of new thinking about conduct between women and men in France before such ideas are developed in the *langue d'oeuil* in the second half of the twelfth century. The only way of establishing more firmly whether or not these letters are written by Abelard and Heloise is to compare their vocabulary and style to that of known texts by this famous couple. The love letters are like fragments of a mosaic of which only certain sections remain, but which allow us to appreciate a larger picture once they are put correctly into position. They record in much greater detail than the *Historia calamitatum* the evolution of a love affair between a celebrated teacher and a young woman of great literary promise.

CHAPTER 5

THE LANGUAGE OF THE LOVE LETTERS

> When you saw these letters from my eager hand
> could your eye recognize the sender
> or did you fail to recognize their author
> until you could read my name, "Sappho"?[1]

The opening lines of *Sappho to Phaon* provoke the question of female authorship in acute form. How do we ever really know that we are listening to a woman's voice? The same question could be posed of the letters copied by Johannes de Vepria. While twelfth-century readers were fascinated by the literature of dialogue, whether it be Cicero's discussions about friendship or Augustine's philosophical conversations about truth, happiness and God, women's voices were rarely encountered except as imagined in scripture or in poems like Ovid's *Heroides*. The exchange copied by Johannes de Vepria is unusual in recording such a lengthy dialogue between a woman and a man. The controversy surrounding the authenticity of the famous Abelard–Heloise correspondence may have had the effect of discouraging scholars from exploring these anonymous love letters. It seems astonishingly bold to suggest that a copy of the intimate correspondence of two famous lovers could survive unnoticed in a municipal library in France without its significance being recognized. The only way to establish whether Johannes de Vepria did come across a copy of their intimate correspondence is to compare the language of these letters with that of other known writings of Abelard and Heloise.

The Process of Dialogue

The dialogue recorded in these love letters is quite different from the formal speeches invented by Abelard in philosophical dialogues which explore a single, unified argument. In his *Soliloquium* (ca. 1122), Abelard invents an imaginary conversation between *Petrus* and *Abaelardus* to explore the common goal of philosophy and religion.[2] He develops these interests further in his *Collationes,* fictional dialogues of an imaginary philosopher with both a Jew and a Christian, written ca. 1126–33.[3] In both these treatises Abelard pursues a theme implicit in the woman's love letters, that the ethical wisdom of the ancients is fully consistent with the message of the Gospel. Abelard never includes a woman's voice in these dialogues, in which different protagonists share the same literary style and vocabulary. Abelard is quite conventional in all his scholastic writing, whether about logic or theology, in consistently presenting arguments in a male voice. One treatise in which a woman's voice does appear is *The Problems of Heloise* (*Problemata Heloissae*), a collection of forty-two questions put by Heloise, many of them dealing with ethical issues raised by scripture, each followed by a response from Abelard. They are introduced by a letter from Heloise in which she presents herself as imitating Paula and Eustochium in questioning Jerome. The use of a Greek word for the title of this work, rather than the standard Latin term, *Quaestiones,* may reflect a deliberate desire on Heloise's part to emulate sophisticated scholastic usage.[4] The questions and answers do not form a continuous dialogue as in the love letters. Heloise supplies a series of questions to which Abelard provides answers.

The love letters do record some elements of a scholastic exchange between teacher and pupil. In letter 5, she articulates her desire to absorb the philosophical gifts which he so richly manifests. In letter *24,* he responds to her question about the nature of love. For most of the correspondence, however, she addresses him not as her teacher, but as her beloved. Her desire is for a relationship of full equality, a goal that proves ultimately beyond his capacity. There is a similar tension in the more famous Heloise–Abelard correspondence. Heloise strives to develop a more philosophical exchange, as she forces Abelard to address the ethical dilemma in which she finds herself. She is plagued by the contrast between her public reputation for piety and religion and her own conviction that she cannot repent of her love for Abelard, which she insists was always true and selfless. To argue, as Schmeidler and others have done, that the correspondence is a literary dialogue invented by Abelard to instruct Heloise in the religious life, is to silence the voice of Heloise. Such claims also fail to recognize the vast stylistic gulf between formal scholastic dialogues and a literary exchange in which two distinct personalities emerge. It is more plausible to argue that Heloise was forcing Abelard to address

ethical issues both in relation to herself and to her community than to insist that Abelard anticipated all these ideas.

Only in letter 112 does the woman address her beloved as her teacher.
She explains that although his letters had once raised her to the heights of
ecstasy, she now has a quite different cause for joy, one which she cannot
put into words. The very act of addressing her teacher as her beloved has
transformed her relationship to him. At the same time, she struggles with
feelings of anxiety that she does not have the technical eloquence to profess her feelings. By letter 23 she is overwhelmed by internal conflict between the desire of her spirit (*animus*) to write and the advice of her ability
(*ingenium*) to advance more cautiously, she exclaims that she lacks the "salt
of learning" to answer him, while he is rich in philosophy. Even in letter
49 she still professes in extravagantly rhetorical phrases that she is unworthy to respond to such a great teacher. In a sense these love letters are the
report of a discussion between a teacher and a student who believed for a
short while that they had transcended these labels through their love. She
is fascinated by the idea that true love (*amor*) imposes all the ideals of
friendship (*amicitia*) as defined by Cicero, except that she sees their friendship as between a man and a woman. While he does once define *amor* in
terms of Ciceronian *amicitia,* he is not as at ease as she is in understanding
amor as an ideal intimacy and sharing between people who have transcended self-concern. His understanding of love in letter *24* is that it is "a
universal thing" which already resides in both of them, proven by his sense
that the two of them already shared the same thoughts. He does not quite
say that they have become one person, as Cicero imagined was the ideal
of friendship, but he thinks that the two of them are "not different."

The argument that these love letters could not be written by Abelard
and Heloise because they document an idealized relationship depends on
reading a phrase in letter 84, "Hitherto you have stayed with me, you have
manfully fought the good fight with me, but you have not taken your reward," as evidence that this relationship was unconsummated. In this letter, however, the woman is using religious imagery to profess the
constancy of her love, a love that looks forward to eternal joy. The religious
imagery in her letters must be taken seriously. She does not yet think that
their relationship has arrived at its goal. In the man's letters, there is more
explicit allusion to sexual gratification (as in letter *26*). Her tendency is to
divert his eagerness with moral exhortation (as in 27). What he construes
as her tendency to delay (*17*) makes him upset. The woman balances her
comments in letter 84 about his not having gained his reward by offering
to reward him with "the obedience of love" for having composed a cer-

tain prologue for her. Even if letter 84 does refer to the promise of sexual favors, this is not in itself an argument against the possibility that the lovers are Heloise and Abelard. In the *Historia calamitatum,* Abelard passes over the period during which he began to get to know Heloise very quickly, in order to dwell on the period of physical debauchery in Fulbert's house. The letters before 87 could have been exchanged before their union was consummated.

In the *Historia calamitatum,* Abelard gives the impression that he deliberately seduced Heloise. He gives no consideration to Heloise's desire to engage in any relationship with her teacher other than to provide him with an opportunity to vent his lust. He mentions the messages they exchanged only as a device by which he could get to know her. In her recollections of their relationship, Heloise does not shrink from talking about their past intimacy as a time of physical pleasure: "When we were uneasily enjoying the joys of love and, to use a rather vulgar but more expressive term, were giving ourselves up to fornication, divine severity spared us."[5] Her attitude toward the relationship is different from his. While she admits to having submitted to carnal desire, she is troubled that she cannot find her way to true repentance.[6] Unable to accept Abelard's castration as the working of providence, she considers that her love for him was not in itself wrong. Abelard, by contrast, has no doubt that his love for her is wrong. Heloise does not deny that they had engaged in sinful physical pleasure, only that their love was not in itself so wrong as to merit the punishment which it received. She is ruthlessly honest in her self analysis. How can it be sinful to remember past pleasure? She wants him to respond to her ideal of love as not concerned with any material reward, one which she thinks they had once shared. Heloise is preoccupied with the obligations of love, which she feels Abelard does not live up to. The same concerns are held by the woman in the love letters. The man in that exchange, overwhelmed by what he sees as her depth in discussing love, tries to respond to her ideals, but eventually retreats behind traditional Ovidian rhetoric about being tricked by love and dazzled by the brilliance of her gifts (*113*).

Rhyming Prose in the Love Letters

A characteristic feature of the woman's prose is regular use of half-rhyming phrases, in which the rhyme does not necessarily involve the last stressed syllable. This is evident from letter 1: *Amori suo precordiali / omnibus aromatibus dulcius redolenti / . . .* (To her heart's love, more sweetly scented than any spice . . .). This style of rhyming prose, quite out of fashion in humanist prose in the fifteenth century, was much cultivated in monastic circles in the eleventh and twelfth centuries.[7] It is used in the women's love letters from Tegernsee, as also in an exchange between an Italian merchant and his wife, written ca. 1132–36.[8] Prose writers more influenced by a classical prose style tended to avoid excessive rhyme in formal writing, following the warnings of the *Rhetorica ad Herennium* against overusing words with similar endings.[9] In scholastic treatises, Berengar of Tours, Peter Abelard, and Gilbert of Poitiers were all more concerned with logical arguments than with the musical effects of language in their prose. The use of unstressed rhyme in the woman's love letters (and in some of the man's metrical verse, but not his prose) is a stylistic feature which falls out of fashion after the first quarter of the twelfth century. Abelard uses the technique in his hymns and laments (*planctus*), but does not imitate the dominant trend of the twelfth century verse toward stressed rhyme, evident in the sequences of Adam of Saint-Victor (d. ca. 1140).[10]

In her monastic letters to Abelard, Heloise reserves rhyming prose for passages of particular intensity:

> Hujus quippe loci tu post Deum solus es fundator, / solus hujus oratorii constructor, / solus hujus congregationis edificator. / Nichil hic super alienum / edificasti fundamentum. / Totum quod hic est, / tua creatio est. / Solitudo hec feris tantum sive latronibus vaccans, nullam hominum habitationem noverat, / nullam domum habuerat. /

> After God, you alone are the founder of this place, alone the builder of this oratory, alone the inspiration of this flock. You have built nothing here on another's foundation. All that is here is your creation. The isolation here, open to wild beasts as much as to brigands, had not known any human dwelling, did not contain any house.[11]

Heloise's half-rhyming phrases have a particular potency when read aloud:

> Que cum siccis oculis neminem / vel legere vel audire posse estimem, / tanto dolores meos amplius renovarunt / quanto diligentius singula expresserunt, / et eo magis auxerunt / quo in te adhuc pericula crescere retulisti.

> Since I think no one can read or hear of these things dry-eyed, they renewed my grief all the more for being each expressed so carefully; they have increased all the more in that you say that dangers you face are still growing.[12]

Heloise uses this rhyming style again in a short letter to Peter the Venerable written sometime after Abelard's death (the authenticity of which has never been questioned). She asks for a formula of absolution to be attached to his tomb, as well as for assistance for Astralabe:

> Visitante nos dei misericordia, / dignationis uestrae nos uisitauit gratia. / . . .
> Est siquidem uestra uisitatio / magna magnis quibuslibet gloriatio. / Norunt alii, quantum eis utilitatis / uestrae contulerit praesentia sublimitatis. / Ego certe non dicam enarrare dictu, / sed nec ipso ualeo comprehendere cogitatu, / quam utilis, quam iocundus uester michi fuerit aduentus. /

> With the mercy of God coming upon us, the grace of your eminence has visited us. . . . Your visit is indeed of great pride for some great people. Others do not know how much advantage for them the presence of your sublime person has brought. I certainly am not able to explain in words, nor am I capable of understanding in thought how useful, how joyful your visit has been to me.[13]

In his response, Peter the Venerable, employs more rhyming prose than is normal in his letters.[14] Heloise was more traditional in her prose style in making her phrases rhyme.

Both the man and the woman employ dramatic antithesis and parallel constructions, such as "as much as/so much" (*tantum/quantum*) in the love letters. While their presence in the letters of both Heloise and Abelard has sometimes been used to argue that Abelard composed Heloise's letters, any medieval writer influenced by Augustine and Gregory the Great employed these stylistic devices.[15] The same observation can be made about the presence of the *cursus* (fixed prose rhythms at the end of sentences) in the letters of both Abelard and Heloise, as well as in both the man's and the woman's love letters. A common stylistic device can easily be shared by two people.[16] While further study is needed of the *cursus* in the love letters, it seems premature to construct arguments which do not recognize that its practice can be traced back to late antiquity.[17]

The Rhetoric of Individuality

A distinctive feature of both the love letters and the monastic correspondence of Abelard and Heloise is the significance attached to formulae of greeting. As Carol Lanham has so well documented, letter writers in the eleventh and twelfth centuries paid particular attention in their personal correspondence to using these greetings to define a more intimate relationship than normal in conventional correspondence.[18] Literary experimentation was a mark of intimacy, showing the extent to which one was prepared to break with convention. In her very first letter, the woman describes herself as "she who is his in heart and body" (*sua corde et corpore*) and offers her love (*Amori suo*) "the freshness of eternal happiness" (*viriditatem eterne felicitatis*). The man does not employ rhyming phrases or scriptural imagery in reply (2), but emphasizes from the outset her uniqueness: "To the singular joy and only solace of a tired mind" (*Singulari gaudio et lassate mentis unico solamini ille*). In his second reply (4), he describes himself as "her only one" (*singularis eius*), an image that recurs in 54. In 56 he offers her whatever good thing is reserved "specifically" (*singulariter*) for lovers. By contrast, she never describes him as *singularis*. The only occasion she uses the word is in letter 23 to explain that a well constructed statement of praise demands one think about "the qualities of individual parts." There is a similar contrast between his fondness for *unicus* to emphasize her uniqueness (2, 31, 37, 47, 63, 75, 89, 99, 110), and her lack of interest in the term. The first time Johannes de Vepria records her as using it in is letter 48, "Farewell, my one salvation" (*Vale unica salus mea*) when she deliberately picks up his conclusion to letter 47: "Farewell . . . my one peace" (*Vale . . . unica quies mea*).

Whereas the woman never describes him as singular, she does call him special. The first time that she does so is in letter 21, in which she makes a bold attempt to employ a number of philosophical concepts. She opens with a greeting that is far from easy to translate: "Dilecto suo speciali, et ex ipsius experimento rei, esse quod est." Literally this can be rendered as: "To her beloved, special from experience of the reality itself: the being which she is."[19] As in some of her earlier letters (3, 5, 9), she does not identify herself at all in this greeting, but offers herself to her beloved. While she attempts to employ philosophical terminology, the effect is rather clumsy. Her use of *res* (thing) to refer to the essence of what he is, is characteristic of the woman's letters (used twenty-two times, against eleven in the man's letters). She concludes letter 21 with another term from dialectic, to explain that she loves him whether he is present or absent: "In either case, I love you" (*equipolenter te diligo*).[20] *Equipolenter* literally means "with equal value." She does not repeat such phrases in subsequent letters, preferring to draw on the vocabulary of classical poets as well as of scripture. His greeting in reply (22) is a more elegant effort in which he compares her to a jewel and hopes that she will shine with natural light.

The woman gives some indication as to why she prefers *specialis* to *singularis* in her own reflection on the meaning of *amor* in letter 25. When observing that we do not love everyone equally, she contrasts charity, which we should show to all people, with the love that is special for certain people. The observation, not in itself original, draws on a commonplace distinction between *generale* and *speciale*. Her definition is very different from that offered by her teacher in the previous letter (*24*), according to which love is "a universal thing" which makes two wills one thing "without difference" (*indifferenter*). The distinction that she draws is between a general love for everyone, and a special love that is shared with a close friend rather than between two unique individuals. She repeats *specialis* in letter 76, when she calls him her "special beloved," usage that echoes Baudri of Bourgueil's phrase, *specialis amicus*.[21] She sends letter 79 "To one deserving to be embraced with the longing of a special love," (*Merito specialis dilectionis amplectendo amore*) by which she is bound to her beloved.

The contrast between the man's use of *singularis* and the woman's preference for *specialis* echoes that contained within the unusual greeting with which Heloise opens her third letter to Abelard: "To him who is hers specially, she who is his singularly" (*Suo specialiter, sua singulariter*).[22] Latin is far more succinct than English. While both St. Bernard and Hato of Troyes (Heloise's bishop and a good friend of Peter the Venerable) use *specialis* and *singularis* effectively as synonyms, Heloise seems to draw a deliberate contrast between the fact that she saw him as "specially hers," while in his eyes she was "singularly his."[23] This is precisely the contrast between the woman and the man in the Troyes love letters. While it has been suggested that Heloise was alluding to a phrase of Abelard in his first letter to her ("Always remember in your prayers that one who is specially yours"), it seems more likely that she was reminding him of the contrasting ways each of them used to single out the other.[24] From a dialectician's perspective, "special" means "of a species," and thus embraces a plurality of individuals, as Abelard explains in glossing Porphyry.[25] His preference for the term "singular" may reflect an idea which he once floated in these early glosses on Porphyry (but never returned to), of adding "individual" to Porphyry's standard list of five broad predicables in the tree of being: genus, species, difference, the particular, accidence.[26]

Heloise's greeting to Abelard in her third letter is itself a carefully thought out response to the earlier greetings in the exchange. There is no conventional epistolary greeting to the *Historia calamitatum*, written as a treatise rather than as a letter. In the oldest manuscripts, it is simply titled: "Consoling things of Abelard to his [male] friend" (*Abaelardi ad amicum suum consolatoria*). By contrast, Heloise's first letter in response to that narrative is carefully constructed so that she begins with the most general and concludes with the most particular:

Domino suo immo patri, conjugi suo immo fratri, ancilla sua immo filia, ipsius uxor immo soror, Abaelardo Heloysa.

To her lord or rather father, to her husband or rather brother, his servant or
rather daughter, his wife or rather sister, to Abelard Heloise.[27]

While the greeting begins by addressing Abelard in standard fashion, "To
my lord," it then picks up the ambiguities in their relationship, moving towards an ever more intimate address. A standard greeting would conclude
with some variant on *salutem*. The absence of any salutation being offered
marks this out as an unusual exchange. Heloise continues the crescendo
initiated in the greeting by then addressing Abelard in her letter as
"beloved" (*dilectissime*) and then "only one" (*unice*). She concludes the letter similarly: *vale, unice*.[28] She wants Abelard to address her not just in general terms, but as an individual. She was angry at the way that Abelard
related to her only from a distance, not communicating in the same way as
he did to the male friend to whom he addressed his autobiographical narrative. She closes her first letter by reminding him of the frequent letters
he had sent her in the past. Her emphasis on *unicus* has a particular significance in the light of the love letters. This was a favorite term of the man
to describe his beloved's uniqueness. In the man's last greeting to her in
that exchange (*110*), he addresses her as *Unice sue*. By repeating *unice* at the
beginning and end of her first response to the *Historia calamitatum*, Heloise
was signaling her desire to return to the intimate dialogue that Abelard had
once lavished on her in the past.

Abelard's first greeting in reply to Heloise modifies her greeting. He
emphasizes that he now relates to her in Christ, rather than as an individual: "To Heloise, his beloved sister in Christ, Abelard, her brother in the
same" (*Heloise, dilectissime sorori sue in Christo, Abaelardus, frater ejus in ipso*).[29]
She responds in her next letter by cleverly combining the notions of sin-
gularity conveyed by *unicus* with his emphasis that they are greeting each
other in Christ: "To her only one after Christ, she who is his alone in
Christ" (*Unico suo post Christum, unica sua in Christo*).[30] She accepts that her
relationship with him is in Christ, but she wants to communicate with him
as an individual, the way he used to speak to her. As if to drive home her
frustration, she then chides Abelard for putting the name of Heloise before
his own, contrary to the convention of how a superior should address an
inferior. If he does not want to engage with her at a personal level, he
should begin "Abelard to Heloise." She points out that he is employing an
epistolary convention normally used by friends in correspondence, but is

not actually addressing her as an individual. Abelard counters in his second reply by re-emphasizing the general terms in which he wishes to address her: "To the Bride of Christ, the servant of the same" (*Sponse Christi, servus ejusdem*).[31] There is an ambiguity here, as he could be defining himself as the servant of Christ or as the servant of the bride of Christ. He repeats this theme in the farewell to his letter. As if in direct rejoinder to such a general greeting, she replaces *unicus/unica* in her earlier greeting by invoking the two different ways they used as lovers to address each other: "To him who is hers specially, she who is his singularly" (*suo specialiter, sua singulariter*). Heloise brought more than her memories with her when she came to the Paraclete in 1129. She brought with her a record of the intense exchange of messages that they had shared in the past. When she reminds Abelard of how he visited her "with frequent letters" (*crebris me epistolis visitabas*), she was forcing Abelard to remember a collection of texts which he had effectively erased from his conscience when writing the *Historia calamitatum*. Her three letters to Abelard all attempted in their different ways to persuade him to engage in the form of intimacy which they had once enjoyed in the past. She is reminding Abelard that he was once fascinated by the rhetoric of individuality, and that he has an obligation to consider Heloise not just as a spiritual daughter, but as a separate person.

Philosophical Vocabulary in the Love Letters

The clearest demonstration of the teacher's skill in philosophical terminology can be seen in letter *24*, when he offers his own definition of love. His answer is delivered in the pedagogical tone of a teacher familiar with Cicero's *De amicitia*. He says that he is not uninformed about *amor* since it has subdued him to its rule:

> cum ita me idem amor imperio suo subiecerit, ut non extranea res, sed multum familiaris et domestica, immo intestina videatur. Est igitur amor, vis quedam anime non per se existens nec seipsa contenta, sed semper cum quodam appetitu et desiderio se in alterum transfundens, et cum altero idem effici volens, ut de duabus diversis voluntatibus unum quid indifferenter efficiatur.

> For that very love has brought me under its own command in such a way that it seems not to be external but very familiar and internal, even visceral. Love is therefore a particular force of the soul, existing not for itself nor content by itself, but always pouring itself into another with a certain hunger and desire, wanting to become one with the other, so that from two diverse wills, one is produced without difference.

After an omission mark, the discussion in letter 24 continues:

> Scias quia licet res universalis sit amor, ita tamen in angustum contractus est,
> ut audacter affirmem eum in nobis solummodo regnare, in me scilicet et in
> te domicilium suum fecisse. Nos enim duo amorem integrum, invigilatum,
> sincerum habemus, quia nichil est dulce, nichil quietem alteri, nisi quod in
> commune proficit; eque annuimus, eque negamus, idem per omnia sapimus.
> Quod inde facile probari potest qui tu sepe meas cogitaciones anticipas;
> quod ego scribere concipio, tu prevenis, et si bene memini tu illud idem de
> te dixisti.

> Know that although love may be a universal thing, yet it has nevertheless
> been condensed into so confined a place that I would boldly assert that it
> reigns over us alone—that is to say, it has made its very home in me and in
> you. For the two of us have a love that is pure, nurtured, and sincere, since
> nothing is sweet or carefree for the other unless it has mutual benefit. We say
> yes equally, we say no equally, we feel the same about everything. This can
> easily be shown by the way that you often anticipate my thoughts: what I
> think about writing, you write first, and if I remember well, you have said
> the same thing about yourself.

He asserts that although true love (*amor*) is "a universal thing" (i.e., able to
be shared by many different individuals), in reality it is so restricted that it
prevails only between the two of them.

He is here drawing on Cicero's definition of friendship (*amicitia*) to help
define love (*amor*). For Cicero, as indeed for the educated Roman establishment of which he was a part, *amicitia* was a social concept, the foundation of
all social relationships, involving men bound by common ideals of virtue, but
not women. Cicero accepted that *amicitia* took its name from *amor*, understood as the cause of benevolence, but he never formally defined *amor* as
such.[32] Cicero defined friendship as existing for its own sake rather than for
personal advantage. A true friend was another self (*alter idem*). When Cicero
spoke of *amor* it was to comment on the natural tendency of all living creatures to love first themselves and then others of their species with an eagerness like human love: "For a man loves himself and searches for another,
whose spirit (*animum*) might thus mix with his own, so that it might become
almost one from two."[33] Cicero believed that true friendship was the fruit of
virtus, and was not driven by need or personal advantage.[34] In letter 24 the
teacher adjusts Cicero's definition to apply to the relationship between a man
and a woman. His addition of "without difference" (*indifferenter*) to Cicero's
statement that friendship creates "one [spirit] from two" is of particular

significance. He is not claiming that there is a common underlying essence between two individuals, only that there are no differences between them. The man uses *indifferenter* similarly in letter *16* to wish her "Affection, the more enduring as the well-being of each of us is made a shared concern without difference" (*quo in unius nostrum salute res communis indifferenter agitur*). This idea that two things could be the same "without difference" was the position that Abelard forced William of Champeaux to admit, according to his recollections of the debate in the *Historia calamitatum*.[35] While Abelard was not the first logician to question the idea that two individuals of the same species were essentially the same, he created an issue out of the topic through the intensity of his rivalry with William of Champeaux.[36]

Cicero had defined the force of friendship as "able to be understood from the fact that from the infinite society of human kind which nature has bound together, it is such a restricted thing led into something narrow, that complete charity joins either two people or a small number."[37] The teacher expands this statement by turning the word "thing" (*res*) which Cicero had used, into "although love may be a universal thing" (*licet res universalis sit amor*), it has nevertheless been condensed into so confined a space that I would boldly assert that it reigns in us alone." With patronizing confidence, he claims that this is proven by the fact that she always anticipated what he intended to write to her, as well as, according to her, the other way round. In other words, the only true identity is that which they share. By implication, the rest of the world is made up of separate individuals. Her teacher is implying that the only universal in a world of individuals was the love that he shared with her. Where Cicero had spoken glibly of love making a single unity, the man adds that this unity is made "without difference," precisely the point that Abelard forced William of Champeaux to accept. William subsequently incorporated into his theological teaching the idea that the humanity of Peter was the same as that of Paul "without difference" rather than by essence in recognition of Abelard's argument.[38]

The man's use of *indifferenter* in letter *24* echoes closely Abelard's terminology in one of his earliest writings on logic, the *Sententie secundum magistrum Petrum*, preserved in a Fleury manuscript (Orléans, Bibl. mun. 266) that reports the lectures of a number of teachers active in Paris ca. 1109–1113. Abelard here defines the way in which Socrates the man was the same as Plato the man, while resisting the idea that Socrates and Plato are the same person:

> Similarly when we say in this argument that the expression "Socrates is a man" enunciates "Socrates is that which he is himself," we utter "that" not

separately according to person, but indifferently according to nature as much as to person. For the proposition does not state that Socrates is that person which he is himself, but we state that he has that human nature, namely that he is a man, just as when we say "Socrates is a man and Plato is the same thing."[39]

Abelard was using *indifferenter* to mean that Socrates and Plato shared the status of being a man without any *differentiae,* although they were not the same person.[40] He subsequently made the same point about the liturgical expression "the woman who damned [us], has saved [us]" in relation to Aristotle's *On Interpretation* (ca. 1120).

> . . . just as when it is said "through woman came death, through the same one life" and "woman who has damned [us], has redeemed [us]," we apply pronouns indifferently, not personally, as if one said "the woman has damned and the same one has redeemed, that is that which is her sex has redeemed [us]," namely similarly, so that it is said according to the non-difference of sex rather than according to the identity of person.[41]

His point is that Eve and Mary are not the same person, although the same term (*mulier*) is applied to both. Abelard's use of *indifferenter* is not found in discussions of the subject by his contemporaries.[42] When Abelard defines the meaning of a term which stands for a noun (a pronoun) and comments on the phrase "a woman damned the world and the same one saved it" in his *Christian Theology* (ca. 1122–26; after the gloss on Aristotle's *On Interpretation*), he does not mention the term *indifferenter.* He simply says that the expression is false in relation to person or number but true in relation to the identity of the definition of "woman."[43]

Abelard uses the expression "universal thing" (*res universalis*) just once in his *Dialectica* (probably written in large part before his castration) and never again in his later writings on logic: "For the quantity of a universal thing consists in its diffusion through inferiors."[44] Such terminology does not necessarily imply conscious philosophical realism, but rather is an example of Abelard reverting, perhaps unconsciously, to traditional usage to refer to that which is signified by a universal. Abelard subsequently rejected the idea that a universal was any kind of "thing" (*res*) in his *Logica Ingredientibus.* Among the views that he rejected in this work was the opinion which he had once forced William of Champeaux to accept, that a universal was a thing shared "indifferently" by different individuals.[45] Abelard avoided this notion when he commented again on the expression "The same woman who damned the world has saved it" in his *Christian Theology.*

Letter *24* is written by someone intimately familiar with Abelard's philosophical vocabulary as recorded in the *Sententie secundum magistrum Petrum*, before it was refined in his later glosses on Porphyry and Aristotle. This parallel provides yet further evidence for arguing that the male partner in this exchange is Peter Abelard. Letter *24* suggests that the one shared reality whose existence he was prepared to admit was the love he shared (or so he believed) with Heloise. The irony of these letters is that Abelard certainly did not share the same ideas as Heloise about the nature of love. The letter has implications for our understanding of the subsequent evolution of Abelard's thinking about logic. The subsequent collapse of his relationship with Heloise may have reinforced his sense that a universal term did not signify a universal thing, only some common characteristic predicated on different subjects. Abelard inherited from Roscelin a fascination with the problem of how to respect the identity of an individual object or person. He distrusted any philosophical language which interpreted universal categories as real substances. In the love letters, he sees Heloise as an individual like no other, through whom he thinks (for a while) that he can transcend the limitations of his own identity. By the end of the exchange, it becomes apparent that the relationship is beginning to come apart at the seams. In the *Historia calamitatum* Abelard completely glides over the inner dynamics of his relationship with Heloise. He does not refer to any difficulties in their relationship before she fell pregnant. That event transformed the situation. Abelard simultaneously blamed these events on his getting carried away by love (*amor*) for a beautiful woman, and then thought that he could resolve the situation by marrying her, a decision he subsequently recognized was a tragic mistake. Abelard's philosophical perspective made him acutely sensitive to what made one individual different from another. In his personal life, he found it difficult to accept that Heloise had ideas different from his own.

The Woman's Imagery in the Love Letters

The woman in this exchange, "the only disciple of philosophy among the young women of our age" (*50*) was no pale imitation of her teacher. Könsgen's careful tabulation of the contrasting modes of address in these letters highlights the distinctiveness of her vocabulary.[46] She is much more fond than he is of speaking about the heart (*cor*), mentioned thirty-one times in her letters, but only thirteen times in those of the man. In her very first letter she identifies herself as his "in heart and body," and addresses him as "my heart and body" in letter 18. In letter *24*, he identifies himself as "flesh," and calls her "his soul" (*anima*). This image, which recurs frequently in his letters (*15, 46, 47, 51, 61, 65*), is itself an echo of the scriptural image used in David's lament over Jonathan (the inspiration for one of Abelard's Laments), that Jonathan was David's own soul (1 Samuel 20.17).[47] Other images the man applies to her are abstract qualities like sweetness, joy, hope, life, Lady (*domina*). Many are passive in nature: quiet (*15, 47, 50*), restoration (*28*), refreshment (*47, 50*), rest (*6, 8, 57, 67*), solace (*2, 105*). Her preferred imagery is more naturalistic and often more bold. In letter 18, after he chides her for not writing (*17*), she breaks with convention by addressing him as "An equal to an equal, to a reddening rose under the spotless whiteness of lilies: whatever a lover [gives] to a lover." She repeats this inversion in letter 48, "A lover to a lover: the viridity of love," and again in letter 84, "A lover to lover: joy . . ." The man never describes himself as a lover (*amans*) except in a general sense when talking about lovers (*56, 61, 63, 87*). He prefers to use images which contrast her to himself, like her being light (*2*), his star (*4, 6, 20*) or the sun (*22*), giving light to the moon or his dark self. His other images of her include heat (*50*), food (*47*), consolation (*4*), delight (*75*), expectation (*37*), lily (*43, 53*), light (*2, 93, 108*).

She applies many different epithets to him, such as fragrance (94), city (9), consort of poets (21), elegance (21, 73), desire (69, 86), half of my heart (86), flower (73, 109), foundation (88), jewel (76, 79), fire (86), happiness (21), medicine (76), grove of virtues (90), a rose (18, 49), a star (76), breath (66). The epithet to which she persistently returns is "most beloved" (*dilectissimus*). This variety in the woman's greetings is characteristic of her general tendency, quite different from that of her teacher, to use a word only once.[48] She sometimes employs rare forms of words, possibly making them up herself by analogy with other words. Thus in letter 49 she uses the relatively rare *cervicositas* (pigheadedness), applied to the Romans by St. Bernard, and to the Jews by Peter the Venerable.[49] She then matches this with the even more unusual *superciliositas* (haughtiness or disdain)."[50] She also creates some rarely used adjectives: *inepotabilis* (86) or "unquenchable" from the verb *epoto*, to drink up; *innexibilis* (94) or "bindable" from *innecto*, to bind; *dulcifer* (98) or "sweetness-bearing."

One neologism employed in letter 53 is of particular significance. She combines the concept of *scibilitas* or "knowability" with imagery that the bride applies to her beloved in the Song of Songs (4.11): "If a droplet of knowability trickled down to me from the honey-comb of wisdom . . ." (*De favo sapiencie si michi stillaret guttula scibilitatis . . .*).[51] *Scibilitas* is not used, to my knowledge, by any major classical or medieval author prior to the mystical philosopher Ramon Llull (ca. 1232–1315) apart from Peter Abelard. In his *Dialectica,* Abelard invokes the concept to explain that every adjective can be related to an abstract form.[52] Thus *scibilis* can apply to something known and to an ideal form of "knowability."[53] He makes a similar point about *scibilitas,* defined as "the power of knowing" in his *Ingredientibus* gloss on Aristotle's *Categories.*[54] The woman turns this abstract concept into a very physical image by speaking of "a droplet of knowability" as like a drop of nectar so as to reinforce her point that she can find no speech (*sermo*) in all Latinity to express the special love (*dilectio*) which she has for the man she loves. The word *scibilis* also occurs in an epitaph reported as having been engraved on Abelard's tomb:

> Est satis in titulo: Petrus hic iacet Abaelardus
>   cui soli patuit scibile quidquid erat.

> It is sufficient as a heading: here lies Peter Abelard
>   To whom whatever was knowable was clear.

The most likely person to have composed this epitaph, placed on his tomb, is Heloise. She remembered him as someone who understood everything capable of being known.[55]

Heloise's practice of creating new words and new combinations of words was singled out by Hugh Metel (d. ca. 1150), an Augustinian canon of Toul, who sought to engage in an epistolary dialogue with her after Abelard's death. Hugh praised not only Heloise's reputation for religion, but also her fame as a writer:

> Your reputation, flying through the void, has resounded to us, worthy of sound from you, it has made an impression on us. It has informed us that you have surpassed the female sex. How? By composing, by versifying, by joining new words, making known words new, and what is more excellent than everything, you have overcome womanly weakness and have hardened into virile strength.[56]

Hugh then sent a second letter to Heloise, repeating the request to enter into correspondence. Hugh, who had written a hostile letter to Abelard ca. 1140 and was an ardent admirer of St. Bernard, William of Champeaux, and Anselm of Laon, saw Heloise as a figure quite different from Abelard. Like Peter the Venerable, he saw her as a woman "of virile strength." Literary genius was perceived as a masculine quality. Hugh's comments about

Heloise's vocabulary are immensely valuable, as he is the only twelfth-century writer who acknowledges her literary reputation. The aspect of her literary gift which he found remarkable, the invention of new words and phrases, is a characteristic feature of many innovative writers in the twelfth century, as they struggled to articulate concepts not available to them in the texts of Latin antiquity. Most new words, however, were generated to address the demands of philosophy, theology, science, and administration. The woman in these love letters is particularly adept at employing new words in an imaginative way. Her remark in letter 53 that she cannot find an expression (*sermo*) in all Latinity to express the intent of her spirit gives voice to her sense that she is exploring the boundaries of language. Hugh's remark provides further support for identifying this woman as Heloise.

The Rhetoric of Inner Disposition in the Love Letters

A key concern of both the teacher and the student in the love letters is a common conviction that words are not as important as their inner meaning. They strive to find words to express their inner intention. In letter *22* her teacher contrasts the words which he delivers to other people with the intention (*intencionem*) he directs to her: "To others I address words, to you my intention. Often I stumble over words, because my thought is far from them." The comment recalls Abelard's remark that at the height of his passion for Heloise, he began to lose inspiration in his lectures, and that he started to compose love songs.[57] In subsequent letters the man prefers *voluntas* to *intencio*, as in letter *89:* "Consider not the words but the will of the sender" (*non verba consule sed mittentis voluntatem*). He uses *intencio* only once again, in letter *72.* By contrast, the woman employs *intencio* seven times in her letters, the first time in letter 23, immediately after he has introduced the term within a long monologue about her uncertainty whether to continue the relationship: "Where does the unthinking intention of your hasty spirit drive you?" Often she employs "intention" to denote her own will, as in letter 76: "My intention has decided this, that further conflict between us should cease." In her next letter (79), *intencio* occurs twice:

> If through reflection a person's inner intention (*hominis interioris intencio*) conceives anything great, it is often not brought to fruition without a certain external force. . . . For a long time, and with a blazing struggle of heart and body, I have considered how I should address you, my graceful jewel, but the difficulty of expected failure has so far defied the intention of my feelings (*intencionem mei affectus*).[58]

Whereas her teacher uses *intencio* in the more precise sense of intention of words, she refers to this term as a metaphor for inner identity. This tendency is particularly marked in her later letters: in 88, "you do not slip from the intention of the mind" (*ab intencione mentis non labescis*); in 102, "I pray with the best intention of the heart" (*summa opto cordis intencione*); in 104, "who never slips from the intention of my mind" (*qui nunquam labescit ab intencione mentis*). Abelard had always paid attention to the different ways in which words could be used, but he does not speak of intention in writing about dialectic except to refer to "the intention of Porphyry." This is a standard scholastic device, employed for example in an introduction to the *Heroides* to refer to Ovid's intention in those poems.[59] Abelard says in the *Historia calamitatum* that "sincere intention and love for our faith" provoked violence from his enemies, but he never justifies his behavior towards Heloise in terms of right intention. In her subsequent letters, she emphasizes the role of intention in her relationship to Abelard. He reminds her of the lustful acts which they had committed.[60] When discussing the religious life, Abelard subsequently expands on Heloise's emphasis that interior disposition was more important than outward observances in relation to food and drink.[61] Only in the *Ethics* (circulated under the title *Scito teipsum* or "Know Yourself"; commenced ca. 1138/39 but never completed), does Abelard reflect more generally on the theme that intention alone can distinguish what is good and bad.[62]

The exchange between Heloise and Abelard reflects a similar contrast to that evident in the later love letters. In the *Historia calamitatum*, Abelard never discusses the intentions behind his behavior towards Heloise, which he identifies quite simply as the fruit of debauchery (*luxuria*). It is Heloise who raises the purity of her intentions towards Abelard. She also raises the theme of purity of intention in relation to the religious life in her third letter, when reflecting on the impulses which drive human nature:

> Nothing is less in our power than the spirit (*animus*), and we are more forced to obey than to rule it. And so when its affections (*affectiones*) provoke us, nobody repels their sudden impulsions so that they do not easily burst out into effects and pour out more easily through words—which are the ever-ready indications of the passions of the spirit: as it is written: "From the fullness of the heart, the mouth speaks."[63]

Heloise's use of *animus* to identify her impulsive spirit is like that of the woman in letter 23, when she contrasts "the burning feeling of the spirit" (*animi fervens affectus*) with the weakness of dried-up talent (*aridi defectus in-*

genii). She supports her psychological discussion of *animus* as an irrepress-
ible dimension of her identity by quoting the saying of Jesus (Luke 6.45;
Matthew 12.34) about the mouth speaking from the abundance of the
heart. In letter *24* the man uses precisely this scriptural quotation to support his comment that "the abundant and yet insufficient richness of your
letter provides me with the clearest evidence of two things, namely, your
overflowing faith and love; hence the saying: 'From the fullness of the
heart, the mouth speaks.'" In his *Christian Theology*, Abelard quoted this
same verse to explain that "speech of the heart" (*locutionem cordis*) was a
scriptural way of defining "a thought of the mind."[64] Heloise also speaks
about the heart as the source of behavior, and alludes to Matthew 5.28 to
insist that evil thoughts, adultery, and homicide stem from nothing external, but from the heart.[65] Although Bernard of Clairvaux frequently alludes to this saying of Jesus when preaching on the Song of Songs, he uses
it only twice in his correspondence. On both occasions, it is to defend his
own right to speak out rather than to praise someone else's directness.[66]
The phrase occurs only once in the letters of Peter the Venerable.[67] In both
letter *24* and the third letter of Heloise, as well as in Abelard's *Christian Theology*, the quotation is used not to justify speaking out, but to comment on
the relationship between words and the heart. It is insufficient to say that
this is simply another "typical" phrase in medieval letters.

Another key term used both in Heloise's third letter and in the woman's
love letters is *affectus* (disposition or feeling), employed nine times in the
woman's letters, but never in his. She first uses the term in letter 7 in a
phrase that is potentially ambiguous: *tota sua re et affectu*. The punctuation
in the manuscript indicates that it describes the greeting she offers and
translates as "with all her being and disposition" rather than as "she who is
completely his in being and disposition." Frequently she uses *affectus* to
emphasize the state of her inner spirit, as in letter 21: "handsome in appearance, yet more distinguished in disposition" (*decorus aspectu, praestabil-
ior affectu*); in 23: "the burning feeling of my spirit" (*animi fervens affectus*);
in 76: "a feeling of inner sweetness encourages me" (*interne dulcedinis me
hortatur affectus*) and "I am unable to reveal in any way at all just how greatly
my feeling burns for you" (*Quantus igitur erga te meus ardeat affectus, ullo modo
tibi manifestare nequeo*); in 79: "the intention of my feeling" (*intencionem mei
affectus*). The expression *affectus animi*, often used by St. Augustine to define
interior disposition, is also a favorite phrase of St. Bernard to describe his
interior state. Abelard himself uses the expression *affectus animi* in his theological writing to relate the term "Holy Spirit" or "Holy breath" to the
breath of human emotion:

Nomine uero spiritus sancti affectus benignitatis et caritatis exprimitur, eo uidelicet quod spiritu oris nostri, id est anhelitu, maxime affectus animi patefiant, cum aut pre amore suspiramus, aut pre laboris uel doloris angustia gemimus.

By the name "Holy Spirit" the feeling of kindness and love is expressed in the same way as by the breath or panting of our mouth the feelings of the spirit are made obvious, when we either sigh out of love or groan out of difficulty of effort or sorrow.[68]

Abelard turned to the experience of making love to explain a theological concept central to his argument about the nature of God.

Heloise uses *animus* in a very similar way when protesting her own innocence of the crime of Abelard's castration:

Que plurimum nocens, plurimum—ut nosti—sum innocens: non enim rei effectus, sed efficientis affectus in crimine est, nec que fiunt, sed quo animo fiunt, equitas pensat.

Wholly guilty though I am, I am also—as you know—wholly innocent; it is not the effect of something which makes the crime, but the disposition of the doer; justice does not consider what happens, but how they happen in the spirit.[69]

Animus, often mistranslated in this passage as "heart," refers to "spirit" or that part of a person which influences rational capacity (as distinct from *anima,* that part which gives life to the body). For Augustine, *animus* and *anima* are two sides of one coin, both immortal.[70] Heloise is saying that true justice is concerned with what goes on in this highest part of the human spirit. Like the woman in the love letters, Heloise dwells at great length on her own inner disposition, making the point that, even if she was not entirely without fault, the devil had not dragged her into sin from consent.[71] This echoes the woman's phrase in letter 5 "in accord with my will" (*ad consensum mee voluntatis*), an Augustinian expression used by Bernard of Clairvaux among others.[72] The word *consensus* does not appear in any of the man's love letters.

Abelard refined his thinking about sin only in the late 1130s. In his *Ethics* he explains that "lusting after a woman is not a sin, only consent to lust, the will to intercourse is not damnable, but consent of the will."[73] In his earlier discussion of sin within commentary on Paul's Epistle to the Romans (probably written in the early to mid 1130s), Abelard does not mention consent, but argues that one deserves reward or punishment from God simply through having a good or bad will. As Marenbon has suggested, this is likely to be one of those aspects of Abelard's thought on which Heloise's influence was decisive.[74] It is quite erroneous to think that Heloise derived her ideas about ethical intention from her studies with Abelard. At the time of his affair with Heloise, Abelard was more a specialist on logic than a theorist of ethics.[75]

Religious Vocabulary in the Love Letters and Concepts of Love

The woman in the love letters employs religious vocabulary far more often than her teacher. In the first letter that Johannes de Vepria copies, she offers him "the freshness of eternal happiness" (*viriditatem eterne felicitatis*). Gregory the Great had often spoken of "eternal freshness" (or eternal greenness) to describe true well-being in relation to the sufferings of Job.[76] When she uses *viriditas* again in a greeting (48), it is to offer him "the freshness of love," an image less dependent on the language of Gregory. The one twelfth-century writer to make extensive use of the word *viriditas* in both naturalistic and spiritual senses is Hildegard of Bingen (1098–1179).[77] The term *viriditas* occurs only once in the writings of Peter Abelard, within a sermon to the nuns of the Paraclete. He remarks that secular life is like chaff, "cut from the earth, without the strength of its viridity."[78] Like Hildegard, the woman in the love letters is more at ease than her male contemporaries in drawing on imagery from the natural world.

In her second letter to him (3) she prays that God watch over them, another characteristic feature of her letters. She often asks God to be her witness (11, 23, 32, 53, 55, 86; cf. Romans 1.9) or gives God thanks (3, 7, 9, 38b, 45, 49, 60, 62, 79, 84, 112). Compared to her twenty references to *deus,* he invokes God only ten times. He does so for the first time in letter *24,* in response to her long reflective letter 23 on the mixed emotions in her heart. She uses invocations such as "God knows" (*Deus scit*) and "I call God as my witness" (*Deum testem invoco*) very like those of Heloise in writing to Abelard.[79] After the man feels burdened by some unspecified guilt, the woman concludes her letter 60 by reciting her version of the Good Friday prayer for souls deceived by the Devil.[80] She then asks that all writing cease between them. In this letter she mentions for the first time "the bond that we had established" (*fedus quod pepigeramus*), a phrase that recalls the bond or covenant between God and his people as well as between David and Jonathan.[81] Her final accusation in letter 60 about his wisdom and learning having deceived her draws on Isaiah's lament (Isa. 47.10) over the degradation and false learning of Babylon.

The woman's use of *dilectio,* employed alongside *amor* in letter 60 as elsewhere, is itself rooted in the Vulgate translation of scripture. She goes beyond scripture, however, to emphasize that there is no discontinuity between the love which comes from her heart (*amor*) and selfless love (*dilectio*). *Amor* occurs fifty-two times and *dilectio* forty-one times in those extracts of her letters copied by Johannes de Vepria. By contrast, *dilectio* occurs just ten times in his letters, whereas *amor* occurs forty-seven times. There is a similar imbalance in their use of the verb *diligere* (to love), occurring twenty-eight times in her letters, but just three times in his letters. His vocabulary reflects a perception, dominant in masculine writing, that love for a woman has little to do with the love enjoined by scripture. She does not see any antithesis between passionate and spiritual love. As early as her second letter (3), she defines her love as true *dilectio* within a religious sense of being watched over by God. He on the other hand prefers words connected to *amo.* She never uses *amabilis* (able to be loved) in her letters, used by him four times. He first employs *dilectio* immediately after her lengthy discussion of love in letter 49. He exclaims in letter *50:* "you seem not to have read Tully, but to have given those precepts to Tully himself." He approves her argument that "true *dilectio* does not bind us the way it customarily binds those who seek their own." The next time he employs *dilectio* is in allusion to the scriptural injunction in letter *52:* "Given that we do not keep the Lord's commandment unless we have love for each other, we should obey divine scripture" (*Quia mandatum domini non observamus, nisi dilectionem ad invicem habeamus, oportet nos divine scripture obedire*). His meaning here may be less than spiritual. By letter *54* he begins to use both *dilectio* and *amor* in a single letter. He never employs *pignus* in his letters; by contrast she speaks in 60: *caritatis pignore* (pledge of charity); in 69, *pignus fidei* (pledge of faith); in 84, *tecum pignus* (a pledge with you); in 104: *inviolabile pignus amoris* (inviolable pledge of love). *Pignus,* a word rich in scriptural association, reinforces her sense of their relationship as sacred, as in 2 Cor. 1.22 and 5.5: *pignus spiritus* (the pledge of the Spirit). The woman similarly twice invokes *f(o)edus* (60 and 88), a term much used in the Vulgate version of the Old Testament to mean "covenant," but another word never used by the man.[82]

The woman emphasizes in her letters that true love is entirely selfless, a theme she adapts from Cicero's argument that true friendship disregards outward advantage. This is Heloise's central theme in her first letter to Abelard, in which she complains about his portrayal of their relationship

in the *Historia calamitatum*. She accuses him of leaving out her arguments
about how she preferred "love to marriage, freedom to chains" (*plerisque
tacitis quibus amorem conjugio, libertatem vinculo preferebam*). Heloise describes
her love for Abelard in terms of both *amor* and *dilectio:* "Would, beloved,
that your love for me trusted in me less, so that it would be more concerned for me" (*Utinam, dilecte, tua de me dilectio minus confideret, ut sollicitior
esset*).[83] Heloise's distress was based on her sense that the love (*dilectio*)
which Abelard now offered her as his sister in Christ was not as intimate
as it had been before. To insist that there had been no selfish desire for
wealth and honor in her love for Abelard, she scorns the wealth of the Emperor Augustus, the same image as the woman had used in letter 82.

   This doctrine of selfless love was one which the woman articulates at
some length in her letter 49. True *dilectio* scorned pleasure and wealth. Too
many people loved each other for the sake of things, rather than for the
sake of each other (*non propter se res, sed se propter res*). The image of selfless love was one which Marbod had used in a poem addressed to an unnamed young woman.[84] Heloise wanted to know whether it was lust or
true friendship which had bound him to her. In his first two replies to
Heloise, Abelard asks her to transfer her devotion to Christ, as his bride,
but does not refer to any redeeming qualities in their past affair. Abelard
recalls an occasion after their secret marriage when he satisfied his lust in
the refectory of Argenteuil, because there was no other place to go.[85]
Heloise remembered this period between their secret marriage and his
castration as a time when they were living chastely.[86] The sense of shared
guilt on which Abelard insists in his second letter to Heloise recapitulates
the same attitudes as the man in the love letters, when he feels guilt over
some unspecified sin, and wishes to introduce a note of caution into their
relationship, as in letter 59. In his second reply to Heloise, Abelard reminds her of their debauchery during Holy Week and of his forcing her
to have sex, even when she was unwilling. He does so to argue that there
was no connection between the *dilectio* shown by Christ for sinful humanity, and his own *amor* which bound both of them into sin. Such *amor*
was not love but lust.[87]

   There are interesting parallels between the man's definition of love in
letter 23 and Abelard's understanding of love as expressed in the opening
of the *Theologia Scholarium*, drafted probably in the early 1130s. Here he
defines *amor* as a good will for the sake of him to whom it ought to be
directed. It is a false love if it is directed purely for personal advantage. The
idea of selfless love is not unique to Abelard. Abelard may have picked up
some aspects of this theme from the *De caritate* of Walter of Mortagne,

perhaps composed in the 1120s. Walter addressed a critical but not un-friendly letter to Abelard when he was still drafting the *Theologia Scholarium*. Marenbon's suggestion that Abelard's ideas of selfless love were prompted by Heloise is plausible.[88] The possibility that Heloise was artic-ulating these ideas at the time of their affair makes it all the more re-markable how unwilling Abelard was to develop these ethical ideas in his early writing. Heloise was voicing attitudes toward love occasionally ex-pressed in some verse from the late eleventh century. By coincidence, the single surviving twelfth-century manuscript of the letters of Walter of Mortagne (possibly assembled by Walter himself) also includes a copy of the poem "from a girl to a friend who promises a reward" that Marbod of Rennes includes within his collection of love poems. This poem in-cludes the line "If you are filled with many riches, you are a rustic who believes I love your things, rather than you yourself."[89] Walter may have been interested in the ethical message of this young woman's argument to her beloved. Abelard was not alone in developing ethical definitions in re-sponse to ideas first raised within a purely secular context.

Allusions to Jerome in the Woman's Love Letters

One of Könsgen's important contributions in his edition was to identify allusions to a wide range of classical, scriptural, and patristic texts in the love letters. The woman's very first letter alludes to the Song of Songs. Elsewhere she draws on phrases and imagery from the books of Job, Psalms, John, Matthew, and the Pauline Epistles. Her knowledge of scrip-ture is evident in her cryptic letter 27, in which she sends to him "the spirit of Bezalel" (a divinely inspired craftsman; Exodus 31.2), "the strength of three locks of hair" (an allusion to Samson; Judges 16.13), "the beauty of the Father of peace" (Absalom, the son of David famed for his beauty, who wore his hair long; 2 Samuel 14.25) and "the profundity of Ididia" (Solomon). She draws these images not just from scripture itself, but from her reading of Jerome (or possibly Isidore).[90] Jerome mentions Samson in his commentary on Ezekiel (also a possible source for the comment on Ididia), a work which Abelard must have drawn upon to complete his own commentary on Ezekiel (now lost), written between 1113 and 1115.[91] In letter *16* he describes her as his seal and himself as the image of that seal, imagery inspired by Ezekiel 28.12. Did the prologue which he composed for her introduce this commentary on Ezekiel in the same way that a let-ter from Abelard to Heloise introduces his commentary on the Hexae-meron, written over fifteen years later? The woman's love letters show that she already had a formidable knowledge of scripture. Whatever the nature of the prologue, it seems that she was certainly interested in his wider academic work.

Könsgen also identified a number of allusions to the correspondence of Jerome in the woman's letters. When she offers her own reflections on the nature of love in letter 25, she does not only allude to Cicero's discussion of friendship. She adapts comments made by Jerome about friendships that wane into comment about true love (*verus amor*) between a man and a woman.[92] She longs to fulfil "the debt of true love" (*vere dilectionis debitum*) but feels unable to do so fully. She applies to herself phrases about the dangers of proximity which Jerome had used in writing to Marcella.[93] Könsgen identifies some eight allusions to Jerome's writing in the woman's letters, but none in those of her teacher.[94] The famous letters of Heloise demonstrate a greater maturity of literary style in the freedom with which they handle traditional ideas, culled from Ovid, Cicero, and the Fathers. In these love letters, her concern is to make a conscious effort to create elegant and original prose by transforming phrases from model letters of the past.

The woman's familiarity with Jerome sheds light on one of the most enigmatic features of the *Historia calamitatum,* the speech about marriage which Abelard attributes to Heloise, in fact culled from Jerome's *Against Jovinian.* It has long been known that all the passages which Abelard attributes to Heloise in the *Historia calamitatum* had already been quoted by Abelard in the second book of his *Christian Theology.*[95] The woman's familiarity with Jerome's correspondence in the love letters raises the possibility that Heloise did indeed raise the arguments of Theophrastus against marriage, reported in Jerome's *Against Jovinian,* in her effort to dissuade Abelard from marriage. It is not clear if the one argument which Abelards recalls having with Heloise was conducted through letter or in person. While it is impossible to assess the extent to which Abelard subsequently elaborated upon her argument, it is significant that she felt that she had not been accurately represented by Abelard in the *Historia calamitatum.* She complained that Abelard had glossed over her insistence on the absolute priority of the ideal of love and her preference for freedom over the chains of marriage. He had not done justice to the overall context of her arguments, in which she used Jerome to present her own very idealistic vision of love. It is not impossible that Heloise presented arguments culled from Jerome in a letter to Abelard, and that he drew selectively from this letter when writing about the greatness of the pagan philosophers in both the *Christian Theology* and the *Historia calamitatum.*

The Final Love Letters

The love letters present a relationship which goes through a number of difficult stages. She wants to break off the relationship in her letter 60, but he then persuades her to continue with their exchange. Troubled by his impulsiveness, she seems to have been upset at his statement in letter 59: "I am guilty, I who compelled you to sin." She sees such attitudes as a betrayal of her true love (vera dilectio) for him. He seems to have alternated between eager enthusiasm for sexual satisfaction and remorse for behavior that he then condemns as sinful. By letter 101, he is wanting to withdraw from seeing her too often because of the notoriety they are acquiring. In letter 106 he seems to be stricken with remorse for his behavior. He confesses that he bears the cost of foolishness because "I have not known how to keep that good, of which I have been completely unworthy, as I ought." This prompts her to go through a major crisis, recorded (unfortunately only in excerpt) in letter 107. These tearful outbursts resolve themselves with an expressive poem from him (108) and a letter from her (109), wishing him to be "clothed with the grace of the virtues, covered with the jewels of wisdom, endowed with honesty of behavior." Her message seems to be that she wishes him every respectable virtue. She simply does not talk about any behavior that he worried was sinful. He in turn cannot put her out of his mind, as she to him is his very spirit (110, 111).

These final letters hint at complexities in the relationship between Abelard and Heloise never touched on in the Historia calamitatum. In that narrative, there is no suspicion of any emotional crisis in their relationship prior to the moment that she got pregnant. Abelard's story line is simply that lust led to pregnancy, which in turn led him choosing to marry Heloise (a decision which does seem strange if Abelard's relationship was simply based on lust). Human relationships are never easy to define. These letters suggest that he was certainly infatuated with her, but that he was unable to understand why he behaved in the way he did. He considered his relationship with Heloise as one of amor, exciting because it seemed to flout the sort of strict moralizing he associated with teachers like William of Champeaux and bishop Galo. He had not developed any alternative ethical system by which to interpret his behavior. Heloise was also fascinated by Ovid, but she saw amor as about much more than the sexual games satirized in the Art of Loving and the Amores. Drawing on ideas already expounded by some of the Loire valley poets in the late eleventh century, Heloise was developing her own code of love, in the same way as poets who performed in a vernacular context.

The woman's tone changes dramatically in letter 112. She greets him not as her beloved (as she had done for the last time in 104), but as her teacher, to whom she respectfully offers "well-being in Him who is both salvation and blessing" (*salutem in eo qui est salus et benedictio*). Why does her tone become so formal? Her first phrase is controlled, "If you are well and moving among worldly concerns without trouble," but then rises to a new excitement: "I am carried away by the greatest exultation of mind." She invokes mystical imagery of St. Paul (2 Cor. 12.2) to describe how she has been carried away by his literary gift and reminds him that he is a philosopher with great poetic talent, but then implies that this is not enough and reminds him of the need to thirst for God alone. She forecasts a brilliant future for him, but then explains her own exultation (*mentis exultacione*) as an experience which she cannot describe in any way. She has reached (literally "obtains" or "holds") the *portum,* the harbor or haven of his *dilectio.* He had used the image of "coming to port" in letter 78 after he had received a letter which he interpreted as implying that the difficulties in their relationship were over. He may here be reiterating a phrase of Virgil about sitting in port.[96] In letter 112 she uses *portum* rather differently. She now has reached a source of joy too wonderful to put into words. Instead of being fixed on him, she has now reached "the haven of his love." All she wants is to be free (*vacare*) to be fully devoted to him. Because Johannes de Vepria indicates four separate omission marks in his copy of letter 112, we cannot tell if the woman originally explained more clearly what she means by this source of great joy. Was there something in this letter which a Cistercian monk could not bring himself to transcribe?

Her words suggest that her happiness stems from much more than his well being. Her formal greeting and comments about her being sure that he has a great professional future ahead of him imply that she wants him to succeed in the world as a teacher. An obvious possibility is that she is now telling him that their relationship can no longer be the same as before, because she has conceived a child. Even in letter 109, when she wishes him wisdom and virtue, she seems to be signaling a desire that their relationship become more like that of spiritual friendship. The fact that she compares the joy his letters had given her in the past with her present, indescribable joy, itself suggests that she has now grown to a new stage of understanding. By bearing his child, she has all that she wants.

Johannes de Vepria provides no explanation when he copies a small note (112a), with the marginal annotation *Ex alia* (From another [letter]), in which she says that he accepts sweet things (*dulcia*) as burdensome (*pro gravibus*) and that she no longer wishes to speak to him. As Johannes de

Vepria supplies no omission mark in his transcription of this message, it may well be that this letter did just contain two sentences. As the message (112a) is so different in tone from 112, there seems no reason to doubt that it is a separate letter, or is from a separate letter. In the transcription which Johannes was copying, the random character of his attempts to distinguish one letter from another suggests that he was copying a text in which one letter followed another without break. He seems to have come across a running register, kept by the woman in the exchange, of messages sent by her and received from her lover.

In this final message from her (112a), she alludes to some response from the man, not recorded by Johannes de Vepria, which makes her less than happy:

> Ubi est amor et dilectio, ibi semper fervet exercicium. Jam fessa sum, tibi respondere nequeo, quod dulcia pro gravibus accipis, ac per hoc animum meum contristaris. Vale.

> Where there is passion and love, there always rages effort. Now I am tired, I cannot reply to you because you are taking sweet things as burdensome, and in doing so you sadden my spirit. Farewell.

The implication of her letter is that she is disappointed her teacher does not share her joy in expecting a child. According to the *Historia calamitatum,* Abelard reacted to her pregnancy by taking her away from her uncle's house and sending her to his sister in Brittany. In his second letter to Heloise, he mentions that he sent her to Brittany disguised as a nun in order to emphasize the deceit in their behavior.[97] Such a reaction may be the cause of the woman's distress in letter 112a. Abelard implies that he stayed in Paris and tried to make amends with Fulbert, her uncle. When he went to Brittany to fetch Heloise and marry her, Abelard reports that they had a major argument in which she urged him against that course of action.

The final item in the exchange is an elegy (*113*) begging forgiveness for his behavior: "I do not love patiently" (*non patienter amo*). He had been driven by *amor* to follow its demands. He had been dazzled by her beauty, family (*genus*), and behavior. The implication of this poem is that the relationship between teacher and student, at least as passionately intense lovers, is at an end. The man's explanation for his behavior is not fundamentally different from that which Abelard records in the *Historia calamitatum* that he put to Fulbert: that he had done nothing unusual in the eyes of anyone who knew the power of love, and that women had always brought the no-blest men to ruin.[98] He had "fallen" in love, away from the pedestal of philosophic behavior expected of him. He interprets his relationship to Heloise as one of superficial attraction, without any reference to her un-derstanding of their love. Abelard's explanation of his behavior, shaped by Ovidian imagery, betrays a very traditional pattern of thought, not incon-sistent with his attitude throughout the love letters. For all his effort to be philosophical about love when she asked for his definition of *amor* (*24*), he never becomes as sophisticated as Heloise in formulating ethical ideas dur-ing his early relationship with her. If this exchange were a literary inven-tion composed by a single author, one might ask why it should conclude in such an unsatisfactory way, with the relationship between the two par-ties still unresolved. There is no attempt to round things off, by proposing that worldly love should be replaced by spiritual friendship. The reader is left to imagine what might have happened.

Conclusion

The relationship between the teacher and his student in these letters shows striking parallels to that remembered in different ways by Abelard and Heloise. To argue that the love letters constitute a literary fiction demands that we postulate the existence of an author with an astonishingly intimate knowledge of their attitudes, vocabulary, and prose style. Könsgen's argu-ment that these are genuine letters between two lovers can be taken fur-ther. These letters must have been written by Abelard and Heloise. When we compare the exchange copied by Johannes de Vepria to poems written about Abelard and Heloise from the twelfth century, or other love letters from the period, we simply do not find anything approaching the depth and sophistication of this exchange. The contrasting perceptions of love in these love letters are so similar to those evident in the Abelard–Heloise let-ters, that it seems most unlikely that they could have been written by a male disciple of Abelard intimately familiar with his master's philosophical vocabulary. The only student of Abelard in a position to record this ex-change was Heloise. The copy she made of her exchanges with Abelard is like any letter collection from the twelfth century, the product of a careful literary process. We cannot say to what extent she may have edited the original messages etched onto wax, just as we do not know for certain whether Johannes de Vepria came across Heloise's own transcription, or a copy some other monk had made of those letters. The fact that an episto-lary exchange uses literary artifice to interpret a relationship does not make that exchange any less authentic. Literature always provides an imaginative response to whatever is perceived as other.

It is dangerous to describe these love letters as "written from the heart." Expressions of mutual devotion are always shaped by cultural convention. Dogmatic assertions that Abelard "was driven by lust" or that Heloise "was motivated by pure love" fail to recognize that these are rhetorical phrases, used by Abelard and Heloise respectively, each fulfilling a certain function. The love letters help us probe beyond Abelard's attempt to distance himself from his past in the *Historia calamitatum*, but they do not provide "the real truth" about their relationship. These letters lend substance to Heloise's argument that her love for him was not based on any desire for material reward. She saw the demands of *amor* as no different from classical ideals of friendship except that she believed them to apply as much to an *amica* as to an *amicus*.[99] Heloise certainly liked to invent dramatic contrasts to make her point, such as when she says that she preferred to be called a prostitute rather than to marry Abelard. She did not want to be a prostitute. Her argument is that true love disregards public opinion. With all its limitations, the transcription prepared by Johannes de Vepria at Clairvaux in the late fifteenth century records an echo of the voices of both Abelard and Heloise.

CHAPTER 6

THE VOICE OF HELOISE

At a time when nearly the whole world is indifferent and deplorably apa-
thetic towards such occupations, and wisdom can scarcely find a foothold
not only, I may say, among the female sex from whom it has been banished
completely, but even among the minds of men, you have surpassed all
women in carrying out your purpose and have gone further than almost all
men. Subsequently you turned your zeal for learning to a better direction
and as a wholly and truly philosophical woman you left logic for the Gospel,
natural science for the Apostle, Plato for Christ, the academy for the cloister, according to the words of the Apostle: "It pleased God who had set you
apart since you were in your mother's womb to call you through his grace."
(Gal. 1.15)[1]

Peter the Venerable does not allude at all to Heloise's early love for
Abelard in this letter, written perhaps one or two years after Abelard's
death (21 April 1142).[2] The abbot of Cluny prefers to recall how he himself once admired her for her learning before she became a nun. His letter
is a carefully tuned panegyric about the transition from philosophical inquiry to the monastic life. St. Bernard's criticism of the theology of Peter
Abelard at Sens in 1141 was still fresh in many people's minds. He expresses delight in reports of her learning and religion and praises her as like
Penthesilea, queen of the Amazons, and Deborah, a leader to her community.[3] She has overcome "the proud prince of this world" and will justly
receive a heavenly reward, when she will be united again with Abelard,
who spent his last years as a humble monk of Cluny and whom God now
keeps in his bosom.

This image of Peter Abelard was not widely known in the twelfth century. The Latin text of this letter, translated into French in the fourteenth
century, is known only through a single fifteenth-century copy and the

1522 edition of Peter the Venerable's letters, based on a lost manuscript of Cluny.[4] Far more widely known in the Middle Ages were letters of St. Bernard about the opinions of Peter Abelard that presented him as an arrogant logician "who disputes with boys and consorts with women."[5] Peter the Venerable's sympathetic portrayal of both Heloise and Abelard is itself colored by rhetorical convention. Heloise protests against her public reputation for piety in her letter of complaint about how Abelard had described her in the *Historia calamitatum*. She wants Abelard to address her as an individual, fully aware of her situation. Accepting the love letters discovered by Johannes de Vepria as those of Heloise and Abelard enables us to appreciate the complexity of a relationship that Abelard grossly oversimplifies in his account of the past. Public criticism did not prevent him from exerting influence in the schools and rejecting the accusations that he provoked.[6] Heloise had a much more difficult task in confronting her admirers. Abelard's remark that the less she allowed herself to be seen in public, the more her admirers sought her out for spiritual conversation, highlights her desire for privacy.[7] At the same time, she could not avoid the publicity that surrounded her relationship with the most famous teacher of the day. Accepting the letters as those of Heloise and Abelard enables us to probe more deeply a private world thrown by force of circumstance into a maelstrom of rumor and gossip.

The End of the Affair

The love letters and poems seem to have been exchanged by Heloise and Abelard over a period of at least a year, perhaps between late 1115 and sometime in 1117.[8] Many of the letters may have been exchanged before Abelard obtained lodging in Fulbert's house. Because they speak so much in ideal terms and lack specific historical allusions it is impossible to be certain. Even if they were living in the same house, Abelard would necessarily have had to live separately from Heloise and communicate with her by written messages, exchanged by a servant. Abelard's account of their physical union in Fulbert's house is itself like a novel, colored by dramatic irony as he imagines their relationship in the past. The contrast in the love letters between his discourse and hers suggests that for all their shared interests, they still inhabited different worlds. Even their prose styles reflected the contrast in their background. He praised the way she shone in her behavior, but had difficulty in understanding what she wanted to say about love, informed by a particular fusion of religious and classical idealism. Although Abelard was an authority on linguistic convention, he could not easily see the extent to which many of his own attitudes were themselves deeply rooted in clerical convention. In letter 60 she tried to break off the relationship after he apologized for "forcing her to sin" (59). He then accused her of sinning against himself in wanting to rupture their relationship (61). Something similar seems to have happened in letter 106 when he exclaims that he bears "the price for stupidity" because he has not known how to keep "that good thing as I ought." He becomes caught in a contradiction between delight in receiving her letters (110) and a sense of the folly of his own behavior. The remorse he expresses in letters 59 and 101 suggest that there was some truth to his later comments that he forced Heloise to have sex with him when she was unwilling. He was stricken with guilt by his own behavior.

Whether Abelard consciously set out to seduce her, as he maintains in the *Historia calamitatum*, is another matter. Initially thrilled by the eloquence of his letters, she gradually begins to define their relationship in a way quite distinct from her teacher. Heloise's ideal of love integrated three normally distinct concepts: *amor*, the passion or subjective experience of love; *dilectio*, an act of choice by which one consciously decided to love another person; and *amicitia*, or friendship. She develops ideas similar to those formulated by Baudri of Bourgueil in poems exchanged with various friends, including nuns at Le Ronceray, Angers. Heloise does not see any inconsistency between her love for Abelard and their shared study of philosophy. The quality which he so much admired in her was that her words were matched by her behavior. Other people's words seemed to him to be empty by comparison.

After their intimacy was discovered by Fulbert, Abelard was forced to move out of his house. The final letters of the correspondence, very difficult to interpret clearly, imply that their relationship was going through various difficulties, even before she sends letter 112, in which she reports an experience of joy that she cannot put into words. The fact that she addresses this letter to her teacher rather than to her lover suggests that she wants to put their relationship on a different footing. She acknowledges that his letters had raised her to heights of ecstasy, and affirms her confidence that he has a glorious future before him. He has a public role, while she now has reached her own source of joy. Her last note (112a) implies that Abelard took the news of her pregnancy badly. In his final poem (113), Abelard falls back on a traditional view of *amor* as an insane passion provoked by fascination with external beauty. While not explicitly blaming his behavior on a woman, he implies that a woman's beauty and reputation is a dangerous trap for a man. Abelard reports that he used very similar arguments to Fulbert after he had sent Heloise to Brittany for the duration of her confinement. He then decides that they should return to Paris to marry in secret, leaving Astralabe to be brought up by his sister in Brittany. His insistence that they should get married in secret, but then live apart, represents a pious hope that he can strengthen their relationship by making it respectable in the eyes of Fulbert. Abelard was afraid of losing control over Heloise. As she recognized, it was a disastrous decision which only put her more firmly than ever under Abelard's authority.

Abelard went back to live in lodgings after a secret ceremony, while Heloise returned to her uncle's house. The idea was that this would be a chaste marriage. When Fulbert started to abuse her and spread rumors about the marriage, Abelard sent her to her old convent at Argenteuil, where she had been raised and educated as a child. Fulbert, who thought this a device by which Abelard could continue to have his way with Heloise, was so enraged by this apparent theft of Heloise that he and other members of her family decided to have him castrated.[9] Abelard does not mention in the *Historia calamitatum* a detail that we know about from a letter from Fulco of Deuil, that Abelard wanted to take legal action in Rome against both the bishop and the canons of Notre-Dame. Fulco warned Abelard that this was unrealistic because of the money necessary to obtain a favorable verdict from a corrupt papal court.[10] Two of the thugs involved in the crime were punished with blinding and castration; Fulbert was sent into temporary exile in 1117 by the cathedral chapter. Abelard then decided to become a monk at Saint-Denis at the same time as Heloise took the veil at Argenteuil. He sought to disassociate himself from his past. Abelard was able to sublimate his energies by returning to the study of logic and starting to write about Christian doctrine. The voice of Heloise became transmuted into his own reflection on the goodness of God. Yet the issues raised in those love letters did not disappear. To grasp the deeper continuities between her love letters and the exchange she initiated with Abelard after she came across the *Historia calamitatum*, we need to understand how their lives were shaped by political developments much larger than themselves.

Abelard at Saint-Denis: Escape through Reason

Abelard's castration marked more than the end of a phase in his career. It signaled a reaction against moral laxity both in the diocese of Paris and in the Latin Church as a whole. While Fulbert's act of revenge turned Abelard into a kind of martyr in the eyes of his admirers, it also reinforced public perception of him as a dangerous outsider. Many people thought of him as an overclever logician who could not be trusted as a teacher of Christian doctrine and morality. Abelard responded to his castration by immersing himself in intellectual study, distancing himself from all association with Heloise. This at least is the picture which he gives in the *Historia calamitatum*. Abelard may not have removed himself from Heloise as much as he claims in that account. Roscelin reports rumors that Abelard was continuing to visit "his prostitute" and bring her money, even though he was now a monk.[11] Abelard did not engage in intimate conversation, however, with Heloise. He was anxious to maintain a public image of respectability in a monastic environment which considered any intimate association with a woman dangerous. By identifying himself as an ascetic teacher like Origen, famous for having castrated himself, he sought to re-assert himself as a teacher, unmoved by feminine distraction. Just as he saw the spirit triumphing over the flesh, so he saw reason as triumphing over the senses.[12]

Becoming a monk at Saint-Denis enabled Abelard to escape from the past. The abbey also boasted an important library and offered connections directly to the royal court, being traditionally independent of the bishop of Paris.[13] According to St. Bernard, Saint-Denis was a hive of activity prior to the reforms implemented by Suger in 1127, its cloister "crowded with knights, with affairs being negotiated, with disputes being conducted, and sometimes open to women." Stephen of Garlande, whom Bernard implies was once friendly with Suger, may have played a role in Abelard's choice of a monastic refuge.[14]

Abelard responded relatively quickly to suggestions that he teach for the service of God rather than for personal gain, as in the past. This brought him into conflict with his fellow monks, whom he accused of worldliness. He withdrew from the abbey to a certain *cella,* a church of Saint-Denis where he was able to teach both logic and theology, drawing on the wisdom of philosophy to illuminate traditional Christian doctrine. In both the *Historia calamitatum* and the preface to his *Theologia Scholarium* (drafted in the early 1130s) Abelard makes the point that he undertook this approach in response to the demands of his students for a rational approach to matters of belief.[15] Heloise was the most articulate of his students. The specific focus of his argument was criticism of the thesis of his former teacher, Roscelin of Compiègne, that the three persons of the Trinity had to be described as separate things to avoid identifying God the Father with God the Son. Abelard insisted that only Roscelin's conclusions were wrong, not his basic method of discussing Christian faith through philosophical argument. He shared Roscelin's conviction that secular philosophy provided a path for understanding Christian belief.[16]

Abelard's eagerness to demonstrate that pagan philosophers had glimpsed
the supreme good has particular significance in the light of Heloise's enthusiasm for classical authors in her love letters. She herself was very interested in fusing the ideas of classical authors about human relationships
with the Christian understanding of the demands of love. Little phrases in
his theological writing suggest reminiscences of her love letters. The
scriptural phrase which he had used to describe Heloise's eloquence (24)
is one he now employs to explain that the Word of God is divine wisdom
flowing out in speech from the abundance of the heart.[17] He speaks little about the meaning of divine omnipotence, traditionally so important
for describing God as the supreme ruler. He is more interested in talking
about divine goodness as glimpsed by the ancient writers. He describes
"Holy Spirit" as a name given to express the *affectus* or disposition of divine kindness and charity, just as breathing expresses a disposition of the
spirit, like sighing in love or groaning in effort or sorrow.[18] When he became a monk, Abelard transferred his attention away from the consolation
offered by Heloise to the consolation offered by divine goodness, in his
view the true meaning of what Plato described as the soul of the world.

These reflections on the meaning of the words *pater, filius,* and *spiritus
sanctus* provoked hostility not just from Roscelin, but from those teachers
who saw themselves as continuing the traditions of Anselm of Laon (d.
1117). Abelard tells the story of their persecution of his treatise at the
council of Soissons (March/April 1121) as if it were an attack against him
personally. Alberic of Rheims and Lotulph of Novara resented the way in
which the Parisian schools were taking over in popularity from those of
Laon and Rheims. William of Champeaux had already sensed future trends
in 1109 by establishing a reformed community at Saint-Victor, just outside
Paris. In his theological lectures, William expanded on the technique for
which Anselm of Laon had become famous, of presenting rational solutions to a range of questions about Christian belief and behavior. William's
admirers were worried by the extent to which Abelard seemed to undermine the solutions of established authorities in his *On the Unity and Trinity of God.* After the death of William of Champeaux in 1120, Alberic and
Lotulf were anxious that the Church should rule against arguments that
seemed to subvert patristic authority. One charge in particular was made
against Abelard, that he defined only the Father as omnipotent, not the Son
or the Holy Spirit. William of Saint-Thierry (ca. 1075–1148), present at
Soissons in 1121, made the same complaint later in his letter to Bernard of
Clairvaux.[19] The charge pinpointed Abelard's unwillingness to view God
as an all-powerful being, able to do as he pleased.[20]

After a short confinement at Saint-Médard, Soissons, Abelard returned to Saint-Denis to set about revising and enlarging his controversial treatise, now calling it his *Christian Theology* (appropriating a Greek word, *theologia*, normally associated with the mystical writing attributed to Denis the Areopagite). He incorporated his own accusations against those who argued that he was relying too much on pagan wisdom and was questioning the omnipotence of God.[21] While researching patristic teaching, which he insisted had to be investigated rationally as it embraced many different opinions, he commented on the common confusion between Denis the Areopagite and Denis bishop of Corinth. This led to accusations that he was questioning the identity of the patron saint of France. In a separate letter to the abbot of Saint-Denis, Abelard explained that he did not doubt the traditional belief, but argued that it had to be defended by reference to the most reliable sources.[22]

Abelard at the Paraclete: Responding to Criticism

Abelard recalls that the hostility of his fellow monks provoked him to escape (in 1122) both from the abbey and from France itself. He took refuge with monastic friends at the abbey of Saint-Ayoul, Provins, in the territory of the Count of Champagne. While abbot Adam of Saint-Denis had wanted Abelard to return to the abbey, Stephen of Garlande played a key role in persuading Suger, Adam's successor, to allow Abelard to withdraw from Saint-Denis, as long as he did not come under the authority of any other abbot. Abelard then set about constructing an Oratory or chapel, which he initially dedicated to the Holy Trinity, on land that he had been given not far from Nogent-sur-Seine. He did so with the blessing of the new bishop of the region, Hato of Troyes, recently arrived from the cathedral of Sens.[23] When describing the community of students of philosophy which gathered at this site, Abelard quoted from Jerome's panegyric of pagan philosophers who spurned the delights of the senses and the assaults of lust which he had earlier quoted in his *Christian Theology:* "If anyone takes pleasure in . . . a woman's beauty, the splendor of jewels and garments . . . the liberty of his soul is captured through the window of the eye."[24]

Intellectually, these were productive years. Abelard distinguished his ideas about words and their signification more clearly from that of Roscelin, within the context of both logic and theology. He gave much more attention than his teacher to the role that a word plays in generating an understanding in the mind, building on ideas Aristotle had raised in his *On*

Interpretation (*Periermeneias*). No word or concept established any final truth. Complete truth was known only to God. When he applied these linguistic principles to pronouncements on Christian doctrine, as in the Prologue to his *Yes and No* (*Sic et Non*), he invited his students to consider that no Church Father had ever delivered the final word on any disputed question.

Abelard was most at home in analyzing patristic definitions of the Trinity. He began his discussions of any subject by pointing out the inconsistencies present within patristic tradition, of which he developed an encyclopedic knowledge. He then gradually worked out a rational solution which embraced the teaching of the most important authorities. The subject matter which Abelard found the most difficult to deal with was that of human behavior. When he was drafting the *Christian Theology* in the early 1120s, his thoughts were still largely guided by his reading of Cicero and other classical authors. While Abelard did not include any of the subtle reflection on love which he had marveled at in the love letters of Heloise, he defended vigorously the value of reading those authors to whom she was so attached. He hinted at the idea that the incarnation provided an opportunity for God to instruct us in wisdom and draw us to the love of those things which he knows, a subject he may have discussed at more length in his lectures during this period.[25] He gave most attention to the Holy Spirit, the comforting goodness or benignity of God. His decision to re-dedicate his Oratory to the Paraclete reflected this concern, a shift which Abelard took pains to justify in the face of criticism that he was lessening respect for God the Father and God the Son. Abelard did not think of God as a Being who could do whatever he willed. His God was the supreme good, manifest in the goodness of creation.

In the *Historia calamitatum*, Abelard blames the collapse of the Paraclete community ca. 1126/27 on false rumors propagated by two "new apostles," whom he identifies as famous for resurrecting the life of regular (i. e. reformed) canons and of monks. There seems little reason to doubt that he had in mind Norbert of Xanten (ca. 1080–1134) and Bernard of Clairvaux (1090–1153).[26] In a sermon written ca. 1127, Abelard is cynical about certain miracles that Norbert attempted to perform after leaving Prémontré to become archbishop of Magdeburg.[27] Bernard, ordained as abbot of Clairvaux by William of Champeaux in 1115, was then already politically aligned with Abelard's critics. In 1126 Bernard wrote to Pope Honorius II (1124–30) to support the promotion of Alberic of Rheims, Abelard's antagonist at Laon, to the bishopric of Châlons-sur-Marne.[28] Bernard was then working with Norbert on various ecclesiastical causes.[29] He was also emerging as an authoritative writer on Christian doctrine. In 1127/28,

Bernard replied to various questions of Hugh of Saint-Victor in Paris about arguments of an unnamed teacher who mocked traditional doctrine about baptism, claimed that righteous people before Christ had full knowledge of the incarnation, and taught that no one could sin through ignorance.[30] Although Bernard may not have known the identity of the teacher about whom Hugh was talking, as he affirms in this letter, Abelard could easily have perceived Bernard as an unfriendly rival. Eleven years younger than Abelard, Bernard was then emerging as a significant figure in Champagne. After Count Hugh of Champagne decided to join the Knights Templar in 1125, Bernard encouraged Count Theobald II of Blois, who had just inherited governance of the County of Champagne (1125–52), to hold a council at Troyes in January 1128. Bernard's role in gaining official recognition for the Templar Order was important in turning him into a figure of public prominence.[31] Bernard was not a politician or diplomat like Suger, but a preacher, able to inspire an audience about great themes of love and self-knowledge in a prose style of great originality. Unlike William of Champeaux, he could exploit popular interest in the theme of love between a woman and a man to talk about the spiritual life. Like Norbert, Bernard saw himself as a spiritual adviser to the powerful. It is perhaps not surprising that Abelard should blame Norbert and Bernard for the collapse of the Paraclete. We have no firm documentary evidence, however, that Abelard was correct in these accusations. The collapse of the Paraclete may have had more to do with the difficulties Abelard experienced in building up a network of support at a time of great political instability in France and Champagne between 1127 and 1132.

The Political Crisis of 1127–32

Abelard's fortunes had already begun to wane in 1123, when the cathedral canons elected as bishop of Paris an outsider to the chapter, Stephen of Senlis (d. 1141). Member of a family long opposed to the Garlande brothers, Stephen of Senlis imposed a more austere life style on the canons of Notre-Dame and obtained from Louis VI significant financial privileges for Saint-Victor.[32] In the process the new bishop came into conflict with Stephen of Garlande over the latter's support for Gualo, a logician who had replaced Abelard at Notre-Dame.[33] Stephen of Senlis excommunicated Gualo and his students, prompting Gualo to appeal to the archbishop of Sens and to Rome itself.[34] The disagreement between Stephen of Senlis and the cathedral chapter over control of the school was related to a larger dispute about the power of archdeacons in general.[35] It led to the bishop's decision in 1127, witnessed by Suger of Saint-Denis and the abbot and prior of Saint-Victor, to transfer the cathedral school from the cloister to the episcopal court, on the south side of the Church. The bishop's plan to introduce canons of Saint-Victor into Notre-Dame was resisted by the king. The bishop also encountered difficulties with the archbishop of Sens to whom Stephen of Garlande had appealed.[36] Stephen of Senlis and the abbot of Saint-Victor had the full support of Bernard of Clairvaux.[37] The bishop's actions helped polarize the Parisian clerical community into two camps, one pro-monastic, the other opposed to monastic influence in the Church.

The immediate cause of Stephen of Garlande's fall from grace in 1127 was the planned marriage of one of his nieces to Amaury IV of Montfort, nephew of Bertrada of Montfort.[38] Stephen had long been disliked by Queen Adelaide, who accused him of wanting to keep the position of seneschal within the control of his own family. Ralph of Vermandois, cousin to Louis VI, took part in the military action against the Montforts, and quickly became senior adviser to the king, although he did not officially become seneschal until 1132. Louis of Senlis, brother of the bishop, took over the post of butler to the king from Gilbert of Garlande.[39] Ralph of Vermandois had played a key role in the expedition of Louis VI against the Emperor Henry V in 1125, and was the true beneficiary of the fall of the Garlandes. Ralph was also involved in a brutal, but ultimately unsuccessful campaign of Louis in 1127 to assert royal authority in Flanders through his support for William Clito (1101–28), after the assassination of the king's cousin, Count Charles.[40] Suger downplays the political significance of these events in his life of Louis VI by never giving prominence to Stephen of Garlande. There can be no doubt, however, that Stephen's fall from grace was a significant event. Angevin culture was seen as a pernicious influence by ecclesiastical moralists, who saw the reform movement in the Church as now gaining the political support of the highest people in the land.

Abelard and Heloise were caught in the slipstream created by these events. Family connections enabled Abelard to take a position as abbot of Saint-Gildas-de-Ruys, in a remote part of Brittany ca. 1126/27. In 1127 Suger implemented reforms at Saint-Denis to ensure that monastic life was not disturbed by secular affairs, while he himself took an active part in political decision making. Early in 1129, Suger forged a charter, supposedly issued by Louis the Pious and his son Lothar, to prove his claim that Argenteuil traditionally belonged to Saint-Denis.[41] Cardinal Matthew of Albano reported to the Pope at a council at Saint-Germain-des-Prés that there had been an outcry over "irregularity and scandal" at an abbey where a few nuns had lived for a long time "polluting all the neighborhood of the place by their foul and debauched way of life."[42] On 14 April 1129, Suger acquired approval from Louis VI and Queen Adelaide, as well as from Ralph of Vermandois, for expelling Heloise and her nuns from Argenteuil. Suger also secured a promise from Louis that he be buried at Saint-Denis rather than at Fleury. Access to Argenteuil provided Suger with a valuable port on the Seine, essential for him to undertake his plans to rebuild the abbey of Saint-Denis. Abelard would never have invited Heloise to take over the Paraclete if Suger had not intervened to take control of Argenteuil. Abelard always insisted that good could come out of bad.

The accusations invoked by Suger were the same as those used at Arras on 10 May 1128 to justify the expulsion of nuns from the abbey of Saint-Jean, Laon. Bernard of Clairvaux spoke approvingly to Haimeric, the papal chancellor, about "the restoration at Laon of a sanctuary to God formerly the brothel of Venus."[43] Pope Innocent confirmed the expulsion of nuns from both Saint-Jean and Argenteuil on 2 November 1130.[44] Just as in 1107, when William of Champeaux and bishop Galo justified the expulsion of nuns from Saint-Éloi on grounds of sexual immorality (an action confirmed in 1134 by Stephen of Senlis), so the rhetoric of pollution was again invoked to justify claims to political control.[45] It served to distract attention from complaints from some quarters that bishops who claimed to advocate reform were in fact serving to legitimize secular authority (precisely the situation that reformers in the eleventh century were fighting against).

The expulsion of Heloise and her nuns from Argenteuil presented Abelard with an opportunity that he interpreted as a gift of the Paraclete, the giver of true consolation. Presumably at her suggestion (he is silent about her initiative in this), Abelard invited Heloise and some of the nuns with her to take over the Paraclete, and transferred to them ownership of the site. Heloise must have written to Abelard demanding that he do something for her community. Those nuns who did not want to lead a life of austerity and hardship, moved to the abbey of Sainte-Marie de Footel, Malnouë, near Champigny. Thirty years later, bishop Maurice de Sully (1163–96) claimed episcopal jurisdiction over Argenteuil and tried to return the nuns who had taken refuge at Malnouë to Saint-Denis, but was not successful in this.[46]

Between 1130 and 1139 Bernard of Clairvaux was closely involved in winning support for Pope Innocent II, elected by a minority of cardinals (led by Haimeric, papal chancellor) on 13 February 1130, after the death

of Honorius II. The majority of cardinals supported the election of Anacletus II, a scion of the important Pierleoni family who enjoyed the support of the city and clergy of Rome. At the same time as Bernard was
soliciting the support of Louis VI, Norbert of Xanten was persuading the
new German emperor, Lothar III (1125–37) to recognize Innocent II as
the legitimate pope.[47] Anjou, ruled by Fulk V (1109–42, son of Bertrada of
Montfort), preferred Anacletus II to Innocent II. Bernard tried to get
Hildebert of Lavardin, archbishop of Tours 1125–33, to recognize Innocent
II as Pope in 1131, but could not prevent Hildebert's successor from being
consecrated by Anacletus. Duke William X of Aquitaine was similarly opposed to Innocent II.[48] Only with the death of Gerard of Angoulême,
papal legate of Anacletus, in 1136 could Innocent II be sure of recognition
by the bishops of Aquitaine.[49] In such an atmosphere, anyone perceived as
not supporting Innocent II could be accused of fomenting schism within
the Church.

Heloise survived the political turbulence of the late 1120s and early
1130s more successfully than Abelard. Her request to take over the Paraclete was a bold move, as she could have followed those nuns who settled
at Malnouë. Abelard pays tribute in the *Historia calamitatum* to her success
in winning support from bishops, abbots, and laypeople.[50] The accusations
made by Suger of sexual profligacy at Argenteuil did not prevent her from
obtaining papal confirmation of the community's possessions at Auxerre
on 28 November 1131. Abelard's own public reputation was beginning to
improve. In January 1131 Innocent consecrated an altar at Morigny in the
presence of many distinguished ecclesiastics, including Bernard of Clairvaux and Peter Abelard. The Benedictine chronicler of Morigny described
him as "a monk and abbot, a most distinguished religious man and teacher
of the schools, to whom educated men flocked from almost the whole
Latin world."[51] While Abelard may have enjoyed more professional connections in Paris than he reveals in the *Historia calamitatum,* he still thought
of himself as an outsider, driven east by the jealousy of the French.

Exactly when Abelard resumed teaching at Sainte-Geneviève is not
known. Stephen of Garlande, re-appointed royal chancellor by October
1132, still faced continued opposition from the bishop of Paris and the
abbot of Saint-Victor. The bishop laid an interdict on the churches of
Sainte-Geneviève in 1132/33.[52] Tensions flared in August 1133 after
nephews of archdeacon Theobald attacked the bishop of Paris as well as
the abbot and prior of Saint-Victor as they returned from "reforming" the
female community at Chelles.[53] Prior Thomas was killed in the fray.
Bernard of Clairvaux complained loudly about the slowness with which

those guilty of Thomas' murder were prosecuted.[54] This was also the year that Adam, the musically gifted precentor of Notre-Dame, left the cathedral to join Saint-Victor.[55] The polemical tone of Abelard's *Historia calamitatum* is directly shaped by the intensity of this conflict between Stephen of Garlande and the bishop of Paris. In order to re-establish himself at Sainte-Geneviève, Abelard needed to distance himself from the taint of his past. At the same time, he needed to explain that he had for years been victim of rumor and false innuendo. In trying to establish the truth as he saw it, he inevitably colored his account in very particular ways.

Heloise and Cistercian Observances at the Paraclete

Unlike Abelard, Heloise was able to establish good connections to individuals from a number of different ecclesiastical networks. Abelard's comments about the admiration she won from ecclesiastics and laypeople alike, coupled with her manifest success in winning gifts for the Paraclete, testify to her skill in handling public matters. She herself remained suspicious of the flattery of admirers. Particularly important was the support that she won from Matilda, Countess of Blois and Champagne.[56] Her capacity to negotiate with a wide range of people was perhaps the most obvious difference between herself and Abelard.

Heloise's relationship to the Cistercian order is of particular significance given Abelard's reserve towards the abbot of Clairvaux. While she professes sympathy for Abelard against the attacks of "those two pseudo-apostles" (perhaps in a tone of gentle irony), she is not hostile to the values of authenticity of religious observance for which the Cistercians stood. The fact that Hugh Metel, a fervent admirer of Bernard of Clairvaux and a stern critic of Peter Abelard, was anxious to win her friendship in the 1140s is itself significant. Hugh saw her as a woman of piety and religion, quite different from Abelard.[57] An important discovery about the Paraclete in recent years has been the finding by Chrysogonus Waddell that the early observances of the Paraclete, the *Institutiones nostrae,* are largely influenced by early Cistercian usage. These observances follow Abelard's Rule in the Troyes MS 802. In the thirteenth century, they were extended with certain additional conciliar decisions about the religious life for women. John Benton was the first scholar to draw attention to a number of discrepancies between Abelard's Rule and the observances established in this document. Waddell's discovery that the observances of the Paraclete draw heavily on Cistercian monastic practices as they existed prior to far-reaching reforms within the Cistercian Order in 1147 is of great significance.[58]

He concluded that the observances were drawn up under the supervision of Heloise in order to establish harmony of observance between the Paraclete and its daughter houses, such as at Trainel and La Pommeraye.

The document is structured around the theme that the nuns should follow the teaching of Christ. They should practice poverty, humility, and obedience in imitation of the apostles. It uses rhyming phrases, characteristic of the prose style of Heloise:

> Domino super nos prospiciente et aliqua loca nobis largiente misimus quasdam ex nostris ad religionem tenendam numero sufficiente. Annotamus autem boni propositi nostri consuetudines, ut quod tenuit mater incommutabiliter, teneant et filie uniformiter.

> With the Lord looking over us and bestowing certain places to us, we have sent some women in sufficient number from among ourselves to observe religion. We are adding however observances for our good plan so that what the mother has adhered to unchangeably, the daughters may adhere to uniformly.[59]

The usage of *religio* rather than *vita monastica* in these observances echoes Heloise's usage in her third letter when she describes what she wanted Abelard to establish at the Paraclete.[60] Religion was an all embracing way of life, not just that practiced by monks. Heloise's whole third letter is about the importance of true *religio*, and the need to avoid any situation which gives rise to hypocrisy. The Paraclete observances do not refer explicitly to the authority of Abelard's Rule. In a few details, they modify Cistercian emphasis on simplicity of dress, such as by prescribing lambskin and linen clothes, as well as those of wool. In her third letter to Abelard, Heloise had observed how awkward it was for women to wear wool next to the skin, given their monthly periods. A few small details, like the use of feather mattresses and linen sheets, echo elements in Abelard's Rule in which he had responded to observations of Heloise. The observances are much simpler than Abelard's Rule, in which broad principles are sometimes overwhelmed by a mass of prescriptive detail and theoretical discussion. For example, the observances simply lay down that meals are without meat, whereas Abelard devotes an involved discussion to the subject, allowing its consumption with certain restrictions. Heloise had asked him what basis there was to forbidding meat not so much to change the diet as to raise a more important principle about the distinction between outward and inward virtue.[61] Just as in her letters, she had insisted that words be backed up by right behavior, so in practical matters she insisted that observances respond to the realities of daily life. The fact that the nuns did not include meat in their diet may have as much to do with economic necessity as anything else.

Waddell's discovery that most of the practical details in the *Institutiones nostrae* are based on early Cistercian usage matched his finding that the calendar, hymns, and prayers of the Paraclete also reflect Cistercian practice.[62] A number of extra saints have been added to the Cistercian calendar as it stood in 1147, notably many women: Adelgund, Margaret, Radegund, Thecla, Faith, the 11,000 virgins, Cirilla, Katherine, Anastasia, Eugenia, and Columba. The collects and antiphons are similarly based on Cistercian usage, as is also the choice of scriptural readings and canticles. Abelard had composed a complete cycle of hymns for the Paraclete, in response to complaints of Heloise about the inadequacy of many traditional hymns and their lack of strict meter, but about a third of these were not used within the Paraclete liturgy. The community paid particular attention to celebrating Pentecost, and employed Abelard's special prayers to the Holy Spirit. Abelard's sermons were read on important feasts, such as during the octave of Pentecost. These liturgical manuscripts of the Paraclete may not affirm the voice of Heloise as an individual, but they give some clues to the liturgical direction that she chose for her community. She drew on the writings of both Abelard and the early Cistercians in order to implement her own vision of the religious life.

Heloise and Bernard of Clairvaux

The complex relationship between Heloise, Abelard, and Bernard of Clairvaux is fully evident in a letter which Abelard sent to the abbot of Clairvaux sometime in the 1130s, after hearing that Heloise had welcomed him at the Paraclete:

> When recently I came to the Paraclete, driven by the need to conduct some business, your daughter in Christ and our sister, who is said to be abbess of that place, informed me with the greatest rejoicing that you had come there for the sake of a holy visitation, something long wanted, and that you had given strength both to her and her sisters by pious exhortations not as a man, but as an angel. In secret she intimated to me that you were a little disturbed—with that charity with which you have embraced me in particular—that in that Oratory [the Paraclete] the Lord's prayer is not customarily recited during the daily services as in other places, and that since you thought that this was my doing, I had made myself distinguished because of this, as if through a kind of novelty. When I heard this, I decided to

write some kind of explanation for you, particularly since I am rightly sorry to offend you above all others.[63]

Abelard's comment about "your daughter in Christ" and Heloise's expectation of this visit suggests that there already existed close ties between Bernard and Heloise. The changes made to the wording of the Lord's Prayer brought tensions to the surface. Abelard argued that it was more authentic to recite the Lord's Prayer according to the version supplied by Matthew 6.9–13 (give us this day our "supersubstantial" bread) than by Luke 11.1–4 (our daily bread), as Matthew wrote his Gospel before Luke, and (it was thought) originally in Hebrew rather than Greek. Such arguments took principles laid out in the prologue to the *Sic et Non* dangerously close to questioning the authority of the Gospels. To the charge of novelty laid against him, Abelard retorted that a number of specifically Cistercian liturgical reforms could be accused of being equally novel. Abelard's detailed knowledge of primitive Cistercian practice could stem, as Waddell has suggested, from their already having been adopted by Heloise in the 1130s. The Order of the Paraclete was never officially part of the Cistercian Order, but it shared Cistercian ideals of simplicity and authenticity with a number of other new women's communities established in the twelfth century.

It is not clear whether the initiative for this reform of the Lord's Prayer came from Abelard or Heloise. Heloise certainly had strong opinions about liturgical texts, as Abelard makes clear in his prologues to the hymnal of the Paraclete. Abelard confessed that he had thought it was superfluous to write new songs when so many were supplied by tradition, but then devoted the rest of the preface to the first book of hymns to rehearsing arguments he reported as having been raised by Heloise:

> While different things were said to me by different people, you put forward among other things, I recall, reasoning like this: We know that the Latin, and particularly the Gallican Church follows custom rather than authority in hymns, just as it does in psalms. For we are still uncertain who is the author of the translation which the Gallican Church uses. If we want to judge from the sayings of those who have exposed the diversities of translations, it departs far from a universal interpretation and carries no weight of authority, as I think. Indeed, long habit of tradition has prevailed in this, so that while with other texts [of scripture] we have copies corrected by blessed Jerome, with the psalter, which we use a great deal, we are following what is inauthentic. There is now so much confusion in the hymns which we use, that there is no or only infrequently a heading to distinguish which or whose they are. . . . You added

that for several feasts, particular hymns were lacking, as for the Innocents and the Evangelists and indeed for those women saints who scarcely lived as virgins or martyrs. Finally, you asserted that there were several in which it was necessary for those who sing them to lie, sometimes because of the necessity of the season, sometimes because of the insertion of falsehood. . . . By these or similar persuasive arguments, the holiness of your reverence has driven our mind to compose hymns for the cycle of the whole year.[64]

Abelard implies that Heloise was particularly interested in having good hymns which were easy to sing, appropriate for a particular time of day. Heloise's comments echo those of the early Cistercians to recover authentic Christian practice, although she went further than the Cistercians in complaining about the texts themselves. She was troubled not only by the frequently uncertain source of the hymns used, but also by the "inequality of syllables," which made it very difficult for them to be supported by a melody.[65] In its strict fidelity to the earliest sources of liturgical tradition, early Cistercian observance ran the risk of monotony. Heloise took greater liberties than the Cistercians in asking Abelard for new hymn texts as well as new melodies (all lost to us, apart from that for *O quanta qualia*). When the Cistercians undertook major liturgical reform under the direction of Bernard of Clairvaux, they replaced the relatively dull Ambrosian melodies with more expressive melodies, while keeping the same texts. Under Heloise's guidance, the Paraclete combined Cistercian reforms with some of Abelard's hymns, although not all of them. Whether she was talking about love or the liturgy, she insisted that the words one proclaimed had to conform to the spirit in which they were spoken or sung. The ideals to which the nuns at the Paraclete were in theory committed were not so different from those revered by the early Cistercians. They remembered the entire Cistercian community in their prayers on 14 December of every year.[66] While Bernard was certainly critical of Abelard at Sens in 1141, he did not extend any such hostility to Heloise. In 1148 he wrote to Pope Eugenius III in 1148 to support an unspecified favor for the abbess of the Paraclete.[67]

Heloise and Vital of Mortain

Although Heloise had been brought up in a wealthy religious community, she seems to have been sympathetic towards simplifying religious observance at an early date. A funerary roll commemorating the death (16 September 1122) of Vital of Mortain includes a poem of unusual sensitivity offered by a nun of Argenteuil.[68] Vital, a friend of Robert of Arbrissel, founded a religious community for men at Savigny in 1112 and a separate community for women at Neufbourg under the guidance of his sister, Adelina, by 1115. These communities were formally admitted into the Cistercian Order in 1147. Vital imitated many of the practices established in the early years of Cîteaux, such as replacing the traditional black monastic habit with clothes of gray, undyed wool. Vital had a reputation for accepting followers from all walks of life, in particular those from an impoverished background. According to Orderic Vitalis, his sermons spared neither rich nor poor, "causing wealthy ladies delicately clad in silk garments and fine lambskins to tremble when he attacked their sins with the sword of God's word."[69] Baudri described Vital as rivaling Cicero in his eloquence and as another Orpheus in his voice.[70] Even Marbod of Rennes, a critic of Robert of Arbrissel, conceded that Vital of Mortain enabled a girl to obtain an education for little cost, in a letter to a woman unable to afford sending her daughter to a traditional religious house.[71]

Compared to the contributions from other religious communities, the poem from Argenteuil is remarkable for its sophistication and interest in human sorrow. The entry begins with a prayer for Vital and the souls of all the faithful departed, and then prayers for "Count Baldwin, Abbess Basilia, Abbess Adela, Abbess Judith, the nun Helvide, the nun Adela, dean (*decana*) Eremburga, Adelaide, Havide, Dodo the lay brother, and for all those whose names God may write in the book of life. Amen."[72]

> Flet pastore pio grex desolatus adempto;
>   Soletur miseras turba fidelis oves.
> Proh dolor! hunc morsu sublatum mortis edaci,
>   Non dolor aut gemitus vivificare queunt.
> Ergo quid lacrime? Quid tot tantique dolores
>   Prosunt? Nil prodest hic dolor, imo nocet.
> Sed licet utilitas ex fletu nulla sequatur,
>   Est tamen humanum morte dolere patris,
> Est etiam gaudere pium, si vis rationis
>   Tristitie vires adnichilare queat.
> Mors etenim talis, non mors sed vita putatur
>   Nam moritur mundo, vivit et ipse Deo.
> Ores pro nobis; omnes oramus ut ipse
>   Et nos ad vitam [*above the line:* Christum] perveniamus. Amen.

> The deserted flock weeps over the shepherd who has been taken away;
>   let the faithful multitude comfort the miserable sheep.

What sorrow! Neither sorrow nor groans can restore to life
    one taken away by the devouring jaws of death.
Therefore why should there be tears? What use so much and so
    widespread sorrow?
    Sorrow here is good for nothing, rather it harms.
But although nothing useful follows from mourning,
    it is human, however, to mourn the death of a father;
it is also pious to rejoice, if the force of reason
    is able to annihilate the powers of sadness.
For such a death is thought not to be death, but life.
    For he dies to the world, living himself for God.
May you pray for us; we all pray that he and we ourselves
    may come to life [*above the line:* to Christ]. Amen.[73]

This poem stands out from the other poems and epitaphs in the funerary
roll by its concern not with the sanctity of Vital, but with the grieving of
the people whom he had left behind. What point was there to being sad?
Sorrow achieved nothing and could be harmful. It was a human quality,
however, to mourn. Rejoicing was a good and pious act if it meant that
the "force of reason" (*vis rationis*) could dispel the power of sadness. The
original version of the final line, "that we may come to life" has been corrected to read "that we may come to Christ." Apart from playing on the
meaning of the name of Vital of Savigny, the poem reflects on the dilemma
of human emotions.

    Less than a quarter of the epitaphs in this funerary roll are written in
verse. Many are simply just names of monks or nuns who wished to
record their sympathy for the loss experienced by the community at Savigny. The poem from Argenteuil demonstrates greater literary skill than
the subsequent contribution from the cathedral of Notre-Dame, which
picked up on the Argenteuil poem's image of a flock abandoned by its
shepherd. It begins with heavy handed word play on the name of Vitalis,
and then offers theological clichés about the redemption, inspired by
some of the vocabulary of the Argenteuil poem, but without its reflection
on human suffering.[74] Given that no other poet is known to have being
living at Argenteuil in 1122, there seems little reason to doubt that
Heloise is its author.

An Unidentified Poem by Heloise?

The comment of Hugh Metel that Heloise was famous for her literary
composition alerts us to the fact that she enjoyed a reputation in her own

right as a poet. Does any of her poetry survive in the mass of little studied anonymous Latin poetry that survives from the twelfth century? Normally such anonymous verse does not make any specific allusion to the gender of the poet. One exception, however, occurs within a twelfth-century verse anthology from Bury St. Edmunds, also containing poems by Hildebert of Lavardin and Marbod of Rennes.[75] The poem in question articulates the frustration of a woman forbidden to practice the craft of writing (*littera*). This woman is an admirer of Aristotle and the discipline of logic. She appeals to Clio in the same way as one of the woman's poems (66) copied by Johannes de Vepria:[76]

Laudis honor, probitatis amor, gentilis
  honestas,
    Cuncta simul quali, quo periere
    modo?
Liuor edax, ignaua quies, detractio
  turpis,
    Quid prosunt regni totius
    imperio?
Caesaribus dilecta uiris hoc tempore
  sordent
    Gratia Pieridum Pegaseusque
    liquor.
Romanae quondam non ultima gloria
  gentis,
    Virgilius, Naso, nomina uana
    iacent.
Pellimur orbe nouo, studium quia
  littera nostrum.
    Clio, fida comes, pellimur,
    egredere!

Principibus si quod placuit noua lectio
  nostris,
    Subque nouis regnat lex noua
    principibus.
Carmine leniri dudum fera corda
  solebant,
    At modo carminibus mollia corda
    tument.
Mitius exilium meruerunt carmina
  uatis

The honor of praise, love of probity,
  pagan virtue
    How, in what way could they all
    perish at the same time?
Gnawing envy, idle inaction, base
  slander,
    What good are they to the rule
    of the whole kingdom?
The grace of the Muses and the
  fountain of Pegasus
    so beloved to the emperors are
    worthless to men nowadays.
Once not the least glory of the
  Roman people,
    Virgil, Ovid lie dead as empty
    names.
We are expelled from the new world
  because our concern is writing.
    Clio, faithful companion, we are
    driven out, leave!

Though new reading [once] pleased
  our leaders,
    Under new leaders a new law
    rules.
Formerly fierce hearts used to be
  softened by poetry,
    But now weak hearts are enraged
    by our poems.
The poems of the poet [Ovid] earned
  a milder exile

Carminibusque fuit Caesaris ira
minor.
Nostris principium dat littera nostra
furoris,
    Nostris nulla placent carmina
principibus.
Accusor, sed enim quo praecedente
reatu?
    Ars michi si quaeras crimen et
ingenium,
Grande mihi crimen genuit mea littera
grandis.
    Clio, [fida comes, pellimur,
egredere!]

O noua relligio uitae discretio sancta

    Iam si quod quid sit littera nosse
scelus!
Illa uel ille bonus cui cernua semper
imago,
    Qui, quoniam nil scit, se putat
esse bonum.
Esse tamen sanctum cui de nihilo
meditari
    Vel cui scire nihil contulit esse
nihil?
Si capitur sense deus et capitur
ratione,
    Plus capiet cui plus iam rationis
inest.

Esse bonum non me prohibebit littera
multa,
    Dat mihi, non prohibet, littera
nosse deum.
Credimus et ratione deum
cognoscimus esse,
    Hoc quoque quod facimus non
prohibere deum.
Quod facimus prohibet, uos quod
facitis prohibemus.
    Clio, [fida comes, pellimur,
egredere!]

And Caesar's anger toward poetry
was less.
Our writing provides a source of rage
to ours,
    No poems now please our
leaders.
I am indicted, but in fact for what
foregoing misdeed?
    If you want to know: art is my
crime, and genius.
My lofty writing gave birth to my
great crime.
    Clio [faithful companion, we are
driven out, leave!]

Oh new religion, holy withdrawal
from life,
    Now if only I knew what
wickedness our writing might be.
She or he is good whose face always
looks to the ground,
    Who, knowing nothing, thinks
that she or he is good.
Yet is that existence holy to which
meditating about nothing
    Or knowing nothing has brought
nothing to be?
If God is grasped by sense and grasped
by reason,
    That person will grasp more in
whom there is already more
reason.
Much writing will not stop me from
being good,
    writing allows me, not forbids me
to know God.
We believe and know rationally that
God exists
    And also that what we do God
does not forbid.
If he forbids what we do, we shall
forbid what you do.
    Clio [faithful companion, we are
driven out, leave!]

Carminibus recitare nouis bene uel
   male gesta:
      Iste fuit noster, si tamen error
   erat.
Detrectare bonis, se quae laudanda
   fuerunt,
      Quoque nequit uestra mens cupit
   arguere,
Si tamen ad laudem uos uel pudor
   impulit illud,
      Heu quam [. . .] esse bonum!
O noua calliditas—sed nobis cognita:
   quaerit
      Sub specie recti liuor habere
   locum.
Non est sanctarum mulierum fingere
   [MS frangere] uersus,
      Quaerere nec nostrum quis sit
   Aristotiles.
Ista uetus probitas, nil carmina
   tempore uestro,
      Nil genus aut species
   rhetoricusue color.
Quid seruare modos iuat, argumenta
   notare?
      Clio, [fida comes, pellimur,
   egredere!]

Scire tamen magis est hoc quod
   reprehendere sanctum:
      Quid carpat nescit, carpit at illa
   tamen.
Quisquis es, hoc quod tam sapienter
   corrigis in me,
      Si uelles in te, uir bone, tunc
   saperes.
Carmina componas, lacertor carminis,
   ut te
      posse quidem se de fingere nolle
   putem.
Et tibi grata forem, si littera grata
   fuisset:
      Par solet ingenium conciliare
   duos!

To recite in new verses good and bad
   deeds—
      That was our mistake, if such it
   was.
Your mind desired to condemn what
   it could not do,
      To disparage the good things, if
   they were worthy of praise.
Yet even if shame compelled you to
   praise it,
      Alas how [. . .] to be good!
O what new cunning—but known to
   us: Envy
      seeks its place under the guise of
   correctness.
It is not for holy women to compose
   verses,
      Nor for us to ask who Aristotle
   might be.
This virtue is ancient, poems are
   nothing in your age,
      Genus or species or rhetorical
   color as nothing.
What good is it to keep measures, to
   record disputes?
      Clio [faithful companion, we are
   driven out, leave!]

Yet knowing this holy thing is better
   than faulting it:
      He does not know what he
   criticizes but still criticizes it.
Whoever you are, what you so wisely
   correct in me
      You would know, good man, if
   you wanted to do so in yourself.
Compose verses, you slanderer of
   verse, so that I may think
      That you of course can create but
   do not want to.
I would be acceptable to you if my
   writing were acceptable:
      Equal genius usually reconciles
   two people!

The poet articulates her gender only through a single word in the penultimate line (*grata*). She is upset that her new poems about "good and bad deeds" have led her to be sent into an exile, a fate she believes to be worse than that suffered by Ovid. She observes that voracious envy (cf. Ovid, *Amores* 1.15.1) and base slander now seem to govern the world in place of the virtues once observed in Antiquity. Mockingly she appeals to Clio, her trusty companion, to leave as she has now been expelled. The implication of her verses is that what she has written has been perceived as a direct challenge to the new authorities. Her wrath is directed against a particular form of religion which elevates ignorance of learning into a worthwhile cause. She sees no point in meditating on nothing. She sees her writing as part of her coming to understand God "by reason." The craft of writing was not opposed by God. She makes fun of remarks apparently made against her: "it is not for holy women to compose (*fingere*, more likely than *frangere* or shatter) verses, to ask who Aristotle might be." This is a woman of unusual learning, an enthusiast for Aristotle and other ancient authors. While she begins by addressing the person responsible for her being driven into exile by the formal *vos*, she changes to the more familiar *tu* in her final verse to invite him to compose verse himself. Her final line, "equal genius usually reconciles two people," voices savage sarcasm against the hypocrisy of this individual responsible for her situation.

There are a number of parallels here with both the Troyes love letters and the more famous letters of Abelard and Heloise. The appeal to Clio as her constant companion recalls the invocation at the outset of the poem which makes up letter 66. Her description of the Muses and the fountain of Pegasus could be drawn from Fulgentius, as in Letter 66. Her comments about the jealousy of the present age persecuting genius (*ingenium*) recall not just comments about *livor* and *invidia* in the Troyes love letters (e.g., 22, 54, 69, 85) but a central theme of the *Historia calamitatum*. The arguments which the woman raises in defense of *littera* as deepening understanding of God are precisely those which Abelard was making in the early 1130s. His *Theologia Scholarium* contains a passionate attack on those "who seek solace in their own ignorance."[77] The stinging nature of the attack in this poem takes on particular significance in light of the political developments shaking France in 1129. The one famous woman writer, deeply versed in classical authors, whom we know to have been expelled from her monastery, is Heloise. The poem is particularly critical of those who do not think it appropriate for women to engage in learned study. She cannot understand why a woman or a man (*Illa uel ille*) is judged good for knowing nothing. Writing (*littera*) was not a crime, but allowed her to know God. These are the arguments that Abelard was making with great force in the intellectually polarized situation of the early 1130s.

The complaint of the woman poet that a new generation of leaders has come to power, opposed to too much intellectualism in religion, mirrors the situation facing Heloise in 1129 very closely. In that year, Suger obtained official sanction to expel Heloise and her nuns from Argenteuil, on the grounds that it had been "defamed by the deplorable conduct of the young women" (*puellarum miserrima conversacione infamato*).[78] While it was conventional for ecclesiastics to invoke sexual misconduct as sufficient reason to replace nuns by monks, the poet is implying that the real reason why she was being driven out is that she had written "about good and bad deeds." When Heloise was expelled from Argenteuil in 1129, Stephen of Garlande, traditionally a protector of the royal abbey, was still in disgrace. The king had been persuaded to grant new privileges to Saint-Denis. His cousin, Ralph of Vermandois, was now the king's principal adviser and military commander. Royal attention was now shifting away from the Loire valley to the great regions north of France. At the same time, new privileges were being given to the Cistercians and to the order of Saint-Victor. The woman's allusions to a change of political direction in the kingdom as well as to the ideals of a "new religion" in which study was considered dangerous make good sense if she was directing her poem against the actions of Suger of Saint-Denis.

There is no obvious clue as to whether this woman poet also composed other verses in the Bury St. Edmunds anthology. Many of these poems reflect a daring and questioning tone, informed by pagan imagery. The two poems immediately preceding the nun's elegy relate to different subjects: (no. xii) a trick by which Aristotle succeeded in begging peace from Alexander the Great, "tricked by the cunning of the man," and (no. xiii) a mistake of nature by which a man was made into a hermaphrodite, whose "Venus" was entered by both sexes.[79] Another (no. xvii) is similar to the elegy in its complaint that while the Muses were once honored, now they were cheap, silent, and scattered.[80] The next one (no. xviii) asks someone why he (or she) thinks the writing sent by the poet was *aliena* (strange or foreign) and holds the writer in suspicion. One poem (no. xxiv) is addressed to "dear Matilda," while another (no. xxvii) is to a woman and complains of the restlessness of love, "Oh what have I done wrong or what have I deserved that for so long our passion does not purify? . . . You are taken with your Mars, under the sign of Phoebus. Revenge has moved him, virgin to be sought by God. . . . If you were found with Mars by the fault of Phoebus, why does wretched Leucothoe purge the acts of God?"[81]

This last poem echoes a number of the themes in Heloise's letters. It also recalls Abelard's comment about Fulbert's discovery of affair with Heloise as like that of Vulcan coming across Mars and Venus. Further research is needed to establish whether a single author is responsible for this group of poems in the Bury St. Edmunds anthology, which apply a detailed knowledge of classical imagery to profound ethical questions.

How this anthology came to Bury St. Edmunds is not known. The presence of poems by Marbod of Rennes and Hildebert of Lavardin make it likely that it is based on an exemplar from Anjou, closely connected to England after 1128, when the Empress Matilda, daughter of Henry I of England, married the Count of Anjou. Suger feared that this Norman-Angevin alliance was dangerous to France. Closely related to the Bury St. Edmunds manuscript is a very similar anthology which begins with verses, attributed to "Serlo of Paris," and addressed to Muriel, a nun. This Muriel, who seems to have lived both at Wilton in England and at Le Ronceray, Angers, is like Heloise in being a famous poet. Her verse has not yet been identified.[82] Serlo shares with the anonymous nun-poet a tone of caustic satire toward established authority. Her poem, *Laudis honor,* deserves much greater attention than it has so far been given. It gives valuable insight into the difficult situation confronting any educated woman daring to pursue the study of philosophy. There were strong pressures on such women not to write or acquire a reputation for being outspoken. Poems that were politically or theologically sensitive might be circulated anonymously to avoid negative repercussions for their author. While none of the other poems in this anthology reveal the name or even the gender of their author, some of them strike a daring note in their familiarity with classical imagery, turned to reflect on personal themes.

Heloise and Abelard as Writers

Heloise undoubtedly wrote far more than the three letters preserved alongside the *Historia calamitatum,* discovered by Jean de Meun in the thirteenth century. The love letters transcribed by Johannes de Vepria suggest that she was an accomplished writer of Latin verse. Like so many other women, however, any verse that she might have written was not acknowledged specifically as hers. Only a single contemporary, Hugh Metel, acknowledges her reputation as a writer. The letters copied by Johannes de Vepria are far more sophisticated than the short love poems between Marbod and the girl he loves, or the Regensburg exchange between a girl and her teacher, from the early twelfth century. While the technical philosophical vocabulary in the man's letters corresponds very closely to that of Abelard's early writings on logic, Heloise is more experimental in her use of language. She longs to fuse philosophical themes with poetic language. Above all she argues for the supremacy of the ideal of selfless love, drawing both on classical ethical philosophy and scripture. The doubts which have been raised about whether Heloise wrote the letters attributed to her, and about whether Abelard and Heloise could have written the love letters preserved at Clairvaux, reflect an unwillingness to accept that such a gifted and independently minded woman could have existed in twelfth-century France.

Heloise emerges in both her early and later letters as a writer profoundly familiar with classical literature, but preoccupied from the outset by ethical concerns. She combines classical rhetoric, such as found in the letters of Peter the Venerable, with an intensely personal interest in self-knowledge, much more reminiscent of the meditative writing of Bernard of Clairvaux. Bernard himself was profoundly aware that his contemporaries were fascinated by the literature of love. Heloise shares these concerns, but was not afraid to draw on pagan literature to pursue these themes.

Abelard's initial reputation was in dialectic. His lyric and melodic gifts, singled out by Heloise as making him so unusual among philosophers, provided him with an opportunity to escape from the rigid expectations placed on him by his professional work. Her comment that he treated such composition like a game is significant, however. He did not, at least in his early years, seek to fuse his philosophical and poetic gifts. He saw himself first of all as an academic eager to establish himself within the schools of Paris. The system worked to the advantage of male intellectuals who were not married. Abelard's life changed after he was castrated. He became a monk at Saint-Denis, but then fled from conventional monasticism. At the Paraclete, he began to develop his ideas about theological language and ethical behavior. His discussions, however, were always with other men. Even after he transferred the Paraclete to women, Heloise complained that he was unwilling to listen too closely to what she was saying. These were difficult years. Accusations of sexual promiscuity could easily be invoked by those who feared that any interaction between men and women in religious life was potentially dangerous.

The writing of the *Historia calamitatum* marked a turning point in Abelard's life. He wanted to exorcise those vices of arrogance and lust with which he was associated in the eyes of many of his contemporaries. He did so by playing up those vices in his past, to emphasize the extent to which he had learned from the calamities which had befallen him. Yet Abelard scarcely acknowledges the significance of the many love letters which he had written over fifteen years earlier. He passes over in silence any literary achievement of Heloise either before or after she took solemn vows at the abbey of Argenteuil. His first concern was to re-establish his reputation as a teacher within the schools of Paris.

The correspondence that Heloise initiated after reading the *Historia calamitatum* resulted in Abelard starting to compose treatises specifically for Heloise and the nuns of the Paraclete. Their dialogue was inevitably very different from that which it had been in Paris over fifteen years earlier. After they resumed contact, Abelard became more attuned to discussing the meaning of scripture with Heloise. His growing interest in the 1130s in explaining the redemption as achieved through the example of Christ's love may reflect the belated influence of Heloise's own longstanding interest in the ideals of love. By urging Heloise to turn her love away from himself to Christ, Abelard was obliged to develop a Christology which responded to her own insistence on the supremacy of selfless love. He projected onto Christ the values which he wished to see in himself. At her request, he composed a commentary on the Hexaemeron, the six days of creation as told in the book of Genesis. He also answered forty-two probing questions that Heloise put to him from her reading of scripture. Whereas in the past he had composed love songs for her, he now turned his attention to composing a complete cycle of hymns for the liturgy. A number emphasize the presence of both sexes among the ranks of the blessed.[83] Perhaps the closest Abelard comes to exploring personal emotion is in his composing a sequence of Laments on scriptural themes for which he wrote both text and music.[84] Abelard's rendering of David's lament over Saul and Jonathan has a particular poignancy in its exploration of David's grief over the death of Jonathan. David's lament that he has lost half his soul echoes those love letters in which Heloise had offered him "half a soul" and described herself as part of his soul (11 and 86, also 97). While writing about the parting of David and Jonathan, Abelard was mourning a relationship with Heloise which had never been allowed to come to fruition.[85]

Chrysogonus Waddell has also argued that Abelard composed an Easter sequence used at the Paraclete: *Epithalamica,* a dramatized version of the Song of Songs, charged with erotic emotion:[86]

Iam video quod optaveram, / iam teneo quod amaveram, / iam rideo quae sic fleveram, / plus gaudeo quam dolueram: / Risi mane, / flevi nocte; / mane risi, / nocte flevi. /

Now I see what I had desired, now I clasp what I had loved, now I laugh at what I had so wept over, I rejoice more than I mourned, I laughed in the morning, I wept at night, in the morning I laughed, at night I wept.

The building up of rhyming imagery recalls that of the woman in letter 84:

diligendo quaesivi, querendo inveni, inveniendo amavi, amando optavi, optando omnibus in corde meo preposui. . . . In te, quod quesivi habeo, quod optavi teneo, quod amavi amplexata sum. . . .

Through loving you, I searched for you; searching for you, I found you; finding you, I desired you; desiring you, I chose you; choosing you, I placed you before everyone else in my heart. . . . In you, I have what I searched for, I hold what I chose, I embrace what I desired. . . .

While Waddell has argued in favor of Abelard's authorship of the *Epithalamica,* the similarity between the sequence and this love letter raises the possibility that it was written by Heloise, or alternatively by Abelard in direct echo of that letter of Heloise. Similar questions need to be raised about two other sequences certainly performed at the Paraclete, which Waddell has attributed to Abelard, *Virgines castae, De profundis,* and perhaps also some of the hymns sung by the nuns.[87]

Although he wrote much for the nuns of the Paraclete, Abelard's principal involvement in the 1130s was with the Parisian schools. He could not avoid being caught up in the theological arguments between himself and the theologians attached to the abbey of Saint-Victor. While he continued to teach logic at a school on the Montagne Sainte-Geneviève, his major intellectual effort was now directed towards the study of scripture and Christology. By the late 1130s he was starting to reconsider some of his ideas about ethics. The voice of Heloise seems to have made its biggest impact on Abelard in these years. Abelard came closer to acknowledging her concerns, without ever explicitly acknowledging her contribution. It is fascinating to observe the extent to which the questions that he confronts in his last major work, his *Ethics* or *Know Yourself* (*Scito teipsum*), commenced ca. 1138/39 but never completed, are issues that Heloise had raised much earlier in his life. Only in these years did Abelard reflect on the difference between a lustful thought and active consent to a lustful thought in the heart, in deliberate contempt of God. He had matured considerably since first establishing himself as a brilliant analyst of language, in relation to both logic and theology. His critics never recognized this evolution in his range of interests. To them, Abelard always remained an over-clever logician with little wisdom about Christian teaching and behavior.

The Final Years

Abelard's position in Paris became increasingly precarious after the death of Louis VI on 1 August 1137. Bishop Stephen of Senlis and Abbot Gilduin of Saint-Victor heard the king's final confession, and Suger then took the body to Saint-Denis for burial. Things had changed much since Philip I was buried at Fleury in 1108.[88] Only two months earlier, Louis VI had asked Suger to accompany Ralph of Vermandois, Theobald of Champagne, and five hundred knights as they took Louis, the king's sixteen-year-old son, to Bordeaux in order to marry Eleanor, the fifteen-year-old daughter of the duke of Aquitaine.[89] Marriage of the young Eleanor to the crown prince was a strategic victory for Suger in that France now gained control of Aquitaine and isolated Anjou. While it has often been claimed that the marriage of Eleanor to Louis introduced Occitan culture into France in the mid-twelfth century, the Poitevin court is likely to have provided a conduit for Occitan culture into the Loire valley since the late eleventh century. Even before 1137, a variety of competing traditions had established themselves in the royal domain, culturally far less unified than Suger liked to imagine. When he completed his biography of Louis VI in the early 1140s, Suger did not know that the situation would change dramatically in 1152 when Eleanor left Louis VII in 1152 to marry Henry Plantagenet, son of Geoffrey V Count of Anjou, and heir to the English throne through his mother, the Empress Matilda. The victory of Angevin culture was then complete.

In 1137, however, Suger could feel confident about the future of France. England was stumbling into a period of protracted conflict, with many barons refusing to accept the authority of the Empress Matilda. Stephen of Garlande retired from his post as royal chancellor with the coronation of Louis VII and the advent of a new generation of advisers to the young king. Abelard's departure from the Montagne Sainte-Geneviève, which seemed so premature to John of Salisbury (only recently arrived from England), may be connected to these events.[90] Abelard was then almost sixty years old, a teacher who had once dominated the schools, but was no longer fully up-to-date with the new texts of Aristotle which were being read in the schools of Paris. Abelard may have retired from Paris simply to engage in his writing. Whether he went to stay at the Paraclete is not known. In any case, he no longer had a friendly ear in the royal court.

In Lent 1140, William of Saint-Thierry asked Bernard to act against Peter Abelard, whose writings he feared were circulating in the curia itself.[91] He had grounds for concern. Master Guy of Castello, an influential Cardinal priest in the curia owned a copy of Abelard's working manuscript of the *Christian Theology* and *Yes and No*. Guy subsequently succeeded Innocent II as Pope Celestine II on 26 September 1143 (but died on 8 March 1144, by poison according to one report). William feared that if Abelard's ideas gained ground in Rome, there was a risk that schism could again tear apart the Latin Church, especially as Innocent II was nearing the end of his pontificate. William was conscious of the political tensions which surfaced at the II Lateran Council, held in April 1139. Arnold of Brescia, expelled from Italy by Innocent II at the Lateran Council, attached himself to Abelard in Paris. Arnold was popular in Rome (particularly among Roman women, it is recorded), and was perceived as fomenting outright conflict with Innocent II.[92] Relying for his information on William of Saint-Thierry, Bernard of Clairvaux played up the risk that Abelard's ideas would tear apart the Church, and that schism would again rear its head. Bernard never mentioned Heloise or the Paraclete in any of the many letters which he sent to Rome. Instead he presented Abelard as a dangerous logician who threatened to tear apart catholic unity with his questioning of Christian doctrine.

Abelard appealed to the archbishop of Sens to ask if he could defend himself against these accusations at a forthcoming Council (held on the octave of Pentecost, probably 1141). A propaganda war developed between the two parties. When Abelard discovered that on the eve of the Council, Bernard had persuaded the bishops to condemn him in advance, he decided to appeal directly to Rome itself. Through Peter the Venerable, we learn that the differences between Abelard and Bernard were settled through a compromise agreement arranged by himself and the abbot of Cîteaux. Bernard's secretary, Geoffrey of Auxerre, subsequently circulated a collection of Bernard's letters to Rome which included the Pope's condemnation of Abelard, but did not mention the lifting of that sentence achieved by Peter the Venerable.[93] The image Geoffrey perpetuated of Abelard as an arrogant logician hostile to a great man of God, was of enormous influence.

Abelard was a sick man when he retired to Cluny. He died at Chalon-sur-Sâone, where he had been moved for the sake of his health, on 21 April 1142. The abbot of Cluny allowed Abelard's body to be brought to the Paraclete. He also promised that the monks of Cluny would offer thirty masses for Heloise after her death.[94] Sometime between 1144 and 1154, she asked him for a formal document of absolution for Abelard, and also asked him if he could help find a position for Astralabe, preferably in the diocese of Paris. Its bishop was now Theobald (1143–58), a less politically vigorous figure than Stephen of Senlis. The abbot of Cluny provided the required document, but expressed his fears that it could be difficult to obtain a post for Astralabe. He remarked that bishops tended to be unwilling to assist in such cases, as it had become illegal for children of ordained clergy to acquire benefices. It is not certain what happened to Astralabe. According to a Breton charter of 1150, an Astralabe was a canon at Nantes, as was his uncle, Porcarius. If this was Heloise's son, then it would seem that she never fulfilled her desire to remove him from Abelard's family and bring him closer to the Paraclete.[95]

When Heloise died on 16 May 1164, the Paraclete had already established itself as a religious community with a number of dependent houses. There is no evidence that she ever established a significant scriptorium which could preserve the voices of its founders in the same way as Clairvaux, some eighty miles distant. What happened to the manuscript books which she owned is a mystery, none more tantalizing than those which contained the record of her exchanges with Peter Abelard. Heloise had no successor at the Paraclete as distinguished as herself in Latin letters.

One person who may have been involved in preserving her exchanges with Abelard is Berengar of Poitiers, whose writings occur alongside those of Abelard in the manuscript acquired by Petrarch.[96] The exact path by which the letters of Abelard and Heloise came to public attention in the thirteenth century can only be speculated upon. One possibility is that Eudes Rigaud (ca. 1215–75), archbishop of Rouen, papal legate, and close adviser to Louis IX, came across them when he visited his sister, newly installed as abbess of the Paraclete in 1248.[97] Eudes was very interested in legislation about religious communities, and was one of the first commentators on the Rule of St. Francis. In the Troyes MS 802, bought from the chapter of Notre-Dame in 1347, a scribe has appended to the original Paraclete observances thirteenth-century conciliar decisions from Rouen about the religious life for women.[98] Whatever the precise path by which these letters surfaced, it was only after Jean de Meun gave them publicity in *The Romance of the Rose* that they started to attract interest. The most copied section of the correspondence was not Abelard's Rule, but the *Historia calamitatum* and the first letters of Heloise.

The path by which the love letters came to be transcribed by Johannes de Vepria at Clairvaux is similarly uncertain. It seems most likely that Heloise always kept a parchment record of those messages which she exchanged with

Abelard on wax tablets during the time that she was staying in the house of her uncle. The original messages which they inscribed on the wax are lost. The manuscript which Johannes de Vepria transcribed appears to record Heloise's memories of her early relationship with Abelard. In a very real sense, it was a literary composition by Abelard's most distinguished student.

The connections between the nuns of the Paraclete and the early Cistercians raise the possibility that either Heloise or her nuns decided to bequeath her record of the love letters to Clairvaux, some eighty miles from the Paraclete to the east of Troyes. Alternatively, a sympathetic monk might have come across these letters from the Paraclete after her death, and deposited a copy at Clairvaux. Heloise keeps her mystery. Whatever happened to those letters between the twelfth and the fifteenth centuries, it was not so extraordinary that a well-read Cistercian monk should become interested in texts that are rich in allusion to scripture and classical literature. Her letters are much concerned with issues of the heart and interior disposition (*affectus*), themes also of great interest to Bernard of Clairvaux. She was more interested than Bernard in drawing on classical literature and philosophy to understand the human condition. Here she was closer to the intellectual interests of Peter Abelard. It was not inappropriate, however, that an abbey so celebrated as a center of reflection on the nature of love should come to acquire a copy of her letters. Clairvaux owned many works written outside the immediate circle of the Cistercian Order. Johannes de Vepria was well placed to appreciate this exchange of letters as an unusually rich example of epistolary art.

These letters have been unjustly ignored by subsequent generations for no other reason than that they do not carry explicit identification of a name to whom they can be attached. Their language is so close to that of other writings of Abelard and Heloise that there seems no reason to doubt their authorship. These letters help confirm the authenticity of the famous correspondence of Abelard and Heloise. They also suggest that the *Historia calamitatum* cannot be relied upon as the final word on Abelard's early relationship with Heloise. Much more than Heloise, Abelard distances himself from his past in order to save his reputation. She, by contrast, was rigorously hostile to hypocrisy both in love and in the religious life. Heloise belonged to one of the last generations of educated women for whom writing Latin prose and verse was a natural facility. By the second half of the twelfth century, French was beginning to rival Latin as the language in which to speak about love. Even in Heloise's own lifetime, it was becoming increasingly difficult for women brought up in old-established monastic houses to maintain close literary contact with male friends, at least in France. The expanding influence of the Parisian schools effectively marginalized women from benefiting from the education which Heloise had once enjoyed at Notre-Dame. The love letters copied at Clairvaux in the late fifteenth century offer a glimpse into a relationship from which Abelard wanted to distance himself. In transcribing those letters, Johannes de Vepria discovered the power of voices all too easily lost.

CHAPTER 7

NEW DISCOVERIES AND INSIGHTS
(1999–2007)

Much has happened since the publication in 1999 of my study of the *Epistolae duorum amantium* (*EDA*), a remarkable and enigmatic collection of over one hundred love letters and poems, discovered by Johannes de Vepria, a bibliophile monk of Clairvaux in the late fifteenth century.[1] New insights continue to emerge about an exchange in which the man reveals himself to be a celebrated and controversial teacher, while the young woman with whom he is infatuated presents herself as an ardent student of philosophy, with a particular interest in ethics. Sylvain Piron has produced a new translation of the entire corpus into French, that fully brings out their originality and great beauty. He brings forward fresh arguments for attributing them to Abelard and Heloise.[2] There have also been new translations into German and Italian, although without detailed analysis of their content.[3] A popular biography by James Burge that draws on these love letters has helped generate wider interest in Heloise as a woman who challenged convention.[4] Umberto Eco silently incorporated extracts from these letters into a historical novel, implying that they were an elaborate hoax of his twelfth-century male hero, writing to the wife of Barbarossa.[5] While there has been positive support for the attribution from a number of scholars, others have expressed caution about accepting arguments too quickly. Could not the imagery about love in these letters be conventional medieval tropes, invented by anybody?[6] Even if the authenticity of the famous monastic correspondence between Heloise and Abelard, questioned periodically by scholars for almost two hundred years in response to public interest in the famous letters, is now largely accepted, some critics have raised widely divergent hypotheses about the authorship of the *EDA*.[7] This postscript reflects on new insights that have emerged relating to these love letters since 1999 and their relationship to the art of letter writing in the late eleventh and early twelfth centuries, as well as on the debate that these letters have provoked.

Discussion of the *Epistolae duorum amantium*

Arguments in favor of Abelard and Heloise as having written the original letters excerpted by Johannes de Vepria were put forward quite independently from myself by C. Stephen Jaeger in 1999 in his important study of ennobling love in medieval literature, a theme that he traces back to the eleventh century and earlier.[8] In a volume of essays about male-female dialogue, Jaeger summarizes his arguments in favor of the authorship of Abelard and Heloise in a chapter that is followed by a short essay from Giles Constable voicing caution about claiming that such polished letters constitute a personal outpouring of the heart, to which Jaeger offers a further response.[9]

In 2003, Peter von Moos published a heavily footnoted study of the *EDA*, arguing against Könsgen that these love letters constitute a unified *Hauptwerk* of the art of epistolary composition (*ars dictaminis*) about "a secular religion of love." He compared them to Boncompagno's *Rota veneris,* a thirteenth-century anthology of love letters showing how one ought to address one's beloved, and Machaut's *Voir dit,* a fictional dialogue written in French from the fourteenth century.[10] Attaching little weight to the argument that teacher's identity is revealed in technical terms, he argues that these are simply medieval commonplaces.[11] He dismisses Könsgen's argument that the contrasting prose styles and vocabulary in the *EDA* suggest two distinct authors, by arguing that the phenomenon of one correspondent developing a phrase used in a previous letter (*enjambement*) is evidence of a single author. Von Moos describes the rhyming prose style used in the women's letters, a style that reached its highpoint in the eleventh century, as "excessive" and "mechanical *elocutio.*"[12]

Making some big claims about the evolution of medieval culture, he suggests that themes of doubt and questioning in the love letters are more characteristic of the skepticism of the fourteenth century than of the twelfth-century cultural renaissance, which he describes as marked by "a sense of harmony between inner and outer," and of contrast between "true and untrue love."[13] He argues that the love letters can provide a key to understanding the intellectual history of the fourteenth and fifteenth century, if one moves away from attributing these letters to Abelard and Heloise.[14] This is despite the fact that they allude to no classical text discovered after the mid-twelfth century, such as the writings of Aristotle who took over from Cicero as the dominant authority in ethics in the mid-thirteenth century. He associates the letters not with the great period of experimentation in writing Latin letters between the late eleventh and mid-twelfth centuries, but with the *dolce stil nuovo* of thirteenth-century Italy. His study, which relies on making a few parallels with love letters quoted by later theorists of letter writing, does not come to terms with the radical differences in perspective about love between the man and the woman in the *EDA*. He claims that the man's definition of love in letter 24 was influenced by Aelred's treatise on friendship, even though the ideas in this letter about love existing between two lovers are very different from the religious ideals of a monastic writer. Aelred follows Cicero in speaking of friendship creating a single mind, without adding the term *indifferenter*.[15] In a subsequent study, von Moos has not pursued this claim further, but has continued to doubt that there could be any private exchanges of letters in the twelfth century—even though both Abelard and Heloise refer to exchanging personal messages, and the seal achieved wide use in the twelfth century precisely to facilitate such private exchanges.[16] It would have been standard practice in such an exchange (as for example with the Regensburg verses) for one party to transcribe onto parchment an exchange originally written on wax tablets.

While von Moos rightly points out that love letters could accompany manuals of letter writing, such as the *Rota veneris* of Boncompagno da Signa, there is no precedent for any epistolary exchange as extended as the *EDA* being composed as an elaborate literary fiction that had no introduction or conclusion. The *Speculum virginum* is an extended fictional dialogue between a priest and a nun from the 1130s, that clearly does offer a systematic and structured vision of religious life.[17] The *Epistolae duorum amantium* offer no such coherent perspective. Rather, they present an exchange of letters, written in contrasting literary styles and presenting two quite distinct personalities, each with their own understanding of love, that do not come to any final resolution.

Peter Dronke has put forward a quite different hypothesis, one he first put forward in 1976, namely that the *EDA* do record a genuine exchange between a twelfth-century teacher and his brilliant female student of philosophy, but that they are a couple different from Abelard and Heloise.[18] Pointing to similarities between these love letters and the Regensburg verses (exchanged between a master and a female student in the early twelfth century), he has suggested that the literary formation of the young woman in the *EDA* could have been Bavarian, but that she pursued studies in France. Giovanni Orlandi argues from slight differences in preferred prose rhythm in sentence endings (the *cursus*) that they are written by two people, different from Abelard and Heloise.[19] Ziolkowski points to the absence in the man's love letters of small function words like *quippe* and *autem,* favored by Abelard in his monastic letters, as pointing to two distinct authors. He also observes that while the man's verse in the *EDA* sometimes relies on internal rhyme, this is not a style found in Abelard's *Carmen ad Astralabium,* written near the end of his life. He holds that the verse within the exchange is of inferior quality, and generally "unworthy" of Abelard.[20] Neither Dronke, Orlandi, or Ziolkowski focus on what the two voices in the exchange have to say about love, and how those ideas relate to those of Abelard and Heloise.

Both the hypothesis put forward by von Moos that the *EDA* constitute a literary fiction by a single author, recreating an archaic style of rhyming prose for the woman's letters, and the very different suggestion of Dronke, that they were composed by an authentic couple, different from Abelard and Heloise, are highly speculative. Because these love letters survive only as excerpts, without any concrete references that permit unequivocal identification of the writers, it is necessary to combine philological, literary, and intellectual analysis, as well as the broader discipline of cultural history, to accomplish this task. No single discipline can claim a monopoly in establishing the "truth" of a text.[21]

New Insights into the *Epistolae duorum amantium*

An excellent example of careful philological analysis of the *EDA* has been that of Francesco Stella, who has made a detailed inventory of textual parallels (two words or more in a single verse) between poetry within the *EDA* and medieval poetry. He shows that the overwhelming influences on the love letters are poets from the late-eleventh or early-twelfth century (Marbod of Rennes, Baudri of Bourgueil, Fulcoie of Beauvais, and Hildebert of Lavardin). Stella also identified a few isolated cases of parallel words within a single verse by a later twelfth-century poet, not matched in the late eleventh-century corpus.[22] Yet these few parallels could also be explained by shared dependence on earlier texts not yet recognized. For example, Abelard's love songs (most of which have not been identified) were apparently widely known, and could have been an unconscious influence on later poets.[23] It is the clustering of regular parallels between the poetry in the *EDA* with poetry from the late-eleventh or early-twelfth century, mostly from the Loire valley, that is the most significant result.

In a detailed statistical study of the *EDA* Stella has confirmed Könsgen's argument that the vocabulary of the woman's letters was so distinct from that of the man that it was impossible for them to have been written by a single author, as claimed by von Moos.[24] Stella notes Ziolkowski's observation about the differing use of a few function words (notably *autem* and *quippe*) between the man's letters and those of Abelard, but also observes that little terms are less useful than distinct terms and ideas on which to build an argument. Stella's lexical analysis leads him to consider that in word frequency the man's love letters are further removed from the monastic and even more from scholastic writings of Abelard, than are those of the woman from Heloise. Yet lexical analysis has to confront the way usage may change over time and be influenced by specific literary genres (the love letter declaring fidelity, the homiletic letter promoting piety and distancing itself from emotion). Words which qualify an argument (like *autem*) are hardly appropriate for declaring emotion. Stella leans toward the notion that the love letters emanate from an authentic couple, connected to Paris in the mid-twelfth century and in contact with Abelard, yet a different person. Yet he also asks which couple could be responsible for such letters other than Abelard and Heloise. While the love letters create a *persona* different from the *persona* presented in the *Historia calamitatum,* can we use slightly differing word usage as evidence of a different person? Lexical analysis needs to be buttressed by awareness of literary genre, and key ideas, as well as cultural and social context, if it is to be persuasive.

The man in these love letters is a brilliant but controversial teacher, whose preferred imagery of love, largely couched in terms of *amor,* or passionate longing in a general sense, is profoundly shaped by Ovidian vocabulary. By contrast, the young woman, whom he singles out as the most brilliant student of philosophy, among all the women of his age, is fascinated by the ethics of love and friendship, and wants him to think in this way. He largely avoids her practice of invoking religious rhetoric to describe his love, and avoids her rhyming prose, more characteristic of a monastic than a scholastic education. The gradual unraveling of the relationship that becomes apparent in the second half of the exchange is the consequence of a breakdown in trust between the two parties. Even if one disregards the question of who these lovers are, their exchange is of exceptional interest in articulating the evolution of a relationship that becomes increasingly difficult to sustain. The young woman, initially infatuated by his teaching and eager to absorb the richness of philosophy, evolves into a tragic figure. She is torn by conflicting emotions of selfless love and disappointment as he is unable to fully reciprocate her ideals. The contrasting ways in which the two voices in the exchange perceive their relationship parallel the contrasting perceptions of Abelard and Heloise with remarkable closeness. The issue then becomes one of how likely it is that another couple, similar to Abelard and Heloise, existed in the early-twelfth century who have otherwise escaped attention.

The parallels between the love letters and the known writings of Abelard and Heloise go much further than I had realized in 1999. For example, in her penultimate letter (112), in which the young woman addresses him for the first time, not as her beloved, but as her "most noble and learned teacher" and sends a conventional religious rather than amatory greeting ("well-being in Him who is both salvation and blessing"), she observes: "It has pleased your nobility to send those letters to my insignificance (*mee parvitati;* literally 'smallness')." In Heloise's first response to Abelard's *Historia calamitatum,* she observes that "your excellence knows better than our smallness (*nostra parvitas*) how many and how large treatises were completed by the holy fathers, and with what care they composed them."[25] In her letter to Peter the Venerable, Heloise employs similar rhyming prose to give glory that "your greatness has descended to our smallness."[26] The young woman's use of *parvitas,* completely out of place in love letters, echoes a patristic modesty topos much used, for example, by St. Anselm and Bernard of Clairvaux, but never employed by Abelard or Peter the Venerable.[27] Although the young woman only uses *parvitas* of herself once in the love letters, she regularly contrasts what she considers to be the modesty or her capacity with what she sees as his greatness, as in her letter 23, in which she debates her capacity to address him adequately, and in her letter 25: "However, if the duty of greeting you according to my meager talents in not enough." (*At si pro parvitate ingenii in te salutandi officio non suffici.*) In letter 49, she contrasts his great virtue and learning with what she claims is her inadequacy to return a stylistically adequate reply. Her sense of modesty, inculcated by tradition, is at odds with her desire, evident from early in the exchange, to offer her own perspective frequently at odds with those of her beloved.

Letters *24* and 25 are particularly significant because they provide a rare moment when the lover is forced to adopt a professorial tone, as he attempts to respond to a question she has apparently put to him about the nature of *amor* (either in conversation or a letter not preserved in the *EDA*). She then answers with her own thoughts on the topic, showing that her strategy of asking a question is a way for her to develop her own thoughts, the same strategy as Heloise would adopt to Abelard in later writings. While I had observed in 1999 that he adapts Cicero's definition of friendship with the vocabulary of dialectic, I had not appreciated that that the passage of Cicero's *De amicitia* paraphrased in letter *24*, about love confining itself so tightly that it seems to exist in two people alone, is the only passage from this treatise that Abelard includes in the *Sic et Non* (138: 21) to debate "whether *caritas* once acquired can ever be lost."[28] Given that the vast bulk of texts quoted in the *Sic et Non* are patristic, this passage from the *De amicitia* was clearly of great importance to Abelard.

The fact that the teacher in letter *24* modifies Cicero's definition of love by referring to it as a "universal thing" (*res universalis*) reveals his particular interest in issues of dialectic. He reflects with some skill on what kind of thing (*res*) love is, by saying that he cannot excuse himself on grounds of ignorance "as if I had been asked about a thing (*res*) unfamiliar to me; for that very love has brought me under its own command in such a way that it seems to be a thing not external (*ut non extranea res*), but very familiar and personal, even visceral." He then presents love as the only true universal thing, shared by the lovers alone, proven by the fact that they share the same opinions on everything. Although Abelard would become well known for asserting in the Porphyry gloss of the *Logica Ingredientibus* (written around 1118) that a universal was not any kind of thing (*res*), this was a significant new step in his thinking. Three times in his *Dialectica* (written between 1111 and 1117), Abelard uses the traditional phrase "universal thing" (*res universalis*) to refer to whatever is universal.[29] Modifying Cicero's claim that love makes from two wills a single will with a term from dialectic that explains they are not different (*indifferenter*) parallels exactly the position that Abelard says he forced William of Champeaux to concede, namely that two identical individuals were the same *indifferenter* rather than *essentialiter*.[30]

Abelard's debate with William about universals occurred not in 1109 (as I had assumed in 1999), but sometime after Easter 1111, when William resigned his position at Notre-Dame and moved to a disused chapel of St-Victor.[31] Abelard took issue, not with the traditional phrase "universal thing," but with William's assumption, as voiced for example in his *Introductiones,* that a universal was a substance essentially the same in two identical individuals. William certainly conceded this in recognizing that two such individuals were the same *indifferenter* in theological sentences delivered at St-Victor between 1111 and 1113. His student, Joscelin (*Goslenus,* subsequently bishop of Soissons, who took over William's teaching at Notre-Dame between 1107 and 1111/1112, but was forced out by William after he offered the position to Abelard), maintained the same idea that two individuals were not different, as distinct from essentially the same, developing the notion that a universal was a collection of things.[32] The small philosophical discussion in letter *24* reflects Abelard's terminology during the period in which he wrote the *Dialectica* (ca. 1111–1117), but before he had developed the more radical position articulated in the Porphyry gloss of the *Logica Ingredientibus,* written around 1118.

The teacher in letter *24* is interested in what sort of thing love is, as if it existed already, rather than in the obligations as an ideal. He bases his definition of *amor* on Cicero's explanation of *caritas* in the *De amicitia* as that which binds only the closest of friends, the only passage of that treatise included by Abelard in the *Sic et Non* (138.21).[33] The teacher's comments about his holding the same thoughts as her allude to a very early definition of Cicero of friendship, articulated in the *De inventione,* that it is "a will towards anyone for the sake of good things for that person who is loved, reciprocated within an equal will," also included by Abelard alongside the text from Cicero's *De amicitia* in the *Sic et Non* (138.20), as if he expected students to appreciate the distinction between the two passages.[34] In the *Theologia 'Scholarium'* (written probably in the early 1130s), Abelard defines *caritas,* not like Augustine as a movement of the soul to enjoy God and one's neighbor for the sake of God, but as pure love (*amor honestus*), directed to its proper end, namely God, rather than for one's own benefit. He supports this definition by quoting from that of Cicero in the *De inventione* of friendship as good will to another, but missing out the words "with equal will," probably because this implied some sort of reciprocity.[35] Cicero had observed the problem of calculating equality of friendship, as implied by this earlier definition, in the *De amicitia,* written towards the end of his life.[36] By comparison with Abelard's mature definition of *caritas,* the teacher in letter *24* seems more interested in his understanding of love as already existing between them than as an ideal.

By contrast, his student thinks about love very differently, with a strong awareness of its ethical demands. Her response, letter *25,* is a carefully worked composition that develops an idea raised by Jerome at the end of his letter (3) to Rufinus: "Friendship that can cease, was never true" (*Amicitia quae desinere potest, vera numquam fuit*). Abelard quotes this final line of Jerome's letter in the *Sic et Non* (138.7), but here it is extended by a discussion of how true friendship seeks the will rather than things (an idea itself culled from Jerome's letter 68) that he mistakenly assumes is part of the letter to Rufinus.[37] In letter *25,* the young woman builds on the final line of Jerome's letter 3 by claiming that because of the smallness of her skill, she does not have the capacity to fulfill the duty of true love, although she hopes that her will (*velle*) to greet him would be sufficient. She quotes from

another letter of Jerome (45) to explain that in her case, regularity of seeing him does not introduce over-familiarity, and thus neglect. Her letter
then introduces a theological point, namely that although there is an obligation to show complete *caritas* to all, in practice what is general for all, becomes special to certain people. She emphasizes the importance of interior
intention. Sitting at the table of a prince is quite different from being
drawn to him by love.

This observation that although all people are to be loved equally, particular attention is given to those we see regularly is made by Augustine in
the *De doctrina Christiana* in a passage that Abelard quotes at the outset of
opening question of the *Sic et Non* (136.1) about whether or not *dilectio*
embraces all people.[38] This question, together with questions 137 (whether
only *caritas* is a virtue) and 138 (whether *caritas* once acquired can ever be
lost), effectively introduces the third section of the *Sic et Non*, about *caritas*
as the foundation of all ethical behavior. While Abelard borrowed many of
the patristic quotations in the *Sic et Non* from the *Decretum* of Ivo of
Chartres, the texts in these three questions are not culled from any known
anthology.[39] All of them deal with the nature of love, whether as *caritas,
dilectio,* or *amor.* Abelard started to compile the *Sic et Non* as a manual for
his teaching about faith, sacraments, and love from relatively early in the
1120s.[40] While the parallels between letters 24 to 25 and questions 136 to
38 of the *Sic et Non* could conceivably be explained in terms of a forger
drawing on this anthology for rival ideas about love, it does seem strange
that it is the woman who has the most patristic allusions. The other possibility is that Abelard and Heloise were already discussing contrasting ideas
about love found in Cicero, Jerome and Augustine during their early relationship, and that Abelard drew on these texts while compiling the *Sic et
Non.* Letters 24 to 25 constitute a reflection on at least four different texts
included within questions 136 to 138.

The young woman's distinction between love as either *generale* or *speciale* is not patristic. Her inspiration is more likely to be Baudri of Bourgueil (1045–1133), who makes the notion of "special love" (*amor specialis*)
a particular theme of verses that he addresses to particular friends, both
male and female.[41] Baudri was aware that his writing about love (*amor*)
to both young women and boys had evoked criticism, but he defends the
practice by observing that his verses pleased both sexes, as he explained
to Godfrey of Reims, "not a common, but a special friend."[42] Whereas
her teacher had defined love as a universal thing that the two of them
had already attained, her student, who had been pestering him to come
up with a definition of love, constructs her argument in more general

terms, drawing not just on Cicero, but on Jerome and Augustine, as well as a notion that had been developed in the late eleventh or early twelfth century by Baudri. The young woman invokes this notion of a "special love" in letters 21 (*Dilecto suo speciali*), 76 (*pre cunctis specialis dilectus*) and 79 (*Merito specialis dilectionis amplectendo amore*), although it is not one which her teacher ever uses. He prefers to identify her as his singular or only love, as in his letters 2 (*singulari gaudio et lassate mentis unico solamini*), 4 (*singularis eius*), 54 (*de fide singularis amici tui*), and 56 (*quicquid boni singulariter amantibus servatum est*). As I argued in 1999, without realizing that Baudri might have inspired the young woman's preference for the term *specialis*, this echoes precisely the contrast that Heloise makes in the greeting to her third letter to Abelard: "To him who is hers specially, she who is his singularly" (*Suo specialiter, sua singulariter*).[43] He had previously urged her to pray for him who is "specially yours," but without speaking of a more personal aspect to their relationship.[44] In each of her three greetings, Heloise had been trying to make Abelard speak to her as an individual, rather than in purely general religious terms. After she responded to the presentation of their relationship in the *Historia calamitatum*, she formulated a greeting that emphasized the intimacy that she wished to achieve: "To her Lord, or rather Father; to her wife, or rather brother; his maidservant, or rather daughter; his wife, or rather sister, to Abelard, Heloise." Abelard answered her with a relatively impersonal religious greeting, "To Heloise, his most beloved sister in Christ, Abelard, his brother in Him," prompting her to respond in a more pointedly personal fashion: "To her only one after Christ, his only one in Christ," to which Abelard responds with a more neutral, "To the Bride of Christ, his/her servant."[45] Her third greeting *Suo specialiter, sua singulariter* introducing her questions about religious life, served to remind him one more time of the personal relationship that she wished to restore. Heloise was drawing on discourse of intimate friendship, in part picked up from Baudri of Bourgueil, to explain that whatever word they used of each other, whether special or singular, she wished to return to the intimacy of her past relationship with Abelard.

While much of the exchange is a rhetorical exercise as both parties compete with each other to express their love, the young woman uses letter 49 to reflect for a second time on the reasons behind love, stimulated in particular by Cicero's comments in the *De amicitia* about true friendship as not based on desire for personal gain or pleasure, but extended to *dilectio* (a term unknown to Cicero). The phrase she comes up with is one of great simplicity. For some people, when wealth and pleasure fail, their *dilec-*

tio also fails, because "they love things not because of each other but each other because of things." She has been awakened by his letters, she reports, but is not yet fully satisfied.

Although he had referred to her from early in the exchange as *dilecte* and *dilectissime,* he had always referred to their love as *amor* rather than in her terms of a fusion of *dilectio* and *amor.* Only in letter *50,* after her particularly important discussion of *dilectio,* does he use this scriptural term, and then simply to refer admiringly to her discussion of friendship (in which he astutely observes that she is giving instruction to Cicero).[46] Apart from his ironic use of *dilectio* in letter *52* ("Since we do not keep the Lord's mandate until we have love for each other, we ought to obey Holy Scripture") and acknowledgement of her *dilectio* in letter *54,* he does not describe their love in this way until letters *85, 96, 101,* and *103.*[47] He never raises her sense of the difficulty of describing fully the nature of this love. In letter 53, she responds to his rather trite and hasty message about obeying Scripture by observing that if a "droplet of knowability" might trickle down to her "from the honeycomb of wisdom," she would try with all her effort to describe her love, but that she had found discourse (*sermo*) in all Latinity to describe the particular character of her love (*dilectio*) for him. The term *scibilitas* is first known to have been coined by Abelard in his *Dialectica,* and used again in his *Logica 'Ingredientibus'* to refer to the abstraction by which anything was knowable, but extremely rare prior to its use by Albert the Great in the mid-thirteenth century.[48] Both Ziolkowski and Dronke have suggested that if Albert devised the term on his own, then an intelligent young woman other than Heloise (equivalent to Abelard and Albert the Great in linguistic inventiveness) could also have invented the term to refer to an ideal of knowledge, of which she wanted only a small droplet in order to describe her love. Both this hypothesis, and the contrary view of von Moos, that a remarkably gifted literary artist has carefully created an exchange that employs rare terminology and texts known to Abelard and Heloise, stretch credulity in the extreme. In a poem (82), the woman remarks that even if she had the wealth of Caesar, these riches would be as nothing to her, an image close to that invoked by Heloise in her first response to the *Historia calamitatum.* After a series of crises, separations, and reconciliations in the later part of the exchange (most acute at letters *93–95* and *106–*107), letter 112—the only one addressed to him as a teacher—implies that she is wishing to change the character of the relationship. He should focus on what will be a great career ("I already see the mountaintops bowing down before you"), while she now has a joy that cannot be put into words. In letter 112a, in fact taken from another letter (according to a rare note from the copyist), she parodies the liturgical chant *Ubi caritas et amor, Deus ibi est* ("Where charity and love are, there God abides"), with the lament that where there is *amor* and *dilectio*, there always rages effort (*exercicium*). This may have been the original ending of the correspondence. It has been suggested that the final poem in the exchange (*113*), in which the man explains that he has been forced to act in the way he has by passion (*amor*), driven by her beauty, but that he fears the murmuring of the crowd, and therefore cannot see her as often as he would wish, is an earlier poem, placed here as a coda to the exchange.[49] Yet the poem is not so much a declaration of love as an explanation of why he has fallen for her: "Beauty, noble birth, character . . . / All make you outstanding in our city. / So is it then surprising if I am lured by their brilliance/ If I succumb to you, conquered by your love." Whether this poem was written earlier or whether it was his subsequent explanation of why he loved her as much as he did, it articulates a sense of *amor* as inspired by external attraction very different from her sense of *amor* as an ethical ideal that disregards external appearance and behavior.

Letter Writing and the Cultivation of Intimacy

The *Epistolae duorum amantium* constitute a major monument in the corpus of epistolary exchanges in medieval Latin literature, so unusual that it is not easy to situate them within a broader practice. Von Moos has rightly drawn attention to the rich development of the *ars dictaminis* in the late twelfth and thirteenth centuries, and there is still much to learn from this literature. It is important to distinguish, however, between the art of writing letters as an epistolary skill, absorbed through conscious imitation of other letters, and the codification of this art by theorists of the *ars dictaminis*, from the time of Alberic of Montecassino and Adalbertus Samaritanus in the late eleventh and early twelfth century.[50] These early theorists did not include guidance in writing love letters, as did those from the second half of the twelfth century, clearly responding to a demand from readers of such manuals.[51] One of the earliest witnesses to usage of an epistolary manual is a letter from a nun of Lippoldsberg in the mid-twelfth century, requesting from her brother, Sindold, a copy of the *ars dictaminis* of Adalbertus Samaritanus.[52] While this nun's letters, like those of her brother, were preserved for their stylistic interest and are replete with literary convention, they do not all follow the strict Ciceronian rules laid down by Adalbertus about the necessary sections of the ideal letter. The fact that private letters were preserved as public documents does not mean that they were not initially intended to be private.

The contrast between the two prose styles within the *EDA* is of great interest. From the second half of the twelfth century, theorists imbued with Ciceronian ideals were familiar with elaborate greetings, but they preferred to follow the warnings of Cicero against excessive use of rhyme, such as became widely popular in the tenth and eleventh centuries (as for example in the writings of Hroswitha of Gandersheim, who combines dramatic motifs from Terence with a very non-classical style of rhyming prose). The woman's style of rhyming prose would continue to be used in a later period "to promote piety and joy," according to John of Garland, and might still be employed in homiletic literature or even in some letters copied with a treatise, but theoreticians did not consider it an educated style.[53] If the love letters are an extended device to teach the art of composition, the author has succeeded brilliantly in evoking the contrast between two prose styles practiced in the early twelfth century. In her later letters (including one to Peter the Venerable, the authenticity of which has never been challenged), Heloise employs prose rhyme to a greater degree than Abelard, although more in passages of special intensity than as a consistent pattern. The prose style of the woman's letters in the *EDA* is marked by the same fusion of traditional prose rhyme and classical imagery, also found in the letters of Hugh Metel, who celebrated Heloise's reputation as a writer and her capacity "to join words in a new way."[54]

The *Epistolae duorum amantium* are noteworthy for the way they do not follow specific rules about what each letter should contain. Rather they demonstrate a conscious desire to experiment with received epistolary tradition. As Carol Lanham has shown in her study of one part of the salutation, the art of letter writing developed significantly in the eleventh century. Following her comments about the importance of the letters of St. Anselm (1033–1109), attention should be given to the possibility that they may have been known to the young Heloise.[55]

The letters of St. Anselm are significant because of the way he uses the greeting to identify a personal relationship with his close friends. Regularly, when writing to friends, he employs the phrase "To my lord and friend" (*Domino et fratri*, a formula not found in any other writer). Anselm once criticized his own teacher, Lanfranc, for not being sufficiently personal in his salutation.[56] Heloise wished Abelard would create an equality and intimacy between themselves in a friendly exchange, such as Anselm wished to create with Lanfranc. Thus in letter 68, Anselm writes to a fellow monk: "To his lord, his brother, his dearest friend, lord Gundulf, brother Anselm sends what is his own for him."[57] There is a similar crescendo in greeting in his letter 85: "To his lord, loving freely, deservedly beloved, not as one unknown, but as a familiar friend, Walter, brother Anselm [offers] what is his own."[58] Anselm regularly replaces the conventional *salutem* with "what is his own" (*quod suus*) in letters to close friends. St. Bernard does so much less frequently, only after he observes its use in a letter he had received, as if it were unusual.[59] Not only may St. Anselm's desire to emphasize intimacy through a greeting have influenced Heloise in her first response to the *Historia calamitatum*, but it echoes a frequent practice early in the *EDA*, of one party offering himself or herself to the other.[60] It may also help unlock the rather enigmatic greeting of letter 21, in which she sends to him, "her special beloved, from the experience of the thing itself, the being that she is [or: the being that is]."[61] Given that both the man and the woman offer themselves to the other, *esse quod est*, she could be trying to offer the being that she is (although one could read the phrase simply as the being that exists).

The woman's interest in linking notions of *caritas, amor,* and *dilectio* in her letters also echoes a common theme of St. Anselm, who writes in a rhyming Latin prose impossible to emulate fully in English:

> Your letter, so full of the wholesome advice by which your sweet love [*dilectio*] and beloved prudence deigned to make yourself known to my poverty, is aglow with such ardor of charity [*caritatis*], scented with such fragrance of kindness, and merry with such sweetness of mind that my eyes will not rest until my eyes have seen his face, my ears have heard his voice and my soul has enjoyed the presence of him who, without knowing me, obscure as I am, freely took me on with such love [*amore*].[62]

In his prayers and meditations, Anselm similarly delights in combining notions of *amor, dilectio* and *caritas*.[63] Augustine had himself drawn these links, but had also observed that *amor* was not necessarily virtuous, and was better called *dilectio* and *caritas*.[64] While not the first writer to combine *amor* and *dilectio*, Anselm was certainly influential in re-asserting a positive sense of *amor* within a religious context in the late eleventh century in letters not just to monks, but also to certain aristocratic and religious women.[65]

There were other writers, however, who similarly explored the language of intimacy within a spiritual context. In around 1080, Goscelin of St-Bertin (ca. 1040–1114) wrote a *Liber confortatorius* addressed to Eve, soon after she had left the aristocratic abbey of Wilton in England, and had settled in Angers, at Saint-Eutrope, a dependency of Le Ronceray.[66]

Goscelin had been a chaplain at Wilton, then aged around forty, while Eve was then in her early twenties. A flurry of recent interest in this work (including two independent translations into English) has highlighted the complexity of his writing, as well as signalling potential parallels with the situation of Abelard and Heloise, some thirty-five years later.[67] The *Liber confortatorius* seems to have been the climax of an exchange of letters mentioned by Goscelin: "Frequent sheets and pages from me brought Christ to you, nor did I lack chaste letters from you."[68] He describes the *Liber confortatorius* as "a private document of two people, sealed with Christ as mediator, touching first on the duty owed by virginal simplicity and pure love."[69] Goscelin's terminology echoes that of the young woman in letter 3, "May the rule of heaven be a mediator between us, and be a companion to our faith." Unlike St. Anselm, however, Goscelin only speaks of *dilectio* and *caritas*, never *amor*, to describe his affection for Eve, possibly because there seems to have been some hint of scandal in their previous relationship, from which he was eager to distance himself. Rejecting false rumors that had arisen about their relationship, Goscelin argues that God has separated them, so that they could long for each other more ardently: "The more distance he has put between us physically, the more inseparably at some time he will join together again one soul of two people."[70] He alludes vaguely to some indiscretion that he hopes writing can heal: "And so, because your soul-friend was not able and did not deserve to visit you in corporeal presence, he seeks you now with anxious letters and long complaints. The provident mercy of God has made this consolation for us, that although far distant in place, we can be present to one another in our faith and our writings."[71]

Given that Eve lived as a recluse for some forty years in Angers between around 1080 and her death in around 1120, she may have kept a copy of the letters and the treatise that Goscelin wrote to her. Yet she is not known to have continued her relationship to Goscelin. She became a recluse at Angers, first at Saint-Eutrope and then at Saint-Laurent, where she lived with another hermit, Hervé, in a relationship defended as spiritual *dilectio* by Hilary of Orléans (a companion of Abelard at the Paraclete) in an epitaph he wrote for her around 1120.[72] The poetic flowering in the Loire valley, associated in particular with Marbod and Baudri of Bourgueil, was clearly facilitated by an environment in which educated women could enter into literary relationships with male clerical and monastic friends, with only occasional voices of suspicion being raised. Fulbert's decision to allow Heloise to study under Abelard reflected a similar acceptance that chaste relationships were possible between educated women and men.

Heloise's connections to the dynamic literary and religious life of the Loire valley in the late eleventh and early twelfth century may well be even closer than I realized in 1999.[73] In 2001, Werner Robl published a study in which he observed that Hersende, mother of Heloise (who died December 1 according to the obituary of the Paraclete), had the same name and date of decease as Hersende, the first prioress of Fontevrault, recorded in its obituary as having died on November 30 (December 1 according to the obituary of Saint-Jean-en-Vallée, Chartres, November 29 according to that of Saint-Père-en-Vallée, Chartres).[74] Hersende's father was Hubert III of Champagne, who had a grandmother called Heloise, and was descended on his father's side from the Montmorency family, traditional lay guardians of Argenteuil (and the family of Heloise of the Paraclete, according to d'Amboise in the early seventeenth century).[75] This explanation of Heloise's family background seems easier to accept than the suggestion offered by Lobrichon, that her father was related to the Garlande family.[76]

Nothing is known for certain about Hersende after the death of her husband William of Montsoreau in 1087 until 1100, when she changed from being a lay disciple (*conversa*) of Robert of Arbrissel to a fully enclosed nun at Fontevrault, a community built on land given by her stepson, Walter of Montsoreau. Robert of Arbrissel started to preach in Angers around 1095, during the time of the highly corrupt bishop, Geoffrey of Mayenne (1094/95–1101). Unusually, Marbod remained as archdeacon at Angers, serving bishop Geoffrey, even though he had been appointed bishop of Rennes in 1095. Robl suggests that Heloise was born in around 1095, but was given up by Hersende to the abbey of Argenteuil in around 1100, when she became a fully enclosed nun at Fontevrault. Through her Montmorency family connection, she would have had direct access to Argenteuil. Fulbert, who acquired a canonry at Notre-Dame between 1099 and 1102, may have been charged with watching over her. The suggestion of Hersende sending her child to Argenteuil is quite plausible. Marbod complained (in around 1098) about Robert's scandalous intimacy with female followers, alluding to a past sexual transgression, as well as to his disciples being accompanied by wailing of children, who could not have been accommodated within a cloistered abbey.[77] Robl also suggested, more boldly, that Robert was himself the illegitimate father of Heloise. Yet it could also be that Heloise was born from an otherwise unrecorded marriage, to a father who did not come back from the first Crusade. Whatever the case, Hersende was clearly a significant figure who played a key role in promoting the cause of religious reform and in building up

Fontevrault. She may well have known Eve, who had exchanged writings with Goscelin of St-Bertin, and became celebrated for her spiritual friendship with Hervé, a monk of Vendôme. Hersende died around 1113, to be succeeded by Petronilla de Chemillé, whom Robert appointed the community's first abbess in 1115, shortly before his own death (February 16, 1116).

Baudri of Bourgueil was commissioned by Petronilla to write the first Life of Robert of Arbrissel sometime between 1116 and 1119. A phrase that Abelard uses of himself in the *Historia calamitatum,* that he went from Brittany to Paris, "wandering through the provinces" may have been directly lifted from Baudri's narrative.[78] In 1120 Abelard defended Robert as a great preacher against accusations made by Roscelin of Compiègne (who viewed Robert as establishing a precedent for Abelard's own behavior with Heloise).[79] Baudri certainly knew William of Montsoreau, for whom he writes an epitaph, and speaks with great reverence for Hersende.[80] We know that Robert had wished to be buried alongside Hersende in a simple cemetery, signaling a very close relationship between the two.[81] As it happened, however, Robert was buried in a place of honor in the newly built church, without the simplicity which he wished to retain.

Baudri, a great admirer of Robert, maintained a wide network of friends through sending epitaphs and poems to a host of correspondents, male and female, throughout the Loire valley and beyond. Although a highly literate Benedictine monk rather than a popular preacher, he cultivated a sense of personal relationship through his poems in the same way as Robert developed such connections with his closest disciples (provoking not a little controversy). In particular, Baudri cultivated aristocratic female friends at Le Ronceray, an abbey at Angers not unlike Argenteuil, north of Paris. Robert was particularly famous for preaching against hypocrisy in religious life, as is evident from his sermon to Ermengard, wife of the Duke of Brittany. Although we do not know of any letters that he wrote, he cultivated a sense of intimacy with his female disciples in a way which was quite different from that of conventional monasticism. In this respect, Heloise's distaste for hypocrisy in religious life may indirectly owe much to the preaching of Robert of Arbrissel as well as to the writings, both religious and poetic, of Baudri of Bourgueil.

The permission Fulbert gave Abelard to tutor Heloise, traditionally perceived as a sign of naivety, makes much more sense in terms of a climate of unusual intimacy between educated men and women in religious life that developed in the Loire valley and northern France between around

1080 and 1115. The complex exchange of letters and poems that we know as the *Epistolae duorum amantium,* shared between a teacher and his brilliant student of philosophy makes perfect sense as a product of an intellectual climate that sought to transform the writing of letters and verse into a more intimate form. To argue that they were written by a couple similar to, but different from Abelard and Heloise, is to postulate a remarkable couple for whom there is otherwise no documented evidence. The easiest way of explaining the many parallels between these letters and the many different writings of Abelard and Heloise, including the *Dialectica* and the *Sic et Non,* is to posit that they are an incomplete copy of the letters that both Abelard and Heloise say they exchanged in their early relationship. There is simply no evidence for the existence of another couple like them. If they are a fiction modeled on Abelard and Heloise, why do they recapture so many subtle connections with their writings, but not provide the most well-known details of their story? There are differences in vocabulary between the love letters and the *Dialectica* because these are texts written for different circles, even if they were produced in the same decade. To argue from minor lexical differences between these love letters and the letters of spiritual guidance exchanged by Abelard and Heloise in the 1130s, that these must be two distinct couples is to fail to recognize that different times and contexts generate different ways of communicating, with different texts providing a stimulus for conversation.

In the late-eleventh and early-twelfth centuries, the exchanging of literary texts between educated men and women was perfectly feasible within the constraints of religious life, in which individuals were in theory committed to ideals of chastity. Within the looser constraints of the secular clergy, there were not as many safeguards. Traditional standards of behavior could not be monitored in the same way as in a monastery. This freedom made it possible for the relationship of Abelard and Heloise to evolve in the way it did, and thus for Fulbert to turn against Abelard and wreak his revenge. The kind of exchange between a teacher and a student that we see in the *Epistolae duorum amantium* (or for that matter, at an intellectually less sophisticated level within the Regensburg verses, from around 1106), was simply not possible after Pope Calixtus II imposed clerical discipline throughout the Church, at the Council of Reims in 1119, and more widely after the I Lateran Council in 1123.[82] It became harder for educated women to maintain regular and sophisticated discourse with their male friends. The story of Abelard's increasing distance from Heloise during the 1120s and renewed devotion to study, reflected a more austere climate, in which such relationships were viewed with suspicion.

The Monastic Correspondence of Abelard and Heloise

The cliché that Abelard's letters articulate an ideal of spiritual love, while those of Heloise in response to the *Historia calamitatum* profess worldly love, has severely impaired our understanding of these letters. It is now becoming much clearer that Heloise has her own ideal of love, as well as a horror of hypocrisy in religion. Growing awareness of issues relating to gender and identity influenced a new wave of scholarship in the 1980s and 1990s, emphasizing the distinctness of the voice of Heloise as well as of her achievement as abbess of the Paraclete.[83] Guy Lobrichon's biography of Heloise has similarly focused on her desire to assert herself, against the preference of Abelard, as an abbess in her own right.[84] There has also been no shortage of interest in the *Historia calamitatum,* as evident from a volume edited by Dag Hasse, that brings together a range of interpretative models that can be applied to this text, all of which are acutely aware of the rhetorical structure both of Abelard's narrative account as well as of the correspondence as a whole.[85] Yet to a public more familiar with psychology than with scholastic theology or monastic spirituality, Heloise is still commonly presented as the heroine of a tragic love affair, in which erotic passion had to be subordinated to an otherworldly religion, while Abelard is often viewed as the intellectual who lives in the mind rather than the body.[86]

Warning against a naïve, "psychological-biographical" reading of the monastic letters, Peter von Moos has emphasized what he sees as the unitary character of the famous correspondence.[87] In a study published in 2002, he withdrew his earlier hypothesis that it was the work of a single author, and argued instead that Heloise had co-operated with Abelard in the construction of an exchange in which Abelard develops the theme that out of suffering and human sinfulness, emerges what is good.[88] His study is highly critical of scholarship that focuses on Heloise as a significant figure in her own right, fearing "the eternal return of hermeneutic naivety." While there is no doubt that the correspondence as a whole serves to provide a conception of the monastic life for women, as Morgan Powell has persuasively shown, this perspective need not be at odds with the observation that there is a subtle contrast between the ethical positions of Abelard and Heloise, in relation to their past relationship.[89] Not only is it impossible to imagine Abelard constructing the letters of Heloise, but no single theological message can be extracted from this correspondence, which effectively offers two distinct points of view about the nature of love (*amor*) and religious life more generally. While there might have been light general editing, when transcribing these letters into a single manuscript, they still represent two distinct voices.[90]

The Contribution of the *Epistolae duorum amantium*

Accepting the *Epistolae duorum amantium* as imperfectly preserved copies of letters by Abelard and Heloise allows us to grasp the complexity of a relationship that Abelard deliberately presents in the *Historia calamitatum* as an example of worldly passion, quite different from the consoling love of God, as mediated through the Paraclete, the Holy Spirit. It also allows us to understand that Heloise really was an unusually gifted student, probably of around twenty in 1115.[91] At the time Abelard was a specialist in dialectic. Tutoring Heloise enabled him to broaden his skills in the study of literature and rhetorical expression. Yet while he seems to have maintained the liaison as a diversion from his intellectual life, Heloise viewed the relationship with great seriousness, as a means for her to develop her own thinking and writing about her favorite theme, that of love.

The fact that the young Heloise drew not just on poetic texts, but on Cicero's *De amicitia* and the letters of Jerome, some of which are included by Abelard in questions 136–38 of the *Sic et Non*, the opening to its section on *caritas* as the foundation of ethical behavior is also significant. Although Abelard devoted himself to issues of dialectic and theology in the years immediately following his castration, he was still interested in collecting patristic texts about ethical questions, and above all the nature of love. A favorite text for Abelard was the saying of Augustine, "Love and do what you will" (*Dilige, et quod vis fac*), which he incorporated into the prologue of the *Sic et Non*, itself containing extended reflection on the importance of love as the foundation for resolving any textual conflict.[92] Abelard was one of the first known authors to make use of the authentic Augustinian version of this text, which would become widely known in the course of the twelfth century. He also quoted a more well known paraphrase of this text, slightly modified from what Augustine wrote, but which he knew from Ivo's quotation of an unknown treatise, *De disciplina Christiana* that he assigned to Augustine: "Have charity, and do whatever you will" (*Habe caritatem et fac quidquid uis*).[93] The earliest known writer to use the authentic Augustinian version was Robert of Arbrissel, in his sermon to Ermengard, in which he attacks many types of hypocrisy in religious life.[94] This may well have been one of those texts that Abelard and Heloise discussed in their early relationship, and that assumed an important role when Abelard started to compile the *Sic et Non*, perhaps sometime around 1120.

The *Historia calamitatum* and the subsequent response of Heloise to Abelard's account of their past are in many ways more sophisticated and carefully structured documents than the *Epistolae duorum amantium*. It is absurd to expect otherwise. The vocabulary of each exchange is inevitably influenced by its particular social and literary context. Nonetheless both Abelard and Heloise were aware that they had exchanged messages of love in the past. Heloise wanted Abelard to return to the kind of intimacy they had once enjoyed within the framework of the religious life. There was much precedent for such letter writing, as the letters of St. Anselm to many friends, both male and female, demonstrated. Abelard was relatively slow to respond in the way she wanted, and insisted on reminding her of the sexually corrupt character of their past relationship. Heloise insisted on recalling the purity of her devotion to him. The issue of the nature of love and whether suffering and evil in this life must be endured for the sake of a heavenly reward is a central feature of their discussion, which prompts Heloise to claim that she does not seek a martyr's crown.[95] Abelard had adopted a traditional position that one must endure hardship for the sake of this reward. Heloise argues that love should never strive for any reward other than one's beloved. In the *Collationes* Abelard sets up a not dissimilar debate between the philosopher, committed to *ethica,* or the path to the supreme good, and the Christian, whose religion teaches him about *divinitas,* or the supreme good itself. He explores the same concept of what it means to speak of an eternal reward as Heloise rejects for herself in her discussion with Abelard.[96] In many ways the arguments that Abelard assigns to the philosopher as concerned with the ethical life and religious observances as helpful only in so far as they lead to both the love of God and the love of neighbor, echo concerns of Heloise.

Abelard's response was to urge her to devotion to Jesus, whose redeeming work he reflected on at length in his Commentary on St. Paul's Epistle to the Romans. This in turn laid a basis for the ideas developed in his *Ethica (Scito teipsum),* in which he presents *caritas* as the foundation of all Christian virtue. The passage of Cicero's *De amicitia* about *caritas* as existing between two close friends, paraphrased in letter *24,* and included alongside many Augustinian texts about *caritas* within the *Sic et Non* (138: 21) provided him with a definition very different from the standard Christian understanding of *caritas* as a transcendent ideal, fully embodied only within the Trinity. While Abelard would radically develop his understanding of *caritas* from the time Heloise originally asked him to define *amor,* he still remained fascinated by the contribution that Cicero could make to a definition of friendship. Controversially, he taught that one need not have lost *caritas* from one's heart, when one fell into fornication or murder, as happened to David, sinning with Bathsheeba.[97] Abelard drew on Augustine to support his claim that *caritas* was the greatest of the virtues, and their foundation. While Abelard seems to have expanded his ethical focus only after resuming dialogue with Heloise during the 1130s, he had already been exposed to some of these ideas during his early conversations with her in 1115/1117.

The Oldest Manuscripts of the
Letters of Abelard and Heloise

A significant recent discovery about the fullest manuscript (Troyes Bibl. Mun. 802) of the letters of Abelard and Heloise, beginning with the *Historia calamitatum* and concluding with Abelard's Rule for the Paraclete followed by monastic observances (*Institutiones nostrae*) compiled between 1140 and 1147, is that it was copied not in the late-thirteenth century, as had long been assumed, but before 1250, even in the 1230s.[98] The redating of the Troyes manuscript, itself bought by Robert de Bardi from the cathedral chapter of Notre-Dame in 1349, makes it much more comprehensible that Jean de Meun should have come across the letters by the 1260s, when he composed his continuation to *The Romance of the Rose*. Jean de Meun subsequently translated the entire correspondence, apart from the Rule, from a lost exemplar of the correspondence, presumably that from which the Troyes copy was made, as well as that which came into Petrarch's possession in the 1330s.[99] Whether or not William of Auvergne was responsible for the copying of the manuscript, as Dalarun suggests, there is little doubt that the original copy of the *Historia calamitatum* and subsequent exchange with Heloise was originally preserved at the Paraclete, but was brought to the Paris region by the 1230s. The Troyes copy must have been commissioned sometime after 1231, as various other texts about the religious life, including certain canons of the Council of Rouen (1231), were then added to the *Institutiones nostrae*.[100]

Dalarun's suggestion that the correspondence itself is an artificial creation, intended to lead into Abelard's Rule and *Institutiones nostre*, in which Abelard wrote the *Historia calamitatum* in order to justify the exchange that follows seems unlikely, given that Heloise herself responds to that narrative. It is easier to view the correspondence as a cumulative compilation of two distinct voices, with only the lightest editing. Whether Abelard's Rule was itself part of the original manuscript containing the letters is not certain. An isolated reference to a manuscript in private possession in the early-fifteenth century records an otherwise unknown manuscript, in which an unbound copy of the Rule (separated from its introductory letter) was separate from the previous letters.[101] Given that a number of other manuscripts conclude with the introduction to the Rule, it is quite possible that the copyist of the Troyes manuscript consciously copied the Rule immediately after the introductory letter, in the way that would be reproduced by Duchesne in his 1616 edition. The Troyes manuscript seems to have been given to the Paraclete by the late fifteenth century, as part of a process of reconstruction of the abbey and a new interest in its founders, but was given away in the early-seventeenth century, as a consequence of strict introduction of Tridentine reforms at the abbey.

One important feature of the *Institutiones nostrae* preserved in the Troyes manuscript, is that they show that Heloise never enforced Abelard's Rule at the Paraclete. As Waddell demonstrated, these observances were influenced by the earliest Cistercian practices, although with a significant reference. While the Cistercians based their way of life on strict observance of the Rule of Benedict, the *Institutiones,* drawn up on the occasion of the first daughter house of the Paraclete (probably that of Mary Magdalene, Trainel, in around 1140), based their way of life on imitation of the example of Christ and the early apostles.[102] The liturgical manuscripts of the Paraclete, from the early thirteenth and late fifteenth century respectively, confirm the picture given by the *Institutiones* that this was an abbey with a most unusual character. While the Paraclete liturgy used the early version of the Cistercian hymnal, supplanted in Cistercian houses by 1147, it also incorporated a good many (though not all) of the cycle of hymns that Abelard had composed for the Paraclete. Building on a suggestion that I had made in 1999, David Wulstan has proposed that Heloise composed, not just the sequence, *Epithalamica* (certainly sung at the Paraclete), but various Easter plays, from which *Epithalamica* seems to have been taken.[103] Although these manuscripts do not go back to the twelfth century, it seems very likely that Heloise carefully combined elements from Abelard with elements of Cistercian tradition to create an original liturgical synthesis, that made the Paraclete an abbey like no other.

These Cistercian connections may help explain why the *Epistolae duorum amantium* should have been preserved at Clairvaux. That she once asked Bernard of Clairvaux to support her interests while visiting Rome in 1148 is a sign that she was not as estranged from Bernard as Abelard had been at the height of the controversy surrounding his writing, at the Council of Sens in May 1141. The nuns of the Paraclete regularly prayed for the monks of the entire Cistercian Order.[104] As Sylvain Piron has observed, Jacques de

Bar, a monk of Clairvaux and confessor to the nuns at the Paraclete, bequeathed two liturgical manuscripts to Clairvaux in 1440.[105] Whether he or another monk may have deposited at Clairvaux a manuscript containing the letters of two lovers, is impossible to say. There were good relations between the two abbeys. It was not inappropriate that Johannes de Vepria, librarian at an abbey, whose founder was so well-known for talking about the ideal of growing in love for God and neighbor, should copy a set of letters that talk with such eloquence about love. Johannes de Vepria was reported to have been generous with manuscripts in his possession, and could have given the original copy of the letters to another scholar, after transcribing them.[106] Perhaps a future discovery within another scholar's notebook might shed more light.

II

From the Letters of Two Lovers

Edited by Ewald Könsgen

Translated by Neville Chiavaroli and Constant J. Mews

THE EDITION

The text of the love letters reproduced here is that established by Ewald
Könsgen in his edition, *Epistolae duorum amantium. Briefe Abaelards und
Heloises?* (Leiden: E. J. Brill, 1974). No effort is made to reproduce the sophisticated analysis of the manuscript and its copyist, Johannes de Vepria,
provided by Könsgen in his introduction. The text of the love letters is
based on a single manuscript (Troyes, Bibliothèque municipale 1452, ff.
159r–167v), copied at Clairvaux probably sometime around 1471, the year
cited in the colophon of another item in the manuscript. As Könsgen de-
termined, the text copied and corrected by Johannes de Vepria is of remarkable quality. In most cases, the scribe correctly distinguishes the
woman's letters from those of the man by adding to the margin of his manuscript M[ulier] or V[ir]. Könsgen's numbering of individual letters is
maintained, with the slight modification that the man's letters are always
cited in italics (a practice Könsgen employs in the invaluable lexical concordance to the letters included at the end of his edition). Johannes de
Vepria does not always identify letters as V and M (MAN and WOMAN).
When there is a series of letters by the man, for example, he often draws
lines from a single letter V to the beginning of each of the subsequent letters. Following Könsgen's method, single angle brackets around V and M
indicate that only a paragraph mark identifies the beginning of a new letter. Double angle brackets indicate that no separation between one letter
and another is given in the manuscript.

Könsgen supplies on pp. 64–67 of his edition detailed discussion of certain textual anomalies in the transcription, which may be the result of
scribal error. It is impossible to be sure whether Johannes de Vepria is at
fault, or whether the text he was copying was less than perfect in spelling,
syntax, and prosody. Könsgen's text has been reproduced with three minor
changes (in letters 23, 49, and 87) for which we assume responsibility.

In letter 23, the unknown word *conorare* can be interpreted in various
ways. One of the possibilities that Könsgen raises (p. 64) is followed here,

that it is a mistake for *honorare*. There is also a problematic phrase in letter 49, given in the manuscript as *invenit erga te mee dilectionis fervens affectio*. Könsgen (p. 66) persuasively suggests adding *inpulit* at the end of the subordinate clause before *invenit*. He also corrects *erga* (toward) to *ergo* (therefore) reading the last part of this sentence as "the ardent feeling of my love has *therefore found you*, so that . . . ." Here *erga te* (cf. M 84) is preserved, reading the Latin as "the ardent feeling of my love for you finds that. . . ."

In letter 112, perhaps the most important and enigmatic in the entire exchange, the manuscript reads *summa effero mentis exultacione* (I bear great things in exultation of mind). Könsgen corrects *effero* to *efferor*, reading *summa* not as neuter plural, but as in agreement with *exultacione:* "I am carried away by great exultation of mind." While the manuscript could be correct here, Könsgen's suggestion is preferred. A brief explanation of these occasional differences in interpretation of the text is included in footnotes to the text of individual letters.

The general impression that emerges from a close reading of the transcription made by Johannes de Vepria is that he must have been copying a manuscript relatively free from scribal error. The corrections that Johannes de Vepria makes suggest that he paid close attention to elucidating obscurities in the text before him. In letter 87 Johannes de Vepria originally transcribed line 17 as *in lumine me fore credo* (I believe myself to be in light). He subsequently added to the margin of his text, *vel nil tunc michi defore* (or nothing to be lacking to me). At the foot of f. 165va he subsequently rewrote the entire line: *His ego quando fruor, nil tunc michi defore credo* (When I enjoy these things, I believe that I lack nothing). The phrases *nil tunc* and *in lumine* could be confused if they had been abbreviated. Although Könsgen follows the original *in lumine* version within his edition, the alternative reading has been adopted here, as the next line seems to offer a deliberate contrast, *His ego cum careo, defore cuncta puto* (When I am denied them, I think that I lack everything).

As is his custom when copying other manuscripts in the library of Clairvaux, Johannes de Vepria takes care to indicate when he is omitting a passage with the sign // (sometimes a single /). Könsgen's identification of scribal ellipses (indicated here as ....., as distinct from . . . to indicate my own abbreviation of a passage) is generally accurate; in only a few cases has it been felt that there is insufficient marking in the manuscript to justify identifying a scribal ellipse (as in *50, 56, 59,* 60, 79, 98). The same mark occurs immediately after the title with which Johannes de Vepria introduced his anthology: "*Ex epistolis duorum amantium.*//" While Könsgen does not consider these two parallel lines to be palaeographically significant, they may indicate another scribal ellipse, indicating that Johannes de Vepria was omitting certain text before the first greeting that he copies.

Johannes de Vepria generally indicates *versus* when he is transcribing metrical poetry. In certain poems of the woman (notably 69 and 82), Könsgen has judged irregularity in the prosody to be evidence that the scribe has omitted a line. The Latin text does make sense, however, as it stands in the manuscript. It is possible that the person who composed the poem was inexperienced in prosody. Johannes de Vepria is normally very careful about indicating ellipses in his transcription. In the final poem (*113*), he twice indicates that he is leaving out certain lines. As in both cases the text surrounding the scribal ellipse has sexual allusions, it is possible that Johannes de Vepria found certain lines too explicit to include.

One last area for which we take responsibility is punctuation. We have not followed Könsgen's practice of placing a comma before every subordinate clause, as is standard in German prose. In the Troyes manuscript, phrases like *ille qui* (he who is) and *illa quae* (she who is) are never interrupted by punctuation, while larger phrases are separated by a *punctus* (presented here as a comma, when it is not followed by a new sentence). Terms of endearment like *dulcissima* (sweetest) are similarly never separated from the surrounding text. On the other hand, a *punctus* is used before *et* (and) and *nec* (neither) for rhetorical effect, to indicate a pause in the way a sentence should be read. The punctuation of the manuscript is particularly important in showing how Johannes de Vepria understands a greeting, which never contains a main verb, but normally comprises three parts: "To X [dative], Y [nominative]: *salutem* (or a variant)." Because Könsgen does not always supply punctuation between the sender and the greeting being sent, it is not always immediately clear just where the break occurs. In the manuscript, there is almost always a *punctus* before the salutation proper (either a noun in the accusative or an infinitive verb). This *punctus* before a salutation is here presented as a colon. One example of punctuation affecting the sense of a greeting occurs in letter 21, punctuated in the manuscript as: "Dilecto suo speciali, et ex ipsius experimento rei, esse quod est." Many readings are possible of this rather obscure greeting, but here we propose: "To her beloved, special from experience of the reality itself, the being which she is." Könsgen omits the comma after *rei*, but adds a comma after *esse*, making it unclear whether or not *esse* belongs to the third part of the sentence. Given that elsewhere she offers him herself (as in 5), it seems likely that she is sending the being (*esse*) which she is, as suggested by the scribe's punctuation. In letter 94, however, a *punctus* occurs before *luna plena innexibilis amoris delicia*. If *luna plena* belonged to the third part of the greeting, the woman might be offering "the delights of love in a full moon." In this case, however, *luna plena,* is interpreted here as a nominative image (a full moon) that the woman uses of herself, following his image of her in letter *91.* In the sentence which follows, she rebukes his fickleness. As with so many other phrases in this exchange, the final interpretation of this greeting must be left open to debate.

Johannes de Vepria seems to transmit two layers of punctuation within his text, unfortunately impossible to distinguish with normal typography. Besides using the punctus to mark the most important clauses in the text, Johannes de Vepria inserts a light stroke to indicate sense units within a phrase or sentence. While it is impossible to be sure whether they correspond to punctuation marks in the manuscript that he was copying, they have been used here as a guide to the sense of the text. In the case of the longer poems that occur in the second half of the manuscript, the scribe uses punctuation sparingly at the end of lines, a practice that is retained here. In the manuscript, there are no paragraph marks within individual letters, and no break is indicated between the greeting and the substance of the letter.

No critical edition can avoid offering an interpretation of the text being transmitted. In the case of the Troyes manuscript, we are dealing with the effort of Johannes de Vepria to come to terms with a text that has been lost to us. Könsgen's painstaking editorial work on the text of these letters must provide the point of departure for any study of their significance. No attempt has been made to reproduce all the details about the scribal erasures and corrections in the manuscript that Könsgen observes in his critical apparatus. The Latin text is offered here as an encouragement to readers to come to terms themselves with a remarkable collection of letters and to engage in ongoing debate about what they mean.

The Translation

This translation is intended to make more broadly available to students of medieval culture, perhaps the most important example of amatory letter writing in the twelfth century. Literary Latin of the kind employed in these letters presents its own challenges to any translator. As the meaning of individual letters is often far from clear, a great deal is left up to the imagination. The reader must often work hard to know what is being discussed. In general we have tried to remain as faithful to the Latin as the English language can tolerate, believing that the way an idea or sentiment is phrased can be as instructive as its content. At times this has meant that we have tried to maintain the original imagery even when the phrase may seem unnatural in English. If the result is one that bears unmistakable traces of having been translated, we are not convinced that this is undesirable; in another context, a different approach may have been warranted. At the same time, we have tried to avoid non-English constructions and outdated words that have for too long rendered medieval texts excessively foreign, if not unintelligible, to modern students forced to rely on translations.

This translation has not endeavored to imitate the prose rhyme used by the woman, nor the poetic metre of the metrical verses. We have also not sought to "improve" the style simply for the sake of euphony in English. When certain words or their derivatives are repeated in the Latin, we have tried to retain this repetition in English, believing that an author's choice of words, particularly in the face of viable synonyms, ought to be respected. We do not see the tendency to avoid such repetition in English as sufficient reason to deviate from the style of the original (see, for example, 37, 100, and 112). Conversely, when the Latin uses synonyms rather than repetition, we have attempted to convey this feature of style. We are thus walking a fine line between fidelity to the original and naturalness of expression. We readily concede that we have not always achieved this to our complete satisfaction. But therein lies both the great joy and frustration of translating.

We have preserved the fundamental structure of the formula of greeting of any letter addressed to someone perceived to be one's superior. In this sentence, the verb "send" or "offer" is implicitly understood: "To X, Y: greeting." A letter from a superior to an inferior follows the form: "Y to X: greeting." The particular form of the greeting defines the nature of the relationship a correspondent wished to establish (pp. 15–16 above). The conventional term *salutem* can be replaced by a more elaborate phrase, like "the best of health" or even a verbal clause depending on the implied verb of wishing, hoping, etc.: "[I want you] to live a long and happy life." This structure is encoded in the morphology of the words, with each component requiring its particular case: the receiver in the dative, the sender in the nominative, the greeting in the accusative. This formal structure was expected and immediately recognizable to the eye (or ear) trained in the art of Latin letter writing, even though it might not be physically separated from the rest of the letter. In our translation, we introduce the greeting wished for by the sender with a colon, following the punctuation of the manuscript. Sometimes the woman does not identify herself in the nominative case at all (as in 3, 5, 7, 9 etc.) or she identifies herself before him, as in 18: "An equal to an equal." Only occasionally have we supplied a verb of wishing (often the weak auxiliary "may"), usually when the greeting contains a verbal clause or when clarity seemed to warrant it.

The closing greeting of these letters also provided an opportunity to develop a particular theme, beyond the traditional *vale* or "farewell." The lovers are particularly fond of exploring different nuances in the term *vale* as meaning both "Farewell" and "Keep well." While we have translated *vale* as "farewell" in most cases, we use "fare well" when the Latin seems to emphasize *vale* as a verb (as in *8* and *28*).

The vocabulary of these love letters inevitably presents many problems for a translator, as the same word may range over concepts for which English uses different words. *Salus* for example means both salvation in a religious sense and good health or well-being in a temporal sense. In a formal salutation, it was conventional simply to offer another person *salutem,* often translated as "greetings." We have adopted the latter term only when the context clearly indicates that *salus* or its derivatives are being used in such a neutral sense. In most cases we have opted for "well-being," which if understood to imply both physical and spiritual well-being, is perhaps not too far removed from the Latin sense. The woman often employs religious language, however, to express the sincerity of her love. Occasionally we have proposed salvation, as in the greeting to letter 112.

A particular problem is presented by the woman's subtle explorations of the nuances between *amor, dilectio,* and *caritas,* which in English can all be rendered by "love." Classical usage recognized only *amor* and *caritas* as separate concepts, while *dilectio* was a particular contribution of the Latin translation of the Christian Bible (pp. 16–19 above). The verb *amo* means "I love" from inclination or passion, whereas *diligo* means "I love" in the sense of "I esteem or prize highly." Often, the difference in nuance in meanings of "love" is indicated simply by a footnote. At other times, *amor* is translated as passion or longing. In a sexual context, it often evokes the idea of something that happens to an individual rather than that which the individual initiates. These writers are similarly careful about using the terms *anima, animus,* and *spiritus.* In traditional understanding, *anima* is the principle of physical life, as distinct from *animus,* the principle of spiritual and intellectual life (and thus subtly distinct from *mens,* the mind). These are distinguished as "soul" and "spirit" respectively, while *spiritus* is generally rendered as breath.

Könsgen meticulously identified many classical and scriptural allusions in the apparatus to his edition, of which only the more important are indicated here. Certain further allusions to scriptural and patristic texts have been added. References to scripture are to the Latin Vulgate, the Psalms according to their Vulgate numbering (Psalms 10–145 corresponding to Psalms 11–146 in subsequent translations). He transcribed metrical verse on separate lines, adding the comment *versus* in his margin. These editorial marks are included in our translation.

Peter Dronke's translations of parts of several letters in *Women Writers* (p. 289 n. 14 above) have been of assistance. Graziella Ballanti's translation of the entire text into Italian (p. 292 n. 9 below) has also been consulted. We would also like to express our profound gratitude to Ewald Könsgen, Gavin Betts, Naomi Norris, Kathryn Mews, Maryna Mews, and John O. Ward for offering their careful attention to drafts of our translation. Responsibility for any errors or misinterpretations is of course entirely our own.

N. C. and *C. J. M.*

The Letters

EX EPISTOLIS DUORUM AMANTIUM

1

M Amori suo precordiali omnibus aromatibus dulcius redolenti,[a]
corde et corpore sua: arescentibus floribus tue juventutis, viriditatem eterne felicitatis.

..... Vale salus[b] vite mee.

2

V Singulari gaudio, et lassate mentis unico solamini, ille cuius vita
sine te mors est: quid amplius quam seipsum quantum corpore et
anima valet.

..... Vale lux mea, vale pro qua mori velim.

3

M Purissimo amori suo, et intime fidelitatis digno: per vere dilectionis statum,[a] care fidei secretum.

..... Celi regnator sit inter nos mediator, et sit socius fidei nostre.[b] Vale, et Christus rex regum, te dulcissimum salvet in evum.
Vale in illo qui cuncta gubernat in mundo.

---

1. a) cf. Song of Songs 4.10: *pulchriora ubera tua vino et odor unguentorum tuorum super omnia aromata:* "Your breasts are more beautiful than wine and the fragrance of your perfumes above all spices."
b) or "salvation" as *salus* embraces both physical and spiritual
senses.
3. a) a punctuation mark after *digno* suggests that *per vere dilectionis
statum* qualifies *secretum* or "hiding place" rather than *digno*. b) M
38b.

FROM THE LETTERS OF TWO LOVERS

1

WOMAN To her heart's love, more sweetly scented than any spice,[a] she who is his in heart and body: the freshness of eternal happiness as the flowers fade of your youth.

..... Farewell, well-being[b] of my life.

2

MAN To the singular joy and only solace of a weary mind, that person whose life without you is death: what more than himself, in so far as he is able in body and soul.

..... Farewell, my light, farewell, you for whom I would willingly die.

3

WOMAN To her love most pure, worthy of inner fidelity: through the state of true love,[a] the secret of tender faith.

..... May the Ruler of Heaven mediate between us and may He accompany our faith.[b] Farewell, and may Christ, King of Kings, save you, my sweetest, for eternity. Farewell in Him who governs all things in the world.

4

V   De die in diem dulciori et nunc quam maxime dilecte et semper super omnia diligende, singularis eius: eandem et immutabilem sincere fidei constanciam.

..... Vale clarissima stella mea, nobilissima dulcedo mea, et sola consolacio mea. ..... Vale o mea valitudo.

5

M   Iocunde spei mee: fidem meam, et cum omni devocione meip-sam quamdiu vivam.

Tocius artis largitor, et humani ingenii largissimus dator, mei pectoris interna philosophie artis impleat pericia, quo te possim dilectissime ita salutare scriptis, ad consensum mee voluntatis. Vale vale, spes juventutis mee.[a]

6

V   Clarissime stelle sue, cuius nuper radiis delectatus sum: ita in-deficienti splendore nitere, ut nulla eam nebula possit offuscare.

Quia tu ita dulcissima domina mea precepisti, vel ut verius dicam, quia ardentissima amoris flamma compellit, se dilectus tuus continere non potuit, quin in vice sue presentie eo quo potest litterarum officio[a] te salutet. Ita ergo salva esto, sicut ego tui salute indigeo. Ita vale sicut in tuo meum constat valere. In te spes mea, in te requies mea. Nunquam tam subito evigilo, quin animus meus[b] te intra se locatam inveniat.

7

M   Hucusque dilecto semperque diligendo:[a] tota sua re et affectu, salutem, gaudium totiusque utilitatis ac honestatis profectum.

---

5. a) Ps. 70.5.

6. a) "the office of letters;" cf. Cicero, *Ep.* 6.6.1 and *17;* see too *HC,* ed. Monfrin, p. 70; ed. Hicks, p. 10; trans. Radice, p. 66. b) *animus* is consistently translated here as "spirit" rather than "mind" to evoke the idea of the seat of human thought.

4

MAN   To one who is sweeter from day to day, is loved now as much as possible and is always to be loved more than anything, her only one: the same unchanging constancy of sincere faith.

..... Farewell, my brightest star, my noblest delight, and my only consolation. ..... Farewell, my well-being.

5

WOMAN   To my joyful hope: my faith and my very self with all my devotion, as long as I live.

May the Bestower of every art and the most bountiful Giver of human talent fill the depths of my breast with the skill of the art of philosophy, in order that I may greet you in writing, most beloved, in accord with my will. Farewell, farewell, hope of my youth.[a]

6

MAN   To his brightest star, whose rays I have recently enjoyed: may she shine with such unfailing splendor that no cloud can obscure her.

Because you, my sweetest lady, have so instructed me, or to speak more truly because the burning flame of love compels me, your beloved could not restrain himself from greeting you as he can, through the agency of a letter[a] in place of his actual presence. Therefore keep well, just as I need your keeping well. And fare well, just as my faring well depends on your doing so. In you is my hope, in you my rest. Never do I wake so suddenly that my spirit[b] does not find you present within itself.

7

WOMAN   To one loved thus far and always to be loved:[a] with all her being and feeling, good health, joy, and growth in all that is beneficial and honorable.

---

7. a) A punctuation mark after *diligendo* suggests that *tota sua* is ablative rather than nominative, as in "she who is his in being and disposition." She here recapitulates his phrase in V 4.

..... Vale vale et tamdiu vale quoadusque regnum dei videatur permanere.

8

V   Dilectissime domine sue, cuius memoriam nulla intercipere potest oblivio, fidelissimus eius tunc primum tui nominis oblivionem, cum mei nominis memor non ero.

..... Vale, in pace in idipsum dormi et requiesce.[a] Dormi dulciter, cuba suaviter, ita firmiter dormias, ut latus non mutes.[b] Vale o requies mea, vale et semper vale.[c]

9

M   Ardenti lucerne, et civitati supra montem posite:[a] sic pugnare ut vincat, sic currere ut comprehendat.[b]

..... Volo et inhianter cupio ut litteris iuxta preceptum tuum intercurrentibus precordialis inter nos firmetur amicicia, donec illa michi nimium felix dies illucescat, qua votis omnibus desideratam tuam faciem videam.[c] Sicut lassus umbram, et siciens desiderat undam, ita te desidero videre.[d] .... Nihil unquam erit tam laboriosum corpori meo, nichil tam periculosum anime mee, quod tue non impendam caritati. .... Vale in deo, quo validior est nemo.

10

V   Preciosissime gemme sue, suo naturali splendore semper radianti, aurum eius purissimum:[a] letissimis amplexibus eandem gemmam circumdare et decenter ornare.

..... Vale que me valere facis.

---

8. a) Ps. 4.9: the Vulgate phrase *in idipsum* is not translated here. b) "that you do not change sides." c) a play on *vale* as meaning both "farewell" and "may you flourish."
9. a) John 5.35; Matthew 5.14. b) 1 Cor. 9.24. c) cf. Proverbs 7.18: *veni inebriemur uberibus donec inlucescat dies et fruamur cupitis amplexibus:* "Come, let us get drunk in abundance until the day dawns and let us enjoy longed for embraces." d) Job 7.12; Psalm 41.2.
10. a) cf. 2 Chronicles 9.1, 9 (the gift of the Queen of Sheba to Solomon) and Ecclesiasticus 32.7.

..... Farewell, farewell, and fare well for as long as the kingdom of God is seen to endure.

8

Man To his most beloved lady, the memory of whom no forgetting can steal away, her most faithful one: may the first time I forget your name be when I no longer remember my own.

..... Farewell, sleep, and rest in peace.[a] Sleep sweetly, lie comfortably, may you sleep so soundly that you do not stir.[b] Farewell, my rest. Farewell and fare well always.[c]

9

Woman To a burning lamp and city set on a hill:[a] may he fight in order to conquer, run in order to win.[b]

..... I wish and eagerly desire that by exchanging letters according to your bidding, the heartfelt friendship between us may be strengthened until that exceedingly happy day shines on me when I shall see your face,[c] the desire of all my prayers. Just as the weary desire shade and the thirsty long for water, so I desire to see you.[d] ..... Nothing will ever be so laborious for my body, nothing so dangerous for my soul, that I would not expend out of care for you. ..... Farewell in God, than whom no one is more strong.

10

Man To his most precious jewel, ever radiant with its natural splendor, her purest gold:[a] may he surround and fittingly set that same jewel in a joyful embrace.

..... Farewell, you who make me fare well.

11

M   Omnium virtutum continentia clarissimo, et super favum mellis iocundo,[a] inter omnes eius fidelissima: dimidium anime,[b] et seipsam in omni fide.

..... Deum testem habeo, quem neque latet, nec latere potest ulla secreti machinacio, quam pure, quam sincere, cum quanta fide te diligo. ..... Nunc igitur, quia ocium in scribendo non habeo, ut valeas centies clamo, ac milies repeto, tuumque vale nulli sit equale.

12

V   Ardenter amate, et ardentius amande,[a] pre omnibus fidelis, et ut verius dicam solus fidelis: quicquid sincerissimi amoris regula exigit.

Non opus esse reor dulcissima ut fidem tuam quam factis evidenter exhibes, verbis dilecto tuo commendes. (f. 159v) Si omnes vires meas in tuum servitium contendam, nichil me fecisse putabo, inanem me operam sumpsisse comparacione tuorum meritorum judicabo. Si quicquid bonorum secularium conferri potest, totum congeratur in unum,[b] ut aut hec aut tuam amiciciam eligere debeam, per fidem quam tibi debeo, nullius ea precii reputabo. ..... Certe fecisse iuvat. Vale decus meum,[c] que omnibus que dulcia sunt, incomparabiliter dulcior es, et omnia tempora ita leta ducas ut ego tibi cupio, quia non melius opus est.

13

M   ..... Grata mentis mee benivolencia, pro se et officio suo tibi semper obnoxia, cum omnes quas vellet salutes expedire non potuit permultas, et iam siluit, ne plures enumerando, offendere sibi

---

11. a) Psalm 18.11; Ecclesiasticus 24.27. b) Horace, *Carmina* 1.3.8.
12. a) modeled on her greeting in M 7. b) Cicero, *Tusculan Orations* 5.117. c) cf. Horace, *Carmina*, 1.1.2.
13. a) Marbod, *Rescriptum ad amicam*, ed. Bulst (1984), p. 186: "*In te namque sita mea mors est et mea vita* (For in you is placed my death and my life)."

11

WOMAN   To one most brilliant in possessing every virtue, more delightful than honey from the comb,[a] his most faithful one of all:
half her soul[b] and her whole self in complete faith.

..... God is my witness, from whom no secret plotting is hidden
nor can ever be hidden, how purely, how sincerely and with how
much faith I love you. ..... Therefore, because I do not have time
for writing now, I cry out a hundred times and repeat a thousand
times my wish that you keep well and that your faring well may
have no equal.

12

MAN   To one loved intensely, and to be loved even more intensely,[a]
one faithful beyond all others, and to speak more truly, the only
faithful one: whatever the rule of sincerest love demands.

I do not think there is any need, sweetest, for you to recom-
mend with words to your beloved the faith that you clearly show
through actions. If I were to exert all my strength in your service,
I would deem that I had done nothing and would consider that I
had undertaken a trifling matter compared with what you deserve.
If whatever is of worldly value could be brought together and gathered up in one place[b] so that I had to choose between them and
your friendship, out of the faith that I owe you I would consider
them to be worthless. ..... Certainly I am glad to have done so.
Farewell, my beauty,[c] you who are incomparably sweeter than all
sweet things. May you prolong your years as happily as I wish for
you, for nothing better is needed.

13

WOMAN   ..... Since the grateful benevolence of my mind, of its own
accord and out of duty always bound to you, could not send all the
greetings that it wished, it has remained silent up to now over
many, lest by listing several it might seem to undermine them all.
I think it neither a burden for you nor difficult for me to write to

videretur universas. Sepe me tibi scribere, eadem iterum atque iterum repetere, nec tibi onerosum reor, nec michi est difficile, quippe quem sicut memetipsam diligo, ita te toto cordis conamine diligere non negligo. ..... Vale carior vita. Scias quod in te mea mors est et vita.[a]

14

V   Si tabulas tuas dulcissima diutius retinere michi liceret, plurima scriberem sicut plurima occurrerent. Nam si semper scribere possem, ita, ut nichil aliud facerem, sufficientem sine dubio materiam haberem: tuam scilicet probitatem, tua merita que circa me tanta sunt, ut quanta sint estimari non possit. Vale certissima spes mea.

15

V   Cordi suo, fidelissimus eius: noctem candidam, et utinam mecum.[a]
   Vale anima mea,[b] quies mea.

16

<V>   Signaculo suo, mentis interioribus artius impresso, ille qui eiusdem signaculi expressa similitudo est:[a] eo tenaciorem affectionem quo in unius nostrum salute res communis indifferenter[b] agitur.
   Tu o dura, anime tue quomodo immemor esse potuisti? Nam ubi mei oblita es, si ego anima tua sum, anime tue quoque oblita es. Vale dulcissima. Totus tecum sum, et ut verius dicam, totus in te sum.

17

<V>   Inexhausto tocius sue dulcedinis vasculo, dilectissimus eius: neglecto celi lumine, te solam indesinenter aspicere.

---

15. a) Ovid, *Heroides* 16.320 (Paris to Helen). b) cf. 1 Samuel (= I Regum, Vulgate) 20.17: *sicut animam sua ita diligebat eum:* "For he (David) loved him (Jonathan) as his own soul."
16. a) Song of Songs 8.6; cf. Ezekiel 28.12 b) cf. V 24.

you often, repeating the same things again and again, for just as I love you as my very self, so I do not neglect to love you with all the effort of my heart. ..... Farewell, dearer than life. Know that in you lies my death and my life.[a]

14

MAN If I may be permitted to keep your writing tablets a while longer, sweetest, I would write many things, just as many things would come to mind. For even if I could write to you continuously so that I did nothing else, I would undoubtedly still have enough material: namely your integrity and your merits, which for me are so many that I could not count them all. Farewell, my surest hope.

15

MAN To his heart, her most faithful: an unclouded night—would that it were with me![a]

Farewell, my soul,[b] my rest.

16

<MAN> To his seal, imprinted very firmly inside his mind, he who is the visible likeness of that seal:[a] affection, the more enduring as the well-being of each of us is made a shared concern without difference.[b]

How could you, unfeeling woman, forget your soul? For whenever you forget me, if I am indeed your soul, you forget your own soul as well. Farewell, sweetest. I am wholly with you, or to speak more truly I am wholly within you.

17

<MAN> To the inexhaustible vessel of all his sweetness, her most beloved: may I gaze endlessly at you alone, having ignored the light of day.

Cum dies in noctem vergeret, ulterius me continere non potui, quin salutandi officium[a] ultro arriperem, quod tu tarda distulisti. Vale, et scias quia sine tua valitudine, nec salus nec vita mea consistit.

18

M   Par pari, rubenti rose sub immarcido liliorum candore: quidquid amans amanti.

Quamvis sit hiems in tempore, estuat tamen pectus meum amoris fervore. Quid ultra? Plura tibi scriberem, sed sapientem pauca monebunt. Vale, cor et corpus meum, et omnis dilectio mea.

19

V   Pauca quidem verba tua sunt, sed ea plura feci sepe relegendo, nec ego penso quantum dicas, sed de quam fecundo corde procedat quod dicis. Vale dulcissima.

20

\<V\>	Stella polum variat, et noctem luna colorat,
versus	Sed michi sydus hebet quod me conducere debet.[a]
	Nunc mea si tenebris oriatur stella fugatis,
	Mens mea iam tenebras meroris nesciet ullas.
5	Tu michi Lucifer[b] es, que noctem pellere debes.
	Te sine lux michi nox,[c] tecum nox splendida lux est.

Vale stella mea que splendoris sui damna non patitur. Vale summa spes mea in qua sola michi conplaceo,[d] quam nunquam reduco ad memoriam, quia nunquam amitto a memoria. Vale.

---

17. a) V 6.
20. a) cf. Ovid, *Fasti* 3.449; Lucan, *Pharsalia* 1.661–62; Ovid, *Metamorphoses* 2.144. In ancient thought, the stars revolve around the north pole; cf. *Carmina burana* no. 169 (*Hebet sidus*). b) the morning star or planet Venus; cf. Ovid, *Metamorphoses* 2.723. *Lucifer* is used in this sense in 2 Peter 1.19 and Job 11.17, without the connotation of a fallen star as in Isaiah 14.12. c) cf. V *38c* line 4. d) cf. Matthew 3.17.

Since day was turning into night, I could not contain myself any longer from seizing the duty of greeting you[a] of my own accord, something which you, tardy one, have put off. Farewell and know that without your good health, neither well-being nor life exists for me.

18

WOMAN An equal to an equal, to a reddening rose under the spotless whiteness of lilies: whatever a lover gives to a lover.

Although it is wintertime, yet my breast blazes with the fervor of love. What more? I would write more things to you, but a few words instruct a wise man. Farewell, my heart and body, and my total love.

19

MAN Indeed your words are few, but I made them many by re-reading them often. Nor do I measure how much you say, but rather how fertile is the heart from which comes what you say. Farewell, sweetest.

20

<MAN>   The star turns around the pole, and the moon colors the
                    night,
               But that star is fading that should be my guide.[a]
               Now if through the retreating shadows my own star should
                    appear,
               No longer will my mind know the darkness of grief.
5   You to me are Lucifer,[b] who must banish the night.
               Without you day is night to me,[c] with you night is splendid day.

Farewell, my star, whose splendor never dies. Farewell, my greatest hope, in whom alone I find favor,[d] and whom I never bring back to mind since you never slip from mind. Farewell.

21

M   Dilecto suo speciali, et ex ipsius experimento rei: esse quod
est.[a]
   Cum mens mea versetur circa plurima rerum negocia, deficit
acuto percussa dilectionis hamo. ..... Sicut ignis inextinguibilis
est, nulla materia rerum superabilis, nisi adhibeatur aqua que nat-
uraliter est ei potens medicina, sic omnibus est amor meus in-
sanabilis, tibi autem soli est medicabilis.[b] Quo munere te ditabo,
mens mea anxiatur ignorando.[c] O decus juvenum, consors poetarum, quam decorus aspectu, sed prestabilior es affectu; tu mea
presens leticia, et est michi meror tui absencia; equipolenter te
diligo. Vale.

22

V   Gemme sue presenti luce gratiori et lucidiori, ille qui sine te
crassis est tenebris obvolutus: quid aliud, nisi ut in tuo naturali fulgore indeficienter glorieris.
   Fateri solent physici, quod luna nisi a sole non luceat. Itaque
cum hoc lumine privatur, omni caloris et splendoris beneficio des-
tituta, orbem suum mortalibus fuscum et pallidum ostendit.[a]
Huius nimirum rei similitudo inter me et te aperte exprimitur. Tu
enim sol meus es, que me vultus tui iocundissimo splendore semper accendis (f. 160r) et illuminas. Ego lumen nisi a te nullum
habeo, sine te ebes, obscurus, enervis et mortuus sum. Et ut
verum fatear, maius est quod tu michi quam quod sol lunari globo
accomodat. Quia luna quo soli propior fit plus obscuratur, ego
quo plus tibi admoveor, quo tibi vicinior sum, plus ardeo et in tantum inflammor, ut, sicut ipsa sepe notasti, cum iuxta te sum, totus
in ignem transeam, totus medullitus urar.[b]
   Quid ergo tuis innumerabilibus beneficiis equum reponam?
Nihil equidem, quia dulcissima verba tua factorum quantitate tran-

---

21. a) a punctuation mark after *rei* suggests that the woman does not
   identify herself in this greeting, but offers her own being. b) cf. Ovid,
   Heroides 5.149. c) While Könsgen reads this as one sentence, the
   MS shows a period here, followed by a new sentence.
22. a) cf. Rhabanus Maurus, *De computo* 1.45, ed. Wesley M. Stevens,
   CCCM 44 (1979): 257; Bede, *De natura rerum* 20, ed. Charles W.
   Jones, CCSL 123A (1975): 211. b) cf. Ovid, *Heroides* 18.177; *Meta-
   morphoses* 1.494. c) cf. V 6. d) Horace, *Carmina* 4.1.36.

21

WOMAN   To her beloved, special from experience of the reality itself: the being which she is.[a]

Since my mind is turning with many concerns, it fails me,
pierced by the sharp hook of love. ..... Just as fire cannot be ex-
tinguished or suppressed by any material, unless water, by nature
its powerful remedy, is applied, so my love cannot be cured by any
means—only by you can it be healed.[b] My mind is bothered by not
knowing through what gift I can enrich you.[c] Glory of young men,
companion of poets, how handsome you are in appearance yet
more distinguished in feeling. Your presence is my joy, your absence my sorrow; in either case, I love you. Farewell.

22

MAN   To his jewel, more pleasing and more splendid than the present light, that man who without you is shrouded in dense
shadow: what else except that you glory unfailingly in your natural
brilliance.

Scientists often say that the moon does not shine without the
sun, and that when deprived of this light, it is robbed of all benefit of heat and brightness and presents to humans a dark and
ashen sphere.[a] Surely the similarity of this phenomenon to you
and me is very plain to see: for you are my sun, since you always
illumine me with the most delightful brightness of your face and
make me shine. I have no light that does not come from you and
without you I am dull, dark, weak, and dead. But, to tell the truth,
what you do for me is even greater than what the sun does for the
sphere of the moon. For the moon becomes more obscure the
closer it gets to the sun, whereas the nearer I am brought to you
and the closer I get, the more on fire I become. So much do I burn
for you, that, just as you yourself have often noted, when I am
next to you I become completely on fire and am burned right
down to the marrow.[b]

What then shall I offer in return to equal your innumerable benefits? Nothing, actually, because you transcend your sweetest

scendis, ipsa amoris exhibicione transgrederis, ita ut pauperior michi in verbis quam in factis videaris. Inter cetera que pre aliis innumera possides, hoc quoque tenes egregium, ut in amicum plus agas quam dicas, in verbis pauper, in factis copiosa; quod eo tibi est gloriosius, quanto facere quam dicere difficilius. .....
In pectore meo immortaliter sepulta es, de quo sepulcro me vivente non emerges; ibi cubas, ibi quiescis. Usque ad somnum me comitaris, in somno me non deseris, post somnum statim ut oculos aperio ante ipsum celi lumen te video.[c] Ad alios verba, ad te intencionem dirigo. Sepe in verbis cado,[d] quia cogitacio mea ab eis extranea est. Quis ergo negare poterit, quin veraciter in me sepulta sis?. ..... Invidum amori nostro tempus imminet, et tu tamen ita differs quasi ociosi simus. Vale.

23

M   Dulcissimo anime sue presidio, et in eius caritatis radice plantato, illa in cuius dilectione firmiter es constitutus, et in cuius[a] mellifluo amoris sapore bene fundatus:[b] quod ab ira distat et odio.

Cum vellem tibi rescribere, reiecit me impar viribus meis[c] rei magnitudo. Volui enim et non potui, incepi et defeci, sustuli et elisis gravitate humeris corrui. Voluit animi fervens affectus, renuitque aridi defectus ingenii. Horum duorum altercaciones plenasque litibus persuasiones sustinui, et perpensa utriusque racione cui pocius cederem[d] examinare nequivi. Ait enim animi affectus: "Quid agis ingrata? Quamdiu suspendis me longa et certe indigna taciturnitate? Nonne te excitat dilecti tui liberalis benignitas, et benigna liberalitas? Contexe plenas graciarum litteras, refer abundanti pietati, quas debes, gracias. Beneficium enim non videtur gratum et acceptum, de quo multum graciarum non fuerit relatum."

Persuasionibus his parendum credidi, et certe parere volui, sed restitit ingenii ariditas temeritatis mee inceptum acri correptionis flagello[e] castigans. "Quo," inquit, "stulta et infirma ruis? Quo te procellit[f] inconsiderata intencio festini animi? Incipiesne, cum sis

23. a) cuius Könsgen) eius MS. b) Expanding on Ephesians 3.17 with three different words for love. c) Ovid, *Metamorphoses* 5.610. d) cederem Könsgen) celerem MS.

words with the number of your actions and you have so surpassed them by the demonstration of your love that you seem to me poorer in words than in actions. Among other things that you possess in infinite number compared with other people, you have this distinction too, that, poor in words, but rich in actions, you do more for a friend than you say; this is all the more to your glory since it is more difficult to act than to speak. .....

You are buried inside my breast for eternity, from which tomb you will never emerge as long as I live. There you lie, there you rest. You keep me company right until I fall asleep; while I sleep you never leave me, and after I wake I see you, as soon as I open my eyes, even before the light of day itself.[c] To others I address my words, to you my intention. I often stumble over words,[d] because my thought is far from them. Who then will be able to deny that you are truly buried in me? ..... Envious time looms over our love, and yet you delay as if we were at leisure. Farewell.

23

WOMAN   To the sweetest protector of her soul, planted at the root of her caring love, she in whose love you are firmly established and in whose honeyed taste of love you are well founded:[a] whatever is far from anger and hate.

Although I wanted to write back to you, the magnitude of the task, being beyond my powers,[b] drove me back. Indeed I wanted to but could not, I began then grew weak, I persisted but collapsed, my shoulders buckling under the weight. The burning feeling of my spirit[c] longed to do so but the weakness of my dried-up talent refused. I endured the numerous disputes and litigious arguments of both, and after weighing up rationally to which of the two I would rather yield,[d] I was unable to decide. For the feeling of my spirit said: *"What are you doing, ungrateful woman? For how long do you keep me in suspense with long and surely undeserved silence? Does not the generous kindness and kind generosity of your beloved stir you? Compose a letter full of thanks, give the thanks which you owe for his abounding integrity. For a kind act does not seem pleasing and welcome when many thanks are not received."*

I thought that I ought to heed these arguments, and certainly I wanted to heed them, but the dryness of my talent resisted, rebuking the attempts of my temerity with the harsh whip of reproach,[e] saying: *"Where are you rushing, you foolish and feeble woman? Where does the unthinking intention of your hasty spirit throw[f] you? Do you begin to speak mighty words, though you are unskilled and have unrefined lips?[g] Surely you are no match for*

rudis et incircumcisis labiis, grandia loqui? [g] Non enim sufficis materie tali et tam magnifice. Quippe qui rem quamlibet assumit laudare, debet tandem in partes distribuere singularumque partium qualitates summa cautione pensare et quamque secundum dignitatem congrue laudis celebritate honorare.[h] Alioquin rei laudande iniuriam facit, qui speciosa eius narracione < ..... >, eleganciam enormi narracione deterit.[i] Sed unde tibi est hec scribendi copia, ut digne dicas sublimia? Attende te et rem, quam affectas. Multiformia et ampla sunt beneficia, quibus tu litteris tuis gracias referre paras. Quid estuas multis cogitacionum procellis?[j] Respice pectus tuum brutum et frigidum, prorsus carens sale sciencie et tantum crassi aeris segnicie turgidum. Contrahe audacie tue vela,[k] lintrem qua imperiosum pelagus[l] tranare paras, cito nisi caves mersura."

Hac hortaminis et dehortaminis alternacione suspensam, hucusque debitam graciarum actionem distuli, parens consiliis, imbecillitatem suam erubescentis ingenii. Quod queso abundans in te divine suavitatis excellencia michi non imputet, sed cum sis vere dulcedinis filius, cognita tibi mansuetudinis virtus super me magis abundet.[m] Scio quidem et fateor ex philosophie tue diviciis maximam michi fluxisse et fluere copiam gaudiorum, sed ut inoffense loquar, minorem tamen quam que me faciat in ea re perfecte beatam. Venio enim sepe aridis faucibus desiderans suavi oris tui refici nectare, diffusasque in corde tuo divitias sicienter haurire. Quid pluribus opus est verbis? Deo teste profiteor, quia nemo in seculo vitali spirat aura quem te magis amare desiderem. ..... Sit tibi vale dilecto meo, medullas interiores dulciter penetrare.

---

e) cf. Judith 8.27. f) procellit MS propellit Könsgen-Schaller g) cf. Exodus 6.12, 30 about Moses' slowness of speech; Daniel 7.20. h) honorare) conorare MS; Könsgen (p. 64) suggests various interpretations of *conorare;* here it is taken as a scribal mistake for *honorare.* i) Könsgen (p. 64) suggests that words have been accidentally omitted between *narracione* and *eleganciam.* A possibility which he considers less likely

such matter so distinguished. For anyone who assumes to praise anything at all must in the end divide it into parts and with the utmost care weigh the qualities of each individual part, honoring[h] each one according to its merit with a suitable tribute of praise; otherwise he who diminishes its brilliance by < ..... > description, its elegance with outrageous description, harms the object to be praised.[i] But from where will you get such ability in writing that you might speak of great things worthily? Look at yourself and at the task you are undertaking. Abundant and various are the benefits for which you are preparing to give thanks in your writing. Why are you tossed about by so many storms of deliberations?[j] Look at your cold and brutish breast, utterly lacking the salt of learning and so inflated with the sluggishness of dense air. Draw in the sails of your audacity,[k] the skiff in which you are preparing to cross the imperious ocean,[l] quickly, for unless you take heed, you will drown."

Suspended between this alternating encouragement and discouragement, I have until now deferred the due act of thanks, yielding to the advice of a mental capacity ashamed of its own ineptitude. I pray that the excellence of divine amiability abundant in you will not blame me for this, but rather, since you are the son of true sweetness, may the virtue of mildness familiar to you flow over me even more.[m] Indeed I know and admit that from the treasures of your philosophy the greatest amount of joys have flown and still flow over me, but, if I may speak freely, still less than what would make me perfectly happy in this regard. For I often come with parched throat longing to be refreshed by the nectar of your delightful mouth and to drink thirstily the riches scattered in your heart. What need is there for more words? With God as my witness I declare that there is no one in this world breathing life-giving air whom I desire to love more than you. ..... May this farewell, my beloved, sweetly penetrate your inner marrow.

---

is that *speciosa eius narracione* was copied by the scribe from a marginal gloss serving to correct *enormi narracione;* in this case the phrase translates as "he who diminishes elegance with specious (or superficially attractive) description. . . ." j) Gregory the Great, *Liber pastoralis* 1.9. k) cf. Ovid, *Tristia* 3.4.32; Horace, *Carmina* 2.10.23. l) Baudri of Bourgueil, *Carmina* 193.64. m) 1 Thess. 4.1, 4.10.

24

V Anime qua nec candidius, nec michi carius terra protulit, caro quam eadem anima spirare facit et moveri: quicquid ei debeo per quem spiro et moveor.

Litterarum tuarum copiosa et tamen insufficiens (f. 160v) ubertas, duarum rerum evidentissimum michi testimonium prebet, redundantis scilicet fidei et amoris. Unde dictum est: "Ex abundancia cordis os loquitur."[a] ..... Ego autem litteras tuas ita avide suscipio, ut michi semper breves sint quia desiderium meum et saturant et accendunt, ad similitudinem in ardore laborantis, quem potus ipse quo plus reficit, plus accendit. Deum testor quod novo modo cum eas diligencius intueor, novo inquam modo commoveor, quia ipse animus leto horrore concutitur, et corpus in novum habitum gestumque convertitur; et tales littere laudabiles sunt, que sensum audientis quocumque volunt impellunt.

Soles a me querere dulcis anima mea quid amor sit, nec per ignoranciam excusare me possum quasi scilicet de re incognita sim consultus, cum ita me idem amor imperio suo subiecerit, ut non extranea res sed multum familiaris et domestica, immo intestina videatur. Est igitur amor,[b] vis quedam anime non per se existens nec seipsa contenta, sed semper cum quodam appetitu et desiderio, se in alterum transfundens, et cum altero idem effici volens ut de duabus diversis voluntatibus unum quid indifferenter[c] efficiatur. .....

Scias quia licet res universalis sit amor, ita tamen in angustum contractus est,[d] ut audacter affirmem eum in nobis solummodo regnare, in me scilicet et in te domicilium suum fecisse. Nos enim duo amorem integrum, invigilatum, sincerum habemus, quia nichil est dulce, nichil quietum alteri, nisi quod in commune proficit; eque annuimus, eque negamus, idem per omnia sapimus. Quod inde facile probari potest quia tu sepe meas cogitaciones anticipas; quod ego scribere concipio, tu prevenis, et si bene memini, tu illud idem de te dixisti. Vale et sicut ego te, ita tu me indefesso amore contuere.

---

24. a) Luke 6.45; Matthew 12.34. b) in the margin: *diffinicio.* c) cf. Cicero, *Laelius (De amicitia)* 81. d) *Laelius* 20.

24

MAN   To a soul brighter and dearer to me than anything the earth has produced, the flesh which that same soul causes to breathe and move: whatever I owe her through whom I breathe and move.

The abundant and yet insufficient richness of your letter provides me with the clearest evidence of two things, namely, your overflowing faith and love; hence the saying: "From the fullness of the heart the mouth speaks."[a] ..... And yet I receive your letters so eagerly that for me they are always too brief, since they both satisfy and stimulate my desire: like someone who is suffering from fever—the more the drink relieves him, the hotter he feels. God is my witness that I am stirred in a new way when I look at them more carefully; in a new way, I say, because my spirit itself is shaken by a joyful trembling, and my body is transformed into a new manner and posture. So praiseworthy are your letters that they direct my sense of hearing to whatever place they wish.

You often ask me, my sweet soul, what love is—and I cannot excuse myself on grounds of ignorance, as if I had been asked about a subject unfamiliar to me. For that very love has brought me under its own command in such a way that it seems not to be external but very familiar and personal, even visceral. Love is therefore[b] a particular force of the soul, existing not for itself nor content by itself, but always pouring itself into another with a certain hunger and desire, wanting to become one with the other, so that from two diverse wills one is produced without difference.[c] .....

Know that although love may be a universal thing, it has nevertheless been condensed into so confined a place[d] that I would boldly assert that it reigns in us alone—that is, it has made its very home in me and you. For the two of us have a love that is pure, nurtured, and sincere, since nothing is sweet or carefree for the other unless it has mutual benefit. We say yes equally, we say no equally, we feel the same about everything. This can be easily shown by the way that you often anticipate my thoughts: what I think about writing you write first, and, if I remember well, you have said the same thing about yourself. Farewell, and regard me with unfading love just as I do you.

25

M   Thesauro suo incomparabili, super omnes delicias seculorum delectabili: beatitudinem sine fine, salutem sine defectione.

Quid sit amor, vel quid possit naturali intuitu ego quoque perspiciens morum nostrorum studiorumque similitudine[a] que maxime contrahit amicicias, et conciliat[b] perspecta vicissitudinem amandi tibi rependere et in omnibus obedire. ..... Si amor noster tam facili propulsione discedit verus amor non fuit[c]; verba mollia et plana que inter nos hactenus contulimus, non fuerunt vera sed amorem simularunt. Amor enim cui semel aculeum infigit, non facile deserit. Nosti o mi amor precordialis, quod tunc veri amoris officia bene persolvuntur quando sine intermissione debentur, ita ut pro amico secundum vires faciamus et super vires velle non desinamus.[d]

Hoc ergo vere dilectionis debitum persolvere studebo, sed proh dolor ad plenum nequeo. At si pro parvitate ingenii in te salutandi officio non sufficit, saltem proficiat apud te meum indesinens velle. Scias enim dilecte mi et vere scias ex quo dilectio tua cordis mei hospiciolum vel tugurium sibi vendicavit, semper grata et de die in diem delectabilior permansit, nec sicut plerumque fieri solet assiduitas familiaritatem, familiaritas fiduciam, fiducia negligenciam, negligencia fastidium peperit.[e] Magno quidem studio tempore inter nos nascentis amicicie me appetere cepisti, sed maiori desiderio ut augeretur et permaneret dilectio nostra contendisti. Unde sicut res tue se habent, noster variatur animus, ut tuum gaudium, meum deputem profectum, et tuam adversitatem meam amarissimam deiectionem. Non idem michi videtur impleri quod ceperis, et augere quod perfeceris, quia ibi additur quod deest, hic cumulatur quod perfectum est. Et nos licet omnibus integram caritatem exhibeamus, non tamen omnes equaliter diligimus,[f] et ita quod omnibus est generale quibusdam efficitur speciale. Aliud est sedere ad mensam principis, aliud eius interesse consilio, et plus est ad amorem trahi quam ad consessum invitari. Non itaque tantum gracie tibi debeo si me non repellas, quantum si obvia manu suscipias. Simpliciter candide menti et purissimo pectori tuo loquar. Non magnum est si te diligo, immo

---

25. a) cf. Cicero, *De officiis* 1.56. b) cf. *Laelius* 100. c) cf. Jerome, *Ep.* 3.6, CSEL 54: 18. d) desinamus Könsgen) desinemus MS. e) Jerome, *Ep.* 60.10.3. f) The contrast is between *integram caritatem exhibeamus* and *non tamen omnes diligimus.*

25

WOMAN   To her incomparable treasure, more delightful than all the pleasures of the world: blessedness without end and well-being without weakening.

I too have been considering with innate reflection what love is or what it can be by analogy with our behavior and concerns[a], that which above all forms friendships,[b] and, once considered, leads to repaying you with the exchange of love and obeying you in everything. ..... If our love deserted us with so slight a force, then it was not true love.[c] The plain and tender words which to date we have exchanged with each other were not real, but only feigned love. For love does not easily forsake those whom it has once stung. You know, my heart's love, that the services of true love are properly fulfilled only when they are continually owed, in such a way that we act for a friend according to our strength and not stop[d] wishing to go beyond our strength.

This debt of true love, therefore, I shall endeavor to fulfil, but alas I am unable to do so in full. However, if the duty of greeting you according to my meager talents is not enough, at least my never ending desire to do so may be of some merit in your estimation. For know this, my beloved, and know it truly, that ever since your love claimed for itself the guest chamber—or rather the hovel—of my heart, it has always remained welcome and day after day more delightful, without, as often happens, constant presence leading to familiarity, familiarity to trust, trust to negligence, and negligence to contempt.[e] Indeed, you began to desire me with much interest at the very beginning of our friendship, but with greater longing you strove to make our love grow and last. And so our spirit fluctuates according to how your affairs turn out, so that your joy I count as my gain and your misfortune my most bitter loss. But your fulfilling what you have begun does not seem the same to me as your increasing what you have completed, because in one case what is lacking is added, in the other what is completed is added on. And even if we show perfect kindness to everyone, we still do not love[f] everyone equally; and what is general for everyone is made particular for certain people. It is one thing to sit at the table of a prince, another to be there in order to advise him, and a greater thing to be drawn out of love, rather than just to be invited to a gathering. So I owe you fewer thanks for not spurning me than for receiving me with open arms. Let me speak plainly to your resplendent mind and heart so pure. It is not a

pessimum si unquam tui oblita fuero.[g] Ergo care mi tam fideli amice rarus esse noli. Hactenus aliquo modo supportare potui, ast nunc tui presencia dum careo cantibus volucrum, viriditate nemorum permota, amore tuo langueo.[h] His omnibus utique congauderem si tui colloquio et presencia secundum velle meum perfrui possem. Sicut tibi cupio, ita michi faciat deus. Vale. (f. 161r)

26

V   Dilecte sue nondum cognite, sed adhuc interius cognoscende, juvenis[a] qui tanti boni noticiam intrinsecus ardet perscrutari: in tam abstruso et inexhausto boni fonte semper redundare, et per eum haustu non deficere.

..... O quam fecundum suavitatis pectus tuum, o quam integra venustate prefulges, o corpus succi plenissimum,[b] o ineffabilis odor tuus, profer quod latet, revela quod habes absconditum, totus ille copiosissime dulcedinis tue fons ebulliat, amor tuus totus in me suas laxet copias, nichil penitus devotissimum servum tuum celes, quia nichil actum credo, dum aliquid restare video.[c] De hora in horam tibi vicinius astringor, sicut ignis qui ligna comburit, plus eo voracior, quo in alimentis est copiosior.[d] ..... Perpetua luce et inextincto fulgore immortaliter coruscas. Vale.

27

M   Oculo suo: Bezelielis spiritum,[a] trium crinium fortitudinem,[b] patris pacis formam,[c] Idide profunditatem.[d]

---

g) cf. Psalm 136.5. h) Song of Songs 2.5; 5.8.

26. a) cf. M 1. b) Terence, *Eunuchus* 318. In classical physiology, the female body was considered more moist than the male. c) cf. Lucan, *Pharsalia* 2.657. d) cf. Ovid, *Metamorphoses* 8.837–40.

27. a) Exodus 31.2: a skilled craftsman inspired by God. b) Judges 16.13–17 (Samson, normally referred to as having seven locks of hair). c) 2 Samuel 14.25 (Absalom). d) Isidore, *Etymologiae* 7.6.65 (Solomon).

great thing if I love you, but rather a wicked thing if ever I shall forget you.[g] Therefore, my dear, do not make yourself so scarce to
your faithful friend. So far I have somehow been able to bear it,
but now, deprived of your presence and stirred by the songs of
birds and the freshness of the woods, I languish for your love.[h]
Surely I would have rejoiced in all these things if I had been able
to enjoy your conversation and presence according to my will.

May God do for me such as I desire for you. Farewell.

26

MAN   To his beloved not yet known, and still to be known more intimately, the young man[a] who deep within yearns to probe the understanding of such a great good: may you always abound in such
a secret and inexhaustible fountain of goodness, and through it
never be without refreshment.

..... How fertile with delight is your breast, how you shine with
untouched beauty, body so full of moisture,[b] indescribable scent
of yours! Reveal what is hidden, uncover what you keep concealed, let that whole fountain of your most abundant sweetness
bubble forth, let all your love release its abundance in me, and
may you keep absolutely nothing from your most devoted servant,
because I believe nothing has been done as long as I see something remaining.[c] Hour by hour I am bound closer to you, just like
fire devouring wood: the more devouring the more plentiful its
fuel.[d] ..... You glitter with perpetual light and inextinguishable
brightness immortally. Farewell.

27

WOMAN   To her eye: the spirit of Bezalel,[a] the strength of the three
locks of hair,[b] the beauty of the father of peace,[c] the depth of
Ididia.[d]

28

V   Dilecte in eterna memoria tenaciter recondite: quicquid ad illud esse conducit, cuius plenitudini nichil deficit.

Qui nobis invident, utinam invidendi longa eis materia detur et utinam nostris opimis rebus diu marcescant[a] quandoquidem ita volunt. Me a te separare, ipsum si nos mare interluat, non potest; ego te semper amabo, semper in animo gestabo. Nec mirari debes si in nostram tam insignem, tam aptam amiciciam prava emulacio suos obliquat oculos, quia si miseri essemus sine omni profecto livida notacione vivere cum aliis utcumque possemus. Rodant ergo detrahant, mordeant,[b] in seipsis liquescant, nostra bona suam amaritudinem faciant; tu tamen mea eris vita, meus spiritus, mea in angustiis recreacio, meum denique perfectum gaudium. Vale que valere me facis.

29

M   Omnibus omissis sub alas tuas confugio,[a] tue dicioni me suppono obnixe tibi per omnia subsequendo. Dicere vix possum tristia verba. Vale.[b]

30

V   Deus tibi dulcissima propicius sit. Ego servus tuus sum, in tua iussa promptissimus. Vale.

31

<V>   Dulcissime sue in omni egritudine unico remedio suo: nichil unquam molestie sentire, nulla temptari egritudine.

..... Collige quantum ipsa presentia tua fecisset, si tantam vim absens habuisti. Certe si uno saltem intuitu in iocundissimam faciem tuam intendissem, nunquam quicquam doloris sensissem. ..... Manda michi quo in loco fortuna mea sit, quia penes te tota est. Vale, et valere non desine. .....

---

28. a) Horace, *Epistulae* 1.2.57. b) Ovid, *Tristia* 4.10.123.
29. a) Ruth 2.12. b) Ovid, *Tristia* 1.3.80.

28

MAN To his beloved, firmly stored in eternal memory: whatever leads to that state in whose fullness nothing is lacking.

May prolonged cause for envy be given to those who envy us, and may they long pine away for our prosperity,[a] since that is what they want. But it is not possible to separate you from me, even if the sea itself should flow between us; I will always love you, I will always carry you in my spirit. Nor should you be surprised that twisted jealousy should turn its eyes towards such a conspicuous and fitting friendship as ours, because if we were miserable, we could undoubtedly live among others however we liked without any malicious attention. Therefore let them backbite, let them drag us down, let them gnaw,[b] let them waste away inside, let them derive their bitterness from our good things; you will still be my life, my breath, my restoration in difficulty, and finally my complete joy. Farewell, you who make me fare well.

29

WOMAN Having given up everything, I take refuge under your wings,[a] I submit myself to your rule, resolutely following you in everything. I can scarcely speak these sad words: "Farewell."[b]

30

MAN May God be gracious to you, sweetest. I am your servant, most ready for your commands. Farewell.

31

<MAN> To his sweetest, his only remedy in every affliction: may you never have worries or be troubled by any affliction.

. . . . . Consider how much you would have achieved by your actual presence if you had such power when absent. Surely if I could have directed my gaze to your most delightful face just once, I would have felt no grief whatsoever. ..... Send me to the place in which lies my destiny, since it is completely within your power. Farewell and never stop faring well.

32

M   Ut convalescis, neminem me letiorem ipse scis. Crede quidem tibi solem oriri meridianum, tue saluti jocundari concentus avium, te propter eadem,[a] dum infirmabaris, elementa non rectum servasse ordinem;[b] cuius rei testis est aeris temperies hucusque debilitata, que iam, ut te sospitari sensit, tibi congratulando est mutata. Ecce quidem hac modica nive liquata reviviscent omnia, arridebunt sibi tempora nobis quoque per dei graciam non insolita leticia. Tu tantum sis incolumis, et omnia adiciuntur nobis.[c]

33

V   Excutienda pigricia est, et cum fervore temporis novus dictandi fervor sumendus. Nisi tu precurras, ego precurram. Vale luna presenti multo lucidior[a] et sole cras orituro gratior.

34

M   Vale et premeditare quod melius est provida dilacio quam incauta mentis festinatio. Aptum colloquio nostro tempus elige, et michi manda. Vale.

35

V   Electe sue dilectus eius: eidem incepto amori fixis insistere vestigiis.
Ego tibi dilectissima facile condonarem, eciam si grave aliquid in me commisisses, quia nimium durus esset, quem sermo tuus tam mollis, tam suavis emollire non posset. Nunc vero venia tibi opus non est, quia nichil in me peccasti. Vale.

---

32. a) eadem Könsgen) eandem MS. b) Marbod of Rennes, *Carmina*, PL 171: 1717A; cf. Song of Songs 2.11–12. c) Matthew 6.33; Luke 12.31.
33. a) cf. Song of Songs 6.9.

32

WOMAN You yourself know that no one is happier than I that you are getting better. Know indeed that the midday sun has risen for you, that the chorus of birds is rejoicing over your health, and that on your account, while you were sick, those same[a] elements did not keep their natural order.[b] The proof of this lies in the weather, which till now has been bleak; but when it sensed that you had been kept safe, it changed by congratulating you.

And look too how, now that this slight snow has melted, all things flourish again; the seasons will smile on them, and by the grace of God there will be for us too a not unfamiliar joy. May you just keep well, and all things are provided for us.[c]

33

MAN This laziness must be shaken off, and along with the fervor of the season, a new fervor for composition must be taken up. If you do not do so first, I will. Farewell, you who are much brighter than the present moon[a] and more welcome than tomorrow's rising sun.

34

WOMAN Farewell and remember that thoughtful delay is better than imprudent haste. Choose a suitable time for our meeting and let me know. Farewell.

35

MAN To his chosen one, her beloved: may you keep with sure step to the same love that has begun.

I would have forgiven you readily, most beloved, even if you had committed some serious act against me, because too hard would he be whom your speech so tender and amiable could not soften. But truly you have no need of forgiveness, because you have not wronged me in any way. Farewell.

36

\<V\> Reverende domine sue, humilis servus eius: devotum servitium.

Sic enim vos appellare iam michi opus est,[a] ut non dicam tu, sed vos, non dulcis, non cara, sed domina, quia non sum familiaris ut antea, et vos michi nimis estis extranea.

37

\<V\> Unice expectacioni sue qui expectans expectat:[a] ut felix sis, sine me tamen felix esse nolis.

Tuus servus sum, ad te corpus totum, ad te totum animum dirigo. Cum te non video, lumen me videre non judico. Miserere tabescentis dilecti tui, et fere deficientis nisi cito michi succurras. ..... Interroga nuncium quid egi, postquam litteras perscripsi: ilico certe in lectum pre inpatiencia me conieci. Vale. (f. 161v)

38a

\<\<V\>\>	Ardorem mentis his cogor pandere verbis,
versus	Qui mentem mordet cordis secretaque torret
	Ut laticesque petit quos[a] ardor solis inurit
	Tangere sic pectus iam gestio temet[b] anhelus
5	Iam facio finem concludens ista sigillo.

38b

\<\<M\>\>	Nolis atque velis tibi corde manebo fidelis
	Celi regnator sit nobis hic mediator

---

36. a) This letter hinges on the difference between the intimate address *tu* (the singular form of "you") and the more respectful address *vos* (the plural form). Dronke uses *tu* and *vous* in his translation of this letter, *Women Writers*, p. 94. "Your Ladyship" is employed here to convey the force of *vos*.

37. a) Psalm 39.2.

36

<MAN>   To his lady, worthy of respect, her humble servant: his de-
voted service.

For this is how I must now address your ladyship:[a] no longer
saying you, but Madam, not "sweet" nor "dear" but "lady" because
I am not the confidant I was before and your ladyship is too much
a stranger to me.

37

<MAN>   To his only longing, he who longs longingly:[a] may you be
happy, but may you not wish to be happy without me.

I am your servant; my whole body, my whole spirit I direct towards you. When I do not see you, I do not feel that I see daylight.
Have pity on your beloved, wasting away and almost fading away,
unless you quickly come to help me. ..... Ask the messenger what
I did after I wrote this letter: there and then I threw myself onto
the bed out of impatience. Farewell.

38a

<<MAN>>   With these words I am compelled to disclose the burning of
                my mind,
             Which gnaws at my mind and scorches the secrets of my heart,
             Just as one parched by the heat of the sun seeks water,[a]
             So now do I, breathless, long to touch your breast and your
                very self.[b]
5   Now I shall close, signing this off with a seal.

38b

<<WOMAN>> Whether you wish it or not, in my heart I shall remain faithful to
                you.
             May the Ruler of Heaven mediate here between us,

---

38a-c.   a) quos MS, Könsgen, p. 65. Isidore relates *latex* (pl. *latices*) to water
         which hides (*lateat*) in the veins of the earth, *Etymologiae* 13.20.4;
         cf. V 26 and Psalm 41.2. b) temet Könsgen-Schaller) tumet MS. c) cf.
         M 3. d) Ovid, *Amores* 1.6.42. e) cf. V 2.

Sit socius fidei[c] que constat amore duali
Hos versus scribo tibi quos carissime dono
5   In quis perpendas quod sum tibi corde fidelis
Namque fides vera repetit bene facta priora.
His autem demptis datur hec pariter quoque ventis[d]
Ergo quicquid amet hec nobis semper inundet
Alma dei dextra te protegat intus et extra.

38c

<<V>>   Vite causa mei, tu clemens esto fideli
Cuncta mee vite quoniam spes permanet in te.
Diligo te tantum non possum dicere quantum
Hec michi lux nox est, sine te michi vivere mors est[e]
5   Sic valeas vivas sic cuncta nocentia vincas,
Ut volo ceu posco ceu totis viribus opto.

39

<<V>>   Dilecte sue super mel et favum dulci:[a] si quid dulcedinis ac-
cedere potest ei que plene totam possidet.
    Tu mea vita es, tu meum desiderium es. Vale.

40

<<V>>   Amice nobili ac multum amabili: precor mecum sis stabilis,
ut ego tecum volo.
    Tu mecum esto, meus animus esto, meum gaudium esto. Vale
ceraso pulcrior et dulcior.

41

<<V>>   Soli in quam mens et oculus inreflexos habet intuitus: quic-
quid meus tota animi et corporis directione valet conatus.

---

39. a) M 11 note a.

May He accompany our faith,[c] which stands firm in mutual love.

These verses which I give to you, dearest, I write
5   So you may perceive that in my heart I am faithful to you,
For true faith rightly looks back to previous actions.
But if these are removed, this faith is equally given to the winds.[d]
Therefore may whatever faith loves always flow over us.
And may the nurturing right hand of God protect you within and without.

38c

\<\<MAN\>\>   My reason for living: be kind to your faithful one,
Since all hope in my life resides in you.
I cannot say how much I love you.
Without you this light is night to me, and to live is death.[e]
5   May you be well, live, and overcome all harm
As much as I wish, ask, and pray with all my strength.

39

\<\<MAN\>\>   To his beloved, sweeter than honey and the honey-comb:[a] if anything at all sweet can come close to the one who possesses all sweetness in full.

You are my life, you are my desire. Farewell.

40

\<\<MAN\>\>   To a noble and very lovable friend: I beg you, be steadfast with me, as I want to be with you.

Be with me, be my spirit, be my joy. Farewell, sweeter and more beautiful than the cherry.

41

\<\<MAN\>\>   To the only one on whom my mind and my eyes hold their undeflected gaze: whatever the effort and application of my entire spirit and body can manage.

Ego preceptum in te non habeo, fac quod vis. Aliquid scribe duo saltem verba si potes. Vale.

42

<<V>>   Amate et semper amande[a] solitarius in tecto[b] merens et curis estuans: salutem quam velim tecum habere, et te sine me non habere.

..... Talis opposicio non amantis est, sed recedere volentis, occasiones frigidas querentis. Non olim in me talis eras, amiciciam ad calculum non vocabas.[c] Ego duricia tecum nequeo contendere, nimis enim in te mollis sum; meas accipe litteras, que tuas michi mittere gravaris. Dic ergo dulcissima quousque torquebor, quousque flammis estuantibus interius ardebo, et nullo dulcissimi sermonis tui refrigerio eas levabo? Multa dicenda supersunt. De die in diem magis in amore tuo ferveo, et tu frigescis. ..... Nil celes, nude dicas. Vale.

43

V   Lilio suo, non illi lilio quod marcescit, sed quod odorem mutare nescit, cor eius: quantum tota vi corporis et animi valet.

Sine dubio quicquid est suavitatis, in te natura transfudit, quia quocumque me verto nusquam aliquid suave nisi te solam reperio. Te ergo pre animo habens vivo, sencio, discerno, iocundor, omnium laborum obliviscor, ad omnia sum negocia fortior. In te igitur qui valeo, perpetuam tibi valitudinem opto vehementer. Vale, in animo me semper habe.

44

<<V>>   Integro gaudio suo quo dum careo vere exul et infortunatus sum: feliciter vivere, summe gaudere, si fas est ut sine me gaudeas.

Vale deum testor quod istud vale oculis stillantibus protuli.

---

42. a) cf. V *12*. b) Psalm 101.8: "I stay awake and have been made like a sparrow alone on the roof." c) Cicero, *Laelius* 58.

I have no instructions for you, do what you wish. Write anything, even a couple of words, if you can. Farewell.

42

\<\<MAN\>\> To one loved and forever to be loved,[a] he "who grieves alone on the roof"[b] and is consumed with troubles: well-being, which I want to have with you, and do not want you to have without me.

..... Such contentiousness is not that of a lover, but of one wanting to withdraw, of one looking for opportunities to be cold. Once you were not like this with me, you used not to call friendship to account.[c] I cannot contend with you in harshness, for I am too soft towards you. Take my letter, you who are unwilling to send me yours. So tell me, sweetest, for how long shall I be tortured, for how long shall I burn inside with blazing flames and not extinguish them with the refreshment of your sweetest speech? Much still remains to be said. Day after day I burn more for your love, while you grow cold. ..... Conceal nothing and speak openly. Farewell.

43

MAN To his lily, not the lily that withers but one that knows not how to change its scent, her heart: as much as he can manage with all the strength of his body and spirit.

Without doubt, nature has poured into you whatever is delightful, for wherever I turn, I find nothing of delight apart from you alone. And so, holding you before my spirit, I live, I feel, I observe, I enjoy, I forget all toils, and I am stronger in all my affairs. Therefore I who keep well through you, fervently pray for perpetual well-being for you. Farewell, and keep me in your heart always.

44

\<MAN\> To his entire joy, whose absence truly leaves me an exile and wretched: may you live happily and enjoy fully—if it is right for you to enjoy without me.

Farewell. God is my witness that I expressed this farewell through tear-filled eyes.

45

M   Cedrine domui sue,[a] eburnea statua, supra quam domus innititur tota:[b] nivis albedinem, lune fulgorem, solis candorem, stellarum splendorem, rosarum odorem, lilii pulcritudinem, balsamique suavitatem, terre fertilitatem, celi serenitatem, et quicquid in eorum dulcedinis comprehenditur ambitu.

Cithara cum timpano tibi serviat dulciter modulando. Si voluntatem meam amantissime consequeretur effectus, quicquid nunc per litteras, totum tecum per corporalem conferrem presenciam. ..... Te discedente tecum discessi spiritu et mente, nec aliud relictum fuit patrie, nisi corpus stolidum et inutile, et quantum longa tue discessionis absencia me cruciarit, illius solummodo novit sciencia qui cuiusque cordis rimatur secreta. Ut enim ardentis tempore Syrii area[c] siciens imbrem expectat e celo,[c] sic mens mea te desiderat merens et anxia. Nunc sit deo in celis gloria, michique gaudium in terra,[d] quod te quem super omnes diligo, vivere scio et valere. Nam quociens fortuna deposuit, tue dulcedinis consolacio me restituit. Tu vadis in rotis virtutum,[e] ideo michi longe preciosior es super aurum et topazium.[f] Non enim me magis possum negare tibi, quam Biblis Cauno, aut Oenone Paridi, vel Briseis Achilli.[g] ..... Quid plura? Tot mando tibi gaudia, quot habuit Antiphila recepto suo Clinia.[h] Ne tardes venire; quanto cicius veneris, tanto cicius invenies unde gaudebis. Vivas, valeas, ut Helye tempora cernas.[i] (f. 162r)

46

V   Desideratissime spei et tali bono, quo habito ulterius nichil desiderari possit: opto ut ego illi bono incorporari merear, quod cum tanta desidero impatiencia, quanta vix dici vel credi potest.

---

45. a) 2 Kings 7.2; 1 Chronicles 17.1 etc. b) cf. Song of Songs 7.4; Judith 16.29. c) area Könsgen, cf. Joel 1.20) ardea MS. d) cf. Luke 2.14. e) Könsgen (p. 23 n.9) suggests an allusion to Jerome, *Ep.* 52.13.3, in which the Ciceronian virtues of prudence, justice, moderation and courage are four wheels of the chariot of Christ. f) Psalm 118.127. g) Ovid, *Metamorphoses* 9.454–665; *Heroides,* 5 and 3. h) Clinia Könsgen (a character with Antiphila in Terence, *Heautontimorumenos*)) oluna MS. i) cf. Malachi 4.5; Ecclesiasticus 48.11.

45

WOMAN To the house of cedar,[a] the ivory statue on which the whole house rests:[b] the whiteness of snow, the gleam of the moon, the brightness of the sun, the splendor of the stars, the scent of roses, the beauty of lilies and the pleasantness of balsam, the fertility of the earth, the serenity of the sky, and whatever sweetness is contained within their compass.

Let the harp be at your service with the sweetly beating tambourine. If the result followed my wish, most beloved, all that I now convey by letter I would discuss with you in person. ..... After you left, I left with you in spirit and mind, and there was nothing left at home, except my stupid and useless body; and just how excruciating your long absence since you left has been for me is known only to the one who looks into the secrets of everyone's heart. For just as the thirsty land[c] of Syria longs during summer for rain from the sky, so does my mind, grieving and troubled, desire you. But glory to God in heaven and joy for me on earth,[d] for now I know that you whom I love more than any one are alive and well. For every time I am struck down by fortune, the solace of your sweetness restores me. You travel with the wheels of the virtues,[e] and for this reason you are far more precious to me than gold or topaz.[f] For I cannot deny myself to you any more than Byblis could to Caunus, or Oenone to Paris, or Briseis to Achilles.[g] ..... What more? I send you as many joys as Antiphila had when she welcomed back Clinia.[h] Do not delay in coming; the quicker you come, the quicker you will find cause for joy. Live and be well, that you may see the time of Elijah.[i]

46

MAN To my most desired hope and good so great that, once attained, nothing else can be desired: I pray that I may deserve to be incorporated into that good which I desire with an impatience such as can scarcely be expressed or believed.

Ego anime mi quantum litteris tuis delecter, quanta animi exultacione tuo in me amori velim occurrere, potius opere volo exhibere, quam verbis demonstrare. Videre te nimis desidero, pre desiderio tabesco. Vale anima mea formosa mea,[a] omne gaudium meum, qua nulla pulcrior meo iudicio, nulla melior.

47

<V>   Anime qua sub celo terra nichil protulit candidius, ille omnium hominum infelicissimus: ita omnem felicitatem sicut ipse qui optat, omni caret felicitate.

O noctem infaustam, o dormitationem odiosam, o execrabilem desidiam meam. Vale sola refectio mea, solus cibus meus, unica quies mea; ubicumque ego sum, tu veraciter es.

48

M   Amans amanti: amoris viriditatem.

Nemo debet vivere, nec in bono crescere, qui nescit diligere, et amores regere. Quid pluribus opus est verbis? Igne amoris tui succensa, te diligere volo per secula. Vale unica salus mea, et solum in mundo quod amem.

49

<M>   Rose immarcessibili beatudinis flore vernanti illa que te super omnes homines diligit: florendo crescere, et crescendo florere.

Nosti o maxima pars anime mee[a] multos multis se ex causis diligere, sed nullam eorum tam firmam fore amiciciam quam que ex probitate atque virtute,[b] et ex intima dilectione proveniat. Nam qui ob divicias vel voluptates sese diligere videntur,[c] eorum nullo-

---

46. a) Song of Songs 2.10. There may be a deliberate linking of *animus* (spirit) and *anima* (soul) to describe her.

49. a) Baudri of Bourgueil, *Carmina* 6.16. b) Cicero, *Laelius* 20. c) Cicero, *De officiis* 3.43; *Laelius* 20. d) Boethius, *De Arithmetica*, Praef. 3.8. e) Persius, *Satires* 1.106. The image of "nibbled nails" contrasts with the previous image of someone "learned to his finger-nails." f) Jerome, *Ep.* 48.3 or 125.6. g) cf. Boethius, *Consolation of Philoso-*

Just how much, my spirit, I am gladdened by your letter and with how much exultation of spirit I would like to meet your love for me, I would rather show through action than describe in words. I desire very much to see you and am wasting away because of this desire. Farewell, my soul, my beautiful one,[a] my every joy, than whom in my opinion no woman is more beautiful, no woman better.

47

<MAN> To his soul, brighter than anything which the earth has produced under the sun, he who is the unhappiest of all men: as much total happiness as he who makes this wish lacks all happiness.

Unlucky night, hateful sleep, cursed idleness of mine. Farewell, my only restoration, my only food, my one peace; wherever I am, truthfully you are.

48

WOMAN A lover to lover: the freshness of love.

No one ought to live, or grow in good, who does not know how to love, and rule his desires. What need is there for more words? Aflame with the fire of desire for you, I want to love you forever. Farewell, my one salvation and all that I love in the world.

49

<WOMAN> To the rose that does not wither, blooming with the flower of blessedness, she who loves you above all men: may you grow as you flourish and flourish as you grow.

You know, greatest part of my soul,[a] that many people love each other for many reasons, but no friendship of theirs will be as constant as that which stems from integrity and virtue,[b] and from deep love. For I do not consider the friendship of those who seem to

---

phy, Proem. 1.2. h) invenit erga MS) Könsgen (p. 66) inserts <inpulit> before invenit and changes erga to ergo. It is suggested here that inpulit should be inserted before licet and that it is not necessary to change erga to ergo. The sentence brings together three different kinds of love (caritas, dilectio, amor), to describe her friendship (amicicia) for her teacher. i) Virgil, Aeneid 1.233.

modo diuturnam arbitror amiciciam, cum res ipse propter quas diligunt, nullam videantur diuturnitatem habere. Quo fit, diviciis vel voluptate deficientibus eorum eciam deficiat simul et dilectio, qui non propter se res sed se propter res dilexerunt.

Sed mea dilectio, pacto longe tibi alio sociata est. Nec enim me ignava opum pondera, quibus nichil est ad nefas instructius, cum habendi sitis incanduit,[d] te diligere compulerunt, sed sola excellentissima virtus, penes quam omnis honestatis, tociusque prosperitatis causa consistit. Illa quidem est que sibi sufficiens, nullius indiga, cupiditates omnes refrenat, amores reprimit, gaudia temperat, dolores extirpat; que cuncta apta, cuncta placentia, cuncta jocundissima sumministrat nichilque se melius reperire valet. Habeo sane repertum in te, unde te diligam, summum scilicet atque omnium prestantissimum bonum. Quod cum constet esse eternum, est michi causa procul dubio, qua eterno maneas in mei dilectione. Crede igitur michi o desiderabilis non opes non dignitates non omnia que sectatores huius seculi concupiscunt, poterunt me a tui dilectione secernere. Non erit vere ulla dies qua mei meminisse valeam, que sine tui memoria possit a me transduci. Quin a te illud idem sperem, nullo me scias scrupulo permoveri.

Magne temeritatis est litteratorie tibi verba dirigere, quia cuique litteratissimo et ad unguem usque perducto, cui omnis disposicio artium per inveterata incrementa affectionum transivit in habitum, non sufficit tam floridum eloquencie vultum depingere, ut iure tanti magistri mereatur conspectui apparere, nedum michi que vix videor disposita ad queque levia, que demorsos ungues non sapiunt, nec pluteum cadunt:[e] magistro inquam tanto, magistro virtutibus, magistro moribus, cui jure cedit francigena cervicositas, et simul assurgit tocius mundi superciliositas, quilibet compositus qui sibi videtur sciolus,[f] suo prorsus judicio fiet elinguis et mutus.[g]

Unde sit michi credula benignitas tua, nisi scirem vere dilectionis indefectam amiciciam tibi insitam esse, impolitas tam rudis stili litteras non tibi mittere presumerem. Sed quia indefective caritatis dulcedinisque stimulus in tue dilectionis amorem me, licet eciam tibi foret ingratum, quod absit <inpulit>, invenit erga[h] te mee dilectionis fervens affectio, ut nunquam potest aliqua interveniente molestia perfecta excludi devocio. Qua de re si mea voluntas expleri potuisset, essent profecto iste pluresque littere tibi directe, ut tibi tantum scriberem si sic mea res exigeret, nec una die curarem stilum feriatum habere, quamvis te pigeat michi scribere.

Certe famem meam litterarum tuarum incepcione suscitasti, non pleniter adhuc exsaciasti. Cum enim more meo, intimo amicorum meorum tabescam desiderio, multum dolorem meum re-love each other for riches and pleasures[c] to be durable at all, since the very things on which they base their love seem to have no durability. Consequently, when their riches or pleasure runs out, so too at the same time love may fail, since they loved these things not because of each other but each other because of these things.

But my love is united with you by a completely different pact. And the useless burdens of wealth, more conducive to wrongdoing than anything when the thirst for possession begins to glow,[d] did not compel me to love you—only the highest virtue, in which lies the root of all honors and every success. Indeed, it is this virtue which is self-sufficient and in need of nothing else, which restrains passion, keeps desires in check, moderates joys and eradicates sorrows; which provides everything proper, everything pleasing, everything delightful; and than which nothing better can be found. Surely I have discovered in you—and thus I love you— undoubtedly the greatest and most outstanding good of all. Since it is established that this is eternal, it is for me the proof beyond doubt that you will remain in my love for eternity. Therefore believe me, desirable one, that neither wealth, distinctions, nor all the things that devotees of this world lust after, will be able to sever me from love for you. Truly there will never be a day in which I would be able to think of myself and let it pass without thinking of you. Know that I am not concerned by any doubt that I may hope the same thing from you.

It is very rash of me to send studied phrases to you, because even someone learned right down to his fingertips, who has transformed every artistic arrangement into habit through long-established practice, would not be capable of painting a portrait of eloquence florid enough to justly deserve being seen by so great a teacher (a teacher so great, I declare, a teacher of virtue, a teacher of character, to whom French pigheadedness rightly yields and for whom at the same time the haughtiness of the whole world rises in respect, that anyone who considers himself even slightly learned[f] would be rendered completely speechless and mute[g] by his own judgement), much less myself, who hardly seem adept at trifles "which neither taste of nibbled nails nor bang the desk."[e]

And so may your generosity trust me: unless I knew the unfailing friendship of true love to be implanted in you, I would not presume to send you inelegant letters of such unrefined style. But because the spur of tireless care and sweetness has driven me into a passion for loving you, although it might be unpleasing for you (heaven

frigeres, si eloquio prolixiore usus fuisses. Hoc tamen tantillum
caritative salutacionis compendium, accipio quasi angelum, atque
per horas singulas legens et relegens. Interdum eciam vice tua de-
osculans, operam do ut ferventissime aviditati mee satisfaciam.
Nichil enim hac in vita michi delectabilius esse existimes quam te
loqui, vel scribere, aut audire loquentem. Heret quippe cordi meo
illa tue scriptionis mellita (f. 162v) dulcedo, que dum recolo a tristicia ad gaudium, a merore vero ad hylaritatem deducit. Quo
verius deus scit nichil credi potest. Sed si forte minime credis, erit
ut estimo dies illa si deo placuerit, qua nichil verius te audivisse
fatebere. Cesset iam exclamacio, quia reddita est racio, qualiter
sit tenenda nostri dilectio.

versus   Sicut in axe poli nil est equabile soli
          Sic tibi consimilis meta non clauditur orbis.[1]
          Dum vivis valeas, post mortem gaudia sumas.

Ne amplius te fatigem sermone impexo, esto cure salvatori al-
tissimo; vale qui in tui recordacione omnes michi molestias ab-
stergis. Vale sine termino.

50

V Soli inter omnes etatis nostre puellas philosophie discipule, soli
in quam omnes virtutum multiplicium dotes integre fortuna con-
clusit, soli speciose, soli graciose, ille qui tuo munere etheriis
auris vescitur,[a] ille qui tunc solum vivit, cum tue certus est gracie:

---

50. a) Virgil, *Aeneid* 1.546. b) The man's first use of *dilectio* in the correspondence. c) cf. 1 Corinthians 13.4–5. d) Ovid, *Ponticae* 2.3.10.

forbid), the ardent feeling of my love for you[h] finds that complete devotion can never be hindered by any intervening difficulty. Therefore, if my will could have been fulfilled, certainly that letter and more would have been sent to you, so that I would write to you only if my situation demanded, nor would I care to give my pen a single day's holiday, even though it might annoy you to write to me.

At the beginning, you certainly aroused my hunger for your letters, and you have not yet fully satisfied it. For when, as is usual, I pine deep inside with longing for my friends, you could have relieved much sorrow if you had delivered a longer speech. Nevertheless I accept this tiny abridgment of a caring greeting as if it were an angel, reading and re-reading it every single hour. Sometimes even kissing it in place of you, I apply myself to satisfying my intense longing. For you might think that there is nothing in this life more delightful to me than to speak or write to you or to hear you speak—indeed, that honey-like sweetness of your writing clings to my heart and, whenever I think about it, leads me from sorrow to joy and even from grief to cheerfulness. God knows, nothing can be considered more true. Perhaps you scarcely believe it, but I believe the day will come—if it pleases God—when you will admit that you have never heard anything more true. But let my declaration come to an end, for I have given an account of how our love should be maintained.

> Just as in the axis of the pole nothing is equal to the sun[i]
> So the ends of the earth do not enclose anything like you.
> While you live, may you fare well, and after death taste joy.

Lest I wear you out any more with my unkempt words, may you be in the care of the supreme Savior; farewell, you who wipe away all troubles from me whenever I think of you. Farewell without end.

50

MAN To the only disciple of philosophy among all the young women of our age, the only one on whom fortune has completely bestowed all the gifts of the manifold virtues, the only attractive one, the only gracious one, he who through your gift is nourished by the upper air,[a] he who lives only when he is sure of your favor:

in ulteriora semper profectum, si proficere potest que ad summum pervenit.

..... Tuum admiror ingenium, que tam subtiliter de amicicie leg-
ibus argumentaris ut non Tullium legisse, sed ipsi Tullio precepta
dedisse videaris. Ut ergo ad respondendum veniam si responsio
jure vocari potest, ubi nichil par redditur, ut meo modo respon-
deam: verum dicis o omnium mulierum dulcissima, quod vere
talis dilectio[b] nos non colligavit, qualis solet colligare qui sua tantum querunt,[c] qui amiciciam questum faciunt, quorum fides cum
fortuna stat et cadit,[d] qui virtutem sui ipsius precium non putant,
qui amiciciam ad calculum vocant,[e] qui id quod ad se rediturum
sit,[f] sollicitis articulis supputant,[g] quibus demum sine lucro nichil
dulce est.[h]

Nos vere alio pacto, ne dixerim fortuna, immo deus[i] coniunxit;
ego te inter multa milia[j] ob innumeras virtutes tuas elegi: nullum
veraciter ob aliud commodum, nisi ut in te quiescerem, nisi ut omnium miseriarum michi lenimen esses, ut de terrenis bonis omnibus, sola tua venustas me reficeret et omnium dolorum oblivisci
faceret. Tu michi in fame saturitas, tu in siti refectio, tu in lassitu-
dine quies, tu in frigore calor, tu in calore umbraculum, tu demum
in omni intemperie saluberrima michi et vera temperies.

Tu eciam me ob aliquam fortasse bonam opinionem quam de
me habuisti, me in tuam noticiam vocare dignata es. Tibi multis
modis impar sum, et ut verius dicam omnibus modis impar sum,
quia in hoc eciam me excedis, ubi ego videbar excedere. Ingenium tuum, facundia tua, ultra etatem et sexum tuum iam virile in
robur se incipit extendere. Quid humilitas, quid omnibus con-
formis affabilitas tua! Quid in tanta dignitate admirabilis tempe-
rancia tua! Nonne te super omnes magnificant, nonne te in
excelso collocant? ut inde quasi de candelabro luceas et omnibus
spectabilis fias?[k] Ego credo et confidenter affirmo quod nemo sit
mortalium non cognatus non amicus, quem michi anteponas, et
ut audacius dicam quem michi conferas. Non enim plumbeus
sum,[l] non stipes sum, non corneum rostrum[m] habeo, ut acute non
olfaciam, ubi verus amor sit, et quis me ex corde diligat. Vale que

---

e) Cicero, *Laelius* 58. f) Ovid, *Ponticae* 2.13.17–18. g) supputant
Könsgen; cf. Ovid, *Ponticae* 2.3.18) suppetant MS. h) Terence,
Heautontimorumenos 234. i) Matthew 19.6; Mark 10.9. j) Song of
Songs 5.10. k) Matthew 5.15. l) Terence, *Heautontimoruemos* 877.
m) Corneum Könsgen) cornicum MS. Literally, "I have no horny
beak," meaning that he is not so insensitive that he cannot sense
where true love is.

may you advance ever further—if she who has reached the sum-
mit can advance any further.

. . . . . I admire your talent, you who discuss the rules of friendship so subtly that you seem not to have read Tully but to have
given those precepts to Tully himself! Therefore, so that I may
come to the reply, if it can rightly be called a reply when nothing
equal is given back, I shall reply in my own manner. What you say
is true, sweetest of all women, that truly such a love[b] does not
bind us as often binds those who seek only their own interests,[c]
who make friendship a source of profit, whose loyalty stands firm
or collapses with their fortunes,[d] who do not consider virtue to be
of value for its own sake,[e] who call friendship to account,[f] those
who with busy fingers keep count of what they ought to get back,[g]
for whom indeed nothing is sweet without profit.[h]

Truly we have been joined—I would not say by fortune but
rather by God[i]—under a different agreement. I chose you among
many thousands[j] because of your countless virtues: truthfully for
no other benefit than that I might rest in you, or that you might
lighten all my troubles, or that of all the good things in the world
only your charm might restore me and make me forget all sorrows.
You are my fill when hungry, my refreshment when thirsty, my rest
when weary, my warmth when cold, my shade when hot, indeed
in every storm you are my most wholesome and true calm.

Perhaps because of some good report you heard about me, you
also thought fit to invite me to make your acquaintance. I am inferior to you in many ways, or to speak more truthfully, I am inferior in every way, because you surpass me even where I seemed
to surpass you. Your talent, your command of language, beyond
your years and sex, is now beginning to extend itself into manly
strength. What humility, what affability you accord to everyone!
What admirable moderation with such dignity! Do not people esteem you more than everybody else, do they not set you up on
high, so that from there you can shine forth like a lamp and be observed by all?[k]

I believe and confidently assert that there is no mortal, no relative, no friend whom you would prefer to me, or to speak more
boldly, whom you would compare with me. For I am not leaden,[l] I
am not a blockhead, I am not so hard-nosed[m] that I cannot scent
acutely where true love exists and who loves me from the heart.
Farewell, you who make me fare well, and in whatever way I stand

me valere facis, et quomodo in gracia tua sim, certum me fac,
quia tua gracia mea sola festivitas est.

51

V   Anime sue toti et integro <gaudio>:[a] diem hanc felicem, et omne
tempus. Manda michi dulcissima quomodo te habeas quia sanus
esse non potero, nisi tua valitudo causam michi sanitatis prebeat.
Vale feliciter, donec iuga montis amabit aper.[b]

52

<V>   Lilio ligustrum: florere perpetuum.
     Quia mandatum domini non observamus, nisi dilectionem ad
invicem habeamus, oportet nos divine scripture obedire.[a] Vale,
donec tua valitudo michi tedio sit.

53

M   Sapiencie lumine per nobilitatis insignia mirabiliter prefulgenti,[a]
candentis lilii et vernantis rose similitudinem pretendenti, tocius
corporis juvenili flore vigenti, tocius expers pericie: omnia que
prospiciunt ad vere dilectionis profectum.
     De favo sapiencie si michi stillaret guttula scibilitatis,[b] aliqua
olenti nectare cum omni mentis conamine, alme dilectioni tue litterarum notulis conarer depingere. Ergo in omni latinitate non est
sermo inventus qui aperte loquatur erga te quam sit animus meus
intentus, quia deo teste cum sublimi et precipua dilectione te
diligo. Unde non est nec erit res vel sors que tuo amore me sepa-
ret nisi sola mors. Quapropter quotidianum michi inest
desiderium et optio, ut presentie tue reficiar refrigerio, et dies
michi mensis, septimana quoque videbitur annus, donec dulcissimus tue dilectionis appareat aspectus. ..... Cordi meo surgit et
virescit dolor tam magnus, ut in eius descriptione saltem nec in-

---

51. a) Könsgen (p. 30) notes that integro could be a mistake for integre,
    but opts for adding gaudio by analogy with V 2, 89 and 105. b) Vir-
    gil, Eclogues 5.76.
52. a) John 13.34.
53. a) Wisdom 6.23. b) cf. Abelard, Dialectica 1.2.3, ed. De Rijk, p. 85.

in your favor, make me certain, for your favor is my only enjoyment.

51

MAN To his whole soul and undivided joy:[a] may this day and every season be happy.

Write to me, sweetest, about how you are, because I shall not be able to be healthy unless your well-being provides a reason for my health. Fare well and be happy, for as long as the wild boar loves the mountain tops.[b]

52

<MAN> To the lily, the privet: may you flourish forever.

Given that we do not keep the Lord's commandment unless we love each other, it behoves us to obey divine scripture.[a] Farewell, until your well-being becomes tedious to me.

53

WOMAN To one shining wonderfully with the light of wisdom[a] through the signs of his nobility, spreading out in the likeness of the radiant lily and the blooming rose, flourishing with the youthful flower of his whole body, she who is totally devoid of skill: all things that provide for the advance of true love.

If a droplet of knowability[b] trickled down to me from the honeycomb of wisdom, I would try with every effort of my mind to portray in the jottings of my letter various things with a fragrant nectar for your nourishing love. But throughout all Latinity, no phrase has yet been found that speaks clearly about how intent on you is my spirit, for God is my witness that I love you with a sublime and exceptional love. And so there is not nor ever will be any event or circumstance, except only death, that will separate me from your love. For this reason every day there is in me the desire and wish that I may be restored by your soothing presence, and one day will seem a month to me and a week a year until that sweetest vision of your love appears. ..... So much pain sprouts and thrives in my heart that not even a whole year would suffice for its description.

teger sufficiat annus. Corpus autem meum contristatum est, animus a solita hilaritate mutatus. Vale. (f. 163r)

54

V Dilecte et semper diligende fidelissimus eius: ut amor noster finem non senciat et semper in melius convalescat.

Si tu o omnium rerum dulcissima de fide singularis[a] amici tui dubitares vel si ego de tua dilectione non essem certissimus, tunc ad commendacionem mutui amoris longiores littere querende, plura argumenta in patrocinium vocanda essent. Nunc quia sic amor invaluit, ut per se sine adiumento luceat, verbis minime opus est, quia in rebus abundantes sumus. Verumtamen non absurdum est si aliquando vel sic nos invicem visitemus et corporalis presencie littera locum suppleat, cum edax malorum hominum invidia, nos pro libito nostro iungi non patitur. Quid multa? sicut cum multis suspiriis frequenter exopto, deus omnipotens te michi incolumem diu conservet. ..... Abire permittamus, quos retinere non possumus. Bonum inde consilium erit.

55

M Viventium carissimo, et super vitam diligendo, intime devocionis amica: queque optima ex toto corde et anima.

Non te ignorare credo o meum dulce lumen quod nunquam superpositi cineres suffocant sopitum ignem,[a] et si prohibent lucere, tamen non vetabunt semper ardere. Ita nulla extrinsecus accidentia aliqua racione poterunt obsolere tui memoriale, quod cordi meo adnexui aureo vinculamine. Quid ultra? Deum enim testem habeo, quod vera et sincera dilectione te diligo. Vale maxima dulcedo mea.

56

V Super omne quod desiderari potest desiderabili unanimis amicus: quicquid boni singulariter amantibus servatum est.

---

54. a) cf. V 2, 4, 56.
55. a) Virgil, Aeneid 8.410.

My body too is sad, my spirit transformed from its usual cheerfulness. Farewell.

54

MAN To one loved and always to be loved, her most faithful: may our love not know an end and always recover for the better.

If you, sweetest of all things, doubted the faith of your particular[a] friend, or if I were not absolutely certain of your love, then a longer letter commending mutual love would be required, and more arguments in its defense called for. But now that our love has grown so strong that it shines forth by itself without help, there is little need for words because we are overflowing with what is real. Nevertheless it is not unreasonable if sometimes or now for example, we alternate between visiting each other and having a letter take the place of physical presence, when the consuming envy of evil men does not allow us to be united according to our desire. What more? Just as I often wish with many sighs, may almighty God keep you safe for me for a long time. ..... Let them go away, those whom we cannot hold back. It will be good advice.

55

WOMAN To the dearest of all living things, to be loved more than life itself, a deeply devoted friend: whatever is best from all my heart and soul.

I believe that you are not unaware, my sweet light, that ashes placed on a sleeping fire never put it out[a] and that, even if they prevent it from giving off light, they cannot keep it from burning for ever. And so not for any reason will external events be able to wipe out the thought of you, which I have bound to my heart with a chain of gold. What else? God is my witness that I love you with a true and sincere love. Farewell, my greatest sweetness.

56

MAN To one desirable over everything that can be desired, a friend of one mind with you: whatever good that is reserved specifically for lovers.

Sermo tuus super mel dulcis[a] sincerissime fidei planissime testis est. Quid dicam tibi dubius sum, quia tantum te amo quod amorem exprimere prout se habet non valeo. Ad hoc o summa vite mee requies, ad hoc inquam res devenit, ut excellentissimis meritis tuis nomen invenire non possim. Cum vales, nichil est quod me contristare possit. Cum egrotas, nichil est quod delectare possit. Si ergo vis dilecto tuo integre consulere, sana esto, tunc et ego sanus ero. Scit deus quem nichil latere potest quod cordi meo ita infra es, ut omnis cogitacio mea in te directa sit. Vale dulcissima non mulierum, immo generaliter omnium rerum.

57

M   Pulcherrimo ornamento suo, virtute, non forma eius amica: summe suavitatis plenitudinem.

Multum uti ipse nosti iam temporis fluxit, in quo nulla nos proh dolor familiaris confabulacio iunxit; scias tamen, quamvis tua presencia ad libitum meum uti nequeam, tamen nulla re impedi-ente, visibus internis te non cesso respicere, tuamque salutem et prosperitatem diligere. Vale dilectissime, et me meo erga te amore dilige.

58

<M>   Amico ut reor, illa olim pre ceteris in verbis dilecta, que im-merito nunc caret amoris privilegio: quod nec oculus visu per-cepit, nec in interiora cordis pertransiit.[a]

Valete,[b] onus meum propensius alleviate.

---

56. a) Ecclesiasticus 24.27.
58. a) 1 Cor 2.9. b) *Valete*, the formal plural (as in *36*), but never used previously by the woman, who always uses the intimate singular, *Vale*. A serious rift has taken place between letters 57 and 58.

Your speech, sweeter than honey,[a] is the clearest proof of your sincerest faith. I am not sure what I should say to you, because I love you so much that I cannot manage to express the extent of my love. The matter has come to such a point, greatest repose of my life, to such a point, I declare, that I cannot even find words for your outstanding virtues. When you are well, there is nothing that can make me sad. When you are ill, there is nothing that can make me happy. If therefore you wish to take full care of your beloved, keep well, and then I shall be well too. God, from whom nothing can be hidden, knows that you are so deep within my heart that my every thought is directed to you. Farewell, sweetest not of all women, but rather of all things in general.

57

WOMAN To her most beautiful ornament, in virtue not appearance, his friend: the fullness of greatest delight.

As you yourself know, much time has passed since we—sad to say—were last joined by any intimate conversation. Yet know that even though I am unable to enjoy your company as much as I would like, nothing can stop me from constantly seeing you with my mind's eye and yearning for your health and prosperity. Farewell, most beloved, and love me with the love I have for you.

58

<WOMAN> To a friend, so I believe, she who was once loved above all others with words, now unjustly deprived of the privilege of love: that which neither the eye has seen by sight nor has pierced the inside of the heart.[a]

Sir, farewell.[b] Lighten my burden more readily.

59

V Dilectissime sue supra omne quod est vel esse potest diligende: continuam salutem, et in omnibus bonis affluentissimos profectus.

Causa necessaria obstitit, que meo desiderio pedem sinistrum opposuit.[a] Ego nocens sum qui te peccare coegi.

60

M Hucusque fideliter adamato postmodum vinculo egri amoris non diligendo: tamen stabilitum vadimonium dilectionis et fidei.[a]

Magno caritatis pignore me tibi intimaveram quamdiu vera dilectio tua firma in radice pendebat; nam et omnem spem meam quasi turrim invictam[b] in te fundaveram. Nosti quoque si tantum dignaris, quod nunquam fui erga te duplici animo, nec esse volo. Nunc cogita et recogita hec et his similia. Ego vere semper pro te supportavi plurima satis plene et perfecte, nunquam possum scribere quam fortiter quam acriter te cepi diligere. Si necesse erat rumpi fedus[c] quod pepigeramus, quamvis in se multum amaritudinis contineat, tamen altera iam vice non frangetur. Clamor tuus recedat a me, verba tua ultra non audiam.[d] Nam unde michi profutura multa speravi bona, inde lacrimabilia cordis creverunt suspiria.

Omnipotens deus qui neminem vult perire qui supra paternum amorem diligit peccatores, illuminet cor tuum gracie sue splendore, et reducat ad viam salutis, ut cognoscas que sit voluntas eius beneplacens et perfecta.[e] Vale, sapiencia et sciencia tua me decepit,[f] propterea omnis nostra amodo pereat scriptura.

---

59. a) Ovid, *Ponticae* 4.6.7–8.
60. a) Three different notions of love are here arranged in a crescendo: *adamato* "to one fallen in love with;" *egri amoris* "infirm desire" or "infirm passionate love;" *vadimonium dilectionis* "guarantee of true love." b) Cf. Ps. 60.4 and Cassiodorus, *Expositio in Psalmos* 60.4, ed. Adriaen, CCSL 97 (1958): 539. c) on bond or covenant in scripture, Deuteronomy 5.2 and 29.1. d) Cf. Deuteronomy 18.16 (recalling the covenant made at Horeb). e) Romans 12.2. f) Isaiah 47.10.

59

MAN   To his most beloved, to be loved more than everything that is
or can be: continuous well-being and abundant success in everything good.

An unavoidable matter has intervened and put its left foot
against my desire.[a] I am guilty, I who compelled you to sin.

60

WOMAN   To one till now faithfully adored, hereafter not to be loved
with the chain of an ailing passion: the firm guarantee nonetheless
of love and faith.[a]

I had revealed myself to you with a great pledge of loving care
while your true love was founded on a firm root; for I had placed
all my hope in you, as though you were an invincible tower.[b] You
also know, if you will only grant this, that I have never been deceitful towards you, nor do I wish to be. Now consider and reflect
on these and other similar matters. I have truly always borne for
you a great many things fully enough and completely, and can
never express how strongly, how intensely I began to love you. If
it was necessary for the bond that we had established[c] to be broken, even though this might contain much bitterness, at least now
it will not be broken again. Take your complaints away from me, I
will not hear your words any more.[d] For where I expected many
good things to be of benefit to me, there emerged instead tearful
sighs of the heart.

May almighty God, who wants no one to perish and who loves
sinners with more than paternal love, illuminate your heart with
the splendor of His grace and bring you back to the road to salvation, so that you may understand that His will is favorable and
perfect.[e] Farewell; your wisdom and knowledge have deceived
me,[f] and therefore from now on may all our writing cease.

61

V   Domine sue amate et semper amande,[a] miserrimus amicus
eius, cuius vite et mortis nullum fere discrimen est: velis, nolis, incepte amicicie talem cursum qui ad finem non veniat.

Nescio quod meum peccatum[b] tam magnum precesserit, ut
tam brevi tempore omnem in me animum misericordie et famil-
iaritatis penitus abicere volueris. Necesse est enim alterum horum
fuisse, ut vel ego nimis in te peccaverim, vel tu parvum antehac
amorem habueris, quem tam facile, tam incuriose abieceris. Ego
nisi diligentius a te sum monitus, nullam (f. 163v) in te culpam
meam recognosco, nisi si culpam vocare vis, miserias suas et anx-
ietates apud eum deplorare, ubi remedium speratur consolacio
expectatur. ..... Non sunt hec dicta amici, non sunt verba eius qui
unquam ex corde benivolus fuerit, sed eius qui occasiones
querit,[c] eius inquam qui diu expectaverit, ut aliquid ad amoris
scissionem cause invenire potuerit. Quo facto, aut verbo, queso
te, tam contumeliosa verba provocavi? Tu semivivum me in
mediis fluctibus[d] involvisti, que vulneribus meis nova vulnera in-
flixisti, et dolorem doloribus addidisti. ..... Si me amares, minus locuta fuisses. Quemvis inter nos constituas judicem, et manifeste
convincam, te plus in me, quam me in te peccasse, et certe
quisquis verba tua diligencius consulit, reperiet ea non esse amantis, sed discidium querentis; nusquam in eis cor molle respicio,
sed pectus durum et amori inexpugnabile adverto.[e] ..... Verumtamen o anima mea sicca lacrimas tuas, quod tamen ego meas non
possum. Vale, cum lacrimis tuis scripta recepi, cum lacrimis mea
scripta remitto.

62

M   Dilecta dilecto: quicquid beatius apud deum, quicquid honestius atque jocundius apud homines esse potest.

Si inesset michi tanta sermonum facecia, ut verbis tuis pru-
denter respondere valerem, quantocunque decentius possem
libenti animo tibi responderem. At tamen licet satisfacere non

---

61. a) cf. M 7, V *12, 42, 54.* b) cf. V *59.* c) cf. V *42.* d) Exodus 14.27. e)
     Ovid, *Metamorphoses* 11.766–67.

61

MAN   To his lady, loved and always to be loved,[a] her most miserable friend, for whom there is scarcely any difference between life and death: whether you want it or not, a path for the friendship begun such as may never come to an end.

I do not know what so great sin[b] of mine preceded, that in such a short time you could wish to throw away completely all feeling of compassion and intimacy for me. For either one or the other of these must have been the case: that I have sinned against you excessively, or that you previously had little love, which you have thrown away so easily, so indifferently. For my part, unless enlightened by you more thoroughly, I admit no guilt of mine towards you except, if guilt you wish to call it, to lament one's misfortunes and troubles before the person from whom remedy is hoped for, consolation expected. ..... These are not the words of a friend, they are not the words of one who was always kind in her heart, but of one who looks for opportunities,[c] of one, I maintain, who for a long time has waited to be able to find some reason for a severing of love. By what action or word, I implore you, did I provoke such reproachful words? You have tossed me half dead into the midst of waves,[d] you who have inflicted new wounds on my wounds and added sorrow to my sorrows. ..... If you loved me, you would have said less. Whoever you appoint as judge between us, I will clearly prove that you have sinned against me more than I have against you. Certainly if anyone examined your words more thoroughly, he would find them to be not those of a lover but of one seeking estrangement. Nowhere in them do I detect a tender heart, but rather I perceive a cruel breast and one impregnable to love.[e] ..... Nevertheless dry your tears, my soul, though I cannot dry my own. Farewell. I received a message containing your tears; I return my message with tears.

62

WOMAN   Beloved to beloved: whatever there can be more blessed in God, whatever more honest and joyful among mortals.

If such cleverness of expression were within me that I could respond prudently to your words, I would reply to you however gracefully I could with a willing spirit. But nevertheless, although I am not capable of doing so satisfactorily, I shall reply as best I can

valeam, pro posse et modulo scienciole mee respondeo. Sic inter nos res agatur, ne et tu periculum, et ego scandalum incurram. O viri duritiam verum est proverbium illud quod vulgo dici solet, pietatem viri talo ligari.[a] Si vincula, si ferrum, si carceres, si cathenas, eciam si gladium pati debuisses,[b] sperabam te abstinere non potuisse, quin quoquo pacto ad me venires, et mecum de his que michi litteris mandasti, una voce presentialiter ageres.

Lacrimas ulterius nolo ab oculis tuis prorumpi, quia indecens est virum flere, cum honesti rigoris debeat in se severitatem tenere. Tempus est carissime ut has amaras atque flebiles descriptiones proiciamus, secundis autem et letioribus manus cere imprimamus. Ergo dilecte mi letum scribe, letum cane, prospere feliciterque vive; fere mei oblite dulcedo mea, quando te videbo? Saltem unam michi horam concede letam.

63

V   Dilectissime sue: quicquid inter unice amantes sincera poscit devocio.

..... In litteris quas misisti, mature fuerunt sentencie, racionalis et ordinata composicio; nunquam certe aptius vidi dispositas. Ego dulcissima multas horas deo volente tibi prestabo dulcissimas et letissimas. Vale, anime mi.

64

<V>   Dilectissime sue: salutem quam ego tibi presens afferre cupio.

Vale et vide ut nunquam lacrimas tuas videam, sed leta sis, certa de fide tui fidelis.

65

<V>   Anime sue, anima eius: in una anima diu unum esse.

---

62. a) A *talus* is an ankle-bone or die with four flat sides, made out of an ankle-bone. b) Hebrews 11.36.

and within the limits of my small learning. Let the matter between us be managed in such a way that neither you face danger nor I scandal. Harshness of man, how true is the proverb that people often say: "A man's integrity is tied to dice."[a] Even if you had had to suffer chains, irons, prison, shackles, even the sword,[b] I had hoped that you could not refrain from coming to me by whatever means to discuss those things about which you wrote to me in your letter, harmoniously with me in person.

I do not want to cause any further tears to flow from your eyes, because it is not proper for a man to cry, since a man of honorable firmness ought to be strict with himself. It is time, dearest, that we dispense with these bitter and tearful discussions; instead let us apply our hands to the wax for favorable and more cheerful ones. Therefore my beloved, write something cheerful, sing something cheerful, live prosperously and happily. You who have almost forgotten me, my sweet, when shall I see you? Allow at least one happy hour for me.

63

MAN To his most beloved: whatever sincere devotion demands of lovers alone.

..... The letter which you sent had a logical and orderly arrangement and contained mature judgements; certainly I have never seen anything more fittingly set out. God willing, I shall keep aside for you, sweetest, many very sweet and joyful hours. Farewell, my spirit.

64

<MAN> To his most beloved: greetings, which I want to convey to you in person.

Farewell, and see that I never see your tears, but that you be happy about the sure faith of your faithful one.

65

<MAN> To his soul, her soul: may we be one in one soul for a long time.

66

M	Omine felici ceptis assis, Clio, nostri,[a]
versus	Carmine sis comens tabulas et suavia promens.
	Mens vigila queso tali ditata patrono
	Organa cuncta Jovis flabris spirate secundis
5	En lux adventat, nox et discedere temptat
	En[b] lux advenit, nox et confusa recedit
	Ecce manus cleri splendescit luce magistri,
	Splendor doctoris noctem fugat <at>que[c] prioris.
	Muse qua causa laudes date voce sonora.
10	Concine prima Clio: "flos cleri semper aveto."
	Dic post Euterpe: "florens felicia carpe."
	Dicque Thalia: "vale, crescunt dum cornua lune."
	Annue Melpomene: "spirant dum frigora brume."
	Addeque Tersicore: "felix per secula salve."
15	Huic quoque Calliope rogo dulcia carmina prome.
	Dic Urania simul: "vivat virtutibus auctus."
	Moribus hunc ornes et honore Polimnia dones.
	Dic et nunc Erato: "felix sit corpore mundo.
	Felix sit mundo sed gaudens postque secundo
20	Quo sibimet grati gaudent sine fine beati."
	"Salve, vive, vige," cuncte resonate Camene.
	"Gaudia tot retine quot habent guttas maris unde.[c]
	Quotque virent herbe quot pisces sunt maris amne."
	Quid plus, quid dictem, pace fruatur, amen.

Vale spiraculum meum.

---

66. a) On Clio and the other Muses named in this poem, Fulgentius
Mythographus, *Mitologiarum* 1.15; see Könsgen, p. 67. Fulgentius
explains Clio as the thought of knowledge to be gained, Euterpe as
seeking knowledge, Thalia as capacity or of planting shoots,

66

WOMAN   Clio, assist my undertaking with an auspicious sign,[a]
Decorating tablets with song and uttering sweet things.
Mind, endowed by such a patron, please pay attention,
Every instrument, blow with the propitious breezes of Jove.
5   Lo, day approaches, and night tries to leave,
Lo,[b] day has come, and confounded night recedes,
See, the throng of the clergy shines with the light of the
    master,
And the teacher's splendor expels[c] his predecessor's night.
Therefore, Muses, give praises with sonorous voices.
10   Sing first, Clio: "Hail, flower of the clergy, forever."
Speak next, Euterpe: "Flourish and gather joys."
Speak, Thalia: "Be strong, for as long as the crescent moon
    grows."
Nod in agreement, Melpomene: "For as long as winter
    breathes cold."
And join in, Terpsicore: "Be well and happy forever."
15   For this also I ask, Calliope, "Utter sweet songs."
Speak also, Urania: "Let him live enriched with virtues."
Adorn him with courtesy and grant him honor, Polymnia.
And now speak, Erato: "May he be happy bodily in this world."
May he be happy in this world, but rejoicing afterwards in
    the next,
20   Where, each welcome to the other, the blessed rejoice for-
    ever.
"Be well, live, and thrive" echo together, Muses all.
"Hold on to as many joys as the waves of the ocean have
    drops,
As many as the grasses that grow, as many as the fish in the
    waters of the ocean."[d]
What more, what shall I compose? Let him enjoy peace.
Amen.

Farewell, my breath.

Melpomene as making meditation last, Terpsicore as delighting in instruction, Calliope as of the best voice, Urania as heavenly, Polymnia
as making deep memory, Erato as what is similar. b) En Könsgen) Et
MS c) fugat <at>que Könsgen) fugatque MS d) Ovid, *Ponticae* 2.7.28.

67

V Vale dulcissima mea, et tuam licenciam dilecto tuo concede. Vale et sencias de me, quod de te ipsa. Tu semper es meta ad quam tendo, tu cursus mei terminus et requies. Vale super omne quod dici potest amabile.

68

V Dulcissime dulcissimus: quicquid dulcius excogitari potest. Vale omnibus dulcior que dulcia esse noscuntur. Precor te obnixe ut michi mandes quomodo te habeas, quia tua prosperitas, est mea summa voluptas. Manda michi quando venire possim. Vale. (f. 164r)

69

M	Littera vade meas et amico ferte querelas,
versus	Dans ex parte mei verba salutis ei.
	Tu licet invitum converte precamur amicum
	Dic, quia pro merito non meritum capio,[a]
	Eius sermonis credula facta dolis.
	Sit memor illarum michi quas fudit lacrimarum
	Cum michi dicebat quod moriturus erat,
	Si tam formose non perfrueretur amore
10	Et tunc laudavit, quod modo vile facit.
	Dic ubi ploratus, ubi sint inquire, rogatus,
	Et pignus fidei quod dedit ultro michi.
	Cur tam raro venit? mea cur precordia ledit?
	Ah! Sic deludi non ego digna fui.
15	Hos rogo ne versus oculus legat invidiosus
	Hosque sciant nolo pectora plena dolo.

Qua dictaminis dulcedine te alloquar dilectissime mentis mee excedit valenciam, quia sicut cor humanum in medio sanguine principalem sedem elegit exultacionis, ita mens mea te sibi summum desiderium in omni genere proposuit dilectionis.

---

69. a) Könsgen judges a line or lines to be missing in the transcription between lines four and five. The fourth line is here translated as a continuation of the imperative verbs in lines one and three. b) Matthew 11.21. c) Jeremiah 14.17. d) cf. Psalm 44.6; Isaiah 5.28 etc.

67

MAN Farewell, my sweetest, and give your permission to your beloved. Farewell, and may you feel about me as you do about yourself. You are always the goal at which I aim, the end and repose of my journey. Farewell, more lovable than anything that can be named.

68

MAN To his sweetest, her sweetest: whatever sweeter thing that can be imagined.

Farewell, sweeter than everything known to be sweet. I earnestly beg you to tell me how you are, because your good fortune is my greatest pleasure. Tell me when I may come. Farewell.

69

WOMAN Go, letter, and take my complaints to a friend,
  Giving him words of greeting on my behalf.
Change this friend, I beg you, even if he be unwilling,
  Speak, because I do not receive my just reward,[a]
5
  I came to believe in the guile of his speech.
May he remember those tears, which he shed for me,
  When he told me that he would die
If he could not enjoy the love of one so beautiful.
10 Then he praised what he now deems worthless.
Say to him, where is the weeping? Ask him, where are the
    pleas
  And the pledge of faith which he gave me of his own accord?
Why does he come so rarely? why does he break my heart?
  Ah! I did not deserve to be so deceived.
15 Let not jealous eyes read these verses, I ask:
  I do not want hearts full of guile to know them.

With what sweetness of composition might I appeal to you, most beloved? It goes beyond the capacity of my mind, for just as the human heart chose the principal seat of its exultation at the center of the bloodstream, so my mind has set you up as its highest desire in every kind of love.

Anima mea incomparabili amore ad fontem visionis tue sitit, neque unquam beatam vitam sine te ducere valet. ..... Quot litteris hec eadem verba componuntur, tot doloris aculei cordi meo cum unda cruoris infiguntur. O pars pectoris mei quid fecisti? Miror quomodo ulla coactus vi a me tam subito mutari potuisses, quem tenaci dilectionis anchora in corde meo sigillavi. Idcirco cultrix cineris facta sum et cilicii[b] et per diem ac noctem lacrimas deducunt oculi mei.[c] Quid plura? Super omnia me acutissima doloris penetrat sagitta,[d] et durior permanebit adamante, quem suspiria mee non movent miserie. Vale in eternum et ultra, si fieri potest.

70

V Expectato desiderio suo et semper expectando: quicquid boni desiderari vel expectari potest.
    Vale.

71

M Dominica sentencia perterrita per quam dicitur: "difficile est contra stimulum calcitrare,"[a] has inornatas litteras tibi mitto, earum probans indicio quam devote in omnibus me tuis preceptis subicio. Multum distat ortus ab occidente,[b] sed fides rependitur fide per multa temporum spacia disiunctis, nec puncto distabit si eos vinculum vere dilectionis[c] concathenavit.[d] Quacunque enim morantur parte, anima tamen juncti erunt et mente. Multa habui loqui,[e] sed nimia mentis amaritudine[f] prepedior. Vellem ad horam tibi collaterari, et tecum confabulari; nam parva liceret[g] tristicia, sed plura cordis increscunt suspiria, dum studiosa mei laboris tempora, in te funditus perpendam neglecta. Unum autem de multis ago, te saluto vere pacis osculo. Vale, et licenciam eundi michi concede.

---

71. a) Acts 26.14, a proverb meaning that resistance is useless. b) Psalm 102.12. c) cf. Jerome, *Ep.* 55.11. d) cf. Romans 8.35. e) cf. John 8.26. f) Job 3.20, 7.20. g) liceret Könsgen) licere MS.

My soul thirsts with incomparable love for the source of your image, and it can never lead a happy life without you. . . . As many as the very letters which make up these words, so many are the stabs of pain driven into my heart with every surge of blood. Part of my heart, what have you done? I marvel at how, without any force of compulsion, you could be removed from me so quickly, you whom I have secured to my heart with the tenacious anchor of love. That is why I have taken to ashes and sackcloth,[b] and why night and day tears drop from my eyes.[c] What more? Above all, I am pierced by the sharpest arrow of pain,[d] and harder than steel would be the man who stands firm, unmoved by my sighs of misery. Farewell for eternity and beyond, if that is possible.

70

MAN   To his longed for desire, always to be longed for: whatever good thing that can be desired or longed for.
Farewell.

71

WOMAN   Terrified by the Lord's judgement, which says: "It is hard to kick against the goad,"[a] I send you this unadorned letter as proof of how devotedly I submit myself to your instructions in all matters. There is a great distance between East and West,[b] but faith is repaid with faith for those separated for long periods of time—yet not for one second will they be distant if the bond of true love[c] keeps them chained together.[d] For in whatever region they may linger, they will still be joined in soul and mind. I had many things to say,[e] but I am hindered by too much bitterness of mind;[f] for I would like to be next to you and be talking with you for an hour. Now some sadness might be acceptable,[g] but many sighs of the heart keep increasing when I consider that times set aside for my work are completely abandoned because of you. But of those many things I had to say, I do one: I greet you with a kiss of true peace. Farewell, and give me license to go.

72

V   Irate, et in ira misericordiam non deserenti, receptus in graciam: ut tamdiu feliciter vivas, donec ego gracia tua carere velim.

Sic amor noster immortalis erit si uterque nostrum felici et amabili concertacione preire laboret alterum, et neutri nostrum constet se ab altero superatum esse. Fit siquidem ut amicus in amando languescat, si se ab amico minus amari videat quam ipse promereatur. Nunquam ergo dixisse velim quod plus te amem, quam me amari sentiam, quia talis vox stulta est, et discidium parit. Immo hoc multo melius dictum recolligo, quod in mutuo amore inferior esse nolo, et uter nostrum alterum vincat dubito. ..... Quidam cum spinam pulcerrimos de se flores proferentem videret, "talis est" inquit "domina mea, qua nulla spina est asperior cum irascitur, nullus flos gratior vel nitidior cum placatur." ..... Vale et ut neminem mortalium michi compares, diligenter observa, quia ego in eadem circa te intencione tenaciter perseverabo. Salve dilectissima, et me semper tuum in memoria habe.

73

M   Salve et tu dilectissime, omni dulcedine digne.

> Flos juvenilis[a] ave, lux et decus imperiale,
>   Imperiale decus, flos juvenilis ave.
> Cum te plasmavit, sat te natura beavit:[b]
>   Viribus interius, laudibus exterius.
> 5 Forme splendorem, tantum dedit atque decorem,
>   Quantum vel nequeo dicere, vel stupeo.
> Plurima narrarem de te si crederet ullus,
>   Quod mea mens sentit de probitate tua.
> Nunc faciam finem licet et plus dicere possem:
> 10   Vivere gaudere, volo te minimeque dolere.
> Quot celo stelle, quot sunt et in orbe puelle,[c]
>   Quot maris undisone, tot tibi dico vale.

---

73. a) cf. M 1, 5, 21, 53. b) Marbod, *Carmen* 24, PL 171: 1660. c) Ovid, *Ars Amatoria* 1.56–59.

72

MAN   To one angered but not forsaking compassion in her anger, he
who is restored to favor: may you live happily until such time as I
might wish to be without your favor.

In this way will our love be immortal: if each of us strives to
outdo the other in a friendly and loving contest and if neither of
us agreed to be outdone by the other. Indeed, it happens that a
friend may grow weary of love if he sees himself loved by a friend
less than he deserves. Therefore I would never want to say that I
love you more than I feel loved, because such a statement is foolish and invites division. On the contrary, I hold this assertion to be
much better: that in a mutual love, I do not want to be the lesser,
and which of us surpasses the other, I do not know. ..... Someone
once said on seeing a thorn sprouting very beautiful flowers from
itself: "Such is my lady: no thorn is sharper when she is angry, no
flower more delightful or beautiful when she is pleased." .....
Farewell, and make sure that you compare no mortal with me, for
I will tenaciously persist with the same intention towards you.
Greetings, my most beloved, and keep me in your memory as forever yours.

73

WOMAN   Greetings to you too, most beloved, worthy of every delight!

> Flower of youth,[a] hail, light, and imperial glory,
>   Imperial glory, flower of youth, hail.
> When she formed you, nature blessed you well enough:[b]
>   Internally with strength, externally with acclaim.
> 5   To your form she gave such splendor and beauty
>   That either I cannot describe or am struck dumb.
> Much more could I say of you, if anyone would believe
>   What my mind feels about your worth.
> Now I shall end, although I could still say more:
> 10   I want you to live, enjoy and suffer little.
> As many as the stars in the sky, as young women in the world,[c]
>   As roaring waves over the sea—so many times do I bid you
>   farewell.

74

V   Nunc demum intelligo dulcissima quod ex toto corde et ex tota anima mea es,[a] cum oblivisci vis omnis iniurie, quam ego stultus et improvidus mente nimis precipiti, et nimium molli ad resistendum doloribus sine omni deliberacione dilectissime mee intuli. (f. 164v) Vox illa cassa fuerit, nichil significans, nichil habens ponderis; et tu anime mi si verba cum factis velis conferre: verba illa vere tantum fuerunt, que nullo opere claruerunt. De valetudine mea requiris? Si tu vales, ego valeo, si gaudes gaudeo, ad omnes demum fortunas tuas me coaptare volo. Vale anime mi.

75

V   Unice suavitati sue: quicquid in vita suavissimum reperiri potest. ..... O stulta promissio, o vox nimium preceps et temeraria, o dictum hominis, qui vel amens vel ebrius aperte videatur. Quis enim tanta sciencia plenus tam labiis circumcisus,[a] tam magnum de se audeat promittere? Pretermitto huius temporis litteratos. Si ipse Tullius de se tale aliquid iactasset, vere copiosa eius facundia in solvendo deficeret, quia nichil tanta promissione dignum afferet. Si ad metrum totas Ovidius vires suas intenderet, in hoc incepto planissime deficeret. Quis ergo sum ego aut que in me facultas, ut tales litteras dictare queam que me aureo sinu tuo, eburneis brachiis tuis,[b] lactea cervice tua[c] dignum exhibeant?

Verba omitto que ventis[d] similia sunt: quis labor, quod opus, tanti sit, ut tam admirandam suavitatem sufficienter mercari possit? Si mare in spe talis boni transeam, exiguus labor est, si Alpes in asperrimo frigore transcendam, vel si de medio igne, cum vite discrimine te petam, in omnibus his nichil fecisse videbor. Rogo igitur suppliciter graciam tuam, ut litteras istas secundum promissa mea non metiaris, ne in proverbium illud incidam: "Parturient montes nascetur ridiculus mus,"[e] quia tam superbo promisso nichil dignum affero.[f] .....

---

74. a) cf. Deuteronomy 6.5; Matthew 22.37.
75. a) cf. M 23. b) Ovid, *Amores* 3.7.7. c) Virgil, *Aeneid* 10.137. d) Ovid, *Amores* 2.19.19. e) Horace, *Ars poetica* 139. f) Horace, *Ars poetica* 138. g) Song of Songs 2.10. h) Horace, *Ars poetica* 389–90. i) Ovid, *Ars amatoria* 2.511. j) cf. Ovid, *Metamorphoses* 4.64.

74

MAN Now at last I understand, sweetest, that you are mine with all
your heart and all your soul,[a] since you are willing to forget all the
wrongs which I, stupidly and thoughtlessly and with a mind too im-
petuous and too weak to resist my sorrows, inflicted on my most
beloved without any consideration. That remark was empty; it
meant nothing and had no weight; and you, my spirit, if you wish
to compare words with deeds, will see that truly they were only
words, not backed up by any action. You ask about my health? If
you are well, I am well, if you are happy, I am happy; in fact, I want
to attach myself to your every fortune. Farewell, my spirit.

75

MAN To his only delight: whatever is the most delightful thing in life
which can be found.
     . . . So foolish a promise, words too impetuous and ill consid-
ered, a remark made by one apparently out of his mind or drunk.
For who is filled with such knowledge and is so refined in speech[a]
as to dare promise such a great thing from himself? Never mind
the educated people of our own time: if Cicero had made such a
claim about himself, even his abundant eloquence would fail to
deliver, for nothing worthy of such a promise would emerge. If
Ovid had focused all his energies on his meter, he would very
clearly have failed in this undertaking. Therefore who am I or what
quality is there in me that I could compose such a letter which
would prove me worthy of your golden breast, your ivory arms,[b]
your milk-white neck?[c]
     I give up on words, which are like the winds;[d] what effort, what
action is great enough to be sufficient to buy such wonderful delight? If I were to cross the sea in the hope of such good, it would
be but little effort; if I were to climb the Alps in the bitterest cold
or search for you in the midst of fire and risk my life, in all this I
would deem that I had done nothing. Therefore, I humbly beg for
your favor and ask that you do not measure that letter according
to my promises, lest the proverb "Mountains will be in labor, but
will give birth to a laughable mouse"[e] should apply to me, because
after such a proud promise I produce nothing of worth.[f] . . .

Aliquanto iam tempore formosa mea[g] de fide dilectissimi tui du-
bitasti propter quedam verba, que subita impulsus contumelia, in
ipso doloris cursu dictavi, et utinam non dictassem, quia tu nimis
ea memoriter signasti, que rogo ut a corde deleas, et apud interi-
ora tua radicem non figant, sicut ego ea deo teste nunquam fixi,
sed ubi ea a manibus dimisi, statim revocare volui, si vox emissa
reverti nosset.[h]

Idem tibi sum qui fueram; noli verba sed facta consulere. Non
michi vetus es; quotidie cordi meo innovaris, sicut anni iocunda
temperies, equaliter semper ingruente vere, nova est. Tempus
ipsum nobis sua commoditate blanditur, temporis oportunitate
fruamur. Sapienter amare poterimus, quod tamen rarum est, cum
quidam dixerit: "quis unquam sapienter amavit?"[i] Nos vere sapienter amare poterimus, quia et fame nostre sollerter consulemus,
et tamen gaudia nostra cum summa suavitate miscebimus. Ille
ignis fortius estuat qui tegitur, quam ille cui exundare conceditur.[j]
Vale amabilis delectacio mea.

76

M   Cunctorum vinculo amoris[a] alligantium carissimo certe sodali-
tatis amica: integerrime dilectionis summam.

Quam intime carus michi sis, plene nullatenus denudare valet
scribentis manus, quia interne dulcedinis me hortatur affectus, ut
sis michi pre cunctis specialis[b] dilectus. Quantus igitur erga te
meus ardeat affectus, ullo modo tibi manifestare nequeo. ..... Vere
fateor dilectissime quod multociens ut pecus ignavum[c] via sub-
sisterem, nisi magisterialis institucionis tui sollercia, me prono di-
gressam assidue revocaret tramite. "Nunc autem claudamus rivos
sat prata biberunt."[d] Decrevit hoc mea intencio ut cesset ultro al-
terna contencio; satis iam dire iactis mutuo sermonibus intu-
muere ire.[e] ..... Quid prolixis moror ambagibus? Unius michi
peticionis annuas effectum: ut scilicet me animam tuam tali nunquam ambiguitate inquietare presumas. Vale mi stella clara, sydus
aureum, gemma virtutum, corpori meo dulce medicamentum.

76. a) cf. M 60, 71. b) cf. M 21, 25. c) Virgil, *Georgics* 4.168. d) Virgil,
Eclogues 3.111. e) Statius, *Thebaid* 1.411–12.

For some time now, my beautiful one,[g] you have doubted the faith of your beloved because of certain words which I wrote, provoked by an unexpected reproach, while in the very throes of sorrow. Would that I had never written them—for you engraved them into your memory too much. I ask that you erase them from your heart and not let them establish roots inside you; just as, God knows, I never let them, but rather after they had left my hands, I immediately wanted to call them back—if only an uttered remark knew how to return.[h]

I am the same towards you as I was; look not to words but deeds. You are not outmoded to me, but each day are renewed in my heart, just as the pleasant period of the year is always and equally renewed by the coming of spring. The season itself favors us with its compliance, let us enjoy the opportunities of the season. We shall be able to love wisely, which admittedly is rare; for as someone once said: "Who ever loved wisely?"[i] But we shall be able to love wisely, because we shall shrewdly look out for our reputation while mixing our joys with the greatest delight. The fire which is sheltered burns more strongly than one left to burn freely.[j] Farewell, my lovable delight.

76

WOMAN To the chain of love,[a] of all that binds the dearest, a friend of sure companionship: fulfilment of the most complete love.

Just how intimately dear you are to me, the hand of this writer is in no way able to fully reveal, because a feeling of inner sweetness urges me to make you my special[b] beloved above everyone else. And so I am unable to reveal to you in any way at all just how greatly my feeling burns for you. ..... Truly I admit, most beloved, that many times I would have halted like an idle sheep[c] along the way, if the masterly skill of your instruction had not kept calling me back as I strayed from the proper path. "But now let us block the streams, the fields have drunk enough."[d] My intention has decided this: that further conflict between us should cease. Dreadful anger has already swelled enough with words thrown at each other.[e] ..... Why do I linger with long-winded ramblings? May you grant the fulfilment of one of my requests; namely, that you never think that I am troubling your soul with such uncertainty. Farewell, my bright star, golden constellation, jewel of virtues, sweet medicine for my body.

77

V   Gaudio suo: gaudium et leticiam.

Quid dicam tibi dulcissima nisi quod sepe dixi? Toto te pectore gero. Interioribus ulnis[a] te amplector, dulcedinem tuam quo plus haurio plus sitio. Omnes copie mee in te unam se congesserunt, omne quod possum tuum est. Ut ergo operas mutuas demus, tu es ego, et ego sum tu.[b] Hoc dixisse satis sit. Vale, protegat te valida manus omnipotentis dei.

78

<V>   Ille sollicite scribat qui non habet, ut quod non habet reperiat.[a] Ego securus sum, ego navigando ad portum veni; qui naufragium patitur vota faciat; ego in portu sedeo, et ideo votis non egeo. Vale.

79

M   Merito specialis dilectionis amplectendo amore, incendium tui amoris: quot ameno tempore redolent flores, tot percipere salutes.

Si grande aliquid meditando concipit hominis interioris intencio,[a] profecto interdum non consumitur sine quadam vi exterioris. Aut enim perficiendi desperacio confundit aut priusquam perficiat nimietas laboris graviter contundit. Unde fit, ut utriusque hominis labor vel studium in se videatur (f. 165r) plerumque deficere, cum ad votum quod cupit non potest pervenire.

Ego tamdiu tractavi cordis et corporis flagranti nisu, qualiter te o gemma decora appellarem, sed intencionem mei affectus hucusque distulit difficultas suspecti defectus. Scio enim et fateor pro singulis quibusque tuis beneficiis quod grates persolvere nullatenus sufficio animi vel corporis officio. Verumtamen pro uno quod auro et topazio[b] preciosius duco, quamdiu hic spiritus in corpore viget, tue dilectioni nunquam scribere piget. Nam quan-

---

77. a) Ovid, *Metamorphoses* 8.818, 11.63. b) Plautus, *Stich.* 731.
78. a) cf. Matthew 25.29; Mark 4.25; Luke 19.26.
79. a) cf. Ephesians 3.16. b) Psalm 118.127. c) Psalm 44.16. d) 1 Corinthians 9.22.

77

MAN   To his joy: joy and happiness.

What shall I say to you, sweetest, except that which I have often said? I hold you with my entire breast. I embrace you with inner arms,[a] and the more I drink of your sweetness, the more I thirst. All my resources have been gathered around you alone; everything that I can do is yours. Therefore, to care for each other, you are me and I am you.[b] May it be enough to have said this. Farewell, may the strong hand of almighty God protect you.

78

<MAN>   Let the man who has not, write anxiously, so that he may recover what he does not have.[a] I myself am safe, I have come sailing into port. He who has been shipwrecked, let him make offerings. I am settled in port and therefore have no need for offerings. Farewell.

79

WOMAN   To one deserving to be embraced with the longing of a special love, a fire of longing for you: may you gather as many greetings as flowers give perfume in the season of delight.

If through reflection a person's inner intention[a] conceives anything great, it is often not brought to fruition without a certain external force. For either it is confounded by despair of ever being completed or it is severely crushed by too much effort before it is completed. As a result, in either case the effort or endeavor itself seems very often to fail when the desired goal cannot be reached.

For a long time, and with a blazing struggle of heart and body, I have considered how I should address you, my graceful jewel, but the difficulty of expected failure has so far defied the intention of my feeling. For I know and confess that I am in no way adequate to render thanks for each and every one of your benefits, through the service of either spirit or body. Except for one way, which I hold more precious than gold or topaz:[b] for as long as this breath thrives in its body, it will never be a burden to write to your love. For no description in a letter or expression of will can reveal the

tum leticie et exultacionis[c] tua mellita michi conferat dilectio, non pandit ulla litterarum descriptio sive voluntatis confessio.

Tuus honor meum geminasse videretur si usque ad finem fatalem nos conversari liceret pariter. Nunc autem satius eligo mortis terminari periculo, quam vivens dulcifluo tui aspectus privari gaudio. ..... Cum omnia factus sis michi[d] excepta solius dei gracia, nil amplius desiderare michi necesse est per durantia seculi spacia, nisi ut vite tue dies augeat ille, qui ut unum eque facile prestare potest et mille.

80

V   Hiberno sole gratiori, et estiva umbra dulciori,[a] ille qui familiarius calore tuo uritur et suavi spiritu leniter reficitur: ut suaviter vivas, nichil nisi quod dulce est experiaris.

Si esurio, tu sola me saturas, si sitio, sola me reficis. Sed quid dixi? Immo reficis et non saturas. Nunquam tui satur fui, ut puto nec ero. Vive in leticia, que nunquam tibi desit. Vale.

81

M   Dilectissimo meo, et ut verum fatear in amore peritissimo, cui non satis ad plenum gracias agere valeo: tamen laudes omnium rerum tibi simul famulantium et tocius pulcritudinis ascribo.

Vale tu, et illi pereant qui nos disiungere temptant.

82

\<M\>	Quam michimet vellem mitti tibi mitto salutem.
versus	Nescio quod magis hac esse salubre queat.
	Si quicquid Cesar unquam possedit haberem,
	Prodessent tante nil michi divitie.[a]
5	
	Gaudia non unquam te nisi dante feram,

---

80. a) Ovid, *Metamorphoses* 13.793.
82. a) cf. Marbod, *Rescriptum ad amicam*, ed. Bulst (1984), p. 185. Dronke also discusses this poem in *Women Writers*, pp. 96–97. Köns-

amount of joy and exultation[c] which your honey-sweet love bestows on me.

Your glory might seem to have doubled mine had we been equally allowed to remain together right to the ordained end. But now I prefer to be confined by the threat of death rather than live and be deprived of the sweet-flowing joy of the sight of you. ..... Since you have become everything to me,[d] except for the grace of God alone, it is not necessary for me to wish for anything more for the span of centuries to come; except that He who can just as easily grant one day as he can a thousand, increase the days of your life.

80

MAN   To one more pleasing than winter sun and sweeter than summer shade,[a] he who burns more intimately by your heat and is gently refreshed by your delightful breath: may you live delightfully and not experience anything except what is sweet.

If I am hungry, only you fill me; if I am thirsty, only you refresh me. But what have I said? Indeed you refresh me, but you certainly do not fill me. I have never had enough of you, nor do I think I ever will. Live in happiness which may never fail you. Farewell.

81

WOMAN   To my very beloved, and to confess the truth, very skilled in love, to whom I am incapable of giving thanks fully enough: nevertheless I assign to you praises of everything both useful and totally beautiful.

May you fare well, and may those who try to separate us perish.

82

<WOMAN>   I send you the salutation which I would like sent to me.
         I know of nothing more salutary than this.
         If I could have all that Caesar ever owned,
         Such wealth would be of no use to me.[a]

5
         I will never have joys except those given by you,

---

gen interprets the metrical irregularity as indicating that the scribe missed out line 5. She seems to be contrasting the passing pleasures

Et dolor et luctus nos tempus in omne secuntur
Ni dederis michi res nulla salubris erit.
De rebus cunctis quas totus continet orbis[b]
10   Denique semper eris gloria sola michi
Suppositi terre lapides velut igne liquescunt
Cum quibus imposita liquitur igne pyra
Sic nostrum late corpus vanescit amore
Sicque vale vive per tempora longa Sibille.[c]
15   Vincas ut metas habuit quas Nestoris etas.

Miserere mei quia vere coartor dilectione tui. Vale.

83

<M>   Dies ista feliciter orta sit tibi, feliciter currat tibi, feliciter occidat tibi. Quid plura? Condicione pari per me te noris amari. Vale, tu vitro es lucidior, et calibe fortior.

84

M   Amans amanti: gaudium cum salute optanti illud dico salutare quod non finiatur, et gaudium quod a te non tollatur per evum.

Post mutuam nostre visionis allocucionisque noticiam, tu solus michi placebas[a] supra omnem dei creaturam, teque solum dilexi, diligendo quesivi, querendo inveni, inveniendo amavi, amando optavi, optando omnibus in corde meo preposui, teque solum elegi ex milibus, ut facerem tecum pignus;[b] quo pignore peracto, dulcedinisque tue melle gustato, sperabam me curis finem posuisse futuris. ..... Nemorum umbrosa diligunt volucres, in aquarum rivulis latent pisces, cervi ascendunt montana,[c] ego te diligo mente stabili et integra. Hactenus mecum mansisti, mecum viriliter bonum certamen certasti, sed nondum bravium accepisti.[d] ..... Si fides illius titubat, vinculumque eius dilectionis non firmiter se continet,[e] in quem omnem spem meam, fiduci-

---

provided by wealth with the joys she receives from him. b) Ovid, *Metamorphoses* 7.59. c) Ovid, *Metamorphoses* 14.132–53.
84. a) Ovid, *Ars amatoria* 1.42. b) Song of Songs 5.10. c) Cf. Psalm 103.18. d) a fusion of 1 Timothy 6.12, 2 Timothy 4.7, 1 Corinthians 9.24. e) continet Könsgen (p. 66)] contineat MS.

And grief and sorrow follow us through every season.
Unless you give it, nothing will be salutary to me.
Of all things which the entire world contains,[b]
10   You will in the end be my only glory forever.
As stones placed on the ground dissolve in fire,
When the pyre set over them dissolves in fire too,
So our body completely vanishes in love.
And so fare well, live the long life of the Sybil.[c]
15   May you accrue and surpass the years that Nestor lived.

Pity me, for I am truly constrained by love for you. Farewell.

83

<Woman>   May this day dawn happily for you, may it pass by happily
for you, may it close happily for you. What more? You know that
you are loved in the same manner by me. Farewell; you are clearer
than glass and stronger than steel.

84

Woman   A lover to a lover: joy with well-being for one desiring that
saving joy, I declare, never ending and never to be taken away
from you.

Ever since we first met and spoke to each other, only you have
pleased me[a] above all God's creatures and only you have I loved.
Through loving you, I searched for you; searching for you, I found
you; finding you, I desired you; desiring you, I chose you; choosing you, I placed you before everyone else in my heart, and picked
you alone out of thousands, in order to make a pledge with you.[b]
With that pledge fulfilled and having tasted the honey of your
sweetness, I hoped to put an end to future cares. ..... Birds love
the shady parts of the woods, fish hide in streams of water, stags
climb mountains,[c] I love you with a steadfast and whole mind.
Thus far you have remained with me, you have manfully fought the
good fight with me, but you have not yet received the prize.[d] .....
If the faith falters of the one in whom I had placed—and still
keep—all my hope and trust, and if the chain of his love should

amque positam habui, et habeo, cui postea credere possim prorsus ignoro.

Velis, nolis, semper meus es et eris, nunquam erga te meum mutatur votum neque a te animum abstraho totum. In te quod quesivi habeo, quod optavi teneo, quod amavi amplexata sum, tui solius conveniunt mores, te nisi mors michi adimet nemo, quia pro te mori non differo. Vale, et in continuis horis memento nostre dilectionis. Prologum tuum quem composuisti michi, cum graciarum actione, cum amoris servitute recompensabo tibi. Cor tibi letetur; desit quod triste vocetur.

85

V Si in eodem corpore ulla potest esse alteritas, vel divisio, tunc divise a se optime parti sui corporis: indivisam dilectionem, incorruptam, et integram, et interminabilem vivacissimi amoris dulcedinem.

Si verba dilecti tui notare perspicaciter velis, aperte notare (f. 165v) potes dulcissima quod plus volo, quam possim, quod verba querendo deficio, quia ita usitatum modum superexcellit affectio mea, ut usitatis verbis exprimi nullomodo ad plenum possit. Si aliqua in me notatur segnicies, si aliquis perpenditur defectus, utique defectus est non in amore frigescentis, sed pre nimia mentis alienatione, quid dignum dicat dubitantis, multa volentis, et minus facientis. Nec dignum est ut verba sufficienter recompensent, quod tu in rebus beneficium prestas.

Si quicquid mundus habet preciosius in unum congeratur,[a] tuis beneficiis collatum omnimodo sordescat, nullius estimari queat. Tanta est suavitas tua, tam mirabilis continuitas tua, tam ineffabilis demum eloquii habitus, et omnium que circa te aguntur pulcritudo et gracia, ut si quis hec verbis equiparare presumat, magna videatur contumacia. Ignis noster novis semper crescat alimentis, quo magis tegitur magis exestuet,[b] invidos et insidiantes decipiat, et semper in dubio servetur, uter nostrum magis alterum diligat, quia ita semper pulcerrima inter nos erit concertacio ut uterque vincat.[c] Vale.

---

85. a) cf. V 12. b) exestuet Könsgen (p. 66)) exestuat MS. c) cf. V 72.

not firmly hold fast,[e] I have no idea at all in whom else I can sub-sequently believe.

Like it or not, you are mine and always shall be. Never shall my desire for you be altered, nor will I ever take back my whole spirit from you. In you I have what I searched for, I hold what I chose, I embrace what I desired; only your qualities will do. Nobody—ex-cept Death—will ever take you from me, because I would not hes-itate to die for you. Farewell and remember our love hour after hour. I shall repay you for your Prologue, which you composed for me, with an act of thanks and the obedience of love. Let your heart be glad; begone whatever may be called sad.

85

MAN   If there can be any alterity or division in the same body, then, to the best part of his body, parted from him: undivided love, un-corrupted and whole, and endless sweetness of the most vigorous love.

If you wish to note closely the words of your beloved, sweetest, you can clearly note that I want to say more than I am able, that I fail when searching for words, because so much does my feeling exceed ordinary measure that in no way can it be fully rendered by ordinary words. If you note any slowness in me, or perceive any weakness, it is certainly not the weakness of one growing cold in love, but the result of too much mental distraction of one unsure of what he should rightly say, of one wanting much but doing less. Nor is it appropriate that words should suffice to repay the bene-fits you provide through actions.

If whatever the world considers precious were gathered up together,[a] compared with your benefits they would be utterly worthless and they would be deemed to have no value. Such is your amiability, so marvelous your constancy, so indescribable even your way with words and the beauty and grace of everything that surrounds you, that it would seem great arrogance if one pre-sumed to match them with words. May our flame always increase with new nourishment, may its blaze[b] be greater the more it is cov-ered, may it defy the envious and those who wait in ambush, and may it always be kept uncertain which of us loves the other more, since this way there will always be between us a most beautiful contest in which both of us will win.[c] Farewell.

86

M   Inepotabili fonti dulcedinis, pars anime eius individua: post sollicitudinem Marthe, et fecunditatem Lie, possidere optimam
partem Marie.[a]

Immensa vis tui amoris, indesinenter, incessanter, indubitan-
ter, inenarrabiliter permanens in statu sui tenoris, secundum
posse meum ac nosse, me cogit pauca ad te dilectissimum
scribere. Sed quid potissimum eloquar prorsus ignoro; tociens me
verbis tuis dulcissimis prevenis, tociens michi tue intime, et sincere dilectionis affectum ostendis, ut absque omni ambiguitate
amor et desiderium tui semper in me ardescat, et nunquam re-
frigescat.

O si nutu dei acciperem volucris speciem quantocius volando
te visitarem.[b] ..... Id enim quod nunc optavi, si salva gracia dei
posset fieri: deo teste cui difficile est verba dare fallacie, nichil est
in omni orbe terrarum quod maius optarem. Impinguat me affectus tuus, sed non potest me implere amor tuus. In tua vita est
salus mea, tu es totum desiderium meum, et omne bonum meum.
Vale cordis dimidium, et tocius leticie ac amoris incendium.

87

V   Et brevis et longus presens michi transiit annus
             Ex quo cara tuus me sibi vinxit amor.
         Nam repetendo tue decus insaciabile forme
             Et bonitatis opus familiare tibi
5   Noticie brevis una tue, vix hora videtur
             Sic semper votis es nova cura meis.
         At repetens quam rara tuo contingis amanti,
             Annos innumeros estimo preteritos.
         Quelibet una dies ter denos continet annos
10   Quam sine te cogor ducere dulcis amor
         Sole carens fluit illa dies, et lucis honore,
             Qua tua ceu michi sol non oritur facies.
         Sol certe meus est vultus tuus, et mea lux est,
             Contingit faciem quando videre tuam.
15   Sidera si queras, duo sunt mea, nescio plura.
             Sidereos oculos hec ego dico tuos.

---

86. a) Genesis 29.31–35; Luke 10.41–42. On the Mary/Martha theme,
     see Giles Constable, "The Interpretation of Mary and Martha" in his
     Three Studies in Medieval and Religious Thought (Cambridge: Cam-
     bridge University Press, 1995), pp. 1–142, especially 74–75. b)
     Psalm 54.7.

86

WOMAN To the inexhaustible fount of sweetness, the indivisible
part of his soul: after the worries of Martha and the fertility of Lia,
may you possess the best part, that of Mary.[a]

The immense strength of my love for you, unceasingly, inces-
santly, unquestioningly and indescribably holding its own course,
impels me to write a few words to you, most beloved, as best I can
or know. But I have no idea at all what is the most important thing
I should say: every time you anticipate me with your sweetest
words, you show me the affection of your innermost and sincere
love, so that passion and desire for you always burn in me without
any uncertainty and never grows cold.

If only with a nod from God I could take the form of a bird, I
would fly to visit you as soon as possible.[b] ..... If it could be done
with the saving grace of God, there is nothing in the whole world
which I could wish for more than that which I just wished for, as
God, to whom it is difficult to give deceitful words, is my witness. I
may grow fat with your affection but your love cannot fill me. My well-
being is in your life, you are my complete desire and all my good.
Farewell, half of my heart and fire of all my happiness and love.

87

MAN   Both short and long has this year seemed to me,
                Since, my dear, your love bound me to itself.
            For when I recall the insatiable glory of your form
                And the work of goodness present within you,
5   It seems barely one short hour since we met:
                So you are always a fresh concern for my desires.
            But recalling how rarely you happen upon your lover,
                I consider countless years to have gone by.
            Any single day I am forced to spend without you,
10   Sweet love, seems like three decades.
            A day without your face rising like the sun over me,
                Goes by without sun or the gift of its light.
            Certainly your visage is my sun and my light,
                Whenever it happens that I see your face.
15   My stars, if you should ask, are two. I know no others:
                I declare them to be those starry eyes of yours.

His ego quando fruor, nil tunc michi defore[a] credo,
His ego cum careo, defore cuncta puto.
Sic dici possum felicior omnibus esse,
20   Sic dici possum nil habuisse boni,
Sic igitur verum, quod diximus ante, probatur,
Qualiter annalis hec mora transierit. (f. 166ra)
Nunc novus est annus, novus est amor incipiendus[b]
Vultque fides aliam nostra tenere viam
25   Non amor ulterius ullis ledendus amaris
Nil mea vita tibi, iam nisi dulce dabo,
Nec dicam nec agam, nisi que tibi nosco placere
Ad nutus domine me cohibebo mee;
In nullis rebus unquam diversa probemus
30   Tu quod vis jubeas protinus ipse sequar.
Corpus sic tenerum, nichil ultra ledat amarum
Carminibus duris, nec locus ullus erit.
Ignoscas formosa tuo, si scripsimus unquam,
Irasci posses unde michi merito
35   Non hoc consilio, non hoc egi racione
Qui male consuluit, impetus ipse fuit[c]
Emissam vocem, si quis revocare valeret
Hanc fateor vocem quod revocasse velim.[d]
Quando tuas animo lacrimas dilecta reduco
40   Non possum lacrimas ipse tenere meas
Suscipias igitur sua qui delicta fatetur
Suscipe, nec culpe sis memor ulterius.
Suscipe, nam lacrimis precor hoc carissima largis.
Orabo flexis hoc eciam genibus
45   Lux oculis hodierna meis extrema sit orta[e]
Femina si vivit, quam tibi pretulerim. (f. 165vb)

88

M Firmissimi amoris fundamento, domus bene superedificata
atque optime consummata: vicinitatem federis et stabilitatem.[a]

---

87. a) nil tunc michi defore) written as a correction in the margin and at
the foot of f.165v. Könsgen prefers the uncorrected version of the text
in the MS: *in lumine me fore* (I believe I am in light). b) cf. Ovid, *Fasti*
1.149–50 and *Remedium amoris* 452. c) Statius, *Thebaïd* 10.704–5.
d) Horace, *Epistulae* 1.18.171; cf. *V 75.* e) Ovid, *Heroides* 9.167.
88. a) on the idea of covenant, see M 60; on the image of a house, see
M 45.

When I enjoy them, I believe that I lack nothing,[a]
    When I am denied them, I think that I lack everything.
Thus can I be said to be happier than everyone,
20   Thus can I be said to have nothing of worth,
Thus what I said before is proven true,
    About how this space of a year has passed by.
Now the year is new, and a new love is to begin,[b]
    And our faith wants to pursue another path:
25 No more bitterness should wound this love, my life;
    Nothing but sweet things shall I now give to you;
Nor say nor do, save what I know pleases you.
    Only the approval of my lady will matter to me.
Let us not differ on anything at all.
30   Command what you will, I shall obey straight away.
May no more bitterness wound a body so delicate,
    Nor will there be cause for any more harsh poems.
Forgive me, fair lady, if something I wrote
    Ever made you justly angry with me:
35 I did not do deliberately or with reason.
    It was Impulse itself which counseled badly.[c]
If one could recall an uttered remark,
    Such words, I confess, I would wish to recall.[d]
When I bring back to mind your tears,
40   Beloved, I cannot hold back tears of my own.
So receive one who confesses his own faults,
    Receive him, and remember his guilt no more.
Receive him, dearest lady, for with many tears do I beg
    And plead with you, even on bended knee.
45 May the day's risen light be the last that I see,[e]
    If there lives a woman I could prefer over you.

88

WOMAN To the foundation of firmest love, the house that is well built upon it and perfectly completed: the closeness and stability of a bond.[a]

Montes et nemora, silvarumque omnia respondent umbrosa,[b] et quomodo michi gloria difficilis esset rescribendi? Fallit enim labor laborantem,[c] animus dum se voluntarius expedit ad rem. Immo nil difficile quod ex voluntate.

Raro quenquam invenimus in hoc salo tam composite felicitatis, tam perfecte virtutis, quin corpus eius non bene politum, deesse sibi peniteat multum, nisi tu solus, qui per omnia et in omnibus extas virtuosus. Igitur cordi meo firmiter infixus semper adheres, et adherebis, nec saltem horam unam dormiendo neque vigilando inde recedis neque recedes.[d]

Non est nec unquam erit dilectio firma, que tam cito flectitur fallacia. Quicquid unquam michi iniurie intulisti, a memoria actenus non recessit cordis mei, sed nunc pure ac sincere et pleniter tibi condonabo omnia, eo tenore ut deinceps a te tali non movear iniuria. Tecum permanebo fida, stabilis, immutabilis, et non flexibilis, et si omnes homines capiendos in unicos scirem, nunquam a te nisi vi coacta, et penitus expulsa, recederem. Non sum harundo vento agitata,[e] neque me a te movebit asperitas ulla, nec alicuius rei mollicia. (f. 166rb)

Ignis enim amoris tui semper in me renovabitur et crescet, altius inardescit et non refrigescit, et quanto interius plus absconditur, et servatur, tanto magis augetur et multiplicatur. Et licet tociens, ut velim, ut optem, ut desiderem, oculis corporeis a me non videaris, tamen ab intencione mentis non labescis. Facilius enim ignis servatur, si caute cineribus sepelitur, nec fumus inde generatur; ita et nos invicem diligamus.[f] Vale interminabili gaudio letare.

89

V   Unico gaudio suo: salutem si tibi dare possum, quod nisi a te non habeo.[a]

Si verba que mitto, aliquantulum pauciora desiderio tuo esse videntur, non verba consule, sed mittentis voluntatem. Inopem me copia facit. Volunt siquidem multa simul erumpere, et ita se in-

---

b) Virgil, *Eclogues* 10.8–9. c) Horace, *Satires* 2.2.12; Ovid, *Metamorphoses* 6.60. d) cf. V *6, 22.* e) Matthew 11.7; Luke 7.24. f) 1 John 4.7.
89. a) cf. V *51.*

The mountains and shady groves of the forests reply:[b] so how can the glory of writing back be difficult for me? For work leads the worker astray[c] while the spirit willingly frees itself for the task. Indeed nothing is difficult which comes from the will.

It is rare to find on these high seas anyone with such composed happiness and such complete virtue that he does not have cause to regret greatly the failing of his unrefined body—apart from you who stand out as virtuous through everything and in everything. Therefore, you cling and will always cling firmly attached to my heart; not even for one hour, whether I am asleep or awake, do you leave or will you ever leave me.[d]

There does not exist nor will there ever be a firm love that is turned away by deceit so quickly. Whatever injuries you inflicted on me have not yet gone from the memory of my heart, but I shall now genuinely and sincerely and fully forgive you for everything connected with them, so that I shall not be upset by such injuries from you again. I shall remain faithful to you, stable, unchangeable and unwavering, and, even if I knew all men as individuals, I would never leave you unless compelled to by force and completely expelled. I am not a reed shaken by the wind,[e] nor shall any severity or weakness of any kind take me from you.

For the fire of love for you will always be renewed and grow within me; it burns deeper and does not grow cold, and the more it is hidden and kept inside, the more it enlarges and multiplies. And even if you are not seen by me with corporeal eyes as often as I wish, hope and desire, nevertheless you do not slip from the intention of my mind. For a fire is kept going more easily if it is carefully buried under ashes and smoke is not produced from it. Let us love each other like this.[f] Farewell, enjoy unending happiness.

89

MAN   To his only joy: well-being, if I can give you that which I do not have except from you.[a]

If the words that I send seem to be somewhat fewer than you desire, consider not the words but the will of the sender. Abundance makes me poor: indeed, many words want to pour out all

vicem officiunt; dum dubitando moras facio tempus fluit. Vale gemma tocius Gallie.

90

M Frondoso nemori omnigenarum virtutum odore redolenti, flos et lilium[a] eius: fidei augmentum, et amoris incrementum.

Libenti animo ac mente devota ad te mi dilecte scriberem multa, nisi quod tot me impediunt cure, que animum meum trahunt diverse, ut pre nimio dolore cordis, vix proferam aliqua verba salutacionis. Nunc autem te obtestor per tuam fidem, et mei amoris sollicitudinem, ut sicut me ab inicio in dilectionem tuam accepisti, acceptam serves, et amorem nostrum ex animo non amoveas. Vale, vive, bene valendo per secula letare.

91

V Lune splendidissime omnes tenebras fuganti, lune inquam cuius splendor non deficit, ille cui sine te nunquam dies est: semper fulgere, semper gratissime lucis incrementis gaudere.[a]

Cure dulcissima quas pro dilecto tuo geris, tanto michi dulciores sunt, quanto maius fidei tue argumentum tribuunt. Si ergo presens essem, ego tibi curas omnes eluerem, ego dulcissimas lacrimas a sidereis oculis tuis abstergerem,[b] amplexibus sollicitum pectus tuum ambirem, leticiam tibi integre reformarem. Vale.

92

M Lumini clarissimo, et solsticio suo,[a] nunquam fuscis tenebrarum labenti, sed semper candoris colorem inferenti, illa quam nullus nisi tu sol uret in die, nec luna per noctem:[b] acrius can-

---

90. a) Song of Songs 2.1.
91. a) cf. V 50. b) Revelations 7.17, 21.4.
92. a) The summer solstice, when the earth is closest to the sun. b) Psalm 120.6. c) Mark 9.49.

at once and so get in each other's way. While I hesitate, I delay, and time flies by. Farewell, jewel of all Gaul.

90

WOMAN   To the leafy grove, scented with the fragrance of every kind of virtue, his flower and lily:[a] increase in faith and growth in love.

With a willing spirit and devoted mind, my beloved, I would write a great deal to you, were it not for the fact that I am impeded by as many different cares as distract my spirit, such that I can barely find any words of greeting because of the great grief in my heart. But now I appeal to you, by your faith and concern to love me, to look after the one whom you have welcomed, just as you welcomed me into your love from the beginning, and not to let our love slip from your spirit. Farewell, prosper, and in faring well, rejoice forever.

91

MAN   To the most brilliant moon, driving away all darkness, a moon whose brilliance, I declare, does not diminish, he for whom without you it is never day: may you always shine and always enjoy an increase of that most gratifying light.[a]

The cares which you, sweetest, bear for your beloved are all the more sweet for me, in that they offer stronger proof of your faith. If I were there, I would wash away all cares from you, I would wipe sweetest tears from your starry eyes,[b] I would surround your troubled breast with my embrace, I would restore your happiness completely. Farewell.

92

WOMAN   To her clearest light and solstice,[a] never falling into the shadows of darkness but always imparting the color of radiance, she whom no sun but you warms by day nor moon at night[b]: may you

descere, splendidius fulgere, in fervore nostri amoris non deficere, salis condimentum habere, conditaque servare.[c]
Vale.

93

V   Splendidissime luci sue, que in mediis tenebris lucere solet: dulcissime lucis nullos sentire defectus.
   Nullus nobis infelicior est, quos amor simul et pudor in diversa
rapiunt.[a]

94

M   Perfecti decoris, et optimi odoris aromati, germine suavitatis in
campo heremi centuplicato,[a] luna plena: innexibilis amoris delicia.[b]
   Verba das ventis.[c] Si me pro talibus lapidas, quid faceres ferenti
iniurias? Ille amicus non est laudandus, nec ex omni parte per-
fectus, qui non est memor amici nisi in tempore usus necessarii.
Vale.

95

M   Navi periclitanti,[a] et anchoram fidei non habenti, illa quam non
movent ventosa que tue infidelitati sunt congrua.
   Tu non equo mecum sentis animo, sed mutasti mores; idcirco
nusquam est tuta fides. Penitet me non modice, quod te solum
pre omnibus cordi meo tam firmiter affixi, quia frustra laborat, cui
laboris mercedem nemo recompensat. Pendula expectacione vix
expectavi. Sed quid hec spes michi profuit, que nullum profectum
attulit? Vale. (f. 166v)

---

93. a) Ovid, *Metamorphoses* 1.618–619; *Heroides* 15.121.
94. a) cf. Matthew 13.8, 13.23; Mark 4.8, 4.20. b) Here *luna plena* is
   taken as an image of herself (picking up his image of her in V *91*).
   c) Ovid, *Amores* 1.6.42.
95. a) Jonah 1.4.

radiate more brightly, shine more brilliantly, not diminish in the fervor of our love, be seasoned with salt and preserve your flavor.[c] Farewell.

93

MAN To his most brilliant light, who is used to shining in the midst of darkness: may you experience no diminishing of your sweetest light.

No one is unhappier than we who are simultaneously pulled in different directions by love and shame.[a]

94

WOMAN To the spice of perfect quality and finest fragrance, multiplied a hundredfold[a] with the seed of sweetness in the wasteland, a full moon: the delights of binding love.[b]

You give words to the wind.[c] If you stone me for such things, what would you do to one inflicting injuries on you? He who does not remember a friend except in time of necessity is no friend deserving of praise nor perfect in every part. Farewell.

95

WOMAN To the imperiled boat[a] not having the anchor of faith, she who is not moved by the winds which fan your faithlessness.

You are not being fair to me, but have changed your ways; and so trust is not secure anywhere. I regret in no small way having fastened you alone over everyone so firmly to my heart, because it is wasted effort when nobody repays the price of that effort. Suspended in hope, I barely kept hoping. But what good has such expectation been to me when it has brought no result? Farewell.

96

V Speciose sue, cuius laudi nec mens nec lingua sufficit: quid aliud, nisi ut totum tibi proveniat, quod dilectissimi tui estuans dilectio iugiter affectat?

Mea verissime in te dilectio de die in diem proficit, nec temporum vetustate minuitur, immo sicut sol quotidie novus est, ita tua suavissima dulcedo novitate sua florescit, germinat, et vivide crescit. Vale martyr mea, ut ego tui sic memor esto mei.

97

<<V>>   Cordi dimidio, parti anime[a] mando, quod sum: tibi sum dum vivo.

Vale quamvis nullum miseris michi salve.

98

M Tyroni[a] et amantium dulcissimo: fundamentum stabilis amicicie infidelitatis fusca nescire, frigidum neque tepidum fieri in dulcifero nostri amoris ardore, sed solito more ardentius estuare, meque promerentem amicabili fomite pectoris semper sine tedio gestare.

Mea vota nil michi prosunt, quia ego et mea tibi vilescunt, et delectacionem desiderati gaudii, tu quasi iratus sustulisti.

99

V Amoris leges bene scienti et optime implenti, amicus idem qui fuerat: eandem unici amoris constanciam.

100

M Fidelis fideli: nodum qui nunquam denodatur amoris integri.

---

97. a) cf. M 11, 49.

98. a) Isidore defines *tirones* as strong boys (*pueri*) chosen to bear arms, *Etymologiae* 9.3.36.

96

MAN   To his beautiful one, whom neither mind nor tongue is capable of praising enough: what else but that everything which the burning love of your most beloved continually strives for, may come about for you.

Most truly my love for you grows from day to day and is not diminished by the passing of time. On the contrary, just as the sun is new every day, so your most delightful sweetness flourishes in its newness, sprouts, and grows vigorously. Farewell, my martyr, be as mindful of me as I am of you.

97

<<MAN>>   To half my heart and part of my soul:[a] I send what I am; I am yours, as long as I live.

Farewell, even though you sent no greeting to me.

98

WOMAN   To a tiro,[a] the sweetest of lovers, the foundation of a stable friendship: may you never know the darkness of faithlessness; may you become neither cold nor lukewarm in the sweet-flowing fire of our love, but rather blaze more ardently than usual; and may you always carry me deservedly in the friendly kindling of your breast without tiring.

My wishes are of no use to me, because I and everything I have are worthless to you, and because you have borne the pleasure of desired joy as if angry.

99

MAN   To one who knows well and is best equipped with the rules of love, the same friend as he had been: the same constancy of a unique love.

100

WOMAN   Faithful to faithful: the knot of an intact love never untied.

Dignum est et benefactum ut possessio que possidetur a possessore attencius exerceatur, neque in corde eius vilescat, sed magis ac magis omni hora crescat.

101

V   Sidereo oculo suo: semper videre quod placeat, nunquam sentire quod displiceat.

Ego sum qui fui. Nichil in me de tuo amore mutatum est, nisi quod in maius quotidie flamma tue dilectionis exuberat. Hec sola mutacio fatenda est, hec sola iuste conceditur quod tuo amori apud me in omni tempore proficitur. Cautius modo te alloquor si notare vis, cautius aggredior, pudor se amori contemperat, amorem verecundia cohibet, ne in immensum proruat, ut et nostris dulcibus votis copiam demus, et famam que de nobis orta est paulatim attenuemus. Vale.

102

M   Lacte et melle mananti,[a] candor lactis et dulcedo mellis: liquorem tocius suavitatis et augmentum gaudii salutaris.[b]

Te dilectissimum cordique meo amantissimum, amori meo aptissimum, voto meo convenientissimum semper valere, et semper dulciter vivere, summa opto cordis intencione. Quod preciocissimum habeo, tibi do, scilicet meipsam, in fide et dilectione firmam, in amore tuo stabilem, et nunquam mutabilem. Vale, letare, nil te offendat, nec me per te ledat.

103

V   Argento nitidiori, omni precioso lapide splendidiori,[a] omnia pigmenta odore et sapore superanti, ille qui semper novis reficitur donis tuis, et gaudiis: blanda semper novitate delectari.

---

102.   a) Deuteronomy 26.15. b) cf. M 84.
103.   a) cf. Proverbs 8.19. b) Gregory the Great, *Hom. in Evangelia* 2.30.2, PL 76:1221B.

It is right and proper that a possession which is possessed by the possessor is utilized attentively and not made worthless in his heart, but grow more and more every hour.

101

MAN   To his starry eye: may it always see what is pleasing and never perceive what is displeasing.

I am the person I have been. Nothing has changed in me concerning my ardor for you, except that every day the flame of love for you rises even more. I admit this change alone, this alone do I rightly concede, that it grows in love for you within me in every season. If you care to note, I am now speaking to you more cautiously, and approaching you more cautiously; shame tempers love, modesty checks love, lest it rush out in its immensity. This way we can fulfil our sweet desires and gradually stifle the rumor that has arisen about us. Farewell.

102

WOMAN   To one flowing with milk and honey,[a] the whiteness of milk and the sweetness of honey: outpouring of every delight and increase of saving joy.[b]

Most loved and most cherished in my heart, so much suited for my love and the complete answer to my prayer, I hope with the greatest intention of my heart that you may always fare well and always live in sweetness. The most precious thing I have I give to you, namely, myself, firm in faith and love, stable in desire for you and never changeable. Farewell, rejoice, may nothing upset you nor hurt me through you.

103

MAN   To one more shiny than silver, more brilliant than any precious stone,[a] and surpassing all spices in aroma and taste, he who is always restored by your new gifts and joys: may you always delight in lovely newness.

Amor ociosus esse non potest.[b] Se enim semper in amicum erigit, semper ad nova obsequia contendit, nunquam dormit, nunquam desidia labascit. Hec anime mi sentencia in te liquido conprobatur que in incepte dilectionis cursu firmiter durans, amico tuo qualis in eum sis, novis semper declaras indiciis. Quanti dona tua faciam vel cuius apud me sint ponderis, tibi familiariter intimabo.

104

M   Insaciabili amoris dulcedini, cuncta delectabilia suavitate superanti, illa cui nichil preciosius in toto mundo conparatur: ut dignitas tua ineffabili gloria renovetur.

Amoris tui incendium quod in me crescit, semper me scribere cogit. Sed quid potissimum dicam ignoro, nisi quod dilectionis indicium cordi meo insitum tibi revelabo. Jure pro illo doleo, quem tam tenere, tam interne diligo, cuius dulcedinis benignitas, suavitates precellit humanas, et illum non datur oculis cernere corporeis, qui nunquam labascit ab intencione mentis. Huius ergo doloris incrementum non est alio modo sanandum, nisi in modo turturis[a] tibi servem inviolabile pignus amoris, illud optans voce et votis, ut tibi multiplicentur anni vite, et adipiscaris quandoque coronam immortalitatis eterne.[b] Vale.

105

V   Summo lassorum animorum solamini, gaudio integro, spei solide, omnium demum que iocunda sunt domicilio, ille cui tuus spiritus mellis est haustus, cui tuus intuitus clarissimum lumen est: quid aliud nisi ut magne suavitati tue longissima vita sufficiat?

Quod amorem meum dulcissima scribendi necessarium tibi causam constituis, ita gratanter accipio, sicut artissima vere dilectionis cathena te firmiter astrictam teneo. Verbis eciam tuis ut facillima fides sit, opera tua probant, que ita frequentibus beneficiis redundant, ut apertum sit amorem tuum frigidum non esse,

---

104. a) Isidore, *Etymologiae* 12.7.60; cf. Song of Songs 2.12.   b) cf. Proverbs 4.10; James 1.12.

Love cannot remain idle.[b] It always rises for a friend, always strives for new ways to be of service, never sleeps, never falls into laziness. These maxims are clearly confirmed in you, my spirit; firmly persisting in the course of the love that has begun, you always indicate to your friend with new signs how you feel about him. How much I value your gifts and how important they are to me, I shall reveal to you privately.

104

WOMAN To the insatiable sweetness of love, surpassing every delight in pleasantness, she for whom nothing in the whole world is more precious: may your excellence be renewed with indescribable glory.

The fire of passion for you which is always growing in me drives me to write. But I do not know what is the most important thing to say, except to show you evidence of the love planted in my heart. Rightly I grieve for him whom I love so tenderly and so deeply, whose generous gift of sweetness surpasses mortal delights and whom it is not granted to see with corporeal eyes, but who never slips from the intention of the mind. An increase of this grief can therefore only be alleviated if, like the turtle dove,[a] I preserve for you an inviolable pledge of love, wishing in word and prayer that the years of your life be multiplied and that some day you will obtain the crown of eternal immortality.[b] Farewell.

105

MAN To the greatest comfort of weary spirits, to untainted joy, solid hope, and home of all things joyful, he for whom your breath is honeyed draught and your gaze the clearest light: what else but a very long life to suffice for your great delightfulness?

I accept just as gladly as I hold you firmly clasped in the tightest chain of true love, the fact that you, sweetest, establish my love as the essential reason for your writing. Indeed, your actions, which overflow with so many recurring benefits that it is obvious that your love is not cold, prove that it is very easy to trust in your

et eum quem te amare testaris, lingua eciam tacente, factis sufficienter loqueris. (f. 167r)

106

<<V>>   ..... Nichil insipiente fortunato gravius est.[a] Nunc primum ante actam fortunam recognosco, nunc leta tempora respexisse vacat, quia spes recedit nescio an unquam recuperanda. Ego precium ob stulticiam fero, quia bonum illud quod retinere sicut decuit nescivi, quo utique indignus fui, illud inquam bonum perdo, alio avolat, me relinquit, quia me sua possessione indignum recognoscit. Vale.

107

M   ..... Cuius animus dividitur in multa, minus valet ad singula. ..... Vidi michi assistere mulierem, etate senem, aspectu decoram, et per omnes compages membrorum ultra humanum modum elegantem, que me torvis oculis inspiciens, iustaque increpacione has voces proferens inquit:[a] "Cur tam negligenter agis? Nonne vides quod nullum nobilitas generis, nec forma decoris, nec aspectus pulcritudinis juvat, nisi quem spiritus sancti gracia prevenit, diviciasque sapiencie et sciencie in se recipit ut his munitus secularibus calliditatibus possit resistere salvus?." ..... Reducto in vires animo, hoc eam allocuta sum responso.....etc. Vale, quot folia queque gerunt arbores, tot mando prosperitates.

108

V	Sol meus atque serena dies mea lux mea salve.
versus	Tu mea dulcedo, te sine dulce nichil
	Si queris quis verba tibi tam dulcia mittat
	Vita manes cuius hoc facit ille tuus
5	Cui potus lacrime te discedente fuere
	Cui dolor et gemitus mixta fuere cibus.

---

106. a) Cicero, *Laelius* 54.
107. a) cf. Boethius, *Consolation of Philosophy* 1.1.

words; and you speak through deeds sufficiently of the one whom you assert you love even with a silent tongue.

106

<<Man>> ..... There is nothing worse than a foolish man blessed by fortune.[a] Now for the first time I realize the good fortune I previously enjoyed, now I have the opportunity to look back on happy times, for hope is fading—I do not know whether ever to be recovered. I am paying the price for stupidity, because I am losing that good thing of which I have been completely unworthy, that good thing which I have not known how to keep as I ought. It is flying elsewhere, forsaking me, because it realizes that I am not worthy of having it. Farewell.

107

Woman ..... A spirit divided over many things is less effective on individual matters. ..... I saw a woman standing near me, advanced in years, graceful in appearance and in every part of her body elegant beyond human measure. Looking at me with stern eyes and speaking these words in rightful reproach,[a] she said: *"Why do you act so negligently? Do you not see that neither nobility of birth nor attractive form nor beautiful appearance helps anyone for whom the grace of the Holy Spirit does not come first and who does not draw in the riches of wisdom and knowledge, so that, protected by these, worldly cunning can be safely resisted?"* ..... My spirit having been restored to strength, I spoke to her with this response. etc. Farewell. As many as the leaves borne by every tree, so many prayers do I send for your prosperity.

108

Man   My sun and my serene day, my light, greetings.
            You are my sweetness, without you nothing is sweet,
            If you should ask who sends words so sweet to you:
            He who is yours does so, whose life you remain,
5   Whose drink has been tears with you away,
            Whose food has been mixed with grief and sighs.[a]

---

108. a) Isaiah 35.10. b) Boethius, *Consolation of Philosophy* 3 m.1.7; Lucan, *Pharsalia* 8.159–60. c) Ovid, *Metamorphoses* 2.272.

Vita gravis mors suavis erat, hanc sepe precabar
Nam nec leta dies, nec michi grata quies
Sepe sequi dominam votum fuit, ire parabam,
10   Sed pudor atque metus continuere viam.
Fama tui reditus simul est audita, reversus,
Spiritus est cari dulcis amica tui.
Incalui totus, horror ferit intima letus,
Erigor, et mea vix gaudia percipio,
15   Nec mirum reduci tibi me dilecta favere,
Namque favent letis tempora blandiciis
Gratius astra nitent, sol clarior exerit orbem,[b]
Blanditur tellus floribus alma suis.[c]
In laudes natura tuas se preparat omnis
20   Cuncta tuas laudes o mea vita canunt.

109

M   Quia uterque nostrum alter alterius conspectui modo in momento presentari valet, littere nostre salutacione non indigent. Cupio te tamen esse salvum, virtutum decore indutum, sophie gemmis circumtectum, morum honestate preditum, omnisque composicionis ornatu decoratum. Vale, fons refrigerii. Vale flos odoris gratissimi. Vale memoria leticie, oblivio tristicie.

110

V   Unice sue: gaudium quod nulla egritudo corrumpat.
Deo teste dilectissima quotiens tuas legere litteras incipio, tanta interius suavitate perfundor, ut litteram quam legi sepe cogar repetere, quia attencionem michi magnitudo aufert leticie. Facile ergo perpendere potes quam iocunda michi sit ipsius gratissime persone tue presencia et quantum in se ponderis habeant viva verba tua, cum tantum me vox eminus missa letificet. Vale.

111

<<V>>   Lucida nox tua sit, preter me nil tibi desit
<versus>   Dum me pulcra cares defore cuncta putes.
Me sopita vide, me dum vigilas meditare,
Et velut ipse tuus sum, michi sis animus.

Life was difficult, death sweet and often prayed for;
　　　Day was not joyful nor sleep pleasing to me.
I often wished to follow my lady, and was preparing to go,
10　　But shame and fear blocked the way.
As soon as news of your return was heard, sweet friend,
　　　The breath of your dear one was restored.
I became hot all over, joyous trembling pounded inside,
　　　I am revived and scarcely grasp my joys.
15　　Nor is it any wonder that I favor your return,
　　　Beloved, for the season favors delightful joys.
The stars shine more pleasingly, the sun shows its orb more
　　　brightly,[b]
　　　Mother Earth delights with its flowers.[c]
All Nature prepares itself for your praises,
20　　Everything, my life, sings your praises.

109

WOMAN　Since each of us is able to see the other in a moment now,
our letters do not need a greeting. Nevertheless I want you to be
well, clothed with the grace of the virtues, covered with the jewels
of wisdom, endowed with honesty of behavior, and decorated with
the adornment of complete composure. Farewell, font of refreshment. Farewell, flower of the most pleasing scent. Farewell, memory of joy, end of sadness.

110

MAN　To his only one: joy which no sickness can destroy.
　　　God is my witness, most beloved, that every time I begin to
read your letters, I am flooded with so much delight inside that I
am often forced to go back over the letter I have read, because
the extent of my happiness takes my attention away. So you can
easily imagine how joyful for me is the very presence of your so
pleasing person, and how important are your living words, when
just a word sent from afar makes me happy. Farewell.

111

<<MAN>>　　May your night be clear, may you lack nothing but me.
　　　And lacking me, beautiful woman, may you feel deprived of
　　　everything.
　　　Imagine me when you sleep, think of me while awake,
　　　And just as I am yours, be my spirit for me.

112

M Magistro suo nobilissimo atque doctissimo: salutem in eo qui est salus et benedictio.

Si bene vales et inter mundana curris sine offensione, summa efferor[a] mentis exultacione. Placuit tue nobilitati eas litteras mittere mee parvitati, in quibus me appellando, et tue dilectionis consolacionem promittendo, pre nimio gaudio sicut michi visum est quadam agilitate mentis, me usque ad tercium celum rapuisti.[b] Evidentius verum dicam: litterarum tuarum immensa iocunditas ex improviso me rapuit, et quasi per internam revelacionem ad voti mei consolacionem instituit. ..... Jam philosophie laribus nutritus,[c] poeticum fontem ebibisti. ..... Sitire deum et illi adherere soli necessarium est omni viventi. ..... Quamvis futurum sit, tamen iam tibi moncium cacumina[d] supplicare conspicio. Nec dubito, quin in te impleatur hoc quod opto divino consilio. Verum nullo genere linguarum, nulla verborum facundia potest sufficienter explicari, quantum gaudeo, quod portum tue dilectionis secura nec ingrata optineo.[e] Cum ergo tanti beneficii meritis dignam rependere vicem nullatenus valeam, tamen desiderio, desidero[f] indeficienter tuo vacare studio. .....

112a[a]

<<M>> Ubi est amor et dilectio, ibi semper fervet exercicium.[b] Jam fessa sum, tibi respondere nequeo, quod dulcia pro gravibus accipis, ac per hoc animum meum contristaris. Vale. (f. 167v)

---

112. a) efferor) Könsgen corrects *effero* in the MS ("I bear [great things]") to *efferor* ("I am carried away [by great . . .]"), a more elegant construction. It is difficult to be certain which is the correct reading. Given a number of scribal corrections in this passage, it seems unusual that the scribe did not notice this mistake. b) 2 Corinthians 12.2. c) cf. Boethius, *Consolation of Philosophy* 1.2; 1.3. d) Genesis 8.5. e) On the image of sailing into port, see V 78. f) Luke 22.15.

112

WOMAN   To her most noble and most learned teacher: well-being in Him who is both salvation and blessing.

If you are well and moving among worldly concerns without trouble, I am carried away by great exultation of mind.[a] It has pleased your nobility to send those letters to my insignificance, in which by naming me and promising me the solace of your love, you snatched me—from so much joy, it seemed to me, and through a certain agility of mind—right up to the third heaven.[b] But I shall speak more plainly: the immense pleasure of your letters has seized me unexpectedly, and, as though by some internal revelation, provided solace for my desire. ..... Already nourished at the hearth of philosophy,[c] you have drunk from the fountain of poetry. ..... To thirst for God and to cling to Him alone is necessary for every living creature. ..... Although it may be in the future, nevertheless I already see the mountaintops[d] bowing down before you. Nor do I doubt that this, which I hope for, will be fulfilled in you by divine plan. But no manner of speech nor way with words can sufficiently express how happy I am, that, secure yet not ungrateful, I am reaching the haven of your love.[e] Therefore, although I am totally incapable of appropriately repaying the worth of such a great benefit, I nevertheless long with desire[f] to be free to be unfailingly devoted to you. .....

112a[a]

<<WOMAN>>   Where there is passion and love, there always rages effort.[b] Now I am tired, I cannot reply to you, because you are taking sweet things as burdensome, and in doing so you sadden my spirit. Farewell.

112a. a) In the margin: *Ex alia* <epistola> "From another <letter>." b) cf. the Maunday Thursday hymn, *Ubi caritas et amor, Deus ibi est* "Where charity and love are, there God abides."

113

<<V>>   Urget amor sua castra sequi[a] sua jura vereri
            Et quod non didici discere cogit amor.[b]
            Non homo sed lapis est quem non tua forma movebit.[c]
            Credo quod moveor, nec lapis esse queo.
5   Cura fuit Veneris effingere membra poetis[d]
            .....
            Sed tibi num finxere pares? Non estimo certe
            Exuperat veras nam tua forma deas.[e]
            Eloquar an sileam?[f] Si sit tua gracia dicam.
10   Dicam nam verbis proditor omnis abest
            Qualia sunt que veste tegis? Vix mente quiesco.
            Que palpasse volo cum subeunt animo.
            Sed fortuna pudorque meis dulcissima votis
            Obstant et populi murmura que timeo.
15   Ut quociens opto te possim cara videre
            (Quod ter quaque die posse velim fieri)[g]
            .....
            Candidior medio nox foret illa die.[h]
            Da veniam quia dictat amor que scribere cogor
20   Da veniam fasso, non patienter amo.[i]
            Tu me vicisti, potuit quem vincere nulla.
            Fortius hinc uror, est quia primus amor;[j]
            Nam non ante meas penetravit flamma medullas.[k]
            Si quis amor fuerat ante fui tepidus.
25   Facundum me sola facis,[l] hec gloria nulli
            Contigit, ut fuerit carmine digna meo.
            Tu nulli similis, in qua natura locavit[m]
            Quicquid precipuum mundus habere potest
            Forma genus mores per que pariuntur honores
30   Urbi te nostre conspicuam faciunt.
            Ergo quid est mirum si me nitor attrahit horum?
            Si tibi succumbo, victus amore tuo?

---

113. a) Ovid, *Amores* 1.2.17–18, 1.9.1, 3.8.26; *Ars amatoria* 3.559. b)
Ovid, *Metamorphoses* 9.515. c) Terence, *Hecuba* 214; Statius, *Sil-
vaid* 2.1.139. d) Könsgen conjectures from the meter a missing line
at this point; the scribe indicates an ellipsis. e) Ovid, *Heroides* 18.68.
f) Virgil, *Aeneid* 3.39. g) Scribal ellipse indicated, although there is
no major lapse in sense. h) Ovid, *Heroides* 16.320. i) Ovid, *Heroides*
19.4; cf. *Ponticae* 1.7.22, 4.2.23. j) Ovid, *Metamorphoses* 1.452. k)
Ovid, *Metamorphoses* 14.351. l) Ovid, *Metamorphoses* 6.469. m) cf.
43, 73. n) Ovid, *Metamorphoses* 1.619; *Heroides* 15.176.

113

<<Man>>   Love urges me to enlist in its service,[a] to respect its laws,
         And what I had not learnt, love forces me to learn.[b]
         No man but stone is he whom your beauty does not move.[c]
         I believe that I am moved, nor can I be stone.
5   Poets have tried hard to portray the body of Venus,[d]
         .....
         But did they ever produce anyone equal to you? Certainly I
             think not.
         For your beauty surpasses even the goddesses themselves.[e]
         Should I go on or be silent?[f] By your grace, I will speak.
10   I will speak, for a traitor is devoid of words.
         What are they like, what you conceal with clothing? My mind
             can scarcely rest.
         I want to stroke them, when they come to mind.
         But fortune and shame and, that which I fear, sweetest,
         The murmuring of people, obstruct my desires.
15   If I could see you, my dear, as often as I wished
         (Three times a day I would want it to be)[g]
         .....
         That night would be brighter than the middle of day.[h]
         Forgive me, since love dictates what I am forced to write.
20   Forgive me, for I admit that I do not love patiently.[i]
         You have conquered me, whom no woman could conquer.
         Thus I burn more strongly, this being my first love;[j]
         For never before has that flame penetrated my marrow.[k]
         If ever there was love before, I was only lukewarm.
25   You alone make me eloquent;[l] such glory has happened to
         No one, that she be worthy of my song.
         You are like no one else, you in whom nature has placed[m]
         Whatever excellence the world can have:
         Beauty, noble birth, character—through which honor is begot-
             ten—
30   All make you outstanding in our city.
         So is it then surprising if I am lured by their brilliance,
         If I succumb to you, conquered by your love?[n]

NOTES

Chapter 1

1. Letter 1, ed. Ewald Könsgen, *Epistolae duorum amantium. Briefe Abaelards und Heloises?* (Leiden: E. J. Brill, 1974). Letters are cited according to the numbering established by Könsgen (italic numerals denoting letters from the man), rather than by page numbers. On the punctuation followed in these letters, see p. 183–84.

2. Isidore of Seville, *Etymologiae* 11.2.4–6, ed. W. M. Lindsay (Oxford: Clarendon Press, 1912); Adolf Hofmeister discusses different systems of understanding age, noting that one could be a *puer* up to twenty-eight, "Puer, Juvenis, Senex. Zum Verständnis der mittalterlichen Altersbezeichnungen," in *Papsttum und Kaisertum. Paul Kehr zum 65. Geburtstag dargebracht,* ed. Albert Brackmann (Munich: Münchener Drucke, 1926), pp. 287–316; see also Georges Duby, "Les 'jeunes' dans la société aristocratique dans la France du Nord-Ouest au XIIe siècle," *Annales: Economies, Sociétés, Civilisations* 19 (1964): 834–46; trans. Cynthia Postan, "Youth in aristocratic society. Northwestern France in the twelfth century," included in a collection of Duby's essays, *The Chivalrous Society* (Berkeley: University of California Press, 1977), pp. 112–22. This translation omits inverted commas around "youth," creating the misleading impression that Duby is talking about young people in the modern sense of the word.

3. Isidore, *Etymologiae* 9.7.12, 20.11.5. Baudri of Bourgueil uses *puella* of both Muriel and Beatrice, nuns with whom he exchanged sophisticated Latin verse, *Baldricus Burgulianus Carmina,* ed. Karlheinz Hilbert, Editiones Heidelbergenses 19 (Heidelberg: Carl Winter, 1979), nos. 137 and 140, pp. 189–90 and 193. I have not been able to consult the new edition and translation of Baudri's *Carmina,* prepared by Jean-Yves Tillette and being published by Les Belles Lettres, Paris; on Baudri, see, pp. 98–101. Carla Casagrande comments on the clerical tendency to divide women into young or old, "The Protected Women," in *A History of Women in the West. II. Silences of the Middle Ages,* ed. Christiane Klapisch-Zuber (Cambridge, Mass.: Belknap Press, 1992), p. 75.

4. Könsgen, p. 10. I follow Könsgen's practice of using the Latin form of his name (*Johannes de Vepria*), given on fol. 41v.Vernet identifies him as Jean de Vepria (n. 21 below), following a vernacular form used in the colophon to his translation into French of a liturgical text (n. 35 below).The catalogues of the BNF and British Library identify him as "LaVéprie, Jean de."

5. *HC*, ed. Monfrin, p. 71; ed. Hicks, p. 10; trans. Radice, p. 66.

6. *Ep.* 2, ed. Monfrin, p. 117; ed. Hicks, p. 53. Radice (p. 118) translates the end of the first sentence as "resounds with my name," as if these songs used the name *Heloysa*, when the Latin simply means that they made her famous as a woman praised by Abelard. For further discussion of these passages, see, pp. 31–36.

7. Könsgen, pp. 97–103, with discussion of kinds of love on pp. 88–90.

8. Ernstpeter Ruhe, *De amasio ad amasiam: Zur Gattungsgeschichte des mittelalterlichen Liebesbriefes*, Beiträge zur romanischen Philologie des Mittelalters 10 (Munich:Wilhelm FinkVerlag, 1975).

9. Graziella Ballanti, trans., *Un Epistolario d'Amore del XII secolo (Abelardo e Eloisa?)* (Rome: Edizioni Anicia, 1988). Ballanti downplays Könsgen's achievement in her introduction (pp. 9–10), unfortunate given that the full richness of Könsgen's commentary is not fully explored. Étienne Wolff only translates some of the love letters in *La Lettre d'amour au moyen âge: Boncompagno da Signa, La Roue de Venus; Baudri de Bourgueil, Poésies; Manuscrit de Tegernsee, Lettres d'amours; Manuscrit de Troyes, Lettres de deux amants (Héloïse et Abélard?)* (Paris: Nil Editions, 1996), pp. 117–51.

10. The only reviews recorded in the Citation Index are those of Edward Little, *Cahiers de civilisation médiévale* 19.2 (1976): 181–82; A. Pattin, *Tijdschrift voor Filosofie* 41.3 (1979): 521; G. Chiarini, *Maia. Rivista di Letterature Classiche* 33.3 (1981): 245–46. Jean Jolivet comments that "the question mark to his subtitle has all its value" in "Abélard entre chien et loup," *Cahiers de civilisation médiévale* 20 (1977): 312 n. 20. Giles Constable observes that "there is no sure evidence of their authorship" in *Letters and Letter-Collections*, Typologie des sources du moyen âge occidental 17 (Turnhout: Brepols, 1976), p. 34 n. 100. The letters are briefly commented on by Annie Cazenave, "Yseut et Héloïse, ou la passion et l'amour éternel," in *Tristan et Iseult, mythe européen et mondial*, ed. Danielle Buschinger (Goppingen: Kummerle, 1987), pp. 87–96.

11. They are mentioned only in passing by JacquesVerger, *L'amour castré. L'histoire d'Héloïse et Abélard* (Paris: Hermann, 1996), p. xiii and not at all by Mariateresa Fumagalli Beonio Brocchieri, *Eloisa e Abelardo* (Milan:Arnoldo Mondadori, 1984), John Marenbon, *The Philosophy of Peter Abelard* (Cambridge: Cambridge University Press, 1997) or Michael T. Clanchy, *Abelard. A Medieval Life* (Oxford: Blackwell, 1998).

12. *Abelard and Heloise in Medieval Testimonies*, W. P. Ker Memorial Lecture 26 (Glasgow: University of Glasgow Press, 1976), pp. 24–26, repr. in Dronke,

Intellectuals and Poets in Medieval Europe (Rome: Edizioni di Storia e Letteratura, 1992), pp. 270–72.

13. Dronke, *ML* 2: 422–47.

14. Dronke, *WW,* pp. 94–95.

15. Wolff, *La Lettre d'amour au moyen âge,* p. 24 (n. 9 above).

16. Jean Charles Payen, *Histoire de la littérature française. Le Moyen Age,* new revised ed. (1990; Paris: GF Flammarion, 1997), p. 58; Neil Cartlidge, *Medieval Marriages: literary approaches 1100 – 1300* (Woodbridge: Boydell & Brewer, 1997), p. 60 n. 142.

17. *Index Scriptorum Novus Mediae Latinitatis ab anno DCCC usque ad annum MCC,* ed. Franz Blatt (Copenhagen: Einar Munksgaard, 1993). There is an entry on *Pierre Abélard* by Jean Jolivet, but none on *Héloïse* in *Dictionnaire des lettres françaises. Le Moyen âge,* eds. Robert Bossuat, Louis Pichard and Guy Raynaud de Lage; new edition by Geneviève Hasenohr and Michel Zink (Paris: Fayard, 1992), pp. 1152–55.

18. Georges Duby, *Dames du XIIe siècle. I. Héloïse, Aliénor, Iseut et quelques autres* (Paris: Gallimard, 1995), pp. 73–110; *Women of the Twelfth Century,* trans. Jean Birrell (Cambridge: Polity Press, 1997), pp. 42–65. He had mentioned these doubts in *Que sait-on de l'amour en France au XIIe siècle?* (Oxford: Clarendon Press, 1983) and *Mâle moyen âge. De l'amour et autres essais* (Paris: Flammarion, 1988), pp. 45, 120; *Love and Marriage in the Middle Ages,* trans. Jane Dunnett (Cambridge: Polity Press, 1994), p. 31, 96. For further discussion of the authenticity question, see, pp. 47–53.

19. Dronke, *WW,* p. x.

20. On frequent visual associations of women with the book, see Lesley Smith, "Scriba, Femina: Medieval Depictions of Women Writing," in *Women and the Book. Assessing the Visual Evidence,* eds. Lesley Smith and Jane H. M. Taylor (London: British Library, 1997), pp. 21–44. On women's writing in Anglo-Norman in the second half of the twelfth century, see Jocelyn Wogan-Browne and Glyn S. Burgess, *Virgin Lives and Holy Deaths. Two Exemplary Biographies for Anglo-Norman Women* (London: J. M. Dent, 1996), pp. xiv-xvi and Wogan-Browne, "Clerc u lai, muïne u dame," in *Women and Literature in Britain, 1150 – 1500,* ed. Carol M. Meale (Cambridge: Cambridge University Press, 1993), pp. 61–85. For wide-ranging anthologies of women's writing, see Marcelle Thiébaux, ed., *The Writings of Medieval Women,* 2nd ed. (New York: Garland Publishing, 1994), much expanded from the 1987 edition, and Carolyne Larrington, ed., *Women and Writing in Medieval Europe* (London: Routledge, 1995).

21. On Johannes de Vepria, see Könsgen, pp. xx-xxvii; on Pierre de Virey, see André Vernet, *La Bibliothèque de l'abbaye de Clairvaux du XIIe au XVIIIe siècle* (Paris: CNRS, 1979), pp. 27–34 and "Un abbé de Clairvaux bibliophile: Pierre de Virey (1471 – 96)," *Scriptorium* 6 (1952): 76–88.

22. Edited by Vernet as the catalogue of Pierre de Virey, *La Bibliothèque de l'ab-baye de Clairvaux*, pp. 67–372. The handwriting of Troyes, Bibliothèque municipale 2299, reproduced by Vernet in Plate II of that volume, is identical to that of MS 1452 reproduced by Könsgen as a frontispiece to his edition; see also Anne Bordérelle-Souchier, *Bibliothèques cisterciennes dans la France médiévale. Repertoire des abbayes d'hommes* (Paris: CNRS, 1990), pp. 91–93, and Jean-Paul Bouhot, "La Bibliothèque de Clairvaux," in *Bernard de Clairvaux. Histoire, mentalités, spiritualité*, eds. Dominique Bertrand and Guy Lobrichon, SC 380 (Paris: Cerf, 1992), pp. 141–53.

23. Josephus-Maria Canivez, *Statuta Capitulorum Generalium Ordinis Cistercien-sis ab anno 1116 ad annum 1786*, 8 vols. (Louvain: Bibliothèque de la Revue d'Histoire Ecclésiastique, 1933–41), 5: 33: "Praecipitur omnibus et singulis patribus abbatibus, quatinus habeant inventoria omnium et singu-lorum librorum et iocalium monasteriorum utriusque sexus sibi subdito-rum." On Cistercian efforts at this time to organize their monastic libraries, see Louis J. Lekai, *The Cistercians. Ideals and Reality* (Kent, Ohio: Kent State University Press, 1977), pp. 89–90.

24. Charles de Visch, *Bibliotheca scriptorum sacri ordinis Cisterciensis* (Cologne: Ioannes Busaeus, 2nd. ed. 1656), pp. 231–32 and 177–78, quoting com-ments made by Johannes de Butrio (Beurreyo) in *De perseverantia religionis* (Paris: Berthold Rembolt, 1511).

25. Sheila J. Heathcote surveys this tradition in relation to Transmundus and John of Limoges, in "The Letter Collections Attributed to Master Trans-mundus, Papal Notary and Monk of Clairvaux in the Late Twelfth Cen-tury," *Analecta Cisterciensia* 21 (1965): 35–109, 167–238, in particular 49–66. See too Transmundus, *Introductiones dictandi*, ed. and trans. Ann Dalzell (Turnhout: Brepols, 1995).

26. Könsgen comments that Johannes de Vepria may not rely on the printed text of the *Epistolae*, first printed in 1476, pp. xii–xiii. On Virulus (Man-neken), see the article of Judith Rice Henderson in *Contemporaries of Eras-mus*, ed. Peter G. Bietenholz, 3 vols. (Toronto: University of Toronto Press, 1987), 3: 401–2. Another connection with a Flemish humanist is suggested by a note in another Troyes manuscript (1226) about a book sent to him by Cornelius Godefridus of Ghent; Könsgen, p. xxiii.

27. Troyes, Bibliothèque municipale 294bis; Könsgen, "Zwei unbekannte Briefe zu den Gesta Regum Anglorum des Wilhelm von Malmesbury," *Deutsches Archiv für Erforschung des Mittelalters* 31 (1975): 204–14.

28. Könsgen (p. xiv) lists the opening and closing phrases of these anonymous letters, still unidentified. They are addressed "to the General Chapter," and to the persecutor of the Church," "to the Counsel of the King," "to Pope J." (perhaps Pope John XXII, 1316 – 34); the last is simply called "Complaint."

29. My account is indebted to Könsgen's detailed analysis, pp. ix–xiv and pp. xxviii–xxxi.

30. Vernet, *La Bibliothèque de l'abbaye de Clairvaux,* p. 577 (no. 1658): "Deflorationes ex epistolis duorum amantium, incipientes *Amori suo."* See also pp. 483 (no. 822b), 545 (no. 1432).

31. Könsgen, *Epistolae,* p. xxv. See *Petrarch's Bucolicum Carmen,* trans. Thomas G. Bergin (New Haven: Yale University Press, 1970), pp. 3, 217 and Petrarch's explanation in *Familiares* 10.41.

32. Troyes, Bibl. mun. 2471; Könsgen, *Epistolae,* pp. xxii–xxiii. A handwritten analysis of this manuscript is kept at the Institut de recherche et d'histoire des textes, Paris. It is not clear if Johannes de Vepria himself added the early printed editions of Tibullus and Sidonius Apollinaris into this manuscript. On the *Epistula Sapphus,* see, pp. 296, n. 42 and 332, n. 29.

33. Könsgen, pp. xxv–xxvi; *Architrenius* was first edited by Thomas Wright, *The Anglo-Latin Satirical Poets and Epigrammatists of the Twelfth Century,* Rolls Series, 2 vols. (London: Longman, 1872), 1: 240–392. A new critical text, prepared in 1974 by P. G. Schmidt, is included alongside a translation by Winthrop Wetherbee, *Architrenius* (Cambridge: Cambridge University Press, 1994).

34. *Die Gesta Militum des Hugo von Mâcon. Ein bisher unbekanntes Werk der Erzählliteratur des Hochmittelalters,* Mittellateinische Studien und Texte 18 (Leiden: E. J. Brill, 1990); see the informative review by Christopher J. McDonough, *Mittellateinisches Jahrbuch* 28 (1993): 186–93.

35. *Les prouerbes communs* (Paris: Estienne Jehanot, 1495), translated into Latin by Gilles le Noyer, *Proverbia gallicana secundum ordinem alphabeti reposita et ab J. Egidio Nuceriensi latinis versiculis traducta* (Troyes: Johannes Lecocq, 1519). A. Vainant mentions that fifty proverbs were censored in 1558 in a concluding note to his unpaginated reprint of the 1539 Lyons edition, *Les Proverbes communs,* Collection de Poésies, Romans, Chroniques publiées d'après d'anciens Manuscrits et d'après des Editions des XVᵉ et XVIᵉ siècles (Paris: Silvestre, 1838). See also *L'Ordinaire de lordre de Cisteaux ceste annee MCCCCXVI corrige et a bonne forme redige par ung moyne du dicte ordre por Englebert et Geufroy de Marnef* (Paris, 1516); it concludes: "Cy fine lordinaire du service divine selon lordre de cysteaux extraict du latin et mis en francois pour les religieuses dudit ordre de cysteaux par frere jehan de vepria Lors prieur de cleruaulx Lan mil cccc iiiixx et xv. Et nouvelement corrige et bien emende par ung moyne dudit ordre et imprime lan mil cccc xvi pour englebert et geuffroy de marnef libraires iures de luniversite de paris demourans au pellican de la rue saint Jacques." See Vernet, *La Bibliothèque de l'abbaye de Clairvaux,* p. 570, no. 1606.

36. Troyes, Bibl. mun. 1447, fols. 7r–27r. Könsgen, p. xxii.

37. Aeneas Silvius Piccolomini (Pius II) and Niklas von Wyle, *The Tale of Two Lovers. Eurialus and Lucretia,* ed. Eric John Morrall, Amsterdamer Publikationen zur Sprache und Literatur 77 (Amsterdam: Rodopi, 1988). Morrall discusses the historical context to this work, as well as a letter of Aeneas in

which he asks his father to adopt a son fathered while attending the Council of Basel. The original Latin text circulated in the Holy Roman Empire, but is not known to have been read at Clairvaux or elsewhere in France; Morrall, pp. 21–24 and 39–42.

38. Könsgen, pp. xxviii–xxx. See also p. 182.
39. Canivez, *Statuta*, 5: 77, 79–80 (n. 23 above). See also Louis J. Lekai, "The Cistercian College of Saint Bernard in Paris in the Fifteenth Century," *Cistercian Studies* 6 (1971): 172–79 and "The College of Saint Bernard in Paris in the Sixteenth and Seventeenth Centuries," *Analecta Cisterciensia* 28 (1972): 167–218.
40. Canivez, *Statuta*, 5: 376 [1476], 421–24 [1481], 445–48 [1482], 481–85 [1484]. The final section of a dialogue between a prior and a subprior, justifying the condemnation of Pierre de Virey, followed by the sentence of excommunication in 1488, is preserved in Dijon, Bibliothèque municipale MS 602. On the centralizing reforms of Jean de Cirey, see Roger de Ganck, "Les pouvoirs de l'Abbé de Cîteaux de la Bulle *Parvus Fons* (1265) à la Révolution Française," *Analecta Cisterciensia* 27 (1971): 3–63, esp. 53–57.
41. Constable, *Letters and Letter-Collections*, pp. 11–12 (n. 10 above).
42. *P. Ovidii Nasonis Epistulae Heroidum*, ed. Heinrich Dörrie (Berlin: De Gruyter, 1971); *Heroides. Select Epistles*, ed. Peter E. Knox (Cambridge: Cambridge University Press, 1995) [*Heroides* 1–15]; *Heroides XVI-XXI*, ed. E. J. Kenney (Cambridge: Cambridge University Press, 1996); trans. Harold Isbell, *Heroides* (Harmondsworth: Penguin, 1990).
43. For the letters of Oenone and Briseis, see *Heroides*, nos. 5 and 3, ed. Dörrie, pp. 83–91 and 64–71; trans. Isbell, pp. 40–45 and 21–25. On Biblis and Cauno, see Ovid, *Metamorphoses* 9.454–665, ed. William S. Anderson (Leipzig: Teubner, 1977), pp. 218–24; trans. Mary M. Innes (Harmondsworth: Penguin, 1955), pp. 234–40.
44. Against the view that the *ars dictaminis* was invented in the late eleventh and early twelfth centuries, see William D. Patt, "The Early 'ars dictaminis' as Response to a Changing Society," *Viator* 9 (1978): 133–55, and more fully Carol Dana Lanham, "Freshman Composition in the Early Middle Ages: Epistolography and Rhetoric before the Ars Dictaminis," *Viator* 23 (1992): 115–34. Major treatises are edited by Ludwig Rockinger, *Briefsteller und Formelbücher des elften bis vierzehnten Jahrhunderts*, Quellen und Erörterungen zur bayerischen und deutschen Geschichte 9, 2 vols. (Munich, 1863, 1864, repr. New York: Johnson Corporation, 1961, 1969), 1: 9–94: Alberic, *De dictamine* [ca. 1087], Hugh of Bologna, *Rationes dictandi prosaice* [1119 – 24]; *Rationes dictandi* [1135; once attributed to Alberic]; see also Adalbert of Samaria, *Praecepta dictaminum* [ca. 1115], ed. Franz-Joseph Schmale, MGH Quellen zur Geistesgeschichte des Mittelalters 3 (Weimar: Hermann Böhlaus Nachfolger, 1961). James J. Murphy translates the *Ra-*

tiones dictandi in *Three Medieval Rhetorical Arts* (Berkeley: University of California Press, 1971), pp. 5–25.

45. Charles Homer Haskins draws extensively on students' letters preserved in these anthologies, "The Life of Mediaeval Students as Illustrated by Their Letters," in *Studies in Mediaeval Culture* (Oxford: Clarendon Press, 1929), pp. 1–35. Richard Sharpe emphasizes the wide use of Latin in conversation as well as in writing in "Latin in Everyday Life," in *Medieval Latin. An Introduction and Bibliographical Guide,* eds. F. A. C. Mantello and A. G. Rigg (Washington, D.C.: The Catholic University of America Press, 1996), pp. 315–41.

46. See Ruhe, *De amasio ad amasiam,* pp. 61–97 with a valuable appendix of edited texts, pp. 297–343 (n. 8 above). Dieter Schaller questions Ruhe's notion that these letters form a genre, in "Erotische und sexuele Thematik in Musterbriefsammlungen des 12. Jahrhunderts," in *Fälschungen im Mittelalter. Internationaler Kongress der Monumenta Germaniae Historica, München 16.–19. September 1986,* Monumenta Germaniae Historica Schriften Band 33, 6 vols. (Hannover: Hahnsche Buchhandlung, 1988 – 90), 5: 63–77 and a review of Ruhe, in *Arcadia* 12 (1977): 307–13; see also Albrecht Classen, "Female Epistolary Literature from Antiquity to the Present: An Introduction," *Studia Neuphilologica* 60 (1988): 3–13 and the essays in *Dear Sister. Medieval Women and the Epistolary Genre,* eds. Karen Cherewatuk and Ulrike Wiethaus (Philadelphia: University of Pennsylvania Press, 1993). Martin Camargo explores vernacular forms of the genre, "The Verse Love Epistle: An Unrecognized Genre," *Genre* 13 (1980): 397–405.

47. Helene Wieruszowski, "A Twelfth-Century 'Ars Dictaminis' in the Barberini Collection of the Vatican Library," *Traditio* 18 (1962) 382–93, repr. in *Politics and Culture in Medieval Spain and Italy* (Rome: Edizioni di storia e letteratura, 1971), pp. 331–45, at 343. Cf. Ovid, *Metamorphoses* 3.316–38.

48. *Boncompagno da Signa: Rota Veneris Facsimile Reproduction of the Strasburg Incunabulum with Introduction, Translation and Notes,* ed. Josef Purkart (Delmar, NY: Scholars' Facsimiles and Reprints, 1975) and *Rota Veneris,* ed. Paolo Garbini (Rome: Salerno Editrice, 1996); part of Purkart's translation is reprinted within Larrington, *Women and Writing,* pp. 61–63. See too Josef Purkart, "Spurious Love Letters in the Manuscripts of Boncompagno's *Rota Veneris,*" *Manuscripta* 28 (1984): 45–55 and on its context, Friedrich Baethgen, "Rota Veneris," *Mediaevalia. Aufsätze, Nachrufe, Besprechungen* (Stuttgart: Anton Hiersemann, 1960), pp. 363–84.

49. Bernard Bray discusses the transformation of letter collections into the novel in *L'Art de la lettre amoureuse. Des manuels aux romans (1550 – 1700)* (The Hague-Paris: Mouton, 1967). See also Janet Gurkin Altman, "The Letter Book as a Literary Institution 1539 – 1789: Toward a Cultural History of Published Correspondence in France," *Yale French Studies* 71 (1986): 17–62, Marie-Claire Grassi, "Friends and Lovers (or The Codification of Intimacy)," ibid., 77–92 and *L'Art de la lettre au temps de la Nouvelle Héloïse et*

du Romantisme (Geneva: Slatkine, 1994); see also Alain Viala, "La Genèse des formes épistolaires en français et leurs sources latines et européennes," *Revue de littérature comparée* 218 (1981): 168–83. A more recent model of the genre is Louis Chauffurin, *Le parfait secrétaire* (1954; Paris: Larousse, 1979).

50. Cf. Mikhail Bakhtin, *François Rabelais and his World,* trans. Helene Iswolsky (1965; Cambridge, Mass.: MIT Press, 1968).

51. Paul Veyne, *Roman Erotic Elegy. Love, Poetry and the West,* trans. David Pellauer (Chicago: University of Chicago Press, 1988), p. 7; originally published as *L'Élégie érotique romaine: L'amour, la poésie et l'Occident* (Paris: Seuil, 1983). On Duby, see n. 18 above.

52. R. Howard Bloch argues that the rise of courtly love in the twelfth century was a new form antifeminism, transformed from earlier Christian antifeminism by being secularised and fused with ideals of suffering, proposing (paradoxically) that romantic love was a reaction "on the part of a marriage-minded nobility against the increasing economic power of women;" *Medieval Misogyny and the Invention of Western Romantic Love* (Chicago: University of Chicago Press, 1991), pp. 10, 195–96. More nuanced doubts about such blanket generalizations are made by Penny Schine Gold in her preface to *The Lady and the Virgin. Image, Attitude, and Experience in Twelfth-Century France* (Chicago: University of Chicago Press, 1985). Laurie Finke comments on a variety of recent interpretations in "Sexuality in Medieval French Literature: Separés, on est ensemble," in *Handbook of Medieval Sexuality,* eds. Vern L. Bullough and James A. Brundage (New York: Garland Publishing, 1996), pp. 345–68.

53. Constable, *Letters and Letter Collections,* p. 11 (n. 10 above).

54. Constable, "Forged Letters in the Middle Ages," in *Fälschungen im Mittelalter* 5: 11–37, especially 33, in which he discusses the explanation of Bernard of Clairvaux about the difference between a sealed and an unsealed letter, *Ep.* 223, *SBO* 7: 90 (n. 46 above). See also Hartmut Hoffman, "Zur mittelalterlichen Brieftechnik," in *Spiegel der Geschichte. Festgabe für Max Braubach,* eds. K. Repgen and S. Skalweit (Münster: Aschendorff, 1964), pp. 141–70. Michael Clanchy discusses the growth in use of seals in the twelfth century in *From Memory to Written Record: England, 1066 – 1307* (Cambridge, Mass.: Harvard University Press, 1979).

55. Roscelin describes Abelard's seal in his *Epistola ad Abaelardum,* ed. Joseph Reiners, in *Der Nominalismus in der Frühscholastik. Ein Beitrag zur Geschichte der Universalienfrage im Mittelalter,* Beiträge zur Geschichte der Philosophie des Mittelalters, Bd 8.5 (Münster: Aschendorff, 1910), p. 80. John Benton suggested that Abelard's seal could have contained a traditional image of Rusticus (bearded) and Eleutherius (unbearded), companions of St. Denis, to whose memory the abbey of Saint-Denis was also dedicated. "A reconsideration of the authenticity of the correspondence of Abelard and Heloise," in *Petrus Abaelardus,* ed. Thomas, p. 47 (see p. 314 n. 95 below).

56. See above n. 13 and pp. 101–102.
57. Richard H. and Mary A. Rouse, "The Vocabulary of Wax Tablets," *Harvard Library Bulletin* 12 (1990): 12–19. On the use of wax tablets, see Elisabeth E. Lalou, "Les Tablettes de cire médiévales," *Bibliothèque de l'école des chartes* 147 (1989): 123–40, and her "Inventaire des tablettes médiévales en présentation générale," in *Les tablettes à écrire, de l'antiquité à l'époque moderne. Actes du colloque international du Centre National de la Recherche Scientifique, Paris, Institut de France, 10–11 octobre 1990*, ed. Elisabeth E. Lalou (Turnhout: Brepols, 1993), pp. 233–88. Parisian ivory writing tablets from ca. 1300 depicting a pair of lovers hawking and exchanging roses for a wreath (British Museum, Ivories 360) are illustrated in Larrington, *Women and Writing*, p. 43 (see above, n. 20).
58. *Carmina*, ed. Hilbert, nos. 12, 144, 148, 148, 196, pp. 42–43, 197–98, 200–201, 262–64 (n. 3 above); see Constable, *Letters and Letter-Collections*, p. 45 (n. 10 above).
59. Pseudo-Boèce, *De disciplina scolarum* 4.1, ed. Olga Weijers (Leiden: E. J. Brill, 1976), p. 110: "Si autem discipulus specialiter magistro suo, ut necessarium est, nequeat exhibere presenciam, tum propter mansionis distanciam, tum propter alterius rei causam, dipticas semper lateri promciores habeat cedulamve, quibus diligenter imprimat quod consciencie sue senserit intimatum eiusque explicite inquirat dubitatum." Weijers dates this Parisian manual to ca. 1230 – 40.
60. Letters *6, 9, 23, 24, 37, 42,* 45, *46,* 49, 53, *54,* 62, *63,* 69, 71, *75,* 79, 109, *110,* 112. Cf. Isidore, *Etymologiae* 19.18.4 and *De differentiis uerborum* 159, PL 83: 27A.
61. Constable observes that only the salutation and subscription are consistent elements of medieval letters, not necessarily the exordium (commonplace generality), narration and petition, as defined by theorists, *Letters and Letter-Collections*, pp. 16–17 (n. 10 above).
62. Carol Dana Lanham, *Salutatio Formulas in Latin Letters to 1200: Syntax, Style, and Theory,* Münchener Beiträge zur Mediävistik und Renaissance-Forschung 22 (Munich: Arbeo-Gesellschaft, 1975), especially pp. 7–12.
63. Modern English translations of Cant. 4.10 (*pulchriora ubera tua vino et odor unguentorum tuorum super omnia aromata*), have the image refer not to the breasts of the bride, but to her love.
64. The relative frequency of use of any word is evident from the immensely useful concordance to the Letters, supplied by Könsgen, pp. 113–37. Also of great value is his comparative list of metaphors, pp. 68–71.
65. See, p. 121.
66. *Liber pastoralis* 1.9, ed. Floribert Rommel, SC 381 (Paris: Cerf, 1992), p. 160: "semper cogitationum procellis nauis cordis quatitur." Cf. Isidore, *Etymologiae* 19.1.25.
67. See, pp. 69–70, 125–28.

68. Augustine, *In Iohannis epistulam ad Parthos tractatus* 8, PL 35: 2038: "omnis dilectio quae carnalis dicitur, quae non dilectio sed magis amor dici solet—dilectionis enim nomen magis solet in melioribus rebus dici, in melioribus accipi—tamen omnis dilectio, fratres carissimi, utique benevolentiam quandam habet erga eos qui diliguntur." This distinction is not commented upon by Pierre Rousselot, *Pour l'histoire du problème de l'amour au moyen âge* (Münster: Aschendorff, 1907) or Irving Singer, *The Nature of Love,* vol. 1, *Plato to Luther,* 2nd ed. (Chicago: University of Chicago Press, 1984).

69. See, p. 138.

70. See, pp. 91–93.

71. Cassiodorus, *Expositio psalmorum* Ps. 60.4, ed. Marc Adriaen, CCSL 97 (1958): 539.

72. Virgil, *Aeneid* 4.630–705; Lucan, *Pharsalia* 8.87–109, 637–793.

73. The words/deeds contrast is often made by Augustine, as in: *Ep.* 246, ed. Alois Goldbacher, CSEL 57 (1911): 585; *In Iohannis euangelium* 42.6, ed. Radbodus Willems, CCSL 36 (1954): 364; *In Iohannis epistulam* 6, PL 35: 2028. See also Abelard, *Commentaria in epistolam Pauli ad Romanos* 3 (9.3), ed. Buytaert, CCCM 11 (1969): 229; *Theologia Summi boni* 2.3, eds. Buytaert and Mews, CCCM 13 (1987): 114; *Theologia christiana* 2.53, 3.3, ed. Buytaert, CCCM 12 (1969): 153, 195.

74. In the manuscript, her phrase reads: "Si bene vales et inter mundana curris sine offensione, summa effero mentis exultacione." Without correcting the Latin, this translates as "I bear great things with exultation of mind." Könsgen corrects the stylistically awkward *effero* to *efferor.* It is surprising that Johannes de Vepria did not correct this mistake, given that he made two corrections to lines of text immediately preceding, *missa* over *emissa* (*110*) and an added *O* to indicate that *pulcra* is a vocative (*112*) as well as correcting his word order after this line.

75. The plural *eas litteras . . . litterarum tuarum* can theoretically refer to "that letter . . . your letter" in the singular, but the context suggests that she is referring to his letters as a whole.

76. Könsgen (p. 44) notes parallels in Virgil's *Aeneid* 7.201 (*portuque sedetis*) and Terence's *Andria* 480 (*Ego in portu navigo*).

77. Könsgen, p. 93. Bernd Scheidmüller, *Nomen patriae. Die Entstehung Frankreiches in der politisch-geographischen Terminologie (10.–13. Jahrhundert)* (Sigmaringen: Jan Thorbecke, 1987), p. 13; Charles T. Wood, "Regnum Francie: A Problem in Capetian Administrative Usage," *Traditio* 23 (1967): 117–47; Elizabeth M. Hallam, *Capetian France 987 – 1328* (London: Longman, 1980), pp. 27–62.

Chapter 2

1. *Le Roman de la Rose* lines 8808–32, ed. Daniel Poirion (Paris: Garnier-Flammarion, 1974), pp. 253–54; the complete passage relating to Abelard

and Heloise occupies lines 8759–832. The translation quoted here is that of Frances Horgan: Guillaume de Lorris and Jean de Meun, *The Romance of the Rose* (Oxford: Oxford University Press, 1994), p. 135. For the Latin text of the passage cited by Jean de Meun, see below, n. 15.

2. *La Vie et les epistres Pierres Abaelart et Heloys sa fame,* ed. Eric Hicks (Paris: Honoré Champion, 1991).

3. Only a single copy survives of his translation of the Abelard–Heloise correspondence, in the hand of Gontier Col (n. 49 below); about twenty each of his translations of Boethius and Vegetius, but none of Aelred or Gerald of Wales; V. L. Dédeck-Héry, "Boethius' *De Consolatione* par Jean de Meun," *Mediaeval Studies* 14 (1952): 165–275 and the introduction of Hicks, *La vie et les epistres,* pp. xxvii–xxix.

4. Kristeva comments on this transition in "The Troubadours: From "Great Courtly Romance" to Allegorical Narrative," *Tales of Love,* trans. Leon S. Roudiez (New York: Columbia University Press, 1987), pp. 280–96.

5. Heather Arden dissects Jean de Meun's presentation of Heloise and of women in general in "Women as Readers, Women as Text in the *Roman de la Rose,*" in *Women, the Book and the Worldly,* pp. 111–117 (p. 293, n. 20).

6. *HC,* ed. Monfrin, p. 107; ed. Hicks, p. 43. Radice (p. 104) translates *ex divina conversatione familiarissime comes* simply as "close friend and long-standing companion."

7. *HC,* ed. Monfrin, pp. 67, 70, 71, 73, 107; ed. Hicks, pp. 6, 9, 10, 12, 43; trans. Radice, pp. 61, 65, 68, 104. See Abelard's *Ep.* 10 to Bernard, ed. Smits, p. 239.

8. *HC,* ed. Monfrin, p. 71; ed. Hicks, p. 10; trans. Radice, p. 66 (translating *adolescentula* as young girl, rather than as young woman): "Erat quippe in ipsa civitate Parisius adolescentula quedam nomine Heloysa, neptis canonici cujusdam qui Fulbertus vocabatur, qui eam quanto amplius diligebat tanto diligentius in omnem qua poterat scientiam litterarum promoveri studuerat. Que cum per faciem non esset infima, per habundantiam litterarum erat suprema. Nam quo bonum hoc literatorie scilicet scientie in mulieribus est rarius, eo amplius puellam commendabat et in toto regno nominatissimam fecerat. Hanc igitur, omnibus circunspectis que amantes allicere solent, commodiorem censui in amorem mihi copulare, et me id facillime credidi posse. Tanti quippe tunc nominis eram et juventutis et forme gratia preminebam, ut quamcunque feminarum nostro dignarer amore nullam vererer repulsam. Tanto autem facilius hanc mihi puellam consensuram credidi, quanto amplius eam litterarum scientiam et habere et diligere noveram; nosque etiam absentes scriptis internuntiis invicem liceret presentare et pleraque audacius scribere quam colloqui, et sic semper jocundis interesse colloquiis."

9. *HC,* ed. Monfrin, p. 64; ed. Hicks, p. 4; trans. Radice, p. 59; cf. Isidore, *Etymologiae* 11.2.3–6 (p. 291, n. 2 above).

10. See n. 68 below. Radice states (p. 66 n. 1) that "as she was a young girl (*ado-lescentula*), it can only be assumed that she was about seventeen at this time, and born in 1100 or 1101," a claim repeated by Verger, *L'amour castré*, p. 42 (p. 292, n. 11). The lack of evidence for her age was pointed out in *Histoire littéraire de la France* 12 (Paris: Huart et Moreau, 1763): 629. Charlotte Charrier thought that she was a teenager, *Héloïse dans l'histoire et dans la légende* (Paris: Honoré Champion, 1933; repr. Geneva: Slatkine Reprints, 1977), p. 52; Enid McLeod was more cautious, *Héloïse. A Biography*, 2nd ed. (London: Chatto & Windus, 1971), pp. 8 and 287–89.

11. *Ep.* 115, ed. Giles Constable, *The Letters of Peter the Venerable* (Cambridge, Mass.: Harvard University Press, 1967), 2 vols, 1:303–4; trans. Radice, pp. 277–78. Constable (2:257) indicates that Peter was born in either 1092 or 1094; it seems likely that the chronicle of Cluny pushed up his age to explain his appointment as abbot in 1122 more respectable. Clanchy rightly criticizes the young age imputed to Heloise, *Abelard: A Medieval Life*, pp. 173–74.

12. *HC,* ed. Monfrin, pp. 72–73; ed. Hicks, p. 10; trans. Radice, p. 67.

13. *HC,* ed. Monfrin, p. 73; ed. Hicks, p. 12; trans. Radice, p. 68.

14. *HC,* ed. Monfrin, pp. 75–78; ed. Hicks, pp. 14–17; trans. Radice, pp. 71–74, alluding to passages in *Theologia christiana* 2.38, 67, 96–97, 101, ed. Buytaert, CCCM 12:148, 159–60, 173–74, 177.

15. *HC,* ed. Monfrin, p. 78; ed. Hicks, p. 17; Radice, p. 74 (translating *amicam* as mistress): "Addebat denique ipsa et quam periculosum mihi esset eam reducere, et quam sibi carius existeret mihique honestius amicam dici quam uxorem ut me ei sola gratia conservaret, non aliqua vinculi nuptialis constringeret." Curiously this central passage is missing from Jean de Meun's translation of *HC.* On the passages from Jerome, see pp. 139 and 353, n. 95 below.

16. Abelard quotes Ovid, *Remedia Amoris* line 369, ed. A. A. R. Henderson (Edinburgh: Scottish Academic Press, 1979), p. 13: "Summa petit livor, perflant altissima venti" in *HC,* ed. Monfrin, p. 66; ed. Hicks, p. 6; trans. Radice, p. 61; in *HC,* ed. Monfrin, pp. 85–86 and 94; ed. Hicks, pp. 23 and 31; trans. Radice, pp. 81 and 90, Abelard quotes classical allusions from Jerome, *Liber quaestionum hebraicarum in Genesim* 1, ed. Paul de Lagarde CCSL 72 (1959): 1: "semper enim in propatulo fortitudo aemulos habet, feriunt que summos fulgura montes [Horace, *Odes* 2.10.11]: me uero procul ab urbibus, foro, litibus, turbis remotum, sic quoque (ut Quintilianus [*Declamationes*, 13.2] ait) latentem inuenit inuidia." Cf. Ovid, *Tristia* 4.10 line 123 and *Epistulae ex Ponto* 3.3 line 101. Jerome speaks of *invidia* in *Ep.* 15.2, 21.2, 36, 45.4, 54.3, 77.12, 78.3, 99.2, 108.18, ed. Isidorus Hilberg, 3 vols. CSEL 54–56 (1910 – 18), 54:63, 112, 136, 325, 468; 55:49, 53, 212, 329.

17. Jean de Meun reads *vestrum* in her opening sentence as *nostrum* and leaves out *forte,* so as to diminish the sense of outrage in her opening remark:

"Your man lately showed me your letter which you sent to our friend as consolation." In *Women Writers*, p. 304 n. 12, Dronke suggests that Jean de Meun might have preserved Heloise's original words, but this has no support in the Latin manuscripts. Hicks (p. 45) notes that *voz homs* and *nostre* in the manuscript of Jean de Meun's translation could be misreadings of *uns homs* and *vostre,* thus agreeing with the Latin text.

18. *Ep.* 2, ed. Monfrin, p. 114; ed. Hicks, p. 49: "Nichil umquam—Deus scit!—in te nisi te requisivi; te pure, non tua concupiscens. Non matrimonii federam non dotes aliquas expectavi, non denique meas voluptates aut voluntates, sed tuas, sicut ipse nosti adimplere studui. Et si uxoris nomen sanctius ac validius videtur, dulcius mihi semper extitit amice vocabulum, aut—si non indigneris—concubine vel scorti; ut quo me videlicet pro te amplius humiliarem, ampliorem apud te consequerer gratiam, et sic etiam excellentie tue gloriam minus lederem. Quod et tu ipse tui gratia oblitus penitus non fuisti in ea directa, ubi et rationes nonnullas quibus te a conjugio nostro et infaustis thalamis revocare conabar exponere non es dedignatus, sed plerisque tacitis quibus amorem conjugio, libertatem vinculo preferebam. Deum testem invoco, si me Augustus universo presidens mundo matrimonii honore dignaretur, totumque mihi orbem confirmaret in perpetuo possidendum, karius michi et dignius videretur tua dici meretrix quam illius imperatrix." As in her translation of Abelard's version of her argument, Radice (pp. 74, 113) renders *amica* as "mistress." Jean de Meun renders it as *amie* in his translation of *Ep.* 2, but does not include this sentence in *The Romance of the Rose,* only her later sentence that she would rather be called "your prostitute" than his empress (n. 1 above).

19. On the epitaph and Hilary's comment, see, pp. 90, 105, 341, n. 107.

20. Michael Calabrese, "Ovid and the Female Voice in the *De Amore* and the *Letters* of Abelard and Heloise," *Modern Philology* 95 (1997): 1–26; see also pp. 90–93.

21. *Ep.* 5, ed. Hicks, pp. 78–79, 84; trans. Radice, pp. 146–47, 153.

22. Although the traditional view has been that the council of Sens was held on the octave of Pentecost 1140 (2 June), it has been convincingly argued that William of St Thierry must have written to Bernard in Lent 1140, and that the council of Sens was held on the octave of Pentecost 1141 (25 May), as Stephen, cardinal bishop of Palestrina (formerly a monk of Clairvaux and recipient of Bernard's *Ep.* 336 on the errors of Abelard) was not made a cardinal bishop until 8 April 1141; see Piero Zerbi, "Les différends doctrinaux," in *Bernard de Clairvaux,* eds. Bertrand and Lobrichon, pp. 429–58 (p. 294, n. 22, referring to research of R. Volpini), and Ferruccio Gastaldelli, "Le piu antiche testimonianze biografiche su san Bernardo. Studio storico-critico sui 'Fragmentum Gaufridi'," *Analecta Cisterciensia* 45 (1989): 3–80, esp. 60–61, and "'Optimus Praedicator'. L'Opera oratoria di San Bernardo," *Analecta Cisterciensia* 51 (1995): 321–418, esp. 339; see also

Adriaan Hendrik Bredero, *Bernard of Clairvaux. Between Cult and History* (Grand Rapids, Mich.: William B. Erdmanns, 1996), p. 285. An 1141 date was originally put forward by S. Martin Deutsch, *Die Synode von Sens 1141 und die Verurteilung Abälards* (Berlin: Weidmann, 1880), pp. 50–54. Constable (2: 317–20) observed that Nicholas of Montiéramy, likely to be *Nicolaus iste meus, immo et vester,* whom Bernard mentioned in a codicil to *Ep.* 330 as able to advise the pope about Abelard (*SBO* 8: 268), was in Rome between 1140 and August/September 1141, and so opted for an 1141 date for the condemnation (issued on 16 July), but an 1140 date for the council. It seems more likely, however, that the council was held on 25 May 1141, and the condemnation issued seven weeks later. Nicholas may have brought Bernard's treatise on the errors of Abelard (*Ep.* 190) to the pope in 1140, but could not have taken *Ep.* 330, written by Bernard to the pope immediately after the council, to Rome. Instructions attached to Innocent's letter of condemnation to have Abelard and Arnold of Brescia thrown into confinement, printed by Jean Mabillon from an unknown Vatican manuscript, were never carried out, *Sancti Bernardi Opera Omnia* 1.1 (Paris: Gaume, 1839), col. 896.

23. *S. Bernardi Vita Prima* 3.5, PL 185: 310D–312A. Bredero observes that Geoffrey's later revision of this passage (after 1163) eliminated description of Abelard as a heretic, *Bernard of Clairvaux. Between Cult and History,* p. 47 (n. 22 above); on his conversion to Bernard, ibid., pp. 93–94. Bredero also discusses the relationship between the *Vita prima* and the push to canonize Bernard in "The Canonization of Bernard of Clairvaux," *Saint Bernard of Clairvaux: Studies commemorating the Eighth Centenary of his Canonization,* ed. M. Basil Pennington, CSS 28 (Kalamazoo, Mich.: Cistercian Publications, 1977), pp. 63–100 and "The Canonization of Bernard of Clairvaux and the Rewriting of his Life," *Cistercian Ideals and Reality,* ed. John R. Sommerfeldt, CSS 60 (Kalamazoo, Mich.: Cistercian Publications, 1978), pp. 80–105. Michael Casey reflects on the limitations of Geoffrey's presentation of Bernard in "Towards a Methodology for the *Vita prima:* Translating the First Life into Biography," *Bernardus Magister. Papers Presented at the Nonacentenary Celebration of the Birth of Saint Bernard of Clairvaux,* ed. John R. Sommerfeldt, CSS 135 (Spencer, Mass.: Cistercian Publications, 1992), pp. 55–70. Excerpts from the *Vita prima,* as compiled by William of St. Thierry, Arnold of Bonneval and Geoffrey of Auxerre (although unfortunately not the passage relating to Abelard) are translated by Pauline Matarasso, *The Cistercian World: Monastic Writings of the Twelfth Century* (Harmondsworth: Penguin, 1993), pp. 19–41.

24. Bernard of Clairvaux, *Ep.* 188–94, *SBO* 8: 10–48. A separate sequence of letters about Abelard, *Ep.* 330–38, *SBO* 8: 266–78 did not circulate until later in the twelfth century. On the development of these collections of letters relating to Abelard see my study, "The lists of heresies imputed to Peter

Abelard," *Revue bénédictine* 95 (1985): 73–110. Leclercq discusses the corpus of letters assembled by Geoffrey of Auxerre ca. 1145, as well as a subsequent collection, in the introduction to *SBO* 7: xii-xvi.

25. *Ottonis et Rahewini Gesta Friderici Imperatoris* 1.49, eds. Georg Waitz and Bernard von Simson, 3rd ed. (Hannover: Hahnsche Buchhandlung, 1912, repr. 1978), p. 69: "Ubi occasione quadam satis nota non bene tractatus monachus in monasterio sancti Dyonisii effectus est." Even John of Salisbury was under the impression that Abelard had been officially condemned, although John was aware that the cardinals of the curia in 1148 were opposed to Bernard's efforts to influence the Pope in this way, *Historia pontificalis*, ed. and trans. Marjorie Chibnall (Oxford: Clarendon Press, 1986), pp. 16–20.

26. *Ep.* 115, ed. Constable, 1: 307: "Sacramenta caelestia, immortalis agni sacrificium deo labore meo, apostolicae gratiae redditus est, pene continuabat." Trans. Radice, p. 282.

27. *Ep.* 98, ed. Constable, 1: 258–59; trans. Radice, pp. 275–76. Only one twelfth-century copy of this letter is known.

28. *Chronicon, Recueil,* 13: 675, re-edited from Paris, BNF lat. 4943, fol. 56v in my introduction to the *Theologia Scholarium,* CCCM 13 (1987): 291. While doubts have been raised about a rubric attributing it to William Godel, monk of Saint-Martial, Limoges (on the grounds that he does not discuss Limoges), there seems no reason to call him pseudo-Godel, as sometimes is the case.

29. Godel's comments about his admiration for Elisabeth of Schönau and Hildegard of Bingen were omitted from the edition printed in *Recueil* 13; ed. Léopold Delisle, *Histoire littéraire de la France,* 32 (Paris: Imprimerie nationale, 1898): 254–55.

30. *Ep.* 9, ed. Edmé Smits, *Peter Abelard. Letters IX – XIV* (Groningen: Bouma, 1983), p. 231: "et dum potestis et matrem harum peritam trium linguarum habetis." On Jerome's knowledge of the three languages, see Augustine, *De Ciuitate Dei* 18.43, ed. Bernard Dombart and Alphonsus Kalb, CCSL 48 (1955): 639 and Isidore, *Etymologiae* 6.4.5 and 9.1.3.

31. Robert of Auxerre, *Chronicon* (ca. 1203), ed. Bouquet, *Recueil,* 12: 294A, ed. O. Holder-Egger MGH SS 26 (1882): 235.

32. *Decrees of the Ecumenical Councils,* canon 27, ed. Josepho Alberigo et al., trans. Norman Tanner, 2 vols. (London and Georgetown: Sheed & Ward and Georgetown University Press, 1990), 1: 203. See Jo Ann Kay McNamara, *Sisters in Arms. Catholic Nuns through Two Millennia* (Cambridge, Mass: Harvard University Press, 1996), p. 221.

33. *Ecumenical Councils,* Canon 27, 1: 203: "Simili modo prohibemus ne sanctimoniales simul cum canonicis vel monachis in ecclesia in uno choro conveniant ad psallendum."

34. *Ep.* 79, *SBO* 7: 211. On Luke de Roucy and the subsequent separation of women from men at Cuissy, see Bruce L. Venarde, *Women's Monasticism and*

Medieval Society: Nunneries in France and England, 890 – 1215 (Ithaca: Cornell University Press, 1997), pp. 69, 164 n. 114.

35. Venarde, *Women's Monasticism,* pp. 70 and 164–65 (n. 34); Sally Thompson, *Women Religious. The Founding of English Nunneries after the Norman Conquest* (Oxford: Clarendon Press, 1991), pp. 134–36; McNamara, *Sisters in Arms,* p. 296. On the separation of monks and nuns that took place at Fontevrault in the second half of the century, see Lorraine N. Simmons, "The Abbey Church at Fontevraud in the Late Twelfth Century: Anxiety, Authority and Architecture in the Female Spiritual Life," *Gesta* 31 (1992): 99–107.

36. Peter Dronke edits the passage from the Chronicle of Tours, composed before 1227 (from Berlin, Deutsche Staatsbibliothek, Phill. 1852) in *Medieval Testimonies,* p. 51 (*Intellectuals and Poets,* p. 286; p. 292, n. 12 above). This passage is also found in Bern, Bürgerbibliothek MS 22, fols. 112v–113r.

37. Constant J. Mews, "La bibliothèque du Paraclet du XIIIe siècle à la Révolution," *Studia Monastica* 27 (1985): 31–67. On the liturgical manuscripts of the Paraclete, see the publications of Waddell (n. 112 below).

38. Monfrin describes this MS in his introduction to the *Historia calamitatum,* pp. 10–13, noting that the date of 1346 given by Robert de Bardi on its flyleaf in fact refers to 1347.

39. Berengar's *Apologia* and other letters are edited by Rodney M. Thomson, "The Satirical Works of Berengar of Poitiers: An Edition with Introduction," *Mediaeval Studies* 42 (1980): 89–138. Charles Burnett has edited the three works of Abelard in this dossier: "Peter Abelard. 'Soliloquium'—A Critical Edition," *Studi Medievali* 25 (1984): 857–94; "'Confessio fidei ad Heloisam'—Abelard's last Letter to Heloise?," *Mittellateinisches Jahrbuch* 21 (1986): 147–55; "Peter Abelard, *Confessio fidei 'Universis':* A Critical Edition of Abelard's Reply to Heresy," *Mediaeval Studies* 48 (1986): 111–38. The correspondence occurs alongside the Berengar corpus in Paris, BNF lat. 2923 and Oxford, Bodleian Library, Add. C.271.

40. Monfrin, pp. 18–19; *Posteritati* in *Prose,* eds. G. Martellotti, P. G. Ricci, E. Carrara, and E. Bianchi (Milan: Riccardo Ricciardi Editore, 1955), p. 14. The Abelard manuscript is not mentioned in a list of Petrarch's books drawn up in 1337, ed. Pierre de Nolhac, *Pétrarque et l'humanisme,* 2 vols. (Paris: Honoré Champion, 1965), 2: 293–96.

41. Paris, BNF lat. 2923, fols. 91–93 and 172–77. Jean Leclercq, "L'amitié dans les lettres au moyen âge. Autour d'un manuscrit de la Bibliothèque de Pétrarque," *Revue du moyen âge latin* 1 (1945): 391–410. Leclercq notes (405–6) that a number complain of financial hardship; one is from a student to his mother saying he wishes to return home for the vacation, followed by his mother's reply. His unsubstantiated remark (391) that the manuscript was probably written in the south of France is repeated by Monfrin (p. 19), who assigns it to the late thirteenth rather than the mid-

thirteenth century. The Parisian origin of the students' letters in the treatises point to Paris as the more likely provenance.

42. Pierre de Nolhac, *Pétrarque et l'humanisme*, 2: 287–92. He edits this list,
spanning 21 April – 23 August 1344, 21–27 July, and 2–25 October 1345,
30 May 1348 – 2 August 1349, without noting the coded nature of the
accompanying dots, dashes, and crosses. On Petrarch's sexual struggles at
this time, see *Posteritati* [ca. 1351], in *Prose*, ed. Martellotti, p. 4. In a letter to Boccaccio (*Seniores* 8.1) written in 1366, Petrarch says that he had
freed himself "more perfectly" from sexual temptation only after the
Great Jubilee, in 1350; in a letter of 11 June 1352 to his brother Gerard,
the Carthusian monk, Petrarch says that he now fears as more serious
than death the company of women, without whom he previously could
not live; "and although I am often disturbed by very sharp temptations,
yet when it comes back to mind what a woman is, all temptation immediately flies away and I return to my freedom and peace" (*Familiares*
10.5). Ernest Hatch Wilkins discusses Petrarch's ecclesiastical career in
the period after 1341 in *Studies in the Life and Works of Petrarch* (Cambridge, Mass.: Mediaeval Academy of America, 1955), pp. 8–13. Petrarch
first came to Parma on 22 May 1341, restored the house he had obtained
there in 1344 and took possession of his canonry at Parma in 1347, his
archdeaconry in 1348; see Fortunato Rizzi, "Date e opere parmense nella
vita del Petrarca," *Parma e Francesco Petrarca (9–10 Maggio 1934). Atti del
Convego. Communicazioni. Memorie* (Parma: Editore Mario Fresching,
1934), pp. 279–88.

43. Dronke comments on these notes of Petrarch in *Medieval Testimonies*, pp.
56–58 (*Intellectuals and Poets*, pp. 290–91; p. TKTK, n. 11 above). Petrarch
refers to Abelard, but not Heloise, in his *De vita solitaria* 2.12, in *Prose*, ed.
Martellotti, p. 528; trans. Jacob Zeitlin, *The Life of Solitude by Francis Petrarch*
(Urbana: University of Illinois Press, 1924), p. 270; see 2.44, ed. cit., p. 434;
trans. Zeitlin, p. 205. Whether Petrarch wrote the paragraph on Abelard in
1346 is not known, as he was still making emendations to *The Life of Solitude* in 1371.

44. Most surviving manuscripts of the correspondence are from the fourteenth
or early fifteenth centuries: Checklist, nos. 131, 154, 99, 37; Monfrin, pp.
20–28. See also a fourteenth-century copy in private possession, described
by Colette Jeudy, "Un nouveau manuscrit de la *Correspondance d'Abélard et
Héloïse*," *Latomus* 50 (1991): 872–81.

45. This comment in the letter of Jean de Hesdin directed against Petrarch,
found in Paris, BNF lat. 16232, fols. 144–49 was noted by Beryl Smalley,
"Jean de Hesdin, O.Hsp.S.Ioh.," *Recherches de théologie ancienne et médiévale*
28 (1961): 293. Petrarch responded to Jean de Hesdin in his *Invectiva contra
eum qui maledixit Italie*, within *Prose*, ed. Martellotti, pp. 678–807 (with
valuable notes on pp. 1175–76).

46. F. Novati, *Epistolario di Coluccio Salutati,* 4 vols. (Rome: Istituto storico italiano, 1891 – 1911), 3: 76 and 146. Pico della Mirandola (1469 – 1533) owned a manuscript of Berengar's *Apologia* which might have included the letters; Checklist, nos. 244, 260.

47. Ed. Éric Hicks, *Le Débat sur le Roman de la Rose* (Paris: Honoré Champion, 1977), p. 146: "Tu ressambles Helouye du Paraclit qui dist que mieux ameroit estre *meretrix* appellee me maistre Pierre Abalart que estre royne couronnee; si appert bien que les voulantés qui mieux plaisent ne sont pas toutes raisonnables." *La Querelle de la Rose: Letters and Documents* (Chapel Hill: North Carolina Studies in the Romance Languages and Literatures, 1978), trans. Joseph L. Baird and John R. Kane, p. 141, based on an earlier, less accurate edition of Christine's text.

48. Earl Jeffrey Richards comments on Christine's avoidance of Heloise in "'*Seulette a part*'—The Little 'Woman on the Sidelines' Takes Up Her Pen: The Letters of Christine de Pizan," in *Dear Sister,* ed. Cherewatuk and Wiethaus, pp. 139–70 (p. 293, n. 46 above). While her use of *meretrix* might indicate familiarity with the Latin, her knowledge of Heloise's letter is shaped by Jean de Meun's quotation from it.

49. Carla Bozzolo, "L'humaniste Gontier Col et la traduction française des *Lettres* d'Abélard et Héloïse," *Romania* 95 (1974): 199–215.

50. He owned a manuscript, valued at 10s., containing *La Exortation Pierre Abalard, avec aultres traitiez* (almost certainly Abelard's lost "Exhortation to my brothers and fellow monks"); an unbound copy of the sermons of Peter Abelard, valued at 24s; a paper copy of the letters of Abelard, valued at 2s; a manuscript valued at 8s, in which Abelard's Rule for the Paraclete was attached on eight gatherings, separated from its letter of introduction; Checklist, no. 212.

51. Benedict XIII [1396], *Cartulaire de l'Abbaye du Paraclet,* no. 44, ed. C. Lalore, Collection des principaux cartulaires du diocèse de Troyes, vol. 2 (Paris: Ernest Thorin, 1878), pp. 60–61: "Cum itaque, sicut accepimus, ecclesia et alia edificia monasterii monialium Paracliti ordinis sancti Benedicti, Trecensis diocesis, propter guerras, que in illis partibus diucius viguerunt, adeo sint destructa quod absque Christi fidelium elemosinis commode reparari non possint: Nos cupientes ut dicta edificia reparentur, et ut Christi fideles eo libentius causa devotionis confluant ad eandem et ad reparationem hujusmodi manus promptius porrigant adjutrices, quo ex hiis ibidem uberioris dono celestis gracie conspexerint se refectos. . . ." See also Lalore, pp. xxi–xxii. Gontier Col (see above, n. 49) was an important member of a royal delegation to Benedict XIII in Avignon in 1395. Given his interest in Abelard and Heloise, it might be worth investigating whether he helped obtain this indulgence for the Paraclete and even helped return Robert de Bardi's manuscript to the abbey.

52. Sometime before 1326 Annebale de Ceccano, a canon of Notre-Dame, bought from the cathedral chapter a twelfth-century copy of Abelard's commentary on Genesis, introduced by a letter of Abelard to Heloise (Vatican, Biblioteca apostolica, Vat. lat. 4214) see Checklist, no. 188. Pierre de Joigny bequeathed sermons of Abelard to Notre-Dame in 1297; Checklist, no. 250. In the late fourteenth or early fifteenth century Simon de Plumetot (1371 – 1443), a humanist moving in the same circle as Gontier Col, Nicolas de Baye and Jean de Montreuil, prepared an elegant copy of the *Theologia Scholarium* (Paris, BNF lat. 14793). Simon also commissioned the only surviving copy (Paris, BNF lat. 14511) of the *Problemata* of Heloise and Abelard's *Ep.* 9 to the nuns of the Paraclete.

53. Ed. Leslie C. Brook, *Two Late Medieval Love Treatises. Heloise's* Art d'Amour *and a Collection of* Demandes d'Amour. *Edited with Introduction, Notes and Glossary from British Library Royal MS 16 F II*, Medium Aevum Monographs New Series XVI (London: Society for the Study of Mediaeval Languages and Literature, 1993). This edition is not known to Véronique Walkerley, "Heloys: André or Andreas? A problem of authorship in MS Royal 16 F II in the British Museum Library," *Nottingham French Studies* 35 (1998): 18–26.

54. Discussed by Charrier, *Héloïse dans l'histoire et dans la légende*, pp. 386–88 (n. 10 above).

55. For further detail of my criticism of Monfrin's hypothesis that the *exemplar Paraclitense* used by Duchesne is an exact duplicate of the Troyes MS, and existed at the Paraclete until it was lost at the Revolution, see Mews, "La bibliothèque du Paraclet du XIIIe siècle à la Révolution," 39–42 (n. 37 above). The epitaphs and formula of absolution are edited by Mews and Charles Burnett in an appendix, 61–67.

56. On this and subsequent re-burials, see Charrier, *Héloïse dans l'histoire et dans la légende*, pp. 304–9 and McLeod, *Héloïse. A Biography*, pp. 229–31 (n. 10 above). Charrier also mentions antagonism between the Paraclete and the bishop of Troyes at ths time over a separate matter, complaints that the nuns danced and sang vernacular song in procession to the *Croix du Maître*, said to have been established by Abelard.

57. These two related paper manuscripts, Paris, BNF lat. 2545 and BNF lat. nouv. acq. lat. 1873, described by Monfrin, pp. 25–28, are important because they include a letter from Fulco to Abelard not found in any earlier manuscript, but which existed in their common exemplar. Monfrin (p. 27) notes that Paris, BNF lat. 2545 includes a rubric specifically about the year of Bernard's death in 1153, the foundation of Cîteaux, and Bernard's age when he became a monk there. This might suggest Cistercian provenance for the manuscript, which also included the letters of Bernard of Clairvaux against Abelard. Late fifteenth-century interest in Abelard's writings for the Paraclete is also demonstrated by the copy of Abelard's sermons *ad virgines*

Paraclitenses et alia quaedam, bequeathed by Jean L'Huillier (d. 1500) to the library of the Sorbonne; Checklist, no. 235, p. 233.

58. Abelard's writings are prohibited in the *Index Auctorum et Librorum . . . Prohibitorum* (Rome: Antonius Bladus, 1559) [unpaginated, under letter P, but in many subsequent editions under A]; see also *Catalogue des ouvrages mis à l'index* (Paris: Edouard Garnot, 2nd ed. 1825), p. 1.

59. Repr. PL 178: 109–112. Monfrin provides an excellent discussion on pp. 31–46 of how the edition was published twice in 1616, once under the name of André Duchesne (the more accomplished scholar) and with different prefatory matter, but an identical text, under the name of François d'Amboise. When d'Amboise's edition was reprinted with additional texts by Jacques-Paul Migne in 1885 as vol. 178 of the *Patrologia Latina,* it was published as *Petri Abaelardi abbatis Rugensis Opera Omnia,* without reference to writings by Heloise.

60. Juan Caramuel y Lobkowitz, O.Cist., *Bernardus Petrum Abailardum eiusque potentissimos sectarios triumphans* (Louvain: Everard de Witte, 1644). Interest in Abelard's theology was maintained during the mid-seventeenth century by a group of English scholars who transcribed then still unpublished works of Abelard from a major fourteenth-century manuscript (Oxford, Balliol College 296), unknown to Amboise or Duchesne; see my introduction to the *Theologia Scholarium,* CCCM 13: 258–61.

61. François de Grenaille, *Nouveau recueil de lettres des dames tant anciennes que modernes,* 2 vols. (Paris: Toussainct Quinet, 1642), 1: 273–381. This translation, unknown to Charrier, has been ignored by subsequent scholars writing about the image of Heloise and the *Lettres portugaises.* On de Grenaille, see Katherine A. Jensen, "Male Models of Feminine Epistolarity; or, How to Write Like a Woman in Seventeenth-Century France," *Writing the Female Voice. Essays on Epistolary Literature,* ed. Elizabeth C. Goldsmith (Boston: Northeastern University Press, 1989), pp. 25–45, especially 35–36 and Linda Timmermanns, *L'accès des femmes à la culture (1598 – 1714)* (Paris: Honoré Champion, 1993), pp. 200–1. Altman discusses the rarity of collections of women's letters in the seventeenth century in "The Letter Book as a Literary Institution 1539 - 1789," 42–49 (p. 293, n. 49 above).

62. De Grenaille, 1: 274.

63. The first letter is quite fictitious (1: 275–300), but the second and third are based more closely on Heloise's first letter (1: 302–34, 336–63). De Grenaille then introduces an invented letter (1: 364–71) and has Heloise introduce the *Confessio fidei ad Heloisam* (1: 374–80) as a letter to a third party.

65. Frédéric Deloffre and Jacques Rougeot argue for the possible influence on Guilleragues of the de Grenaille translation, in their edition of his writing, *Chansons et bon mots, Valentins, Lettres portugaises* (Geneva: Droz, 1972), pp. 106–8, developing arguments of Leo Spitzer, "Les Lettres por-

tugaises," *Romanische Forschungen* 65 (1954): 94–135, repr. in *Romanische Literaturstudien 1936 – 1956* (Tübingen: Niemeyer, 1959), pp. 210–47, and translated into English by David Bellos, "The *Lettres portugaises,*" *Essays on Seventeenth-Century French Literature* (Cambridge: Cambridge University Press, 1983), pp. 255–83 and by Guido Waldman, *The Love Letters of a Portuguese Nun* (London: The Harvill Press, 1996). Dronke had earlier defended Marianne's authorship in "Heloise and Marianne: Some Reconsiderations," *Romanische Forschungen* 72 (1960): 223–56, arguing against Spitzer (both unaware of the de Grenaille translation) that they could not have been based on the letters of Heloise given that Bussy-Rabutin's translation only appeared in 1687. Yves Florenne argues for Marianne's authorship in his edition of the *Lettres portugaises* (Paris: Librairie générale française, 1979).

66. Charrier discusses this novel and subsequent translations in *Héloïse dans l'histoire et dans la légende,* pp. 406–32, with detailed bibliography on pp. 605–13 (n. 10 above); *Les Amours d'Abailard et d'Héloïse* (Amsterdam: Pierre Chayer, 1695), p. 8. I have not found a copy of the first edition, which Charrier reports (pp. 407 and 450) was published in Amsterdam in 1675.

67. *Les Lettres de Messire Roger de Rabutin, comte de Bussy,* 2 vols. (Paris: Florentin et Pierre Delaulne, 1697), 2: 116–51; *Correspondance,* ed. Ludovic Lalanne, 6 vols. (Paris: Charpentier, 1858 – 59), 6: 61–63 (letters of 16–18 April 1687); see Durant W. Robertson Jr., *Abelard and Heloise* (London: Millington, 1974), pp. 156–64.

68. *Lettre d'Héloïse à Abailard* (Amsterdam: Pierre Chayer, 1693), p. A.3: "L'Amour est aisée à persuader à une fille, surtout à l'age de dix-huit ans." Rémond des Cours produced a study and a translation *Histoire d'Éloïse et d'Abélard, avec la Lettre passionnée qu'elle lui écrivit* (The Hague: Louis et Henry van Dole, 1693), reprinted many times subsequently under the name of F.-N. Du Bois, that was in turn based on that of Rabutin. The Amsterdam translation was published alongside the Portuguese letters, *Recueil de Lettres galantes et amoureuses d'Héloïse à Abailard, d'une Religieuse portugaise au chevalier ****; avec celles de Cléante et de Bélise, et leur Réponse* (Amsterdam: François Roger, 1699).

69. The letters were among books seized in Paris in 1694, 1696, 1701; Anne Sauvy, *Livres Saisis à Paris entre 1678 et 1701* (The Hague: Martinus Nijhoff, 1972), nos. 481, 518, 942, 1111, 1113; see also nos. 183, 202 as well as many other examples of such literature, seized by the authorities.

70. Bayle is reported as attributing the 1693 (The Hague) translation to a woman because of their subtlety of perception, in the introduction to *Letters of Abelard and Heloise* (London: J. Watts, 1718), p. iv, but I have not located this remark in his articles on *Abélard* and *Héloïse* in *Dictionnaire historique et critique* (Rotterdam: Reinier Leers, 1697; 4th revised ed. Paris: P. Brunel, 1730), 2 tomes in 4 vols, 1.1: 23–31 and 2.1: 40–48.

71. P.-F. G. de Beauchamps, *Les Lettres d'Héloïse et d'Abailard, mises en vers françois* (Paris: J. Estienne, 1714, expanded in 1721); see also Charrier, pp. 424, 606, nos. 49, 53–54.

72. V. Malherbe, *La langue françoise expliquée dans un ordre nouveau* (Paris: Nicole Lebreton, 1725), p. 244: "ce n'est point l'art, c'est la nature qui s'exprime." The translations of letters 2–5 occur on pp. 245–74.

73. Wing Catalogue of Early English Books, 1641 – 1700: Ann Arbor, Mich.: University Microfilms International, reel 1400: 26, p. 5. Charrier's listing of English translations of the correspondence (p. 614) is very incomplete.

74. *The Letters of Eloïsa and Abelard*, translated by John Hughes (London: J. Watts, 1714) from the version attributed to Du Bois (n. 68 above).

75. Pope's esteem for Hughes is evident in a letter of 7 October 1715, *The Correspondence of Alexander Pope*, ed. George Sherburn, 5 vols. (Oxford: Clarendon Press, 1956), 1: 316. See Maynard Mack, *Alexander Pope. A Biography* (New Haven-London: Yale University Press, 1985), pp. 302–6, 319–31 and Ellen Polak, *The Poetics of Sexual Myth. Gender and Ideology in the Verse of Swift and Pope* (Chicago: University of Chicago Press, 1985), pp. 183–87.

76. *Letters of Abelard and Heloise: to which is prefix'd a particular account of their lives, amours and misfortunes, extracted chiefly from Monsieur Bayle, by John Hughes. To which are added the poem of Eloisa to Abelard by Mr Pope and Abelard to Eloisa by Mrs Madan* (London, 1773). Durant W. Robertson Jr. emphasises the links between Pope's composition and Ovid's *Sappho to Phaon*, in *Abelard & Heloise*, pp. 182–214 (n. 67 above). The poem by Mrs Madan is not mentioned by Charrier or Robertson, but was published alongside the Hughes translation many times between 1773 and 1818; see Lonsdale, *Eighteenth-Century Women Poets*, pp. 93–96, 520 (n. 75 above).

77. Colardeau's translation of Pope's *Eloisa to Abelard* was printed alongside a reply from Abelard to Heloise by a M. C★★, as well as versions by M. Feutry, M. Dorat, M. Mercier. M. G★★ Dourxigné, M. Saurin; *Les Lettres et Epitres amoureuses d'Héloïse et d'Abeillard, traduits librement en vers et en prose* n. d. (Au Paraclet: [1774]); Charrier, p. 609 no. 82. According to Charrier (p. 607, nos. 61), the first translation of Pope into French was published in Berlin in 1751, prompting that of Colardeau in 1758; Charrier, pp. 440–92 and pp. 607–8 (nos. 58–91).

78. *Julie, ou la Nouvelle Héloïse. Lettres de deux Amans, Habitans d'une petite Ville au pied des Alpes receuillis et publiées par Jean-Jacques Rousseau*, ed. René Pomeau (Paris: Garnier Frères, 1960), lettre 24, p. 60; trans. Judith H. McDowell, *La Nouvelle Héloïse. Julie or the New Eloise. Letters of Two Lovers, Inhabitants of a small town at the foot of the Alps* (University Park and London: Pennsylvania State University Press, 1968), p. 68.

79. Eric Walter, "Le Complexe d'Abélard ou le célibat des gens de lettres," *Dix-Huitième Siècle* 12 (1980): 127–52; Charrier lists works inspired by Rousseau, pp. 644–45.

80. Charrier, pp. 310–11. The stone statue was described by Dom Martène and Dom Durand in 1706 as comprising three figures of the same size, one with the inscription *Filius meus es tu*, another *Pater meus es tu*, and a third *Utriusque spiraculum ego sum*, in *Voyage littéraire de deux religieux bénédictines*, 2 vols. (Paris: Florentin Delaulne, 1717), 1: 85.

81. *La vie de Pierre Abeillard, abbé de Saint-Gildas-de-Ruis, de l'ordre de Saint-Benoist, et celle d'Héloïse son épouse, première abbesse du Paraclet*, 2 vols. (Paris: Jean Musier, 1720), and *Les Veritables Lettres d'Abeillard et d'Heloise*, 2 vols. (Paris: Jean Musier, 1723), discussed by Charrier, pp. 432–37. In 1718 Richard Rawlinson reprinted the 1616 Latin text with spurious manuscript variants, *Petri Abaelardi Abbatis Ruyensis et Heloissae Abbatissae Paraclitensis Epistolae. A prioris Editionis Erroribus purgatae, et cum Cod. MS collatae* (London: E. Curll & W. Taylor, 1718); see Monfrin, pp. 46–49.

82. Charrier, pp. 313–14. In 1780 the bones of Abelard were completely reduced to dust; the skull of Heloise was well preserved, but one tooth was taken out by the abbé Pernitti.

83. Mews, "La Bibliothèque du Paraclet," 56–57 (n. 37 above).

84. Valuable documentation about the reputed house of Fulbert (11 Quai des Fleurs) is given by Charrier, pp. 76–82 and 504–505. Charles de Rémusat describes the house, demolished in 1849, recorded by local tradition as that of Fulbert, in *Abélard* (Paris: Ladrange, 1845), p. 51. Charrier (p. 78 n. 6) notes that the claim made for this site is very likely an eighteenth-century invention.

85. Maurice de Gandillac, "Sur quelques images d'Abélard au temps du roi Louis-Philippe," in Jean Jolivet, ed., *Abélard en son temps* (Paris: Belles Lettres, 1981), pp. 197–209; Michel Lemoine observes that Cousin did not initiate this enthusiasm in "Un philosophe médiévale au temps des Lumières: Abélard avant Victor Cousin," in A. Cazenave, J.-F. Lyotard, H. Gouhier eds., *L'art des confins: Mélanges offerts à Maurice de Gandillac*, (Paris: Presses Universitaires de France, 1985), pp. 571–84.

86. *Abélard*, 2 vols. (Paris: Ladrange, 1845), 1: 148–63, commenting on Heloise's outward obedience to Abelard, 1: 160.

87. Ignaz Aurelius Fessler, *Abälard und Heloise*, 2 vols. (Berlin: Friedrich Maurer, 1806, 1807), p. 623; see Peter von Moos, *Mittelalterforschung und Ideologiekritik. Der Gelehrtenstreit um Héloïse* (Munich: Wilhelm Fink Verlag, 1974), with further detail on Fessler in "Le silence d'Héloïse et les idéologies modernes," in *Pierre Abélard—Pierre le Vénérable: les courants philosophiques, littéraires et artistiques en occident au milieu du XIIe siècle* (Paris: CNRS, 1975), pp. 441–42.

88. *HC*, ed. Monfrin, p. 101; ed. Hicks, p. 37; trans. Radice, p. 98; *Ep.* 2, ed. Hicks, p. 51; trans. Radice, p. 116.

89. Jo. Caspar Orelli, ed. *Magistri Petri Abaelardi epistola quae est Historia calamitatum . . .* (Zurich: Officina Ulrichiana, 1841); Ludovic Lalanne, "Quelques

doutes sur l'authenticité de la correspondance amoureuse d'Héloïse et d'Abailard," *La Correspondance littéraire* 1 (Nov. 1856 – Oct. 1857): 27–33 and 109, summarized by von Moos, *Mittelalterforschung und Ideologiekritik*, pp. 45–49 (n. 87 above); Octave Gréard, *Lettres complètes d'Abélard et d'Héloïse* (Paris: Garnier, 1869), pp. xli–xlviii.

90. Henry Adams, *From Mont St Michel to Chartres* (1904; Harmondsworth: Penguin, 1986), pp. 270–71.

91. Bernhard Schmeidler, "Der Briefwechsel zwischen Abälard und Heloise einer Fälschung?," *Archiv für Kulturgeschichte* 11 (1914): 1–30; "Der Briefwechsel zwischen Abälard und Heloise als eine literarische Fiktion Abälards," *Zeitschrift für Kirchengeschichte* 54 [3.F.5] (1935): 323–38; "Der Briefwechsel zwischen Abälard und Heloise dennoch eine literarische Fiktion Abälards," *Revue bénédictine* 52 (1940): 85–95. See also S. Martin Deutsch, *Peter Abälard. Ein kritischer Theologe des zwölften Jahrhunderts* (Leipzig: S. Hirzel, 1883), pp. 43–44.

92. *Héloïse dans l'histoire et dans la légende*, pp. 573–90 (n. 10 above).

93. Georg Misch, *Geschichte de Autobiographie*, 3.1 (Frankfurt: G. Schulte-Bumke, 1959), pp. 523–719; Ruhe, *De amasio ad amasiam*, pp. 56–57 (p. 292, n. 8 above).

94. Durant W. Robertson Jr, *Abelard and Heloise*, pp. 121–24 (n. 67 above).

95. "Fraud, Fiction and Borrowing in the Correspondance of Abelard and Heloise," in *Pierre Abélard-Pierre le Vénérable*, pp. 469–511 (n. 87 above); "A Reconsideration of the Authenticity of the Correspondence of Abelard and Heloise," in *Petrus Abaelardus (1079 – 1142). Person, Werk und Wirkung*, ed. Rudolf Thomas (Trier: Paulinus Verlag, 1980), pp. 41–52; "The Correspondence of Abelard and Heloise," in *Fälschungen im Mittelalter*, 5: 95–120 (p. 297, n. 46 above).

96. "Réflexions sur la thèse de J.F. Benton relative au dossier 'Abélard et Héloïse'," *Recherches de théologie ancienne et médiévale* 44 (1977): 211–16; "L'idylle d'Abélard et Héloïse: la part du roman," *Bulletin de la classe des sciences morales et politiques*, 5ᵉ sér. 71 (1985): 157–200; "Die Liebesgeschichte zwischen Abaelard und Heloise; der Anteil des Romans," in *Fälschungen im Mittelalter*, 5: 121–65 (p. 297, n. 46 above); "Héloïse et le témoignage du 'Carmen ad Astralabium'," *Revue d'Histoire Ecclésiastique* 88 (1988): 635–60.

97. Helen C. R. Laurie, "The 'Letters' of Abelard and Heloise: A Source of Chrétien de Troyes?," *Studi Medievali* 3ᵃ ser. 27 (1986): 123–46; *The Making of Romance. Three Studies* (Geneva: Slatkine, 1991), pp. 95–119 ["Heloise and her achievement"]; "'Cligès' and the Legend of Abelard and Heloise," *Zeitschrift für Romanische Philologie* 107 (1991): 324–42; "The Letters of Abelard and Heloise: Classical, Patristic and Medieval Models. A Reconsideration," *Mittellateinisches Jahrbuch* 28 (1993): 35–45.

98. Gilson, *Héloïse et Abélard*, 3rd revised ed. (Paris: Vrin, 1978).

99. Dronke, *WW,* pp. 107–43.
100. Peter von Moos, "Le silence d'Héloïse et les idéologies modernes," (n. 87 above); "Palatini quaestio quasi peregrini. Ein gestriger Streitpunkt aus der Abaelard-Heloise-Kontroverse nochmals überprüft," *Mittellateinisches Jahrbuch* 9 (1973): 124–58; "Die Bekehrung Héloïses," *Mittellateinisches Jahrbuch* 11 (1976): 95–125.Von Moos also contributed valuable studies on classical exempla within the correspondence, notably derived from Lucan: "Cornelia und Heloise," *Latomus* 34 (1975): 1024–59 and "Lucan und Abaelard," in *Hommages à A. Boutemy,* ed. G. Cambier, Collection Latomus 145 (Brussels, 1976), pp. 413–43; "*Post festum*—Was kommt nach der Authentizitätsdebatte über die Briefe Abaelards und Heloises?," *Petrus Abaelardus,* ed. Thomas, pp. 75–100 (n. 95 above); "Heloise und Abaelard," in *Gefälscht. Betrug in Politik, Literatur, Wissenschaftliche Kunst und Musik,* ed. Karl Corino (Nördlingen: Greno, 1988), pp. 150–61.
101. Peter von Moos, *Consolatio, Studien zur Mittellateinischen Trostliteratur über den Tod und zum Problem der Christlichen Trauer,* 4 vols. (Munich: Wilhelm Fink, 1971), especially 1: 212–20.
102. Ileana Pagani, "Epistolario o dialogo spirituale? Postille ad un'interpretazione della corrispondenza di Abelardo ed Eloisa?" *Studi Medievali* 27 (1986): 241–318.
103. Karl Schmid, "Bemerkungen zur Persona – und Memorial Forschung nach dem Zeugnis von Abaelard und Heloise," in *Memoria in der Gesellschaft des Mittelalters,* eds. Dieter Geunich and Otto Gerhard Oexle (Göttingen:Vandenhoek and Ruprecht, 1994), pp. 74–127.
104. See above, p. 293, n. 18 and Duby, *Le chevalier, la femme et le prêtre. Le mariage dans la France féodale* (Paris: Hachette, 1981), trans. Barbara Fey, *The Knight, the Lady and the Priest* (Harmondsworth: Penguin, 1983).
105. Paulette Hermite-Leclercq, "The Feudal Order," in *A History of Women. Silences of The Middle Ages,* p. 203.
106. David Edward Luscombe, "From Paris to the Paraclete: the correspondence of Abelard and Heloise," *Proceedings of the British Academy* 74 (1988): 247–83. Other major Abelard specialists all accept their authenticity, as for example Verger, Beonio Brocchieri and Marenbon (p. 292, n. 11 above).
107. The studies of Charrier and McLeod are cited p. 302, n. 10 above. Barbara Newman, "Authority, authenticity, and the repression of Heloise," *The Journal of Medieval and Renaissance Studies* 22 (1992): 121–58, repr. in *From Virile Woman to WomanChrist. Studies in Medieval Religion and Literature* (Philadelphia: University of Pennsylvania Press, 1995), pp. 46–75.
108. Peggy Kamuf, *Fictions of Feminine Desire: Disclosures of Heloise* (Lincoln: University of Nebraska Press, 1982). See Juanita Feros Ruys, "Role-playing in the *Letters* of Heloise and Abelard," *Parergon* 11 (1993): 53–78. Feros Ruys is submitting a Ph.D thesis being prepared at the University of Sydney, *Genre, Gender, and Authenticity: Reading Heloise in the Twentieth Century.*

109. See for example Andrea Nye, "Philosophy: A woman's thought or a man's discipline? The letters of Abelard and Heloise," *Hypatia* 7.3 (Summer 1992): 1–22; Glenda McLeod, "'Wholly guilty, wholly innocent': Self-definition in Héloïse's letters to Abélard," in *Dear Sister*, eds. Cherewatuk and Wiethaus, pp. 64–86 (p. 297, n. 46 above); Catherine Brown, "*Muliebriter*: Doing Gender in the Letters of Heloise," in *Gender and Text in the Later Middle Ages*, ed. Jane Chance (Gainesville: University Press of Florida, 1996), pp. 25–51. Elizabeth Freeman, "The public and private functions of Heloise's letters," *Journal of Medieval History* 23.1 (1997): 15–28. Mary Ellen Waithe contributes a chapter on Heloise within a volume she edits, *A History of Women Philosophers Volume II. Medieval, Renaissance and Enlightenment Women Philosophers A.D. 500 – 1600* (Dordrecht: Kluwer Academic Publishers, 1989), pp. 67–83. On Abelard, see the essays of Martin Irvine, "Abelard and (Re)writing the Male Body: Castration, Identity, and Remasculinization," and Bonnie Wheeler, "Origenary Fantasies: Abelard's Castration and Confession," in *Becoming Male in the Middle Ages*, eds. Jerome Cohen and Bonnie Wheeler (New York: Garland Publishing, 1997), pp. 87–106 and 107–28. Martin Irvine makes good points about Heloise's linking of *amor* and *amicitia*, "Heloise and the gendering of the literate subject," in *Criticism and Dissent in the Middle Ages*, ed. Rita Copeland (Cambridge: Cambridge University Press, 1996), pp. 87–114.

110. Linda Georgianna, "Any Corner of Heaven: Heloise's Critique of Monasticism," *Mediaeval Studies* 49 (1987): 221–53.

111. The original text was printed in PL 178: 313C-317B, with the erroneous reading of *Instructiones* for *Institutiones*, reprinted with translation by Gréard, *Lettres d'Abailard*, pp. 453–81; Chrysogonus Waddell, ed., *The Paraclete Statutes. Institutiones Nostrae. Introduction, Edition, Commentary*, CLS 20 (Gethsemani Abbey, Trappist: Cistercian Publications, 1987).

112. Chrysogonus Waddell, "Peter Abelard as Creator of Liturgical Texts," in *Petrus Abaelardus*, pp. 267–86 (n. 95), and in more detail in E. Rozanne Elder and John R. Sommerfeldt, eds., "Saint Bernard and the Cistercian Office at the Abbey of the Paraclete," *The Chimaera of his Age. Studies on Bernard of Clairvaux*, Cistercian Studies Series 63 (Kalamazoo, Mich.: Cistercian Publications, 1980), pp. 76–121. His editions of Paraclete liturgical texts were published as volumes 3 – 7 of the Cistercian Liturgy Series, published in 1985 by Gethsemani Abbey, Trappist, Kentucky: *The Old French Paraclete Ordinary and the Paraclete Breviary I. Introduction and Commentary* [CLS 3]; *The Old French Paraclete Ordinary II. Edition* [CLS 4]; *The Paraclete Breviary IIIA Edition, Kalendar and Temporal Cycle. IIIB Edition. The Sanctoral Cycle. IIIC Edition of the Saints, Varia, Indices* [CLS 5 – 7].

113. *Stealing Heaven* (Heaven Productions Ltd, 1988), directed by Clive Donner and produced by Amy International/Jadran Films, was based on Marion

Meade, *Stealing Heaven: The Love Story of Heloise and Abelard* (New York: William Morrow, 1979).

114. Richard William Southern, "The Letters of Abelard and Heloise," *Medieval Humanism and Other Studies* (Oxford: Blackwell, 1970), p. 95.

115. Hilary Davies includes a major poem about Abelard and Heloise, "In a Valley of this Restless Mind," within a collection of her verse, *In a Valley of this Restless Mind* (London: Enitharmon Press, 1997), pp. 50–73.

116. Radice, *The Letters of Abelard and Heloise,* p. 68 n. 1.

117. Peter von Moos announces a project on the study of Latin dialogue in the Middle Ages in "Zwischen Schriftlichkeit und Mündlichkeit: Dialogische Interaktion im lateinischen Hochmittelalter (Vorstellung des neuen Teilprojekts H im SFB 231)," *Frühmittelalterliche Studien* 25 (1991): 300–314.

118. Guillaume de Saint-Thierry, *De natura et dignitate amoris* 3, 18–23, ed. M.-M. Davy, *Deux traités de l'amour* (Paris:Vrin, 1953), pp. 72–74, 94–98.

119. On this theme, see Martha G. Newman, *The Boundaries of Charity. Cistercian Culture and Ecclesiastical Reform, 1098 – 1180* (Stanford, Calif.: Stanford University Press, 1996).

Chapter 3

1. My account of the geography and politics of Paris is indebted to Robert-Henri Bautier, "Paris aux temps d'Abélard," in *Abélard en son temps,* ed. Jean Jolivet (Paris: Les Belles Lettres, 1981), pp. 21–77, especially 42–43 and 56 n. 1 on the chronology of the affair, which he sees as perhaps beginning in the winter of 1115/16 with the castration quite possibly in 1117 rather than 1118, as traditionally thought.

2. Bautier, art. cit., 28–29 and Jean Hubert, "Les origines de Notre-Dame de Paris," in *Huitième Centenaire de Notre-Dame de Paris (Congrès de 30 Mai – 3 Juin 1964),* ed. Gabriel Le Bras (Paris:Vrin, 1967), pp. 1–22, especially 14–16; see also Jacques Boussard, *Nouvelle histoire de Paris. De la fin du siège de 885 – 886 à la mort de Philippe Auguste* (Paris: Hachette, 1976).

3. On Adam, precentor of Notre-Dame 1107 – 1134, then canon of Saint-Victor until his death in the late 1140s, see Margot Fassler, *Gothic Song.Victorine Sequences and Augustinian Reform in Twelfth-Century Paris* (Cambridge: Cambridge University Press, 1993), pp. 197–210.

4. Louis VI defined the area of jurisdiction of the bishop between 1112 and 1117 after a dispute with the chapter, Dufour, no. 121, 1: 247–52.

5. Astrik L. Gabriel, "Les écoles de la cathédrale de Notre-Dame et le commencement de l'université de Paris," in *Huitième Centenaire,* pp. 145–66, especially 145–46. *Cartulaire de l'Église Notre-Dame de Paris,* ed. M. Guérard, Collection des Cartulaires de France 7, 4 vols. (Paris: Crapelet, 1850), 1:338.

6. Fulco of Deuil, *Ep. ad Petrum Abaelardum,* PL 178: 371D; ed. Cousin, 1: 87–88.

7. Fulbert is mentioned in an act of 31 March 1099, in *Cartulaire générale de Paris*, ed. Robert de Lasteyrie (Paris: Imprimerie nationale, 1887), no. 122, p. 147; see also: 1102, no. 130, p. 154; 1107, no. 145, p. 163; 1107/8, nos. 147–48, p. 168.

8. *HC*, ed. Monfrin, p. 78; ed. Hicks, p. 16; trans. Radice, p. 70: "te clericum atque canonicum." His canonry at Sens is reported by Geoffrey of Courlon (de Collone), a thirteenth-century chronicler of Sens, *Chronicon Senonense*, cited by V. Le Clerc, *Histoire littéraire de la France* vol. 21 (Paris: Imprimerie Nationale, 1845), p. 12. Abelard enjoyed the support of another canon of Sens: Hato, canon, archdeacon and eventually dean of Sens between 1095/96 and 1122, before becoming bishop of Troyes (1122 – 45/46). Hato, a good friend of Peter the Venerable, gave Abelard permission to establish the Paraclete; Constable, *The Letters of Peter the Venerable*, 2: 97–98.

9. *HC*, ed. Monfrin, pp. 70, 81; ed. Hicks, pp. 9, 19; trans. Radice, p. 65, 77.

10. *HC*, ed. Monfrin, p. 79; ed. Hicks, p. 17; trans. Radice, p. 74.

11. Roscelin mentions that Fulbert, her maternal uncle, was noble (n. 15 below). François d'Amboise claimed in his preface to the 1616 edition (repr. PL 178: 74) that Heloise was related to the powerful family of Montmorency, but provided no evidence for this; André Duchesne made no such claim in his detailed notes to the *Historia calamitatum* or in a separate history of the Montmorency family. Bautier repeats Amboise's claim without citing further evidence, apart from suggesting alliances with the Garlande family, art. cit., 76 (n. 1 above); see McLeod, *Héloïse*, pp. 9–10 (p. 302, n. 10).

12. According to the Paraclete obituary, Hersindis died on December 1 of an unknown year, *Hubertus, canonicus, domine Heloise avunculus,* presumably a copyist's mistake for *Fulbertus,* on 26 December; *Recueil des historiens de la France. Obituaires de la province de Sens. Diocèses de Meaux et de Troyes,* ed. Boutillier du Retail and Piétresson de Saint-Aubin, vol. 4 (Paris: Imprimerie nationale, 1923), pp. 428–29. The significance of Fulbert being her maternal uncle is picked up by Enid McLeod, *Héloïse. A Biography,* pp. 8–9 (p. 302, n. 10 above). Bautier notes that the absence of mention of Heloise's father may not signify illegitimacy, as the same record remembers Abelard's mother, but not his father, art. cit., 75 n. 6.

13. Lasteyrie, nos. 139 and 185, pp. 159–60 and 209–10; Luchaire, no. 192 and 284. Durand is still a priest in 1119, Lasteyrie, no. 182 (p. 204). On Berner's pronouncement of 1115, Dufour, no. 8, 3: 458–60. A date of late March 1115 for the marriage is argued by Andrew W. Lewis, "La date du mariage de Louis VI et d'Adélaïde de Maurienne," *Bibliothèque de l'école des chartes* 148 (1990): 5–16.

14. Beleth comments on these legal privileges in relation to the Parisian cloister, *Summa de ecclesiasticis officiis* 2, ed. Heribert Douteil, CCCM 41A (1976): 6.

15. Roscelin, *Ep. ad Abaelardum,* ed. Reiners, p. 78 (p. 298, n. 55; PL 178: 369BC): "Vidi siquidem Parisius, quod quidem clericus nomine Fulbertus te ut hospitem in domo sua recepit, te in mensa sua ut amicum familiarem et domesticum honorifice pavit, neptim etiam suam, puellam prudentissimam et indolis egregiae, ad docendum commisit. Tu vero viri illius nobilis et clerici, Parisiensis etiam ecclesiae canonici, hospitis insuper tui ac domini, et gratis et honorifice te procurantis non immemor, sed contemptor, commissae tibi virgini non parcens, quam conservare ut commissam, docere ut discipulam debueras, effreno luxuriae spirit agitatus non argumentari, sed eam fornicari docuisti, in uno facto multorum criminum, proditionis scilicet et fornicationis, reus et virginei pudoris violator spurcissimus. Sed *deus ultionum dominus, deus ultionum libere egit* [Ps. 93.1], qui eam qua tantum parte peccaveras te privavit."

16. Abelard alludes to the injunction of Leviticus 22.24 and Deuteronomy 23.1 about the ritual exclusion of those whose testicles have been crushed or removed, in *HC,* ed. Monfrin, p. 80; ed. Hicks, p. 19; trans. Radice, p. 76. On this punishment, see Mathew S. Kuefler, "Castration and Eunuchism in the Middle Ages," in *Handbook of Medieval Sexuality,* ed. Bullough and Brundage, pp. 279–306 (p. 298, n. 52). Yves Ferroul observes that castration was never of the penis in the medieval period; see "Abelard's Blissful Castration," in *Becoming Male* (p. 316, n. 109).

17. Orderic Vitalis, *The Ecclesiastical History* 6, ed. and trans. Marjorie Chibnall, 6 vols. (Oxford: Clarendon Press, 1969 – 78), 3: 336–38 (with chronological notes on 3: 365–66). Orderic had previously explained how an earlier French king had unjustly stolen the relics of St. Évroul from Normandy, 3: 306–22.

18. Fulco of Deuil to Abelard, PL 178: 375B; ed. Cousin, 1: 707: "Ille autem qui per se factum abnegat, iam ab omni possessione sua bonorum suorum comportatione exturbatus est."

19. All the canons apart from Fulbert sign a charter in 1117, Lasteyrie, no. 174, p. 200, suggesting to Bautier that his exile was in this year, art. cit., 56 n. 1. Fulbert witnesses charters on: 1 April 1119, no. 182, p. 204; 1122, no. 194, p. 217 and 1124, before 3 August, no. 203, p. 223, but is no longer subdeacon later that year, no. 205, p. 226.

20. On Bishop Galo, see *Gallia christiana* (Paris: Typographia regia, 1744), 7: 54–58; P. Paris, "Galon, évêque de Paris," *Histoire littéraire de la France* 10 (1868): 94–99; T. de Morembert, "Galon, évêque de Paris," *DHGE* 19 (1981): 911, and *Dictionnaire de biographie française* 15 (1982): 266–68.

21. On Stephen's significance and his many appointments, see Luchaire, pp. xliii–lvi and Dufour, 1: 38–40. He is first mentioned as archdeacon in 1095, in Guérard, *Cartulaire de Notre-Dame de Paris,* 1: 305, for the last time in 1146/47, Lasteyrie, no. 344, p. 302; on the duties of an archdeacon, see Hugh of Saint-Victor, *De Sacramentis* 2.4.17, PL 176: 431B.

22. Ivo, *Ep.* 89, PL 162: 110C: "utpote nondum subdiaconum, hominem illiteratum, aleatorem, mulierum sectatorem, publice olim de adulterio publico infamatum, et ob hoc a Domino Lugdunensis archiepiscopo tunc temporis sedis apostolicae legato, Ecclesiae communione privatum;" see too *Ep.* 87, 92 and 95, PL 162: 108A, 113AB and 115A–116D. On Galo's claim to Beauvais, see Bernard Monod, *Essai sur les rapports de Pascal II avec Philippe I* (1099 – 1108) (Paris: Honoré Champion, 1908), pp. 87–92.

23. *HC,* ed. Monfrin, pp. 64–65; ed. Hicks, pp. 4–5; trans. Radice, p. 59.

24. Fulk had married Bertrada "out of love" according to a speech quoted by Orderic Vitalis, *Ecclesiastical History* 8.10 and 20, ed. and trans. Chibnall, 4: 184 and 260–62. They had a son (Fulk V) in 1090. Michel-Jean-Joseph Brial provides a detailed discussion of all known sources relating to Bertrada in *Recueil* 16 (1814): xxviii–cxiv.

25. *Yves de Chartres. Correspondance I, Ep.* 50, ed. Jean Leclercq (Paris: Les Belles Lettres, 1949), pp. 200–206.

26. Orderic Vitalis claimed that the interdict lasted for fifteen years, from 1093 until Philip's death, and remembered this as a great period of mourning in France, *Ecclesiastical History* 8.20, ed. and trans. Chibnall, 4: 262.

27. *Vita Ludovici* 18, ed. Waquet, p. 122; trans. Cusimano and Moorhead, p. 81: "Mater etiam, his omnibus potentior viragoque faceta et eruditissima illius admirandi muliebris artificii, quo consueverunt audaces suis etiam lascessitos injuriis maritos suppeditare. . . ."

28. Orderic Vitalis, *Ecclesiastical History* 11.9, ed. and trans. Chibnall, 6: 50–54.

29. On the difficulties facing Louis in 1108 and the fate of his brothers and sisters, see Andrew W. Lewis, *Royal Succession in Capetian France: Studies on Familial Order and the State* (Cambridge, Mass.: Harvard University Press, 1981), pp. 50–54 and p. 245 n. 28–29.

30. Brigitte Bedos Rezak, "Women, Seals and Power in Medieval France, 1150 – 1350," in Mary Erler and Maryanne Kowaleski, eds., *Women and Power in the Middle Ages* (Athens: University of Georgia Press, 1988), pp. 61–82. She notes that while this is the first French seal of a woman at royal level, the first German woman to use a seal was the Empress Kunegund in 1000. See too M. Facinger, "A Study of Medieval Queenship: Capetian France, 987 – 1237," *Studies in Medieval and Renaissance History* 5 (1986): 6–7, 28. Bertrada and Louis jointly established a priory of Fontevrault at Hautes-Bruyères in 1112 (confirmed by Pope Paschal II in 1119). Bertrada transferred there from Fontevrault in 1115, but died not long after; Dufour, nos. 75, 113 and 153, 1: 168–69, 234 and 317–18.

31. Ivo of Chartres, *Ep.* 144 and 146, PL 162: 150–151; Bautier, art. cit., 60–61. *Annales capituli Cracoviensis,* ed. Richard Roepell, MGH SS 19 (1856): 588.

32. Lasteyrie, no. 136, pp. 157–58.

33. Eadmer, *Historia novorum in Anglia* 4, ed. Martin Rule, Rolls Series 81 (London: Longman, 1884), p. 162; *Vita Sancti Anselmi* 55, ed. and trans.

Richard Southern, *The Life of St Anselm Archbishop of Canterbury* (London: Thomas Nelson, 1962), pp. 132–34. Louis' letter of invitation is *Ep.* 432 among the letters of St. Anselm, ed. Schmitt, 5: 279; Dufour, no. 11, 1: 16.

34. Suger, *Vita Ludovici* 9, ed. Waquet, pp. 44–50; trans. Cusimano and Moorhead, pp. 43–46.

35. Suger, *Vita Ludovici* 8, ed. Waquet, p. 38; trans. Cusimano and Moorhead, p. 41; see Luchaire, pp. xxvii-xxxi and 21.

36. *Vita Ludovici* 11, ed. Waquet, pp. 68–77; trans. Cusimano and Moorhead, pp. 55–58. In notes to their translation of *The Deeds of Louis the Fat*, p. 176 n. 5, Cusimano and Moorhead observe that while Suger claims the marriage was annulled at the Council of Troyes in 1107 on grounds of consanguinity, the chronicle of Saint-Pierre-le-Vif of Sens reported that Lucienne of Rochefort was not acceptable to the counts of the kingdom, as if this marked a victory for allies of the Montfort dynasty. Suger describes Louis' attack on Hugh of Crécy in c. 15, ed. Waquet, pp. 88–96; trans. Cusimano and Moorhead, pp. 64–68.

37. *Actes de Philippe I*, ed. M. Prou (Paris: Imprimerie nationale, 1908), nos. 154, 157, pp. 388, 392. On the rise of these families, see Jean Lemarignier, *Le Gouvernement royal aux premiers temps Capétiens* (Paris: Picard, 1959), pp. 124–25, 154–58 and Hallam, *Capetian France*, pp. 90–91 (p. 300, n. 77 above). Gilbert (Païen) of Garlande holds the position 1095–1101, Anselm 1101–1118 (apart from 1104 7), William 1118-20, Stephen 1120–27. Moorhead and Cusimano provide a useful summary of their dynastic ambitions, noting that Suger never describes Stephen as *nobilis* like Guy of Rochefort in end-notes to *The Deeds of Louis the Fat*, pp. 208–9. The family became connected in marriage to a powerful noble family, however, through the marriage of Anselm's daughter to Amaury IV of Montfort; see above, p. 154.

38. *Gallia Christiana* 7: 706.

39. *La Chronique de Morigny (1095–1152)*, ed. Léon Mirot (Paris: Alphonse Picard, 1912), pp. 33–35 and 42–43. Stephen was not hostile to all monks. Thomas, abbot of Morigny, had a particular grievance against Stephen, who had not wanted monks of Morigny to take control of the churches of Vieilles-Étampes and had been persuaded by abbot Boso of Fleury (Saint-Benoît-sur-Loire) to grant them to that abbey (1118/27); Luchaire, no. 402, pp. 186–87. See too Lindy Grant, *Abbot Suger of St-Denis* (London: Longman, 1998), pp. 55–57.

40. Bautier assumes that William was already an archdeacon in 1102/3 when Ivo wrote to the Pope about the appeal of Vulgrin and Stephen of Garlande in favor of Fulco, dean of Notre-Dame to the bishopric, art. cit., 60. William is not mentioned by Ivo of Chartres in the letter he writes about this contested election, *Ep.* 139, PL 162: 147AB. Bautier does not repeat the claim in "Les origines et les premiers développements de l'abbaye

Saint-Victor de Paris," in *L'Abbaye parisienne de Saint-Victor au moyen âge*, ed. Jean Longère, Bibliotheca Victorina 1 (Paris: Brepols, 1991), pp. 23–52.

41. Bautier, art. cit., 34. William is first identified as an archdeacon in 1107, alongside Stephen and Rainaldus (having replaced Vulgrin after 1102/3); Lasteyrie, nos. 143–44, pp. 161–64, improving on the text in PL 162: 725C-728D (in which Fulbert is cited as Guilbert).

42. The same rituals as related in the charter about Saint-Éloi are discussed by Penelope D. Johnson in relation to Poitiers, as well as attempts to restrict such public activity, *Equal in Monastic Profession. Religious Women in Medieval France* (Chicago: University of Chicago Press, 1991), pp. 140–41. John Beleth, writing in Paris in the mid-twelfth century, describes how nuns take part in the Rogationtide processions of major churches, after monks and canons, but before different categories of lay folk, *Summa de ecclesiasticis officiis* c.123b, ed. Douteil, CCCM 41A: 235.

43. See Pope Paschal II, *Ep.* 149 (PL 163: 158A), Lasteyrie, no. 134, pp. 156–57. The action of Galo and William is described in a letter, Lasteyrie, nos. 143–44, pp. 161–64; Dufour, no. 14, 1: 23–24. The bishop claims that "moved by the devil, that weak sex has fallen into such disgusting wretchedness, adhering without shame to general worldliness, having broken the vow of chastity and having completely thrown away the commitment to the religious life; it has turned the temple of God into a cave of fornication and has not listened at all to our words of warning and correction."

44. Lasteyrie, no. 130, pp. 153–54 and Dufour, no. 5, 1: 6–7; see Boussard, *Nouvelle histoire de Paris*, p. 148 (n. 2 above).

45. Dufour, no. 96, 1: 209–10 [1114, after 3 August].

46. Bautier, art. cit., 42.

47. Lasteyrie, no. 144, p. 164; on the unfaithfulness of Hugh of Crécy, described by Suger as "a skilled and valiant young warrior, equally adept at plundering and burning and very quick to make trouble for the whole kingdom," see Suger, *Vita Ludovici* 8, ed. Waquet, pp. 88–96, 128–36; trans. Cusimano and Moorhead, pp. 64–68, 84–88. Constable discusses whether this is the same Hugh of Crécy who became a monk at Saint-Martin-des-Champs and an advisor to Louis VII, *The Letters of Peter the Venerable*, 2: 311–15.

48. Edited by Uta-Renata Blumenthal, *The Early Councils of Pope Paschal II 1100 – 1108* (Toronto: Pontifical Institute of Mediaeval Studies, 1978), pp. 92–97. Blumenthal notes the presence of William of Champeaux as archdeacon on pp. 80–81.

49. The exact translation of this statute is far from clear; it is edited without commentary by Blumenthal, *The Early Councils of Pope Paschal II*, p. 94, c.8: "Presbyteris et diaconibus longos capillos, rostratos sotulares, fixas uestes, laqueos in blialdis [MS blialibus] uel camisiis habere uel aleis seruire pro-

hibemus."The phrase *rostratos sotulares* ("toes in the form of a beak") is presumably the same as the *acutissimos subtolares* ("very pointed toes") spoken about by Orderic Vitalis (n. 109 below). The Old French *bliaud* (*bliaut, bleaunt* or *bliadus*) is discussed in *Bildwörterbuch der Kleidung und Rüstung*, ed. Harry Kühnel (Stuttgart: Alfred Kröner Verlag, 1992), p. 34.

50. *Ep.* 70, ed. Leclercq, pp. 310–12 (n. 25 above). Leclercq notes that the transfer of Faremoutiers to the monks of Marmoutier, from whom he heard these rumors, as well as from the Countess of Blois, might have provoked this letter. In *Ep.* 10 (pp. 40–48) Ivo had warned the nuns of Saint-Avit against indulging in conversation with men.

51. Penelope Johnson argues from the evidence of Eudes Rigaud in the thirteenth century that lapses in chastity have been much exaggerated, *Equal in Monastic Profession*, pp. 112–33 (n. 42 above). She questions the extent of sexual dissolution portrayed by Graciela S. Daichman, *Wayward Nuns in Medieval Literature* (Syracuse: Syracuse University Press, 1986).

52. Bautier, art. cit., 33–39.

53. Guibert of Nogent, *Monodiae* 2.5; ed. Edmond-René Labande, *Autobiographie* (Paris: Les Belles Lettres, 1981), p. 248; Robert Chazan comments on the absence of pogroms in France, *Medieval Jewry in Northern France* (Baltimore: The Johns Hopkins University Press, 1973), pp. 24–26. There are translations of Guibert's *Monodiae* by John Benton, *Self and Society in Medieval France* (Toronto: University of Toronto Press and Medieval Academy of America, 1984) and by Paul J. Archambault, *A Monk's Confession. The Memoirs of Guibert of Nogent* (Philadelphia: University of Pennsylvania State Press, 1995).

54. Lasteyrie, nos. 151–52, pp. 171–74; the letter accompanying this gift is addressed to Galo and Stephen of Garlande and is dated to 1108 in PL 162: 729–32; Geneviève [Bresc-]Bautier, "L'envoi de la relique de la vraie Croix à Notre-Dame de Paris en 1120," *Bibliothèque de l'école des chartes* 129 (1971): 384–97 and on the fairs, Anne Lombard-Jourdain, "Les foires de Saint-Denis," ibid. 145 (1987): 273–338.

55. Dufour, no. 184, 1: 384–85.

56. *Cartulaire de Notre-Dame*, ed. Guérard, 1: 246–47 [1108]; 1: 223 [1114].

57. Guérard, 1: 449; see too Lasteyrie, nos. 179–80, pp. 202–203 [1118], in which Stephen produces a similar authorization for Gibelina, daughter of Burdini de Funtaneto.

58. Suger, *Vita Ludovici* 13, ed. Waquet, p. 84; trans. Cusimano and Moorhead, p. 62.

59. Suger, *Vita Ludovici* 8, ed. Waquet, p. 38; trans. Cusimano and Moorhead, p. 41.

60. Hallam, *Capetian France*, pp. 43–50 (p. 300, n. 77).

61. On the rise of royal authority in France, see Karl Ferdinand Werner, "Kingdom and Principality in Twelfth-Century France," in *The Medieval Nobility*,

ed. Timothy Reuter (Amsterdam: North-Holland Publishing Co., 1978), pp. 243–90.

62. *HC,* ed. Monfrin, p. 63; ed. Hicks, p. 3; trans. Radice, p. 57. Abelard is said to be sixty-three at his death on 23 April 1142, according to an Old French Paraclete obituary list, cited by André Duchesne in his notes to the *Historia calamitatum* (repr. PL 178: 176C). On Berengar, see n. 64 below.

63. *HC,* ed. Monfrin, p. 67; ed. Hicks, p. 7; trans. Radice, p. 62.

64. *Chronicon,* ed. Georg Waitz, MGH SS 26 (1882): 81. As Richard was already a monk at Cluny in 1141 when Abelard became a monk there, his testimony is worthy of credence.

65. In 1087 Alan IV had been married to Constance (d. 1090), daughter of William the Conqueror, but this marriage was without issue; *Gesta Normannorum Ducum* 8.34, ed. and trans. Elisabeth M. C. Van Houts, 2 vols. (Oxford: Clarendon Press, 1995), 2: 260. On these divisions, see Noel-Yves Tonnerre, "Le comté nantais à la fin du XIᵉ siècle," *Abélard en son temps,* pp. 11–20 and Mews, "In search of a name and its significance: a twelfth-century anecdote about Thierry and Peter Abaelard," *Traditio* 44 (1988): 175–200. Anti-breton sentiment is still evident in a chronicle written in the 1150s by a member of Nantes cathedral, *La Chronique de Nantes,* ed. René Merlet (Paris: Alphonse Picard, 1896).

66. *HC,* ed. Monfrin, p. 98; ed. Hicks, p. 35; trans. Radice, p. 95. Cf. Abelard, *Dialectica,* ed. De Rijk, p. 128.

67. Jacques Boussard, "La vie en Anjou aux XIᵉ et XIIᵉ siècles," *Le Moyen Age* 5 (1950): 29–68; Hironori Miyamatsu, "A-t-il existé une commune à Angers au XIIᵉ siècle?" *Journal of Medieval History* 21 (1995): 117–52; Jean Vézin, *Les scriptoria d'Angers au XIe siècle* (Paris: Honoré Champion, 1974), pp. 1–17.

68. *HC,* ed. Monfrin, p. 64; ed. Hicks, p. 4; trans. Radice, p. 58. Roscelin, *Epistola ad Abaelardum,* ed. Reiners, pp. 64–65: "Neque vero Turonensis ecclesia vel Locensis, ubi ad pedes meos magistri tui discipulorum minimus tam diu resedisti, aut Bizuntina ecclesia, in quibus canonicus sum, extra mundum sunt, quae me omnes et venerantur et fovent et, quae dico, discendi studio libenter accipiunt."

69. Anselm, *De incarnatione verbi,* ed. Franciscus Salesius Schmitt, *Anselmi Opera Omnia,* 7 vols. (Edinburgh: Nelson, 1938 – 70), 2: 9–10.

70. Roscelin, *Ep. ad Abaelardum,* ed. Reiners, p. 63: "Si Christianae religionis dulcedinem quam habitu ipso praeferebas vel tenuiter degustasses, nequaquam tui ordinis tuaeque professionis immemor, et beneficiorum quae tibi tot et tanta a puero usque ad juvenem sub magistri nomine et actu exhibui oblitus . . ."

71. Charters of Fontevrault are printed in PL 172: 1052D and 1053D, as well as PL 162: 1087D–1118D. Jacques Dalarun has uncovered a sixteenth-century French translation of an early Life of Robert, *L'Impossible Sainteté. La*

vie retrouvée de Robert d'Arbrissel (v. 1045 – 1116), fondateur de Fontevraud (Paris: Editions de Cerf, 1985). See Penny Schine Gold, *The Lady and the Virgin*, pp. 93–115 (p. 298, n. 52 above); *DHGE* 14: 961–3 and W. Scott Jessee, "Robert d'Arbrissel: Aristocratic patronage and the question of heresy," *Journal of Medieval History* 29 (1994): 221–35. Constable mentions Robert's influence on Peter the Venerable's mother, *The Letters of Peter the Venerable*, 2: 239.

72. *Ep.* 14, ed. Smits, p. 280.

73. *Ep. ad Abaelardum,* ed. Reiners, p. 67. A lost treatise of Roscelin against Robert of Arbrissel is mentioned in a list of books from an unidentified abbey, Paris, Bibliothèque Sainte-Geneviève, MS 1042, fol. 113v (s. xii/xiii): *Roscelinus contra Robertum liber I.* I am indebted to François Dolbeau for this reference.

74. Marbod, *Ep.* 6, PL 171: 1481B and 1482D-83A.

75. Geoffrey of Vendôme, *Ep.*11 to Rainaud, PL 157: 114A: "Mima quaedam et mulier publica quae vos garruliter acclamabat;" a number of these details, although not that about the "actress and public woman," are mentioned by Hildebert of Lavardin in *Ep.* 5, 6 (PL 171: 211D-213A).

76. *HC,* ed. Monfrin, p. 64; ed. Hicks, p. 4; trans. Radice, p. 58.

77. Baudri of Bourgueil, *Vita B. Roberti Arbrisselli,* PL 162: 1047A, 1048B: "Perambulabat regiones et provincias irrequietus, et in litterarum studiis non poterat non esse sollicitus. Et quoniam Francia tum florebat in scholaribus emolumentis copiosior, fines paternos, tanquam exsul et fugitivus, exivit, Franciam adiit, et urbem, quae Parisius dicitur, intravit, litterarum disciplinam, quam unice sibi postulaverat, pro voto commodam reperit, ibique assiduus lector insidere coepit. . . . Reddebat etenim scholasticis, quod scholasticorum erat, nec propterea se Dei servitio minus coaptabat." Robert's studies in Paris took place between 1079 and 1089.

78. *HC,* ed. Monfrin, p. 105; ed. Hicks, pp. 40–41; trans. Radice, p. 101.

79. Guibert, *Monodiae* 3.17, ed. Labande, pp. 428–34; see also Mews, "An excerpt from Guibert of Nogent's *Monodiae* (III, 17) appended to Augustine's *De haeresibus,*" *Revue des études augustiniennes* 33 (1987): 113–27.

80. Guibert thought that when Clement reminded the bishop of the verse in scripture *Beati eritis,* he erroneously thought scripture said "Blessed are the heretics" by confusing *eritis* with *haereticos.* Labande identifies the verse as part of John 13.17, but *Beati eritis* makes better sense as a reference to Luke 6.23: "Beati eritis cum vos oderint homines." Robert quoted this verse in a sermon to Ermengarde, countess of Brittany quoted by Dalarun, *L'Impossible sainteté,* p. 218.

81. *Liber Ordinis Sancti Victoris Parisiensis* 19, 22, ed. Luc Jocqué and Louis Milis, CCCM 61 (1984): 78–86, 103–110.

82. Lasteyrie, no. 148, p. 168.

83. Dufour, 3: 77, no. 1 [private acts agreed to by Louis VI]; see n. 38 above.

84. *Vita Goswini, Recueil*, 14: 444; see Mews, "Philosophy and Theology 1100 – 1150: The Search for Harmony," in *Le XIIe siècle: Mutations et renouveau en France dans la première moitié du XIIe siècle*, ed. Françoise Gasparri (Paris: Le Léopard d'Or, 1994), pp. 182–83.

85. The most important such records occur within a manuscript from Fleury, Orléans, Bibliothèque municipale, MS 266, described in detail by Lorenzo Minio-Paluello, *Twelfth-Century Logic. Texts and Studies II. Abaelardiana Inedita* (Rome: Edizioni di Storia e Letteratura, 1958), pp. xli-xlvi. The manuscript contains fragments of two works by Abelard, the *Positio vocum sententie* and *Secundum magistrum Petrum sententie*. Minio-Paluello edits the latter work, while the former treatise has been edited by Iwakuma Y., "'Vocales,' or Early Nominalists," *Traditio* 42 (1992): 66–73, Another is also from Fleury, Paris, BNF lat. 13368, described by Bernhard Geyer, *Peter Abaelards Philosophische Schriften. II Die Logica 'Nostrorum petitioni sociorum'* (Münster: Aschendorff, 2nd ed. 1973), pp. 592–97. There is an edition of so-called 'literal glosses' of Abelard (erroneously confused with the *Introductiones parvulorum*, a lost work to which Abelard refers in the *Dialectica*) by Mario Dal Pra, *Pietro Abelardo. Scritti di logica* (Florence: La Nuova Italia, 2nd. ed. 1969), pp. 3–203.

86. John of Salisbury, *Metalogicon* 2.17, ed. J. B. Hall, CCCM 98 (1991): 83; trans. Daniel D. McGarry, *The Metalogicon of John of Salisbury* (Gloucester, Mass.: Peter Smith, 1955), p. 115.

87. Anselm expressed sympathy for Walerann's thwarted desire to enter the monastic life at Saint-Martin des Champs in *Ep.* 161–62 to bishop Geoffrey in 1093, ed. Schmitt, 3: 351–54, trans. Walter Fröhlich, *The Letters of Saint Anselm of Canterbury*, vol. 2 (Kalamazoo, Mich.: Cistercian Publications, 1993), pp. 48–52. Walerann must subsequently have left Paris, if this is the same person as the Walerann who writes to Anselm ca. 1107 about diversity of eucharistic practice (ed. Schmitt, 2: 233–38), and to whom Anselm sends his *Epistola de sacramentis ecclesiae* (2: 229–42) and *De processione spiritus sancti contra Graecos* (5: 362–63).

88. *HC*, ed. Monfrin, p. 65; ed. Hicks, p. 5; trans. Radice, p. 60.

89. Lasteyrie, no. 155, p. 175–76 and Dufour, 3: 77.

90. Robert of Meulan intervened on Bec's behalf to obtain significant tax exemptions for their boats when travelling along the Seine in 1095, renewed sometime between 1100 and 1108, Dufour, no. 18, 1: 31–32. Véronique Gazeau observes the role of Robert of Meulan in "Le Domaine continental du Bec. Aristocratie et monachisme au temps d'Anselme," in *Les mutations socio-culturelles au tournant des XIe – XIIe siècles*, ed. Raymonde Foreville, Spicilegium Beccense 2 (Paris: CNRS, 1984), pp. 259–71.

91. *Vita Ludovici* 16, ed. Waquet, pp. 98–112; trans. Cusimano and Moorhead, pp. 69–75; Luchaire, no. 103, p. 56; Sally N. Vaughn, *Anselm of Bec and Robert of Meulan. The Innocence of the Dove and the Wisdom of the Serpent*

NOTES 351

(Berkeley: University of California Press, 1987), pp. 351–53 and Judith Green, "Lords of the Norman Vexin," in *War and Government in the Middle Ages: Essays in Honour of J. O. Prestwich,* ed. John Gillingham and J. C. Holt (Suffolk: Boydell and Brewer, 1984), pp. 47–63.

92. Luchaire, no. 111, pp. 59–60.
93. Louis VI issues many charters from Paris between 1110 and 1117: Dufour, nos. 40, 41, 43, 50, 56–57, 64–65, 70, 72–74, 89–90, 96–97, 101–103, 116–119, 123–128.
94. Dufour, no. 50, 1: 100–102.
95. Dufour, no. 80, 1: 173–80.
96. *S. Bernardi Vita prima* 1.7, PL 185: 245C-246A.
97. Philippe Buc argues that Anselm of Laon introduced an egalitarian dimension into scriptural exegesis in the early twelfth century, *L'Ambiguïté du livre. Prince, Pouvoir et peuple dans les commentaires de la Bible au Moyen âge* (Paris: Beauchesne, 1994), pp. 30–33.
98. Guibert, *Monodiae* 3.4–9, ed. Labande, pp. 280–357. Gaudry's Norman links are mentioned by Orderic Vitalis, *Ecclesiastical History* 11.20, ed. and trans. Chibnall, 6: 90.
99. Guibert, *Monodiae* 3.14, ed. Labande, p. 394.
100. Bautier, art. cit., pp. 63–64.
101. On papal politics in this period, see J. N. D. Kelly, *The Oxford Dictionary of Popes* (Oxford: Oxford University Press, 1986), pp. 163–64 and Ian S. Robinson, *The Papacy 1073 – 1198. Continuity and Innovation* (Cambridge: Cambridge University Press, 1990), pp. 63–64, pp. 430–32.
102. *HC,* ed. Monfrin, p. 71; ed. Hicks, p. 10; trans. Radice, pp. 65–66.
103. *HC,* ed. Monfrin, p. 74; trans. Hicks, p. 13; trans. Radice, p. 69. The full name, *Petrus Astralabius magistri nostri Petri filius* is given in the necrology of the Paraclete as having died on 30 October, *Obituaire de la province de Sens* 4: 425 (n. 12 above).
104. *Theologia christiana* 5.50, ed. Buytaert, CCCM 12: 369; *Commentaria in epistolam Pauli ad Romanos* 3 (13.10), ed. Buytaert, CCCM 11 (1969): 290.
105. See above, p. 293, n. 14.
106. *Ep.* 2, ed. Monfrin, p. 115; ed. Hicks, p. 51; trans. Radice, p. 115.
107. *HC,* ed. Monfrin, pp. 74–75; ed. Hicks, p. 13; trans. Radice, p. 70.
108. *Autobiographie* 1.12, ed. Labande, pp. 78–80.
109. *Ecclesiastical History* 8.10, ed. and trans. Chibnall, 4: 188; Orderic explains earlier (p. 186) that Fulk established the fashion for pointed shoes ("pulley-shoes" in Chibnall's translation, or *souliers à la poulaine,* still popular in the fourteenth and fifteenth centuries, in the seventeenth century according to Chibnall, p. 187 n. 4), although it was a certain courtier of William Rufus who bent these shoes into the shape of a ram's horn. Geneviève Brunel-Lobrichon and Claudie Duhamel-Amado discuss contemporary fashion in *Au temps des troubadours XIIe – XIIIe siècles* (Paris: Hachette,

1997), pp. 169–80; Orderic's evidence indicates that these new fashions should be dated to earlier than 1150, as they suggest (p. 175).

110. *Gesta Regum* 4.314, ed. William Stubbs, Rolls Series 90 (London: Longman, 1889), 2: 369–70.

111. Rodulphus Glaber, *Historiarum libri quinque* 3.40, ed. and trans. John France (Oxford: Clarendon Press, 1989), p. 166 with similar comments in his Life of St. William (p. 290 of the same volume). On perception of a distinct culture in Occitania, see Linda M. Paterson, *The World of the Troubadours. Medieval Occitan society, c. 1100 – c. 1300* (Cambridge: Cambridge University Press, 1993), pp. 6–9.

112. Henri Platelle, to whom I am indebted for much of what follows, "Le problème du scandale: les nouvelles modes masculines aux XIᵉ et XIIᵉ siècles," *Revue Belge de Philologie et d'Histoire* 53 (1975): 1071–96 at 1074. In Germany, new fashions were also blamed on the influence of Theophanu, wife of Otto II; see C. Stephen Jaeger, *The Envy of Angels. Cathedral Schools and Social Ideals in Medieval Europe, 950 – 1200* (Philadelphia: University of Pennsylvania Press, 1994), pp. 200, 210–211, 244.

113. *Ep.* 257, ed. Schmitt, 4: 169–70; trans. Fröhlich, 2: 248–49. Eadmer reports these rulings in *Historia novorum* 3, ed. Rule, p. 143; Eadmer, *Historia novorum* 1, ed. Rule, p. 48; PL 159: 576.

114. *De restauratione S. Martini Tornacensis* 3, 6, ed. Georg Waitz, MGH SS 14 (1883): 276–77; *The Restoration of the Monastery of Saint Martin of Tournai*, trans. Lynn H. Nelson (Washington DC: Catholic University of America, 1996), pp. 16, 21.

115. Orderic Vitalis, *Ecclesiastical History* 9.3, 11.11, ed. and trans. Chibnall, 5: 22 and 6: 64–66; Platelle, "Le problème du scandale," 1081.

116. Council of Rheims (1046), J.-D. Mansi, *Sacrorum Conciliorum nova et amplissima collectio,* 31 vols. (Venice: Antonium Zata, 1725 – 98; repr. Graz: Akademische Druk 1960 – 66), 19: 741–42: "Ne quis sine electione cleri et populi ad regimen ecclesiasticum proveheretur"; trans. Brian Tierney, *The Crisis of Church and State 1050 – 1300* (Englewood Cliffs, N.J.: Prentice-Hall, 1964), p. 31.

117. Mansi, 19: 873, 898; MGH Constitutiones et Acta, 1 ed. L. Weiland (1893), p. 547; trans. Tierney, *The Crisis of Church and State,* p. 43.

118. *Vita S. Galterii Abbatis* 2.9, *Acta Sanctorum* 8 April, p. 752D and *II Vita S. Galterii,* p. 756D, *Bibliotheca Hagiographica Latina,* 2 vols. (Brussels: Société des Bollandistes, 1900 – 1901), nos. 8798 and 8796; repr. Mansi, 20: 437–38; Charles-Joseph Hefele, *Histoire des Conciles,* vol. 5 (Paris: Letouzey et Ané, 1912), pp. 111–14; see Orderic Vitalis, *Ecclesiastical History* 4, ed. and trans. Chibnall, 2: 200. On the debate, see: Anne Llewellyn Barstow, *Married Priests and the Reforming Papacy: the Eleventh-Century Debates* (New York: Edward Mellen Press, 1982), pp. 67–77; Charles A. Frazee, "The Origins of the Clerical Celibacy in the Western Church," *Church History*

41 (1972): 140–67; Christopher N. L. Brooke, "Gregorian Reform in Action: Clerical marriage in England 1050 – 1200," in *Cambridge Historical Journal* 12 (1956): 467–75, repr. *Change in Medieval Society: Europe North of the Alps,* ed. Sylvia Thrupp (New York: Appleton Century Crofts, 1964), pp. 49–71.

119. Ivo of Chartres, *Ep.* 200, PL 162: 206D-207B.
120. *Ep.* 257, ed. Schmitt, 4: 169–70; trans. Fröhlich, 2: 249.
121. Serlo, *Defensio pro filiis presbyterorum,* ed. Ernst Dümmler, MGH Libelli de lite 3 (1897): 579–83; see Barstow, *Married Priests and the Reforming Papacy,* pp. 105–73.
122. Theobald of Étampes, *Epistola ad Roscelinum,* ed. H. Boehmer, MGH Libelli de lite 3: 605; PL 163: 767D: "Plus itaque prodest bene vixisse, quam de justis parentibus originem duxisse. Deus enim vitam hominis, non nativitatem attendit." Cf. Marbod, *Ep. ad Ingilgerium,* ed. Boehmer, *MGH Libelli de Lite* 3: 692–94.
123. On the council of Rheims, see Orderic Vitalis, *Ecclesiastical History* 12.21, ed. and trans. Chibnall, 6: 252–76; Hesso reports popular murmuring against the Pope's firm management of the council, *Relatio de concilio Remensi,* ed. W. Wattenbach, MGH Libelli de Lite 3 (1897): 22–28 and Robinson, *The Papacy 1073 – 1198,* pp. 131–33 (see above, n. 101).
124. Orderic Vitalis, *Ecclesiastical History* 12.25, ed. and trans. Chibnall, 6: 290–94. Cf. Paul of Bernried, *Gregorii VII Vita* 116, in *Pontificum Romanorum Vitae,* ed. Johann Matthias Watterich, 2 vols. (Leipzig, 1862; repr. Aalen: Scientia, 1966) 1: 543.
125. Ivo, *Decretum* 8.77, 82 and 8.205, PL 161: 600B, 601A, 626C. See James A. Brundage, *Law, Sex and Christian Society in Medieval Europe* (Chicago: University of Chicago Press, 1987), pp. 189, 205–6.
126. John M. Riddle suggests that Marbod of Rennes, author of a treatise on medicinal stones, *De Lapidibus,* may have also written *De virtutibus herbarum,* attributed to Macer Floridus, in *Aemilius Macer De herbarum virtutibus cum Joannis Atrociani commentariis* (1530), in *Contraception and Abortion from the Ancient World to the Renaissance* (Cambridge, Mass.: Harvard University Press, 1992), pp. 114–16. See also Riddle, "Contraception and Early Abortion in the Middle Ages," in *Handbook of Medieval Sexuality,* ed. Bullough and Brundage, pp. 261–77 (p. 298, n. 52).
127. Luchaire, no. 221, p. 108; Dufour, no. 437, 2: 374.
128. Herman of Tournai, *De restauratione S. Martini Tornacensis* 18, ed. Waitz, p. 282; trans. Nelson, pp. 35–36.
129. PL 178: 372D-373A, 373D (on sodomites); ed. Cousin, 1: 88–89.
130. *HC,* ed. Monfrin, p. 71; ed. Hicks, p. 10; Radice (p. 66) translates *laicarum conversationem* as "secular way of life."
131. John W. Baldwin, *The Language of Sex. Five Voices from Northern France around 1200* (Chicago: University of Chicago Press, 1994), pp. 81–82.

132. *Carmen ad Astralabium* ll. 221–234, ed. José M. A. Rubingh-Bosscher (Groningen [privately published], 1987), p. 119.
133. *Ep.* 257 (as in n. 120 above). On Christian teaching on sodomy in this period, see Mark D. Jordan, *The Invention of Sodomy in Christian Theology* (Chicago: University of Chicago Press, 1997).
134. See for example, *Medieval Latin Poems of Male Love and Friendship,* trans. Thomas Stehling (New York: Garland Publishing, 1984).
135. John Boswell translates this poem in *Christianity, Social Tolerance and Homosexuality. Gay People in Western Europe from the Beginning of the Christian Era to the Fourteenth Century* (Chicago: University of Chicago Press, 1980), pp. 261–62.
136. *Ep.* 66, ed. Leclercq, p. 296 (n. 25 above): "Quidam enim concubi sui appellantes eum Floram, multas rythmicas cantilenas de eo composuerunt, quae a foedis adolescentibus, sicut nostis miseriam terrae illius, per urbes Franciae in plateis et compitis cantitantur, quas et ipse aliquando cantitare et coram se cantitari non erubuit. Harum unam domno Lugdunensi in testimonium misi, quam cuidam eam cantitanti violenter abstuli."
137. *Ep.* 65, ed. Leclercq, pp. 282–97 (n. 25 above), with detail about the boast of Philip I that he had slept with John (282), and about Baudri's failed effort to acquire the bishopric (288).
138. Guibert of Nogent, *Monodiae* 1.4, ed. Labande, p. 26.
139. *Ep.* 2, ed. Monfrin, p. 115; ed. Hicks, p. 50; trans. Radice, p. 115.

Chapter 4

1. *Carmina Leodiensia* no. 4, ed. Walther Bulst, Sitzungsberichte der Heidelberger Akademie der Wissenschaften, 1975, Abh. 1 (Heidelberg: Carl Winter, 1975), p. 13, edited from Liège, Bibliothèque de l'Université 77 (47), fol. 72r-v. M. Delbouille suggested that the poet who sent the anthology was a friend of Marbod called Walter, "Un mystérieux ami de Marbode," *Le Moyen Age,* 4th ser. 6 (1950 – 51): 205–40. Bulst is cautious about the claim that Walter wrote all the poems in the anthology. That he came from France is suggested by no. 8, ed. Bulst, p. 18 (*miratur Francia dulcis*).
2. *Metamorphoses* 2.272.
3. The earliest known troubador lyrics are edited and translated by Gerald A. Bond, *The Poetry of William VII, Count of Poitiers, IX Duke of Aquitaine* (New York: Garland Publishing, 1980).
4. Collected in translation by Magda Bogin, *The Woman Troubadours* (New York: Paddington Press, 1976).
5. Reto R. Bezzola, "Guillaume IX et les origines de l'amour courtois," *Romania* 66 (1940): 145–237 and *Les origines et la formation de la littérature courtoise en Occident* (Paris: Honoré Champion, 1966), 2ᵉ partie, 2: 275–315. Jacques Dalarun comments on Michelet's vision of Robert of Arbrissel, *L'Impossible sainteté,* pp. 120–34 (p. 324, n. 71 above).

6. Bezzola, *Les origines,* 2: 323–26 (n. 5 above).
7. Denis de Rougemont, *Love in the Western World* (Princeton: Princeton University Press, 1983), trans. Montgomery Belgion, with a postscript of 1972; originally published as *L'Amour en Occident* (Paris: Plon, 1940).
8. René Nelli, *L'Erotique des troubadours* (Toulouse: Privat, 1963).
9. Patterson, *The World of the Troubadours,* pp. 220–28 (p. 328, n. 111).
10. Apart from Dronke, *ML* and *WW* (see List of Abbreviations, p. xv), see Dronke, *Poetic Individuality in the Middle Ages: New Departures in Poetry 1000 – 1150* (Oxford: Oxford University Press, 1970).
11. See above, p. 292, n. 12.
12. Tony Hunt, "Aristotle, Dialectic, and Courtly Literature," *Viator* 10 (1979): 95–129.
13. Gerald Bond, *The Loving Subject. Desire, Eloquence, and Power in Romanesque France* (Philadelphia: University of Pennsylvania Press, 1995). For a fuller version of one chapter, see his essay, "'Iocus amoris': the Poetry of Baudri of Bourgueil and the Formation of the Ovidian Subculture," *Traditio* 42 (1986): 143–93.
14. *Geschichte der Lateinischen Liebesdichtung im Mittelalter* (Halle: Max Niemeyer, 1925; repr. Tübingen: Max Niemeyer, 1979), pp. 8–19.
15. *Carmina Burana,* ed. Alfons Hilka, Otto Schumann and Bernhard Bischoff, 2 vols. in 4 parts (Heidelberg: Carl Winter, 1933 – 70). There have been numerous translations into English, including David Parlett, *Selections from the Carmina Burana* (Harmondsworth: Penguin, 1986) and P. G. Walsh, *Love Lyrics from the Carmina Burana* (Chapel Hill: University of Carolina Press, 1993).
16. Walsh voices caution about this image in his *Love Lyrics from the Carmina Burana,* pp. xiv-xvii. Scholars rarely allude to Helen Waddell, *The Wandering Scholars* (London: Constable, 1927), *Medieval Latin Lyrics* (London: Constable, 1929) and *Peter Abelard* (London: Constable, 1933), but these were books of enormous influence in shaping popular perception of twelfth-century culture, like John Addington Symonds, *Wine, Women, and Song* (London: Chatto and Windus, 1884) and George F. Whicher, *The Goliard Poets* (Westport, Conn.: Greenwood Press, 1949). The origins of the *Carmina burana* are studied by Olive Sayce, *Plurilingualism in the Carmina Burana,* Göppinger Arbeiten zur Germanistik 556 (Göppingen: Kümmerle, 1992).
17. *Hilarii Aurelianensis Versus et Ludi, Epistolae, Ludus Danielis Belouacensis,* ed. Walther Bulst and M. L. Bulst-Thiele (Leiden: E. J. Brill, 1989), nos. 1–5, pp. 21–29; see also no. 14, *De papa scolastico,* p. 48; nos. 16, 17 (ed. Bulst, pp. 59–61) occur as nos. 95 and 117 of the *Carmina burana.* Hilary's connections with Sainte-Croix, Orléans are evident in an exchange of letters with his teacher there, a certain Hugo, *Ep.* 2–3, ed. Bulst, pp. 82–83.
18. *Carmina burana,* no. 169: *Hebet sidus leti visus . . . ;* trans. Walsh, *Love Lyrics from the Carmina Burana,* p. 192: "The bright star of my joyful countenance

is dulled by my heart's cloud." Dronke suggested Abelard's authorship in *ML* 1: 313–18.

19. Gerald Bond examines the wide range of authors who dedicate writing to Adela of Blois in *The Loving Subject*, pp. 129–57; see below, n. 72.

20. On Hildebert, see A. B. Scott, "The Poems of Hildebert of Le Mans," *Medieval and Renaissance Studies* 6 (1968): 42–83 and his edition, *Hildeberti Cenomannensis Carmina minora* (Leipzig: Teubner, 1969), nos. 4 to Queen Matilda, 10, 15 to Adela, 19 about Lucretia, 26 to Muriel of Wilton, 27 on the virgin Bona, 30 on a certain matron, 35 to Queen Matilda, 46 to Cecilia, abbess of Caen, 52 on a virgin married to an old man, 53 on Bertha. The major study of Hildebert's literary output is Peter von Moos, *Hildebert von Lavardin, 1056 – 1133. Humanitas an der Schwelle des höfischen Zeitalters* (Stuttgart: Hiersemann, 1965).

21. Carl Erdmann studied these themes in detail within eleventh-century letter collections, especially one from Hildesheim, in *Studien zur Briefliteratur Deutschlands im elften Jahrhundert* (Leipzig: Karl W. Hiersemann, 1938), pp. 117–224. See also Brian Patrick McGuire, *Friendship and Community: the Monastic Experience, 350 – 1250* (Kalamazoo, Mi.: Cistercian Publications, 1988).

22. See, p. 296, n. 43.

23. *Ars Amatoria* 2.281–86.

24. *Amores* 1.11.19–28.

25. *Remedia amoris* 717–20.

26. Stanley K. Stowers, *Letter Writing in Greco-Roman Antiquity* (Philadelphia: Westminster Press, 1986), discussing letters of friendship on pp. 58–70. A letter survives from Taus to her lover, Apollonius, a married man and civil governor in Egypt in the second century C.E., *Select Papyri* 1, ed. A. S. Hunt and C. C. Edgar, Loeb Classical Library (London: Heinemann, 1949), no. 115, 1: 309–31.

27. *Saturae* 6.277–78; see also 6.141 and 6.234 on women writing love letters.

28. *Tristia* 3.7.53–54.

29. On Ovid's debt to Sappho, and the legacy of the *Heroides*, see Linda S. Kauffman, *Discourses of Desire. Gender, Genre, and Epistolary Fictions* (Ithaca: Cornell University Press, 1986), pp. 50–61, as well as pp. 64–89 on the letters of Heloise. Ovid's authorship of *Heroides*, no. 15 (*Epistula Sapphus*); Heinrich Dörrie discusses the dubious grounds for such skepticism in *P. Ovidius Naso. Der Brief der Sappho an Phaon* (Munich: C. H. Beck, 1975), p. 4. Knox attributes the *Epistula Sapphus* to an unknown author in *Heroides. Select Epistles*, pp. 78–85 (p. 296, n. 42), arguing (pp. 7, 12–14) that it may be an imitation of a lost poem of Ovid, if the reference to Ovid's version of a poem of Sappho in *Amores* 2.18.26 is not an interpolation. Isbell (p. xvi) had written in 1990 that "scholarly opinion is nearly unanimous in seeing this letter as of genuine authenticity." The *Epistula Sapphus* occurs as

part of the *Heroides* in the oldest witnesses to its text, twelfth-century anthologies from the Loire valley; it is displaced from other *Heroides* in the earliest surviving complete manuscript of the poems, from the thirteenth century (see below, n. 49).

30. Veyne, *Roman Erotic Elegy,* pp. 83, 188 (p. 298, n. 51).

31. For a full survey of testimony about Roman women, see Mary R. Lefkowitz and Maureen B. Fant, eds., *Women's Life in Greece and Rome,* 2nd ed. (London: Duckworth, 1992).

32. Juvenal, *Saturae,* 6.434–37.

33. *Albii Tibulli aliorumque carminum libri tres,* ed. Fridericus Waltharius Lenz and Godehardus Carolus Galinsky (Leiden: E. J. Brill, 1971); extracts from her verse letters are translated by Lefkowitz and Fant, *Women's Life in Greece and Rome,* pp. 8–9.

34. For an introduction to the large literature on Augustine and women, see Kim Power, *Veiled Desire. Augustine's Writing on Women* (London: Dart, Longman and Todd, 1995).

35. William S. Anderson, ed., *Ovid. The Classical Heritage* (New York: Garland Publishing, 1995), pp. xii–xviii.

36. Birger Munk Olsen, *L'Etude des auteurs classiques latins aux XIe et XIIe siècles,* 3 vols. (Paris: CNRS, 1982 – 89), 2: 126, 127, 145, 158, 251, 255 (copies from central Italy, Germany, Corbie, Tegernsee and Toul from the ninth to the eleventh centuries).

37. These poems, *De excidio Thoringiae* and an epistle to her nephew Artachis, are edited as an appendix to those of Venantius by Friedrich Leo, MGH Auctores Antiquissimi 4.1 (1881): 271–79 and translated as poems of Radegund by Marcelle Thiébaux, *The Writings of Medieval Women,* pp. 30–56 (p. TKTK, n. 20). See too the translations of Jo Ann McNamara and John E. Halborg, *Sainted Women of the Dark Ages* (Durham: Duke University Press, 1992), pp. 70–105.

38. Karen Cherewatuk, "Radegund and Epistolary Tradition," in *Dear Sister,* ed. Cherewatuk and Wiethaus, pp. 20–45 (p. 297, n. 46). Dronke discusses her poems in *WW,* pp. 26–29, commenting on Ovid's influence pp. 85–86 with refutation of the argument that Fortunatus, a much younger man, invented her poems, p. 298 n. 14.

39. Peter Godman, *Poetry of the Carolingian Renaissance* (London: Duckworth, 1985), p. 8. Godman translates Theodulf's verse on pp. 150–75 and comments on his self-identification with Ovid in *Poets and Emperors: Frankish politics and Carolingian Poetry* (Oxford: Clarendon Press, 1986), pp. 101–106, suggesting that Ovid inspired the idea of verse epistles to be read aloud among friends on pp. 11 and 72.

40. On this manuscript (Oxford, Bodleian Library: Auct. F. 4. 32), see E. J. Kenney, "The Manuscript Tradition of Ovid's *Amores, Ars amatoria* and *Remedia amoris,*" *Classical Quarterly,* N.S. 12 (1962): 1–31 and *Texts and Transmission,*

p. 261 n. 12. Its glosses are studied by Ralph Jay Hexter, *Ovid and Medieval Schooling: Studies in Medieval School Commentaries on Ovid's Ars amatoria, Epistulae ex Ponto and Epistulae Heroidum* (Munich: Bei der Arbeo-Gesellschaft, 1986). Hexter comments on Carolingian interest in "The Poetry of Ovid's Exile," in *Ovid. The Classical Heritage*, pp. 37–60 (n. 35 above).

41. Dörrie, *Der Brief der Sappho an Phaon*, pp. 52–54 (p. 332, n. 42) and Richard H. Rouse, "Florilegia and Latin Classical Authors in Twelfth- and Thirteenth-Century Orléans," *Viator* 10 (1979): 131–60; see also Ruhe, *De amasio ad amasiam*, pp. 44–50 (p. 292, n. 8 above).

42. *Monodiae* 1.17, ed. Labande, p. 134.

43. *Dialogus super auctores*, ed. R. B. C. Huygens, *Accessus ad Auctores. Bernard d'Utrecht. Conrad d'Hirsau* (Leiden: E. J. Brill, 1970), p. 114.

44. *Theologia christiana* 2.21, CCCM 12: 141, quoting *Amores* 3.4.17. This verse is also quoted by Abelard in his Rule for the Paraclete, *Ep.* 8, ed. McLaughlin, 275; trans. Radice, p. 239.

45. *HC*, ed. Monfrin, p. 66; ed. Hicks, p. 6; trans. Radice, p. 61, quoting *Remedium Amoris* 1.369.

46. For example, *Tristia* 4.10.23; see also Marbod, *Contra invidum*, PL 171: 1719D.

47. *Ep.* 6, ed. Hicks, pp. 89–90; trans. Radice, pp. 160–61.

48. Many commentaries of Arnulf of Orléans on Lucan and Ovid are still unedited; see F. Ghisalberti, "Arnolfo d'Orléans, un cultore di Ovidio nel sec. XII," *Memorie del Reale Istituto Lombardo di scienze e lettere* 24 (1932): 157–234 and Bruno Roy, H. Schooner "Querelles de maîtres au XIIe siècle: Arnoul d'Orléans et son milieu," *Sandalion* 8–9 (1985–86): 315–41. See too B. M. Marti, "Hugh Primas and Arnulf of Orleans," *Speculum* 30 (1955): 233–38 and H. V. Schooner, "Les 'Bursarii Ovidianorum' de Guillaume d'Orléans," *Mediaeval Studies* 43 (1981): 405–24. There is a vast literature on Ovid's influence in the Middle Ages; for general surveys: n. 36 above; James H. McGregor, "Ovid at School: From the Ninth to the Fifteenth Century," *Classical Folia* 32 (1978): 29–51; Dorothy M. Robathan, "Ovid in the Middle Ages," in *Ovid*, ed. J. W. Binns (London: Routledge & Kegan Paul, 1973), pp. 191–209; Winfried Offermans, *Die Wirkung Ovids auf die literarische Sprache der lateinischen Liebesdichtung des 11. und 12. Jahrhunderts*, Mittellateinisches Jahrbuch, Beiheft 3 (Wuppertal: Henn, 1970).

49. Besides "Sappho to Phaon," the *Florilegium Gallicum* included works of Valerius Flaccus, Tibullus, Petronius, and over a dozen orations of Cicero as well as the *De oratore* and *Epistulae ad familiares*, a copy of which Petrarch discovered at Verona in 1345, thinking it had been lost since antiquity. See Birger Munk Olsen, "Les classiques latins dans les florilèges médiévaux antérieurs au XIIIᵉ siècle," *Revue d'histoire des textes* 9 (1979): 47–121 (especially 75–83 and 103–115) and 10 (1980): 115–64, and Rosemary Burton,

Classical Poets in the "Florilegium Gallicum," Lateinische Sprache und Literatur des Mittelalters 14 (Frankfurt am Main: Peter Lang, 1983).

50. M. A.-F. Sabot, "Ovid's Presence in the Twelfth Century: Latin Elegiac Poetry, Provençal Lyric," and Leslie Cahoon, "The Anxieties of Influence: Ovid's Reception by the Early Troubadours," in *Ovid. The Classical Heritage,* pp. 61–83 and 85–117 (n. 35 above).

51. Marbod did not relinquish his position at Angers until 1102/3; see Oliver Guillot, *Le Comté d'Anjou et son entourage au XIe siècle,* 2 vols. (Paris: Picard, 1972), 1: 260–62, 275 and 2: 206.

52. Könsgen, pp. 93–95; cf. letter 13 and Marbod, "In te namque sita mea mors est et mea vita" in *Rescriptum ad amicam,* ed. Bulst (1984) p. 186 (see n. 56 below); cf. Letter 32 and Marbod, "Et formam mentis mihi mutuor ex elementis ipsi naturae congratulor" in *Carmina,* PL 171: 1717A; cf. Letter 73 and Marbod, *Carmina* 24, PL 171: 1660.

53. His saints' lives and other writings are collected in PL 171. One of his major compositions was the *Liber decem capitulorum,* ed. Walther Bulst (Heidelberg: Carl Winter, 1947), more recently edited with detailed commentary by Rosario Leotta (Rome: Herder, 1984); see André Wilmart, "Le Florilège de Saint-Gatien. Contribution à l'étude des poèmes d'Hildebert et de Marbode," *Revue bénédictine* 48 (1936): 235–58; Bond, *The Loving Subject,* pp. 70–98, with a valuable bibliographical survey on pp. 231–32.

54. *Liber decem capitulorum* 1, ed. Bulst, p. 5; ed. Leotta, pp. 59–62. His discussion of woman comes in c.3 "On the prostitute," ed. Bulst, pp. 12–15 (PL 171: 1698B-99D).

55. *Carmen* 17 ("Repentance for lascivious love"), PL 171: 1633D-36B.

56. *Liber Marbodi quondam nominatissimi presulis Redonensis . . . ,* ed. Ivo Mayeuc (Rennes: Johannes Baudouyn-Johannes Mace, 1524), used by Bulst, "Liebesbriefgedichte Marbods," in *Liber Floridus. Festschrift Paul Lehmann,* ed. Bernhard Bischoff and Suso Brechter (St. Ottilien: Eos Verlag der Abtei, 1950), pp. 287–301, repr. [with typographical corrections] in Bulst, *Lateinisches Mittelalter. Gesammelte Beiträge,* ed. Walter Berschin (Heidelberg: Carl Winter, 1984), pp. 182–96. Bulst observed that four of these poems had been printed as anonymous poems from a twelfth-century MS, Zurich, Zentralbibliothek C 58, by Jakob Werner, *Beiträge zur Kunde der lateinischen Literatur des Mittelalters,* 2nd ed. (Aarau: Sauerländer, 1905; repr. Georg Olms: Hildesheim, 1979); see Ruhe, *De amasio ad amasiam,* pp. 23–34 (p. TKTK, n. 8 above).

57. No. 24 in the 1524 edition, *Ad amicam repatriare parantem,* ed. Bulst (1984), p. 2184.

58. Dronke discusses them in *ML* 1: 213–16. Bulst suggested that she may have been from Le Ronceray, like the women to whom Baudri of Bourgueil sent poems.

59. *Carmina Leodiensia* 6, ed. Bulst, p. 16 from Liège, Bibliothèque universitaire, MS 77, fol. 73, and Paris, BNF lat. 14193, fol. 1v. Charles S. F. Burnett observes that the text of the *Confessio fidei 'Universis'* in this latter manuscript, perhaps preserved by Walter of Mortagne himself, is our closest witness to the archetype of Abelard's text, "Peter Abelard, *Confessio fidei 'Universis'*: A Critical Edition of Abelard's Reply to Accusations of Heresy," *Mediaeval Studies* 48 (1986): 111–38, esp. 117–19 and 128–29.

60. *Puella ad amicum munera promittentem,* ed. Bulst (1984), p. 185: "Gaudia nimpharum, violas floresque rosarum, / Lilia candoris miri quoque poma saporis / Parque columbarum, quibus addita mater earum, / Vestes purpureas, quibus exornata Napeas / Vincere tam cultu possim quam transeo vultu, / Insuper argentum, gemmas promittis et aurum. / Omnia promittis, sed nulla tamen mihi mittis. / Si me diligeres et que promittis haberes, / Res precessissent et verba secuta fuissent. / Ergo vel es fictus nescisque cupidinis ictus / Vel verbis vanis es diues, rebus inanis. / Quod si multarum sis plenus diuiciarum, / Rusticus es, qui me tua, non te credis amare."

61. See above, p. 303, n. 18.

62. *Rescriptum ad amicam,* ed. Bulst (1984), p. 185: "A te missa michi gaudens, carissima, legi, / Namque tenetur ibi me placuisse tibi. / Si scirem verum quod ais, pulcherrima rerum, / Quam si rex fierem, letior inde forem. / Non facerem tanti thesauros Octauiani / Quam placuisse tibi, sicut habetur ibi. / Littera me vicit, que dulcem me tibi dicit, / Basia que recitat, cor michi sollicitat."

63. See above, p. 303, n. 18.

64. *Rescriptum rescripto eiusdem,* ed. Bulst (1984), p. 186: "Pro quo verba patris toleres et iurgia matris, / Pro quo ieiunes noctibus et vigiles."

65. *Ad puellam adamatam rescriptum,* ed. Bulst (1984), p. 187: "Sum felix tandem, qui nunc scio quid tibi mandem, / Cum iam non timeam, ne tibi displiceam. / Quod spes suadebat, metus hactenus impediebat, / At modo sum letus, transiit ille metus. / Per pharetram Veneris, qua tu quoque lesa videris, / Iuro per atque faces, sub quibus ipsa iaces: / Ex quo te noui, cunctas a corde remoui / Protinus inque tui totus amore fui. / Nam tuus aspectus lesit michi vulnere pectus / Et renitens facies vt sine nube dies. / Crinis erat pexus nulloque ligamine flexus, / Longus et auricolor, candida frons vt olor, / Et decliue latus et venter continuatus / Quodque stat in primis, ilia stricta nimis, / Hec et que restant, ex tunc michi vulnera prestant, / Que nisi contigero, viuere non potero."

66. *Ad amicam sub custodia positam,* ed. Bulst (1984), p. 194: "Viuere non possum sine te neque viuere tecum, / Istud namque metus impedit illud amor. / O vtinam sine te vel tecum viuere possem, / Sed mallem tecum viuere quam sine te." Cf. *Letter 2:* "cuius vita sine te mors est" and *38c:* "sine te michi vivere mors est."

67. Fulcoius of Beauvais intertwined biblical history with Virgilian imagery in *De nuptiis Christi et ecclesiae,* ed. Mary I. J. Rousseau (Washington: Catholic University of America Press, 1960) 1.20–24 and 6.206–14.

68. Twenty-six poetic letters to a wide variety of figures are edited by Marvin L. Colker, "Fulcoii Belvacensis Epistulae," *Traditio* 10 (1954): 191–273 with summaries of these letters in English on 198–204.

69. *Ep.* 10.82–84, ed. Colker, 237: "Potamus uinum; portamus candida, linum; Mitibus et Veneris uicibus, plerunque seueris, Vtimur—utamur passi quo compatiamur." Sexual humor and advice also occur in: nos. 9 to an adulterer friend; 10 to Fulcrad, archdeacon of Laon, whose homosexuality is contrasted unfavorably with the author's own married state; 16 and 17 more deferentially to matron Ida; 18 to Gervaise, archbishop of Rheims advising him not to be too amorous or greedy; 20–23 about foolish relationships.

70. *Ep.* 19.79–108, ed. Colker, 258–59, with English summary on 203.

71. Fulcoius, *Ep.* 26.1–2, ed. Colker, 196 and 267.

72. While Hilbert's edition of Baudri's poems is followed here (p. 291, n. 3 above), that of Phyllis Abrahams is still valuable for its extensive notes, *Les oeuvres poétiques de Baudri de Bourgueil* (Paris: Honoré Champion, 1926). References to these poems are given by Hilbert's numbering, followed by line numbers, with page numbers in round brackets. On Baudri, see Gerald Bond, "'Iocus amoris'" and *The Loving Subject,* pp. 42–69 (n. 13 above). Most of his writings are collected in PL 166: 1049–1212.

73. See pp. 82, 330, n. 137.

74. Bond notes that of eighty-seven direct or indirect participants of the letter poems, there were only two abbots, three priors, and three bishops, "Iocus amoris," 187.

75. The longest of his poems to women is no. 134 (pp. 149–87) to Adela of Blois, describing the tapestries in her chamber as a synthesis of learning, discussed by Jean-Yves Tilliette, "La chambre de la comtesse Adèle dans le c. cxcvi de Baudri de Bourgueil," *Romania* 102 (1981): 145–71; see too nos. 135–36 (pp. 187–89) to Adela and to Cecilia, daughter of William I and a nun at Caen. The Muriel to whom he writes no. 137 (p. 189) may be Muriel of Wilton (perhaps then resident at Le Ronceray). See also poems to Agnes, no. 138 (pp. 191–92); to Emma, *magistra* of the nuns, nos. 139 and 153 (pp. 192–93 and 203–4); to Constance, nos. 142 and 200 (pp. 194–96 and 266–71); on Constance's death, no. 213 (pp. 284–85). Baudri also wrote an epitaph for a recluse named Benedicta, no. 171 (245). Bond notes that the names of these women occur in documents of Le Ronceray, including an *Emma grammatica* listed in a charter of 1118, *art. cit.,* 168 n. 74. An Emma is listed by Jean Verdon as a widow who took the veil at the abbey in 1100 in "Les moniales dans la France de l'Ouest au XIe et XIIe siècles: Étude d'histoire sociale," *Cahiers de civilisation médiévale* 19 (1976):

247–64 at 248. In no. 139.21 (p. 192) to Emma, Baudri asks to greet "my Godehilde;" Verdon's list mentions Godehold, a daughter of Ralph viscount of Sainte-Suzanne as consecrated around 1100 and Agnes, daughter of Walter consecrated around 1110, but not Muriel, Constance or Beatrice.

76. Verdon, "Les moniales," 261. Boussard ("La vie en Anjou," 43; see p. 324, n. 67 above) believes that a nun of Le Ronceray probably wrote the history of an ambitious serf, Constant le Roux, who acquired property from the nuns (bequeathed them by a widow whose daughter had been murdered by her husband), but then became a monk at Saint-Aubin while his wife became a nun at Le Ronceray.

77. Ed. Hilbert, nos. 140–41 (pp. 193–94). Baudri's verse of complaint is followed by a witty four-line verse: "The mountain has brought forth a mouse, because mute Beatrice speaks. She has written, composed, spoken almost nothing. Either it is nothing which she says, or she protects what she has written and defends her poems with poems." This may be the Beatrice, *magistra* of the countess of Anjou, who signs a charter of Aremburga, wife of Fulk V (PL 162: 1102B).

78. On Muriel of Wilton, remembered as *inclyta versificatrix*, see J. S. P. Tatlock, "Muriel: the earliest English poetess," *Proceedings of the Modern Language Association* 48 (1933): 317–21 and André Boutemy, "Muriel: Note sur deux poèmes de Baudri de Bourgueil et de Serlon de Bayeux," *Le Moyen Age*, 3rd ser. 6 (1935): 241–51. Serlo's poem *Ad Murielem sanctimonialem*, is edited by Thomas Wright, *The Anglo-Latin Satirical Poets and Epigrammatists of the Twelfth Century*, Rolls Series, 2 vols. (London: Longman, 1872), 2: 233–40.

79. Ed. Hilbert, no. 139.15–16 (p. 192); see also nos. 153 (pp. 203–4).

80. Ed. Hilbert, no. 200.37–44 (p. 267): "Crede michi credasque uolo credantque legentes: / In te me nunquam foedus adegit amor. In te conciuem uolo uirginitatem, / In te confringi nolo pudiciciam. / Tu uirgo, uir ego; iuuenis sum, iunior es tu. / Iuro per omne, quod es: nolo uir esse tibi. Nolo uir esse tibi neque tu sis femina nobis; / Os et cor nostram firmet amiciciam." The whole poem is translated by Bond, *The Loving Subject*, pp. 170–81 (n. 13 above). Jean-Yves Tilliette discusses this poem and that attributed to Constance in "Hermès amoureux, ou les métamophoses de la chimère. Réflexions sur les *carmina* 200 et 201 de Baudri de Bourgueil," *Mélanges de l'école française de Rome. Moyen âge* 104 (1992): 121–61.

81. Ed. Hilbert, no. 201.60–64 (p. 273): "Me miseram, nequeo cernere, quod cupio. / Afficior desiderio precibusque diurnis; / In cassum fundo uota precesque Deo." This translation is based on that of Bond, *The Loving Subject*, pp. 182–93.

82. Ed. Hilbert, no. 201.113–116, 121–24 (p. 274): "Casta fui, sum casta modo, uolo uiuere casta; O utinam possim uiuere sponsa Dei. / Non ob id ipsa tamen uestrum detestor amorem; / Seruos sponsa Dei debet amare sui. . . .

Ius et lex nostrum semper tueatur amorem; / Commendet nostros uita pu-
dica iocos. / Ergo columbinam teneamus simplicitatem / Nec michi pre-
tendas quamlibet ulterius."

83. Ed. Hilbert, no. 201.175–79 (p. 276): "Grande tibi crimen, nisi paueris es-
urientem, / Oranti si non ipse satisfatias. Expectate, ueni nolique diu re-
morari; / Sepe uocaui te, sepe uocate, ueni."

84. Baudri, no. 97.51–60 (p. 105): "Naturam nostram plenam deus egit amoris;
/ Nos natura docet, quod deus hanc docuit. Si culpatur amor, actor culpatur amoris; / Actor amoris enim criminis actor erit. / Quod sumus, est
crimen, si crimen sit, quod amamus; / Qui dedit esse, deus prestat amare
michi. / Nec deus ipse odium fecit, qui fecit amorem; / Namque, quod est
odium, nascitur ex uicio. / Tu recitator eras nec eras inuentor amoris; /
Nulla flamma magisterio flamma reperta tuo est." Trans. Bond, *The Loving
Subject*, p. 52.

85. Baudri of Bourgueil praised Godfrey of Rheims (d. 1095) for combining
"the seriousness of Virgil and the lightness of Ovid, no. 99 (112); see also a
short verse letter to Geoffrey, complaining that he had not yet received verses
in reply, and the series of five epitaphs on his death, describing him as "a
happy treasure of great philosophy," nos. 100 and 35–39 (118 and 56–58).

86. The Regensburg love verses were edited and translated by Dronke, *ML* 2:
422–47 and re-edited by Anke Paravicini, *Carmina Ratisponensia* (Heidelberg: Carl Winter, 1979). Dronke comments further on Paravicini's edition
in *Sandalion* 5 (1982): 109–17. The complexity of the texts in these folios
of the manuscript is such that there is considerable disagreement as to exactly which verses form part of the exchange; Ruhe, *De amasio ad amasiam*,
pp. 34–41 (p. 292, n. 8).

87. Paravicini, *Carmina Ratisponensisia*, p. 13.

88. Paravicini, no. 40. Paravicini notes (p. 14) that the three communities for
women in Regensburg were all technically Benedictine rather than foundations for canonnesses: Niedermünster (founded ca. 760), Mittelmünster
(founded 974) and Obermünster (founded 1010).

89. Paravicini, no. 1; the translation of these verses is my own, although here as
elsewhere I am indebted to the always poetic rendering of Dronke, *ML* 2:
422. The habit of training students by getting them to summarize a fable
is commented upon by Ruth Morse, *Truth and Convention in the Middle
Ages. Rhetoric, Representation and Reality* (Cambridge: Cambridge University Press, 1991), pp. 40–43.

90. Paravicini does not include this verse within the exchange, included by
Dronke as no. 2 in *ML* 2: 422. Preceding no. 3 is an outline of the stories
of Phyllis and Demophoon, Meleager and Atalanta, Briseis and Achilles.

91. Paravicini, nos. 3–5; Dronke, nos. iii–iv, *ML* 2: 424.

92. Dronke suggests that certain verses are written by different men and
women, *ML* 1: 225–26 and *WW*, pp. 91–92.

93. Paravicini, nos. 3–5; Dronke, nos. iii–iv, *ML* 2: 424: "Simia dicaris, vel spinx, quibus assimularis / Vultui deformi, nullo moderamine comi!"

94. Paravicini, no. 16; Dronke, no. xiv, *ML* 2: 426: "En ego quem nosti, sed amantem prodere noli! / Deprecor ad vetulam te mane venire capellam. Pulsato leviter, quoniam manet inde minister. / Quod celat pectus modo, tunc retegit tibi lectus."

95. Paravicini, nos. 62 and 63; Dronke, nos. xlvii and xlix. Paravicini includes four short verses (nos. 64–68) beyond those published by Dronke, *ML* 2: 442–43.

96. These letters are edited and translated by Dronke, *ML* 2: 472–82, with description of the manuscript (Munich, Bayerisches Staatsbibliothek, Clm 19411) on 2: 566–67, but does not discuss them in *Women Writers*. They occur alongside *The Play of the Antichrist*, excerpts from Otto of Freising's *Deeds of Frederick I*, other letters to and from the abbey of Tegernsee, and a treatise about letter writing by Alberic of Montecassino. On the texts in this manuscript, *Du bist mîn, ih bin dîn. Die lateinischen Liebes- (und Freundschafts-) Briefe des clm 19411*. Abbildungen, Text und Übersetzung, ed. Jürgen Kühnel (Göppingen: Kummerle, 1977).

97. Dronke, *ML* 2: 474–75: "Accipe scriptorum o fidelis, responsa tuorum. Quid dignum digno valeam scribere ignoro—presertim cum doctoris aures pudor sit inculto sermone interpellare, et nefas sit silentio preterire; tamen prout potero tibi respondebo. Duorum mihi videtur ac difficile quod conaris a me inpetrare, scilicet integritatem mee fidei, quam nulli unquam mortalium promisisti. Attamen si sciero me casto amore a te adamandam, et pignus pudicie mee inviolandum, non recuso laborem vel amorem.—Si consistat absque dolore, non potest dici amor, unde constat maximus labor.—Cave ne quis videat ista dicta, quia non sunt ex autoritate scripta."

98. Dronke, *ML* 2: 475–76.

99. Dronke, *ML* 2: 476–77: "C. Cara karissime . . . quamvis nos disiungant maxima intervalla locorum, tamen coniungit nos equanimitas animorum, et veras amicicia, que non est ficta, sed cordi meo infixa. . . . Te amare volo quousque luna cadat de polo, quia ante omnes qui sunt in mundo cordis mei fixa es profundo. . . . Salutat te, dulcis margarita, et conventus iuvencularum."

100. Dronke, *ML* 2: 473–74: "Anima mea consummabitur dolore et merore repleta, quia a memoria tua funditus video deleta, que fidem et dilectionem semper a te sperabam, usque ad vite consummationem. Que est enim, H., fortitudo mea, ut sustineam pacienter et non defleam nunc et semper? Numquid caro mea est enea, aut mens mea saxea, aut oculus mei lapidei, ut non doleam malum infortunii mei? Quid feci? Quid feci? Numquid prior te abieci? In quo invenior rea? Vere abiecta sum absque culpa mea. Si culpam queris, ipse, ipse, culpabilis haberis! Nam sepe et sepissime meam

ad te direxi legationem, sed numquam in maximo vel in minimo verborum tuorum percepi consolationem. Ideo mortales cuncti dicedant, fidem et dilectionem a me ulterius non querant! Cave diligentius, ne tercius interveniat oculus. Vale, vale, meliora sectare."

101. Dronke, *ML* 2: 463–64. The prose letters are followed by a poem, *Instar solis ave*, expressing desire for a sublimely beautiful woman. By making a small correction to the text and giving the title "To Mary mother of God," a fourteenth-century scribe has changed it from a secular to a religious poem, *ML* 2: 518–19.

102. The verses in Zurich, Stadbibliothek C.58 were edited by Werner, *Beiträge zur Kunde der lateinischen Literatur des Mittelalters*, pp. 1–151 (n. 56 above). Werner noted an earlier opinion of Wackernagel that identified the scribe as a monk of Schaffhausen, although he did not commit himself to this (pp. 1 and 151). Its contents are discussed by Jean-Yves Tilliette, "Le sens et la composition du florilège de Zurich (Zentralbibliothek, ms. C58). Hypothèses et propositions," in *Non recedet memoria eius. Beiträge zur Lateinischen Philologie des Mittelalters im Gedenken an Jakob Werner (1861 – 1944)*, ed. Peter Stotz, Lateinsche Sprache und Literatur des Mittelalters 28 (Bern: Peter Lang, 1995), pp. 147–67.

103. Werner, nos. 60 and 61, p. 26, translated in Boswell, *Christianity, Social Tolerance and Homosexuality*, p. 217 (p. 330, n. 135).

104. Werner, no. 19, p. 17 about Poiters; nos. 46 and 133, pp. 21 and 54 about Orléans; nos. 101 and 138, pp. 40–41 and 58 lamenting the departure of Galo. No. 94 (p. 39) is an epitaph for Suger of Saint-Denis (d. 1152), while the last major item is a sequence in honor of Thomas à Becket (d. 1170, canonized in 1173). It includes too (no. 153, pp. 63–64) the *Moralium Dogma Philosophorum*, a summary of moral teaching by pagan philosophers sometimes attributed to William of Conches, and a version of the *Verbum abbreviatum* of Peter the Chanter (no. 290, pp. 115–116; PL 205: 369–528), as well as a commentary on Gratian (no. 289, pp. 114–115) possibly by the same teacher, a master of theology in Paris from about 1173 to 1191/92.

105. Werner, no. 48, p. 22: "Omine felici te Musa salutat amici, / Te mea musa canit, tibi soli ludere gestit." translated by Dronke, *ML* 1: 260; see no. 66 in the Troyes anthology: "Omine felici ceptis assis, Clio, nostri, / Carmine sis comens tabulas et suavia promens!"

106. Werner, no. 49, p. 23: "Dulcis amica mea, specior es Galatea, / Gloria, flos, speculum, lux atque decus mulierum, / Unica spes vitae, dulcis amica, meae, . . . / Lucifer ut stellis, sic es prelata puellis; . . . / Hec tu ne vento tradas, dilecta, memento: / Vive vale semper, te plus me non colit alter."

107. The epitaph's location is mentioned in a late fifteenth-century manuscript copied at precisely the moment that the remains of Abelard and Heloise were transferred to a new church at the Paraclete, Bern, Bürgerbibliothek 211, fol. 161. Dronke expands the letter V in the Zurich MS as: "V<ersibus

hic> studium coniunxit philosophie," *Medieval Testimonies,* p. 50 (*Intellectuals and Poets,* p. 251; p. 292, n. 12 above) *Versificandi* fits the meter more closely.

108. Werner, no. 66, p. 27: "Sepe tibi scripsi, semel et tua scripta recepi: / Te precor, ut nobis non levis esse velis; / Aut si versus amor tuus est in tedia nostri, / Et breviter scribas tu mihi, quid cupias. / Ulterius animum noli suspendere nostrum. Si te vis ut amem—fateor—te semper amabo, / Et, quamvis nolis, cura perennis eris." Dronke prints the first part of the poem, subsequently turned into a poem to the Virgin Mary, from the Tegernsee MS, Dronke, *ML* 2: 518–519.

109. Werner, no. 116, pp. 45–46, commented on briefly by Dronke, *ML* 1: 253: "Omnia vilescunt, artusque dolore liquescunt, / Non opus exponi, tolerent que dura coloni, / Sensus marcescit, corpus, vox, atque tabescit; / Ergo revertaris, ne mortem promerearis. . . . / Oro deum vivum, quod te mihi reddat amicum, / Insanae menti tu consule iam pereunti. / . . . / Scripta mihi desunt, quia cordi tristia presunt. / Quid loquar absenti, me, pro dolor! et fugienti? / Quid iuvat absentes lacescere versibus aures? / Durior es lapide factus, dum quereris a me: / Non te saxosum valeo superare remotum. / Convenias mecum, faciam te non fore tecum; / Multa loqui vellem tecum, si tempus haberem / Et loca, quae nostris congruerent lacrimis. / Haec quia non dantur, pro me mea scripta loquantur, / Et sit pro viva kartula voce mea. / Ei mihi, quid merui, quod nulla licencia fandi / Tecum secretis est habitura locis. / Si mihi privatim non vis concedere, saltim / Concedas kartae dicere pauca meae: / Flava prius Rhenum sua flumina rebar in Histrum / Vertere, quam soli te mihi nolle loqui. / Qua ratione tibi modo sim magis ipsa pudori / Quam prius, omnino dicere non potero. / Venerat hoc ex te, quicquid tibi displicet in me: / Nonne probasti mea? cur modo carpis ea? / Tunc ego gemma fui, tunc flos, tunc lilia campi; / Tunc quoque nulla fuit orbe mei similis. / Illud idem, quod eram, modo sum, nisi virgo; nec umquam / Id fieri potero; quod sine fine fleo. / Hoc ego nocte die fleo, quod non fata tulere / Cum dulci vitam virginitate meam. / Fraude triumphare nichil est nisi laude carere. / Pollicitando mihi bona plurima sepe dedisti / Proque bonis sumpta sunt mihi multa mala. / Sepe tui causa mihi sunt data verbera plura / Mollibus et membris vix pacienda meis. / Verbera quam membris nocuit plus fama pudoris, / Verbera sunt levius quam mihi verba pati. / Quod dedit ante iocum, modo dat mihi fundere fletum."

110. Werner, no. 120, p. 48: "Omnia postpono, te pectore diligo toto, / Tu mundanarum fons vivus deliciarum. / Te colo, te cupio, peto te, lassatus anhelo, / Ad te suspiro moribundus, teque requiro . . ."

111. Werner, no. 121, p. 48: "Carmina misisti, quod amat mea Musa dedisti; / Es, aurum squalent, carmina sola valent."

112. John Benton, Peter Dronke, and Elisabeth Pellegrin, "Abaelardiana," *Archives d'histoire doctrinale et littéraire du moyen âge* 49 (1982): 273–95.

113. Dronke edits and translates the poem in *Medieval Testimonies*, pp. 19, 45 (*Intellectuals and Poets*, pp. 263, 280; p. 292, n. 12 above). I reproduce Dronke's translation with modification of line 5 (*Damnosum tenere minus or<r>endeque puelle*), which he renders as "destructive for a tender, not at all venerable girl."

114. Dronke identifies this Mathias with count of Nantes, suggesting that it might have been written by somebody who knew Abelard's home region, and edits the poem with the subsequent verse, "Sola tamen Petri coniunx est criminis expers, / Consensus nullus quam facit esse ream," in "Abaelardiana," 278–79, and with translation in *Medieval Testimonies*, pp. 19, 45–46 (*Intellectuals and Poets*, pp. 263, 281).

115. Ed. Dronke, "Abaelardiana," 280: Aut me cecatum furor excusabbit amoris / Aut reus immense proditionis ero. / Omnia preter te mihi tradidit hospes supellex: / Nil volo preter te, nec Iosep<h> alter ero!" In the Zurich anthology these verses are introduced with the phrase "Peter about his host, who entrusted everything to him," Werner, no. 54, p. 25: "Petrus de hospite suo, qui sibi omnia commendabat. / Aut me cecatum furor excusabit amoris / Aut reus immense prodicionis ero. / Omnia preter te mihi tradidit hospes supellex: / Nil volo preter te, nec Ioseph alter ero." In the Zurich MS, *mihi . . . Nil volo* is omitted.

116. Ed. Dronke, "Abaelardiana," 280: "Re<m> mona<c>hi, Roberte, tenes, si nomen aborres? / Aut vero gaudes nomine canonici? Orret—ni fal<l>or tibi, frater, sola cuculla. . . ." "Saepe, soror, rogo te preciosas spernere vestes, / Quas cui nupsisti non amat, immo vetat."

117. Lioba's letter is no. 29 with the corpus of Boniface's letters, ed. Michael Tangl, *Die Briefe des Heiligen Bonifatius und Lullus*, MGH Epistolae Selectae 1 (Berlin: Weidmann, 1955). Dronke, *ML* 1: 196–99 and *WW*, pp. 30–35, discusses the correspondence with Boniface and Lul of Aelffled, Egburg, Eangyth, Bugga and Lioba, preserved with their letters. Cf. *Vita Leobae abbatissae Bischofesheimensis auctore Rudolfo* 11, ed. Georg Waitz, MGH SS 15.1 (1887): 126.

118. See too Mary Skinner, "Benedictine Life for Women in Central France, 850 – 1100: A Feminist Revival," in *Distant Echoes. Medieval Religious Women, I*, ed. John A. Nichols and Lillian Thomas Shank, CSS 71 (Kalamazoo, Mi.: 1984), pp. 87–119. Philibert Schmitz, *Histoire de l'Ordre général de Saint Benoît*, 7 (Maredsous: Editions de Maredsous, 1956), pp. 255–71.

119. An eleventh-century glossed manuscript of Terence from St. Ursula, Augsburg (Oxford, Bodleian Library, Auct. F. 6. 27), carries a note on fol. 112v: "Adelbert, Hedwich, Matthilt curiales aduluscentule unum par sunt amiciciae"; Adelbert could be Adelheit or Adelaide (d. 1043), daughter of Otto II and Theophano, later abbess of Quedlinburg (999) and then of

Gandersheim (1039); Munk Olsen, *Auteurs classiques,* 2: 624 (n. 36 above). Demoit was a famous woman scribe and recluse at the male monastery of Saint-Pierre Wessobrun, who copied many of its books in the first half of the twelfth century (ibid. 3: 272 for further references). An inventory of books, including a Cicero, was copied and annotated by Margareta of Lippoldsberg in the mid-twelfth century (ibid. 3.1: 140).

120. Verdon, "Les moniales," 261 (n. 75 above); Johnson, *Equal in Monastic Profession,* pp. 96–97 (p. 322, n. 42 above). See for example the poems edited by Léopold Delisle, *Rouleaux des morts du IXe au XVe siècle* (Paris: Jules Renouard, 1866), pp. 182, 187, 222, 242–44, 262; see also pp. 162–163.

121. The ruling of 789 is in MGH Cap. I, 63, c. 19. Jane Tibbetts Schulenberg documents a range of this legislation in "Strict Active Enclosure and Its Effects on the Female Monastic Experience (ca. 500 – 1100)," in *Distant Echoes,* pp. 51–86.

122. Dronke mentions these condemnations in relation to these *kharjas* preserved in a manuscript of the eleventh century, but possibly dating back many centuries, even to before the Arab conquest of Spain, *ML* 1: 26–32. Doris Earnshaw discusses whether these could be male compositions in *The Female Voice in Medieval Romance Lyric* (New York: Peter Lang, 1988), pp. 1–2.

123. Gerhoch of Reichersberg, *In Psalmos,* 4 at 39.4, PL 193: 1436AB, mentioned by Giles Constable, *The Reformation of the Twelfth Century* (Cambridge: Cambridge University Press, 1996), p. 66.

124. The translation from the Icelandic is that of Dronke, *WW,* p. 105.

125. *Carmina Cantabrigiensia,* ed. Walther Bulst (Heidelberg: Carl Winter, 1950), no. 25, pp. 50–51: "Sponso sponsa karissimo se ipsam in coniugio . . ."

126. On parallels between the Cambridge Songs and other vernacular traditions, see Dronke, *ML* 1: 271–81. Dronke reconstructs and offers a translation of a badly damaged dialogue as *Suavissima nunna* in 2: 353–55. One of the oldest surviving Latin love poems is "May God love a girl, bright and gracious," tucked into a monastic manuscript of the early tenth century, *ML* 1: 264–68.

127. *Liber X Capitulorum* 1, ed. Leotta, pp. 69–70; see Janet Martin, "Classicism and Style in Latin Literature," *Renaissance and Renewal in the Twelfth Century,* ed. Robert L. Benson and Giles Constable (Oxford: Clarendon Press, 1982), pp. 537–68, esp. p. 545.

128. See n. 18 above.

129. Könsgen, pp. 64–66.

130. *Mitologiarum Libri Tres* 1.15, ed. R. Helm, *Fabii Planciadis Fulgentii Opera* (Stuttgart: Teubner, 1970), pp. 25–26. Könsgen notes this parallel in an appendix on this poem (p. 67). Fulgentius alluded to a wide range of Greek and Latin authors, not all of whom can be verified; see Barry Baldwin, "Fulgentius and his Sources," *Traditio* 44 (1985): 37–57.

131. *Philosophiae consolatio* 1 carmen 1, ed. Ludwig Bieler, CCSL 94 (1958): 1. Ernst Robert Curtius passes over the eleventh and twelfth centuries in his discussion of the Muses in *European Literature and the Latin Middle Ages*, trans. William Trask (London: Routledge & Kegan Paul, 1953), pp. 228–46 and in "Die Musen im Mittelalter," *Zeitschrift für romanische Philologie* 59 (1939): 129–88 and 63 (1943): 256–68. Among examples of invocation of the Muses cited by Curtius is an eleventh-century hymn to St. Martial, in which the nine Muses are individually named, ed. Guido Maria Dreves, *Analecta Hymnica* 19 (Leipzig, 1895; repr. New York: Johnson Corporation, 1961), no. 367, 207. See also Jan M. Ziolkowski, "Classical Influences on Medieval Latin Views of Poetic Inspiration," *Latin Poetry and the Classical Tradition*, ed. Peter Godman and Oswyn Murray (Oxford: Clarendon Press, 1990), pp. 15–38.

132. Ed. Hilbert, no. 154.151–164, p. 209. Bond notes that Baudri did not repeat Fulgentius' comments about "mendacious Greeks," but rather was very interested in the relationship between myths and moral truth, so anticipating the theory of *fabula* with which the humanists of Chartres came to be associated, "Iocus Amoris," 179–180 and *The Loving Subject*, p. 58. See Robert Edwards, "The Heritage of Fulgentius," in *The Classics in the Middle Ages*, ed. Aldo S. Bernardo and Saul Levin (Binghampton, NY: Center for Medieval and Early Renaissance Studies, 1990), pp. 141–51.

133. Hildebert, *Hactenus, O Musae*, no. 17 in PL 171: 1448BC.

134. Dyan Elliott comments on the potentially destabilizing aspect of chaste unions in *Spiritual Marriage. Sexual Abstinence in Medieval Wedlock* (Princeton: Princeton University Press, 1993), p. 141.

135. John T. Noonan, "Power to Choose," *Viator* 4 (1973): 419–34.

Chapter 5

1. *Epistula Sapphus ad Phaonem, Heroides. Select Epistles* 15, ed. Peter E. Knox, p. 78 (p. 296, n. 42): "Ecquid, ut aspecta est studiosae littera dextrae, / protinus est oculis cognita nostra tuis? an, nisi legisses auctoris nomina Sapphus, hoc breue nescires unde ueniret opus?" Trans. Isbell, p. 133.

2. Charles Burnett, ed., "Peter Abelard 'Soliloquium'," *Studi Medievali*, 3ª Ser. 25 (1984): 857–94.

3. Rudolf Thomas, ed., *Dialogus inter philosophum, Iudaeum et Christianum* (Stuttgart-Bad Canstatt: Frooman, 1970); Pierre J. Payer, ed., *A Dialogue of a Philosopher with a Jew, and a Christian* (Toronto: Pontifical Institute of Mediaeval Studies, 1979). A new edition and translation is being prepared by Giovanni Orlandi and John Marenbon; see also Constant J. Mews, "Peter Abelard and the Enigma of Dialogue," in *Beyond the Persecuting Society. Religious Toleration Before the Enlightenment*, ed. John Christian Laursen and Cary J. Nederman (Philadelphia: University of Pennsylvania Press, 1998), pp. 25–52.

4. PL 178: 677B–730B, translated by Elizabeth Mary McNamer, *The Education of Heloise. Methods, Content, and Purpose of Learning in the Twelfth Century* (Lewiston: Edwin Mellen Press, 1991), pp. 111–83. *Problemata* are defined by Isidore as propositions or questions having something to be resolved by disputation, *Etymologiae* 6.8.14. John of Salisbury discusses *problemata* as philosophical questions in his *Metalogicon* 3.5–7, 9, ed. Hall, CCCM 98: 120–23, 128.

5. *Ep.* 4, ed. Monfrin, p. 120; ed. Hicks, p. 63; trans. Radice, p. 130: "Dum enim solliciti amoris gaudiis frueremur et—ut turpiore sed expressiore vocabulo utar—fornicationi vaccaremus, divina nobis severitas pepercit."

6. *Ep.* 4, ed. Monfrin, p. 121; ed. Hicks, p. 65; trans. Radice, p. 132.

7. Könsgen (p. 81) observes that the Troyes correspondence strictly speaking uses "imperfectly rhymed prose." Karl Polheim, *Die lateinische Reimprosa* (Berlin: Weidmannsche Buchhandlung, 1925), p. 362. Polheim (pp. 201–26) describes how prose rhyme in Latin was used in the second and third centuries by African Christian writers such as Tertullian and Cyprian, following a style developed by Apuleius of Madaura. Augustine of Hippo favored prose rhyme much less, except in certain sermons such as those in which he drew on Tertullian.

8. Dronke, *ML* 2: 472–82 (p. 340, n. 96). The exchange between the merchant and his wife, preserved within an anthology from Lombardy, is edited by Ruhe, *De amasio ad amasiam*, pp. 310–11 (p. 292, n. 8). She asks him to return from doing business in Cremona and Bologna for her sake and that of the children. He replies by sending money, explaining that he had to attend a forthcoming papal council at Piacenza, dating the exchange to ca. 1132 – 36.

9. *De ratione dicendi ad C. Herennium* 4.32, ed. and trans. Harry Caplan (London: Heinemann, 1954), p. 309. On Cicero's reaction to the rhetorical style of Georgias, see Polheim, *Reimprosa*, pp. 133–200 and Michael Grant's introduction to *On the Orator*, in his translation of various works of Cicero, *On the Good Life* (Harmondsworth: Penguin, 1971), pp. 228–35.

10. Peter Dronke makes this point in "Virgines caste," in *Lateinische Dichtungen des X. und XI. Jahrhunderts. Festgabe für Walther Bulst zum 80. Geburtstag*, ed. Walter Berschin and Reinhard Düchting (Heidelberg: Lambert Schneider, 1981), pp. 97–98; see also Chrysogonus Waddell, who suggests that *Virgines caste* is by Abelard, rather than an eleventh-century composition, "*Epithalamica*: An Easter Sequence by Peter Abelard," *The Musical Quarterly* 72 (1986): 239–71 at 255.

11. *Ep.* 2, ed. Monfrin, p. 113; ed. Hicks, p. 47; trans. Radice, p. 111.

12. *Ep.* 2, ed. Monfrin, p. 111; ed. Hicks, p. 46; trans. Radice, p. 110. Dronke documents other examples of rhymed prose in the letters of Heloise in an appendix to "Heloise's *Problemata* and *Letters*: Some Questions of Form

and Content," *Petrus Abaelardus,* ed. Thomas, pp. 53–73 (p. 312, n. 95), repr. *Intellectuals and Poets,* pp. 295–322 (p. 292, n. 12).

13. *Ep.* 167, ed. Constable, 1: 400–1; trans. Radice, p. 285.

14. On Peter's classicizing prose style, see Constable, 2: 38–41, and Martin, "Classicism and Style in Latin Literature," in *Renaissance and Renewal* (p. 344, n. 127), pp. 541–43. Martin implicitly counters Constable's view that there is no definite use of rhymed prose in his letters (acknowledging divergent views on the matter). Deliberate rhyme is certainly not used extensively, although it is evident in *Ep.* 115 to Heloise, ed. Constable, 1: 303: "Visum est ut affectui tui erga me quem et tunc ex litteris, et prius ex michi missis xeniis cognoveram, / saltem uerborum uicem rependere festinarem, / et quantum in corde meo locum tibi dilectionis in domino seruarem, / ostenderem." Similarly in *Ep.* 168 to Heloise, ed. Constable, 1: 401: "Gauisus sum et hoc non parum, / legens sanctitatis uestrae litteras, in quibus agnoui aduentum meum ad uos non fuisse transitorium, / ex quibus aduerti non solum me apud uos fuisse, / sed et a uobis nunquam postmodum recessisse."

15. Charrier lists occurrences of *quantus / tantus,* and a few other constructions in the letters of Abelard and Heloise to support the hypothesis that Abelard was its sole author in *Héloïse dans l'histoire et dans la légende,* pp. 573–82. Lodewijk Engels notes the influence of Augustine in his excellent study of the literary style of Abelard, "Abélard écrivain," *Peter Abelard. Proceedings of the International Conference, Louvain May 10 – 12, 1971,* ed. Eligius-Marie Buytaert (Leuven: University Press, 1974), pp. 12–37, especially 35–36.

16. Dronke explains the significance of Janson's work on the *cursus* in relation to the Abelard-Heloise correspondence in "Heloise's *Problemata* and *Letters*" (n. 12 above) and *Women Writers,* pp. 110–111. See also N. Denholm-Young, "The *Cursus* in England," *Collected Papers of N. Denholm-Young* (Cardiff: University of Wales Press, 1969), pp. 42–73, and Terence O. Tunberg, "Prose Styles and *Cursus,*" in *Medieval Latin,* ed. Mantello and Rigg, pp. 111–21 (p. 297, n. 51).

17. Janson questioned Dronke's hypothesis about the influence of Adalbert of Samaria on Heloise's use of the *cursus* in "Schools of *Cursus* in the XIIth cent. and the letters of Heloise and Abelard," *Retorica e poetica tra i secoli XII e XIV. Atti del secondi Convegno internazionale di studi dell'Associazione per il Medioevo e l'Umanesimo latini (AMUL) in onore e memoria di Ezio Franceschini, Trento e Rovereto 3 – 5 ottobre 1985,* ed. Claudio Leonardi and E. Menesto, (Florence: Centro per il Collegamento degli Studi Medievali e Umanestici nell'Università di Perugia, 1988), pp. 171–200.

18. Lanham, *Salutatio Formulas* (p. 299, n. 62).

19. In this translation, *esse* (rendered here as "true being") is interpreted as in apposition to her beloved, rather than to herself or to what she offers him.

20. Abelard discusses equipollence in *Dialectica* 2.2, ed. De Rijk, pp. 198–99, 207 etc.

21. *Carmina* 99.131, ed. Hilbert, p. 116, noted by Könsgen, p. 43 n. 4. St. Bernard uses the phrase *specialis amicus,* not used by any major patristic author, when writing to Haimeric, *Ep.* 157, *SBO* 7: 364.

22. *Ep.* 6, ed. Hicks, p. 88. Jean de Meun provides the correct translation "Ou sien specialment, la sieue senglement." While the correct reading of *Suo* rather than as *Domino* (the 1616 reading, repr. PL 178: 213A) was given by Muckle in *Mediaeval Studies* 17 (1955): 241 (p. xvii above), Radice (p. 159) persisted in translating the erroneous text as "God's own in species, his own as individual"). Georgianna discusses the various interpretations and translations of this greeting in "Any corner of heaven," 238–40 (p. 316, n. 110).

23. Bernard, *Sermo* 23, *SBO* 1: 138: "Sine mora aperitur ei, tamquam domesticae, tamquam carissimae, tamquam specialiter dilectae et singulariter gratae." (It is opened to him without delay, as if to an intimate, as if to a dearest, as if to a specially one beloved and singularly pleasing.") Hato of Troyes, bishop responsible for the Paraclete and thus personally familiar with Heloise, writes to Peter the Venerable in March 1138, *Ep.* 71, ed. Constable, 1: 205: "Salutat uos Odo archidiaconus nepos meus, tam specialiter uester, quam singulariter noster." (My nephew, archdeacon Odo, as much specially yours as particularly ours, greets you.)

24. *Ep.* 3, ed. Hicks, p. 57; trans. Radice, p. 123, an allusion suggested by Dronke, *WW,* p. 127.

25. *Editio super Porphyrium,* ed. Mario dal Pra, *Scritti di Logica,* 2nd ed. (Florence: La Nuova Italia Editrice, 1969), p. 16.

26. Ibid., ed. Dal Pra, p. 3.

27. *Ep.* 2, ed. Monfrin, p. 111; ed. Hicks, p. 45; trans. Radice, p. 109.

28. *Ep.* 2, ed. Monfrin, p. 117; ed. Hicks, p. 53; trans. Radice, p. 118.

29. *Ep.* 3, ed. Hicks, p. 54; trans. Radice, p. 119.

30. *Ep.* 4, ed. Hicks, p. 61; trans. Radice, p. 127.

31. *Ep.* 5, ed. Hicks, p. 70; trans. Radice, p. 127.

32. Cicero, *Laelius* [*De amicitia*], ed. and trans. L. Laurand (Paris: Belles Lettres, 1965); trans. Michael Grant in *On the Good Life,* pp. 172–227 (n. 9 above); see especially *Laelius* 80–81, trans. Grant, pp. 216–217.

33. Cicero, *Laelius* 81: "qui et se ipse diligit, et alterum anquirit, cuius animum ita cum suo miscet, ut efficiat paene unum ex duobus." I translate this more literally than Grant, p. 216.

34. *Laelius* 100; trans. Grant, pp. 225–26.

35. *HC,* ed. Monfrin, p. 65; ed. Hicks, p. 5; trans. Radice, p. 60.

36. I relate Roscelin's ideas to those on the *Glosule* on Priscian in "Nominalism and Theology before Abaelard: New Light on Roscelin of Compiègne," *Vivarium* 30 (1992): 4–33 and "The trinitarian doctrine of Roscelin of Com-

piègne and its influence: twelfth-century nominalism and theology re-considered," in *Langages et philosophie. Hommage à Jean Jolivet,* ed. Abdelali Elamrani-Jamal, Alain Galonnier, Alain De Libera (Paris: Vrin, 1996), pp. 347–64.

37. Cicero, *Laelius* 92 (trans. Grant, p. 221): "Nam cum amicitiae uis sit in eo, ut unus quasi animus fiat ex pluribus . . ." Ibid. 20 (trans. Grant, p. 187): "Quanta autem uis amicitiae sit, ex hoc intellegi potest, quod ex infinita societate generis humani, quam conciliauit ipsa natura, ita contracta res est et adducta in angustum, ut omnis caritas aut inter duos aut inter paucos iungeretur."

38. William of Champeaux, *Sententiae,* ed. Odon Lottin, *Psychologie et Morale au XIIe et XIIIe siècles,* vol. 5 (Gembloux: Ducoulot, 1959), pp. 192–94.

39. *Secundum magistrum Petrum Sententie* xxvii [sophisms about 'totum'], ed. Laurenzo Minio-Paluello, *Twelfth-Century Logic. Texts and Studies. II Abaelardiana Inedita* (Rome: Edizioni di Storia e Letteratura, 1958), p. 118: "Similiter, cum in ista argumentatione dicimus hanc enuntiationem 'Socrates est homo' enuntiare 'Socratem esse id quod ipse est,' istud 'id' non secundum personam discrete proferimus, sed indifferenter tam secundum naturam quam secundum personam illud accipimus. Non enim propositio proponit Socratem esse illam personam que ipse est, sed enuntiamus illum humanam naturam habere, hoc est hominem esse, sicut et cum dicimus 'Socrates est homo et Plato est idem.'"

40. For an excellent summary of Abelard's position on *differentiae,* see Marenbon, *The Philosophy of Peter Abelard,* pp. 117–37 (p. 292, n. 11 above).

41. *Logica 'Ingredientibus',* ed. Bernhard Geyer, *Peter Abaelards Philosophische Schriften,* Beiträge zur Geschichte der Philosophie und Theologie des Mittelalters Bd 21 (Münster: Aschendorff, 1919 – 1923), p. 397: " . . . sicut et cum dicitur: 'per mulierem intravit mors, per eandem vita' vel 'mulier quae damnavit, ipsa salvavit, scilicet similiter, ut videlicet eadem secundum indifferentiam sexus, non secundum identitatem personae dicatur."

42. C. H. Kneepkens discusses Abelard's interpretation at length, alongside that of his contemporaries in an invaluable study, presenting all the relevant texts, "'Mulier Quae Damnavit, Salvavit': A Note of the Early Development of the Relatio Simplex," *Vivarium* 14 (1976): 1–25.

43. *Theologia christiana* 3.144, CCCM 12: 250.

44. *Dialectica,* ed. De Rijk, p. 186; see Yukio Iwakuma, "The *Introductiones dialecticae secundum Wilgelmum* and *secundum G. Paganellum,*" *Cahiers de l'Institut du Moyen-Age Grec et Latin* 63 (1993): 59. I argue against a late date for the *Dialectica* in "On dating the works of Peter Abelard," *Archives d'histoire doctrinale et littéraire du Moyen Age* 52 (1985): 73–134, a view supported by Marenbon in *The Philosophy of Peter Abelard,* pp. 40–42 (p. 292, n. 11 above); I am now inclined to accept his view that much of the *Dialectica* recapitulates positions arrived at before he became a monk at Saint-Denis.

45. *Logica 'Ingredientibus',* ed. Geyer, pp. 13–14 and *Logica 'Nostrum petitioni sociorum',* ed. Geyer, p. 518.

46. Könsgen, pp. 68–71: Appendix 7 (Anrede-Metaphern). Also invaluable for comparing frequency of word usage by the man and the woman is the index on pp. 113–37.

47. Abelard develops this image from 1 Samuel 20.17, when he expands upon David's lament for Saul and Jonathan (2 Samuel 1.19–27) in his version of this lament: *Plus fratre mihi Jonatha / In una mecum anima* (More than a brother to one, [you are] in one soul with me) and *Nec ad vitam anima / Satis est dimidia* (Nor is half a soul enough for life); ed. Dronke, *Poetic Individuality,* pp. 202–209 (p. 327, n. 10 above).

48. If occasions are counted of single occurrences of words in the letters of the woman and compared to those of the man within the first few columns of Könsgen's concordance (pp. 113–37), the following statistics are arrived at: 17/9 (i.e., 17 words used once by the woman, compared to 9 words by the man); 15/11; 15/8; 16/14; 25/12; 25/11; 26/8; 18/21; 23/13; 13/14; 19/7; 17/11; 8/4; 18/12; 11/14; 18/18; 17/3 (words from *abicere* to *fatalis*).

49. Bernard of Clairvaux, *De consideratione* 4.2, *SBO* 3: 449; Peter the Venerable, *Aduersus Iudaeos* 3, ed. Yvonne Friedman, CCCM 58 (1985): 67.

50. Rupert of Deutz (ca. 1075 – 1129/30) speaks of the scribes and pharisees as *superciliosi* or disdainful, *De gloria et honore filii hominis super Matheum* 4, ed. Haacke, CCCM 29 (1979): 131; *supercilium* is defined as brow (as in the protrusion above the eye) by Isidore, *Etymologiae* 11.1.42. The files of the Comité Du Cange reveal just two usages of *superciliositas,* Guibert of Nogent, *Tropologiae* 4.15, PL 156: 418B, and the Life of St. Vital of Savigny by Stephen of Fougères (d. 1178), ed. E. P. Sauvage, "Vitae BB. Vitalis et Gaufridi," *Analecta Bollandiana* 1 (1882): 357–90, at 368.

51. I have searched the databases of the *Patrologia Latina, Corpus Christianorum* and of Yukio Iwakuma, rich in texts of twelfth-century logic. According to the CLCLT3 CD-ROM database (Turnhout: Brepols, 1996) Ramon Llull (ca. 1232 – 1315) employs *scibilitas* thirty-three times. *Scibilis* is used just once by Augustine, in *De trinitate* 9.12, ed. William J. Mountain, CCSL 50 (1968): 309, and by Boethius, *In librum Periermeneias,* II 5.11, ed. C. Meiser, 2 vols. (Leipzig: Teubner, 1880), 2: 376.

52. *Dialectica* 1.2.3, ed. De Rijk, p. 85: "Sicut enim dicitur scibile *scientia scibile,* ita etiam uidetur bene dici scibile *scibilitate scibile* ac magis etiam proprie, cum hoc sit propria forma *scibilis,* ut iam uidelicet contingat secundum Platonem idem duo relativa habere aut fortasse etiam plura."

53. Marenbon, *The Philosophy of Peter Abelard,* pp. 138–49 (p. 288, n. 11 above).

54. *Logica 'Ingredientibus,'* ed. Geyer, p. 214.

55. See p. 19.

56. Hugo Metellus, *Ep.* 16, ed. Charles-Louis Hugo, *Sacrae Antiquitatis Monumenta,* 2 vols. (Saint-Die: Joseph Charlot, 1731), 2: 348–49: "Helvidi Abbatissae Venerabilis Paracleti: Fama sonans per inane volans apud nos sonuit,

quae digna sonitu de vobis, nobis intonuit. Foemineum enim sexum vos excessisse nobis notificavit. Quomodo? Dictando, versificando, nova junctura, nota verba novando, et quod excellentius omnibus est his, muliebrem mollitiem exuperasti, et in virile robur indurasti."
57. *HC,* ed. Monfrin, p. 73; ed. Hicks, p. 12; trans. Radice, p. 68.
58. Letter 79: "Si grande aliquid meditando concipit hominis interioris intencio, profecto interdum non consumitur sine quadam vi exterioris. . . . Ego tandiu tractavi cordis et corporis flagranti nisu, qualiter te, o gemma decora, appellarem, sed intencionem mei affectus hucusque distulit difficultas suspecti defectus."
59. Alistair J. Minnis, *Medieval Theory of Authorship* (Aldershot: Wildwood House, 2nd ed. 1988), pp. 55–57.
60. *Ep.* 5, ed. Hicks, p. 78; trans. Radice, p. 147.
61. *Ep.* 8, ed. McLaughlin, 276; trans. Radice, p. 241.
62. *Ethics,* ed. David Edward Luscombe (Oxford: Oxford University Press, 1971), p. 28.
63. *Ep.* 3, ed. Hicks, p. 88. Radice (p. 159) translates *animus* as heart in this passage.
64. *Theologia christiana* 1.16, CCCM 12: 78.
65. *Ep.* 5, ed. Hicks, pp. 102–3; trans. Radice, pp. 174–75.
66. Bernard, *Ep.* 231.1 and *Ep.* 505 (*SBO* 8: 101, 463). Cf. *Sermones super Cantica Canticorum* 7.2, 24.4, 24.8, 42.1, 67.2–3, 70.7, 78.8, 85.11 (*SBO* 1: 2, 155; 2: 33, 189–90, 212, 271, 314).
67. *Ep.* 182, ed. Constable, 1: 426.
68. *Theologia Summi boni* 1.17, CCCM 13: 92, reproduced with slight variation in *Theologia christiana* 2.32, CCCM 12: 85 and *Theologia Scholarium* 72 and 1.65, CCCM 12: 430 and 13: 343. Augustine speaks of *affectus animi* in *Confessiones* 2.9 and 9.4, ed. Louk Verheijen, CCSL 27 (1981): 25, 137.
69. *Ep.* 2, ed. Monfrin, p. 116, ed. Hicks, p. 51. My translation is more literal than Radice (p. 114), "It is not the deed but the intention of the doer which makes the crime."
70. Augustine, *De immortalitate animae* 4.6–6.11, ed. W. Hörmann CSEL 89 (1986), repr. with translation by Gerard Watson, *Soliloquies and Immortality of the Soul* (Warminster: Aris and Philips, 1990), pp. 134–40 (translating *animus* as soul).
71. *Ep.* 2, ed. Monfrin, p. 121; ed. Hicks, p. 65; trans. Radice, p. 131.
72. Bernard, *Liber de gratia et de libero arbitrio* 4, 9, 38, 45 (*SBO* 3: 168–69, 172, 193, 198). Cf. Augustine, *De diuersis quaestionibus* 1.2.12, ed. Almut Mutzenbecher, CCSL 44 (1970): 36; *Contra Iulianum* 3, 5, PL 44: 733, 796.
73. *Ethics,* ed. Luscombe, p. 14: "Non itaque concupiscere mulierem sed concupiscentiae consentire peccatum est, nec uoluntas concubitus sed uoluntatis consensus damnpablis est."

74. *Comm. in epist. Pauli ad Romanos* 1 (2.9), CCCM 11: 81. On this evolution in vocabulary see Marenbon, *The Philosophy of Peter Abelard,* pp. 258–64 (p. 292, n. 11 above).

75. Radice's footnote (p. 115 n. s) about the "ethic of pure intention" as strongly held by both Heloise and Abelard is misleading in this respect.

76. E.g. *Moralia in Iob* 14.55, ed. Marc Adraien, CCSL 143A-143B, 3 vols. (1979 – 81), 143A: 742: "Through moments in the seasons, we see bushes loosing the viridity of leaves, ceasing from bearing fruit; and behold, suddenly we may see leaves springing out of the withering branch as if in a kind of resurrection, fruit growing, and the whole tree being clothed in restored magnificence." Gregory refers to "the viridity of eternal life" in *Moralia in Iob* 12.4, 143A: 631: "the teaching of eternal viridity" in 29.26, 143B: 1469; cf. 30.14.3, 143B: 1524.

77. Mews, "Hildegard of Bingen: The Virgin, the Apocalypse and the Exegetical Tradition," in *Wisdom Which Encircles Circles. Papers on Hildegard of Bingen,* ed. Audrey Ekdahl Davidson (Kalamazoo, Mi.: Medieval Institute Publications, 1996), p. 34 and "Religious Thinker: 'A Frail Human Being' on Fiery Life," in *Hildegard of Bingen: Voice of the Living Light,* ed. Barbara Newman (Berkeley: University of California Press, 1998), pp. 57–58.

78. Abelard, *Sermo* 32, PL 178: 584D: "Quae enim ad saecularem pertinent vitam feno comparanda sunt, quod abscisum de terra suae viriditatis vigorem amisit."

79. *Ep.* 2, 4, ed. Hicks, pp. 49, 67.

80. Roman Missal, Prayers for Good Friday, as in *Liber sacramentorum Augustodunensis,* ed. O. Heiming, CCSL 159B (1984): rubrics 515, 519.

81. Used of the bond between God and his people (Genesis 15.8; Deuteronomy 29.1; 1 Kings [= III Regum, Vulgate] 8.9; 2 Kings [= IV Regum] 11.17), the king and his people (2 Chronicles 23.16) and between Jonathan and David (1 Samuel [= I Regum] 20.16).

82. Tilliette comments on Baudri's use of the phrase *foedus amor,* also found in *Metamorphoses* 10.319 in "Hermès amoureux, ou les métamorphoses de la chimère," 154–55 (p. 338, n. 80 above).

83. *Ep.* 2, ed. Monfrin, pp. 114, 116; ed. Hicks, pp. 48, 52; trans. Radice, pp. 114, 117.

84. See p. 96.

85. *Ep.* 5, ed. Hicks, p. 78; trans. Radice, p. 146.

86. *Ep.* 4, ed. Monfrin, p. 120; ed. Hicks, p. 78; trans. Radice, p. 130.

87. *Ep.* 5, ed. Hicks, pp. 80, 83; trans. Radice, pp. 147, 153.

88. Robert Wielockx, "La Sentence De caritate et la discussion scolastique sur l'amour," *Ephemerides theologicae lovanienses* 58 (1982): 50–86 [edition 69–73], 334–56; 59 (1988): 26–45. Marenbon discusses Abelard's debt to the *De caritate* and his subsequent distancing from this work in *The Philosophy of Peter Abelard,* pp. 299–303 (p. 292, n. 11 above).

89. See, p. 95.
90. Jerome, *Ep.* 72.3, CSEL 54: 10. He mentions Bezalel in *Ep.* 60.12, CSEL 54: 564; cf. Isidore, *Etymologiae* 7.6.65.
91. *Comm. in Ezechielem* 14.48 and 8.27, ed. Franciscus Glorie, CCSL 75 (1964): 734, 381. A phrase in the woman's Letter 49 (*qui sibi videtur sciolus*) is slightly closer to a phrase in this commentary of Jerome 22.6 (75: l. 485) (*qui sciolus sibi uidetur*) than to Jerome's *Ep.* 48.3 (*uidentur sibi scioli*).
92. Jerome, *Ep.* 3.6, CSEL 54: 18, noted by Könsgen, p. 15 n. 1: "Amicitia, quae desinere potest, vera numquam fuit."
93. Jerome, *Ep.* 60.10, CSEL 54: 559; also *Ep.* 45.2, CSEL 54: 324.
94. Könsgen, p. 83. He notes possible such allusions in: letters 25 (Jerome, *Ep.* 3.6, 45.2. 49.1, 53.11 and 60.10.3; CSEL 54: 18, 324, 350, 464, 559), 27 (*Interpretation of Hebrew names; CCSL 72: 105*), 45 (*Ep.* 52.12.3, CSEL 54: 437), 49 (*Ep.* 48.3, CSEL 54: 382), 69 (*Ep.* 108.1, CSEL 55: 307). The allusion in the man's letter *41* to Jerome, *Ep.* 31.3 (CSEL 54: 251) seems too remote to be plausible. One could add the woman's use of *vinculum dilectionis* in letter 71, perhaps a reminiscence of *Ep.* 82.11 (CSEL 55: 118).
95. *HC,* ed. Monfrin, pp. 75–78; ed. Hicks, pp. 14–17; trans. Radice, pp. 71–74, drawing on *Theologia christiana* 2.38, 67, 96–97, 101, CCCM 12: 148, 159–60, 173–77. See Philippe Delhaye, "Le Dossier anti-matrimonial de l'*Adversus Jovinianum* et son influence sur quelques écrits latins du XIIᵉ siècle," *Mediaeval Studies* 13 (1951): 65–86 and Mews, "Un lecteur de Jérôme au douzième siècle," in *Jérôme entre l'Occident et l'Orient,* ed. Yves-Marie Duval (Paris: Études Augustiniennes, 1988), pp. 31–44.
96. Könsgen (p. 44) notes parallels in Virgil's *Aeneid* 7.201 (*portuque sedetis*) and Terence's *Andria* 480 (*Ego in portu navigo*).
97. *HC,* ed. Monfrin, p. 74; ed. Hicks, p. 13; trans. Radice, p. 69; *Ep.* 5, ed. Hicks, p. 79. Radice translates *te . . . transmisi* as "I took you," but the Latin clearly demands "I sent you," indicating that Abelard did not accompany Heloise to Brittany.
98. *HC,* ed. Monfrin, p. 75; ed. Hicks, p. 13; trans. Radice, p. 70.
99. *HC,* ed. Monfrin, p. 78; ed. Hicks, p. 17.

Chapter 6

1. *Ep.* 115, ed. Constable, 1: 304–5; ed. Hicks, pp. 156–57. Radice (pp. 277–78) leaves out the phrase *pro physica apostolum* (the apostle for natural science) from her translation of this passage.
2. On its date, see Constable, 2: 177.
3. *Ep.* 115, ed. Constable, 2: 305–6; trans. Radice, p. 280. Penthesilea was depicted as queen of the Amazons on tapestries in Dido's chamber according to Virgil, *Aeneid* 1.491–94; on Deborah, see Judges 4: 4–10.
4. Constable, 2: 55–59; ed. Hicks, pp. 156–61.

5. *Ep.* 332, *SBO* 8: 270; see, p. 304, n. 24.

6. The extent of his influence is well documented by David Edward Luscombe, *The School of Peter Abelard* (Cambridge: Cambridge University Press, 1969) and "The School of Peter Abelard Revisited," *Vivarium* 30 (1992): 127–38.

7. *HC*, ed. Monfrin, p. 101; ed. Hicks, p. 37; trans. Radice, p. 97.

8. She alludes to winter in letter 18 (1115/16?); he refers to the passing of a complete year in letter 87, perhaps (but not necessarily) implying that the final letters belong to the first part of 1117; see above, p. 317, n. 1.

9. *HC*, ed. Monfrin, p. 79; ed. Hicks, p. 18; trans. Radice, p. 75; see p. 319, n. 16.

10. See, p. 319, n. 18.

11. *Ep. ad Abaelardum,* ed. Reiners, p. 79 (p. 298, n. 55).

12. Carole Straw provides an excellent visual summary of these traditional distinctions in *Gregory the Great: Perfection in Imperfection* (Berkeley: University of California Press, 1988), p. 54.

13. *Vita Ludovici* 9, ed. Waquet, p. 52; trans. Cusimano and Moorhead, p. 47 and p. 179 n. 4.

14. Bernard, *Ep.* 77, *SBO* 7: 203, 210.

15. *HC*, ed. Monfrin, p. 81; ed. Hicks, pp. 19–20; trans. Radice, p. 77.

16. For a summary of the argument and context of the *Theologia Summi boni,* see my introduction to the work in CCCM 13: 39–71.

17. See, p. 351, n. 64.

18. See, p. 351, n. 68.

19. *HC*, ed. Monfrin, p. 88; ed. Hicks, p. 25; trans. Radice, p. 83; William of Saint-Thierry's presence at Soissons was discovered by Benton, "Fraud, Fiction and Borrowing," p. 486 n. 41 (p. 314, n. 95).

20. *HC*, ed. Monfrin, p. 88; ed. Hicks, p. 25; trans. Radice, p. 83.

21. *Theologia christiana* 4.78, 83, CCCM 12: 301–2, 304; *HC,* ed. Monfrin, pp. 84–85; ed. Hicks, pp. 22–23; trans. Radice, p. 80. Michael Clanchy argues that St. Anselm's arguments were used by Alberic against Abelard at Soissons, in "Abelard's Mockery of St Anselm," *Journal of Ecclesiastical History* 41 (1990): 1–23.

22. *HC*, ed. Monfrin, p. 90; ed. Hicks, p. 28; trans. Radice, p. 86; cf. *Ep.* 11, ed. Smits, pp. 249–55.

23. On Hato's connections to Sens, see Constable, 2: 97–98 and p. 318, n. 8 above.

24. *HC*, ed. Monfrin, p. 93; ed. Hicks, p. 30; trans. Radice, p. 89; cf. *Theologia christiana* 2.61–63, ed. Buytaert, CCCM 12: 156–57.

25. *Theologia christiana* 4.66, ed. Buytaert, CCCM 12: 292.

26. *HC*, ed. Monfrin, pp. 97–98; ed. Hicks, pp. 34–35; trans. Radice, pp. 93–94. Radice (p. 93) follows Muckle, "Abelard's Letter of Consolation to a Friend (Historia calamitatum)," *Mediaeval Studies* 12 (1950): 212–13 in ar-

guing against the traditional identification, on the grounds that no texts attacking Abelard survive by Norbert, elected archbishop of Magdeburg in 1126, or Bernard from this time. Edward Little developed this argument, "Relations between St Bernard and Abelard before 1139," in *Saint Bernard of Clairvaux. Studies commemorating the eighth centenary of his canonization,* ed. Basil Pennington (Kalamazoo, Mich.: Cistercian Publications, 1977), pp. 155–68.

27. *Sermo* 33, PL 178: 605C.

28. *Ep.* 13, *SBO* 7: 62–63.

29. Bernard, *Ep.* 8, 38, 78, *SBO* 7: 49, 97, 201–10.

30. *Ep.* 77, *SBO* 7: 184–200. Hugh Feiss provides a complete translation of this letter in his valuable study, "*Bernardus Scholasticus:* The Correspondence of Bernard of Clairvaux and Hugh of Saint Victor on Baptism," in *Bernardus Magister,* ed. Sommerfeldt, pp. 349–72 (p. 304, n. 23 above).

31. *Ep.* 31, 37–41, *SBO* 7: 85–86, 94–100.

32. PL 173: 1421A-1422D.

33. PL 173: 1418A-1420B (wrongly dated to 1134), *Recueil* 15: 329–30. Gualo (or Walo, Galo, not to be confused with Galo, bishop of Paris) is praised as "another Aristotle" in the two poems of the Zurich anthology (see p. 109). No other teacher at Notre-Dame is recorded after Abelard's departure in 1117/18. Bautier notes that he may be the Gualo, cantor at Beauvais from 1108 to 1114/17, in "Paris au temps d'Abélard," pp. 66–67. It is not clear if this is the same Gualo as wrote an *Invectio in monachos,* ed. Thomas Wright, *Satirical Poets of the Twelfth Century,* 2 vols. (London: Longman, 1872), 2: 201–7; see Jan Ziolkowski, "A Bouquet of Wisdom and Invective: Houghton MS. Lat. 300," *Harvard Library Bulletin* 1 (1990): 29–30.

34. Émile Lesne presented this as a dispute between Gualo and Algrin (d. 1150), *Les Écoles de la fin du VIIIe siècle a la fin du XIIe,* Histoire de la propriété ecclésiastique en France V (Lille: Facultés catholiques, 1940), pp. 208–9. A canon of Étampes and archdeacon of Orléans (as well as canon of Notre-Dame in 1120, with a house outside the cloister), Algrin had been an associate of Stephen of Garlande and served as chancellor in 1132 prior to Garlande's restoration (Luchaire, nos. 254, 268, 284, 497, pp. 122, 127, 133, 229); in 1132, Algrin was associated with opposition to subdeacon Archibald, thought to have been murdered by friends of Stephen of Garlande. Algrin replaced Stephen of Garlande as royal chancellor in 1137 with the accession of Louis VII; see Luchaire, no. 505, pp. 233 and 305–306 and Constable, 2: 309–310.

35. Matthew of Albano resolved this dispute in Rome, PL 173: 1263B-64C; see p. 317, n. 5 above.

36. See an exchange between Stephen of Senlis and the archbishop of Sens, as well as with Geoffrey of Chartres, the papal legate, PL 173: 1411A-14B.

37. *Ep.* 45–49, *SBO* 7: 133–41; see Luchaire, no. 424, p. 196.

38. *Vita Ludovici* 31, ed. Waquet, p. 254; trans. Cusimano and Moorhead, pp. 144–45 and notes on pp. 208–9 (with a mistaken reference to the niece as Stephen's daughter). Stephen was dismissed as royal chancellor sometime between 3 August 1127 and 10 March 1128, when the new royal chancellor is Simon, Bautier, "Paris au temps d'Abélard," p. 68 n. 4 (p. 317, n. 1 above). John Benton doubted Bautier's suggestion that this Simon was Suger's nephew Simon (d. ca. 1178/80), royal chancellor 1150 – 51, as he would have to have been a young man when he took this office in 1128, "Suger's Life and Personality," in *Abbot Suger and Saint-Denis: A Symposium*, ed. Paula Lieber Gerson (New York: Metropolitan Museum of Art, 1986), p. 5 and n. 22. Michel Bur argues (against Benton) that Suger was not directly involved in the ousting of Stephen, *Suger. Abbé de Saint-Denis, régent de France* (Paris: Perrin, 1991), pp. 133–34, as does Lindy Grant, *Abbot Suger*, pp. 124–29 (p. 321, n. 39).

39. Luchaire calls this a *coup d'État*, p. lii and 304; see also Hallam, *Capetian France 987–1328*, pp. 159–60 (p. 300, n. 77) and Boussard, *Nouvelle Histoire de Paris*, p. 138 (p. 317, n. 2 above).

40. Dufour, no. 263, 2: 59–62 and Galbert of Bruges, *De multro, traditione, et occisione gloriosi Karoli comitis Flandriarum* 47–52, ed. Jeff Rider, CCCM 131 (1994): 97–102; trans. James Bruce Ross, *The Murder of Charles the Good Count of Flanders* (New York: Columbia University Press, 1950), pp. 186–98. Suger comments on Louis' support for William Clito, *Vita Ludovici* 30, ed. Waquet, p. 246; trans. Cusimano and Moorhead, p. 140, as does Orderic Vitalis, *Ecclesiastical History* 12.1, 12.45, ed. and trans. Chibnall, 6: 184, 368–78. On Clito's hostile attitude to knights and burgers, see Herman of Tournai, *De restauratione monasterii Tornacensis* 36, trans. Nelson, pp. 52–53.

41. *HC*, ed. Monfrin, p. 100; ed. Hicks, p. 35; trans. Radice, p. 96; Abelard's accusation is supported by the close study of the suspect document offered by Thomas G. Waldman, "Abbot Suger and the nuns of Argenteuil," *Traditio* 41 (1985): 239–72, and Grant, *Abbot Suger*, pp. 190–93 (p. 321, n. 39 above). Luchaire, no. 97, p. 53; Suger, *Vita Ludovici* 27, ed. Waquet, pp. 216–18; trans. Cusimano and Moorhead, pp. 126–27.

42. PL 173: 1265CD, quoted by Waldman, "Abbot Suger and the nuns of Argenteuil," 252, n. 62. For the royal charter, see Dufour, no. 281, 3: 100–106.

43. *Ep.* 48, *SBO* 7: 138: "An certe quod Lauduni de prostibulo Veneris suum Deo sanctuarium restitutum est?" Luchaire, no. 410, pp. 190–91. Dufour observes political factors behind their replacement by monks, no. 263, 2: 61.

44. PL 179: 64, 66, nos. 15 and 17; see also Matthew of Albano, PL 173: 1268AB.

45. Stephen's confirmation of the 1134 charter, repeating claims about the sexual immorality of the nuns of Saint-Éloi, is printed in PL 173: 1424D–1427A.

46. Duchesne prints a document from 1207 revealing these events, PL 178: 169D-70A; *DHGE* 4.25–26.
47. *Vita Ludovici* 32, ed. Waquet, pp. 256–68; trans. Cusimano and Moorhead, pp. 145–51 and Bernard, *Ep.* 124–127, *SBO* 7: 305–21; see Mary Stroll, *The Jewish Pope: Ideology and Politics in the Papal Schism of 1130* (Leiden: E. J. Brill, 1987). Robinson notes the sympathy of the Pierleone family for Rome, but questions the traditional idea that the majority faction supporting Anacletus were either predominantly Roman or in favor of older models of reform, as distinct from the party of Innocent, *The Papacy 1073–1198*, pp. 69–78 (p. 327, n. 101).
48. Bernard, *Ep.* 124, 150–51, *SBO* 7: 305–307, 354–58; Philip of Tours was degraded by Innocent II in 1139; John of Salisbury, *Historia Pontificalis* 16, ed. and trans. Chibnall, p. 43 (p. 305, n. 25).
49. Two letters from the Duke of Burgundy to William X of Aquitaine, perhaps written by Bernard in 1131, are preserved as *Ep.* 127–28, *SBO* 7: 320–22, alongside *Ep.* 126, *SBO* 7: 309–319, to the bishops of Aquitaine; see Robinson, *The Papacy 1073–1198*, pp. 158–59.
50. *HC,* ed. Monfrin, p. 101; ed. Hicks, pp. 36–37; trans. Radice, p. 97.
51. *Chronicon Mauriniacensis,* ed. Mirot, p. 54 (p. 321, n. 39).
52. Luchaire, no. 420, p. 194. Letters of the archbishop and of Stephen of Senlis (PL 173: 1416) reveal that the archbishop warned the bishop of Paris to come to Provins to examine the case of Stephen of Garlande, but the bishop refused. Threats against the life of Stephen of Senlis are mentioned in an anonymous letter to Stephen (PL 173: 1415AB). The atmosphere of violence and political confusion are well illustrated in a letter from a certain *frater P.* to Geoffrey of Chartres written ca. 1132/33, in support of the bishop of Paris and lamenting the behavior of certain canons who do not conduct themselves properly, Edmé R. Smits, "An Unedited Letter (1132–1133) to Geoffrey de Lèves, Bishop of Chartres, concerning Louis VI and the Reform Movement," *Revue bénédictine* 92 (1982): 407–417.
53. Innocent's reply is printed as *Ep.* 552 among his letters, PL 179: 620BC. The events were reported by Stephen of Senlis to Geoffrey of Chartres, PL 173: 1416B-1417D. The nephews of archdeacon Theobald were vassals of Stephen of Garlande. In February 1133, Archembald, subdean at Orléans, had been killed by supporters of archdeacon John, in turn loyal to Stephen of Garlande; Bautier, "Paris au temps d'Abélard," p. 70.
54. Bernard wrote *Ep.* 158 to the Pope about the murder; *Ep.* 159 and 160 are written in the name of bishop Stephen but seem to be written by Bernard or his secretary (*SBO* 7: 365–69). On the related murder in 1133 of subdean Archibald of Orléans, opposed by archdeacon Ralph and Stephen of Garlande, dean of the cathedral at Orléans, see Constable, 2: 308–309.
55. Fassler, *Gothic Song,* pp. 203–206 (p. 317, n. 3 above).

56. Many of the early charters are translated into French, including that the very detailed 1147 charter of Eugenius III (Checklist, no. 420), and commented upon by Charrier, *Héloïse dans l'histoire et dans la légende,* pp. 256–70 (p. 302, n. 10 above). On the gift of Matilda see Checklist, no. 434; trans. Theodore Evergates in *Medieval France. Documents from the County of Champagne* (Philadelphia: University of Pennsylvania Press, 1993), pp. 62–63.

57. *Ep.* 2, ed. Monfrin, p. 111; ed. Hicks, p. 45; trans. Radice, p. 109; on Hugh Metel, see above, p. 350, n. 56.

58. See, p. 316, n. 111.

59. PL 178: 313D; *The Paraclete Statutes,* ed. Waddell, p. 9 with commentary on p. 77 and conclusions on pp. 199–203 (p. 316, n. 111).

60. *Ep.* 6, ed. Hicks, p. 106; trans. Radice, p. 178.

61. Waddell, *The Paraclete Statutes,* pp. 86–87; see Heloise's *Ep.* 6, ed. Hicks, p. 89 and *Ep.* 8, ed. McLaughlin, pp. 268–69; trans. Radice, pp. 160 and 245–46.

62. See, p. 316, n. 111.

63. *Ep.* 10, ed. Smits, p. 239.

64. *Peter Abelard's Hymnarius Paraclitensis,* ed. Joseph Szövérffy, 2 vols. (Albany, New York: Classical Folia Editions, 1975) 2: 9–13.

65. Ibid. 2: 10.

66. Ed. Boutillier du Retail and Piétresson de Saint-Aubin, *Recueil des historiens de la France, Obituaires de la province de Sens,* 4: 429 (p. 318, n. 12 above). The Paraclete also had a confraternity of prayer with Fontevrault, noted by Johnson, *Equal in Monastic Profession,* p. 98 (p. 322, n. 42). In the obituary of Clairvaux, there is no reference to the Paraclete; see the edition of C. Lalore in *Le Trésor de Clairvaux du XIIe au XVIIIe siècle* (Troyes: Thorin, 1875), pp. 174–85.

67. Bernard, *Ep.* 278, *SBO* 8: 190. This message was taken to Rome by a certain master Garnerius.

68. This poem was edited by Léopold Delisle, "Des documents paléographiques concernant l'usage de prier pour les morts," *Bibliothèque de l'école des chartes,* 2e ser. 3 (1846): 361–411 and more fully in *Rouleaux des morts du IXe au XVe siècle* (Paris: Imprimerie nationale, 1866), p. 299 and *Rouleau mortuaire du B. Vital, abbé de Savigny* (Paris: Imprimerie nationale, 1909), pp. 22–24. Delisle (*Rouleaux des morts,* p. 262) edits also a shorter, less sophisticated poem from Argenteuil in honor of Matilda, first abbess of Sainte-Trinité, Caen (d. 6 July 1113). In its list of nuns *Helvidis monacha* is mentioned twice, whereas there is only one *Helvidis* mentioned at Argenteuil in 1122. This could mean Heloise only moved to Notre-Dame in 1113, when Abelard was already teaching there.

69. Orderic Vitalis, *Ecclesiastical History* 8.27, ed. and trans. Chibnall, 4: 332. Vital and Robert of Arbrissel are mentioned as leaders of a group of hermits in

the Loire region in the *Vita B. Bernardi Tironensis,* PL 172: 1381A; on the Life of Vital, see p. 350, n. 50 above. The chronology of the foundation of Savigny and Neufbourg (re-dated to 1115, rather than to 1105) is considered by Jacqueline Buhot, "L'abbaye normande de Savigny, chef d'ordre et fille de Cîteaux," *Le Moyen Age* ser. 3, 7 (1936): 1–19, 104–21, 178–90, 249–72 (with note on 111 that all communities founded by Vital were dedicated to the Holy Trinity, unlike Cistercian houses, customarily dedicated to the Virgin Mary).

70. Ed. Hilberg, no. 195.14, p. 262.
71. *Ep.* 4, PL 171: 1474AB.
72. The records of Argenteuil prior to its being taken over in 1129 by monks of Saint-Denis are so scanty, identification of these individuals is difficult. Dépoin identifies abbess Judith with the daughter of Charles the Bald, seduced by and then married to Count Baldwin, before being given the abbey of Argenteuil, *Une élegie latine d'Héloïse suivie du Nécrologe d'Argenteuil et autres documents inédits* (Pontoise: Société du Vexin, 2nd ed., 1897), p. 4.
73. McLeod discusses the text and translation in *Héloïse. A Biography,* pp. 87–91, with reproduction of the original document as a frontispiece to the book (p. 302, n. 10 above). Her comment that "the sentiments it expresses are not in any way original" (p. 89) perhaps goes too far in the opposite extreme to the enthusiasm of older scholars. A translation by Patrick T. McMahon, O. Carm. is provided without detailed commentary within Penelope Johnson's excellent study of twelfth-century female religious communities, *Equal in Monastic Profession,* pp. 145–46 (p. 322, n. 42 above).
74. Delisle, *Rouleaux des morts du IXe au XVe siècle,* no. 47, p. 301 (n. 69 above).
75. The manuscript in which this occurs, (British Library, Add. 24199, fol. 77v) is a twelfth-century verse anthology that includes poems of Hildebert of Lavardin and Marbod of Rennes, perhaps coming from the region around Bury St. Edmunds, edited by André Boutemy, "Recueil poétique du manuscrit Additional British Museum 24199," *Latomus* 2 (1938): 30–52 at 42–44; Boutemy discusses its provenance in his earlier study, "Notice sur le recueil poétique du manuscrit Cotton Vitellius A xii, du British Museum," *Latomus* 1 (1937): 278–313 at 293–95.
76. No. xiv.1–10, ed. Boutemy, 42–43. The translation is that of Gerald Bond, given as an appendix to *The Loving Subject,* pp. 166–69 (p. 331, n. 13 above), to which I have made small modifications (*gentilis* as gentile rather than noble) and the first person plural maintained for *pellimur,* rather than turned into the singular.
77. *Theologia Scholarium* 2.1–61, ed. Buytert and Mews, CCCM 13: 406–38.
78. See, p. 64.
79. No. xii.10, ed. Boutemy, 42: "Dat pacem, lusus callidate uiri"; no. xiii, ed. Boutemy, 42: "In cuius Venerem sexus uterque uenit."

80. No. xvii.7–10, ed. Boutemy, 46: "Tunc musae celebres et erant in honore poetae, / Nunc isti uiles, illaeque silent quasi spretae. / Tunc clari reges et eorum gloria multa, / Nunc est istorum cum uita fama sepulta."

81. No. xxvii.1–2, 13–14, 23–24: "Heu quid peccaui uel quid potui meruisse, Quod non illa diu [est] passio nostra luat? . . . Es deprensa tuo cum Marte, sub indice Phoebo; Vltio mouit eum: uirgo petenda deo. . . . Si culpa Phoebi cum Marte reperta fuisti, Leucothoe misera cur luit acta Dei."

82. Thomas Wright edits this poem as well as those of Serlo which follow from British Library, Cotton, Vitellius A. xii in *Satirical Poets of the Twelfth Century*, pp. 233–58 (n. 33 above); see also Boutemy, "Deux poèmes inconnus de Serlon de Bayeux," *Le Moyen Age* 51 (1938): 241–69.

83. E.g. *Peter Abelard's Hymnarius Paraclitensis*, ed. Szövérffy, 2: 102–104, 117, 2: 206 "cum viris amazones."

84. Lorenz Weinrich, "'*Dolorum solatium*'. Text und Musik von Abaelards "«Planctus David»," *Mittellateinisches Jahrbuch* 5 (1968): 59–78 and Dronke, *Poetic Individuality in the Middle Ages*, p. 146 (p. 331, n. 10 above).

85. See above, p. 129.

86. Ed. Chrysogonus Waddell, "Epithalamica: An Easter Sequence by Peter Abelard," *Musical Quarterly* 72 (1986): 239–71 at 249.

87. For reference to the extensive manuscript sources for these sequences, entirely based on the work of Waddell, see Mews, *Peter Abelard* (London: Variorum, 1995), pp. 69–71.

88. *Vita Ludovici* 34, ed. Waquet, pp. 282–84; trans. Cusimano and Moorhead, pp. 158–59.

89. *Vita Ludovici* 34, ed. Waquet, pp. 280–82; trans. Cusimano and Moorhead, pp. 156–57.

90. *Metalogicon* 2.10, ed. Hall, CCCM 98: 70–71.

91. Bernard, *Ep.* 189, *SBO* 8: 12–16; on the date of the council of Sens, see, p. 303, n. 22. On the nature of the manuscript of the *Theologia christiana* owned by Cardinal Guy (a copy of which survives at Montecassino), see Mews, CCCM 13: 210–217, with references to further literature.

92. John of Salisbury, *Historia pontificalis* 31, ed. and trans. Chibnall, p. 64 (p. 305, n. 25 above). On the persistent claims of the city of Rome to appoint the prefect, apparent in a revolt of 1116, a conflict which spilled into open warfare with the papacy, see Robinson, *The Papacy 1073–1198*, pp. 12–14 (p. 327, n. 101).

93. See, p. 38.

94. Heloise's letter and Peter's reply are edited as *Ep.* 167–68 by Constable, 1: 400–402; trans. Radice, pp. 285–87. The discrepancy observed by Constable (2: 210) between the comment of Richard of Poitiers that Abelard's body was brought to the Paraclete soon after his death and Heloise's comment that Peter gave him Abelard's body could be explained if Peter simply allowed the body to be transported, rather than brought it in person.

95. McLeod, *Héloïse*, pp. 283–84 (p. 302, n. 10).

96. See p. 306, n. 41.
97. Eudes visited the Paraclete 15–17 June 1249, and twice again later that
    year, [4 Kal] October and [xvii kal] February, as well as once in 1253 [17
    kal February], *Regestrum Visitationum Archiepiscopi Rothomagensis*, ed. Th.
    Bonnin (Rouen, 1852), pp. 39, 52, 53, 177.
98. John Benton, "The Paraclete and the Council of Rouen of 1231," *Bulletin
    of Medieval Canon Law*, n.s. 4 (1974): 33–38, anticipated in n. 72, appended
    to his article "Fraud, Fiction and Borrowing in the Correspondence of
    Abelard and Heloise," p. 502 (p. 314, n. 95 above).

Chapter 7

1. This chapter completely rewrites the *Postface* published in French (trans.
   M. Lejbowicz), included within *La voix d'Héloïse. Un dialogue de deux
   amants* (Fribourg-Paris: Academic Press Fribourg-Éditions du Cerf, 2005),
   pp. 287–321, translated by Emilie Champs, with the collaboration of
   François-Xavier Putallaz and Sylvain Piron, of *The Lost Love Letters of
   Heloise and Abelard* (New York: St. Martins Press, 1999). I am indebted to
   Sylvain Piron for discussion of many themes in this chapter.
2. Sylvain Piron, *Lettres des deux amants, attribuées à Héloïse et Abélard* (Paris:
   Gallimard 2005), with a significant discussion about their authorship (pp.
   175–218).
3. *Und wärst du doch bei mir. Ex epistolis duorum amantium. Eine mittelalterliche
   Liebesgeschichte in Briefen. Lateinisch-deutsche Ausgabe. Übersetzt und mit einem
   Nachwort von Eva Cescutti und Philipp Steger* (Zurich: Manesse Verlag, 2005).
   They have been translated afresh into Italian as *Lettere di due amanti. At-
   tribute a Eloisa e Abelardo*, trans. Claudio Fiocchi, with a preface by Maria
   Teresa Fumagalli Beonio Brocchieri (Archinto: Collana, 2006).
4. James Burge, in his *Heloise & Abelard: A Twelfth-Century Love Story* (London:
   Profile, 2003). See for example Cristina Nehring, "Abelard and Heloise:
   Love Hurts," in the *New York Times*, February 13, 2005, and Priya Jain, "Lust,
   Revenge and the Religious Right in 12th- Century Paris," printed in
   http://dir.salon.com for December 18, 2004.
5. Umberto Eco, *Baudolino* (Milan: Bompiani, 2000), pp. 84–85; trans. William
   Weaver (London: Secker & Warburg, 2002), pp. 79–80. See Ewald Köns-
   gen, "*Der Nordstern scheint auf dem Pol*. Baudolinos Liebesbriefe an Beatrix,
   die Kaiserin—oder *Ex epistolis duorum amantium*," in *Nova de veteribus. Mit-
   tel- und neulateinische Studien für Paul Gerhard Schmidt*, ed. A. Bihrer, E. Stein
   (Munich-Leipzig: Saur, 2004), pp. 1113–21.
6. Positive comments on the attribution have been made by: Michael
   Clanchy in *Times Literary Supplement* (25 February 2000), pp. 24–25, W. P.
   Gerritsen in *NEC Handelsblat* (6 May 2000), p. 49; Barbara Newman, in
   the on-line review journal, *The Medieval Review* (6.1.2000); Albrecht
   Classen, "Abaelards Historia Calamitatum, der Briefwechsel mit Heloise

und Gottfrieds von Strassburg Tristan," *Arcadia* 35 (2000): 225–53; John O. Ward and Neville Chiavaroli, "The Young Heloise and Latin Rhetoric: Some Preliminary Comments on the 'Lost' Love-Letters and Their Significance," in *Listening to Heloise: The Voice of a Twelfth-Century Woman,* ed. Bonnie Wheeler (New York: St. Martin's Press, 2000), pp. 53–119; Paola de Santis, *I Sermoni di Abelardo per le monache del Paracleto* (Louvain: Leuven University Press, 2002), pp. xxv–xxviii; Juanita Ruys, "Eloquencie vultum depingere: Eloquence and Dictamen in the Love Letters of Heloise and Abelard," in *Rhetoric and Renewal in the Latin West 1100–1540. Essays in Honour of John O. Ward,* ed. Constant J. Mews, Cary J. Nederman and Rodney M. Thomson (Brepols: Turnhout, 2003), pp. 99–112; Jane Stevenson, *Women Latin Poets. Language, Gender, and Authority, from Antiquity to the Eighteenth Century,* Oxford 2005, pp. 474–75, and p. 121. The publication of Piron's translation of the *Lettres de deux amants and of La voix d'Héloïse* has also elicited positive responses in reviews by Laurent Cornaz, "Des nouvelles d'Héloïse," *Agenda de la pensée contemporaine,* (2005): 45–66 ; Damien Boquet, Médiévales, 51 (2006): 185–88, and Elisabeth Lalou, "Quid sit amor ?," in *Critique,* 716/717 (January 2007): 80–90. Guy Lobrichon, *Héloïse. L'amour et le savoir* (Paris: Gallimard, 2005), pp. 43–48, recognizes the closeness between the EDA and Abelard and Heloise, but concludes that the question remains open.

7. For more critical views, see n.10 (Peter von Moos), n. 18–19 (Peter Dronke), and n. 20 (Jan Ziolkowski). See also, Sylvain Piron and Réka Forrai, who have produced an unpublished paper for a seminar on the *EDA* held at Arezzo, "The debate on the *Epistolae duorum amantium.* Current status quaestionis and further research" (March 9, 2007), available online at http://www.monnalisagarden.com/tdtc/personale/materiale_didattico/ stella/Piron-status%20quaestionis.pdf, and Sylvain Piron, "Heloise's literary self-fashioning and the Epistolae duorum amantium," in *Memory Constructions,* ed. Lucie Dolezalova (Berlin: LIT Verlag, 2008) (forthcoming).

8. C. Stephen Jaeger, *Ennobling Love. In Search of a Lost Sensibility* (Philadelphia: University of Pennsylvania Press, 1999), pp. 157–73.

9. C. Stephen Jaeger, "The 'Epistolae duorum amantium' and the Ascription to Heloise and Abelard," and Giles Constable, "The Authorship of the *Epistolae duorum amantium. A Reconsideration,*" in *Voices in Dialogue: New Problems in Reading Women's Cultural History,* ed. Linda Olson and Kathryn Kerby-Fulton (Notre Dame: University of Notre Dame Press, 2005), pp. 125–66, and 167–78, with Jaeger, "A Reply to Giles Constable," on pp. 179–86 of the same volume. The response of Constable first appeared as "Sur l'attribution des *Epistolae duorum amantium,*" *Académie des Inscriptions et Belles-Lettres* (Nov.-Dec. 2001): 1679–93.

10. Peter von Moos, "Die *Epistolae duorum amantium* und die säkulare Religion der Liebe. Methodenkritische Vorüberlegungen zu einem einmaligen Werk mittellateinischer Briefliteratur," *Studi Medievali* 3a ser. 44 (2003): 1–115.

11. Ibid., p. 44, n. 137.

12. Ibid., pp. 13, 43.

13. Ibid., p. 97.

14. Ibid., p. 99, n. 300: "Sie könnten zu einem Schlüssel der 'intellectual history' des 14 und 15 Jhs.werden, wenn man sie von der dilettantischen Zuschreibungen Heloise und Abaelard befreien konnte und andererseits Mediävisten und Renaissanceforscher aufhorten, sich in zwei vershiedenen Booten zu fühlen."

15. Ibid., p. 81, n. 249, referring to Aelred, *De spiritali amicitia* 1.19, ed. A. Hoste and C. H. Talbot, CCCM 1 (Turnhout: Brepols, 1971), p. 292. Aelred speaks of friendship creating a single mind in 2.11, p. 304, but without *indifferenter*. Although von Moos claims that *indifferenter* is a favorite term of Aelred of Rievaulx, it occurs only once in Aelred's entire corpus, in *Dialogus de anima* 2.34, ed. Hoste and Talbot, CCCM 1: 87.

16. Peter von Moos, "Kurzes Nachwort zu einer langen Geschichte mit missbrauchten Liebesbriefen: *Epistolae duorum amantium*" included as an appendix to "Abaelard, Heloise und ihr Paraclet" (see n. 88 below), printed in von Moos, *Abaelard und Heloise. Gesammelte Studien zum Mittelalter,* Band 1, ed. Gert Melville, Geschichte: Forschung und Wissenschaft, 14 (Münster: Lit, 2005), pp. 282–92; "Vom Nutzen der Philologie für den umgang mit anonymen Liebesbriefen. Ein Nachwort zu den *Epistolae duorum amantium*," forthcoming in: *Schrift und Liebe in der Kultur des Mittelalters,* ed. by M. Schnyder, Trends in Medieval Philology (Berlin: De Gruyter) available on-line http://centri.univr.it/RM/biblioteca/

17. See the essays collected in Constant J. Mews, ed., *Listen Daughter. The Speculum Virginum and the Formation of Religious Women in the Middle Ages* (New York: Palgrave, 2001).

18. Peter Dronke, in a review of Bonnie Wheeler, ed., *Listening to Heloise* (n. 6 above), *International Journal of the Classical Tradition* 8/1 (2002): 134–39. Dronke bases his argument on a few verbal similarities (of classical inspiration) with the Tegernsee letters and the Regensburg verse exchange, also a record of a male-female exchange from the early twelfth century.

19. Peter Dronke, Giovanni Orlandi, "New Works by Abelard and Heloise," *Filologia mediolatina* 12 (2005): 123–177, with discussion by Orlandi on pp. 146–77.

20. Jan Ziolkowski, "Lost and Not Yet Found: Heloise, Abelard, and the *Epistolae duorum amantium*," *Journal of Medieval Latin* 14 (2004): 171–202.

21. François Dolbeau offers a methodology based on more strictly positivist lines, "Critique d'attribution, critique d'authenticité. Réflexions préliminaires," *Filologia mediolatina* 6–7 (1999–2000): 33–62.

22. Francesco Stella, "Le *Epistolae Duorum Amantium*: Nuovi Riscontri Intertestuali" (Toronto 2–6 agosto 2006) http://www.monnalisagarden.com /tdtc/personale/materiale_didattico/stella/EDA-Loci%20similes.pdf.

23. *HC*, ed. Monfrin, p. 73; *Ep.* 2, ed. Monfrin, p. 115.

24. Francesco Stella, "Analisi informatiche del lessico e individuazione degli autori nelle *Epistolae duorum amantium* (XII secolo)," delivered *Late and Vulgar Latin Conference,* Oxford 6–9 September 2006, available at http://www .monnalisagarden.com/tdtc/personale/materiale_didattico/stella/EDA-Statistiche%20Lingua.pdf. Stella argues that from statistical analysis independent from the chi-square factor that the variations in percentages of types of *cursus* between the two sets of correspondence are not statistically significant.

25. Heloise, *Ep.* 2, ed. Monfrin, p. 113; ed. Hicks, p. 48: "Quot autem et quantos tractatus in doctrina vel exhortation seu etiam consolation sanctarum feminarum sancti patres consummaverint, et quanta eas diligentia composuerint, tua melius excellentia quam nostra parvitas novit."

26. *Ep.* 167 among the letters of Peter the Venerable (ed. Constable, 1: 400): "Gratulamur pater benignissime, et quod ad paruitatem nostram magnitudo uestra descenderit, gloriamur."

27. St. Anselm uses variations on *parvitas mea/nostra* in his correspondence, *Anselmi Opera Omnia,* ed. F. X. Schmitt (Edinburgh: Nelson, 1946–1961); *Ep.* 2 (3: 99), 10 (3: 113), 65 (3: 181), 85 (3: 210), 86 (3: 211), 92 (3: 219), 107 (3: 240), 126 (3: 266); 159 (4: 27), 321 (5: 321), 430 (5: 376). Bernard uses the phrase in *Ep.* 2.8 (*SBO* 7: 19), 6.1 (7: 29); 45.2 (7: 134), 59 (7: 152), 61 (7: 154), 62 (7: 155), 76 (7: 183), 79.1 (7: 211), 82.1 (7: 214), 98.1 (7: 248), 123 (7: 304), 144.3 (7: 345), 357.1 (8: 301), 368.1 (8: 326), 377.2 (8: 341), 391 (8: 360), 457 (8: 433). The phrase is used by Jerome in his *Ep.* 21.42 (CSEL 54: 142), 102.1 (55: 323), 138 (56: 266), 142 (56: 291), 155.2 (58: 131).

28. Some of the subsequent argument I develop in "Cicero and the Boundaries of Friendship in the Twelfth Century," *Viator* 38/2 (2007): 369–84, but take further in "Discussing Love: the *Epistolae duorum amantium* and the *Sic et Non*"

29. *Dialectica,* ed. Lambert Marie De Rijk (Assen : van Gorcum, 1970), p. 185: "Et utrumque [*omne* et *totum*] quidem quantitatis signum esse potest, illud quidem quantitatis *universalis rei* secundum comprehensionem singularum specierum. Hoc vero individui compositi secundum constitutionem componentium partium. . . . ; (p. 186) Nam *universalis rei* quantitas in diffusione sua per inferiora consistit ; (p. 574): In distributione enim *rei universalis* non quantitatis eius vel integritatis comprehensio, sed sola participationis diffusio per inferiora monstratur."

30. Abelard, *HC,* ed. Monfrin, p. 65 : "Sic autem istam tunc suam correxit sententiam, ut deinceps rem eamdem non essentialiter sed indifferenter diceret."

31. See Mews, "The Foundation St.Victor (Easter, 1111) and the Evolution of Abelard's Early Career," in Irène Rosier-Catach (forthcoming). The key document requiring a change from the traditional date (1108) assigned to

the foundation of St. Victor is a charter describing William as still an archdeacon in 1110; Dufour, *Actes de Louis VI*, no. 43, 1: 81 . Other signatories are Bernier, dean of Notre-Dame, Reinaldus de Cala (the other archdeacon of Paris), precentor Adam (subsequently a canon of Saint-Victor) and an otherwise unknown figure, Ratherius de Dongione.

32. Abelard does not identify William's initial successor by name, only that William turned against him; *HC*, ed. Monfrin, p. 66. That Joscelin was already a significant teacher at this time is implicit in the *Vita Goswini, Recueil*, 14: 444, a narrative that never mentions William of Champeaux, who may have ceded his position to Joscelyn after becoming archdeacon of Paris by 1107 (when Goswin first came to Paris).

33. Peter Abelard, *Sic et Non* 138: 20–21, ed. Blanche Boyer and Richard McKeon (Chicago: Chicago University Press, 1976–77), p. 473, quoting Cicero, *De amicitia* 20: "Quanta autem vis amicitiae sit, ex hoc intelligi maxime potest, quod ex societate infinita generis humani, quam conciliavit ipsa natura, ita contracta est res et adducta in angustum, ut omnis caritas aut inter duos aut inter paucos iungeretur."

34. Cicero, *De inventione* 2.55.166: "Amicitia est voluntas erga aliquem bonarum rerum illius ipsius causa, quem diligit, cum eius pari voluntate." Although the passage from the *De amicitia* is quoted in the *Florilegium Gallicum*, an influential twelfth-century anthology of classical texts, the definition of friendship from Cicero's *De inventione* is not found there, making it less likely the love letters could have been inspired by that anthology; Johannes Hamacher, ed., *Florilegium Gallicum. Prolegomena und Edition der Exzerpte von Petron bis Cicero, De oratore*, Lateinische Sprache une Literatur des Mittelalters 5 (Frankfurt: Peter Lang, 1975), p. 359. Passages from the *De inventione* (but not that about friendship) are edited on pp. 255–58. This anthology seems to have been composed near Orleans, Rosemary Burton, *Classical Poets in the 'Florilegium Gallicum'*, Lateinische Sprache und Literatur des Mittelalters 14 (Frankfurt: Peter Lang, 1983), p. 31.

35. *Theologia 'Scholarium'* 1.3–4, CCCM 13: 319. This is a more detailed version of a passage found in the *Sententie Magistri Petri Abaelardi*, ed. David E. Luscombe et al., CCCM 14 (Turnhout: Brepols, 2006), pp. 5–6. This record of Abelard's teaching explains *caritas* more fully in *Sententie* 243 (p. 127–28). In 245 (p. 129), Abelard also supplies the Augustinian definition; in one manuscript the additional point is made that although the wording is different, the fundamental teaching is the same.

36. Cicero, *De amicitia* 16.58: "Altera sententia est quae definit amicitiam paribus officiis ac voluntatibus. Hoc quidem est nimis exigue et exiliter ad calculos vocare amicitiam, ut par sit ratio acceptorum et datorum."

37. Jerome, *Ep.* 3.6 (CSEL 54: 18). *SN* 138. 7 begins with this final line of Jerome, but then continues with a passage inspired by a quotation in Jerome's *Ep.* 68.1 (54: 675: *In amicis enim non res quaeritur sed voluntas*) and

various other sources (summarized by Boyer-McKeon, p. 471): "Amicitia quae desinere postest, vera numquam fuit. In amico non res quaeritur sed voluntas. Amicitia quae finiri potest, nunquam vera fuit. Magis enim in insidiis nostrorum periclitamur quam aliorum."

38. Letter 25: "Et nos, licet omnibus integram caritatem exhibeamus, non tamen omnes equaliter diligimus." Cf. Augustine, *De doctrina Christiana* 1.61 (28), ed. W. M. Green (CSEL 80: 23): "Omnes autem aeque diligendi sunt. Sed cum omnibus prodesse non possis, his potissimum consulendum est qui pro locorum et temporum vel quarumlibet rerum opportunitatibus constrictius tibi quasi quadam sorte iunguntur."

39. Evident from the tables given by Boyer-McKeon, *Sic et Non*, p. 643.

40. Questions 136–138 all occur in the version *CT* of the *Sic et Non* (manuscripts that also contain the *Theologia Christiana*, and incorporate passages from this version of the *Sic et Non*). On the chronology of the *Sic et Non*, see Mews, "Peter Abelard's *Theologia Christiana* and *Theologia 'Scholarium'*" re-examined," in *Recherches de théologie ancienne et médiévale* 52 (1985): 109–58, esp. 127–29 ; reprinted in *Abelard and his Legacy* (Aldershot, Hants: Ashgate, 2001).

41. In his edition, Baldricus Burgulianus, *Carmina*, 2 vols (Paris: Belles Lettres, 1998, 2001), Jean-Yves Tilliette follows the reading of *speciale* in the sole surviving manuscript as *spetiale* in some places; for example: *Carmina* 200 (vv. 77–80), ed. Tilliette 2: 125: "Ergo patet liquido quoniam genus istud amoris / Non commune aliquid, sed spetiale sapit. Est spetialis amor, quem nec caro subcomitatur, / Nec desiderium sauciat illicitum." This theme is also raised in no. 138, ed. by Tilliette, 2: 47: "Non est communis quae speciale sapit, / Haec speciale sapit, quia carmen cantat amoris." No. 142 (v. 2), 2: 50: "Fac speciale tibi Burguliensis aue."

42. Baudri, *Carmina*, no. 99 (vv. 185–86, 213–14), to Godfrey of Reims, ed. Tilliette, 1: 110: "Nam scripsi quaedam quam complectuntur amorem / Carminibusque meis sexus uterque placet. . . . Tu magis alter ego, non ut communis amicus, / Sed specialis, aue."

43. Ep. 6, ed. Hicks, p. 88. Jean de Meun provides the correct translation: "Ou sien specialment, la sieue senglement." While the correct reading of *Suo* rather than as *Domino* (the mistaken reading in Duchesne's 1616 edition, reprinted in PL 178: 213A) was given by Muckle in his edition of this letter in *Mediaeval Studies* 17 (1955): p. 241, Betty Radice, *The Letters of Abelard and Heloise* (Harmondsworth: Penguin, 1974), p. 159, persisted in reading it as *Domino,* translating the greeting as "God's own in species, his own as individual." The correct reading is given in the revised and expanded edition of Radice's translation, published in 2003 (p. 93).

44. Ep. 3, ed. Hicks, 57: "Memento itaque semper in orationibus tuis ejus qui specialiter est tuus."

45. Ep. 3, ed. Hicks, p. 54: "Heloise, dilectissime sorori sue in Christo, Abaelardus, frater ejus in ipso."

46. Ep. *50*: "verum dicis, o omnium mulierum dulcissima, quod vere talis dilectio nos non colligavit, qualis solet colligare, qui sua tantum querunt."
47. Ep. *52*: "Quia mandatum domini non observamus, nisi dilectionem ad invicem habeamus, oportet nos divine scripture obedire." In Ep. *54*, he speaks *de tua dilectione*. The first time he speaks of himself sharing in an undivided *dilectio* is in Ep. *85*.
48. Ziolkowski, p. 185, quoting Dronke's review of Wheeler, *IJCT* 8/1 (2001): 136 (n. 18 above). Albert the Great employs *scibilitas* in his commentary on the *Metaphysics* 7.1, ed. B. Geyer, *Alberti Magni Opera Omnia* 16.2 (Münster: Aschendorff, 1964), p. 331, and in his *Summa theologiae*, ed. D. Siedler, 34 (1978), p. 796. Albert the Great, a voracious reader, could have come across the notion of *scibilitas* through Abelard's *Dialectica*, preserved at Saint-Victor, during his studies in Paris. The term was used more extensively by Ramon Lull, who quite likely had access to Albert the Great.
49. This suggestion is made by Piron, *Lettres des deux amants*, pp. 25–26. He persuasively suggests that the exchange ended abruptly because Abelard sent Heloise to his sister to have the child. Whenever the final poem was written, it does seem to have been added as a coda.
50. See William D. Patt, "The Early 'ars dictaminis' as Response to a Changing Society," *Viator* 9 (1978): 133–55, and more fully Carol Dana Lanham, "Freshman Composition in the Early Middle Ages: Epistolography and Rhetoric before the Ars Dictaminis," *Viator* 23 (1992): 115–34.
51. A recent summary of treatises on the *ars dictaminis* is that of Anne-Marie Turcan-Verkerk, "Répertoire chronologique des théories de l'art d'écrire en prose (milieu du XI s.–années 1230)," *Archivum Latinitatis medii aevi* 64 (2006): 193–239; on love letters attached to these manuals, see Ernstpeter Ruhe, *De amasio ad amasiam. Zur Gattungsgeschichte des mittelalterlichen Liebesbriefes*, Beiträge zur romanischen Philologie des Mittelalters, 10 (Munich: Wilhelm Fink, 1975). The publication of the thesis of Turcan-Verkerk on the early treatises on letter writing of Bernard of Bologna, and his student Guido of Arezzo, is eagerly awaited, as well as critical editions of these texts.
52. *Die Reinhardsbrunner Briefsammlung*, ed. Friedel Peeck, MGH Epistolae Selectae 5 (Munich, 1952; reprinted 1978), Ep. 97, ed. Peeck, p. 81. She also requests the herb gentian for medical reasons, a modest example of a private letter. The manuscript containing the Reinhardsbrunn letters (Pommersfelden, Schönbornsche Bibliothek, MS 31, formerly MS 2750, ff. 2v–50), also contains copies of Adalbertus Samaritanus' *De praeceptis dictaminum* (on ff. 50–57), and (on ff. 57–69v) the *Rationes dictandi prosaice* of Hugh of Bologna.
53. Peter von Moos (p. 45, n.141) quotes from the as yet unpublished thesis on prose rhyme of Anne-Marie Turcan-Verkerk, *Forme et réforme. Le Grégorianisme du moyen âge latin. Essai d'interprétation historique du phenomène de la*

rime dans la prose latine des XIe et XIIe siècles (Paris, 1995). She observes that prose rhyme effectively disappears from the *ars dictaminis* in France after the second half of the twelfth century, although continuing in some hagiographic texts. I am grateful to Turcan-Verkerk for providing a copy of her thesis summary.

54. Constant J. Mews, "Hugh Metel, Heloise and Peter Abelard: The Letters of an Augustinian Canon and the Challenge of Innovation in Twelfth-Century Lorraine," in *Viator* 32 (2001): 59–91.

55. Carol Dana Lanham, *Salutatio Formulas in Latin Letters to 1200: Syntax, Style and Theory* (Eugene, Oregon: Wipf & Stock, 2004 (originally published 1975), pp. 49–52. Arguing against Roscelin, Abelard singled out St. Anselm for praise in around 1120, *Ep.* 14, ed. Smits, p. 280, and is familiar with his writing, though more critical on a point of detail, in *Theologia Christiana* 4.83 (CCCM 12: 304). Anselm had exchanged letters with members of Notre-Dame in the 1090s (*Ep.* 161–62, ed. Schmitt, 4: 32–34), and was invited to France in 1104–1107 by prince Louis, *Ep.* 432 (ed. Schmitt, 5: 279). See Mews, "St. Anselm and the Development of Philosophical Theology in Twelfth-Century Paris" in *Anselm and Abelard. Investigations and Juxtapositions* ed. Giles E. M. Gasper and Helmut Kohlenberger (Toronto: Pontifical Institute of Mediaeval Studies, 2006), pp. 196–222. On the early diffusion of manuscripts of the letters, see Walter Fröhlich, in his introduction to *The Letters of Saint Anselm of Canterbury*, 1 (Kalamazoo: Cistercian Publications, 1990), pp. 26–52.

56. Anselm, *Ep.* 57 (3: 171): "Domino et patri suo, reverendo archiepiscopo Lanfranco: frater Anselmus suus quod suus. . . . sic mihi ad inculcandum quis cui et quo anime loquatur, libet ut tam saepe epistolae nostrae, quas vestrae dirigo paternae celsitudini, in fronte pictum praeferant: 'domino et patri' et 'suus quod suus'."

57. Anselm, Ep. 68 (3: 188): "Suo domino, suo fratri, suo amico carissimo domno Gondulfo: frater Anselmus quod suo suus." Fröhlich translates this, in *The Letters of Saint Anselm*, vol 1: 221. as " . . . sends his whole self." H. M Canatella observes that Anselm's letters, especially to Gundulf and Ida, articulate a strong sense of friendship as love, "Friendship in Anselm of Canterbury's Correspondence: Ideals and Experience," *Viator* 38/2 (2007): 351–67.

58. Anselm, *Ep.* 85 (3: 209): "Domino sponte diligenti, merito dilecto, non ut ignoto, sed ut familiari amico Waltero: frater Anselmus quod suus." Fröhlich, (1: 220) renders this as "To his lord Walter, . . ." losing the effect of contrasting the impersonal *Domino* with the more intimate *Waltero*.

59. Anselm, *Ep.* 23 (3: 130), 25 (3: 132), 26 (3: 134), 27 (3: 134), 49 (3: 162), 57 (3: 171) [x 2], 66 (3: 186), 85 (3: 209), 127 (3: 269), 144 (3: 290). Although Fröhlich rightly translates *quod suus* in *Ep.* 23 as "sends his whole self" his translation of the same phrase in subsequent letters, "brother

Anselm, who is in everything totally his" does not capture *quod suus* fully. St. Bernard singles out this greeting in a letter that he has received in *Ep.* 86, ed. Leclercq, *SBO* 7: 223: "Frater Bernardus de Claravalle suo illi quod suo. Hanc mihi tu salutationis formulam tradidisti, scribendo: 'Suus ille quod suus." Bernard then used the greeting *quod suus* in *Ep.* 147 (7: 350) to Peter the Venerable, and 178 (7: 397) to the Pope.

60. Letters 2 (*quid amplius quam seipsum*); 5 (*meipsam, quamdiu vivam*), 11 (*et seipsam*).

61. Piron, *Lettres des deux amants,* p. 44 discusses this ambiguity, but prefers to translate it as equivalent to the the first (i.e., divine) being, "l'être qui est."

62. Anselm, *Ep.* 85 (3:210): "Tanto namque flagrant caritatis ardore, tanto fragrant benignitatis odore, tanta suavitatis sunt iucundae, sic sunt salubris admonitionis fecundae litterae, quibus meae parvitati vestra dignata est se notificare dulcis dilectio et dilecta prudentia, ut nolit quiescere mens mea, donec videant oculi mei vultum eius et audiant aures meae vocem eius et fruatur anima mea praesentia eius, qui me tanto ignotus ignotum amore gratis anticipavit . . ." with debt to the translation of Fröhlich, *The Letters of Saint Anselm,* 1: 220–21.

63. Anselm, *Oratio* 18 (3: 71): "Tu scis, domine, qua dilectionem quam iubes amo, amorem diligo, caritatem concupisco."

64. Augustine, *En. in Psalmos* Ps. 9.5, CCSL 38 : "pes animae recte intelligitur amor; qui cum pravus est, uocatur cupiditas aut libido; cum autem rectus, dilectio uel caritas". *De diversis quaestionibus* 35(CCSL 44A:) : "amor autem rerum amandarum caritas uel dilectio melius dicitur."

65. Mia Münster-Svendsen shows how such intimate discourse between teachers and students (often highly erotic) can be found in the Carolingian period, "The Model of Scholastic Mastery," in *Teaching and Learning in Northern Europe 1000–1200,* ed. Sally N. Vaughn and Jay Rubenstein (Turnhout: Brepols, 2006), pp. 307–42. She quotes (p. 312) a poetic letter of Froumund: "Salve confrater mihi dulcis semper amore / Dulcior es mihi tu quam mellis gustus in ore. /Nescit amare loquor, sed amor dulcescit et ad cor / Intrat et alterius coniungit foedere pectus. / Omnibus exceptis mihi tu sis carior istis." *Tegernseer Briefsammlung,* p. 28.

66. "The *Liber confortatorius* of Goscelin of St-Bertin," ed. C. H. Talbot, in: *Analecta Monastica* series 3, ed. by M. M. Lebreton, J. Leclercq and C. H. Talbot, Studia Anselmiana 37, (Rome 1955), pp. 1–117.

67. The *Liber confortatorius* [LC] has been translated by W. R. Barnes and Rebecca Hayward, in *Writing the Wilton Women,* ed. Stephanie Hollis (Turnhout: Brepols, 2004), pp. 97–212. There is also a translation by Monika Otter, *Goscelin of St. Bertin, The Book of Encouragement and Consolation (Liber confortatorius)* (Woodbridge: Boydell and Brewer, 2004).Why Eve chose to go to Angers is not certain, although there may have been pre-existing connections between Wilton and Le Ronceray. Given that hers is not an

English name, she could have been brought by her mother to Wilton from the continent in around 1065, when Queen Edith rebuilt Wilton abbey church; see Hollis in *Writing the Wilton Women*, p. 225. Rebecca Hayward comments on parallels with Abelard and Heloise, "Spiritual Friendship and Gender Difference in the *Liber confortatorius*" (*Writing the Wilton Women*, pp. 341–54), as does Monika Otter, pp. 7–10.

68. *LC*, ed. Talbot, p. 29: "Afferebant tibi Christum frequentes membrane et scedule nostre, nec tue uacabant castissime littere." Trans. Barnes and Hayward, p. 104.

69. *LC*, ed. Talbot, p. 26: "Archanum duorum est Christo medio signatum, virginee simplicitatis et candide dilectionis prelibans officium." Trans. Barnes and Hayward, p. 99 (who translate *dilectio* as affection, rather than love, as here).

70. *LC*, ed. Talbot, p. 27: "Quo autem longius corpore remouit, eo inseparabilius unicam aliquando duorum animam resolidabit." Trans. by Barnes and Hayward, p. 101.

71. *LC*, p. 27: "Vnde, quia nec potuit nec meruit unanimis tuus te accessibus uisitare corporeis, querit nunc anxiis litteris et longis querelis. Parauit nobis hanc consolationem prouida miseratio Domini, ut locis elongati, fide et scriptis possimus representari. Et que meis debebantur sceleribus, hec separationis tormenta, alligare et refouere nos poterit intercurrens epistola." Trans. by Barnes and Hayward, p. 101.

72. Geoffrey of Vendôme writes *Ep.* 48 to Eve and Hervé (PL 157: 184A–186A). He also writes two subsequent letters in a more friendly tone to Hervé as *amico suo* and as *dilecto suo, Ep.* 49–50 (PL 157: 186A–188A); Œuvres, ed. by Geneviève Giordanengo (Paris: CNRS, 1996). *Hilarii Aurelianensis Versus et ludi. Epistolae. Ludus Danielis Belouacensis*, ed. Walther Bulst and M. L. Bulst-Thiele (Leiden : Brill, 1989), p. 23: "Ibi vixit Euua diu cum Herueo socio / Qui hec audis, ad hanc uocem te turbari sentio; / Fuge, frater, suspicari, nec sit hic suspicio, / Non in mundo, sed in Christo fuit hec dilectio." Bulst observes that most of the datable letters of Hilary were written in the time of Tiburg, abbess of Le Ronceray 1104–22.

73. For further detail on what follows, see Mews, "Negotiating the Boundaries of Gender in Religious Life: Robert of Arbrissel and Hersende, Abelard and Heloise," *Viator* 37 (2006): 113–48.

74. Werner Robl, *Heloisas Herkunft. Hersindis Mater* (Munich: Olzog, 2001), summarized in his chapter "Hersindis Mater. Neues zur Familiengeschichte Heloisas mit Ausblicken auf die Familie Peter Abaelards," in *Peter Abaelard. Leben, Werk, Wirkung*, ed. Ursula Niggli (Freiburg im Breisgau: Herder, 2003), pp. 25–89. *Obituaire du Paraclet*, ed. A. Boutillier du Retail and P. Piétrisson de Saint-Aubin, *Obituaires de la province de Sens, IV. Diocèses de Meaux et de Troyes* (Paris: Imprimerie nationale, 1923), p. 428.

The Fontevrault necrology is recorded in *Gallia Christiana*, vol. 2 (Paris, 1720) col. 1313; see also *Obituaires de la province de Sens, II. Diocèse de Chartres*, ed. A. Molinier (Paris: Imprimerie nationale, 1906), p. 198 [*Obituaire de Saint-Père-en-Vallée*] and p. 661 [*Obituaire de l'abbaye de Saint-Jean-en-Vallée*]. The awareness of Hersende of Fontevraud in Chartres may be connected to the proximity of Haute-Bruyère, where Bertrada de Montfort, queen of France and nun of Fontevraud from 1108, established a daughter house of Fontevraud.

75. Robl provides a useful family tree in "Hersindis mater," p. 89; cf. Amboise, PL 178: 74A. Heloise was not mentioned by Duchesne, however, in his 1624 history of the Montmorency family, presumably because this was an oral tradition of the Paraclete, rather than officially documented.

76. Lobrichon, *Héloïse. L'amour et le savoir*, pp. 121–25. The suggestion that Heloise gained access to Argenteuil through the Montmorency or Garlande connections of an illegitimate father was made by Bautier, "Paris au temps d'Abélard," p. 76. Bautier, unaware of Hersende of Fontevrault, did not think of Hersende as having a Montmorency family connection to Argenteuil.

77. Marbod's letter is edited and translated into both English and French in a definitive collection of texts relating to Robert of Arbrissel, *Les deux vies de Robert d'Arbrissel, fondateur de Fontevraud. Légendes, écrits et témoignages*, ed. Jacques Dalarun, Geneviève Giordanego, Armelle Le Huërou, Jean Longère, Dominique Poirel, Bruce L. Venarde (Turnhout: Brepols, 2006), pp. 526–57. The English versions of these texts, translated by Bruce Venarde, had previously been published within *Robert of Arbrissel: a Medieval Religious Life* (Washington: Catholic University of America, 2004). On Robert's reputation for having sinned sexually, and the presence of infants alongside his followers, see Marbod, *Deux vies*, pp. 530–32: "Mulierum cohabitationem, in quo genere quondam peccasti, dicere plus amare . . . Quod quam periculose sit factum, ut compendiose dicam, vagitus infantium prodiderunt."

78. Baudri's Life of Robert is edited and translated within *Deux vies*, pp. 124–87; cf. *HC*, ed. Monfrin, p. 64: "Proinde diversas disputando perambulans provincias" and Baudri, *Deux vies*, p. 144: "Perambulat regiones et provincias irrequietus et in litterarum studiis non poterat non esse sollicitus." Jacques Dalarun observes that a copy of this Life, followed by the early statutes of Fontevrault, was preserved at Saint-Denis in the early seventeenth century, *Deux vies*, pp. 46–47.

79. Abelard, *Ep.* 14, ed. Smits, p. 280, cited in *Deux vies*, p. 631 (no. 17). The royal abbey of St-Martin of Tours, where Roscelin was a canon was engaged in a legal battle with Fontevraud between 1117 and 1119 over land of St-Martin, given to Bertrada as a dower by Philip, that Bertrada had given to Fontevrault; Dufour, *Recueil des Actes*, no. 155, 1: 319–21.

80. Baudri, *Carmina*, no. 26, ed. Tilliette 1: 45–46 and 175; Baudri in *Deux vies*, p. 72: "Constituit igitur ex sororibus unam responsis et operibus assistricem et magistram, Hersendim nomine, quae, spreta sua qua praelucebat nobilitate, choris foeminarum adhaeserat imo prior conversa fuerat. Vivebat autem Hersendis et magnae religionis et magni partier consilii." A poem that Baudri sent a poem addressed to Peter, "a boy of outstanding intellect" may be addressed to the young Abelard; no. 113 (1: 119–20).

81. *Supplementum historiae vitae Roberti*, in *Deux vies*, p. 252 : "Ibi jacet Hersendis monacha, bona coadiutrix mea, cujus consilio et opere construxi Fontis Ebraudi aedificia."

82. On the importance of these reforms, see Mary Stroll, *Calixtus II (1119–1124). A Pope Born to Rule* (Leiden: Brill, 2004), pp. 400–405.

83. Peggy Kamuf, translator of Jacques Derrida, argued that Heloise's letters subvert those of Abelard, without making any biographical claims about Heloise, in *Fictions of Feminine Desire: Disclosures of Heloise* (Lincoln: University of Nebraska Press, 1982). Barbara Newman by contrast argues that attributing the correspondence as a whole to Abelard, continues a repression of her voice, "Authority, Authenticity, and the Repression of Heloise," *The Journal of Medieval and Renaissance Studies* 22 (1992): 121–58, repr. in *From Virile Woman to WomanChrist. Studies in Medieval Religion and Literature* (Philadelphia: University of Pennsylvania Press, 1995), pp. 46–75. See also the range of perspectives assembled in Bonnie Wheeler (ed.), *Listening to Heloise* (n. 6 above).

84. Lobrichon, *Héloïse. L'amour et le savoir* (n. 6 above), pp. 318–28.

85. *Abaelards "Historia calamitatum". Text-Übersetzung-literaturwissenschaftliche Modellanalysen*, ed. Dag Nikolaus Hasse (Berlin: Walter de Gruyter, 2002).

86. An extended psychological reading of the correspondence is offered by Roland Oberson, *Abélard mon frère. Essai d'interprétation* (Lausanne: L'Age d'homme, 2001). A recent novel exploring the story of their relationship, with a preface by Jean Jolivet, is that of Suzanne Bernard, *Le Roman d'Héloïse et Abélard* (Pantin: Le temps des cerises, 2001). I am grateful to all these authors for sharing their work with me.

87. Many of the most important studies of Peter von Moos are reprinted in Peter von Moos, *Abaelard und Heloise. Gesammelte Studien zum Mittelalter*, Band 1 (n. 16 above).

88. Von Moos put forward the single author hypothesis in "Heloise und Abaelard," in *Gefälscht. Betrug in Politik, Literatur, Wissenschaftliche Kunst und Musik*, ed. Karl Corino (Nördlingen: Greno, 1988), pp. 150–61, rewritten with an explanation of his shifting position as "Das Abaelard und Heloise zugeschriebene Briefwerk. Am Nullpunkt der Zuschreibungsversuche?" in *Abaelard und Heloise*, pp. 199–21. He is much more nuanced in "Abaelard, Heloise und ihr Paraklet: ein Kloster nach Mass. Zugleich eine Streitschrift gegen die ewige Wiederkehr hermeneutische Naivität," in *Das Eigene und*

das Ganze. Zum Individuellen im mittelalterlichen Religiosentum, ed. Gert Melville and Th. Schürer, Vita regularis (Münster, 2002), pp. 563–620; reprinted in *Abaelard und Heloise,* pp. 233–301.

89. Morgan Powell, "Listening to Heloise at the Paraclete: Of Scholarly Diversion and a Woman's 'Conversion'," in *Listening to Heloise,* ed. Wheeler, pp. 255–86.

90. Two small phrases might possibly indicate such cross references: Letter 5, ed. Hicks, p. 83 (*quibus etiam ut iam supra memini scriptum est: Mulieres sedentes ad monumentum lamentabantur flentes Dominum*), although this could refer back to earlier (p. 72) in the same letter, or to Letter 3 (p. 60); his comment about the Apostle's devotion to women (*ut iam satis alibi meminimus*) in Abelard's Rule, p. 258, which may refer back just to the previous letter, and does not necessarily constitute evidence of the exchange as a unified whole.

91. The claim that Heloise was born in 1100 has no foundation. The reminiscence of Peter the Venerable (1092/94–1156) that he remembered Heloise as a learned *mulier* before she became a nun, suggests they may have been of about the same age; Peter the Venerable, *Ep.* 115, ed. Constable, 1: 303 and 2: 257. Piron, *Lettres des deux amants,* p. 27, plausibly suggests that the affair might have begun in autumn 1114, rather than 1115 as I had suggested in 1999, and that Abelard's statement that he taught quietly at the cathedral school for several years (*HC,* ed. Monfrin, p. 70) refers to the period until his castration. He suggests the relationship was discovered in 1116, with Astralabe being born later in that year. Because Fulbert is not mentioned in a charter issued between March/April and May 15, 1117 (Dufour, *Actes de Louis VI,* no. 123, 1:256), it is quite possible that he had gone into exile, as attested by Fulk of Deuil (*Ep.* 16, PL 178: 375B), during this period, and that the castration was thus in early 1117. Fulbert is not mentioned in a similar list from 1118, but reappears in a charter of April 1, 1119, Lasteyrie, *Cartulaire,* nos. 179, 182, pp. 202, 204.

92. *Sic et Non,* Prol., p. 98, quoting Augustine, In Iohannis epistulam ad Parthos tractatus 7, PL 35: 2033C; also used in Sermon 107 (PL 39:1958A) attributed to Augustine: "Dilige ergo, et quidquid volueris, fac" and sermon 5 (PL 46: 985A): "dilige et quidquid vis fac."

93. Abelard borrowed this form of the quotation from Ivo of Chartres, *Decretum,* Prol., PL 161: 48B in *SN* Prol., p. 98, 138:16, in *Commentarium ad Romanos* 4 (13.10), CCCM 11: 293, and in his *Ethica,* ed. Luscombe, p. 38; ed. Rainer Ilgner, CCCM 190 (Turnhout: Brepols, 2001), p. 25. On the history of this saying, see Giles Constable, *"Love and Do What You Will": The Medieval History of an Augustinian Precept* (Kalamazoo: Medieval Institute, 1999).

94. *Sermo domni Roberti,* in *Deux vies,* pp. 460–79, esp. p. 464 : "dilige et quicquid vis fac."

95. Heloise, Letter 4, ed. Hicks, p. 69.

96. Abelard, *Collationes*, ed. John Marenbon and Giovanni Orlandi (Oxford : Oxford University Press, 2001), pp. 104–106.

97. *Sententie* 249–51, ed. Luscombe et al., p. 131–32.

98. Jacques Dalarun, "Nouveaux aperçus sur Abélard, Héloïse et le Paraclet," *Francia* 32 (2005): 19–66, correcting the date of Troyes, Bibl. mun. 802, given by Monfrin, *HC*, p. 11.

99. On the manuscripts of the correspondence, see Monfrin's introduction to *HC*, p. 58 and that of Hicks, p. li. The manuscript belonging to Petrarch, Paris, BNF lat. 2923, also dated by Monfrin (p. 19) to the late thirteenth century is similarly needing to be redated to the mid thirteenth century, or even a little earlier.

100. The additional texts are printed immediately after the authentic texts from the Paraclete copy seen in 1616, reprinted in PL 178 : 317B–326A. Jacques Dalarun suggested it was copied by William of Auvergne, bishop of Paris from 1228 to 1249. John Benton observed that Eudes Rigaud, archbishop of Rouen, visited his sister, Marie, abbess of the Paraclete, in June 10–12, 1249, the year after he became archbishop. Eudes had a known interest in reforming religious life for women, and could have obtained the Abelard-Heloise letters from his sister while she was simply a nun at the abbey, and he was a teacher in Paris, perhaps even attending the Council of Rouen in 1231; see John Benton, "The Paraclete and the Council of Rouen of 1231," *Bulletin of Medieval Canon Law* 4 (1974): 33–38, reprinted in John F. Benton, *Culture, Power and Personality in Medieval France*, ed. Thomas Bisson (London: Hambledon Press, 1991), pp. 411–416.

101. Although Abelard's Rule (erroneously identified as Letter VIII in the 1616 edition, reprinted in PL 178: 255A–314B) is copied without a break after Abelard's letter of introduction, Nicolas de Baye owned a copy of the letters in the early fifteenth century that also including eight unbound gatherings of the Rule (*Tripertitum* . . . ; printed immediately after *Valete in Christo, sponsae Christi* in PL 178: 258A, exactly as in Troyes, Bibl. mun. 802) separately from the letters. This may be the original collection of letters, from which the other copies were made that contain only Abelard's letter of introduction, not his Rule, such as Paris, BNF lat. 2923, obtained by Petrarch in the 1330s, probably through his friend, Roberto de Bardi; see Julia Barrow, Charles S. F. Burnett and David Edward Luscombe, "A Checklist of the Manuscripts Containing the Writings of Peter Abelard and Heloise and Other Works Closely Associated with Abelard and his School," *Revue d'Histoire des Textes* 14–15 (1984–85): 183–302, here no. 212 (p. 229) and Mews, "La bibliothèque du Paraclet du XIIIe siècle à la Révolution," *Studia Monastica* 27 (1985): 31–67; reprinted in Mews, *Reason and Belief in the Age of Roscelin and Abelard* (London: Ashgate, 2002).

102. Mews, "Heloise and Liturgical Experience at the Paraclete," *Plainsong and Medieval Music* 11.1 (2002): 25–35, and two chapters, "Liturgy and Identity

at the Paraclete: Heloise, Abelard and the Evolution of the Cistercian Reform" and "Liturgy and Monastic Observance in Practice at the Paraclete," in *The Poetic and Musical Legacy of Heloise and Abelard,* ed. Marc Stewart and David Wulstan (Westhumble, Surrey-Ottawa: Plainsong and Medieval Music Society-Institute of Medieval Music, 2003), pp. 19–33, 100–112 and p. 143 in chapter 10.

103. David Wulstan, "Heloise at Argenteuil and the Paraclete," and "Sources and Influences: Lyric and Drama at the 'School of Abelard'," in *The Poetic and Musical Legacy,* pp. 67–90 and 113–39. The plays of Vic, which he attributes to Heloise, have been edited by Peter Dronke, *Nine Medieval Latin Plays* (Cambridge: Cambridge University Press, 1994), pp. 92–105. Dronke (p. 85) thinks *Epithalamica* was composed by one of the sisters of the Paraclete, inspired by the one of the plays of Vic.

104. See above, Chapter 6, n. 66 and 67.

105. *La bibliothèque de l'abbaye de Clairvaux du XIIe au XVIIIe siècle. I Catalogues et répertoires,* ed. André Vernet (Paris: CNRS, 1979), p. 317; mentioned by Piron, *Lettres des deux amants,* p. 210.

106. See above, Chapter 1, n. 24.

SELECT BIBLIOGRAPHY

This bibliography lists only the more important primary sources, either in Latin or in translation, as well as major secondary sources useful for students to pursue further research. For more detailed bibliographies, see my volume, *Peter Abelard,* Authors of the Middle Ages 2.5 (London:Variorum, 1995), pp. 45–88, and for commentary on items published before 1988, Jean Jolivet and Constant J. Mews, "Peter Abelard and his Influence," *Contemporary Philosophy: A new survey,* ed. Guttorm Fløstad (Amsterdam: Kluwer Academic Publishers, 1990), vol. 6 *Philosophy and Science in the Middle Ages,* 1:105–40.

Writings of Abelard and Heloise

Ballanti, Graziella, trans., *Un Epistolario d'Amore del XII secolo (Abelardo e Eloisa?)* (Rome: Edizioni Anicia, 1988).

Boyer, Blanche B. and Richard McKeon, ed., *Peter Abailard, Sic et Non: A Critical Edition* (Chicago: University of Chicago Press, 1976–77).

Burnett, Charles S. F., ed. [with translation], "Peter Abelard, 'Soliloquium'. A Critical Edition," *Studi Medievali* 3ª Ser. 25 (1984), 857–94.

———"'Confessio fidei ad Heloisam'—Abelard's Last Letter to Heloise? A Discussion and Critical Edition of the Latin and Medieval French Versions," *Mittellateinisches Jahrbuch* 21 (1986): 147–55.

———"Peter Abelard, *Confessio fidei 'Universis':* A Critical Edition of Abelard's Reply to Accusations of Heresy," *Mediaeval Studies* 48 (1986): 111–38.

Buytaert, Eligius-Marie, ed., *Petri Abaelardi Opera Theologica I-II,* CCCM 11–12 (Turnhout: Brepols, 1969) [CCCM 11: *Commentaria in Epistolam Pauli ad Romanos;* CCCM 12: *Theologia christiana* and early versions of *Theologia Scholarium*].

———and Constant J. Mews, *Petri Abaelardi Opera Theologica III,* CCCM 13 (Turnhout: Brepols, 1987) [*Theologia Summi boni* and *Theologia Scholarium*].

Cousin, Victor, ed., *Petri Abaelardi opera hactenus seorsim edita,* 2 vols. (Paris, 1849, 1859).

Dal Pra, Mario, ed., *Pietro Abelardo. Scritti di Logica,* 2nd ed (Florence: La Nuova Italia Editrice, 1969).

De Rijk, Lambert Marie, ed., *Petrus Abaelardus. Dialectica,* Wijsgerige Teksten en Studies 1, 2nd ed. (Assen:Van Gorcum, 1970).

Geyer, Bernhard, ed., *Peter Abaelards Philosophische Schriften. 1. Die Logica 'Ingredientibus'; 2. Die Logica 'Nostrorum petitioni sociorum',* Beiträge zur Geschichte der Philosophie und Theologie des Mittelalters, Band 21.1–3 (Münster: Aschendorff, 1919 – 27); Band 21.4 2nd ed. (1970).

Hicks, Eric, ed., *La vie et les epistres Pierres Abaelart et Heloys sa fame* 1 (Paris: Honoré Champion, 1991).

Könsgen, Ewald, *Epistolae Duorum Amantium. Briefe Abaelards und Heloises?,* Mittellateinisches Studien und Texte 8 (Leiden: E. J. Brill, 1974).

Luscombe, David Edward, ed. and trans, *Peter Abelard's Ethics* (Oxford: Oxford University Press, 1971).

McLaughlin, T. P., ed., "Abelard's Rule for Religious Women," *Mediaeval Studies* 18 (1956): 241–92.

McNamer, Elizabeth Mary, trans., "The Problems of Heloise" in *The Education of Heloise. Methods, Content, and Purpose of Learning in the Twelfth Century* (Lewiston: Edwin Mellen Press, 1991), pp. 111–83.

Migne, Jacques-Paul, ed., *Petri Abaelardi Abbatis Rugensis Opera Omnia, Patrologia Latina* 178 (Paris: Garnier, 1885).

Minio-Paluello, Lorenzo, ed., *Twelfth Century Logic. Texts and Studies II: Abaelardiana inedita,* Edizioni di Storia e Letteratura, 1958).

Monfrin, Jacques, ed., *Abélard. Historia calamitatum. Texte critique avec une introduction,* Bibliothèque des textes philosophiques (Paris:Vrin, 1959).

Morin, Patrick, ed. and trans., *Abélard. Des intellections* (Paris:Vrin, 1994).

Muckle, J. T., ed., "Abelard's Letter of Consolation to a Friend," *Mediaeval Studies* 12 (1950): 163–213.

——"The Personal Letters between Abelard and Héloïse," *Mediaeval Studies* 15 (1953): 47–94.

——"The Letter of Héloïse on the Religious Life and Abelard's First Reply," *Mediaeval Studies* 17 (1955): 240–81.

Radice, Betty, trans. *The Letters of Abelard and Heloise* (Harmondsworth: Penguin, 1974).

Smits, Edmé, ed., *Peter Abelard. Letters IX – XIV* (Groningen: [privately published], 1983).

Szövérffy, Joseph, ed., *Peter Abelard's Hymnarius Paraclitensis,* 2 vols. (Albany, NY: Classical Folio Editions, 1975).

Thomas, Rudolf, ed., *Petrus Abaelardus, Dialogus inter philosophum, Iudaeum et Christianum* (Stuttgart: Friedrich Fromman, 1970).

Waddell, Chrysogonus, ed., "Epithalamica: An Easter Sequence by Peter Abelard," *Musical Quarterly* 72 (1986): 239–71.

——*The Paraclete Statutes. Institutiones Nostrae. Introduction, Edition, Commentary,* CLS 20 (Gethsemani Abbey, Trappist: Cistercian Publications, 1987).

——*Hymn Collections from the Paraclete*, Cistercian Liturgy Series 8–9, 2 vols. (Gethsemani Abbey, Trappist, Ky: Cistercian Publications, 1989).

Wolff, Étienne, trans., *La Lettre d'amour au moyen âge: Boncompagno da Signa, La Roue de Venus; Baudri de Bourgueil, Poésies; Manuscrit de Tegernsee, Lettres d'amours; Manuscrit de Troyes, Lettres de deux amants (Héloïse et Abélard?)* (Paris: Nil Editions, 1996), pp. 117–51.

Other Primary Sources

Anselm of Canterbury, *Anselmi Opera Omnia*, ed. Franciscus Salesius Schmitt, 7 vols. (Edinburgh: Nelson, 1938 – 70).

Baudri of Bourgueil, *Baldricus Burgulianus Carmina*, ed. Karlheinz Hilbert, Editiones Heidelbergenses 19 (Heidelberg: Carl Winter, 1979).

Bernard of Clairvaux, *Sancti Bernardi Opera*, ed. Jean Leclercq, 8 vols. (Rome: Editiones Cistercienses, 1957 – 75).

Cicero, *On the Good Life* [including *De amicitia*], trans. Michael Grant (Harmondsworth: Penguin, 1971).

Dufour, Jean, ed., *Recueil des Actes de Louis VI roi de France (1108 – 1137)*, 4 vols. (Paris: Diffusion de Boccard, 1992 - 94).

Guérard, M. ed., *Cartulaire de l'Église Notre-Dame de Paris*, Collection des Cartulaires de France 7, 4 vols. (Paris: Crapelet, 1850).

Guibert of Nogent, *Monodiae*, ed. Edmond-René Labande, *Autobiographie* (Paris: Les Belles Lettres, 1981); *Self and Society in Medieval France*, trans. John F. Benton (1970; Toronto: University of Toronto Press, 1984).

Isidore of Seville, *Etymologiarum siue Originum libri XX*, ed. W. M. Lindsay (Oxford: Clarendon Press, 1912).

John of Salisbury, *Historia pontificalis*, ed. and trans. Marjorie Chibnall, 2nd ed. (Oxford: Clarendon Press, 1986).

Lasteyrie, Robert de, ed., *Cartulaire générale de Paris* (Paris: Imprimerie Nationale, 1887).

Marbod of Rennes, *Carmina*, ed. Walther Bulst, "Liebesbriefgedichte Marbods," in Walther Bulst, *Lateinisches Mittelalter. Gesammelte Beiträge*, ed. Walter Berschin (Heidelberg: Carl Winter, 1984).

Mirot, Léon, ed., *La Chronique de Morigny (1095 – 1152)* (Paris: Alphonse Picard, 1912).

Orderic Vitalis, *The Ecclesiastical History*, ed. and trans. Marjorie Chibnall, 6 vols. (Oxford: Clarendon Press, 1969 – 78).

Ovid, *The Erotic Poems* [including *Amores* and *Ars Amatoria*], trans. Peter Green (Harmondsworth: Penguin, 1982).

——*Heroides*, trans. Harold Isbell (Harmondsworth: Penguin, 1990).

——*The Poems of Exile [Tristia, Epistulae ex Ponto]*, trans. Peter Green (Harmondsworth: Penguin, 1994).

Otto of Freising, *Ottonis et Rahewini Gesta Friderici Imperatoris,* ed. Georg Waitz and Bernard von Simson, 3rd ed. (Hannover: Hahnsche Buchhandlung, 1912, reprinted 1978).

Peter the Venerable, *The Letters of Peter the Venerable,* ed. Giles Constable (Cambridge, Mass.: Harvard University Press, 1967).

Roscelin of Compiègne, *Epistola ad Abaelardum,* ed. Joseph Reiners, in *Der Nominalismus in der Frühscholastik. Ein Beitrag zur Geschichte der Universalienfrage im Mittelalter,* Beiträge zur Geschichte der Philosophie des Mittelalters, Bd 8.5 (Münster: Aschendorff, 1910), pp. 63–80.

Suger, *Vie de Louis VI le Gros,* ed. Henri Waquet (Paris: Les Belles Lettres, 1964); *The Deeds of Louis the Fat,* trans. Richard C. Cusimano and John Moorhead (Washington D.C.: Catholic University of America, 1992).

Werner, Jakob, ed., *Beiträge zur Kunde der lateinischen Literatur des Mittelalters,* 2nd ed. (Aarau: Sauerländer, 1905; reprinted Georg Olms: Hildesheim, 1979).

Select Secondary Sources

Barrow, Julia, Charles S. F. Burnett and David Edward Luscombe, "A Checklist of the Manuscripts Containing the Writings of Peter Abelard and Heloise and Other Works Closely Associated with Abelard and his School," *Revue d'Histoire des Textes* 14–15 (1984 – 85): 183–302.

Bautier, Robert-Henri, "Paris aux temps d'Abélard," in *Abélard en son temps,* ed. Jean Jolivet (Paris: Les Belles Lettres, 1981), pp. 21–77.

Benson, Robert L. and Giles Constable, eds., *Renaissance and Renewal in the Twelfth Century* (Oxford: Clarendon Press, 1982).

Beonio Brocchieri, Mariateresa Fumagalli, *Eloisa e Abelardo* (Milan: Arnoldo Mondadori, 1984).

Bond, Gerald, *The Loving Subject. Desire, eloquence and power in Romanesque France* (Philadelphia: University of Pennsylvania Press, 1995).

Charrier, Charlotte, *Héloïse dans l'histoire et dans la légende* (Paris: Honoré Champion 1933; reprinted Geneva: Slatkine Reprints, 1977).

Clanchy, Michael T., *Abelard: A Medieval Life* (Oxford: Blackwell, 1998).

Cherewatuk, Karen and Ulrike Wiethaus, eds., *Dear Sister. Medieval Women and the Epistolary Genre* (Philadelphia: University of Pennsylvania Press, 1993).

Constable, Giles, *Letters and Letter-Collections,* Typologie des sources du moyen âge occidental 17 (Brepols: Turnhout, 1976).

Dronke, Peter, *Medieval Latin and the Rise of the European Love-Lyric,* 2 vols., 2nd ed. (Oxford: Oxford University Press, 1968).

——*Abelard and Heloise in Medieval Testimonies,* W. P. Ker Memorial Lecture 26 (Glasgow: University of Glasgow Press, 1976).

——*Women Writers of the Middle Ages. A Critical Study of Texts from Perpetua (†203) to Marguerite Porete (†1310)* (Cambridge: Cambridge University Press, 1984).

———*Intellectuals and Poets in Medieval Europe* (Rome: Edizioni di Storia e Letteratura, 1992).

Gilson, Étienne, *Héloïse et Abélard,* 3rd revised ed. (Paris: Vrin, 1978); *Heloise and Abelard,* trans. L. K. Shook (Ann Arbor, Mich.: University of Michigan Press, 1960).

Johnson, Penelope D., *Equal in Monastic Profession. Religious Women in Medieval France* (Chicago: University of Chicago Press, 1991).

Jolivet, Jean, *Arts du langage et théologie chez Abélard* (Paris: Vrin, 1969).

———and René Louis, eds., *Pierre Abélard—Pierre le Vénérable: les courants philosophiques, littéraires et artistiques en occident au milieu du XIIe siècle* (Paris: CNRS, 1975).

———ed., *Abélard en son temps* (Paris: Les Belles Lettres, 1981).

Kauffman, Linda, *Discourses of Desire: Gender, Genre, and Epistolary Fictions* (Ithaca: Cornell University Press, 1986).

Kristeva, Julia, *Tales of Love,* trans. Leon S. Roudiez (New York: Columbia University Press, 1987).

Lanham, Carol Dana, *Salutatio Formulas in Latin Letters to 1200: Syntax, Style, and Theory,* Münchener Beiträge zur Mediävistik und Renaissance-Forschung 22 (Munich: Arbeo-Gesellschaft, 1975).

Luchaire, Achille, *Louis VI le Gros. Annales de sa vie et de son règne* (Paris, 1890; reprinted Brussels: Culture et Civilisation, 1964).

Luscombe, David Edward, "From Paris to the Paraclete: the correspondence of Abelard and Heloise," *Proceedings of the British Academy* 74 (1988): 247–83.

Marenbon, John, *The Philosophy of Peter Abelard* (Cambridge: Cambridge University Press, 1997).

McLeod, Enid, *Héloïse. A Biography,* 2nd ed. (London: Chatto & Windus, 1971).

Mews, Constant J. "La bibliothèque du Paraclet du XIIIᵉ siècle à la Révolution," *Studia Monastica* 27 (1985): 31–67.

———"An excerpt from Guibert of Nogent's *Monodiae* (III, 17) appended to Augustine's *De haeresibus,*" *Revue des études augustiniennes* 33 (1987): 113–27.

———"In search of a name and its significance: a twelfth-century anecdote about Thierry and Peter Abaelard," *Traditio* 44 (1988): 175–200.

———"Un lecteur de Jérôme au douzième siècle," in *Jérôme entre l'Occident et l'Orient,* ed. Yves-Marie Duval (Paris: Études Augustiniennes, 1988), pp. 31–44.

———"Philosophy and Theology 1100 – 1150: The Search for Harmony," in *Le XIIᵉ siècle: Mutations et renouveau en France dans la première moitié du XIIᵉ siècle,* ed. Françoise Gasparri (Paris: Le Léopard d'Or, 1994), pp. 159–203.

———*Peter Abelard,* Authors of the Middle Ages 2.5 (London: Variorum, 1995).

———"Peter Abelard and the Enigma of Dialogue," in *Beyond the Persecuting Society. Religious Toleration Before the Enlightenment,* ed. John Christian Laursen and Cary J. Nederman (Philadelphia: University of Pennsylvania Press, 1998), pp. 25–52.

Moos, Peter von, *Mittelalterforschung und Ideologiekritik. Der Gelehrtenstreit um Héloïse* (Munich: Wilhelm Fink Verlag, 1974).

Newman, Barbara, "Authority, authenticity, and the repression of Heloise," *Journal of Medieval and Renaissane Studies* 22 (1992): 121–57.

Ruhe, Ernstpeter, *De amasio ad amasiam: Zur Gattungsgeschichte des mittelalterlichen Liebesbriefes,* Beiträge zur romanischen Philologie des Mittelalters 10 (Munich: Wilhelm Fink Verlag, 1975).

Ruys, Juanita Feros, "Role-playing in the *Letters* of Heloise and Abelard," *Parergon* n.s. 11 (1993): 53–78.

Schine Gold, Penny, *The Lady and the Virgin. Image, Attitude, and Experience in Twelfth-Century France* (Chicago: University of Chicago Press, 1985).

Southern, Richard William, "The Letters of Abelard and Heloise," *Medieval Humanism and Other Studies* (Oxford: Blackwell, 1970), pp. 95–104.

Verger, Jacques, *L'amour castré. L'histoire d'Héloïse et Abélard* (Paris: Hermann, 1996).

BIBLIOGRAPHY SINCE 1999

This bibliography contains significant publications relating to the *Epistolae duorum amantium*, or more generally to Abelard and Heloise, but is not exhaustive.

Epistolae duorum amantium

Cescutti, Eva and Philipp Steger, trans., *Und wärst du doch bei mir. Ex epistolis duorum amantium. Eine mittelalterliche Liebesgeschichte in Briefen. Lateinisch-deutsche Ausgabe* (Zurich: Manesse Verlag, 2005).

Fiochi, Claudio, trans., *Lettere di due amanti. Attribute a Eloisa e Abelardo,* with a preface by Maria Teresa Fumagalli Beonio Brocchieri (Archinto: Collano, 2006).

Piron, Sylvain, ed. and trans. *Lettres des deux amants, attribuées à Héloïse et Abélard* (Paris: Gallimard 2005).

Other Primary Sources

Abelard:

De Santis, Paola, ed., *I Sermoni di Abelardo per le monache del Paracleto* (Louvain: Leuven University Press, 2002).

Ilgner, Rainer M., ed. *Scito te ipsum,* CCCM 190 (Turnhout: Brepols, 2001).

Luscombe, David E. et al., *Sententie Magistri Petri Abaelardi,* CCCM 14 (Turnhout: Brepols, 2006).

Marenbon, John and Giovanni Orlandi, eds., *Collationes* (Oxford : Oxford University Press, 2001).

Romig, Mary and David Luscombe, *Expositio in Hexaemeron,* CCCM 15 (Turnhout : Brepols, 2004).

Baudri de Bourgueil:

Tilliette, Jean-Yves, ed. and trans., Baldricus Burgulianus, *Carmina,* 2 vols. (Paris: Belles Lettres, 1998, 2001).

Goscelin of St-Bertin:

Hollis, Stephanie, ed. and trans. *Writing the Wilton Women* (Turnhout: Brepols, 2004)

Otter, Monika, trans. *Goscelin of St. Bertin, The Book of Encouragement and Consolation (Liber confortatorius)* (Woodbridge: Boydell and Brewer, 2004).

Robert of Arbrissel:
Dalarun, Jacques, Geneviève Giordanego, Armelle Le Huërou, Jean Longère, Dominique Poirel, Bruce L. Venarde, eds., *Les deux vies de Robert d'Arbrissel, fondateur de Fontevraud. Légendes, écrits et témoignages,* ed. (Turnhout: Brepols, 2006).

Venarde, Bruce, trans., *Robert of Arbrissel: A Medieval Religious Life* (Washington: Catholic University of America, 2004).

Secondary Sources

Classen, Albrecht, "Abaelards *Historia Calamitatum,* der Briefwechsel mit Heloise und Gottfrieds von Strassburg *Tristan,*" *Arcadia* 35 (2000): 225–53.

Constable, Giles, "Sur l'attribution des *Epistolae duorum amantium,*" *Académie des Inscriptions et Belles-Lettres* (Nov.–Dec. 2001): 1679–93.

——"The Authorship of the *Epistolae duorum amantium.* A Reconsideration," in *Voices in Dialogue: New Problems in Reading Women's Cultural History,* ed. Linda Olson and Kathryn Kerby-Fulton (Notre Dame: University of Notre Dame Press, 2005), pp. 167–78.

Dalarun, Jacques, "Nouveaux aperçus sur Abélard, Héloïse et le Paraclet," *Francia* 32 (2005): 19–66.

Dronke, Peter, review of Bonnie Wheeler (ed.): *Listening to Heloise,* in *International Journal of the Classical Tradition* 8/1 (2002): 134–39.

Dronke, Peter and Giovanni Orlandi, "New Works by Abelard and Heloise," *Filologia mediolatina* 12 (2005): 123–77.

Findley, Brooke Heidenreich, "Sincere Hypocrisy and the Authorial Person in the Letters of Heloise," *Romance notes,* 45/3 (2005): 281–92.

——"Does the Habit Make the Nun? A Case Study of Heloise's influence on Abelard's Ethical Philosophy," *Vivarium,* 44 (2006): 248–75.

Hasse, Dag, ed., *Abaelards "Historia calamitatum". Text-Übersetzung-literaturwissenschaftliche Modellanalysen,* ed. Dag Nikolaus Hasse (Berlin: Walter de Gruyter, 2002).

Jaeger, C. Stephen, *Ennobling Love. In Search of a Lost Sensibility* (Philadelphia: University of Pennsylvania Press, 1999).

——"The 'Epistolae duorum amantium' and the Ascription to Heloise and Abelard," and "A Reply to Giles Constable," in *Voices in Dialogue: New Problems in Reading Women's Cultural History,* ed. Linda Olson and Kathryn Kerby-Fulton (Notre Dame: University of Notre Dame Press, 2005), pp. 125–66 and 179–86.

Lobrichon, Guy, *Héloïse. L'amour et le savoir* (Paris: Gallimard, 2005).

Mews, Constant J. "Thèmes philosophiques dans les *Epistolae duorum amantium:* les premiers lettres d'Héloïse et Abélard?" in Biard, Joel, ed., *Langage, sciences, philosophies au XIIe siècle* (Paris: Vrin, 1999), pp. 23–38.

——"Philosophical Themes in the *Epistolae duorum amantium:* Early Letters of Heloise and Abelard?" in *Listening to Heloise,* ed. Wheeler, pp. 32–58.

——"Hugh Metel, Heloise and Peter Abelard: the Letters of an Augustinian Canon and the Challenge of Innovation in Twelfth-Century Lorraine," in *Viator* 32 (2001): 59–91

——"Les lettres d'amour perdues d'Héloïse et la théologie de Pierre Abélard," in *Pierre Abélard. Colloque international de Nantes,* ed. Jean Jolivet and Henri Habrias (Rennes: Presses Universitaires de Rennes, 2003), pp. 137–59.

——"Heloise and Liturgical Experience at the Paraclete," *Plainsong and Medieval Music* 11.1 (2002): 25–35.

——"Liturgy and Identity at the Paraclete: Heloise, Abelard and the Evolution of the Cistercian Reform" and "Liturgy and Monastic Observance in Practice at the Paraclete," in *The Poetic and Musical Legacy,* ed. Stewart and Wulstan, pp. 19–33, 100–112.

——*La voix d'Héloïse. Un dialogue de deux amants* (Fribourg-Paris: Academic Press Fribourg–Éditions du Cerf, 2005), pp. 287–321, trans. Emilie Champs.

——*Abelard and Heloise* (Oxford : Oxford University Press, 2005).

——"St. Anselm and the Development of Philosophical Theology in Twelfth-Century Paris" in *Anselm and Abelard. Investigations and Juxtapositions* ed. Giles E. M. Gasper and Helmut Kohlenberger (Toronto: Pontifical Institute of Mediaeval Studies, 2006), pp. 196–222.

——"Negotiating the Boundaries of Gender in Religious Life: Robert of Arbrissel and Hersende, Abelard and Heloise," *Viator* 37 (2006): 113–48.

——"Cicero and the Boundaries of Friendship in the Twelfth Century," *Viator* 38/2 (2007): 369–84.

——"Discussing Love: the *Epistolae duorum amantium* and the *Sic et Non*," *Journal of Medieval Latin,* 19 (2009) (forthcoming).

——"William of Champeaux, the Foundation of Saint-Victor (Easter, 1111), and the Evolution of Abelard's Early Career," in *Actes du Colloque "Glosulae in Priscianum" (Paris, 15–17 février 2007),* ed. Irène Catach-Rosier and Anne Grondeux (Turnhout: Brepols, forthcoming).

Moos, Peter von, "Die *Epistolae duorum amantium* und die säkulare Religion der Liebe. Methodenkritische Vorüberlegungen zu einem einmaligen Werk mittellateinischer Briefliteratur," *Studi Medievali* 3a ser. 44 (2003): 1–115.

——"Kurzes Nachwort zu einer langen Geschichte mit missbrauchten Liebesbriefen: *Epistolae duorum amantium*," in von Moos, *Abaelard und Heloise.* pp. 282–92.

——"Das Abaelard und Heloise zugeschriebene Briefwerk. Am Nullpunkt der Zuschreibungsversuche?" in von Moos, *Abaelard und Heloise,* pp. 199–21.

——"Abaelard, Heloise und ihr Paraklet: ein Kloster nach Mass. Zugleich eine Streitschrift gegen die ewige Wiederkehr hermeneutische Naivität," in *Das Eigene und das Ganze. Zum Individuellen im mittelalterlichen Religiosentum,* ed. Melville, Gert and Th. Schürer, Vita regularis (Münster: Lit, 2002), pp. 563–620; in von Moos, *Abaelard und Heloise,* pp. 233–301.

——*Abaelard und Heloise. Gesammelte Studien zum Mittelalter,* Band 1, ed. Gert Melville, Geschichte: Forschung und Wissenschaft, 14 (Münster: Lit, 2005).

——"Vom Nutzen der Philologie für den umgang mit anonymen Liebesbriefen. Ein Nachwort zu den *Epistolae duorum amantium*," in: *Schrift und Liebe in der Kultur des Mittelalters,* ed. M. Schnyder, Trends in Medieval Philology (Berlin: De Gruyter, 2008).

Münster-Svendsen, Mia "The Model of Scholastic Mastery," in *Teaching and Learning in Northern Europe 1000–1200,* ed. Sally N. Vaughn and Jay Rubenstein (Turnhout: Brepols, 2006), pp. 307–42.

Piron, Sylvain, "Heloise's literary self-fashioning and the Epistolae duorum amantium," in *Memory Constructions,* ed. Lucie Dolezalova (Berlin: LIT Verlag, 2008) (forthcoming).

Powell, Morgan, "Listening to Heloise at the Paraclete: Of Scholarly Diversion and a Woman's 'Conversion'," in *Listening to Heloise,* ed. Wheeler, pp. 255–86

Robl, Werner, *Heloisas Herkunft. Hersindis Mater* (Munich: Olzog, 2001).

——"Hersindis Mater. Neues zur Familiengeschichte Heloisas mit Ausblicken auf die Familie Peter Abaelards," in *Peter Abaelard. Leben, Werk, Wirkung,* ed. Niggli, Ursula (Freiburg im Breisgau: Herder, 2003), pp. 25–89.

Ruys, Juanita, "*Eloquencie vultum depingere:* Eloquence and *Dictamen* in the Love Letters of Heloise and Abelard," in *Rhetoric and Renewal in the Latin West 1100–1540. Essays in Honour of John O. Ward,* ed. Constant J. Mews, Cary J. Nederman and Rodney M. Thomson (Brepols: Turnhout, 2003), pp. 99–112.

Stella, Francesco, "Le *Epistolae Duorum Amantium:* Nuovi Riscontri Intertestuali" (Toronto 2–6 agosto 2006) (forthcoming).

——"Analisi informatiche del lessico e individuazione degli autori nelle *Epistolae duorum amantium* (XII secolo)," *Late and Vulgar Latin Conference, Oxford 6–9 September 2006,* ed. Roger Wright (Leiden: Brill, 2008) (forthcoming).

Stewart, Marc and David Wulstan, eds., *The Poetic and Musical Legacy of Heloise and Abelard* (Westhumble, Surrey–Ottawa: Plainsong and Medieval Music Society–Institute of Medieval Music, 2003).

Ward, John O. and Neville Chiavaroli, "The Young Heloise and Latin Rhetoric: Some Preliminary Comments on the 'Lost' Love-Letters and Their Significance," in *Listening to Heloise,* ed. Wheeler, pp. 53–119.

Wheeler, Bonnie, ed., *Listening to Heloise. The Voice of a Twelfth-Century Woman* (New York: Palgrave, 2000).

Wulstan, David, "Heloise at Argenteuil and the Paraclete," and "Sources and Influences: lyric and drama at the 'School of Abelard'," in *The Poetic and Musical Legacy,* ed. Stewart and Wulstan, pp. 67–90 and 113–39.

Ziolkowski, Jan, "Lost and Not Yet Found: Heloise, Abelard, and the *Epistolae duorum amantium*," *Journal of Medieval Latin* 14 (2004): 171–202.

INDEX

abp.= archbishop; abs. = abbess; abt. = abbot; ard. = archdeacon; bp. = bishop. Latin spellings are standardized in this index, so that *amicicia* is listed as *amicitia* etc. Individual letters of the *Epistolae duorum amantium* are identified in bold type, those of the man in italics. References to footnotes to the letters are cited as **1**a (i.e., letter **1** note a). For a full concordance to these letters, see Könsgen, pp. 113–37.

Abelard, *see* Peter Abelard
Absalom, 18, 138, **27**
Achilles, 12, 91, **45c**
Adalbertus Samaritanus, 190
Adam of Saint-Victor (precentor of Notre-Dame 1107–34), 57, 119, 157
Adams, Henry, 48
Adela of Blois (daughter of William I), 61, 65
Adelaide of Maurienne (queen of France, m. Louis VI 1115), 58, 80, 154–55
adolescentula /-us (young woman / man), 32
Aelred of Rievaulx, 181
Aeneas Sylvius Piccolomini (1405–64), 10
affectus (disposition, feeling), 133–35, 150, 176, **7**, *21*, **23** (x2), **76** (x2), **79**, **86** (x2)

Alberic of Montecassino (d. 1088), 190
Alberic of Rheims (abp. of Bourges 1136–41), 72, 150, 152
Albert the Great (d. 1280), 189
Alluis, Jacques, 44–45
amare (to love), **23**, **25**, *28*, **38b**, **48**, *51*, *56*, *61*, *72* (x4), *75* (x3), **83**, **84** (x3), ***105***, ***113***
Amboise, François d', 43–44, 46
amica (friend), 33–35, 38, 95, 103, 113, 144, **25**, *40*, **55**, **57**, **76**, **108**
amicitia (friendship) 16–19, 22, 26, 99, 113–14, 117, 124–25, 144, 147, 186–88, **9**, *12*, **25** (x2), *28*, *42*, **49** (x3), *50* (x3), *61* (x2), **98**
amicus (friend), 144, *22*, **25**, **49**, *50*, *54*, *56*, **58**, *61* (x2), **69** (x2), *72*, **94** (x2), ***99***, ***103*** (x2)
amor (passionate love), 6, 16–19, 21–26, 31, 54, 60, 76, 84, 92, 99, 101, 103, 114, 116–17, 124–28, 136–37, 140–44, 147, 183, 187, 189, 191–93, 197, 228 **1**, *3*, *6*, *12*, **18**, **21**, *22* (x2), **23**, *24* (x7), **25** (x9), *26*, *35*, **38b**, *42*, *46*, **48** (x3), **49** (x2), *50*, **53**, *54* (x3), *56*, **57**, **58**, **60** (x2), *61* (x3), **69** (x2), *72* (x2), **76**, **79** (x2), **81**, **82**, **84**, *85* (x2), **86** (x4), **87** (x4), **88** (x2), **90** (x3), **92**, *93*, **94**, **98**, ***99*** (x2), **100**, *101* (x4), **102** (x2), ***103***, **104** (x3), ***105*** (x2), **112a**, *113* (x6)
Andreas Capellanus, 42, 89

Printed in the United States
204469BV00002B/70-825/P

9 780230 608139